STUDIES IN EARLY CHRISTIAN, MEDIEVAL, AND RENAISSANCE ART

RICHARD KRAUTHEIMER

STUDIES IN
EARLY CHRISTIAN,
MEDIEVAL,
AND RENAISSANCE
ART

NEW YORK   NEW YORK UNIVERSITY PRESS
LONDON   UNIVERSITY OF LONDON PRESS LIMITED
1969

Editorial Committee: James S. Ackerman, Elisabeth B. Mac Dougall, Richard Pommer; assisted by John Coolidge, Naomi Miller, Cecil L. Striker, Patricia Waddy

Translators: Alfred Frazer, Joachim Gaehde, Marjorie M. Licht, Howard Saalman, Cecil L. Striker
Indexers: Charlotte Lacaze, Constance Lowenthal

EDITORS' PREFACE

THE republication of these essays, chosen by the author and his students on the occasion of his seventieth birthday, makes more accessible some of the major contributions of one of the eminent art historians of our time. Several of the papers have been translated, but otherwise all are presented as they originally appeared, with only minor editorial changes and some additions and replacements of illustrations. The author has added postscripts in which he reexamines the original articles in the light of recent contributions and of changes in his own interpretation of the material.

Most of the studies are on architectural subjects. Though a majority represent basic discoveries and concepts presented in this form for the first time, they can be read with pleasure by nonspecialists. Krautheimer's scholarly achievement is distinguished by the span of his interests, which in this collection encompasses archaeology, history, liturgy and theology, literature and philology, criticism and Renaissance humanism.

Richard Krautheimer was born on July 6, 1897, in Fürth, Bavaria. On graduating from the Gymnasium there in 1912, he entered the University of Munich, where for two years he studied law before being attracted to the history of art by the celebrated lectures of Heinrich Wölfflin and, more profoundly, by the imaginative teaching of Paul Frankl, whose insistence on rigorous verbal description and whose concept of the "layers" of historical monuments were to become cornerstones of Krautheimer's method. From Munich he moved to Berlin to study with Adolf Goldschmidt, whose meticulous and loving examination of objects of art provided a counterweight to Wölfflin's generalizations on style. In 1923 he received his doctorate *summa cum laude* from the University of Halle, and prepared the publication of his first book, on German churches of the mendicant orders.

In the following year, Krautheimer participated in the preparation at Erfurt of the Inventory of Monuments for the province of Saxony, and there, in the museum library, he met his future wife and collaborator, Trude Hess, who in the following years shared his work as well as his leisure both as a scholar and as a counsellor of students. After their marriage in 1924, the Krautheimers set out on their first Italian trip, a year's visit that combined intensive travel with study in Rome at the Hertziana Library. They returned in 1927, 1929–1930 and 1931–

1932, joining a group of contemporaries and older scholars that included G. C. Argan, Ludwig Curtius, Adolph Goldschmidt, Theodor Klauser, Karl Lehmann, Pietro Toesca, Wolfgang Stechow, Ellis Waterhouse, and Rudolf Wittkower. Ever since, Rome has been their second home.

Krautheimer's interest in early Christian architecture, stimulated by the first Italian visits, prompted travels to Yugoslavia, Greece, Turkey and at this time Asia Minor, and in 1933 he undertook his major life's work, the directorship of the Corpus of Early Christian Basilicas in Rome, sponsored by the Pontifical Institute for Christian Archaeology. In that year the Nazis terminated his appointment as Privatdozent at Marburg University, a post he had held since 1928, and in 1934 he was invited to lecture at the Courtauld Institute of London University.

In December of 1935, Krautheimer emigrated to the United States, and a few weeks later began teaching as the first professor of the newly formed department of fine arts at the University of Louisville, Kentucky. Two years later he accepted a visiting professorship at Vassar College, where he was appointed professor in 1938. In the fifteen years of his teaching there, he helped to form one of the strongest undergraduate curricula in the country, one which prepared a large number of its graduates for further professional study.

At frequent intervals beginning in 1938, Krautheimer offered graduate courses as visiting professor at the Institute of Fine Arts of New York University, and in 1952 he moved permanently to a post at the Institute where, in 1965, he became the first holder of the Jayne Wrightsman Professorship. Krautheimer's great success in training a generation of scholar-teachers at the Institute has been due to his capacity to stimulate adventurousness and individuality. His students have contributed to knowledge of the arts of every epoch from late antiquity to the nineteenth century; they have become teachers, museum directors, curators, and field archaeologists, and they have shared and passed on to their own students his firm conviction in the interdependence of teaching and scholarship.

Nearly all of Krautheimer's American publications, and notably the book on Lorenzo Ghiberti, which was written with Trude Krautheimer, the Pelican *Early Christian and Byzantine Architecture,* and recent volumes of the *Corpus,* represent the extension of various studies that had occupied him since his student years, and it is in part this consistency and depth of experience that accounts for their richness. His contribution as a scholar and teacher has been recognized by honorary degrees and awards from the American Academy in Rome, the Pontificio Istituto di Archeologia Cristiana, and the Universities of Louisville and of Frankfürt a. M.

The subjects covered by the essays in this volume represent only a portion of the spectrum of Krautheimer's interests. He has lectured often on Byzantine, Gothic, Baroque, and modern architecture, and his course on the City of Rome from Constantine to the Present Day has long been for students at the Institute of Fine Arts a model of twentieth-century humanism. To each of the epochs he has studied, Krautheimer has brought a perspective that reveals the arts in the context of the cultural environment—religious, political, economic, literary; his work has become a model of the method and of the potentialities of contextual analysis and criticism.

No evaluation of Krautheimer's scholarly credo could be more succinct than the one he framed himself, in addressing the commencement convocation at Vassar College in 1945:

> The world of knowledge, past and present, can be likened to a sphere which is continuously and rapidly expanding; so rapidly, indeed, that we simply cannot catch up with it. New facts are gleaned, new fields are being added, new laws of nature are being discovered, new historical prospects, new problems arise continuously. This expanding sphere of human knowledge cannot be understood by jumping from one fact, from one field, to the other like a raving grasshopper, or by attempting to survey its entire surface: we must enter into the interior of the sphere and work down until the radii are closer together, to an inner sphere, as it were, where the connection between the various aspects becomes more clearly evident and where it becomes possible to transfer, from one field to the other, knowledge, principles, experiences and conclusions.

More should be said of Krautheimer the scholar, teacher, and colleague, but his students have seen him in such diverse ways, and have gained from him so many different benefits, that it proves impossible for any of us to characterize him in just the way another wants it, and this leaves agreement only on the factual record. If he taught the One Way and had disciples rather than younger associates, his contribution could be delineated more clearly in a foreword, but he has the preferable gift of encouraging individuals to arrive at as many perspectives as there are objects of study.

AUTHOR'S PREFACE

COLLECTED *essays more often than not are published after the author's demise. To me this seems not quite fair. It deprives the author of the chance of selecting among his progeny—for scholars ought to be cruel fathers—those he considers fit for survival or, better, revival. It deprives him of the pleasure of seeing a goodly number of his children assembled under one roof, even though some have to be refused admittance because of old age, congenital defects, or simply overlarge size. It deprives him of the opportunity a man ought to have of finding out how after many years he feels about those chosen—now that he has grown away from them, rather than they from him—and even of saying in a few words how he would handle the problem today. And it deprives the reader of the knowledge he is entitled to have as to how the author as an older and—so he hopes—more mature man views questions posed twenty, thirty, and forty years ago.*

Once I had recovered from my surprise, I was therefore greatly pleased to learn that my friends and former students intended to present me with this volume while I am still among the living. Now I can look at the papers I wrote in the past at leisure and with a critical eye—almost, if not quite, as if they were written by someone else—a reasonably gifted student, let us say. I wish I could say that I like all of them equally well or that I stand by every word I have ever put down. But I cannot, and it is not my way. I have looked on my scholarly production as a kind of serial publication and on its components as stepping stones in a development to be used, revised, or discarded when found faulty. Thus I asked my friends for permission to go over these essays critically and to state in a postscript, where necessary, my present position. Where further research—others' or mine—has knocked out an example, a date, or an argument, or on the contrary confirmed it, I shall say so. Where my own approach has changed in direction or in breadth, I shall sum up my present position as briefly as possible. Where I have pulled a regular boner, I shall admit it with good grace—I would rather do so myself than have others do it. Thus these postscripts at times may turn into a dialogue between myself today and the youngster who wrote the papers, and I shall not be able to avoid a personal note. Such self-criticism should be enjoyable; it should be instructive to me as a means of judging the distance I have traveled; it should be healthy as a cure against the disease scholars easily suffer from—the belief in their infallibility; and it should result in a kind of autobiography of myself as a scholar.

That all this comes to pass is due entirely to the dedicated efforts of my friends and former students. They have collected these papers—unearthing in the process a few the existence of which I had quite forgotten; they have edited them and translated into English those originally written in German or Italian and often, I fear, in an involved style; they have obtained the publisher's permission to add to the original text my retrospective musings; they have supervised the printing; and they have somehow found ways to finance the volume—never an easy or enjoyable task. I want to thank them—every single one.

RICHARD KRAUTHEIMER

BIBLIOGRAPHY 1925–1967

1925. *Die Kirchen der Bettelorden in Deutschland* ("Deutsche Beiträge zur Kunstwissenschaft," II [Cologne]).

1927. *Mittelalterliche Synagogen* (Berlin).

1928. "Un disegno di Jacopo della Quercia?" *La Diana*, III, No. 4, 3–6.

1928. "Lombardische Hallenkirchen im XII. Jahrhundert," *Jahrbuch für Kunstwissenschaft* (1928), pp. 136–91.

1928. Review of A. Mettler's *Mittelalterliche Klosterkirchen und Klöster der Hirsauer und Zisterienser in Württemberg*, in *Oberrheinische Kunst*, III, 15–17.

1928. Review of R. Schultze's *Basilika, Untersuchungen zur antiken und frühmittelalterlichen Baukunst* ("Römisch-Germanische Forschungen," II), in *Denkmalpflege und Heimatschutz*, XXX, 101.

1929. "Die Anfänge der Kunstgeschichtsschreibung in Italien," *Repertorium für Kunstwissenschaft*, L, 49–63.

1929. "Zur venezianische Trecentoplastik," *Marburger Jahrbuch für Kunstwissenschaft*, V, 193–212.

1929. Review of A. Riegl's *Spätrömische Kustindustrie*, 2nd ed., in *Germania*, XIII, 97–100.

1930. Contributions to *Sachwörterbuch der Deutschkunde*, Leipzig and Berlin, pp. 82, 112–13, 119–21, 144 45, ??2, 381–82, 528–29, 537, 540–41, 593–94, 610, 637–41, 661–62, 667, 694–97, 698–702, 744, 751, 765–66, 767, 778, 791–92, 892, 901, 985–86, 1040, 1065, 1120, 1191–92, 1262, 1272, 1285.

1932. "Bericht über die Sitzungen des dritten Kongresses für christliche Archäologie in Ravenna," *Die Denkmalpflege*, VI, 233–36.

1932. "Die Erforschung der frühchristlichen Baudenkmäler Italiens," *Zeitschrift für Kunstgeschichte*, I, 172–74.

1932. "Plastik aus Holz und Stein. Vierzehntes Jahrhundert," *Religiöse Kunst aus Hessen und Nassau. Kritischer Gesamtkatalog der Ausstellung Marburg 1928* (Marburg), pp. 21–52, Nos. 13–74.

1932. Review of E. Gall's *Karolingische und ottonische Kirchen*, in *Die Denkmalpflege*, IV, 196–97.

1932. Review of E. Gall's *Karolingische und ottonische Kirchen*, in *Germania*, XVI, 65–67.

1932. Review of J. Oberst's *Die mittelalterliche Architektur der Dominikaner und Franziskaner in der Schweiz*, in *Zeitschrift für Kunstgeschichte*, I, 54–56.

1932. Review of K. Wilhelm-Kästner's *Das Münster in Essen*, in *Die Denkmalpflege*, VI, 197–98.

1933. Review of H. Egger's *Römische Veduten*, in *Zeitschrift für Kunstgeschichte*, II, 120–23.

1934. "Contributi per la storia della basilica di S. Lorenzo fuori le mura," *Rivista di archeologia cristiana*, XI, 285–334.

1934. "San Nicola in Bari und die apulische Architektur des 12. Jahrhunderts," *Wiener Jahrbuch für Kunstgeschichte*, IX, 5–42.

1935. "Basiliche paleocristiane di Roma: San Lorenzo in Lucina," *L'Illustrazione vaticana*, VI, 667–68.

1935. "La façade ancienne de Saint-Jean de Latran à Rome," *Revue archéologique*, Ser. 6, V, 231–35.

1935. "Santo Stefano Rotondo a Roma e la chiesa del Santo Sepolcro a Gerusalemme," *Rivista di archeologia cristiana*, XII, 51–102.

1935. Review of A. Petrignani's *La Basilica di S. Pudenziana in Roma*, in *Rivista di archeologia cristiana*, XII, 184–86.

1936. "Die Doppelkathedrale in Pavia," in Richard Salomon, *Opicinus de Canistris. Weltbild und Bekenntnisse eines avignonesischen Klerikers des 14. Jahrhunderts* ("Studies of the Warburg Institute," IA [London]), 323–37.

1936. "An Oriental Basilica in Rome: S. Giovanni a Porta Latina," *American Journal of Archaeology*, XL, 485–95.

1936. "Terra Cotta Madonnas," *Parnassus*, VIII, No. 7, 4–8.

1937. *Corpus basilicarum christianarum Romae*, I (Vatican City).

1937. "Ghibertiana," *The Burlington Magazine*, LXXI, 68–80.

1938. "Art and Society," *Social Research*, V, 350–59.

1938. Contributions to *A Bibliography of the Survival of the Classics*, II (London), Nos. 169, 666, 671–73, 675, 678–81, 683–88, 708, 709, 713–15, 726, 729, 746, 754, 755, 766, 767.

1938. Review of W. Weisbach's *Geschichtliche Voraussetzungen der Entstehung einer christlichen Kunst*, in *Rivista di archeologia cristiana*, XV, 181–83.

1939. "The Beginning of Early Christian Architecture," *Review of Religion*, III, 127–48.

1939. With W. Frankl. "Recent Discoveries in Churches in Rome," *American Journal of Archaeology*, XLIII, 388–400.

1939. Review of R. Kautzsch's *Kapitellstudien*, in *The Art Bulletin*, XXI, 403–408.

1939. Review of *Antioch-on-the-Orontes*, II. *The Excavations 1933–1936*, ed. R. Stillwell, in *Rivista di archeologia cristiana*, XVI, 355–58.

1940. Review of J. Adhémar's *Influences antiques dans l'art du moyen âge français*, in *The Art Bulletin*, XXII, 280–81.

1941. "S. Pietro in Vincoli and the Tripartite Transept in the Early Christian Basilica," *Proceedings of the American Philosophical Society*, LXXXIV, 353–429.

1941. "San Pietro in Vincoli," abstract, *American Journal of Archaeology*, XLV, 439–40.

1941. Review of M. S. Bunim's *Space in Medieval Painting and the Forerunners of Perspective*, in *The Art Bulletin*, XXIII, 178–80.

1942. "The Carolingian Revival of Early Christian Architecture," *The Art Bulletin*, XXIV, 1–38.

1942. "Introduction to an 'Iconography of Mediaeval Architecture,'" *Journal of the Warburg and Courtauld Institutas*, V, 1–33.

1942. "Recent Publications on S. Maria Maggiore in Rome," *American Journal of Archaeology*, XLVI, 373–79.

1942. Review of J. W. Crowfoot's *Early Churches in Palestine*, in *Review of Religion*, VI, 328–32.

1945. "On Liberal Education," *Bulletin of Vassar College*, XXXV, No. 2, 3–11.

1946. Review of W. Weisbach's *Religiöse Reform und mittelalterliche Kunst*, in *The Art Bulletin*, XXVIII, 203–204.

1947. "Early Christian Art at the End of Late Antiquity," *Folia. Studies in the Christian Perpetuation of the Classics*, II, 5–13.

1947. "Ghiberti and Master Gusmin," *The Art Bulletin*, XXIX, 25–35.

1948. "The Tragic and Comic Scene of the Renaissance: The Baltimore and Urbino Panels," *Gazette des Beaux-arts*, Ser. 6, XXXIII, 327–46.

1948. Review of F. Antal's *Florentine Painting and its Social Background*, in *Magazine of Art*, XLI, 318.

1949. "Some Drawings of Early Christian Basilicas in Rome: St. Peter's and S. Maria Maggiore," *The Art Bulletin*, XXXI, 211–15.

1950. With W. Frankl and E. Josi. "Le esplorazioni nella basilica de S. Lorenzo nell'Agro Verano," *Rivista di archeologia cristiana*, XXVI, 9–48.

1951. Review of L. Goldscheider's *Ghiberti*, in *The Burlington Magazine*, XCIII, 97–98.

1952. "A Drawing for the Fonte Gaia in Siena," *Bulletin of the Metropolitan Museum of Art*, n.s. X, 265–74.

1952. With E. Josi and W. Frankl. "S. Lorenzo fuori le Mura in Rome: Excavations and Observations," *Proceedings of the American Philosophical Society*, XCVI, 1–26.

1953. Review of A. Calderini's *La Basilica Maggiore di San Lorenzo in Milano*, in *The Art Bulletin*, XXXV, 152–54.

1953. Review of A. Grabar's *Martyrium. Recherches sur le culte des reliques et l'art chrétien antique*, in *The Art Bulletin*, XXXV, 57–61.

1954. "Ghiberti," in *Les sculpteurs célèbres*, ed. P. Francastel (Paris), pp. 212–15.

1954. "Sancta Maria Rotunda," *Arte del primo Millennio* (Atti del II° convegno per lo studio dell'alto medioevo tenuto presso l'Università di Pavia nel settembre 1950 [Turin]), pp. 21–27.

1955. "Aggiunte alla relazione 'Le esplorazioni nella basilica di S. Lorenzo nell'Agro Verano,'" *Rivista di archeologia cristiana*, XXXI, 51–52.

1955. "Ghiberti-Architetto," *Bulletin of the Allen Memorial Art Museum, Oberlin College,* XII, 48–67.

1956. With T. Krautheimer. *Lorenzo Ghiberti* ("Princeton Monographs in Art and Archaeology," 31 [Princeton]).

1956. Review of L. Birchler *et al. Frühmittelalterliche Kunst in den Alpenländern* ("Akten zum III. Internationalen Kongress für Frühmittelalterforschung"), in *The Art Bulletin,* XXXVIII, 130–33.

1957. With E. Josi and S. Corbett. "Note lateranensi," *Rivista di archeologia cristiana,* XXXIII, 79–98.

1957. "Il transetto nella basilica paleocristiana," *Actes du Ve Congrès international d'archéologie chrétienne, Aix-en-Provence, 13–19 septembre 1954* ("Studi di antichità cristiana," 22 [Vatican City]).

1957. Review of G. Forsyth's *The Church of St. Martin at Angers,* in *The Art Bulletin,* XXXIX, 147–50.

1958. With W. Frankl and G. Gatti. "Excavations at San Lorenzo f.l.m. in Rome, 1957," *American Journal of Archaeology,* LXII, 379–82.

1958. With E. Josi and S. Corbett. "Note lateranensi," *Rivista di archeologia cristiana,* XXXIV, 59–72.

1958. "Redefinitions of Style. Introductory Note," *The College Art Journal,* XVII, 104.

1959. With W. Frankl and S. Corbett. *Corpus basilicarum christianarum Romae,* II (Vatican City).

1960. With S. Corbett. "The Constantinian Basilica of the Lateran," *Antiquity,* XXXIV, 201–206

1960. "Mensa-Coemeterium-Martyrium," *Cahiers archéologiques,* XI, 15–40.

1961. "Alberti's Templum Etruscum," *Münchner Jahrbuch der bildenden Kunst,* Ser. 3, XII, 65–72.

1961. "The Architecture of Sixtus III: A Fifth-Century Renascence?" *Essays in Honor of Erwin Panofsky* ("De Artibus Opuscola xl," ed. M. Meiss [New York]), pp. 291–302.

1963. "Alberti and Vitruvius," *Studies in Western Art, II: The Renaissance and Mannerism* ("Acts of the Twentieth International Congress of the History of Art" [Princeton]), pp. 42–52.

1964. "The Crypt of Sta. Maria in Cosmedin and the Mausoleum of Probus Anicius," *Essays in Memory of Karl Lehmann* (*Marsyas,* Supplement I [Locust Valley, New York]), pp. 171–75.

1964. "Zu Konstantins Apostelkirche in Konstantinopel," *Mullus, Festschrift Theodor Klauser* (*Jahrbuch für Antike und Christentum,* Supplement I [Münster]), pp. 224–29.

1964. "A Note on Justinian's Church of the Holy Apostles in Constantinople," *Mélanges Eugène Tisserant, II* ("Studi e testi," 232 [Vatican City]), pp. 265–70.

1965. *Early Christian and Byzantine Architecture* ("Pelican History of Art" [Harmondsworth]).

1965. "Riflessioni sull'architettura paleocristiana," *Atti del VI congresso internazionale di archeologia cristiana, Ravenna, 23–29 settembre, 1962* (Vatican City), pp. 567–79.

1965. Review of R. F. Hoddinot's *Early Byzantine Churches in Macedonia and Southern Serbia,* in *The Art Bulletin,* XLVII, 145–46.

1966. "Die Decanneacubita in Konstantinopel. Ein kleiner Beitrag zur Frage Rom und Byzanz," *Tortulae. Studien zu altchristlichen und byzantinischen Monumenten* (*Römische Quartalschrift für christliche Altertumskunde und Kirchengeschichte,* Supplement 30 [Rome-Freiburg-Vienna]), pp. 195–99.

1966. Review of A. M. Romanini's *L' Architettura gotica in Lombardia,* in *The Art Bulletin,* XLVIII, 260–61.

1966. "Letter to the Editor," *The Art Bulletin,* XLVIII, 124–25.

1967. With W. Frankl and S. Corbett. *Corpus basilicarum christianarum Romae,* III (Vatican City).

1967. "A Christian Triumph in 1597," *Essays in Honor of Rudolf Wittkower,* II (London), 174–78.

1967. "The Constantinian Basilica," *Dumbarton Oaks Papers,* XXI, pp. 151–140.

1967. With S. Corbett, R. Malmstrom, and R. Stapleford. "La basilica constantiniana al Laterano. Un tentativo di ricostruzione," *Rivista di archeologia cristiana,* XLIII (1967; *Miscellanea . . . Enrico Josi,* II), 125 ff.

In preparation:

With S. Corbett. *Corpus basilicarum christianarum Romae,* IV, V.

Review of S. Kostof's *The Orthodox Baptistery of Ravenna,* in *Archaeology.*

CONTENTS

CONTENTS

LIST OF TEXT FIGURES

LIST OF PLATES

ABBREVIATIONS

AB	The Art Bulletin
ActaA	Acta Archaeologica
AJA	American Journal of Archaeology
AM	Athenische Mitteilungen (Mitteilungen des deutschen archäologischen Instituts, athenische Abteilung)
AttiPontAcc	Atti della Pontificia Accademia Romana di Archeologia
BCH	Bulletin de correspondance hellénique
BdA	Bollettino d'Arte
BMMA	Bulletin of the Metropolitan Museum of Art
BMon	Bulletin monumental
BSA	British School of Athens, Annual
BSR	British School of Archaeology at Rome, Papers
BurlM	Burlington Magazine
BZ	Byzantinische Zeitschrift
Cabrol-Leclerq	*Dictionnaire d'archéologie chrétienne et de liturgie,* Paris, 1907 ff.
CahArch	Cahiers archéologiques
CIL	*Corpus Inscriptionum latinarum*
Corpus	R. Krautheimer and others, *Corpus Basilicarum Christianarum Romae* (Vatican City, 1939 ff.)
CRAI	Comptes-rendus Académie des inscriptions et belles-lettres
CSEL	*Corpus Scriptorum Ecclesiasticorum Latinorum*
DissPontAcc	Dissertazioni della Pontificia Accademia Romana di Archeologia
DOPapers	Dumbarton Oaks Papers
GBA	Gazette des Beaux-Arts
ILCV	Inscriptiones Latinae Christianae Veteres
JdI	Jahrbuch der österreichischen byzantinischen Gesellschaft
JKS	Jahrbuch der kunsthistorischen Sammlungen in Wien
JKSK	Jahrbuch der kunsthistorischen Sammlungen des allerhöchsten Kaiserhauses
JKunstW	Jahrbuch für Kunstwissenschaft
JÖAI	Jahreshefte des österreichischen archäologischen Instituts

JÖBG	Jahrbuch der österreichischen byzantinischen Gesellschaft
JPKS	Jahrbuch der preussischen Kunstsammlungen
JRS	Journal of Roman Studies
JSAH	Journal of the Society of Architectural Historians
LP	L. Duchesne, *Le Liber Pontificalis* (Paris, 1881–92)
MGH	*Monumenta Germaniae Historica*

	SS.	*Scriptores*
	LL.	*Leges*
	Poet. L.	*Poetae Latini*
	Epist.	*Epistolae*

MünchJb	Münchner Jahrbuch der bildenden Kunst
PG	J. P. Migne. *Patrologia Graeca*
PL	J. P. Migne, *Patrologia Latina*
RA	Revue archéologique
RACrist	Rivista di archeologia cristiana
RE	Pauly-Wissowa. *Real Encyclopaedie der klassischen Altertumswissenschaft*, Stuttgart, 1894–1919
RepKunstW	Repertorium für Kunstwissenschaft
RomA	Mitteilungen des deutschen archäologischen Instituts, römische Abteilung
RQuSchr	Römische Quartalschrift
Venturi	A. Venturi. *Storia dell'arte italiana,* Milan, 1901–1937
VorWarb	Vorträge der kunstwissenschaftlichen Bibliothek Warburg

STUDIES IN EARLY CHRISTIAN, MEDIEVAL, AND RENAISSANCE ART

THE BEGINNING OF
EARLY CHRISTIAN ARCHITECTURE *

WHEN WE think of the origins of Early Christian architecture, the first thing that comes to mind is the normal Early Christian basilica. Indeed, it is this form which appears in some of the most important churches, and which, in the course of centuries, has grown more and more important in Christian architecture: an edifice consisting of a nave, and two or four aisles separated from one another by rows of columns, a transept and an apse. It is this form which dominates the imagination of the historian when he thinks back to the Early Christian period, and the assumption is that it is this form which from the very beginning dominated Early Christian architecture.

There remain, however, several questions. First, was this highly developed form really the beginning of Christian church architecture, or did there exist any earlier edifices belonging to Christian congregations? Second, if any did exist—what did they look like? Was the developed basilica the only type, in either the Roman Empire or in Rome itself, or did there exist other variations? Was it, at least, the dominating one? And third, since the Early Christian basilica form has become so important in the course of history, how did it originate?

The question of whether Christian edifices existed before the recognition of Christianity under Constantine is answered for the first period, the decades that followed the death of Christ and the foundation of Christianity as a religion under Paul, in the Acts of the Apostles,[1] and in the Epistles of St. Paul. From them it appears that the small communities of this earliest period, communities of friends, based on personal relationships as well as on a common creed, assembled in the house or apartment of some more well-to-do member of the group— in any room large enough to shelter them.[2] This situation seems still to have prevailed in the second century; again the community probably assembled in some privately owned house. The Elder presided, he or a wandering preacher (such as Paul had been) gave a sermon, prayers were offered, the memoirs of the

*This article, from *Review of Religion*, III, 1939, 127-148, represents a paper read at a meeting of the New York Chapter of the American Archeological Institute on March 14, 1938. Despite its preliminary character, I am publishing it without alterations, adding footnotes only, in order to provoke discussion on some of the more important problems involved. I am planning two more detailed studies on "The Pre-Constantinian Churches in Rome," and "The Imperial Character of the Early Christian Basilica."

apostles or the writings of the prophets were read, a common meal was eaten, and a discussion on religious or administrative matters may have ensued.[3]

But this situation could no longer be maintained after the communities had grown, and had been consolidated, as was the case during the late second and third centuries. The Christian community of Rome apparently consisted, by the middle of the third century, of about 50,000 members, or five per cent of the population of Rome.[4] In the Eastern provinces sometimes a majority of the population was Christian.[5] Larger assembly rooms were needed for regular meetings, and an administration had to be created; a regular clergy (no longer a lay clergy) had to be installed, and an organization for the administration of charities had to be set up, as well as archives, a legal office, etc. Such a set-up was created in Rome between 230 and 250.[6] But where were the assembly rooms, the "churches" of this growing community? Private homes had certainly become too small for such a purpose. The earlier assumption was that, in Rome at least, the communities assembled in the catacombs, the vast subterranean cemeteries outside the city, because of the continuous persecutions. But this theory has been disproved. Catacombs seem to have existed only in a few places, in Rome, in Lower Italy and Sicily, and in North Africa (Cyrene). Furthermore, the Christian communities did not suffer from continuous persecutions: during the third century there took place in Rome only two persecutions which lasted two years each. It was during these persecutions that small groups of Christians were arrested in the catacombs, and thus the legend of the use of the catacombs as hiding and worshipping places has grown up. Under normal conditions the catacombs were not at all a suitable place for divine services. The network of the galleries was much too complicated, and the "chapels" in the catacombs (which are really tomb chambers) were far too small for the large Christian communities of the third century. The largest of these chambers, the so-called Chapel of the Popes, offers room for fifty people at the most. And the catacombs themselves were too far from the city. For the same reasons the small trefoil chapels which sometimes are situated above the catacombs could not serve for regular meetings. There must have existed within the city regular assembly-rooms for the community. Thus there remains the problem of determining what they looked like.

About twenty years ago, Monsignor J. P. Kirsch, Director of the Pontifical Institute for Christian Archeology, pointed out that below numerous Roman churches there were preserved remains of Roman houses. Since some of these houses were decorated with murals showing Christian symbols, it was a splendid hypothesis to assume that these very houses represented the ecclesiastical centers, the so-called *tituli,* of the third-century Christian communities.[7] As the result of a campaign of research undertaken two years ago, I think I can establish more definitely in at least one case—namely SS. Giovanni e Paolo—the appearance of such a community house.[8]

The church which now exists on this site shows in the interior a remodelling of the seventeenth and eighteenth centuries, while the basic structure, which is visible from the outside, shows fifth-century features. It is clear that below the church, and in its side walls, are preserved the remains of at least four private houses, three of them erected about the middle of the second century and later remodelled several times, while the fourth one may have been entirely a construction of the third century. This last house, under the front part of the church, as well as the one situated under the present apse, can be disregarded, since they did not form part of the community house, which made use of only the two houses situated under the western half of the present nave and aisles. One of these houses, situated in the rear, was a private residence; the larger one, situated along the street, the Clivus Scauri, showed the normal plan of a Roman apartment house with a row of shops on the ground floor (Text Fig. 1). Both houses were

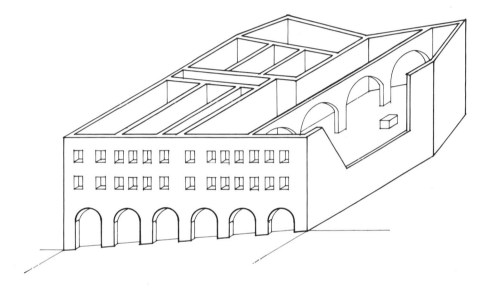

Text fig. 1. Rome, SS. Giovanni e Paolo, titulus, reconstruction (Frankl)

certainly not originally Christian. But about the middle of the third century, as can be seen from the masonry of the new parts (the masonry can be clearly characterized as to period, since it changes continually, both as to the materials used, and as to the thickness and consistency of the mortar beds, the houses were joined by covering the narrow, oblique by-lane between them, and remodelled by erecting some new walls in the interior and a common façade towards the street; as mentioned above, a third house with shops was erected on the right at about the same period. The façade of the main building shows that it belonged to a large three-storied edifice: on the ground floor level are arcades with a portico behind, which opened onto the former shop rooms, while on the second and third floor levels are windows. From the exterior it seems to be a normal Roman apartment house. But while the windows on the second and third floor of the left half of the façade fall very clearly into groups which represent an interior division into two rooms on the left and a single room, possibly a hallway, in the middle of the building, the seven windows on the right show quite a different pattern. The distances between these windows are too small to allow for partition walls dividing the width of the floor on this side into smaller rooms. Only a large hall could have existed in this part of the house, and the existence of such a vast room seems to be confirmed by the existence of a wall on the ground floor, which was erected during this remodelling, and which runs through the whole width of the house up to the façade. This wall must have been erected in order to support a strong upper wall, namely, the west wall of the large room on the second floor, while an even stronger wall under its middle axis may have supported its floor, and perhaps a row of piers along its axis.[9] So large a room, however, would have been of no use in an apartment house; it was suitable only for a large meeting room. It was fifty feet wide and forty to sixty feet long, and may have been two stories high.

It cannot, of course, be definitely proved that at the time of the remodelling, about the middle of the third century, this strange house, with its large hall suitable for assemblies on the right, and a number of smaller rooms which would be suitable for administrative and similar purposes on the left, was already in the possession of a Christian community. It is certain, however, that the building was in Christian hands by the beginning of the fourth century, when the older rooms on the ground floor of the house were decorated in fresco with Christian symbols, and a staircase and a Confessio (a small room for preserving relics) were constructed on a mezzanine above the former by-lane, immediately under the floor of the hall on the second storey.[10] Above this Confessio stood an altar, the place of which is still marked in the middle of the nave of the present church at a place where normally no altar would be found. This must be the place where, in the community house, the altar was erected, and this place would have been situated exactly in the middle of the hall at a short distance from its east wall. Thus the early fourth-century plan of the house is quite clear; the rooms on the ground floor were accessible from the street and evidently served as a vestibule, offices, etc. On the second (and probably also on the third floor) there were more small rooms, possibly offices, on the left, while the large hall on the right contained an altar set not far from the wall. This seems to have been the typical arrangement of a Christian community house of the period immediately before Constantine: a house of normal aspect, the interior of which was adapted to the needs of the Christian community.

I think this arrangement indicates also the position of the Christian communities in Rome at that time. The periods of persecution were rare and short, and in most cases of a more or less local character, and the intermediary periods were peaceful. Christianity was certainly not a *religio licita*—i.e., a religion officially recognized by the State; but it was a *religio tolerata* with which the state did not interfere.[11] It maintained a semi-legal status, and was thus enabled to own property [12] (perhaps through an intermediary in whose name the property was purchased); it was enabled to own a house, and to remodel this house so as to adapt it to religious needs; and its members were able to meet regularly for service. As long as the meeting place preserved the façade of a private house (and the meeting therefore preserved the character of a private meeting) the state evidently saw no reason to interfere.

These conclusions can, of course, not be based on SS. Giovanni e Paolo alone. They rest on documentary evidence as well,[13] and also on the existence of a number of similar pre-Constantinian *tituli* in Rome, the remains of which would lead to similar conclusions if they were reconstructed.[14] These semi-private community houses existed also during the third century outside Rome, in the provinces of the Empire. One of them was excavated by the Yale Expedition a few years ago in the small town of Dura, not far from the Persian border,[15] this one dated 232 (Fig. 1). On the other hand, this type of house was in no way limited to the Christian communities; Jewish communities constructed a certain type of synagogue in about the same way,[16] and so frequently did the Mithraic communities.[17] It is a type in perfect conformity with the position of tolerated, semi-legal, but not officially recognized communities.

It will thus be readily comprehended that the Edict of Milan of 313 A.D. immediately affected the arrangement of the churches, since it changed the status of the Christian communities. The history of this Recognition Act, and the reasons for it, cannot be discussed here; nor is the rather controversial question of Constantine's conversion of any importance in this study. To us the important factor is that, through the various decrees issued at this time, the Christian creed was officially recognized, and the status of the Christian communities legalized. Thus, they were entitled to erect public places of worship which were impressive enough to emphasize the importance of the newly recognized community. It is understandable that, besides the new public places of worship, the tradition of the older semi-public and semi-private "house of the community" still continued; its diffusion declined gradually, of course, while the number and importance of places of public worship grew in the Christian communities of the Empire. But it would be a mistake, I think, to assume that all the newly erected churches followed one type only—that of the Early Christian basilica. On the contrary, there exist quite a number of variations, and for an understanding of the development of the new Early Christian architecture, these secondary types are extremely important.

The previous tradition of Early Christian architecture had created during the third century a very definite type of assembly hall within the houses of the community, the *tituli*: plain large rooms with an altar to one side. The natural first step for the Christian communities, after their recognition, was to isolate these halls as separate buildings, to make them more conspicuous, and (because of the increasing number of the faithful) to enlarge them. A typical example of such a simple large assembly hall is the church excavated at S. Crisogono in Rome about twenty-five years ago.[18]

The excavated church is a relatively late structure, of the fifth century, single-naved with an apse and side rooms, and with a narthex (an entrance hall) in the front part of the nave. Within this building, however, the remains of an older building are preserved, still discernible because of the differences in the masonry. This older construction was a simple hall, with three arched openings in its façade and with doorways probably leading into open porticoes, or side rooms, along the flanks of the church (Text Fig. 2). That this simple hall was

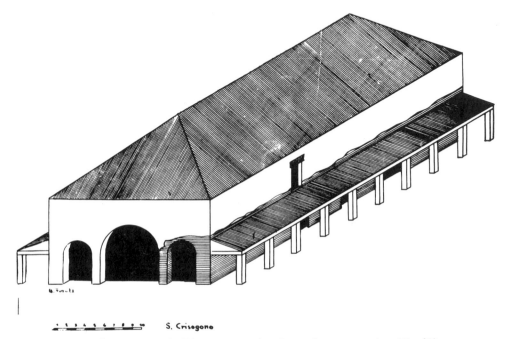

S. Crisogono

Text fig. 2. Rome, S. Crisogono, exterior, isometric reconstruction (Frankl)

a church is proved by the tradition of the site, by the existence of choir screens which separate a "nave" for the faithful from a "choir" for the clergy, and by the openings in the side walls, which would also fit the ecclesiastical character; the porticoes (or courtyards or side rooms) along the church could serve for the catechumens who had to attend part of the service outside the church. This arrangement recalls two passages in Eusebius' description of the basilica of Tyre:

> . . . Then he considered the rest and the parts outside the church, artfully equipping it with lateral rooms (*exedrai*), and with vast halls on each side which were linked to the flanks of the royal hall and united with the entrances to the central edifice. . . .
>
> . . . Others he arranged under the first outside columns around the quadrangular hall initiating them into the first elements of the letter of the four gospels. Those, however, he joins on both sides to the royal house; catechumens who are still growing and progressing, yet not far away, not a long

way separated from the sight of the divinity which possess the faithful innermost.[19]

But this type of hall itself is in no way distinguished as an ecclesiastical edifice. It is a common Roman type of assembly hall used in administrative and other buildings, such as the single-naved halls at Urspring and Wiesbaden,[20] and the Curia of Diocletian in Rome. It is this type of plan which is found in quite a number of early churches, mostly of the fourth and early fifth centuries, in the more distant provinces of the Christian world such as Dalmatia,[21] Istria,[22] Carinthia,[23] Germany,[24] and Syria.[25]

The diffusion of this type makes it quite evident that in the first decades after the recognition of Christianity by Constantine, when the Christians first appeared in public and erected public edifices, they used for their churches the usual type of secular public building without transforming it in any considerable way. To them a meeting was first of all a meeting, and evidently it made no great difference to their architects whether its purpose was ecclesiastical or secular. Were it not for the choir screens, and for the priests' bench which sometimes appears, the special function of the edifice would not be evident. These features, however, are important, for they show the separation of a more and a less important part within the assembly room, and thus a hierarchic separation quite different from the design of a common lay-brotherly congregation room as it existed in SS. Giovanni e Paolo. A step in the same direction was the general adoption of the longitudinal (instead of the transverse) plan, by which the altar became the dominating feature of the edifice, instead of a simple piece of furniture. The assembly hall was subordinated to the altar; the place set apart for the clergy became more important than the place for the congregation; the first signs of the transformation from the assembly hall into what a developed Catholicism would call a true church now became evident.

How earlier types of assembly halls were taken over by the Church, and transformed in varied ways, is shown also in the church of Sta. Croce in Rome, founded about 350 A.D. Under the Baroque decoration numerous older structures are hidden.[26] The interior walls of the nave are clearly twelfth-century, to judge by their masonry, and this is confirmed by the fact that Lucius II remodelled the church between 1144 and 1146. But the exterior walls of the building are much earlier, even older than the transformation into a church in the fourth century. Their masonry shows that they are early third-century, and we know that the edifice originally formed a part of the Sessorian palace. In this original state it presented itself as a large oblong transverse hall with five large archways opening onto a courtyard, and above them a series of five large windows (Text Fig. 3). A similar row of arches in the rear opened into a back room, also with five windows in the upper wall. On the shorter sides were two rows of windows, one above the other, and some secondary rooms. This older palace hall was given to the church, and was transformed, in the second half of the fourth century, for its new ecclesiastical purpose, by adding an apse to one of the short side walls. This, of course, involved the shifting of the axis from a transverse to a longitudinal direction. While those facts are generally known,[27] a new and rather surprising feature was discovered during our recent investigations: simultaneously with the addition of the apse the interior of the edifice had been altered by the addition of two series of transverse arches which crossed the width of the nave. Remains of these arches are still preserved, and although their traces are very small they are sufficient for a reconstruction of the arrangement. Three pieces of walls, later than the original walls of the building and contemporaneous with the apse, show the places where the transverse walls had been inserted in the flanks of the older building, and the remnant of an arch, visible under and within the twelfth-century interior wall of the nave, shows that each of these transverse walls was supported by three arches. Even the columns on which these arches rested are still preserved in the present building. Thus the Early Christian transformation of Sta. Croce appears as a hall with an apse and with two series of arches, arranged in a rhythmical pattern, with two wider bays flanking a narrow one. It is a design unique in Roman churches, which finds its only parallels in a quite distant province of Early Christian architecture, in the Djebel Hauran in Southern Syria,[28] in the pagan (?) basilica of Shakka, and in a few churches, e.g., at Tafha, at Nimreh, and in the church at Kanawat which was attached to the south flank of the atrium of an older pagan (?) basilica. This last was also remodelled at the same time by constructing transverse arches across its nave and aisles, and in this remodelling a rhythmical pattern was created similar to the one used at Sta. Croce in Rome.

Aside from the importance of this discovery from the point of view of the history of architecture, the interesting fact about Sta. Croce is that the audience hall of a palace was used in the middle of the fourth century to fit the needs of the Church. Apparently, even by 350 A.D. the Church had not yet developed any one type of Christian edifice which exclusively dominated ecclesiastical architecture. A secular type at hand could be used, with the addition of only a few features which were evidently considered indispensable for the conception of a Christian church,—the apse, and the shifting of the edifice from a transverse to a longitudinal axis. While the latter element had appeared before, e.g., at S. Crisogono, and in the group of related churches, the apse is certainly a feature which stresses even more the subordination of the part of the building reserved for the congregation to that reserved for the clergy. But even this element of subordination, the apse, is taken from Roman pagan architecture, where it appears frequently from the first century on in public buildings, and in the audience halls of the imperial palaces, such as the audience hall of Domitian on the Palatine, two halls of the Domus Aurea, and any other audience hall where a dominating man or a dominating group—a law court, for example—received a crowd of common people, as in the three halls at the Forum of Pompeii, or in the "auditorium" of Maecenas in Rome. That it is taken up in ecclesiastical architecture shows quite clearly that God is conceived to be more and more like an

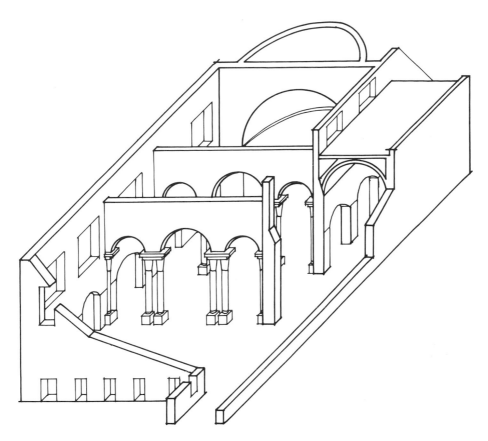

Text fig. 3. Rome, Sta. Croce in Gerusalemme, interior, isometric reconstruction (Frankl)

earthly ruler, similar to the Emperor, and that the clergy is conceived as a body representative of God, just as the high officials of the state represent the Emperor. It is during the second quarter of the fourth century, shortly before the death of Constantine, that Christ, surrounded by the Apostles, is depicted like an Emperor surrounded by his Senate; it is about this time that He is addressed as Basileus, as King of Kings, and is represented with a halo, an imperial attribute, and in imperial dress.[29] This assimilation of the image of God to that of the Emperor makes it understandable that His house also should no longer be conceived of as a simple meeting place, but as an audience hall. Indeed, the development of state philosophy had led more and more to the conception of the audience hall of the imperial palace as a sacred place, a temple, the idol of which was the Emperor's person.[30] This idea is carried over into the Church, and it is quite characteristic that in some edifices of the period, for instance in the church of Sta. Balbina, it is still uncertain whether the edifice was built as a church, or whether it was an audience hall and only later taken over by the church.

There are other unusual types to be found in Roman architecture of the fourth century. The first church at Sant' Anastasia had, in all likelihood, a single nave, a wide transept and a semi-circular apse, thus forming a cross-shaped edifice of a type which seems to be unique in Rome. Its apse and transept are still preserved today,[31] although they have been remodelled in the eighth, fifteenth, seventeenth and eighteenth centuries.

While these different types of congregational and audience halls dominated the ecclesiastical architecture of the city of Rome, other church buildings, again different from the Early Christian basilica, were evolved in the catacombs. There also, in the vast burial grounds of the Christian communities, with their network of galleries at different levels underneath the ground, structures had to be erected in the first half of the fourth century in order to single out the tomb of some martyr buried in the catacombs, and to provide a room for the prayers of the faithful, for occasional services, and also for the agape, all of which, up to the end of the fourth century, took place over the tomb.[32] It is obvious that these catacomb churches were normally relatively small buildings, since they did not have to shelter either very large congregations or regular meetings; indeed, the buildings are often mere chapels (as is the one at SS. Nereo ed Achilleo in Domitilla, datable 366-84, which we excavated a year ago, and which is only twenty feet square). They seem to have developed, not from congregational or audience halls, but from larger tomb chambers in the catacombs such as the "Chapel of the Popes," and like these, they were originally built immediately over the tomb of the saint in the catacomb proper, i.e., underground.

As soon, however, as they grew larger (and that was the case from the second quarter of the fourth century on) a new problem arose. On the one hand, the floor level had to reach the tomb of the saint which was situated deep in the ground, on the first, second, or third level of the catacombs. On the other hand, they had to be provided with light and air, and to be made accessible to larger crowds, who could no longer be led through the dark, narrow labyrinths of the catacomb. This technical problem was solved by the "invention" of the cemeterial basilica, a structure whose floor was kept underground, at the catacomb level, while its upper parts emerged from the ground. The remains of a very early catacomb church of the period immediately after Constantine, datable 335-51, are preserved under the present seventh-century church of Sant' Agnese. It was a rather long and narrow single-naved edifice, about thirty by ninety Roman feet, with an apse, and surrounded by chapels,[33] similar to the somewhat later catacomb church of S. Ermete, and to cemeterial basilicas outside Rome.[34] Again it is a solution quite different from the normal Early Christian basilica, and so is the even more unusual cemeterial church of S. Sebastiano, where the aisles not only accompany the nave, but also encircle the apse, forming an ambulatory through which the congregation might pass to see the sacred place, the *memoria Apostolorum*.[35]

Thus, numerous types of ecclesiastical buildings appeared in Early Christian architecture under Constantine. Among these ecclesiastical edifices which are so different in type, there originated in the early fourth century the Early Christian basilica. Strangely enough, it is this type which is best known, although the earliest examples (those dating from the period of Constantine) are no longer extant, either in the West or in the East of the Empire. In Rome, both St. Peter's and the basilica of the Lateran were destroyed in the sixteenth and seventeenth centuries respectively, when the modern constructions of Michelangelo and Borromini were substituted for them. The ancient drawings and descriptions are, however, quite sufficient to give a clear idea of their original appearance, especially when they are combined with the results of the excavations undertaken by Professor E. Josi at the Lateran,[36] and the results of a thorough investigation of the extant remains of that basilica. Both edifices were enormous basilicas (about 500 Roman feet long), consisting of a nave and four aisles, separated from each other by columns; the columns at St. Peter's carried an architrave, at the Lateran arcades, and above them there were wall paintings and a clerestory with wide windows. The whole interior was magnificently decorated. An atrium extended in front of the nave, and at the opposite end was a transept with a semicircular apse; the transept contained the main altar, the apse, the seats of the bishop and of his presbyters.

Numerous explanations have been proffered to explain the origin of this new type in Early Christian architecture: the Roman house with its atrium;[37] the *oikos*, the large dining room of the Roman house; the private basilica;[38] the Greek peristyle;[39] the *schola;*[40] the Roman secular basilica;[41] the Jewish temple;[42] the *cella trichora*[43]—in brief, practically every building of antiquity. It seems to me that none of these explanations can rest on safe ground unless a few facts are kept in mind. First, that *all* the different types of Christian edifices, after Christianity had become a recognized religion and its constructions had received a public character, are definitely connected, not only with Roman architecture in general, but with Roman assembly halls in particular. Second, that throughout the Roman Empire during the first half of the fourth century, the basilica as represented by St. Peter's and the Lateran (Figs. 2, 12, 79; 5), or by the corresponding basilicas in the East—the one near the Holy Sepulchre or the Church of the Nativity, or the Eleona—is only one, and almost an exceptional form among numerous Christian edifices of different pattern. Third, that it appears in different parts of the *Orbis Christianus,* at Jerusalem, Rome, Mambre, Bethlehem, Orléansville, Naples, Capua,—and that wherever it appears (except for a few cases where the fact cannot be proved)[44] its foundation is related to Constantine's personal influence. Fourth, that Constantine wanted to make the churches which he erected as lavish and beautiful as possible, with the express intention of having them surpass in splendor all other public edifices,[45] and thus emphasize the importance of the new state religion. And fifth, that while single features, such as the transept and the atrium in Rome, or the circular *memoria* and the precinct wall in the East, are evidently local features and can thus be disregarded as far as the question of the origin of the type proper is concerned, the general arrangement is surprisingly uniform.

Seen from this angle, the problem acquires a different aspect. The basic similarity of the first real Early Christian basilicas, whether they stood in the East or in the West of the Empire, combined with the fact that nearly all of them were personal foundations of Constantine; the contrast, on the other hand, in which these imperial churches stand to the numerous other ecclesiastical edifices erected by the Christian communities at the very same time; all this lends itself to the conclusion that the first basilicas were modelled according to definite directions, issued by the imperial office of works for the erection of imperial ecclesiastical buildings, directions within the limits of which the local executive architect enjoyed a certain liberty of action. On the other hand, it is also likely that these imperial churches were modelled after the pattern of some secular assembly hall, transformed for the new ecclesiastical purpose, assembly halls of a pretentious kind, however, so that the transformation would reflect the greatness of the imperial founder and offer room for the largest possible public gatherings.

In any town of the Roman Empire there existed secular basilicas, the official halls for large public gatherings.[46] They were meeting places which might be used as law courts, stock exchanges, bazaars, or for hundreds of similar purposes. Whoever knows Italy knows the last descendant of these basilicas:—the *gallerias,* which are to be found in any fairly large city of Italy, and which still serve the foremost of the purposes of the Roman secular basilica—everyone knows that between noon and one o'clock he can meet his friends somewhere in the *galleria.* But a basilica was something more than a simple meeting place: first, it was in most cases an imperial foundation, and very often named after the reigning Emperor, a highly official edifice (incidentally the modern *galleria* resembles the ancient basilica even on this point: it is always called after the king reigning during its construction). From the early imperial period on, the basilica was used for all kinds of state functions. To give just one instance: Augustus' dead body, when carried from Nola to Rome, lay in state in the basilica of the town where the funeral procession spent the night.[47]

For our problem, however, it seems even more important that the basilica was not merely a public official edifice, but that at least one religious, or semi-religious, function was connected with it. For it usually contained in an adjoining room, in an apse, or in the building itself, the tribunal where the praetor administered the law.[48] Now it is sufficiently known how the essence of Roman state religion is focussed more and more in the Emperor's person, and in his genius, from Augustus' time on.[49] Temples were erected to him throughout the Empire, and the official oath had to be sworn by invoking his genius.[50] In the sanctuaries of military camps, where the military oath was sworn and where the eagles were kept, the presence of an image of the Emperor was even obligatory.[51] On the other hand, these military sanctuaries were quite frequently connected with the military basilicas of the camps [52] in the same way in which the tribunal was connected with the forensic basilicas of the cities. Thus the connection of the Emperor's divine personality with the tribunal of a civic basilica becomes rather likely. Indeed, as early as the time of Christ the tribunal in Vitruvius' basilica of Fano was situated within a niche which linked the basilica to a shrine of Augustus, thus placing the court immediately under the protection of the Emperor's genius.[53] It is also well known how, in the trial against Christians, the defendants are always asked to swear by the Emperor's genius,[54] and to sacrifice to the Emperor's statue. Since, however, the trials took place in the tribunal, is it not likely that a statue of the Emperor was present at the very spot, so that the sacrifice could be made to it then and there, before the eyes of the investigating official? [55] One might even say that, because of this fact, the connection between the tribunal in the basilica and the image of the Emperor must have been particularly strong in the minds of the Christians.

To sum up:—the secular basilica was not merely a secular building, an element of governmental power; the tribunal was connected with it, and the conceptions of Emperor and basilica were closely linked up with each other. Thus, a religious or semi-religious element was connected with the conception of the civic basilica. The Emperor represented to late antiquity, pagan and Christian, a divine power; with the rise of Christianity to the rank of state religion, an assimilation of the Christian cult and of Christian conceptions to the cult of the Emperor's genius took place.[56]

On the other hand, it must be remembered that, to the Early Christian mind, the ecclesiastical assembly hall did not represent a sacred edifice in the sense which later became dominant. In the third century it is stated several times that the hall where the congregation meets is not at all a "temple," [57] and although this attitude changes under Constantine through the formation of the new conception of Christ,[58] the differentiation between the more sacred memorial buildings erected on the venerated spots proper, and the less sacred congregational hall, the basilica, is still clear in many of the ecclesiastical edifices of his period.[59] Only in the later years of Constantine's reign is this conception gradually replaced by a more sacred idea of the congregational hall proper. The formation of the Early Christian basilica belongs to this transitional period. Thus it must have seemed natural to the architects of Constantine, when they were called on to create the new Christian churches, to refer to the secular basilicas of the Roman tradition, which had been pretentious public meeting places, very often imperial foundations, and at the same time closely connected with the idea of state religion. When Constantine founded the first monumental edifices of the new state religion, Christianity, he not only turned to a well-known monumental type of public building, but to public buildings which were intimately linked up with the conception of the identity of religion and state. That this religion was now Christianity instead of paganism did not influence the basic conception, and one ought not to forget that the older identification of the Emperor with the divinity was an idea which in Constantine's philosophy was still a decisive issue; his self-stylization as Sol Invictus, the invincible sun, is a definite proof of this.

Proofs of the connection between the secular and the ecclesiastical basilica are frequently offered in the way the word basilica is used. Constantine, in ordering the Bishop of Jerusalem to erect a church at the Holy Sepulchre, writes that he wants this basilica to be "more beautiful than any of the others anywhere." [60] The Pilgrim from Bordeaux who, in 333, visited the Holy Land, in speaking about the Constantinian church at the Holy Sepulchre, qualifies the word "basilica" by saying "basilica id est dominicum," a basilica, that is to say, a house of the Lord.[61] Everyone knew what a basilica was. If the Pilgrim had to add the explanation "dominicum," it can only mean that he wanted to make it clear that the new edifice was not just any basilica, but a basilica for Christian worship.

Of course, it would be entirely fallacious to assume that the architects of Constantine simply took over the type of the secular basilica. That type was only a working basis on which something new had to be created, and the Early Christian basilica, instead of being a derivative from the secular basilica, had better be considered as a free variant on the old theme. Even so, however, the new Christian type is but the transformation of a Roman basic pattern; again Christian architecture reveals itself as an outgrowth of the architecture of the late Roman Empire.[62] As to the form of the Roman secular basilicas,[63] there existed certain conventions which were broken only in exceptional cases; it was always an oblong building, normally with one of its long sides along the market place, the forum. Its entrance was generally from the forum; only in a few groups of basilicas, in Italy,[64] in Africa [65] and in the Near East,[66] does the small side contain the entrance, while other basilicas, such as the Aemilia in Rome and the Basilica at Ostia, had two entrances, one from the forum on the long side, and one from the street on the small side. The interior of the basilica consisted of a nave, which was normally accompanied by two aisles, or surrounded on all four sides by aisles. The aisles sometimes had galleries above them. The whole design of the building was centered on the nave, the aisles playing only a subordinate role. If apses were included in the construction, there were frequently two or three, attached to the two small sides, or to the two small sides and one long side of the edifice; usually they were separated from the nave by the aisles or by a series of columns. Variations occur, but never in the basic design, and it seems that the type was maintained relatively intact from the earliest instances in the first half of the first, or in the second century B.C.,[67] until the end of the third century A.D.

It will be obvious that some of these features are likewise essential to the Early Christian basilica: the nave and the aisles exist in both structures, the apse is present, and sometimes the galleries also make their appearance. But, of course, the type had to be transformed. First of all, the centralization of the secular basilica was eventually changed. The entrance, which frequently had been on one of the long sides, was now mostly transferred to one of the short sides. The forum itself, which in most cases had been on the long side, migrated to the small side and became the atrium. The aisles, instead of surrounding the nave on its four sides, as had been usual in most Roman basilicas, accompanied it only on its long sides; the apse, instead of being cut off from the nave, was made to open directly onto it, or onto the transept. The clerestory became much higher. Thus the Early Christian basilica is certainly not a copy of the secular, nor is it directly derived from it. It is a new creation based on a traditional type, and adapted to a new function. In the process of this transformation, different variants were created in the different provinces of the Empire, employing the galleries in the Near East, the double apses in North Africa, or arranging in one instance four aisles, in another two, along the nave.

The process of this transformation is still visible in quite a number of Constantinian Christian basilicas. In Old St. Peter's, for example, there seem still to have been preserved some traces of the centralizing conception of the Roman secular basilica (Fig. 2). The large cornice was protected by a railing so that one could walk on it,[68] and it surrounded the nave even on its entrance side, thus showing a certain similarity to the galleries which, in the secular basilicas, were frequently arranged above the aisles, and which together with the aisles surrounded the nave on all four sides.[69] At S. Clemente, it was the aisles which continued on the entrance side of the basilica,[70] as though it were a secular one; and as the aisles had opened with a series of wide entrances onto the forum in a secular basilica, the aisles on the short side of S. Clemente opened directly onto the atrium, and created an immediate connection between the exterior and the interior of the edifice. A similar arrangement of an aisle on the entrance side of the nave is found at Sta. Sabina, as late as the second quarter of the fifth century.

Some other rudiments in a number of Early Christian basilicas point in the same direction: the windows are often arranged in such a way as to surround the nave like a continuous band on all its sides, at the entrance side as well as above the triumphal arch; the entrances, instead of being limited to the short flank, are often also located on the long flanks, at times even exclusively.[71] Only gradually, during the fourth and fifth centuries, does the longitudinal tendency definitely replace the older centralizing arrangement of the Roman secular basilica.

The question of the causes and purposes of these transformations still remains. It is obvious that quite a number of them may be accounted for by the new function of the buildings; the apse had to open directly into the nave instead of being cut off, since it normally held the altar, and was therefore the center of the service; and one might say that, consequently, the side opposite had to become the entrance wall, and the centralized character had to be replaced by a longitudinal arrangement. I wonder sometimes whether this is not too much of a rationalization, and whether everything can really be explained in this way. There may be other trends which might account for the decisive transformation through which the secular basilica became an ecclesiastical edifice.

It is perfectly possible that other types of late antique architecture which were common in religious and secular buildings exercised a considerable influence in this transformation. The *oikos corinthios,* with its nave and two aisles, and a rectangular or semicircular apse,[72] played evidently an ever growing role in late antique architecture, influencing other secular types such as *nymphaea,*[73] audience halls,[74] private basilicas,[75] and sacred edifices such as the mystery temples of certain sects.[76] Simultaneously the *oikos corinthios* became more and more assimilated to the plan of the secular basilica. But to go into the details of these questions would lead too far. My problem has been to show how in pre-Constantinian times the Christian communities adapted their religious edifices from a non-public type of building; how later under Constantine, when Christianity had been recognized as an official religion, numerous forms of public places of worship arose side by side; and how, among all these varied types, the Early Christian basilica developed probably under the direct initiative of Constantine, as a monument to both the imperial conception of God and the divine conception of the Emperor.

Notes

1. See, for instance, *Acts* 1:13; 16:15; 20:7 ff.; 21:18 ff.

2. The synagogues of the Jewish communities seem to have become unavailable for the newly developing Christian sects as early as the period of St. Paul. See *Acts* 9:20 ff.; 14:1 ff.

3. *C. Plinii Secundi Epistularum libri decem,* ed. E. T. Merrill, X (Leipzig, 1922), 97; Justin Martyr, *First Apology,* Ch. 65–67; *Didache* 8–14. For these see J. C. Ayer, *A Sourcebook for Ancient Church History* (New York, 1913); Tertullian, *Apologeticus adversus gentes,* XXXIX (*PL,* I, col. 538; *The Ante-Nicene Fathers,* III, 47): "de solo triclinio Christianorum refractatur . . . ;" the interpolation "modest supper-room" in the translation of the *A.N.F.* seems not to be justified.

4. Letter of Pope Cornelius to Bishop Fabius, in Eusebius, *Eccles. Hist.,* VI, 43 (*The Nicene and Post-Nicene Fathers,* Second Series, I, 286 ff.)

5. A. Harnack, *The Expansion of Christianity,* trans. J. Moffat (New York, 1904–1905), II, 200 ff.

6. E. Caspar, *Geschichte des Papsttums* (Tübingen, 1930–33), I, 50 ff.

7. J. P. Kirsch, *Die römischen Titelkirchen im Altertum* (Paderborn, 1918).

8. Earlier attempts were made by Germano di S. Stanislao, *La casa celimontana dei SS. martiri Giovanni e Paolo* (Rome, 1894); E. Junyent, *Il titolo di S. Clemente* (Rome, 1932), pp. 107 ff.

9. See also Junyent, *op. cit.,* p. 111.

10. Although the paintings on the walls of the staircase and the Confessio are hardly earlier in date than the middle of the fourth century, the masonry of these walls points definitely to the first half of the century.

11. The persecutions seem to have been directed more against individuals who refused to bring the due sacrifices, than

against the communities *qua* communities. See Ayer (above, note 3) and R. Knopf, *Ausgewählte Martyrerakten* (Leipzig, 1901).

12. See Lampridius, *Vita Alexandri Severi* (*Scriptores historiae Augustae*), Ch. 49.

13. Kirsch, *op. cit.*, pp. 175 ff.

14. Junyent, *op. cit.*, pp. 86 ff.

15. *Excavations at Dura-Europos. Preliminary Report of Fifth Season of the Excavations (1931–1932) Conducted by Yale University. The Christian Church at Dura-Europos,* by C. Hopkins and P. V. C. Baur (New Haven, Conn., 1934).

16. E. Renan, "La synagogue de Hammam-Lif," *RA,* I (1883), 157 ff.; II (1884), 273 ff.; *Excavations at Dura-Europos, Report of Sixth Season (1932–1933)* (New Haven, 1936); E. L. Sukenik, "The Ancient Synagogue of El-Hammeh," *Journal of the Palestine Archeological Society* (1935).

17. For instance, in the house with the mithraeum below the apse of S. Clemente in Rome, Junyent, *op. cit.*, pp. 66 ff.

18. M. Mesnard, *La basilique de St. Chrysogone à Rome* (Vatican City, 1935); R. Krautheimer, *Corpus,* I.

19. Eusebius, *op. cit.,* X, Chap. IV, 45, 63 (*PG, XX,* cols. 868, 873 ff.; *The Nicene and Post-Nicene Fathers,* Second Series, I, 375 ff.).

20. *Germania romana,* ed. F. Koepp, I, *Die Bauten des römischen Heeres* (2nd ed., Bamberg, 1924), Pl. XII, 1; XIV.

21. W. Gerber, R. Egger, and E. Dyggve, *Forschungen in Salona,* I (Vienna, 1917): Oratory in the North Thermae.

22. W. Gerber, *Altchristliche Kultbauten Istriens und Dalmatiens* (Dresden, 1912); R. Egger, *Frühchristliche Kirchenbauten im südlichen Norikum* (Sonderschriften des österr. archäol. Inst., [Vienna, 1916]); K. Lanckoronski-Brzezie and G. Niemann, *Der Dom von Aquileia* (Vienna, 1906); C. Cecchelli *et al., La basilica di Aquileia* (Bologna, 1933); A. Gnirs, "Frühe christliche Kultanlagen im südlichen Istrien," *Jahrbuch . . . der KK Zentralkommission,* V (1911), *Beiblatt,* 1 ff. (1911); regarding Nesactium, north church; and Parenzo, south buildings. Sometimes the roof is carried by interior rows of supports: Aquileia; Parenzo, south church; Brioni; Pola.

23. Egger, *op. cit.*: Hemmaberg, before middle of fifth century; Gratzkogel near Virunum (Zollfeld); Aguntum near Linz, Tyrol (with side entrance).

24. E. J. R. Schmidt, *Kirchliche Bauten des frühen Mittelalters in Südwestdeutschland* (Mainz, 1932); H. Lehner and W. Bader, "Baugeschichtliche Untersuchungen am Bonner Münster," *Bonner Jahrbücher,* Heft 136-37 (1932); W. Bader, "Ausgrabungen unter dem Xantener Dom," *Germania,* XVIII (1934), 112 ff. Mainz, St. Alban; Bonn, Cathedral; Xanten, Cathedral.

25. H. C. Butler, *Early Churches in Syria* (Princeton, 1929): chapels at Kasril Muddakhkhin, 'Anz; Dâr Kitâ, Banâkfur, Il-Ubêr.

26. H. Hübsch, *Die altchristlichen Kirchen* (Carlsruhe, 1862–1863); A. Stegensek, "Architektonische Untersuchung von S. Croce," *RQuSchr,* XV (1900), 176 ff.; G. Biasiotti and S. Pesarini, "Pitture del XII secolo . . . nella basilica di S. Croce," *Studi romani,* I (1913); Krautheimer, *Corpus,* I, 165 ff.

27. Hübsch, *loc. cit.*; Stegensek, *loc. cit.*; Biasiotti and Pesarini, *loc. cit.*

28. Butler, *op. cit., passim.*

29. See particularly J. Kollwitz, "Christus als Lehrer und die Gesetzesübergabe an Petrus," *RQuSchr,* XLIV (1936), 45 ff.; W. Weisbach, *Geschichtliche Voraussetzungen der Entstehung einer christlichen Kunst* (Basel, 1937).

30. A. Alföldi, "Die Ausgestaltung des monarchischen Zeremoniells am römischen Kaiserhof," *RM,* XLIX (1934) 1 ff.; *Idem,* "Insignien und Tracht der römischen Kaiser," *ibid.,* L (1935), 3 ff.

31. Krautheimer, *Corpus,* I, 42 ff.

32. Augustines, *Epistles,* XX, Ch. 1, 34; XXIX, *passim* (*PL* XXXIII, cols. 91, 114 ff.); St. Augustine, *Select Letters,* ed. J. H. Baxter ("Loeb Classical Library" [Cambridge, Mass., 1930]), p. 44, where other references from Cyprian and Ambrose are quoted, and p. 84.

33. Krautheimer. *Corpus,* I, 14 ff.

34. Salona, Manastirine, second phase, 313–60: see R. Egger and F. Bulic, *Forschungen in Salona,* II (Vienna 1926); Damus el Karita, see J. Vaultrin, "Les

basiliques chrétiennes de Carthage," *Revue africaine*, LXXIII (1932).

35. F. Fornari, "Il rilievo . . . di San Sebastiano . . . ," *Atti del III° Congresso di archeologia cristiana* (1934), pp. 315 ff.; P. Styger, *Märtyrergrüfte* (Berlin, 1935); A. Prandi, *La memoria Apostolorum* (Vatican, 1936).

36. E. Josi, "Scoperte nella basilica Constantiniana al Laterano," *RACrist*, XI (1934), 335 ff.

37. G. Dehio and C. Bezold, *Die Kirchliche Baukunst des Abendlandes*, I (Stuttgart, 1887–1901).

38. P. Crostarosa, "Le basiliche cristiane," *DissPontAcc*. s.2, IV (1891–1892), 311 ff.

39. V. Schultze, *Archäologie der altchristlichen Kunst* (Munich, 1895).

40. G. B. Brown, *From Schola to Cathedral* (Edinburgh, 1886).

41. K. Lange, *Haus und Halle* (Leipzig, 1885).

42. O. Puchstein, "Die Säule in der assyrischen Architektur," *JdI*, VII (1892), 11 ff., n. 32.

43. E. H. Freshfield, *Cellae Trichorae* (privately printed, 1913); J. P. Richter, *Der Ursprung der abendländischen Kirchengebäude* (Vienna, 1878); G. B. de' Rossi, *Roma sotterranea* (Rome, 1864–1877), III, *passim*.

44. Such as Orléansville and Tyre; I am, however, not quite sure whether Tyre was a basilica proper.

45. See his letter to Makarios, in Eusebius, *Life of Constantine*, III, 31 (*PG*, XX, col. 1091; *The Nicene and Post-Nicene Fathers*, second series, I, 528).

46. A. Zestermann, *Die antiken und die christlichen Basiliken* (Leipzig, 1847); R. Schultze, *Basilika* (Berlin, 1928).

47. Suetonius, "Divus Augustus," Chap. 100, ed. E. S. Shuckburgh (Cambridge, 1896), p. 172; ". . . in basilica cuiusque oppidi vel in aedium sacrarum maxima . . ."; see A. Mau "Basilica," in *RE*, III, 84.

48. Mau, *loc. cit.*; Schultze, *op. cit.*

49. L. R. Taylor, *The Divinity of the Roman Emperor* (Middletown, Conn., 1931); Alföldi, *op. cit.*

50. Taylor, *op. cit.*, p. 241; Th. Mommsen, *Römisches Staatsrecht*, II, no. 2 (Leipzig, 1887), 809 ff.

51. Mommsen, *op. cit.*, pp. 814 ff.; Alföldi, *op. cit.*, pp. 67 ff.

52. Schultze, *op. cit., passim*.

53. Vitruvius, *De Architectura libri decem*, Lib. V, Ch. I; the question of how to reconstruct this niche does not concern this study. See, however, Alföldi, *loc. cit.*; Mau, *loc. cit.*; Prestel, *Des Markus Vitruvius Pollio zehn Bücher über Architektur* (Strassburg, 1912); Schultze, *op. cit.*, pp. 39 ff.

54. "Passio Martyrum Scilitanorum," in Ayer, *op. cit.*, pp. 67 ff.

55. Pliny's statement (Ep. 97. See above, note 3) that he had an image of the Emperor brought in to have the Christians swear the oath of allegiance to it would be contrary to this assumption, if it could be proved that the inquiry took place at a regular court session; but the interpolation "brought into court" which is given by Ayer, *loc. cit.*, is not in any way justifiable: Pliny says simply: ". . . cum imagini tua quam propter hoc iusseram cum simulacris deorum adferri, . . . ture ac vino supplicarent. . . ." The whole tenor of the report seems to indicate rather a semi-private, not a highly official inquiry.

56. Alföldi, *op. cit.*, pp. 73 ff.; Kollwitz, *op. cit., passim*; to quote some problems: proskynesis and adoration; Christ with the imperial insignia, etc.

57. Minucius Felix, *Octavius*, Chaps. X, XXXII: ". . . cur nullas aras habent, templa nulla . . . ; . . . delubra et aras non habemus . . ." (*PL*, III, cols. 274, 353 ff.; *The Ante-Nicene Fathers*, IV, 178, 193); Tertullian, *Apologeticus*, XXXIX (see above, n. 3).

58. See above, *passim*.

59. Architecturally, the distinction between the congregational hall and the memorial building is obvious in almost all the ecclesiastical edifices of the Near East (Jerusalem, Holy Sepulchre; Bethlehem), and in some of the West (Rome, Sta. Croce). Philologically it is confirmed, e.g., in Eusebius, *Life of Constantine*, III, 43 (*PG*, XX, col. 1105): ". . . ἱερὸν οἶκον ἐκκλησίας . . . νεών τε . . ." The "congregational hall" (namely the basilica of the Eleona) and the "temple" (namely the

Rotunda of the Ascension) are obviously contrasted with each other.

60. Eusebius, *ibid.*, III, 31 (*PG*, XX, col. 1091; *The Nicene and Post-Nicene Fathers*, I, 528). The passage has been interpreted controversially either to imply that there existed other Christian basilicas which Constantine wanted to excel by his own building, or that he compared the "ecclesiastical basilica" to the existing "secular basilicas" throughout the Empire. The context seems to favor this latter interpretation. See also L. v. Sybel, *Christliche Antike* (Marburg, 1906–1909), pp. 281 ff.

61. *Anonymi Itinerarium a Burdigala Hierusalem usque* (*PL*, VIII, col. 791).

62. Sybel, *loc. cit.*; G. Leroux, *Les origines de l'édifice hypostyle* (Paris, 1913).

63. R. Schultze, *loc. cit.*; V. Müller, "The Roman Basilica," *AJA*, XLI (1937), 250 ff.

64. Pompeii, Saepinum, Egnacia: Schultze, *op. cit.*, pp. 1 ff.; Lange, *op. cit.*, p. 163.

65. Tipasa, Sigus, Djemila: S. Gsell, *Monuments antiques de l'Algérie* (Paris, 1901).

66. Pergamon, Kremna, Perge: C. Texier, *Description de l'Asie Mineure* (Paris, 1839–1849), *passim;* Lanckoronski-Brzezie, *Städte Pamphiliens und Pisidiens* (Vienna, 1890–1892).

67. Basilica of Ardea: E. Wikén, *Bolletino dell'associazione per gli studi mediterranei* (1934), pp. 7 ff.

68. Drawings: Grimaldi, *Cod. Barb. Lat.* 4410; Ciampini, *De sacris aedificiis* (Rome, 1693), Pl. VIII.

69. Basilica Julia, Basilica Ulpia.

70. Rome: S. Clemente, SS. Giovanni e Paolo, S. Vitale, Sta. Sabina; Constantinople: St. John of the Studion; Salonica: H. Paraskevi, H. Demetrius.

71. North Africa: Orléansville; Matifou; Menas City; Apollonia. Syria: Basufân; Serdjibleh; Kasr Iblisu; Dâr Kitâ, St. Paul and Moses; Burdj-ed-Derun, chapel; and many others. Transjordania: Geras, chapels flanking St. John. See H. Glück, "Der Breit-und-Langhausbau in Syrien," *Zeitschrift für Geschichte der Architektur*, Beiheft 14 (1916).

72. Herculaneum, Casa dell'atrio a mosaico.

73. Unknown nymphaeum, reproduced in eighteenth-century drawing, Windsor Royal Library, vol. 176, no. 9751.

74. Flavian palace on the Palatine: C. Hülsen, *Forum und Palatin* (Munich, 1926), p. 79. Palace of Diocletian, Spalato: E. Hébrard and J. Zeiller, *Spalato* (Paris, 1912), pp. 120 ff.

75. Villa Adriana.

76. Basilica at Porta Maggiore: J. Carcopino, *La basilique pythagorienne de la Porte Majeure* (Paris, 1926); Pesch: Schultze, *op. cit.;* Basilica of Matronae Vacallinehae, pp. 61 ff.

Postscript

The beginnings of Christian architecture in general and the origins of the Christian basilica in particular have, of course, been a main theme in my work over these past thirty years. In the course of this time the ideas laid down in 1938 in this first summary draft have, I trust, broadened and become both more differentiated and more precise. In particular, they are no longer focused primarily and almost exclusively on church building in Rome and on "regular" churches to boot. The Christian centers in the East, in Africa, in North Italy, and north of the Alps have moved to the fore. The differences between churches for regular services and for the martyr cult, and between churches proper and covered cemeteries, have become important. So have the distinctions between Constantinian and later Christian architecture. These questions I have tried to sum up both in a paper read at Ravenna in 1962 and in my *Early Christian and Byzantine Architecture*. But a number of the ideas outlined in this early paper have remained basic to my thinking through all this time: the fundamental contrast between Christian architecture before and under Constantine, the former domestic, the latter public in function and design; the religious connotations inherent in the function of all "secular" Roman basilicas; the formation of the Christian basilica as a variant on rather than a derivative of Roman public meeting halls; and the variety of church planning under Constantine. Clearly, I would have to modify my views as of 1938 on a few points of import. I have long abandoned the idea that in an early phase of church planning the prayer room customarily was laid out along a transversal axis to be replaced only later by a longitudinal layout—a difference to be explained (if, indeed, it existed) along regional rather than chronological lines. With John Ward Perkins (1954) I would stress within the realm of Roman basilicas the variety in function and design rather than focussing exclusively on the forum basilica of the "Italic" type. On the other hand, in contrast to him, I would bring out even more strongly than I did in 1938 the character of the Christian basilica as just one more among many non-Christian variants—palace basilicas, funerary basilicas, religious basilicas, forum basilicas, thermae basilicas, and so forth. Also, I have come to doubt two assumptions I then made: that the majority of Constantinian basilicas were based on a standard type; and that this was due to specific directives for planning new churches distributed by a special agency. On the contrary, I would stress that architects and church leaders had a pretty free hand in developing regionally different types for different functions: churches for the use of the court; for the regular services of a congregation; for the cult of a *martyrium*, as at Bethlehem and Jerusalem; and for the cult of a martyr and burial of the faithful—S. Croce, the Lateran, St. Peter's. These differences I then did not and possibly could not see.

Three details of significance require revision: the Constantinian basilica at the Lateran had no transept (see below, pp. 21 ff.) and its nave colonnades carried an entablature rather than arcades; for the remodelling of the Roman palace hall into the church of Sta. Croce I now prefer a date between 320 and 330 to the one proposed in 1938, "after 350"; and, in reconstructing the *titulus* of SS. Giovanni e Paolo, I have now overcome my doubts regarding the existence of a row of supports along the transversal axis of the meeting room (*Corpus* I, 295, Fig. 158).

Needless to say, I never wrote the two papers promised in the first footnote. Their content, however, is outlined together with my present views on the beginnings of Christian architecture in my *Early Christian and Byzantine Architecture* and in a couple of papers I am working on at this very moment.

Additional Bibliography

Krautheimer, R. *Corpus*, I (Vatican City, 1937), pp. 267 ff. (1957).

———, "Riflessioni sull'architettura paleocristiana," *Atti VI Congresso internazionale di archeologia cristiana* (Vatican City, 1965), pp. 567 ff.

———, *Early Christian and Byzantine Architecture*, Pelican History of Art (Harmondsworth, 1965).

———, and Corbett, S. "La basilica costantiniana al Laterano," *RACrist* on press.

———, "The Constantinian Basilica," *DOPapers,* XXI, 1957, pp. 115 ff.

Perkins, J. B. Ward. "Constantine and the Origins of the Christian Basilica," *BSR*, 22 (n.s. 9), 1954, pp. 60 ff.

Prandi, A., *Il complesso . . . della basilica . . . dei SS. Giovanni e Paolo* (Rome, 1953).

Apollonj-Ghetti B. M., *S. Crisogono (Le Chiese di Roma illustrate, 92 [Rome, 1966]).*

2

THE CONSTANTINIAN BASILICA
OF THE LATERAN

in collaboration with Spencer Corbett *

RECENT INVESTIGATIONS at the Lateran by the present writers, with the indispensable collaboration of Professor Enrico Josi, and under the auspices of the Pontifical Institute of Christian Archaeology, have added considerably to our knowledge of the Constantinian basilica. The fourth-century foundation walls of this church are easily identifiable. They consist of bulky masses of concrete made principally with big fragments of grey-white marble which are obviously the product of the breaking-up of some quite important building, since pieces of architectural mouldings, capitals, ashlar, etc., frequently appear. During the past century (the first significant excavations date from 1851) such foundation walls have been exposed in many places, and an extensive system of vaults has been formed beneath the floor of the church as one investigation after another has added to our knowledge of the Constantinian building; to say nothing of the earlier structures on top of which the basilica was built, namely the *Castra Nova Equitum Singularium* of the early third century, and certain rich private mansions which lie at a still lower level.[1]

Prior to the studies which are briefly summarized in this article,[2] the following parts of the Constantinian church were known: (*a*) the main apse foundations (Text Fig. 5); (*b*) part of the foundation of the end-wall of the inner south aisle, close to the left shoulder of the apse; (*c*) the foundations of both main nave colonnades from points close to their junction with the apse, for about one-eighth of the total length of the nave; (*d*) two more short lengths of the main nave colonnade foundations on the right hand (north) side of the nave.

A new examination of a cellar which lies beneath the pavement of Galilei's portico has now revealed four blocks of the characteristic marble foundation material projecting into the cellar from its west side (Text Fig. 5). Evidently these are the eastern extremities of the foundation walls of the four colonnades which divided the original basilica into a central nave and four side aisles. Their breadth corresponds with the known thickness of the nave foundation walls. Their spacing corresponds with that of the present aisles and shows, what was hitherto uncertain, that the seventeenth-century aisles have exactly the same breadth as the Constantinian ones, all four of Borromini's rows of pillars standing in the

---

*From *Antiquity*, XXXIV (1960), 201–206.

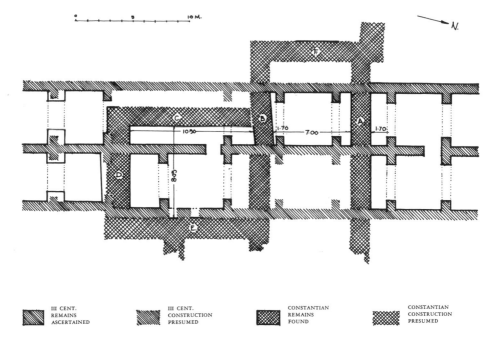

Text fig. 4. Rome, S. Giovanni in Laterano, structure underlying the transept, plan (Corbett)

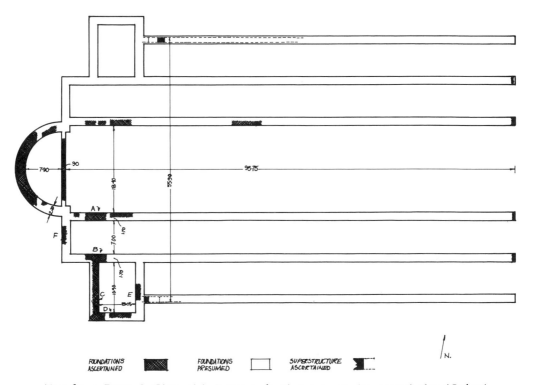

Text fig. 5. Rome, S. Giovanni in Laterano, fourth-century remains, general plan (Corbett)

alignment of the original colonnades and using the original foundations. The extension of the original foundations eastward to a point which is nearly 5 m. outside the east façade has yet to be explained. It may be that Constantine's basilica was longer than the medieval one [3] or, alternatively, that its foundations continued underground beyond the line of the façade for some structural reason which escapes us. As yet no trace of the original façade foundations has appeared.

A sounding in the area beneath the south transept has produced important results (Text Fig. 4). The transept happens to lie on top of a vaulted third-century building which fortunately enables us to approach the church substructures without the inconvenience of raising the floor. The third-century building consists of two parallel underground galleries, roofed with concrete cross vaults, which are undoubtedly the cellars of a long barrack building belonging to the *Castra Nova*. The portion of these cellars which lies beneath the central zone of the transept has long been known, and so too has the extension of the same cellars which lies under the twelfth-century cloisters to the south, but the intervening portion under the south part of the transept has not. When the Constantinian foundation wall of the south nave colonnade (A on the plan) was pierced during the excavations of 1934–1938,[4] the vaults to the south were found to be full of rubble and no further excavations were then undertaken. This rubble has now been partly removed, enabling us to enter the third-century cellars beneath the south part of the transept and examine the Constantinian foundations which intersect them.

At a distance of 7 m. from the south side of wall A the third-century gallery is intersected by another foundation wall (B), also apparently Constantinian, though constructed in masonry rather different from the usual concrete of marble fragments. Although B is not quite parallel with A, it stands nearly enough in the alignment of the outer south colonnade. Whereas the main nave foundations A pass through the barracks vaulting, which was cut away from them, wall B merely impinges on the underside of the vault. We presume that the stylobate above rests on the extrados. The difference between walls A and B reflects the fact that the main nave colonnade bore a much greater weight than the outer one. The slight obliquity of wall B is no more than a builders' mistake; as the preexisting vault was not pierced they were less able to check the wall's straightness than was the case with A.

Continuing our investigations, a hole was cut through wall B (its thickness, 1.70 m., is the same as that of wall A) enabling us to enter the part of the third-century cellar which lies beneath the south end of the transept. Here we were surprised to find a typical Constantinian foundation wall built with the usual marble fragmtnts (C on the plan) lying parallel with the axis of the cellar and thus at right angles to the two foundation walls which we have traversed. After proceeding in a north-south direction for nearly 11 m. the masonry forms a right angle and becomes wall D. Wall D lies directly underneath the south wall of the transept. The southern, or external face of wall D, and the angle between C and D is also seen in the southward continuation of the cellar, under-neath the cloisters.[5]

Wall D crosses the western gallery of the cellar and continues for the full breadth of the parallel eastern gallery. Walls B, C, and D thus form three sides of an approximately rectangular compartment and, in order to establish the eastern limit of the compartment, we made two small openings in the east side wall of the gallery. The fourth wall immediately appeared (E on the plan) touching the exterior of the barrack building.

So much for the foundations. Of the superstructure of the Constantinian church very little has yet been found. Certainly the original colonnades and clerestory walls of the main nave have perished; everything that can be seen behind and above the seventeeth-century decorations is evidently of late medieval date. But the side walls of the outer aisles, where they have not been removed to make entrances to successive side chapels, seem here and there to include fragments which survive from the Constantinian structure. Two such fourth-century fragments are especially important because they contain the remains of windows, one on each side of the basilica, both near the point where the basilica walls are interrupted by the lateral projections of the transept (Fig. 4). We surmise that there was a row of windows in each side wall, spaced to correspond with the arcading of the outer colonnades. The northern fragment also discloses a side entrance to the north aisle close to the angle now formed by the transept.[6]

The main outlines of the plan of Constantine's basilica can thus be recon-structed with some confidence (Text Fig. 5). In its western part the original church is now seen to differ fundamentally from all the hypothetical plans that have hitherto been advanced. It is certain that there was no transept in the usual sense of the word; and it may be noted in passing that the masonry of the present structure (wherever it can be seen) is all of late medieval date. Neither was it a simple basilica of four aisles continuing for the whole length of the nave and terminating against an end-wall in line with the apse front.[7] Nor, for that matter, was there a tri-partite or a quin-partite transept[8] as was once proposed in explanation of the continuous nave stylobates beneath the transept. We now know that the original church had the following features. The stylobates of the main nave colonnades continued, apparently uninterrupted by a triumphal arch, right up to the apse front. The inner aisles had the same length as the main colonnades; witness the foundations of the end-wall (F) on the south side of the apse. The outer aisles, on the other hand, were some 15 m. shorter than the inner ones, ending at wall E. To the west of wall E there was a projecting, wing-like chamber which extended some 4 m. beyond the alignment of the aisle wall. Its increased breadth suggests that the roof of the wing chamber was higher than the aisle roof. It seems likely to have appeared on the outside of the basilica as a lateral annex, having some of the characteristics of a transept, but unconnected with the nave. It might perhaps be termed an aisle-transept (Fig. 5).

Inside the church the means of communication between the aisle-transept and the adjacent aisles must remain an open question. Our ignorance of what stood on top of the foundation walls allows several hypothetical combinations of archways, doors, solid walls and colonnades. Likewise, the function of the chamber remains obscure; though it may seem not unreasonable to guess that it could have served for the reception of offerings at the beginning of the *missa fidelium*.

Our studies have been confined to the south half of the basilica and the existence of corresponding features on the north is, as yet, hypothetical. However, the massive scale of the foundations discovered proves that they supported buildings of monumental character and, as there is nothing to suggest that the Lateran Basilica was asymmetrical, we presume the existence of corresponding foundations underneath the pavement in the north half of the transept.

Notes

1. The fullest account of all excavations at the Lateran up to 1944 is given by A. M. Colini, "Storia e topografia del Celio nell' Antichità," *Memorie della Pont. Acc. rom. di archeologia,* VII (1944), 343-77.

2. Detailed accounts of these studies have appeared in *RACrist,* XXXIII (1957), 79-98; XXXIV (1958), 59-72.

3. The medieval east wall of the basilica is still intact, though it is hidden by Borromini's and Galilei's additions.

4. E. Josi, "Scoperte nella basilica costantiniana al Laterano," *RACrist,* XI (1934), 335 ff.

5. *RACrist,* XXXIII (1957), 84-94.

6. *Ibid.,* pp. 79-84.

7. J. B. Ward Perkins, "Constantine and the Origins of the Christian Basilica," *BSR,* XXII (1954), 84 ff.

8. See below, pp. 61 f.

Postscript

Further study of Borromini's survey drawings of the Lateran church, at the Albertina in Vienna, in Berlin and in the Vatican Library, of contemporary and earlier descriptions and of the building itself has provided additional information regarding the elevation of the Constantinian basilica: the nave colonnades carried entablatures rather than arcades; the aisles differed in height, the inner one rising seven meters above the outer one; semicircular windows, as indicated also by a fresco at S. Martino ai Monti (Fig. 84), placed in the upper part of its wall lit the inner aisle; and the slope of the roof over the inner aisle indicates a minimum height for the sills of the nave windows, no less than twenty meters above floor level.

We have incorporated these features in the appended reconstruction drawing (Fig. 5).

Additional Bibliography

Krautheimer, R., and Corbett, S. "La basilica costantiniana al Laterano," *RACrist,* XLIII (1967; *Miscellanea . . . Enrico Josi,* II), 125 ff.

Malmstrom, R., "The Building of the Nave Piers at S. Giovanni in Laterano," *ibid.,* 155 ff.

3

ON CONSTANTINE'S CHURCH OF
THE APOSTLES IN CONSTANTINOPLE *

DEAR HERR KLAUSER:

When we met once again after thirty years at the Congress in Ravenna in September, 1962, you mentioned in passing in your fine lecture that you doubted the authenticity of Eusebius' *Vita Constantini*.[1] In my lecture the following day, I depended, likewise in passing, on the *Vita* for my reconstruction of the Church of the Apostles, and for its dating in the last years of Constantine. The controversy about the *Vita* is familiar to all of us: forgery about 370[2]; revision of an authentic *Vita* after 340[3]; or attribution to Eusebius and dating in the years 337/340 between Constantine's and Eusebius' deaths.[4] For the entire *Vita* this can only be decided by a philologist, not by me. But I believe that only an eyewitness about 337 or shortly thereafter could have written the description of the Church of the Apostles (Book IV, Chap. 58–60), and the account of the Emperor's funeral (Book IV, Chaps. 70 and 71); and that consequently, as stated in the *Vita,* the church was built by Constantine as his burial church. A revision of the text is possible; but it could not have been a fundamental one, nor could it have taken place after 359. The reasons for a late dating of the chapter and the attribution of the building to Constantius about 356/57,[5] or even just the completion of the building to him,[6] do not appear sound to me. Neither the absence of a ν in the name κωνσταντι(ν)ος in a group of manuscripts of the *Vita,* nor the statements of later Byzantine historians, beginning with Philostorgius and Procopius, appear important to me when compared to the consistent evidence of the fourth- and fifth-century sources such as Socrates, Sozomenos, and Paulinus of Nola. The account of the building and foundation of the Church of the Apostles is thus, in my opinion, not a forgery. For this lack of skepticism I owe you an explanation.

The description of the church in the *Vita* (IV : 58) begins by establishing that the building was erected in memory of the Apostles and that it rose to an indescribable height. It glittered—the author stood inside—from floor to ceiling with the polychrome of variegated stone: the reference here is undoubtedly to marble revetment. The ceiling was divided into coffers and gilded. The roof was covered with gilt bronze plates. In the next sentence, at the end of the chapter, the author describes railings, worked in bronze, that encircle a δωμάτιον,

*Translated by Cecil L. Striker, from *Mullu, Festschrift Theodor Klauser* (Münster, 1964), pp. 224–29.

27

a small house. This could refer to a structure inside the church, to a screen around an altar or a grave, or to a small structure over such. But since the author is evidently concerned here with the exterior, it is equally possible that by the "small round house" is meant a tambour with grille windows and conical roof, rising on the exterior over the roof.

To be sure, the chapter which follows directly upon this, Chapter 59, deals with the exterior of the building and its surroundings. The church stood in the middle of a large court, surrounded by four porticoes, and farther out, by basilicas (οἶκοι βασίλειοι),[7] baths, and concave niches or fountains, apartments, and guard houses. All of this is clear: the church, the decoration of the interior, the enclosure by the *temenos* and its subsidiary buildings. The plan of the church itself is not described. I am convinced that it was laid out as a Greek cross, with four arms of equal or almost equal length, and perhaps with a tambour, the δωμάτιον, over the crossing. I am led to this belief not so much by the well-known passage in Gregory of Nazianz—"the flanks are in the form of a cross, divided into four"—which could mean anything.[8] Much more am I inclined to this by the filiation of the Apostle churches of the fourth century in the West as well as in the eastern part of the Empire, beginning with the Church of the Apostles in Milan and the first Church of St. John in Ephesos, and ending with Justinian's successor building. But I would prefer to speak of this elsewhere.

To continue, then, the *Vita Constantini* does not describe the plan. On the other hand, Chapter 60 deals with the intentions of the founder; and with this the difficulty really begins. The Emperor, so the author says, consecrated "all of this" to the memory of the Apostles. Then he continues—and I had best cite the first sentence in the original, and then translate further word for word—ὠκοδόμει δ' ἄρα καὶ ἄλλο τι τῇ διανοίᾳ σκοπῶν; "and while at first this was kept secret, in the end it was evident to all." Thus clearly the Emperor chose this place for his burial in order that his catafalque (this seems to me to be the best translation of σκῆνος) would be present in the company of devotion to the Apostles, and together with them would receive the prayers offered to them. In fact he ordered that in this place—still referring to σκῆνος—Mass be read (ἐκκλησιάζειν), and he laid out in the middle of it an enclosed chancel (θυσιαστήριον). Here he erected twelve θῆκαι as holy stelai to the honor and memory of the Apostles.[9] In the middle he placed his catafalque so that he would have six Apostles to each side. Thus he consecrated—that is the end of the description—the Temple to the Apostles in the belief that their commemoration would benefit his soul. The account of his funeral runs along the same lines, and corresponds exactly—apart from the Christian elements—to the usual ceremonial of an emperor's funeral in late antiquity.[10] The coffin was brought by Constantius with military escort to the Temple of the Apostles. Then the military withdrew, presumably because of the presence in their ranks of pagan officers and soldiers, and "the clergy and the congregation of the faithful performed the rites of worship as the service required. Thus to this day the catafalque of this thrice-blessed soul is glorified together with devotion to the Apostles, a gathering place for the people of God, and considered worthy of the services and the Holy Mass and the congregation who give prayer to the Holy Apostles" (ἔστι εἰσέτι καὶ νῦν τὸ μὲν τῆς τριομακαρίας ψυχῆς τῷ τῶν ἀποστόλων προσρήματι συνδοξαζόμενον καὶ τῷ λάῳ τοῦ θεοῦ συναγελαζόμενον θεσμῶν δὲ καὶ θείων καὶ μυστικῆς λειτουργίας ἀξιούμενον καὶ κοινωνίας ὁσίων ἀποστόλων εὐχῶν).

The sentence ᾠκοδόμει δ' ἄρα καὶ ἄλλο τι τῇ διανοίᾳ σκοπῶν has, as far as I can see, always been interpreted as though the Emperor "built something different from that which he had conceived." Reference is then made to the passage about the mausoleum near the church which we know from the descriptions of the Porphyrogenetos and Nicolas Mesarites, and where Constantine's sarcophagus still stood in the tenth and thirteenth centuries respectively; and the whole description in Book IV, Chapter 60, of the *Vita*—catafalque, θῆκαι of the Apostles, chancel and Mass is referred to the mausoleum.[11] Of further consequence is, then, the general attribution to Constantine of the erection of the mausoleum: a domed rotunda with eight or twelve niches; while the construction of the church is occasionally given to Constantius.[12] It seems to me—I agree completely with Egger—that it is more likely to assume that the reverse was true. No author of the late fourth or fifth centuries—even if he is confused by subsequent events (more about this below), or if he attributes the building to Constantius—leaves the slightest doubt that Constantine was buried in the church itself: "laid to rest in the Church of the Apostles which he built"[13]; "buried in the church where earlier Constantine had prepared his grave."[14] Thus I believe, together with Egger, that the passage ᾠκοδόμει δ' ἄρα καὶ ἄλλο τι τῇ διανοίᾳ σκοπῶν does not prove that the Emperor built something else. Rather I would refer the καὶ ἄλλο to the διανοίᾳ σκοπῶν and interpret it to mean that in building the Church of the Apostles, which alone is spoken of, he also had other intentions. Only in this way does the entire description make sense. Only if the author is speaking of the church itself, not of a nearby separate mausoleum, can he say that the Emperor's intention to partake in the devotion brought to the Apostles became evident to all only in the end. And only then is he able to say that Constantine consecrated the Temple to the Apostles so that through them benefit would be brought to his own soul; only if the imperial catafalque stood in the church dedicated to them, surrounded by their θῆκαι and inside an enclosure where Mass was read at an altar, not only at the funeral, but καὶ νῦν—even now—at the time of the writing of Chapter 71: thus if Eusebius is the author, still between 337 and 340, the year of his death; or a few years thereafter in the event that the chapter was written or at least revised later.[15] Under no circumstances can the "even now" refer to the period around 370 [16]—but more about this below. If, however, as I hope to have made appear probable, the respective passage in the *Vita* properly represents the facts, and Mass was celebrated there at the funeral of Constantine, then the church must already have been dedicated by, or was dedicated at that time. The later dedications which are reported, for example 370 under Valentinian and Valens, were new dedications.[17]

As it stood in 337, the Church of the Apostles was in the eyes of the author or reviser of the *Vita* and—if he renders correctly the Emperor's intention—in the eyes of Constantine, a martyrium simultaneously for the Apostles and for Constantine himself. Equal to the Apostles, and the thirteenth among them, he erected his catafalque surrounded by the ϑῆχαι of the Apostles in the middle of an enclosure where likewise stood the altar, and ordained that at his catafalque or close nearby Mass be read regularly: not just at the funeral or on the anniversary of his death. Specifically the regular services at the catafalque of the Emperor must have—more so even than the symbiosis or synthanatosis of the imperial corpse with the empty ϑῆχαι of the Apostles—appeared to the author or reviser of the *Vita* as exceptional; and one has the impression that he sensed this—should one say?—personality cult, as being improper. It evidently disturbed him that a mortal, be it even the Emperor, should make his sarcophagus the focal point of a regular service, which only nominally honored the Disciples of Christ. The situation was evidently still tolerable in Constantinian times. But perhaps already in the last years of Constantine's life it had become questionable; and that explains why, in the words of the *Vita,* he kept secret his intentions, which only in the end became evident to all.

This leads also, it seems to me, to an understanding of the history of the Church of the Apostles after the middle of the fourth century. What seemed to the author or reviser of the *Vita* about 337, or shortly thereafter, as exceptional and perhaps improper, was perhaps already to others at the burial and certainly soon after the death of the Emperor a source of irritation and it became increasingly so with time. Finally the situation became intolerable, as Constantius brought the relics of the Apostles Andrew and Timothy and the Evangelist Luke to Constantinople in 356 and 357, and buried them under the floor of the chancel in the middle of the Church of the Apostles, that is to say near or under the altar and close by the catafalque of Constantine.[18] Therein, in my opinion, lies the explanation of the events of 359 which took place at the Church of the Apostles.[19] At that time the Patriarch Makedonios attempted to move the remains of the Emperor elsewhere, since—as was said—the building (οἶχος) over the sarcophagus threatened to collapse, and the faithful who came there to pray feared for their lives. By the οἶχος could have been meant a part of the church that was weakened by an earthquake in 358,[20] perhaps the δωμάτιον, that is either the tambour over the crossing, or possibly a small structure over the grave under the crossing. Regardless of what the damage was, a part of the populace of Constantinople regarded the restoration work as little more than a pretext for removing the body of Constantine from the church. Nor is it altogether impossible that the actual damage and the necessary repairs offered the pretext to the party led by Makedonios to end a situation that had been an irritant for so long: the celebration of Mass at the sarcophagus of Constantine and his identification with the Apostles, who no longer were represented merely by stelai, but by relics that gave them a particular claim to be worshipped alone. In any case, the planned moving of Constantine aroused tempers. The Orthodox Party (οἱ τοῦ ὁμοουσίου φρονήματος) opposed the plan as a *violatio sepulcri,* while their opponents, evidently the Arians, supported it. Disregarding the opposition, Makedonios, himself an Arian and chosen Patriarch over the objections of the Orthodox, had the sarcophagus of Constantine brought to the nearby church of H. Akakios; and there in the courtyard the issue was brought to a bloody clash between the opposing rabble. The reasons for opposition, specifically by the Orthodox, to the move and the support for it by the Arians, are not entirely clear. The opposition by the Orthodox to the Arian Patriarch may have to do with the unclear feeling that ultimately the Council of Nicaea, under Constantine's leadership, took a position against Arius. But the question had best be left open.

The position of the reigning Emperor Constantius in the controversy over his father's remains is likewise unclear. However, he broke with the Patriarch who "dared without his (Constantius') consent (or knowledge? παρὰ τὴν αὐτοῦ γνώμην) to remove the corpse of his father." [21] On the other hand it was he, himself, who had brought the relics of the Apostles to the church, perhaps thereby unintentionally sharpening the existing conflict about the cult centered on his father's remains. Possibly in principle he was not even against the move, and broke with Makedonios only because, as alluded to by Socrates, the Patriarch acted without orders. He might well have had his own ideas about a new resting place for the remains of his father, and have been angered with the Patriarch for having acted like the proverbial bull in the china shop. Now, after the precipitous action of Makedonios and the consequent unrest, Constantius was compelled to act. It is only after 359, as Egger has already noted, that the sources speak of a separate imperial mausoleum built by Constantine: the domed rotunda adjoining the church that survived the rebuilding by Justinian, where Constantine Porphyrogenetos and Nicolas Mesarites saw the sarcophagi of the Emperors of the fourth and fifth centuries, beginning with Constantine and Constantius. With the building of the mausoleum and with the transfer of Constantine to it, the church, itself, could have been newly dedicated, as the burial of the relics of the Apostles would have allowed. When this new dedication took place is not quite clear. Possibly it was in 359 or shortly thereafter, when the damage caused by the earthquake of 358 had been repaired. However the first report of a dedication is on Easter Sunday 370,[22] and it is therefore possible that the restoration work was completed only then. It is quite possible that Constantius began this work in 359, and this could be the reason for the widespread belief shortly thereafter that it was he who built the church. When Philostorgius says that Constantius built the Church of the Apostles where he likewise established the grave of his father, it is evidently no longer clear to him whether this refers to the original burial in the church or to a new burial in the mausoleum.[23] To me it seems certain that Constantius began the building of the mausoleum. But since he died as early as 360, it is possible that the building was still unfinished at his death. In fact the mausoleum appears to be clearly mentioned for the first time only in 398,[24] and Constantius' remains could have rested in H. Akakios for ten years or more.

In any case, however, the removal of Constantine from the church itself removed the irritation over his burial with the Apostles and the regular services held at his catafalque. With the building of the new mausoleum and, following its completion, the reburial of Constantine there, all was well again. Now he lay near the Apostles, yet outside the church, and this was in no way out of the ordinary. On the contrary, the building of the mausoleum in front of one of the entrances to the church—John Chrysostomus makes this appear probable [25] —restored a situation that had been normal for imperial mausolea from the twenties of the century on: the mausoleum of Helena at Tor Pignattara— probably originally planned by Constantine as his own mausoleum—was iden- tically situated in front of the narthex of the *coemeterium subteglatum* of SS. Marcellino e Pietro.[26] At the same time, another objective was achieved with the building of the mausoleum: it was no longer the tomb of Constantine alone, but rather the mausoleum of the dynasty.

But the parity of Emperor and Apostle that Constantine had in mind, although nullified in fact, still lingers in the sources of the late fourth and early fifth centuries. Socrates still says that Constantine erected stately graves in the Church of the Apostles "for Emperor and Patriarch so that they would be so jointly honored only slightly less than the relics of the Apostles." [27] Sozomenos states similarly that in the burial of Constantine in the Church of the Apostles orig- inated the practice of burying there Christian emperors who die in Constantinople —that is in this church.[28] The work of John Chrysostomus, *Adversus Judaeos et Gentiles,* written in 398, clearly reflects the conflict that was terminated with the building of the mausoleum and the transfer to it of Constantine. The Em- perors, as he says in a well-known passage,[29] are the "doorkeepers of the fisherman" (and therefore I would like to believe that the mausoleum was built in front of one of the entrances to the church); they rest "not within with the Apostles, but are satisfied to lie without before the threshold." The allusion to the original location of Constantine's grave in the midst of the Apostles seems clear to me.

This brings me again to the question regarding the authenticity of the descrip- tion of the building and of the account of the foundation of the Church of the Apostles as given in the *Vita Constantini.* In their essence, they could only have been written by an eyewitness, in other words around, or shortly after 337. That they were revised is quite possible, and the expression that even now—καὶ νῦν—Mass is read at the grave of Constantine in the middle of the chancel, may indicate a later date. But no one could state this after 359, since after the removal of Constantine from the church Mass was no longer celebrated at his grave. Thus 359 is the latest possible date for a revision—and for this reason I believe in the basic authenticity of the account.

Notes

1. I. Heikel, *Eusebius Werke*, I ("*Die griechischen christlichen Schriftsteller,*" 7 [Leipzig, 1902]). As first published by H. Valesius in 1659 and reprinted in *PG*, XX, cols. 905 ff., the text of the *Vita* was incomplete.

2. Of first importance is H. Gregoire, "Eusèbe n'est pas l'auteur de la 'Vita Constantini' dans sa forme actuelle, et Constantin ne s'est pas 'converti' en 312," *Byzantion*, XIII (1938), 561–83, and *ibid.*, XIV (1939), 341–51; as well as G. Downey, "The Builder of the Original Church of the Apostles at Constantinople," *DOPapers*, VI (1951), 53–80; recently further Ph. Grierson, "The Tombs . . . of the Byzantine Emperors," *ibid.*, XVI (1962), 1 ff.; C. Nordenfalk, "The Apostolic Canon Tables," *Gazette des Beaux-Arts*, LXII (July, 1963), 12 ff., esp. 29 ff. The last two articles reached me only after the printing of this manuscript.

3. W. Seston, "Constantine as a Bishop," *JRS*, XXXVII (1947), 127–31; F. Scheidweiler, "Nochmals die Vita Constantini," *BZ*, XLIX (1956), 1–23.

4. Generally the case until 1928, and more recently J. Vogt, "Der Erbauer der Apostelkirche in Konstantinopel," *Hermes*, LXXXI (1953), 111–17; *Reallexikon für Antike und Christentum*, III, 307–10; F. Vittinghoff, "Eusebius als Verfasser der Vita Constantini," *Rheinisches Museum*, XCVI (1953), 330–73; A. Kaniuth, *Die Beisetzung Konstantins des Grossen*, (*Breslauer Historische Forschungen*, XVIII [Breslau, 1941]).

5. Primarily Downey, *op. cit.*

6. R. Egger, "Die Begräbnisstätte des Kaisers Konstantin," *JÖAI*, XVI (1913), 212 ff.; A. Grabar, *Martyrium*, I (Paris, 1946), 227–34.

7. Grabar, *op. cit.*, I, p. 228, translates as "imperial residences," but this does not convince me.

8. Ἐνύπνιον περὶ τῆς Ἀναστασίας ἐκκλησίας, V, 59 ff. (*PG*, XXXVII, col. 12).

9. For the form of the stelai, see most recently Kaniuth, *op. cit.*

10. *Ibid.*

11. As A. Heisenberg, *Grabeskirche und Apostelkirche*, 2 (1910), *passim*; as well as others. The only exception is Egger, *op. cit.*, whose interpretation of the passage was curiously enough not accepted.

12. Heisenberg, Grabar, Kaniuth, *op. cit.*, and others attribute the church and the mausoleum to Constantine. H. Koethe, "Das Konstantin-Mausoleum und verwandte Denkmäler," *JdI*, XLVIII (1933), 185 ff., gives the mausoleum to Constantine and the church to Constantius; Downey, *op. cit.*, gives both to Constantius.

13. Socrates, *Historia Ecclesiastica*, I, 40 (*PG*, LXVII, col. 180); see also *ibid.*, I, 16 (*PG*, LXVII, col. 117).

14. Sozomenos, *Historia Ecclesiastica*, II, XXXIV (*PG*, LXVII, col. 1032); also *idem., Kirchengeschichte*, ed. J. Bidez and C. G. Hansen (*Die griechischen christlichen Schriftsteller*, L, [Berlin, 1960]), 100.

15. See above, n. 3 and 4.

16. See above, n. 2.

17. Egger, *op. cit.*, speaks of a dedication under Constantius in 359, probably with reference to Theodorus Lector, *Excerpta ex Ecclesiastica Historia*, II, LXI (*PG*, LXXXVI, cols. 212 ff.). But this is a late source.

18. For the translation of the relics, see Philostorgius, *Historiarum Epitome*, III, 2 (*PG*, LXV, cols. 480 ff.) and *Chronicon Paschale*, ad ann. 356 and 357 (*PG*, XCII, col. 783); for their discovery in Justinian's reign under the altar enclosure, see Procopius, *Buildings*, I, iv, 9–11 ("Loeb Classical Library," Procopius, VII, ed. G. Downey, 48 ff.). The burial of the

relics under the altar (*Chronicon Paschale, loc. cit.*) would refer to this situation.

19. Socrates, *op. cit.*, II, 38 (*PG, LXVII*, cols. 329 ff.); Sozomenos, *op. cit.*, IV, 21 (*PG, LXVII*, cols. 1177 ff. and *Kirchengeschichte*, as above, n. 14, pp. 171 ff.).

20. Ammianus Marcellinus, *The surviving books of the History*, XVII, 7, 1 ff. (ed. J. C. Rolfe, "Loeb Classical Library," I [1956], 340 ff.); also V. Grumel, *La chronologie* (*Traité d'études byzantines*, ed. P. Lemerle [Paris, 1958]), pp. 4 ff.

21. See n. 19.

22. *Chronicon Paschale*, ad ann. 370 (*PG, XCII*, col. 760).

23. Philostorgius, *op. cit.*, 3, 2 (*PG, LXV*, cols. 480 ff.).

24. See below, n. 29.

25. *Ibid.*

26. F. W. Deichmann, "Das Mausoleum der Kaiserin Helena," *JdI, LXXII* (1957), 44–110; R. Krautheimer, "Mensa-Coemeterium-Martyrium," *CahArch, XI* (1960), 15–40; Krautheimer, W. Frankl, S. Corbett, *Corpus, II* (1959), 191–204; and earlier Kaniuth, *op. cit.*

27. Socrates, *op. cit.*, I, 40 (*PG, LXVII*, col. 180).

28. Sozomenos, *loc. cit.*

29. *Adversus Judaeos et Gentiles*, I, 9 (*PG, XLVIII*, col. 823); see also *idem, Epistula ad Corinthios*, hom. 26 (*PG, LXI*, col. 582).

4

MENSA-COEMETERIUM-MARTYRIUM *

HALF A CENTURY AGO two epitaphs came to light on the Verano cemetery in Rome. They were found some fifty meters south of the basilica of S. Lorenzo f. l. m. which in its rear half, in the sixth-century east basilica of Pelagius II, shelters the tomb of St. Lawrence. The front half, the west basilica, dates from about 1200.[1] Both inscriptions concern the purchase of graves: Flavius Eurialus in 405 acquired a tomb *"ad mesa beati Laurenti descindentibus in cripta parte dextera";* at about the same time or, to judge by the lettering, slightly earlier, Lucillus Pelio bought a tomb *"in basilica maiore ad domnu Laurentium* in *mensu e situ presbiteriu"* (Fig. 6, a, b)

A fair amount of ink has been spilled over the finds, since they apparently refer to two favorite topics in the running discussions regarding the architectural history of S. Lorenzo f. l. m. From the *Liber Pontificalis* it was known that Constantine had built *"gradus ascensionis et descensionis"* leading to the tomb of the saint; the same source, in a number of passages, spoke of the existence at S. Lorenzo of a *basilica maior.* Reference to a *basilica maior* was also made in seventh-century pilgrim guides and was confirmed by a third epitaph of fifth- or sixth-century date found on the Verano, in which an unknown mentions his having purchased a tomb *"in basilica maxior"* (Fig. 6b). Unsupported by archeological evidence, the dispute raged furiously regarding the aspect and the relative location of the several elements mentioned in these sources: the stairs, the catacomb (*cripta*) with the tomb of the saint, the *basilica maior.* The terms *mesa* and *mesu* were never discussed. Both stand apparently for *mensa,* also the strange form *mesu:* the reversal of A (without crossbar) into V is frequent enough. But the term *mensa* held little interest, as long as it was interpreted to mean simply altar.

Two excavations carried out since 1947 have thrown light on some of these questions. In the first place, it became clear that prior to the building of the east basilica of S. Lorenzo in the sixth century, the hill which still encloses it on two sides covered its entire site. The galleries of the catacomb, well preserved in the remaining portions of the hill, had apparently started in this lost part; the remnants of a lavishly constructed nucleus of galleries and chambers were traced near the tomb of the saint which apparently still stands at the site it used

*From *CahArch,* XI (1960), 15–40.

to occupy in the catacomb.[2] This was only to be expected. But it was a surprise when on the Verano plain, where the epitaphs of Flavius Eurialus and Lucillus Pelio had been found, the walls of the *basilica maior* came to light, first observed in 1950 by Wolfgang Frankl.[3] It turned out to have been a huge structure over 300 feet long and 120 feet wide. Since the site lies on the modern cemetery, only small parts of the building could be dug up, but luck would have it that they were key points (Text Fig. 6). Divided into a nave and two aisles, the structure was supported by columns closely spaced and apparently surmounted by an entablature. The entrance side, facing east, seems to have opened in a series of arcades. On the other hand, the aisles continued as an ambulatory around the apse and this ambulatory opened in seven entrances westward towards the Roman highway, the Via Tiburtina. Small chapels, apparently mausolea, were built against the flanks of the structure and dense rows of graves, some still covered by inscribed slabs, paved whatever part was excavated, the nave, the aisles, the ambulatory. While all were subsequently inserted, they all date from the fourth and fifth centuries. Fragments of roof tiles were found all over the site, as well as fragments of vessels, epitaphs, marble and stucco decor. Under the circumstances, the graphic reconstruction was easy. (Text Fig. 7).

The discovery of the *basilica maior ad domnu Laurentium* coincided with that of two other buildings of the same type in Rome. One was excavated in 1956 by Messrs. Deichmann and Tschira at Tor Pignattara, on the imperial estate *ad duos lauros* near the Via Labicana, above the catacomb of Marcellinus and Petrus.[4] Slightly smaller than the structure on the Verano, it presented the same plan: nave, aisles, and ambulatory. The supports between the nave and aisles and those encircling the apse were piers, rather than columns and thus in all likelihood supported arches. The mausoleum of the Empress Dowager Helena, Constantine's mother, was built against its short east end; a small tomb chapel, supposedly that of Saints Tiburtius, Marcellinus, and Peter (Fig. 8a) against its north flank. Deichmann was also the first to recognize another structure of the type.[5] Known as the *basilica* or *coemeterium Agnetis,* it rose on the Via Nomentana, apparently again an imperial estate, thirty odd meters south of the church which in the seventh century was inserted into the hill over the tomb of Saint Agnes, thus, as at S. Lorenzo, destroying part of the catacomb. The tall south flank and the curved ambulatory wall of the huge building overlooking the valley to the west are well preserved, as is Sta. Costanza, the mausoleum of Constantine's daughter, Constantina, which leans against the south flank of the main structure.[6] A few soundings made in 1955 have clarified the plan of the huge building, at least in its outlines.[7] Again the aisles continued as an ambulatory around the apse (Fig. 7). The supports, whether columns or piers, remain unknown; but the outer walls of the ambulatory, well preserved as they are, show that from the outset they were pierced by rectangular windows. A long inscription known from two sixth-century syllogai clarifies the foundation of the structure and its dedication to Saint Agnes by Constantina.[8]

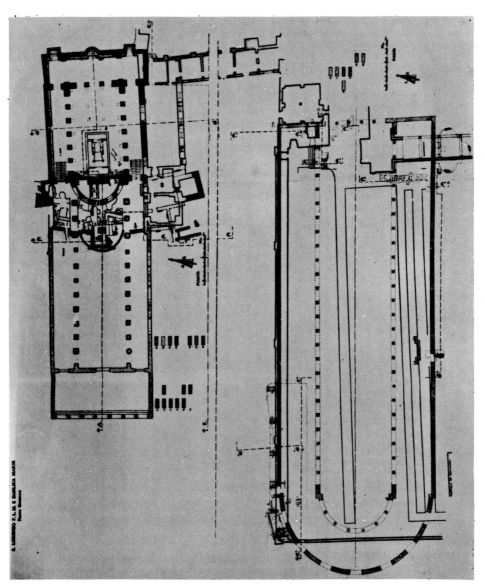

Text fig. 6. Rome S. Lorenzo f.l.m., excavation plan (Frankl)

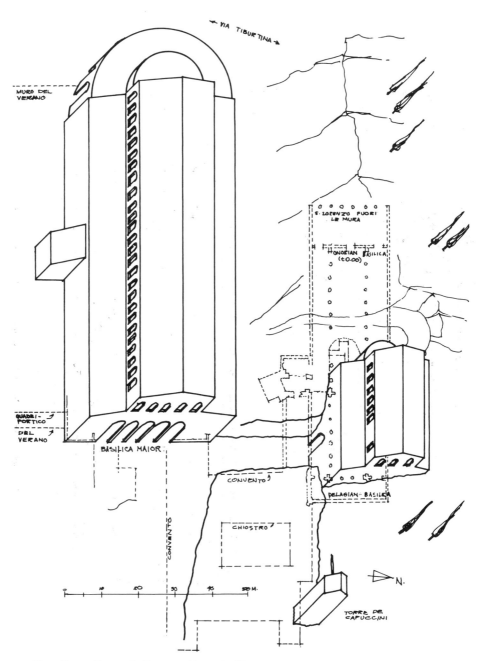

Text fig. 7. Rome, S. Lorenzo f.l.m., *basilica maior,* ca. 330, and *basilica ad corpus,* 579-90, isometric reconstruction (Frankl)

The close relationship of all three buildings, on the Verano, at Tor Pignattara, and at Sant' Agnese, has been brought out by Deichmann [9] (Text Fig. 7; Figs. 7, 8a). All are huge and nearly the same size, between eighty and one hundred meters long. In all three, the aisles continue as an ambulatory around the apse. The nave as well as the aisles were apparently roofed, as witness the finds of tiles, the greater strength of the foundation walls of the naves, and the references to roof repairs scattered through the *Liber Pontificalis*.[10] Whether or not the nave was higher than the aisles and lit by the windows of a clerestory, is from the finds not immediately clear. One could assume that a continuous roof covered the nave and aisles.[11] But the comparison with S. Sebastiano, where the original clerestory has survived, suggests that all the buildings of the group were provided with a window zone in the nave (Fig. 9a, b).

In all three structures mausolea lean against the outer walls: the great mausolea of the imperial ladies at Tor Pignattara and in the *coemeterium Agnetis,* smaller ones at S. Lorenzo as well as at Tor Pignattara, apparently of wealthy members of the congregation. Tombs of the less affluent paved the entire floor in all three buildings: in the structures on the Verano and at Tor Pignattara these dense rows of tombs have been found *in situ;* [12] at Sant' Agnese some tombs were uncovered in the early nineteenth century,[13] and *loculi,* hewn later into the inner wall of the ambulatory are visible to this day. Finally, a martyr's tomb, sheltered by a catacomb close by, was accessible from the large structure or from its forecourt over *gradus ascensionis et descensionis;* those at Sant' Agnese may have survived more or less on the original site, though obviously enlarged.

A few remarks supplement these observations, which coincide with those made by Deichmann. In the structure near Sant' Agnese, the tall outer wall of the ambulatory high above the valley, with its huge buttresses, may have been erected in a first period of building, while the inner foundation walls were possibly inserted later, perhaps during construction. In brief, it is possible that here, as an afterthought, a structure originally open to the sky was transformed into a basilical building divided into nave and aisles. Secondly, not only do all these structures lie *extra moenia,* a mile or so from the city, but two of them certainly rose on an imperial estate. In all likelihood, this was also true of the one on the Verano. Finally, in all three the galleries of a catacomb extended below the structure. At SS. Marcellino e Pietro these galleries are still accessible; at S. Lorenzo and Sant' Agnese their existence is ascertained by sixteenth-century eyewitnesses; [14] in both cases they seem to have extended from an older nucleus in the hill to the north of the structure.

As Deichmann has pointed out, and as is evident, the three newly discovered structures throw light on the fourth building, well-known for many years, S. Sebastiano *ad Catacumbas* on the Via Appia (Figs. 9a, b). The plan with ambulatory is the same; the use of piers and arcades instead of an entablature parallels these same features at Tor Pignattara. Again, the structure was roofed including the nave; the masonry of the windows of the clerestory is identical with that of the aisles, leaving no doubt as to their common date. As in the other structures of the group, the floor was paved with tombs, the flanks encircled by densely crowded mausolea.[15] The only essential difference is that here the μαρτύριον, the venerated spot, was situated right in the middle of the structure, rather than at some distance from it; also it was not a martyr's tomb but the *memoria apostolorum,* set up presumably in 258 to commemorate the transfer, either of relics or simply of the festival of Saint Peter and Saint Paul to this site.[16] Prior to the seventh century, the structure was apparently known simply as *ad catacumbas* or as *memoria apostolorum.*[17]

All four buildings can be safely dated during the years of Constantine's reign in the West, with a possible margin of a few years before or after. The structure at Tor Pignattara, since it appears to be slightly earlier than the mausoleum of Helena, has been assigned a date certainly prior to 330 and possibly before 320–325.[18] The *basilica maior* on the Verano may date from the twenties or early thirties.[19] The *coemeterium Agnetis* seems to have been built, or possibly remodelled into a church, during the years of Constantina's widowhood and residence in Rome, 338–350. Its dedication may even have taken place after 354, since after that date the *martyrologium Hieronymianum* lists in addition to the original festival of Saint Agnes, January 21, a second one on January 28: hence, the first may refer to the celebration at her tomb, the second to the dedication of her church.[20] S. Sebastiano, on the other hand, since it does not occur in the Constantinian or for that matter in the later donation lists in the *Liber Pontificalis,* yet is undoubtedly of early fourth-century date, has been suspected to date from about 320 or possibly from prior to 313.[21]

Of equal importance to the early foundation dates of these buildings is the short life span of the majority of them. The structure of Sant' Agnese was no longer known to the seventh-century pilgrim guides; SS. Marcellino e Pietro at Tor Pignattara is still mentioned in the eighth century.[22] The *basilica maior* on the Verano survived until after 850, but during the eighth century its dedication had been changed to the Virgin, apparently because its original function and dedication as a second church of Saint Lawrence next to his tomb had become meaningless. Only the structure on the Via Appia has survived to this day; but again its original name as early as the seventh century gave way to that of Saint Sebastian.[23] Apparently, all four structures were either abandoned or had their dedications changed during the seventh and eighth centuries; evidently they had lost their *raison d'être* and their original purpose was no longer understood.

What, then, was the function of these huge fourth-century structures, *extra moenia,* near the catacombs in the Roman Campagna? Beyond any doubt, they were ecclesiastical buildings and Mass was celebrated in them. If the Constantinian donation lists incorporated into the *Liber Pontificalis* can be trusted—and

there is no reason to distrust them *a limine*—at least the structures at Tor Pignattara, at Sant' Agnese and on the Verano were provided with all the appurtenances needed for Mass. To the building at Tor Pignattara, the Emperor
specifically gave a silver altar in addition to the altar erected in the adjoining
mausoleum; he also donated to the basilica a complete set of altar vessels, two
patens of gold, and two of silver, a huge golden chalice with his name engraved
on it and a smaller one, five chalices of silver for the celebrants and twenty
for communion (? *pro servitio*) and four pitchers (*amae*). For the Verano
basilica and for that at Sant' Agnese, no altars are specifically mentioned; but
both buildings received sets of altar vessels, patens, chalices both for celebrants
and for communion, and pitchers for the Mass. At Sant' Agnese, even a baptismal
font seems to have existed. To be sure, the listing among the gifts attributed by
the *Liber Pontificalis* to Constantine of a lamp *"supra fontem"* may be doubtful.
But by the early fifth century, when Pope Boniface I celebrated the Easter
baptism *in basilica martyris Agnae,"* a baptistery must have existed, though
certainly it was not at any time identical with the mausoleum of Constantina-
Constantia.

Yet, the four structures were not ordinary churches such as those *intra moenia,*
designed to serve the religious assemblies of the faithful on Sundays or on the
great feast days. Indeed, the present position is that, broadly speaking, they must
be considered as *martyria,* with the understanding that the center of veneration,
the μαρτύριον proper, as a rule lies outside the structure. Indeed, the tomb of
the martyr, be it Saint Lawrence, Saint Agnes, or Saints Peter and Marcellinus,
or the sarcophagus of the founder, whether Helena or Constantina, rises outside
the building in a catacomb or an adjoining mausoleum. In the structure *ad catacumbas,* the third-century shrine of the apostles was buried below the floor of the
new building and remained inaccessible. This separation of the assembly building from the center of veneration is viewed as occurring not infrequently in
fourth-century martyria, beginning with the buildings on Golgotha. Given the
lack of space around the μαρτύριον inside the catacomb or the imperial mausoleum, so the reasoning continues, the memorial services at the anniversary of
the martyr or, for that matter, the founder, would have taken place in the
huge building; hence, they would have contained the altar for celebrating Mass
and they would be the repositories of the altar vessels and communion chalices
listed in the *Liber Pontificalis.* No altar would have risen over the tomb of the
martyr in the catacomb, at least not until the later fifth century. This seems
to be roughly the position prevailing at this point.[24]

In part, no doubt, the position is correct. But it seems to me that it should
be modified on several counts. A passage in the life of Melania the Younger
elucidates the situation as it existed in the last years of the fourth century at
S. Lorenzo.[25] The events fall some time between 397 and 400, or possibly in
402. Melania was pregnant, but wanted to attend the feast of Saint Lawrence,
in sancti martyris basilica on the vigil of his *dies natalis* and spend the night

in prayer. Forbidden by her parents to do so, she passed the night in devotion in her house chapel, but went next morning with her mother *"ad martyrium beati Laurentii"*. When she returned home, labor started and she nearly died. Thereupon, her husband, Pinianus, rushed to Saint Lawrence *"ad sanctum martyrem"*—this being the customary term for the martyr's grave—and *prosternens se sub altare,* in proskynesis below the altar, implored God to save her life. In short, the huge structure on the Verano is clearly distinguished from the *martyrium* where apparently prayers offered to the martyr are of greater efficacy, since obviously his tomb is enclosed within the *martyrium.* An altar rises in the *martyrium,* and since Pinianus prostrated himself *ad sanctum martyrem* below the altar, this latter rose, presumably, over the martyr's grave. The date of this altar remains uncertain; it could have been set up by Damasus, 368–384, who decorated an altar of Saint Lawrence, either in the basilica or at his tomb, but it might as well have gone back as far as Constantine.[26] Moreover, the passage suggests that the vigil and night-long prayers preceding the feast of the martyr took place in the basilica. The *martyrium* and his tomb, on the other hand, were apparently visited on his feast day proper, August 10. To be sure, if an altar rose over the tomb of Saint Lawrence in his *martyrium* in the catacomb, another altar might well have stood in the basilica, just as in the group of buildings at Tor Pignattara where the basilica as well as the mausoleum of the Empress Dowager each sheltered an altar. But neither at the Verano nor at Sant' Agnese can the existence of an altar in the basilica proper be proven so far.

Indeed, it is strange that prior to the fifth century and even later, none of the four structures *extra moenia* seem to have been quite on a par with regular church buildings, either juridically or in the eyes of the contemporaries. Despite their huge size and their undeniable popularity, no permanent clergy was assigned to them, but like any catacomb they were supervised and serviced by the staff of the city churches. Occasionally, to be sure, one or the other was put to uses ordinarily reserved for parish churches or for the bishop's cathedral in the Lateran. But this occurred only under exceptional circumstances, and indeed, such illicit transgressions are always remarked upon by the contemporary sources. The people of Rome, opposed to Pope Damasus, in 366 held religious meetings without benefit of clergy *"stationes per coemeteria martyrum sine clericis cele-brabant . . .".* When congregating *". . . ad sanctam Agnem . . .",* apparently in the huge structure near Sta. Costanza, they were massacred by a mob of the papal faction.[27] The irregularity of celebrating a "statio", that is, keeping a solemn fast interspersed with hymns and scriptural readings in the absence of the clergy is apparent from the overtones of the report. Or else the *Liber Pontificalis* reports that Pope Liberius, prevented from entering the city, *"habitavit in cymiterio sanctae Agnae."* [28] *Cymiterium* in this context can only mean a sizable building above ground, presumably again the large structure; thus one would like to interpret the term "habitavit" as meaning "to reside," "to use as a cathedral." Late as they are, the *Gesta Liberii* of about 500 probably reflect a good tradition with the correct

42

overtones of irregularity when reporting that Liberius baptized at Easter *"sicut consuetudo in eodem coemeterio."* [29] The same overtones pervade the *Liber Ponti-ficalis* when it reports how the schismatic Pope Boniface I (418–422) *"celebravit baptismum Paschae in basilica beatae martyris Agnae . . . ,"* [30] and how he resided *"habitavit . . . in coemeterio sanctae Felicitatis . . . ,"* [31] or when it refers, much later, to John III (561–574) who *"retinuit se in cymiterio . . . Tiburtii et Valeri-ani* (should this be emended to *Marcellini?*) *et habitavit illic multum temporis ut etiam episcopos ibidem consecraret . . ."* [32]

The sources call these structures *extra moenia* either *basilicae* or *coemeteria.* The term basilica is colorless; it simply means assembly hall. Within this broad generic concept it has no specific significance, neither functionally nor structurally. *Coemeterium,* on the contrary, is functionally a specific term, meaning graveyard and nothing else: a graveyard underground, that is a catacomb, or a graveyard under the open sky. Why not, then, a covered graveyard? Indeed, all the struc-tures in question were densely paved with tombs: S. Sebastiano, as demonstrated by the excavations of 1915; the Verano basilica, as shown by the soundings in 1957; the structure at Tor Pignattara as evidenced by the findings in 1956; Sant' Agnese, as witnessed by a small sounding in the early nineteenth century. In all, mausolea were built against the outer walls (Fig. 9a). All goes to indicate that the structures were neither churches in the ordinary sense, nor simply *martyria.* They were, in our opinion, as much as anything, huge covered burial grounds, *coemeteria subteglata, coemeteria cooperta.* But they were more than just that.

Smaller covered *coemeteria* likewise existed in Rome and its vicinity. The *coe-meterium* built near Velletri by one Faltonia Hilaritas and given to the local congregation *". . . coemeterium a solo sua pecunia fecit et hunc religioni don-avit . . ."* [33] may have been small; but apparently it was a covered burial place, perhaps originally private, but then donated for public use. Of greater interest is an epitaph noted first in the sixteenth century in the pavement of S. Paolo f. l. m. and now in the Lateran collections.[34] On the basis of its lettering and spelling, it used to be attributed to the seventh century; present opinion seems to lean towards an earlier, possibly fifth-century date.[35] In any event, the arrange-ments described are so characteristic of the martyr cult of Constantinian and post-Constantinian times, that the text cannot possibly date after 430. The titular of the epitaph, Eusebius, had repaired the entire cemetery including the columns in the *porticus,* *". . . cymiteriu(m) totu(m) et columnas in porticos . . .";* the paintings and the roof with tiles, laths, nails, and wood-work, *". . . (tec)tu cum tegulas et tabl(inas) et acutos et materi(ata) . . .";* the marble bath with low benches and the window panes in the clerestory, *". . . (fenes)tras speclara item in s(up)eriora . . .";* and the fenced-in cloister, *"pal(atiu) clostra . . ."* The text has been taken to refer to an area *sub divo,* a *basilica discoperta,* surrounded by colonnaded porticoes.[36] But *porticus* in early Christian Latin means aisles as well as porticoes, and the singular *tectum* seems to fit a basilica or a small three-aisled hall as well as the quadriporticus of an open area with its four roofs. Likewise, the reference to upper windows evokes the clerestory of a basilica rather than a small bath building. Hence, the structure may as well have been a covered *coemeterium.* Be this as it may, the heirs of Eusebius later built the entrance to the martyrs from the public road, *"introitu(m) at martyres (qu)od est in publicu . . .";* the round *mensae* of the martyrs, *"mesas at martyres rotas(s)"* and the dining room (or perhaps the dining couch) for the banquet, *". . . at con(vivi)a cubiculu(m) . . ."* In short, the *coemeterium,* whether roofed or *sub divo,* was accompanied by a funeral banquet room with round *mensae* and this *cubiculum ad martyres* had a separate entrance. The situation, *mutatis mutandis,* compares with that at S. Lorenzo or Sant' Agnese where the huge *coemeterium* is distinct from the *martyrium,* the site *ad martyrem* down in the catacomb.

The covered *coemeteria* of Rome should, it seems to me, be distinguished from the cemeterial basilicas so frequent in the early Christian world from the latter fourth through the sixth centuries. "Cemeterial basilicas" should be defined correctly as *basilicae ad corpus.* They are built over the tomb of a martyr and indeed the previous existence of the tomb on the site is the *raison d'être* for their construction. The specific situation matters little. The tomb may lie in a catacomb and thus enforce the building of a church sunk down into the hill, as is the case when in the sixth and seventh centuries, *basilicae ad corpus* were set up in the Roman catacombs over the tombs of the martyrs, sometimes remodelled from smaller *martyria,* to use the terminology of the *Vita Melaniae:* Ermete in Bassilla, Sta. Generosa, and Sant' Ippolito represent the latter case; Sta. Petronilla in Domitilla, and the basilicas with galleries at S. Lorenzo (Fig. 10) and Sant' Agnese are large *basilicae ad corpus* enclosing the martyr's grave at the level of a catacomb gallery.[37] Or else the tomb of the martyr may have been situated originally on a graveyard under the open sky and was later enclosed within a *basilica ad corpus.* In this case, the Christian or pagan tombs and mausolea of the preexisting cemetery on the site to be occupied by the new structure were razed. Only the grave (or the *memoria*) of the martyr, sometimes together with its sheltering apse, was singled out to become the focal point towards which the new *basilica ad corpus* was oriented. Set aside from the nave and aisles, it was sheltered by a structure of its own, frequently the apse of the new building.

Such *basilicae ad corpus* above ground are numerous all over the Christian world, in Spain, in North Africa, in Dalmatia, at Rome, and presumably, all over the East. In architectural type they vary. In Rome, both the Constantinian basilica of St. Peter and the late fourth-century structure of St. Paul outside the walls evolve a special type; the shrine of the saint is enclosed in a transept, a transverse structure joined to the apse and set apart from the nave and aisles which were reserved for the congregation.[38] In Salona, the basilica at Manastirine, dated about 400, takes up this "Roman" type; but other *basilicae ad corpus* in the same city, such as the Basilica of the Five Martyrs at Kapljuc of the late fourth century, the south basilica of the Anastasius complex at Marusinac, *circa* 426

(Fig. 11), and presumably the basilicas at the south and east cemeteries, adopt the plan of an ordinary basilica *intra moenia,* with nave, aisles and apse, the latter housing the martyr's grave.[39] The type of the regular basilica was replaced only occasionally, as in the north building of the Anastasius complex, by an area terminating in the apse with the martyr's grave and surrounded by colonnaded porticoes, a *basilica discoperta.*[40]

Architecturally, then, because they shelter the martyr's shrine inside the building, the *basilicae ad corpus,* whether in Rome or Salona, are fundamentally different from the *coemeteria* of Constantinian Rome where the *martyrium* lies, as a rule, outside in the catacomb. They are equally different in function and in origin. They rise in cemeteries, be they *sub divo* graveyards or catacombs, but they are not cemeteries, primarily. Their focal point and *raison d'être* is the martyr's grave. When at a later point ordinary graves were scooped into their floors, it was an *ex post facto* development. They are regular *martyria,* martyrs' shrines, very different both in function and type from the covered *coemeteria* of Constantinian times in Rome whose primary function is to serve as a graveyard.

North Africa like Rome, in contrast to Dalmatia, seems to have known both *basilicae ad corpus* and covered *coemeteria.* The church of St. Sala at Tipasa rises on a preexisting cemetery.[41] From among its graves, that of the saint was isolated and turned into the focal point both of the fourth-century church and its mid-fifth-century enlargement. While burials on the surrounding cemetery were numerous through the fourth and fifth centuries, inside the basilica they became frequent only after the early sixth century. Similarly, at Carthage, the basilica of St. Cyprian was focused, probably in the fifth century, on what was presumably a *memoria* of the martyr isolated from among the tombs of an older cemetery.[43] Again, burials inside the church were rare while both the surrounding cemetery and the atrium of the church were paved with graves. But it seems that in Africa the *basilicae ad corpus* developed at an early point into covered cemeteries; the tomb of the martyr attracted burials of ordinary mortals. The two successive buildings at Uppenna (Henchir Chigarnia) illustrate this situation: numerous graves are arranged throughout the nave and aisles, while the *martyrium* of the martyrs occupies a small enclosure opposite the apse.[44] (At a still later point in churches erected on cemeteries, a reliquary casket took the place of the martyr's tomb while nave and aisles were filled with ordinary graves.[45]) On the other hand, North Africa did have covered *coemeteria.* The large basilica at Tabarka[46] was filled with graves, while mausolea flanked its outer walls, but so far no trace of a martyr's tomb has been established. (In Spain, always closely related to North Africa, a similar structure has come to light at Vega del Mar.[47]) Finally, the chapel of Bishop Alexander at Tipasa is clearly a *coemeterium subteglatum,* including numerous graves and at least one *mensa* for funeral banquets.[48]

Indeed, the true character of these roofed cemeteries, whether in North Africa or in Rome, can be understood only against the background of the funerary ritual which was alive around the graves both of ordinary mortals and of martyrs in the fourth and into the fifth century. If not its main focus, an essential part of this ritual was the funeral banquet carried over from pagan times. On given days during the first year of mourning, afterwards on the anniversary of the death, the *dies natalis,* the family and friends of an ordinary mortal would assemble for a funeral banquet, just as their pagan ancestors had done and as their pagan contemporaries did. The character of these Christian *refrigeria* is known both from inscriptions and from early Christian writings. It has been described in recent times so frequently that a brief summary should suffice here.[49] The mourners would recline around a *mensa,* a sigma-shaped, round or rectangular stone table, built over the tomb or more frequently near it.[50] If placed over the tomb, the plaque was occasionally pierced by holes for pouring libations; at times, especially in North Africa, it bore scooped into it the reproduction of plates and dishes.[51] Wine, bread, oil, and possibly other foods were placed on the grave or on a small round table nearby,[52] while the survivors, assembled around the main table, would feast to their hearts' desire and recount the deeds and the virtues of the beloved one, as at any good wake—Tyrolian, Irish, or Jewish. The epitaph of one Aelia Secundula has been quoted more than once: she died in 299 and her children "set a stone mensa over her grave where foods, goblets, and *couverts* were laid, late in the evening (*scil.* at the vigil of her *dies natalis*) while we swapped tales about our good mother and sang her praise . . ." [53]

The date of the first observances of Mass and communion at these private celebrations is not quite clear.[54] On the other hand, solemn Mass at the tomb of a martyr was said on his *dies natalis* as early as the second century.[54] The *Oratio ad sanctorum coetum,* whether or not pronounced by Constantine, leaves no doubt; hymns were sung, psalms and praise to the Lord recited, Mass was said ". . . and often a modest meal is prepared for the poor and the wretched." [56] In Rome and in Africa, certainly in the late fourth century, this modest meal was a huge feast on the vigil of the *dies natalis,* different from a private funeral banquet only in the far greater number of the participants. Quite naturally, the banquets became noisy, the mobs got out of hand, and rowdiness was rampant. The often quoted attacks of Saint Augustine against such abuses [57] render a vivid picture of the goings-on—drunkenness, brawls, gobbling, bawdy songs, dancing —at the *mensae* of the martyrs in North Africa. But the situation by 400 was no different in Rome. Augustine himself, in some embarrassment had to admit the "daily tippling" (*cotidianae vinulentiae*) going on inside St. Peter's in Rome; [58] another structure outside the walls, needless to say, enclosing a martyr's shrine, and by then, filled with graves and flanked by rows of mausolea. A famous letter of Paulinus of Nola describes a funeral banquet given in 397 in the atrium and in the nave and aisles of St. Peter's for all the poor of Rome, though in memory not of the martyr, but of an ordinary mortal, Pammachius' wife, Paula.[59] Banquets in honor of the martyr were customary at the same time at Nola-Cimitile in Campania.[60]

Funeral banquets in memory both of martyrs and of ordinary mortals originally seem to have been customary all over the Christian world, and they survived for a long time. Saint Ambrose in Milan had set out to abolish the feasts at least at the graves of the martyrs.[61] A characteristic incident has often been quoted: in 384, Monica, Augustine's mother, when about to take an offering of wine, cakes, and bread to the tombs of some martyrs in Milan, was told by the doorkeeper of the bishop's having forbidden such practices.[62] But the opposition progressed slowly and many churchmen closed an eye, as did Paulinus of Nola, when, in 402, commenting on the noisy feasts in honor of the local martyr St. Felix.[63] Augustine, in North Africa, was able to forbid banquees at the *mensae* of the martyrs in 395, at least in his bishopric and to replace them by the celebration of the Eucharist alone.[64] But the fight was hard. Time and again he stressed, as he once put it, that the *mensa* of Cyprian was neither a place where the martyr had feasted nor was it a place to feast with the martyr (as presumably had been the case formerly), but to say Mass ". . . *non in qua pascat sive pascatur*", but ". . . *in sacrificium Deo offeratur . . .*"[65] Throughout the greater part of Italy and in most countries across the sea, too, according to him, banquets at the martyrs' graves were gradually being eliminated.[66] Indeed, after the beginning of the fifth century, apparently few traces of feasting at the graves of martyrs were left in Rome.

On the other hand, private banquets in memory of ordinary mortals continued for some time undisturbed. Augustine himself, while opposing them, was indulgent.[67] In his old age, in 412, he only pointed out that at least "the better Christians" had abandoned the custom.[68] In Nola, the custom apparently continued. Since the tombs of ordinary mortals, however, were located near the graves of the martyrs, such private banquets continued to take place near the martyrs, though not specifically in their honor. But simple minds could hardly be expected to draw a clear line of distinction.

In the long run, the Church succeeded in stamping out two different elements of the ritual for ordinary mortals and martyrs respectively. The feasts at the tombs of the martyrs disappeared, but their *mensae* over or near their graves survived transformed into altars. On the other hand the *mensae* have disappeared from the tombs of ordinary mortals, but the feasts have continued to this day, including at times even the feeding of the defunct: in Serbia where still some forty years ago, the priest poured a glass of wine into the tomb;[69] in Greece where on All Souls' Day a dish of wheat is placed on the grave; among Polish gypsies who on that day bury a ham and pour *raki* on the cemetery;[70] at Naples where a picnic is held over the tomb; and of course, in any wake.

The relationship between the martyr's tomb, a burial ground for the faithful, and the celebration of funeral banquets both in honor of the martyr and of ordinary mortals seems to be the source of the huge covered structures outside the walls of Rome. Had it been merely a question of gaining room for the burials, the mere enlargement of a cemetery *sub divo* would have sufficed where such cemeteries were customary, as they were in by far the largest part of the Christian world. But the funeral banquets would require a covered space. Hence, in North Africa, the *martyrium,* the building which enclosed the martyr's tomb as well as the graves of such faithful as could acquire a spot in the coveted vicinity of his *mensa,* became both burial ground and banquet hall. Where, as in Rome, catacombs were the favorite, though not the only burial places, the need for huge structures for both burial and banquet was felt even more strongly. Burial in the catacombs, because of the labor involved, was costly and the space insufficient, as the number of faithful rapidly increased during the fourth century. Funeral banquets inside the catacomb, still possible for small family gatherings, became entirely impossible at the feast of the martyr.

For the huge crowds gathered on the vigil of the festivals of one of the great saints—be it Cyprian in North Africa, Peter, Lawrence, or Agnes in Rome —to be regaled with food, drink, and presumably a eulogy of the martyr, a huge building would have been required. In Carthage, one such structure was known simply as the *basilica tricliarum.*[71] At St. Peter's, the shrine was enclosed within the structure, albeit within the transept, the *martyrium* part proper; thus the feasting would have been relegated to the nave and aisles and the atrium.[72] Where the saint rested outside, as at S. Lorenzo, at Sant' Agnese, or at Tor Pignattara, it would take place in the huge structure, the *basilica,* the *coemeterium.* The tomb in the catacomb where space was limited would hardly have been involved in these festivals of the vigil. It became the center of attention presumably of a smaller crowd of serious worshippers on the feast day proper. One understands why her parents prevented Melania when she was pregnant from attending the big *kermesse* in the *"basilica beati Laurentii"* on the vigil, but did not interfere with her going next day to his *martyrium* in the catacomb, where the crowd was apparently more orderly; or why, for that matter, Jerome warned Laeta not to let her young daughter from her side "even an inch" during vigils and night-long prayers *"vigiliarum dies et sollemnes pernoctationes sic . . . celebret ut ne transversum quidem unguem a matre discedat . . . ,"*[73] obviously in the crowded *coemeteria.*

The large structures with ambulatories *extra moenia* in Rome, at S. Lorenzo, Sant' Agnese, S. Sebastiano and Tor Pignattara, served, in my opinion, these very functions. They rose near a martyr's tomb or a venerated spot. They were huge covered burial grounds, and they seem to have served as funerary banquet halls. Indeed, in the ruins of the Verano building, numerous sherds have been dug up, fragments of *amphorae,* drinking bowls, dishes. Some were fire-charred at the bottom; they may have belonged to cooking pots. Finally, all the buildings, from what we know, were provided with altar vessels for celebrating Mass and distributing communion to the faithful. They were, in short, *coemeteria-basilicae—* not cemeterial basilicas—with the connotation of funeral banquet halls. Jointly with the tomb of the martyr in the catacomb, and with the mausolea built against their flanks, they form the sanctuary precinct of the martyr.

When the floors of the *coemeteria-basilica* were all covered with graves, leaving no space, and when at the same time the custom of funeral banquets fell into disuse and was frowned upon, the structures, in the course of the late fifth and sixth centuries, lost their *raison d'être.* Their original function was forgotten, even more so since *basilicae ad corpus,* beginning with the late sixth century, began to rise alongside them over the graves of the martyrs. Hence the *coemeteria* were abandoned, as was the *coemeterium Agnetis* in the course of the sixth century. Or else, the local guides re-interpreted them as housing the tombs of innumerable martyrs, real or fictitious, as happened in the *basilica maior* at S. Lorenzo. Finally, as far as they survived into the seventh century and beyond, they were rededicated; the *basilica apostolorum* became S. Sebastiano, the *basilica maior* at S. Lorenzo the church of the Virgin.

This leads back to the epitaphs found on the Verano site, in which Lucillus Pelio and Flavius Eurialus claim the ownership of tombs " . . . *in basilica maiore . . . in mesu et situ prebiteriu . . .*" and ". . . *ad mesa beati Laurenti descindentibus in cripta . . .* " But what does the term *mensa* mean in this context?

Conventionally, *mensa* has been accepted to mean altar. Hence both inscriptions as a rule have been interpreted as referring to graves near the altar of St. Lawrence. On the other hand, this altar is known to have risen over his tomb in the catacomb; prayers were offered "at the tomb below the altar." [74] In consequence, both Flavius Eurialus and Lucillus Pelio were assumed to have been buried in the catacomb, the μαρτύριον, or on a stair leading to it.

But the accepted equation *mensa* = altar is an oversimplification. In Early Christian parlance, the altar on which Mass was celebrated is termed *mensa* far less frequently than is generally thought. The customary fourth-century term in the Latin West is *altare.* In evidence of this Braun has collected passages from patristic writings [75] and supplementary material is easily found. Thus the fourth-century donation lists incorporated into the *Liber Pontificalis* use *altare* whenever clearly referring to an altar, whether or not erected over the tomb of a martyr;[76] so does Damasus (366–384) in his epigrams; [77] so does, finally, the author of the *Vita Melaniae junioris.*[78] To be sure, *mensa,* at least in the writings of the fathers, does occur with the meaning altar. But it occurs less frequently and, in contrast to the East where τράπεζα is the customary term for an altar,[79] in the West, it may, but it need not mean altar. It takes on this meaning only late in the fourth century and slowly [80] and often elucidates it by an adjective, such as *mensa dominica, venerabilis,* or by the explanatory *mensa Dei.*[81] If unaccompanied by such an epithet, *mensa* in epitaphs and other inscriptions is rarely employed so as to demand the interpretation altar; in practically all cases, it either clearly means a funeral banquet table set up over or near the tomb of a martyr or of an ordinary mortal, or else lends itself to an interpretation as such.[82] The fourth century was apparently a time of transition during which the funeral

49

banquet table of the martyr was slowly replaced by the altar, while concomitantly the term *mensa* absorbed the meaning of *altare.*

In the epitaph of Flavius Eurialus, then, *mensa* might refer to the altar over his tomb down in the catacomb, as the consensus of opinion so far has it. But this is not necessarily the case. On the other hand, the grave of Lucillus Pelio cannot have been near the tomb of St. Lawrence in the catacomb, nor can the *mensa* mentioned in its text be synonymous with the altar over that tomb, for Lucillus Pelio had purchased his burial place *". . . in basilica maiore in mesu et situ presbiteriu. . . ."* He was buried inside the huge *coemeterium* on the Verano some fifty meters south of the hill in which the tomb and altar of St. Lawrence were placed. Within the *coemeterium-basilica* he was laid to rest *in presbiteriu,* in the chancel. The words *in mesu* which intervene between *in basilica maiore* and *et situ presbiteriu* obviously cannot mean that this grave was in an altar or in a funeral banquet table, whatever the term *mensa* may mean. They are explanatory in nature, and linked either to the preceding words *"in basilica maiore"* or to the following *"et situ presbiteriu".* Both interpretations are possible.

If the second explanation is accepted, chancel and *mensa* will be equivalent; the chancel *pars pro toto* will be termed *mensa* because a *mensa* stood in it. By about 400, this *mensa* might have been a regular altar set up in the *basilica maior* but it might as well have been a funeral banquet table in memory of the saint. *Refrigeria* on the original *mensa* over his tomb in the narrow space of the catacomb had by then become impossible. Hence it may have become necessary to set up in the huge covered *coemeterium* on the Verano a substitute *mensa.* This *mensa,* possibly placed inside an enclosure, would have served to receive food offerings for the saint. At the same time, it would serve as an altar for celebrating Mass. After all, the years around 400 were years of transition during which the funeral banquet table of the saint gradually became assimilated to the altar of the regular churches *intra moenia.*

What such a *mensa* and its enclosure looked like remains a matter of conjecture. However, one clue may have survived. Inside the *coemeterium Agnetis,* an enigmatic enclosure has come to light, freestanding in the center axis of the nave at the very entrance to the apse (Fig. 7). It looks like a small chapel, rectangular and terminated by an absidiole. The walls are comparatively strong, but at the outset only the absidiole seems to have existed. Only further excavations can possibly clarify its purpose. But it seems possible that it was a protecting screen, sheltering the *mensa martyris* which had been set up in the *coemeterium* as a substitute for the original *mensa* in the catacomb.

It is not quite so likely that the term *in mesu* was meant to elucidate the preceding words *in basilica maiore.* But if this interpretation holds, it is possible that the entire *coemeterium* would have been known, again *pars pro toto,* as *mensa.* The term is appropriate for a funeral banquet hall holding not only the substitute *mensa* of the saint (as we think it possibly did), but beyond any doubt the *mensae* over the tombs of the faithful serving their *convivia.* It simply parallels similar terms for the funeral banquet room, employed in ever new variations in late antiquity.[83] At Dougga in North Africa, three donors offered to the most blessed martyrs a *symposium* with four *cubicula* "AD C.P.M." [84] *Cubiculum* here refers presumably to dining couches as it does in many other inscriptions, such as perhaps the one from S. Paolo f. l. m.[85] But in other cases *cubiculum* may as well mean *pars pro toto* the banquet room, for example, when it appears as *"cubiculum ad confrequentandam memoriam quiescentium."* [86] Certainly a banquet room is described in an inscription from Fano in which one Fl. Concordius dedicated, about 360, *"cenationem . . . ita ut nulli liceat in aeodem aedificio corpus sepulture mandare sed tantummodo convivium copulantibus vel refrigerantibus pateat . . ."* [87] Hence, *mensa* might as well apply to a building which housed *mensae* or, for that matter, the *mensa* of a martyr.

If the *basilica maior* at S. Lorenzo was known as *mensa,* the two epitaphs of Lucillus Pelio and Flavius Eurialus would mean that they were buried, the former in the *mensa* that is the basilica, inside the chancel, the latter *"ad me(n)sa(m) beati Laurentii",* near the flank of the basilica on a staircase leading into the catacomb.

This explanation is hypothetical, to be sure. But if it stands, the three terms: *mensa,* as in *ad mensam beati Laurentii; memoria,* as in *memoria apostolorum* for S. Sebastiano; *coemeterium,* as in *coemeterium Agnetis;* all apparently refer to the various interlocking aspects of the building type: as *martyrium,* as burial place, as funeral banquet hall.

There remains a last question, but I doubt that it can be answered at this point. It concerns the design of these *coemeteria-basilicae,* with aisles carried around the apse so as to form an ambulatory. Generally speaking, the plan represents, of course, but one more variant on the type of the basilica, whether *forensis* or *palatina,* of which all Early Christian basilicas are variants. But no other fourth-century Christian basilica in Rome is provided with an ambulatory, be it one of the city churches or a *basilica ad corpus* enclosing the shrine of a saint, such as St. Peter's or, towards the end of the century, St. Paul's.

Ambulatories are altogether rare in Early Christian architecture, aside from the Constantinian *coemeteria-basilicae* of Rome. Of the few that have come to light so far, none date before the fifth century, nor do they fall into any regional, functional, or indeed architectural patterns. The ambulatory at S. Giovanni in Laterano is not Early Christian, but dates from the thirteenth century; its *tufelli* masonry leaves no doubt. The ambulatory of the Asklepieion basilica at Miletus was perhaps contemporary with the rest of the structure which may date from the fifth or early sixth century.[88] A sixth-century church with ambulatory, Siagu (Bir-bou-Rekba) in Tunisia, is known only from fragmentary notes and a ground-plan, apparently largely reconstructed.[89] Finally, it has been suggested that the eleventh-century colonnade of the ambulatory in the church of S. Giovanni on the island of Rab (Arbe) off the Dalmatian coast rests on foundations contemporary with the Early Christian mosaic pavement found throughout the building.[90]

The function of the ambulatory at Miletus may have been to allow the faithful to pass from one wing of the tripartite transept to the other, after having deposited their offerings, and without impeding the influx of newcomers. At Siagu, on the other hand, the ambulatory seems to lead to a huge baptistery in the rear, in the main axis of the building complex. In short, no common purpose can be established. Nor are the ambulatories of the same architectural type. The one at Miletus accompanies the solid wall of the apse on the outside and thus was not visible from the nave or the chancel of the church. Architecturally speaking, it is a mere adjunct. At Siagu and at Rab, on the other hand (if this latter was Early Christian) the wall of the apse was pierced by the openings of an arcade. Hence the ambulatory communicated with the interior of the apse and was integrated into the architectural design of the entire building, as it was in the Roman *coemeteria-basilicae* of the first half of the fourth century. Given the late date of Siagu, one even wonders whether it was perchance derived from the Roman prototype.

Functional reasons no doubt exerted their impact on planning the ambulatories of the huge *coemeteria extra moenia* of Rome. An ambulatory would offer additional space for burials and, if needed, for *mensae* around the apse and the *mensa martyris*. Its outer wall would provide more space for joining to them mausolea, or in the case of the *basilica maior* on the Verano, for badly needed entrances from the public highway. Its curved interior would be a favorite place from which to view the *mensa martyris* in the apse. Finally, it would lend itself splendidly to processions of pilgrims being led around the *mensa,* and thus solve a traffic problem ever present in the minds of Early Christian architects.

Still, reasons of a very different nature may well have played their part. Three come to mind, but all are mere hypotheses, and presented only for discussion's sake.

Given both their plan and the site of three of the *coemeteria* with ambulatories on imperial estates, one is tempted to link them to the *circi ambulatorii* which formed a common feature of the great Roman villas: huge circus-shaped gardens, surrounded by porticoes and frequently provided with windows in the terminating curved wall. The sunken "stadium" on the Palatine is indeed closely reminiscent of what is left of the *coemeterium Agnetis.* Indeed, it seems possible that this *coemeterium* was actually started as such a *circus ambulatorius:* the position overlooking the valley; the enormous wall with its buttresses; the windows in the wall of the ambulatory—all recall the stadium in the Imperial Palace on the Palatine.[91] Only during construction may the foundation walls of nave and apse have been inserted, thus transforming the *circus ambulatorius* into a roofed *coemeterium.* After all, the transformation of a garden, a παραδεῖσος, into a Christian burial ground, seems eminently fitting. But even if this hypothesis holds, it represents a singular case among the *coemeteria-basilicae* of Rome. None of the three others shows any evidence of having been evolved from a *circus ambulatorius;* the *basilica apostolorum,* S. Sebastiano, was not even situated, as far as our present knowledge goes, on an imperial estate. Nor can the *coemeterium Agnetis,* in all likelihood the last building of the group, have been the source for the type. If anything, the plan of the *circus ambulatorius* could have exerted an indirect impact on the formation of the covered *coemeteria.* But not even this is likely; all the *coemeteria-basilicae* in the group were roofed from the outset. Hence it is only a resemblance in plan. Archeologists, accustomed to looking at plans, have fallen time and again into the trap of such pseudo-resemblance. But the plan as an abstraction is less evident to the builder who sees on one hand a garden surrounded by low porticoes, on the other a roofed structure, its center nave high, and lit by clerestory windows, its aisles low, subordinate, and presumably dark.

In fact, a resemblance in plan only and thus equally treacherous underlies a second hypothesis: that the *coemeteria-basilicae* are derived from Roman circuses.[92] At first glance, the hypothesis is tempting. The *agon* in its very beginning was part of the funeral rite and the link of circus games to funerals was bound to be much in the mind of a period which had seen, preparatory to his funeral, the golden statue of Pertinax on a chariot drawn into the circus by four elephants.[93] Augustine was well aware of the link between games and funerary rites,[94] and Tertullian compares and contrasts the life and death of a Christian with a circus race.[95] A circus erected for funerary games and dedicated to the memory of Maxentius' young son, Romulus, rises on the Via Appia, opposite and nearly contemporary with S. Sebastiano. Yet, its resemblance is in plan only.

However, the *coemeteria-basilicae* of the fourth century in Rome are, I think, linked to the tradition of Roman funerary architecture. Pagan funerary basilicas have come to light in recent years. The two best known so far are the basilica of Julius Piso at Makhtar and the funerary basilica at St. Irénée [96] in Lyon, the latter identified through an inscription and containing a sarcophagus. Both buildings are small and designed for the burial of a wealthy individual and his immediate family, but their plans as well as the inscription of the structure at Lyon, *"sarcophagus cum basilica";* leave no doubt as to their designation as basilicas and their function. Hence, the development on a large scale of a basilica type for mass burial seems to be but a natural development. On the other hand, mausolea for centuries had been provided with circular, semicircular, or even rectangular corridors circling both the tomb chamber and occasionally the funeral banquet room, the *cubiculum,* on the upper floor.[97] Where the banquet area was placed in front of the tomb chamber, the corridor would start from and return to this area. Designed presumably for the solemn triple procession around the grave, the corridor was originally placed outside the tomb chamber, lacking any communication. Later, it was frequently transferred inside and turned into an ambulatory on columns, encircling the center room; the mausoleum of Costantina, Sta. Costanza, is a convenient example. The procession survived into Christian times. To this day, it forms part of the funeral rite of the Catholic Church when at the end of the funeral service the priest walks three times around the catafalque, asperging the coffin with Holy water. Hence the survival of the ambulatory from pagan into Christian funerary architecture seems natural enough.

The design of the covered *coemeteria-basilicae* outside the walls of Rome presented itself, it seems to me, as a two-fold task. In the first place, a huge assembly hall had to be laid out to serve for the celebration of the Eucharist, as a graveyard, and as a funeral banquet hall. For all these purposes, the basilica, the assembly hall κατ' ἐξοχὴν, offered itself as the self-evident solution to any architect of the fourth century, the more so since funerary basilicas were a type customary of old. At the same time, this hall was to serve for the funeral procession, an outstanding element within the funerary rite. Thus the ambulatory, by then part and parcel of funerary architecture, had to be fused into the design of the basilica.

This, to me, seems the most plausible hypothesis.[98]

Notes

1. *Corpus,* II (1959), 35 ff.

2. *Ibid.,* II, 70 ff.

3. *Ibid.,* pp. 93 ff., and E. Josi and W. Frankl, "Ulteriori trovamenti presso S. Lorenzo," *RACrist* XXVI (1950), 48 ff.

4. F. W. Deichmann and A. Tschira, "Das Mausoleum der Kaiserin Helena und die Basilica der Heiligen Marcellinus und Peter an der Via Labicana vor Rom," *JdI,* LXXII (1957), 44 ff. (hereafter quoted as Deichmann-Tschira, 1957).

5. F. W. Deichmann, "Die Lage der Konstantinischen Basilika der Heiligen Agnes . . .," *RACrist,* XXII (1946), 1 ff. (hereafter quoted as Deichmann, 1946).

6. See most recently H. Stern, "Les mosaiques de Sainte-Costance à Rome," *DOPapers,* XII (1958), 159 ff.

7. R. Perrotti, "Recenti ritrovamenti presso S. Costanza," *Palladio,* N.S., VI (1956), 80 ff.

8. Deichmann (1946), p. 3, with reference to older bibliography.

9. Deichmann-Tschira (1957), pp. 81 ff.

10. *LP,* ed. L. Duchesno, I (Paris, 1886 ff., and 1955), 399: Gregory II ". . . Sancti Laurenti ecclesiam foris muros sitam, quae trabibus confractis ruinae iam erat vicina reparabit;" ibid., 1, 500: Hadrian I, ". . . cimiterium . . . beatorum Petri et Marcellini renobavit . . . et tectum eius id est sancti Tiburtii et eorundem sanctorum Petri et Marcellini noviter fecit . . . ," ibid., I, 222: Innocent I, ". . . constituit et basilicam sanctae Agnae a presbyteris Leopardo et Paulino solicitudini gubernari et tegi et ornari . . ."

The emphasis which this last passage possibly places on the roofing of the structure at Sant'Agnese might be interpreted as supporting the contention made orally by Professor Axel Boëthius that the structure was originally open to the sky. However, the comparison with S. Sebastiano with its clerestory militates against the hypothesis of reconstructing any of the structures as a *basilica discoperta.*

11. The possibility has been suggested, tentatively, in a letter by Professor André Grabar.

12. Deichmann-Tschira (1957), pp. 53 ff., consider these graves early medieval; they assume, correctly in our opinion, that an early Christian cemetery preceded this medieval one.

13. G. Valadier and L. Canina, *Aggiunte e correzioni all'opera sugli edifizi antichi di Roma dell'architetto A. Desgo-*

detz, I (Rome, 1843), Pls. 7, 8, and p. 14.

14. *Corpus,* I, 19 and Pl. III, 2; II, 33 ff.

15. P. Styger, "Scavi a S. Sebastiano," *RQuSchr,* XXIX (1915), 75, Fig. 1; F. Tolotti, *Memorie degli apostoli in catacumbas* (*Collezione amici delle catacombe* [Vatican City, 1953]), Fig. 2, after Styger.

16. H. Delehaye, *Les origines du culte des martyres* (Brussels, 1933), pp. 264 ff.; T. Klauser, *Die römische Petrustradition* . . . (Cologne-Opladen, 1956), pp. 73 ff.; E. Kirschbaum, *Die Gräber der Apostelfürsten* (Frankfurt a. M., 1957), pp. 199 ff.

17. *LP,* I, 212: Damasus, ". . . *in catacumbas ubi iacuerunt corpora sanctorum apostolorum Petri et Pauli versibus exornavit."* Gregory the Great, *Epistolae,* IV, ep. 30: "(the bodies of Saints Peter and Paul) . . . *in loco dicitur catacumbas collocata sunt"* (*PL,* LXXVII, col. 703).

18. Deichmann-Tschira (1957), pp. 74 ff.

19. Deichmann-Tschira (1957), p. 84, lean towards a late date for the Verano structure. The development of the apse type which they postulate seems slight ground for this dating.

20. *Ibid.,* p. 83. My interpretation of the fourth- and fifth-century documents in the *Corpus,* I, 16 ff., 34 ff., insofar as I referred them to the catacomb chapel at the tomb of Saint Agnes, has obviously been rendered obsolete by the finds in the *coemeterium Agnetis.* The existence of a first catacomb chapel contemporaneous with the huge structure above ground remains, nonetheless, very possible.

21. Orally suggested by Enrico Josi. Deichmann-Tschira (1957), p. 82, seem to incline toward a Constantinian date.

22. *LP,* I, 500.

23. *Ibid.,* I, 508, and above, n. 17.

24. Deichmann-Tschira (1957), pp. 92 ff.

25. *Vita S. Melaniae Junioris,* ed. C. Smedt, *Analecta Bollandiana,* VIII (1889), 16 ff., esp. 23 f.; *S. Melaniae Junioris Acta Graeca, ibid.,* XLVIII (1930), 5 ff., esp. 10 f.; see also A. d'Alès, *Les deux vies de sainte Mélanie la Jeune, ibid.,* XXV (1906), 401 ff. The Greek text, much shorter than the Latin version, omits the reference to the basilica.

I am greatly indebted to Enrico Josi for calling my attention to the passage to which he had alluded in passing in *Roma Nobilis* (ed. I. Cecchetti [Rome, 1952], p. 361), a publication which had escaped my attention. He dates the event described in the *Vita Melaniae* 402, rather than 397–400.

26. Deichmann (Deichmann-Tschira [1957], pp. 92 ff.) is inclined to think that "the true altar tomb was known to the first half of the fifth century only in exceptional cases" (*ibid.,* p. 105). Regarding the situation at S. Lorenzo, he wonders whether the tomb of the martyr was not isolated from the rock of the catacomb only by Sixtus III (432–440) or perhaps by Damasus, rather than by Constantine (*ibid.,* p. 95). I myself used to have doubts regarding the authenticity of the passage in which the *LP* describes the building activity of the Emperor in the catacomb of S. Lorenzo (see Deichmann, *ibid.,* p. 95, n. 19). But these doubts have been removed through the more recent excavations.

27. *Epistolae Imperatorum Pontificum* . . . , ed. O. Guenther, *CSEL,* 3 (Vienna, 1895), 4.

28. *LP,* I, 207.

29. *PL,* VIII, col. 1392.

30. *LP,* I, 227.

31. *Ibid., loc. cit.*

32. *Ibid.,* I, 365.

33. *Notizie degli scavi* (1922), p. 250; E. Diehl, *ILCV* (Berlin, 1924 ff.) no. 3681a.

34. First published by A. Bosio, *Roma sotteranea* (1650 ed.), p. 201; for the latest edition of the text, complemented and emended, see A. Silvagni, *Inscriptiones Christianae Urbis Romae,* N.S., II, 138, no. 4794, Pl. XXXIII, 5a.

35. Both Father Antonio Ferrua, S.J., and Professor Josi in front of the original pronounced themselves in favor of a fifth-century date for the lettering.

36. R. Egger in E. Dyggve and R. Egger, *Der altchristliche Friedhof Marusinac* (*Forschungen in Salona,* III [Vienna, 1939]), 118.

37. S. Ermete: *Corpus*, I, pp. 196 ff.; S. Generosa: G. B. de Rossi, *Roma sotteranea*, III, pp. 651 ff.; S. Ippolito: P. Styger, *Römische Märtyrergrüfte* (Berlin, 1935), pp. 185 ff.; Sta. Petronilla: O. Marucchi, *Monumenti del cimitero di Domitilla* (*Roma sotteranea*, n.s., I, 1 [Rome, 1914]); S. Lorenzo: *Corpus*, II, 44 ff.; S. Agnese: *ibid.*, I, 14 ff.

38. J. B. Ward Perkins and J. Toynbee, *The Shrine of Saint Peter* (London, 1956), esp. pp. 200 ff.

39. Kapljuc: J. Brødsted and E. Dyggve, *Recherches à Salone*, I (Copenhagen, 1928), 36 ff.; Manastirine: *Forschungen in Salona*, II, 18 ff.; Marusinac: *ibid.*, III, 14 ff.

40. Summaries in E. Dyggve, *History of Salonitan Christianity* (Oslo, 1951).

41. S. Gsell, "Tipasa," *Mélanges de l'Ecole française de Rome*, XIV (1894), 291 ff.; *idem, Monuments antiques de l'Algérie*, II (Paris, 1901), 323 ff.; E. Albertini, "L'archéologie chrétienne en Algérie," *Atti del III° Congresso internazionale di archeologia cristiana* (Rome, 1934), pp. 411 ff., esp. 420 ff.

42. Gsell, *op. cit.* (1894), pp. 385 ff.

43. J. Vaultrin, "Les basiliques chrétiennes de Carthage," *Revue africaine*, LXXIII (1932), 188 ff., esp. 279 ff.

44. M. Robin, "Note sur la basilique byzantine d'Uppena," *Bull. archéol.* (1905), pp. 368 ff.

45. A. Berthier, *Les vestiges du christianisme dans la Numidie centrale* (Algiers, 1942), pp. 193 ff. and *passim*.

46. Benet, "Les fouilles de Tabarka," *Bull. archéol.* (1905), pp. 378 ff.; P. Gauckler, "Mosaiques tombales d'une chapelle de martyrs," *Monuments Piot*, XIII (1907), 175 ff.

47. E. Junyent, in *Atti del III° Congresso internazionale di archeologia cristiana*, pp. 258 ff.

48. *Bulletino comunale*, XX (1892), 466 ff; Gsell, *Monuments antiques de l'Algérie*, II, 333 ff.; *Bulletino comunale*, LXVI (1938), 422 ff.

49. F. van der Meer, *Augustinus als Seelsorger* (Cologne, 1953), pp. 487 ff., with references to the sources and to the older bibliography.

50. Summary of the evidence with special regard to Salona: Dyggve, *History of Salonitan Christianity*, pp. 106 ff. For the monumental evidence in Spain, see J. Serra Villaro, *Excavaciones en la necropolis de Tarragona (Junta superior de excavaciones y antiguidades*, 104, 1928 [Madrid, 1929]); E. Junyent, "I monumenti cristiani di Spagna," *Atti del III° Congresso* (Rome, 1934), pp. 255 ff., esp. p. 271; for North Africa, see Albertini, *op. cit.*, pp. 421 ff.

51. Gsell, *Les monuments antiques de l'Algérie*, II, 48; Cabrol-Leclerq, XI, 1, cols. 113 ff., s.v. *mensa;* both with reference to bibliography.

52. A. M. Schneider, "Mensa oleorum," *RQuSchr*, XXXV (1927), 287 ff.

53. E. Diehl, *ILCV*, no. 1570; see also van der Meer, *op cit.*, pp. 517, 665.

54. J. A. Jungmann, *Missarum Solemnia* I (Freiburg, 1952), 286, refers to the fifth or sixth century.

55. H. Delehaye, *Le culte des martyrs* (Brussels, 1933), pp. 34, 41.

56. *P.G.*, XX, col. 1272; see also Delehaye, *op. cit.*, p. 42.

57. *Ep.* 22 and 29(*PL*, XXXII, cols. 90 ff. 114 ff.); *Sermones* 252, 310, 311 (*PL*, XXXVIII, col. 1413, 1415); see also van der Meer, *op. cit.*, pp. 532 ff., 674 (notes).

58. Augustinus, *Ep.* 29, *loc. cit.*

59. Paulinus of Nola, *Ep.* XIII, 11–13 (*PL*, LXI, cols. 213 ff.).

60. *Ibid., Poema* xxvii (*PL*, LXI, cols. 660 ff.).

61. Ambrosius, *De Elia et Jejunio*, cap. 17 (*PL*, XIV, col. 754).

62. Augustinus, *Confessionum libri* XIII, lib. vi, cap. 2 (*PL*, XXXII, cols. 719 ff.).

63. See n 60 above, and van der Meer, *op. cit.*, pp. 528, 667.

64. Augustinus, *Sermo* 310, cap. 2 (*PL*, XXXVIII, col. 1413) and *Ep.* 29 (*ibid.*, XXXIII, cols. 114 ff.); see the vivid presentation of the situation by van der Meer, *op. cit.*, pp. 536 ff.

65. Augustinus, *Sermo* 310, *loc. cit.*

66. *Idem, Ep.* 22 (*PL*, XXXIII, col. 91).

67. Van der Meer, *op. cit.*, pp. 540 ff.

68. Augustinus, *De Civitate Dei*, VII, 27 (*PL*, XLI, col. 255).

69. F. J. Doelger, *Ichthys*, II (Münster, Westf., 1922), 571.

70. *New York Times*, April 12, 1959.

71. F. van der Meer, *op. cit.*, p. 530; see also *PL*, XXXVIII, col. 364, note c.

72. Paulinus, *Ep.* XIII (*PL*, LXI, cols. 213 ff.).

73. Jerome, Ep. 10 (*Select Letters of St. Jerome*, ed. F. A. Wright, "Loeb Classical Library" [Cambridge, Mass. and London, 1954], p. 358).

74. *Vita Melaniae junioris, op. cit.;* see above, text pp. 40 ff. and n. 25.

75. J. Braun, *Der christliche Altar* (Munich, 1924), I, 27 ff.

76. *LP, passim,* and Index, III, pp. 192, 214.

77. A. Ferrua, *Epigrammata Damasiana* (*Sussidi allo studio delle antichità cristiane*, 2 [Vatican City, 1942]), *passim,* and index, pp. 265 ff.

78. See above, n. 74.

79. Braun, *op. cit.*, p. 25.

80. I am quoting from a letter by Father Anselm Strittmater, O.S.B., to whom I am greatly indebted for much good advice.

81. Braun, *op. cit.*, p. 29.

82. E. Diehl, *ILCV, passim.*

83. R. Egger, "Der christliche Friedhof von Manastirine," *Forschungen in Salona,* II (Vienna, 1926).

84. P. Monceaux, "L'inscription des martyrs de Dougga," *Bull. archéol.* (1908), 87 ff. The interpretation of the letters CPM as *"convivia pro martyribus"* is doubtful, but the rest of the inscription is clear.

85. See above, n. 34.

86. G. B. de Rossi, "Memorie degli apostoli Pietro e Paolo," *Boll. arch. crist.,* 3rd ser., II (1877), 97 ff.

87. E. Diehl, *ILCV,* no. 3827.

88. T. Wiegand, *Abhandlungen Preuss. Akad. der Wissenschaften* (1908), *Anhang,* pp. 28 ff.

89. P. Gauckler, *Basiliques chrétiennes en Tunisie* (Paris, 1913), pp. 17 ff. (without plan); plan in R. de Lasteyrie, *L'architecture religieuse en France a l'époque romane* (Paris, 1929), p. 188. A building with ambulatory at Oum-el-Abouab is presented by Gauckler, Pl. XII, without text and with a question mark as "chevet de basilique."

90. D. Frey, "S. Giovanni Battista in Arbe," *Jbh. des Kunsthist. Inst. der K. K. Zentralkommission,* V (1911), *Beiblatt,* cols. 49 ff. The Early Christian church excavated at Cilli-Celeja (G. Schön, "Mosaikinschriften aus Cilli," *Jahreshefte des österr. archäol. Inst.,* I [1898], *Beiblatt,* cols. 29 ff.) had no ambulatory, but a clergy bench; see Egger, *Forschungen in Salona,* I, 93. I suspect the same to be true of the Early Christian predecessor of the eleventh century church at Rab.

91. Deichmann, 1946, p. 14, has excluded the possibility that the *coemeterium Agnetis* could ever have been an area surrounded by porticoes, largely because of the windows in its outer walls. But the stadium on the Palatine has just such rectangular windows in the wall facing the valley.

92. The suggestion has been made orally and in the most tentative manner by Professor Frank E. Brown of the American Academy in Rome, to whom I am grateful for many a stimulating talk.

93. Dio Cassius, *Roman History,* Epitome, Book LXXV, ed. E. Cary, Loeb Classical Library, IX (London and New York, 1927), 167.

94. Augustinus, *De Civitate Dei*, VIII, 26. 2 (*PL*, XLI, col. 153).

95. Tertullian, *De Spectaculis,* cap. XXIX (*PL*, I, col. 735).

96. G. Picard, "La basilique funéraire de Julius Piso à Mactar," *Comptes rendus de l'Académie des inscriptions et belles lettres* (1945), pp. 185–212; W. Seston and C. Perrat, "Une basilique funéraire païenne à Lyon d'après une inscription inédite," *Revue des études anciennes* XLIX (1947), 139.

97. See "Introduction to an Iconography of Medieval Architecture," below, pp. 115 ff., esp. pp. 134 f.

98. A building of the type of the *coemeteria-basilicae,* but not necessarily Christian, was excavated in 1958–1959 in the Villa dei Gordiani by Dr. G. Gatti. When published it may answer some questions regarding the origin of the type.

Postscript

I can add but a few supplementary notes to this paper.

First: in writing it, I had overlooked a text which beyond any doubt proves the synonymity in early Christian parlance of the terms *coemeterium* and *basilica subteglata*. It is found in the biography of pope Marcus (336) in the *LP* (I, 202: ". . . *Ex huius suggestione obtulit Constantinus Augustus basilicae quem cymiterium constituit* [i.e., the pope] *Via Ardeatina . . . sepultus est in cymiterio Balbinae via Ardeatina quem ipse insistens fecit.*") and supplemented by the epitaph of one Felix Fastinianus who purchased a grave "*in Balbines basilica . . . subteglata . . .*" (*ibid.*, I, 203, n. 4). Site and plan of the building have never been exactly established. But it was apparently located near the Quo Vadis, where in 1640 were seen the remains of a huge structure, comprising a nave and two aisles (*tre navi*) and being filled with graves and sarcophagi (*pili antichi ed altre sepolture*; see De Rossi, *Roma sotterranea*, III [Rome, 1864–1877] 8 ff.). Thus it might well have belonged to our group of large covered cemeteries with ambulatory. The texts in any event provide the technical term "*basilica subteglata*" or, by ellipsis, "*coemeterium subteglatum.*"

Second: regarding S. Sebastiano, Father Ferrua inclines toward dating the construction between 337 and 350 because of his discovery on the threshold of one of the atrium doors of a monogram which he reads as "Constans." I am not sure of his reading, and I would still prefer a prior date for the building; but this date may well be early Constantinian rather than pre-Constantinian. For my argument I refer to *Corpus basilicarum*, IV, in press. I also think it possible, as does my collaborator Spencer Corbett (*ibid.*), that the *memoria apostolorum* at S. Sebastiano for some time remained accessible from the higher level of the nave of the church; only later, a few decades after the *basilica-coemeterium* had been completed, did this "sunk *memoria*" disappear under layers of graves extending in the direction of the apse and maintaining the higher nave level.

Third: I may have been too definite in excluding the possibility that Sta. Costanza ever served as a baptistery. But this is a minor point.

Finally, the "*coemeterium-basilica*" in the Villa dei Gordiani, mentioned in the last footnote, has been published in a preliminary note by the excavator, G. Gatti; but the excavation has not been completed, and exact date, function, and—if Christian—dedication of the building remain unknown at this writing.

Additional Bibliography

Ferrua, A., S.J., "Lavori a San Sebastiano," *RACrist,* XXXVII (1961), 203 ff.
Gatti, G. "Una basilica di età costantiniana recentemente riconosciuta presso la via Prenestina," *Capitolium,* XXXIV (June 1960), 3 ff.
Krautheimer, R., and Corbett, S., *Corpus,* IV, in press.

5

THE TRANSEPT IN
THE EARLY CHRISTIAN BASILICA*

"IL TRANSETTO NELLA BASILICA PALEOCRISTIANA" is the title of an essay published in 1937 by the then *spiritus rector* of our congresses, Mons. Johann Peter
Kirsch. I would like to dedicate these pages to his memory.

Kirsch's article, though brief, was fundamental. He recognized that, from
the fourth to the sixth century, the transept was an exceptional element in the
Early Christian basilica, and that it did not originate in classical Roman architecture.[1] He therefore posed the question of the transept's function both in
the architectural context of the Christian basilica and in the Christian liturgy as
it developed with regional differences throughout the *Orbis Christianus*. This
latter particular aspect of the problem was examined at the same time and in
subsequent years by Klauser, Dyggve and Grabar.[2] Taking the Lateran as his
point of departure, Klauser explained the transept as a space for the presentation
of offerings by the congregation. Grabar and Dyggve, on the other hand, held
the transept, in general, to have been a *memoria-martyrium*. As a result it
became possible and necessary to distinguish among various architectural types
of transepts. These types are by now well known; but it might be helpful to
list them once more. They are *a*) the *continuous transept,* such as that in St.
Peter's in Rome (Figs. 12, 13), an uninterrupted rectangular spatial unit placed
at right angles to and inserted between the apse and the nave; *b*) the *tripartite
transept,* as it appears in Sta. Tecla in Milan (Fig. 14), at S. Pietro in Vincoli
in Rome (Fig. 15), at Nikopolis and elsewhere in Greece, in which the central
arca in front of the apse was separated from the arms by colonnades, huge
arches, or, more simply projecting piers;[3] *c*) the *cross-transept* in which the
aisles were continued from the nave into the arms of the transept, as in the
basilica of St. Menas in Egypt (Fig. 16); and *d*) an *abbreviated version of
the cross-transept* in which aisles were limited to one or two sides of the transept's

---

*Translated by Alfred Frazer, from *Acts du Vᵉ Congrès internationale d'archéologie
chrétienne* (Aix-en-Provence, 1954; Vatican City and Paris, 1957), pp. 283–90.
The author wishes to inform the reader that the purpose of the paper read to the Congress was not to present final conclusions, but rather to define certain ideas in a preliminary form. It is his eager hope that, from discussion with colleagues in the history of
architecture and the liturgy, some of the problems indicated might be clarified. The
friendly exchange of ideas during the Congress, particularly with Professors Grabar,
Josi, Orlandos, and Ward Perkins, has already been of great value.

arms.[4] I have omitted the transepts of churches having aisleless naves since the type seems to me to be different in origin and function.

These various types of transepts have been frequently explained simply as formal architectural variants. To me such an explanation seems unconvincing. In my opinion they are, on the contrary, closely linked to the liturgical acts performed in that area inserted before the apse and distinct from the nave where the faithful gathered. These liturgical functions may have varied widely: the veneration of a *memoria;* the celebration of the Mass; the offering of gifts by the congregation; or perhaps, as Sotiriou maintains, the area may have been designed to shelter the *schola cantorum.*

Lemerle, in a recent article, has enumerated and classified the transepts known to him. His list, though incomplete, is valuable, and based on it, he has raised some interesting questions. He employed a terminology slightly different from mine in that he spoke of independent rather than continuous transepts and of transepts *à nefs enveloppants* instead of cross-transepts.[5] However, the problem is not one of terminology but of the function of these types; and in this respect, two closely related observations seem to me essential for any possible solution to the problem of the transept. First, since we are dealing with architecturally different types of transepts, we should consider as possible and even probable that they were designed to fulfill different liturgical requirements, and that the various architectural types acquired their original significance primarily from the liturgical functions they were intended to serve. Thus it appears inappropriate to intermingle the types as Lemerle does by classifying as independent transepts the tri-partite as well as the continuous type. Second, I think it necessary to insist that the various types did not originate at one and the same time. Their coexistence does not refute this argument. For this reason, the chronology of the various forms is of primary importance. Indeed, it seems to me quite possible that between the fourth and the sixth centuries different types of transepts followed one another and that each, in turn, influenced its successor in such a way that a pattern originally created for a particular function or for a number of specific functions may have been adopted subsequently for quite different uses with or without changes in the architectural type.

The placement of the chancel railings, the level and character of the pavement, the location of entrances to the transept both from the nave and aisles and from the exterior constitute, without a doubt, important evidence for determining the function of the transept. Up to now such evidence has received surprisingly little study. Yet the liturgical and architectural situation prevailing in the tripartite transepts of Greece is quite clear. In Basilica A at Nikopolis (Fig. 17), for example, the central bay of the transept was spatially continuous with the nave; but liturgically it was closely linked to the apse. On its northern, western, and southern sides it was enclosed by chancel railings from which a *solea* extended further into the nave. The floor of the enclosed area was of simple stone slabs. On the other hand, the arms of the transept, while related to the center bay, are separate from it. They communicate not with the center bay, but with the aisles, and were paved with the elegant figural mosaics recently discussed by my friend Ernst Kitzinger.[6] Thus, in Basilica A the function of the tri-partite division was clarified by the plan of the chancel railings and by the pavement. It is likewise apparent that the central bay must have served functions different from those accommodated in the lateral bays of the transept. The first was reserved for the clergy and the Divine Office; the others, accessible to the laity and the clergy alike, must have served a liturgical function for which the clergy and the faithful had to come into direct contact. The hypothesis that such a function was the presentation of offerings by the faithful is confirmed by the layout of other Greek basilicas of the same tri-partite type. In Basilica B at Nikopolis (Fig. 18) and at Corinth this purpose is apparent beyond doubt. In the former, each arm of the transept was connected to the aisles—two on either side—by doors instead of arches, and at least one of these doors was closed by a railing. Moreover, a long railing ran parallel to the east wall leaving but a narrow corridor free along that wall. This corridor was possibly reserved for the deacons; presumably they received there the offerings of the faithful who were admitted to the area in the transept arm in front of the railing. Hence, in this group of Greek basilicas, the purpose of the tri-partite transept was no doubt the following: the central bay served as the sanctuary, while the lateral bays were pastophories in the proper meaning of the term—areas where offerings were presented by the faithful and received by the clergy.

The group of basilicas thus far considered is restricted apparently to a limited region—Greece—and late. (The appearance of the same type at Korykos is important only as evidence for the probably close relations between Cilicia and Greece.) Indeed, contrary to opinions held a decade ago, none of these churches may be ascribed a date prior to the end of the fifth century. Kitzinger has proved that the Basilica A at Nikopolis was built in the second quarter of the sixth century. Likewise, the majority of the others appear to be datable around the end of the fifth century and the beginning of the sixth. Thus, most of the churches in the Greek group are much later than comparable examples in Italy; S. Pietro in Vincoli was built between 430 and ca. 450, while the cathedral of Sta. Tecla in Milan, in its first phase, probably is to be placed around 380. Thus it would appear, at first glance, that the scheme of the tri-partite transept may have originated at Milan; and that, in the middle of the fifth century, it spread to Rome and, toward the end of the century, to Greece. Such an hypothesis, however, may be too simple, for already toward the end of the fourth century the basilica at Epidauros possessed a transept similar to the tri-partite pattern. Its plan is of unusual interest. It was a five-aisled basilica. The apse as well as the central and lateral bays of the transept—the latter corresponding in width to that of the nave and the inner aisles—were paved with marble and thus distinguished from the nave and the outer aisles, where the paving is different. Moreover, the ends of the transept were separated both from its arms proper, by colonnades, and from the side aisles, by small doors. Thus, these outer areas give the impression of having served as sacristies. On the other hand, the central bay of the transept was separated from the nave by a chancel railing and from the lateral bays of the transept by low walls each of which supported a single column. The lateral bays, on the contrary, opened freely into the inner aisles through arches without railed enclosures. It would seem, therefore, that the central bay along with the apse formed the sanctuary and that the inner lateral bays, linked to the sanctuary though separate from it, may have served the rite of the offertory.

The tri-partite, or better the five-part transept at Epidauros may be nearly as early as that of Sta. Tecla in Milan, and it is certainly earlier than that of S. Pietro in Vincoli in Rome. This again raises the question whether the type originated in Greece or in Italy or whether it appeared simultaneously in both regions toward the close of the fourth century.

There is no evidence at either Sta. Tecla or S. Pietro in Vincoli for determining the function of the arms of their tripartite transepts. There are indications, however, in a basilica of the Constantinian period that permit at least hypotheses concerning both the existence and the function of a tri-partite transept. It has been doubted for some time that S. Giovanni in Laterano in its original state had the continuous transept one sees today. Recently Ward Perkins has called attention to the continuation of the foundation walls of the nave colonnades across the present transept; in the light of this fact he has concluded that originally the transept was not continuous.[7] As to its original form, three possibilities remain: the side aisles continued and there was no transept; the transept was tri-partite with its arms separated from the central bay by columns standing on unbroken foundation walls; or it had five divisions with the extremities distinct from the lateral bays, as at Epidauros. Several years ago I suggested a tri-partite scheme, a solution recently more strongly advanced by Forsyth.[8] If such an hypothesis could be proven, it would be of exceptional interest, for it would support Klauser's earlier suggestion that the seven altars given to the Lateran by Constantine, six of them destined for the offertory, were placed in the transept. If the transept of the Lateran Basilica was originally really tri-partite, it is probable that as early as the Constantinian period the tri-partite scheme corresponded to a threefold function, combining an enlarged sanctuary with two lateral pastophories accessible to the congregation for offerings. The decision, nonetheless, must be left to the spade—*ultima ratio archaeologi.*

The arrangement of the sanctuary in basilicas with cross-transepts is totally different, but in those, too, the placement of the chancel enclosure is the decisive element. It is still uncertain whether the type originated in the Constantinian basilica of the Holy Apostles in Constantinople.[9] The basilica of St. Menas surely provides a perfect example from the first decade of the fifth century. The center of the transept sheltered the chancel precinct, enclosed on all four sides and reserved for the clergy. On the other hand, the transept arms were completely open to the aisles and thus afforded free access to the faithful. Such a pattern would have been natural in a pilgrimage sanctuary where the central precinct was used for the display of a relic. And indeed, in the pre-Justinianic basilica of St. John at Ephesus it is quite clear that the cross-transept occurred in connection with a pilgrimage shrine. The central precinct encompassed the tomb of the Evangelist; the arms opened to the aisles and, moreover, were accessible from the exterior through doors in the northern and southern walls. Such a plan is almost surely linked closely to the aisleless cruciform *memoriae*, such as the fourth-century *martyria* at Kaoussié, Sichem, and SS. Apostoli in Milan (Fig. 19).[10]

The transept of Basilica A at Philippi (Fig. 20), published by Lemerle, appears from a strictly formal point of view to be simply a variant of the complete cross-transept—a reduction in which only one or two of the three original aisles were retained in the transept. (The same is true of such basilicas as St. Demetrios at Saloniki (Fig. 21), et-tâbga in the Sea of Galilee, Tropaion in Bulgaria, and Basilica A at Perge.)[11] The plan by itself, however, gives a false impression. The placement of the chancel railings and the relation of the chancel area to the nave and aisles at Philippi are not that characteristic of churches with true cross-transepts. Instead they correspond exactly to those in contemporary Greek churches with tri-partite transepts. I therefore think it likely that also the liturgical function was the same. Indeed, not only Philippi, a century later than the Menas basilica (Fig. 16), but also other later churches with cross plans present a mixed type. To be sure, St. Demetrius—whose date, despite Sotiriou's recent publication, remains uncertain—or the basilica on the Sea of Galilee display a tri-partite arrangement of the chancel railings, but they also preserve the characteristics of *memoriae*. Indeed, they contain in the one case the stone of the Multiplication of the Loaves and in the other a small cruciform crypt. Hence, they may represent mixed types in which the commemorative element, so clear at Ephesus, was associated with the tri-partite arrangement comprising a sanctuary and pastophories.

The few continuous transepts of the pure type, likewise, possessed a commemorative character. The transepts of St. Peter's (St. Paul's-without-the-walls) and the Lateran (Figs. 12, 13, 79, 81, 82), are commonly cited. But with that of the Lateran eliminated, only St. Peter's and St. Paul's remain in the group, and the latter is almost surely a duplicate of the former. Ward Perkins has clarified the problem of the location in the fourth century of the railings surrounding the aedicula over the tomb of St. Peter. And while the exact placement of the original altar remains in doubt (was it movable?), it is clear in any event that it stood in the transept, either near the tomb or eastward toward the triumphal arch.[12]

Gregory of Tours, in discussing St. Peter's, is the first author to transmit to us a term designating the transept. For this purpose he used the word *altare*, thereby specifying the transept as the location of the altar.[13] Hence, the transept of St. Peter's had at least a dual function: it contained both the chancel and the *memoria* precinct whose veneration was the transept's *raison d'être*. Apparently the faithful, even if excluded from the precinct, were permitted to enter the arms of the transept. As far as we know there were never barriers separating the aisles from the arms of the transept, although the openings between aisles and transept were screened by columns. It is not improbable, therefore, that the transept arms were used also for the offerings of the faithful. The arrangement at St. Paul's, toward the end of the fourth century, was almost identical. It may be noted, moreover, that outside of Rome continuous transepts were a rarity. Among those few, the transept of Manastirine-Salona, of around 400, would seem to have absorbed some of the characteristics of the tripartite transept in the disposition of its chancel railings. Other basilicas in the East with continuous transepts, such as the two as Sagalassos, Topkapu Saray, and the recently-discovered basilica at Side, should be restudied with respect to both their functions and their dates.[14]

One of the major problems in religious architecture during the fourth century was presented by the necessity of finding sufficient accommodation within a single area for at least two and, at times, three liturgical functions—the celebration of the Divine Office within the altar enclosure reserved to the clergy, the presentation of offerings in which the congregation and the clergy came into direct contact, and at times the veneration of a *memoria* either incorporated in the altar or placed near it. All three of these diverse functions were accommodated within one and the same area in the transept of St. Peter's. The problem, then, was to concentrate such intimately related yet different functions into a single unified ambience which was liturgically, though not architecturally divisible. This difficulty would seem to account also for the rarity of this type of continuous transept, which survived in the West at Rome and perhaps at Salona, but evidently not beyond the end of the fourth century.[15] It is, in fact, permissible to regard also the cross- and tri-partite transept types as originating coevally with the continuous transept of St. Peter's, i.e., in Constantinian times. The basilica of the Holy Apostles at Constantinople probably was formed like a cruciform *martyrium* with four arms, each divided into nave and aisles. The Lateran Basilica may have had a tri-partite transept whose bays were divided for the sanctuary and the presentation of offerings. The diffusion and the successive assimilations among these various Constantinian types is documented toward the end of the fourth century.

The cross-transept basilica develops, it seems to me, from the cruciform *martyrium* type through a fusion with elements purloined from other transept types. This becomes clear even in the first known example of the cross-transept plan, the Menas basilica. The central enclosure upon which three formal elements, the nave and the transept arms, converged was retained from the cruciform scheme. On the other hand, the substitution of the apse for the fourth arm of the cruciform type and the diminished length of the transept arms in relation to the nave suggests a compromise with the scheme of the continuous transept as it existed in Rome in St. Peter's and St. Paul's. The fusion of the two types is seen very clearly in the basilica at Apollonia in Libya. Upon hasty inspection, its transept appears to be continuous, yet the central placement of the altar enclosure and the location of the doors to the exterior show these elements to have been derived from a cross-transept of the St. Menas type.[16] A similar, though not identical, assimilative process may have prevailed in the development of the tripartite transept. Assuming the type to have had its origins in the Lateran Basilica, its spread to Milan, to S. Pietro in Vincoli and to Epidauros would be easily explained. Yet both S. Pietro in Vincoli and Epidauros represent variants on the pure type. At the former the archetype was modified during construction with the suppression of the columns between the central and flanking bays, thereby assimilating the tri-partite with the continuous transept type. Similarly, the isolation of the rooms at the ends of the transept arms in the five-part transept at Epidauros curiously recalls the comparable disposition in the continuous transept of St. Peter's. This raises two questions: whether the transept of Epidauros was not, in fact, created under the influence of St. Peter's, and whether the identity of the divisions at Rome and Epidauros do not reflect comparable functions.

The transept, in its various forms, was relatively rare during the greater part of the fifth century. Only toward the end of the century and then in the sixth century did the tripartite form spread throughout Greece from Milan, Rome, or Epidauros. In the provinces of the East, a true renascence of the various forms of the transept must be presumed between 470 and 550. The shortened cross-transept with its aisles restricted to one or two sides of the arms and adapted to the requirements of the Mass and the presentation of offerings spread during this period to Greece, Asia Minor, and even the Holy Land—from the Sea of Galilee to Philippi. In the West, on the other hand, transepts of all forms virtually disappeared after the middle of the fifth century. With the exception of the seventh-century S. Pancrazio in Rome, surely copied from St. Peter's, there was no renascence of the transept prior to the Carolingian period. Only then did the form become an integral element of medieval architecture in the West.

All of these ideas are no more than the trial hypotheses of an architectural historian, hypotheses that may be confirmed only through a collaboration with historians of liturgy. To this end I appeal to colleagues in that field to show us the way to a clearer understanding of the succession and the change of liturgical demands in the different regions of the *Orbis Christianus* between the fourth and the sixth centuries.

Notes

1. Johann Peter Kirsch, "Il transetto nella basilica paleocristiana," *Scritti in onore di Bartolomeo Nogara* (Vatican City, 1937), pp. 205 ff.; see also *idem*, "Das Querhaus in den stadtrömischen . . . Basiliken," *Pisciculi: Studien F. J. Doelger dargeboten* (Münster, 1939), pp. 48 ff.

2. Theodor Klauser, "Die konstantinischen Altäre der Lateransbasilika," *RQuSchr*, XLVIII (1935), 179 ff.; Einar Dyggve, *Das Heroon von Kalydon* (Copenhagen, 1934); André Grabar, *Martyrium* (Paris, 1948), esp. I, 293 ff.

3. Alberto de Capitani d'Arzago, "Cenni sullo scavo della basilica di S. Tecla," *Scritti in onore di A. Giussani* (Como, 1944), pp. 185 ff.; Krautheimer, "S. Pietro in Vincoli and the Tripartite Transept," *Proceedings of the American Philosophical Society*, LXXXIV (1941), 411 ff. For the Greek basilicas see Georgios Sotiriou, Αἱ παλαιοχριστιανικαὶ βασιλικαὶ τῆς Ἑλλάδος (Athens, 1930); Anastasios Orlandos, Ἡ ξυλοστέγος παλαιοχριστιανικὴ βασιλικὴ (Athens, 1952–1954), and the detailed bibliography in these books.

4. For *martyria* and cross-transepts in general: Grabar, *op. cit.*, and Samuel Guyer, *Grundlagen mittelalterlicher Baukunst* (Einsiedeln-Zürich, 1950).

5. Paul Lemerle, "Saint-Démétrius de Thessalonique et les problèmes du martyrion et du transept," *BCH*, LXXVII (1953), 60 ff.

6. Ernst Kitzinger, "Studies on Late Antique and Early Byzantine Floor Mosaics," *DOPapers*, VI (1951), 83 ff.

7. John Ward Perkins, "Constantine and the Origins of the Christian Basilica," *BSR*, XXII (1954), 69 ff.

8. George Forsyth, "The Transept of Old St. Peter's in Rome," *Late Classical and Medieval Studies in Honor of A. M. Friend* (Princeton, 1955), pp. 56 ff, especially p. 57, n. 6.

9. For the reconstruction of the church of the Holy Apostles in Constantinople in this respect see Hans Christ, "Zur Erklärung des T-förmigen Grundrisses," *RACrist* XII (1935), 293 ff.

10. Above, n. 4, and E. Villa, "La Basilica Apostolorum," *Arte del primo Millennio*, ed. E. Arslan (Turin, 1952).

11. Paul Lemerle, *Philippes et la Macédoine orientale* (Paris, 1945); Georgios and Maria Sotiriou, Ἡ βασιλικὴ τοῦ ἁγίου Δημητρίου (Athens, 1952); Alfons Maria Schneider, *Die Brotvermehrungskirche von et-tâbga* (Paderborn, 1934), who, however, assigns a date to the church in the fourth century instead of the late fifth century.

12. John Ward Perkins, "The Shrine of St. Peter's and its Twelve Spiral Columns," *JRS*, XLII (1952), 21 ff.; George Forsyth, *loc. cit.*, emphasized the role of St. Peter's transept as a *memoria* and as the audience hall of Christ the King.

13. Gregory uses the phrase *'in altario'* in his description of the basilicas of Tours and Clermont-Ferrand: *"habet finestras in altario XXXII, in capso* (i.e., the nave) *XX; parietes ad altarium opere sarsurio."* Thus in the description of St. Peter's in Rome it seems that the expression *'altare'* refers to the transept: *". . . quattuor ordines columnarum . . . numero nonaginta sex habens. Habet etiam quattuor in altari, quae sunt simul centum, praeter illas quae ciborium sepulcri sustentant."* The four columns *in altari* therefore would have been those placed at the ends of the transept arms; see my note, "Some Drawings of Early Christian Basilicas in Rome," *AB*, XXXI (1949), 211 ff., especially 213; José Ruysschaert, "Réflexions sur les fouilles vaticanes," *Revue d'histoire ecclésiastique*, XLIX (1954), 41 ff.

14. Rudolf Egger, *Forschungen in Salona*, II (Vienna, 1926); Hans Rott, *Kleinasiatische Denkmäler* (Leipzig, 1908); Alfons Maria Schneider, "Funde in Konstantinopel," *Archäologischer Anzeiger*, LXIII (1943), 249 ff.

15. I am happy to be able to rectify an error—*mea maxima culpa*—which has crept into certain recent publications. It concerns a continuous transept in the pre-Pelagian basilica of S. Lorenzo f. l. M. in Rome whose existence on the site of the Pelagian church I formerly presumed. Neither the basilica nor its transept ever existed.

16. John Ward Perkins, "The Christian Antiquities of the Cyrenaica-Pentapolis," *Bulletin de la Société, archéologique copte*, IX (1943), 123 ff.

Postscript

The main aims of this lecture were to distinguish between the various and basically different transept types which occur in Early Christian church planning; to clarify their chronological relationships and their possible dependencies on each other; and to investigate the links that might exist between these types and the liturgy locally or regionally prevailing and the possible impact exerted by the latter on the former. The first point came out clearly enough. The second could have been presented more fully and may require some revisions. The third was presented at the time tentatively and in the hope that thorough research might lead to more positive results. This hope has not been fulfilled. A majority of scholars have preferred the perilous borderland of architectural iconography to the study of church planning in relation to its liturgical function—a field difficult to hoe because of the art historian's ignorance of the history of what has been called the external liturgy. Serious publications of early date concerning the interplay of liturgy and church building are lacking; Liesenberg's thesis of 1928 does not really count, and among recent work I can name only an excellent paper on a specific problem by one of my latter-day students, Fr. Thomas Mathews, S.J. (1962), and a condensed survey of the field by Joseph Rykwert, *Church Building*. The need for more work seems to me as urgent as ever, and I sometimes wonder whether I ought not to try myself.

Details in the paper obviously require revision. While St. John's in the Lateran had no tri-partite transept, its projecting "aisle transepts" (see above, pp. 21 ff.) may well forecast the wings of such a transept, presumably in liturgical function and possibly in design. The existence at S. Pietro in Vincoli of an early church with similar "aisle transepts," datable about 400, was in 1954 still unknown (see now, *Corpus Basilicarum*, III, 178 ff., esp. 214 ff.). Since this first church may have received its decoration only between 432 and 440, its remodelling with a tri-partite transept may date as late as 450–455. The cross-transept of the Menas basilica, according to recent incomplete reports Schläger [1963], p. 118; [1965], p. 125), may have been built as late as the last quarter of the fifth century, instead of 412. On the other hand, I am now inclined to place Sta. Tecla in Milan and its transept in the third quarter of the fourth century (*Early Christian and Byzantine Architecture*, p. 58) rather than 380 as I did twelve years ago. The reconstruction of Constantine's St. Peter's by Frazer should be revised in accordance with proposals recently made by Christern (see additional bibliography). Finally, I am no longer certain that the four arms of Constantine's Apostle Church were divided each into a nave and two aisles; they could have been aisleless, like Ambrose's *Apostoleion* in Milan. But thereby hangs another tale.

Additional Bibliography

Christern, Jürgen "Der Aufriss von Alt-St.-Peter," *RQuSchr,* LXII (1967), 133 ff.

Frazer, A. K. "A Graphic Reconstruction of Old St. Peter's circa 423," M. A. thesis, Institute of Fine Arts (New York University, 1957).

Krautheimer, R. *Corpus.*

———. *Early Christian and Byzantine Architecture* (Pelican History of Art, Harmondsworth, 1965).

Liesenberg, K. *Der Einfluss der Liturgie auf die frühchristliche Basilika,* (Neustadt a.d.H., 1928).

Mathews, T., S. J., "An Early Roman Chancel Arrangement and Its Liturgical Functions," *RACrist,* XXXVIII (1962), 73 ff.

Rykwert, J. *Church Building,* "Faith and Fact Books," 120 (London, 1966).

Schläger, H. "Abu Mena. Vorläufiger Bericht," *Mitteilungen des deutschen archäologischen Instituts, Abteilung Kairo,* XIX (1963), 114 ff., esp. 118; XX (1965), 122 ff., esp. 125.

6

SANTO STEFANO ROTONDO IN ROME AND THE ROTUNDA OF THE HOLY SEPULCHRE IN JERUSALEM *

I. History and Reconstruction.

WE HAVE very few ascertained facts concerning the history of Santo Stefano Rotondo in Rome.[1] From the *Liber Pontificalis* we know that Simplicius I (468–483) dedicated a church to St. Stephen on the Celian Hill (*"hic dedicavit basilicam Sco. Stephano in Coelio monte"*). Since there is no other church of this name on the Celian Hill,[2] it is obvious that this reference must apply to the church of Santo Stefano Rotondo. Inscriptions that have come down to us in the *Sylloge I of Lorsch,* an eighth-century collection of inscriptions—speak of the marbles and mosaics of the church, that is, the embellishment executed by order of John I (523–526) and Felix IV (526–530).[3] Under Theodore I (642–649) the relics of SS. Primus and Felicianus were translated from their catacomb on the via Nomentana to Santo Stefano and the church was newly consecrated. An inscription on a mosaic in the small eastern apse of the church records this translation while another inscription, which has now disappeared but which is conserved in the *Lorsch Sylloge,* mentions the decoration of the vault executed by order of Pope Theodore I.[4] Other restorations of uncertain nature were carried out under Hadrian I (772–795) (*" . . . basilicam . . . Stephani sitam in Coelio monte, que per olitana tempora marcuerat, maximas in ea deferens trabes, tam mole basilicae quamque portica mirifice intrinsecus et extrinsecus noviter renovavit . . ."*). A further campaign of repairs under Innocent II (1140–1143) is referred to in the *Liber Pontificalis* (*" . . . ecclesiam Sancti Stephani in Celio monte pro nimia vetustate quassatam optime reparavit . . ."*).[5] Inscriptions of Nicolas V (1447–1455), remarks by Francesco di Giorgio Martini[6] and the list of building expenses published by Müntz[7] refer to a final, more important restoration. With the frescoes executed in the church under Gregory XIII (1572–1585),[8] and with the assignment of the building to the Collegium Germanicum, documented facts concerning the building history of Santo Stefano Rotondo are complete.

*Translated by Howard Saalman from *RACrist*, XII (1935), 51–102.

It is not surprising that a church should have been dedicated to Saint Stephen in Rome in the fifth century. The body of the saint had been discovered in 415 near Jerusalem, and from the middle of the century on his cult rapidly had spread everywhere and also to Rome. Around 450, Leo the Great had consecrated on the Via Latina a church to Saint Stephen while Hilarus I (461–468) had dedicated to him an oratory in the Lateran. Between 468 and 483, under Simplicius I, followed Santo Stefano on the Celian Hill and a church of Santo Stefano near San Lorenzo fuori le mura. Two other churches dedicated to Saint Stephen may also go back to the fifth century, Santo Stefano degli Abessini located behind the basilica of Saint Peter, and another near Saint Paul's.[9] But the church on the Celian Hill is strikingly different from all these buildings and from Early Christian churches in Rome in general. It is a huge round building (Fig. 22) with a high drum supported by twenty Ionic columns (Figs. 23 and 24). Two T-shaped pilasters are inserted between these columns on a transverse axis. These pilasters and two huge granite columns support a diaphragm wall running across the central space. It rests on three arches, the one in the middle higher than those on the sides, and is pierced above the arches by five arched window-like openings. Twenty-two large windows pierce the drum on the axes of the intercolumniations and a flat ceiling covers the central space. A wide first ambulatory (Text Fig. 8) surrounds this central space—we shall call it the inner ambulatory. At first glance it seems that a series of blind arcades on half columns decorates the inside walls of this ambulatory, but it is clear that originally these were open arches. They opened onto a second ambulatory the major elements of which can still be identified. Four deep rooms on the principal axes (Text Fig. 8, *b*)—the eastern one, divided by two thin partition walls of late date, still stands—alternating with four shallow spaces in the diagonal axes (Text Fig. 8, *c*). In front of these shallow spaces extended four equally shallow courtyards (Text Fig. 8, *d*). The outer walls of these courtyards are continuous with those of the deep rooms in the major axes. Together they form the outer ring wall of the entire building. This ring wall is preserved, partly to its full height, partly in traces along its entire circumference. Likewise preserved are traces of the rooms and areas between this ring wall and the first inner ambulatory. Hence the central nave and the first ambulatory are obviously but a fragment of the original structure.[10]

A few words suffice to identify more recent additions to the building (Text Fig. 8). The chapel to the right of the eastern deep chapel—now the chancel—dates from the eighteenth century, the chancel screens in the center room, the wall paintings in the ambulatory and some minor features from the late sixteenth century. The following can be attributed with assurance to the restoration undertaken in the years 1452–1453 by Nicholas V: the blocking of fourteen out of the original twenty-two windows in the central drum, the tracery and the remnants of glass panes in the remaining eight windows; the flat ceilings with their beautiful foliage brackets in the central area and the first ambulatory; in the deep eastern

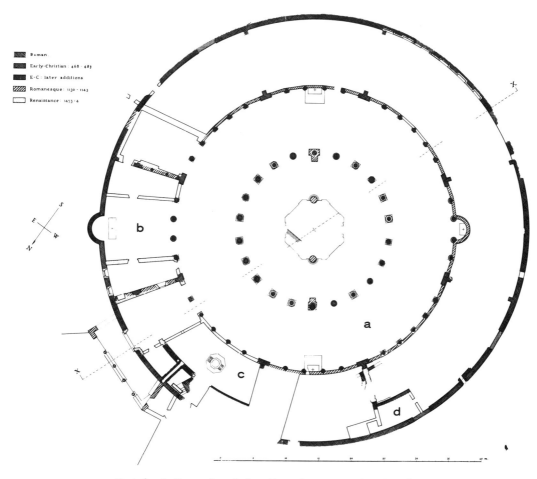

Roman.
Early-Christian: 468-483
E-C: later additions
Romanesque: 1130-1143
Renaissance: 1453-4

Text fig. 8. Rome, Sto. Stefano Rotondo, present plan (Frankl)

chapel, the piercing of the outer wall by three tracery windows and the insertion of partition walls to cut off a sacristy to the left, another room to the right; the lavabo and tabernacle in the sacristy; finally, in the entrance area the righthand wall and the double portal with its dedicatory inscriptions.[11] The arcades between the first and the second ambulatory were closed up in the twelfth century under Innocent II (not in the fifteenth century as generally stated). The small western apse and the outer narthex also were built at this time, and the central drum was raised around 70 cm. with the addition of a cornice.[12] The diaphragm arch across the central space was built in a still earlier period, perhaps under Hadrian I, as were the supporting piers in which were enclosed two of the twenty-two columns of the original inner circle of supports. Shafts, capitals, and bases of these two columns were recently uncovered.[13]

This structure is so strange, and so different from the norm of Early Christian

71

architecture in Rome, that one can understand the hesitancy to place it among church buildings of the end of the fifth century.[14] Even the expression used by the *Liber Pontificalis, " . . . dedicavit basilicam . . . ,"* instead of " . . . *fecit* . . . ," or *". . . erexit . . . ,"* would seem to support the hypothesis that we are dealing with a pagan construction which was merely consecrated as a church by Simplicius. In fact, from the fifteenth century onward the building was considered a pagan temple, dedicated either to Divus Faunus, or to the Emperor Claudius. Another theory, as early as the seventeenth century and still current today, identifies Santo Stefano Rotondo with the Macellum Magnum of Nero. On closer examination, however, it appears that this identification is founded principally on the fact that the Macellum Magnum was situated on the Celian Hill (we have no precise indications concerning its position) and that it was represented on coins as a circular building. The Macellum hypothesis was maintained in particular by nineteenth-century students of classical archaeology such as Isabelle[15] and Lanciani.[16] According to Lanciani, the present church is but a reconstruction of the Macellum built around the end of the fourth century on Neronian foundations. The inner area, he claimed, was unroofed as was the first ambulatory (*a*); adjoining this first ambulatory in the diagonal axes, other ambulatories opened, two-storied and double-naved, in place of the later shallow areas and the equally shallow courtyards (*c, d,*). The place of the four deep main chapels was, according to this reconstruction, occupied by open courtyards and these would have been roofed and closed by outer walls only when the Macellum was transformed into a church. This reconstruction was seconded by Hülsen,[17] by Homo [18] and more recently by Wulzinger.[19] Wulzinger in particular attempted to reconstruct the Macellum of Nero from coin representations. He supported his reconstruction—which coincided on many points with that of Lanciani—by pointing to two remains of wall, uncovered by Valadier and surveyed by Canina [20] in the area of the deep main chapel to the north.[21] We would not wholly reject the hypothesis that a central building of the classic period previously existed on this site.[22] But there are no traces of such a construction with the exception of the aforementioned walls, and these have no connection with the present building. Nevertheless Wulzinger, in agreement with Lanciani, maintained that the present building from its foundations up (*"von den seichten Fundamenten an"*) is a Macellum of the late Roman period (*"nachantik,"* or post-antique), that is, from the end of the fourth century, and he accepted the reconstruction proposed by Lanciani for this Macellum.

Beginning after the middle of the nineteenth century, a number of scholars, such as Hübsch,[23] Dehio and Bezold,[24] and De Rossi [25] joined in opposing this hypothesis, and strongly defended the thesis that Santo Stefano was an organic construction built under Simplicius I and intended from the beginning as a church. Indeed, an examination of the structure leaves no doubt that the church as we see it today was built as an organic whole and in one building period, with a covered central nave, an ambulatory around it, large chapels in the main axes and with narrow corridors and outer courtyards in the secondary axes. Thus the reconstruction proposed by Lanciani with central space and ambulatory unroofed, and with courtyards uncovered in the main axes, open towards the exterior and placed between two-storied, double-naved corridors in the diagonal axes, cannot be maintained. First, the entire outer ring wall is an organic entity (Fig. 22; Text Fig. 8). The high walls of the main chapels (b) continue without interruption in the walls of the narrow courtyards (d) and the original height of both the chapel walls (10.45 m.) and the courtyard walls (6 m.) can be ascertained on both sides. The radial walls, which run from this outer ring wall toward the interior and which separate the areas in the major axes from those in the secondary axes, also bond on either side with the outer ring wall as well as with the wall of the interior ambulatory. Therefore Lanciani's hypothesis, according to which the outer walls of the main chapels were added at a later period, is unacceptable. Nor can we accept his other hypothesis that the spaces in the diagonal axes (d, c,) were two-storied.[26] At a level of 1.50 meters above the arches of the interior ambulatory the springing of a vault can be clearly seen on the outside; it is constructed of light amphorae, embedded in a layer of mortar, about 50 centimeters high. A series of beam holes is visible about 80 centimeters above this vault. There is no room for an upper floor in the space that remains between these holes and the ambulatory roof. It is clear that there was a shed roof above, and therefore we must exclude Lanciani's hypothesis that these corridors were double-storied. Nor can the hypothesis be sustained that these corridors were double-naved. Had this been the case, traces of beam holes or vaults corresponding to those on the ambulatory wall would be visible on the inside of the outer ring wall where it is preserved to its full height, as for instance in its northwest sector. But there are no such traces. From the beginning, therefore, there were narrow, vaulted corridors in the diagonal axes with vaults adjoining the inner ambulatory, and in front of these, narrow courtyards. Given these premises, it is clear that the areas in the major axes, that is, between the corridors just discussed, can never have been courtyards as Lanciani assumed. Rather they must always have been deep roofed chapels. Otherwise we could not explain the windows which pierce the walls of these chapels above the roofs of the narrow corridors as well as towards the courtyards. The outlines of these windows can still be seen today in the righthand wall of the main chapel (Fig. 25), the only one preserved.[27] The same conclusion holds for the central nave. Its windows are integral elements of the wall. Their existence makes it clear that the space was always roofed. There are not the slightest traces of horizontal joints.[28]

There can therefore be no doubt that the building is a wholly organic structure, dating from a single building period. We may go yet further in determining the time of construction and the original purpose of the building. The crosses carved on the imposts of some of the capitals of the inner ambulatory likewise prove that the building was intended from the very beginning as a church. The form of these imposts has its parallels in Roman buildings of the fifth century, for example, at Sant' Agata dei Goti around 470, at Santo Stefano in Via Latina around 450, and at S. Vitale at the foot of the Quirinal Hill around the year 410. These imposts do not yet have the flat form or the form of a truncated pyramid found in the sixth century (S. Lorenzo fuori le mura, S. Apollinare in Classe, Parenzo, S. Apollinare Nuovo, S. Vitale in Ravenna, Grado, Sant' Agnese fuori le mura). To argue that these imposts were added at a later time, one would have to assume that the columns and the Ionic capitals of the columns, both in the nave and the ambulatory, were added at a later period. The columns are spoils of varying diameter and varying height with differing bases all combined with the greatest nonchalance. The capitals surmounting the columns also vary in height and are crudely carved: the necking between shaft and capital is high, resembling a chalice; the volutes are irregular and look as if pasted on; a flat ovolo band runs between the volutes and there are no palmettes in the corners. Similar capitals are found at Santo Stefano in Via Latina around the middle of the fifth century.[29] The Ionic capitals of Santo Stefano Rotondo are certainly not earlier than the fifth century, and this period is also indicated by the flat architrave which runs smoothly over the columns of the nave, and is composed of only slightly profiled bands, but little differentiated among each other.

Some technical details of the building allow us to fix a more precise date. The arches of the windows in the nave are slightly set back from the jambs and the windows differ in their width, height and spacing (1.60 × 3.10 × 1.90 m.) from the rather larger windows of the beginning of the fifth century (Sta. Maria Maggiore: 2.22 × 3.40 × 0.90 m.); (Figs. 66, 68), while resembling the form of the windows of Sant' Agata dei Goti of around 470 (1.70 × 2.80 × 1.35). However, the greater distance between the individual windows at Santo Stefano, as well as their slimmer form, may already represent a later phase of development. The masonry of large and regular bricks with broad layers of mortar (the width of the bricks varies between 2.5 and 4 cm., that of the mortar beds between 3 and 4 cm.), and the beautiful long bricks of the arches immediately recall buildings of the fifth century. The technique of the vaults in the diagonal axes constructed with light amphorae cannot be dated precisely; in any event, it is not found in Rome except between the third and the sixth centuries. These factors suggest that the vague expression of the *Liber Pontificalis* need not be given much weight, and that it is sounder to follow De Rossi in attributing the entire construction to the pontificate of Simplicius I (468–483), as an organic structure, intended from the outset for the Christian cult.

Using these architectural data and old drawings and omitting insignificant particulars, we are in a position to reconstruct the original form of the building (Text Figs. 9, 10, 12, 13). Twenty-two Ionic columns, regularly spaced, surround the inner cylinder and are separated from the drum by the horizontal of the architrave. An order of twenty-two pilaster strips—as shown by a drawing of

Cronaca (Fig. 26)[30]—surmounted the columns and were, immediately under the windows, topped by a cornice. In the panels between the pilaster strips there may have been incrustation or mosaics.[31] Higher up, in the axes of the twenty-two intercolumniations, followed the series of windows. Above the windows, the drum continued and carried probably not a flat ceiling but a truncated conical roof; certainly it never had a masonry vault. The first ambulatory ran around this central space, lower than the main area but spacious and also unvaulted. Its outer perimeter was comprised of an order of supports much lower than the columns of the first circle and these supports carried arches instead of an architrave. Thus we already note a contrast between the first and second order of supports. However another contrast becomes more important: while the columns of the inner order are spaced in regular intervals, the supports of the second order are grouped in a clear rhythm. Four columns each in the principal axes, and five each in the diagonal axes, are separated by heavy T-shaped piers. Thus, the arithmetical correspondence of the forty-four supports in the second order to the twenty-two columns in the nave is less important than the contrast between this simple circle and the rhythmical grouping of piers and columns in the ambulatory. This contrast is further strengthened by the relationship of these grouped supports and of the areas of the third outer circle into which the inner ambulatory opens (Text Figs. 9, 10, 13; Figs. 22, 24, 28).

The groups of four columns in the major axes are higher than those of five columns in the diagonal axes and lead into the main chapels (b). Disposed in the form of a cross, these chapels project from the inner ambulatory. They are large and high spaces, 10 m. deep, and like the ambulatory, unvaulted. Since their outer walls have the same height as those of the ambulatory and since a common shed roof over the chapels and ambulatories could not be constructed without employing a rather complicated system of supports, we must suppose that they were covered by laterally projecting three-part shed roofs (Text Figs. 10, 12). The outer walls of the chapels were pierced by two large, round windows. These are still preserved, though walled up, over the fifteenth-century windows in the main chapel to the east, where still another cross-shaped window can be seen. In the side wall of each chapel (Fig. 25), a large door with a flat architrave abutted the outer wall; next to it a tripartite passage was articulated by columns carrying an arch in the central opening and lintels on the sides. This portal and the tripartite opening may still be seen in the righthand wall of the eastern chapel, while higher up on this wall the outlines of three rectangular windows may be discerned as drawn by Canina.[32] The groups of five columns in the diagonal axes are lower than those of four in the major axes. These columns stand on high bases and face low and narrow spaces (c). These are little more than 6 m. deep and are interposed between the main chapels. The curve of their outer walls appears to be preserved in the pilasters of the little cloister to the right of the anteportico; indeed, according to Hübsch, the pilasters of this cloister are set on antique foundations. These spaces communicate on either

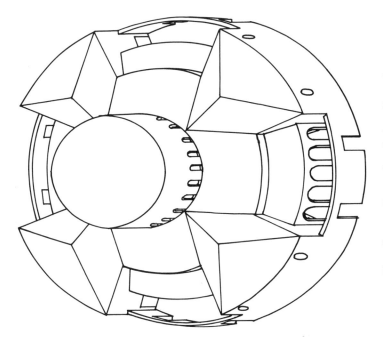

Text fig. 10. Rome, Sto. Stefano Rotondo, original exterior, bird's eye isometric reconstruction (Frankl)

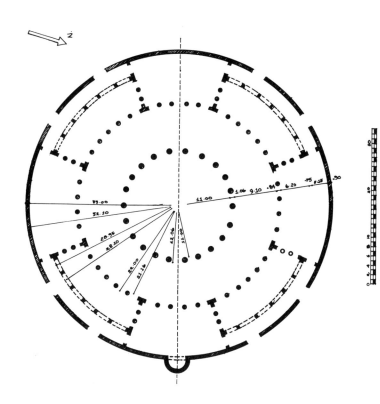

Text fig. 9. Rome, Sto. Stefano Rotondo, original plan, reconstruction (Frankl)

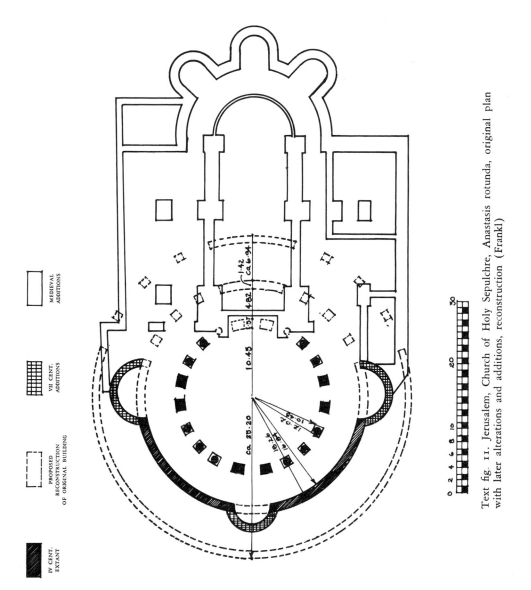

MEDIEVAL
ADDITIONS

VII CENT.
ADDITIONS

PROPOSED
RECONSTRUCTION
OF ORIGINAL BUILDING

IV CENT.
EXTANT

Text fig. 11. Jerusalem, Church of Holy Sepulchre, Anastasis rotunda, original plan with later alterations and additions, reconstruction (Frankl)

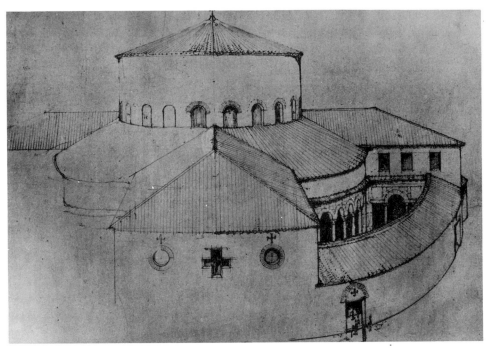

Text fig. 12. Rome, Sto. Stefano Rotondo, original exterior, alternative perspective reconstruction (Corbett)

Text fig. 13. Rome, Sto. Stefano Rotondo, original interior, perspective reconstruction (Corbett)

side with the main chapels through the large tripartite passages in the side walls of the main chapels. Their vaults (we have already mentioned their traces) must have been segmental half barrels. The extremes of the curvature of these vaults are fixed: 1) at the top by the impost of the vault; 2) in the middle by the sill of the second window in the side wall of the main chapel (which must have lain above the vault); and 3) at the foot of the vault by the height of the tripartite passage. These narrow spaces with their low vaults appear to have been corridors with the sole function of connecting the main chapels. This function is also stressed by the way in which these spaces opened towards the exterior. Indeed, their outer walls were pierced either by a series of large windows or portals or by an arcade, carried by either piers or columns. Such an arrangement is indicated by the T-shaped piers known from the excavations of Valadier,[33] Palladio and Hübsch. In any event, spaces as narrow as these with barrel vaults and probably with openings in four walls could never have served as chapels. They must have been intended to serve as lateral communication corridors between the main chapels. In front of the corridors extended four narrow courtyards (d), closed by an outer wall six meters high, provided with two large portals each (they are preserved in nearly every case). These courtyards led to the street. Thus the visitor entering one of these four courtyards found himself in front of a low, barrel-vaulted entrance hall, with openings set on supports, framed on the right and left by the high walls of the main chapels, and above by the roof and by the high drum of the central nave (Text Fig. 10). Turning to the right or to the left, he could enter through one of the two large doors abutting the ring wall into one of the main chapels (b) and continue from there into the interior ambulatory (a); or, turning again to the right or the left, he could enter from the chapel into the low corridor (c) which connected the main chapels and at the same time opened toward the inner ambulatory. At this point the complex grouping of closed and open communicating spaces finally ended, and a harmonious view of the whole presented itself as one entered, the nucleus of the building rising vigorously and serenely, all pervaded by light. Here was concentrated the rich ornamentation of the structure, the marble incrustation with its pilasters and the mosaics (certainly intended from the very beginning, although executed only at the beginning of the sixth century). The entire central space was immersed in light, while the ambulatory remained in semi-darkness. Likewise, the darkness of the corridors contrasted with the full light of the courtyards. The main chapels alone repeated the luminosity of the central area.

It is evident that the whole building is animated by the visible contrast between the sober and serene rhythm of the central space and its ambulatory and the complex and agitated rhythm alternating in crescendo and decrescendo of the outer spaces. At the line of the supports which enclose the main ambulatory (a), the two contrasting complexes meet. The outer spaces are agitated, rich, and varied; seen from the outside, the outlying parts of the building form a group of volumes alternating between highs and lows (Text Fig. 10). The spaces themselves vary correspondingly: they push toward the interior, imposing on the arcade the rhythmic distribution of eight piers between the 36 columns, the grouping of these columns, the crescendo of the groups of four in the principal axes, and the decrescendo of the groups of five in the diagonal axes (Fig. 24). In the first ambulatory, however, another concept of space appears. The sequence of arches is calmer and the impression of a quiet repose is increased yet further by the regular order of the large Ionic columns that support the architrave of the central nave, by the upper order of pilasters in the marble incrustation, and by the regular spacing of windows above these pilasters (Fig. 26). The two inner circles are characterized by a spatial concept of Early Christian architecture as we know it from the fourth- and fifth-century buildings of Rome. It has been repeatedly stated that Santo Stefano is a "round basilica" and, speaking *cum grano salis,* this assertion contains some truth. The center room actually has the spaciousness of the nave of Early Christian basilicas in Rome. As in the Constantinian basilicas with five naves, the columns of the central nave support an architrave, and those of the side aisles (that is, between the second and the third circle) arcades. Also, a longitudinal axis runs through the building from west to east. The groups of four columns at the east and the west have much higher columns and arcades than those of the groups in the north-south axis, and the group in the east is again higher than that in the west. The openings are much wider than those of the chapels in the transverse axis, while the eastern chapel, by virtue of its larger opening, is emphasized more than the western. Since we observe further that the eastern and western columns of the inner circle have a wider intercolumniation than the other columns, and since the western window in the upper wall is situated notably higher than the others (Text Figs. 8, 9), the greater importance of the longitudinal axis and, within the longitudinal axis, the emphasis on the eastern chapel becomes apparent. Perhaps we may assume from this that the altar was situated here from the very beginning; this, in turn, seems to support the hypothesis that Santo Stefano is a "round basilica." [34]

There is no doubt then that the style of Santo Stefano allows us to place this building in a certain sense within the framework of the Early Christian architecture of Rome. However, the theory of a "round basilica" may oversimplify the problem. Dehio [35] already has suggested that the idea of a basilica transformed into a rotunda is inspired primarily by transverse section drawings of modern architects. However, a central structure is not a longitudinal building. It is based on an architectural principle of wholly different nature. To be sure, the transverse section of a central building resembles that of a longitudinal building, but this resemblance in presentation has no analogy in real space. In a central building, the width of the space is not related to length as in a basilica but plays a much more important role. A central building is, so to speak, and again speaking *cum grano salis,* more spacious than a basilica of the same width. A comparison of two such buildings must be made with the greatest caution, and the resemblance of Santo Stefano to Early Christian basilicas in Rome cannot be based solely on the existence of a high, central space and a low ambulatory, and on the relative widths of these spaces.

The difference between Santo Stefano Rotondo and traditional fourth- and fifth-century architecture of Rome comes into full view when we turn our attention from the inner nucleus to the construction and arrangement of the outer elements of the building (Text Figs. 9, 10, 13). Then it becomes clear that their complicated layout, spaces, and architectonic volumes intended to be seen in groups are far removed from the customary Early Christian architecture of Rome. Within the architecture of Early Christian Rome, since the Constantinian period, buildings were articulated by a sober sequence of elementary and uncontrasting prisms that provide a simple and clear rhythm, without any attempt at exterior effects. The exterior design of Santo Stefano aimed at a wholly different effect, involving complex grouping and lively superimposition of elements varied in shape and in height. Above the walls of the courtyards the eye passed over the roofs of the corridors in the diagonal axes, then over the high main chapels, and from there over the roof of the inner ambulatory. From the ambulatory roof the drum of the central nave rose sharply, terminating in a conical roof. In like manner the interior spaces interpenetrate in intricate patterns. The light binds and interconnects them and an alternation of light and dark creates contrasts between adjoining spaces. It seems as if the simple main theme of the building, the inner rotunda with its ambulatory, were evolved from a much more complicated original kernel. The very motif of the central building does not fit into the framework of our conception of Early Christian architecture in Rome. It is in fact difficult to find a precedent within the architecture of the city for the complicated form of Santo Stefano with its impressive grouping of interpenetrating volumes and spaces. From the time of Constantine on, it is difficult to find a building in Rome comprising an arrangement of volumes and masses similar to those built during the third century (Minerva Medica). Within the Greek eastern provinces of the Empire, however, such concepts had remained alive. Even after Constantine and in church buildings, many examples of such structures with grouped volumes and complicated interior chiaroscuro effects were found rising along the shores of the eastern Mediterranean. Various types of central buildings (particularly adapted for the formation and development of complicated architectonic ideas) were created and we know how under Justinian these types with their rich formations finally led to the perfect form of Hagia Sofia in Constantinople and of S. Vitale in Ravenna.

This is but a hint for a possible delineation of the sources of Santo Stefano. Its design still remains unusual and unique among fifth-century churches. In order to go further we must analyze the elements which comprise the construction of Santo Stefano. The decisive motif is the interconnection of the inner rotunda, of the first ambulatory and of the secondary rooms and areas of the outer circle which radiate from the first ambulatory. Among these latter we must further distinguish two motifs: the chapels situated in the principal axes, which project in the form of a cross (Text Fig. 8, *b*); and the interrmediary corridors with their barrel vaults which are situated in the diagonal axes (*c*). We have already observed that these corridors are not structural elements. Their function seems to be precisely that of connecting the main chapels with each other. It might actually be better to consider them as a continuous circular corridor interrupted by the four main chapels. The vaults of the corridors in fact are segments of a circle demanding a continuation towards both sides. They ought to encircle the entire building as a true annular corridor. The high chapels in the main axes interrupt this corridor, leaving only fragments. The chapels then belong to a different type—a central building with secondary elements projecting in the form of a cross. Circular and cross-shaped elements, then, interpenetrate in this outer zone, and both unite with the central nave and its low ambulatory. Thus three different architectural types are fused within the church of Santo Stefano. The first type: *a central building with outer annular corridor;* the second type: *a central building with chapels projecting in the form of a cross;* and the third type: *a central building with wooden roof and with inner ambulatory.* These building types have already been observed by Dehio.[36] While he did not refer them directly to Santo Stefano, he proposed an opposition between the central building with interior ambulatories and the central building in the form of a cross.[37]

In Santo Stefano these building types are both fused and transposed into the architectural idiom of Rome in the fifth century. The single elements blend into a grandiose whole, complex but clear in every respect. However, in order to define the origin of this conjunction and thus the position of Santo Stefano Rotondo within the history of art, we first must turn our attention from this fusion of elements to the derivation of the component parts.

II. The Component Parts

The Outer Corridor. Among the single components of Santo Stefano, as outlined, the first problem concerns the origin of the barrel-vaulted corridor which runs at the rear of the courtyards and around the inner ambulatory interrupted only by the main chapels (Text Figs. 9, 10). This form of corridor is found already in classic Roman architecture. Roughly a hundred years before Santo Stefano Rotondo we find it in Santa Costanza where traces of a barrel vault still are clearly visible on the outside wall of the circular aisle, evidently designed to cover a second, outer ambulatory (Figs. 7, 29). This outer ambulatory, however, did not communicate with the interior space. The doors in the niches in the transverse axis of Santa Costanza were—as is well known—late additions, as is also the blocked opening in the large niche in the rear where the sarcophagus was located. The barrel-vaulted ambulatory was, therefore, a proper exterior corridor encircling the inner nucleus. Only some details remain in doubt. Among sixteenth-century drawings of the building,[38] at least two[39] show an order of twenty-two columns comprising the outer circle of this corridor. While one of these drawings is notably exact in detail, it is nevertheless uncertain whether it is based on remains actually seen or whether it represents an arbitrary reconstruction based on the discovery of a column.[40] Remains still preserved at the bottom of the encircling wall and already mentioned by Valadier[41] might even suggest the conclusion that an order of piers rather than columns supported the barrel vault of the corridor. In any event, Sta. Costanza, a century before Santo Stefano, presents an example of an exterior corridor.

Sta. Costanza was built, as is known, around the year 350 as a mausoleum for two princesses of the family of Constantine, Constantina (or Costantia) and her sister, Helena. Given the dependence of Constantinian on earlier Roman art, we are not surprised to find the motif of the circular corridor in classical funeral monuments. Indeed, barrel-vaulted corridors encircling tombs are common in Roman funeral architecture. The corridor, as a rule, is connected with the tomb by means of a single small door. The tomb thus is composed of two different elements: the interior sepulchre, sometimes two storied, and in that case elevated; and the round or rectangular exterior corridor, which is always low and barrel vaulted. A few examples will suffice: the tomb of the Furii family near Frascati,[42] and that of the Vigna Cavalieri (Fig. 59),[43] both evidently of early date; the tomb of Munatius Plancus in Gaeta;[44] and that of the Servilii on the Via Appia.[45] While in these examples the ambulatory is enclosed by a wall, we find it transformed at a later period into an exterior ambulatory supported by columns and sometimes covered by a flat ceiling, thus approaching the form of a monopteros. In this form the type is found in the Mausoleum of Diocletian in Spalato. As a rule, however, the annular barrel-vaulted corridor appears to remain the rule, also in Christian mausolea up to the fourth and fifth centuries; sometimes with an order of supports and open towards the exterior, sometimes closed by a wall, but always separate from the interior of the tomb. At a later time the motif became detached from mausolea as such and occasionally appeared in baptisteries: we may cite the Bapistery in Djémila in Northern Africa, built around the year 411.[46] Other examples are not hard to find, for instance at Ephesus, in the Baptistery adjoining the Church of the Virgin. Elsewhere, it became rare and in Rome it reappeared in modified form only at Santo Stefano on the Celian Hill.

Indeed, while in the antique mausolea, as well as in Sta. Costanza (Fig. 29) and at Djémila (Fig. 54), the corridor does not communicate with the central nucleus, at Santo Stefano it opens towards the interior. This is a fundamental difference and it is not easy to relate the form of the corridor created at Santo Stefano with the other, only apparently similar one at Santa Costanza. It would seem that other concepts have entered to prepare the transformation of the circular corridor which now opens towards the interior of the building.

The Cross-shaped Type. In the first place we must emphasize that at Santo Stefano the motif of the circular corridor is not preserved in its pure form: it has been blended with the motif of the chapels disposed in the form of a cross (Text Fig. 8, *b*), which intersect the circular corridor and thus form a new entity with it. But if the circular corridor is a common motif in Roman funeral art, such cross chapels are found in the Western Empire not before the fifth century. Even afterward, they always remain exceptional. We find them, however, in the church of Sant'Angelo in Perugia:[47] a central building with a wide ambulatory and with an inner order of sixteen columns supporting a sixteen-sided drum with large windows. Four chapels radiate outwards from the ambulatory and thus create its cross axes. Three of these chapels are square, the fourth one on the eastern side has a horseshoe plan. This arrangement suggests that of Santo Stefano, and therefore Sant'Angelo in Perugia is usually considered to be a construction of the sixth century inspired by Santo Stefano in Rome, though reduced through the omission of corridors and courtyards between the arms of the cross. We must ask ourselves, however, if this view corresponds to the facts. Certain details as, for example, the impost blocks in the form of a cornice or the large windows of Sant'Angelo seem to date the building in the fifth century rather than in the sixth. Likewise, the strong accentuation of the cross form within the inner circle of supports by means of higher columns in the major axes and lower columns in the diagonal ones seems to indicate an earlier phase of the type. Possibly Sant'Angelo represents the purest version of the type of the central building with chapels radiating in the form of a cross, and is earlier than Santo Stefano. But the mere observation of these relationships has only limited significance. It will be necessary to delve yet further into the origins of the motif of chapels arranged in the form of a cross.

However, not every monument in which the supports of an inner circle or niches in the wall are arranged in the form of a cross belongs in the ancestral lineage of Santo Stefano Rotondo. The placing of niches in cross shape around a central space and hence the primacy of the major axes over the diagonal axes is a fundamental element common to almost all Roman central building in the east and the west of the Empire. The motif is found in the *frigidarium* of nearly every thermae and in many mausolea since the first century A.D. It is likewise found in the Domus Aurea[48] of Nero and in the Domus Augustana,[49] on the Palatine as well as in the Baths of Thenae[50] and in the Mausoleum of Diocletian in Spalato. Similar emphasis on the major axes appears in the articulation of the supports of an inner circle through higher arches or through piers as at Sta. Costanza in Rome and in the Rotunda of the Holy Sepulchre in Jerusalem. At Santo Stefano and at Sant'Angelo in Perugia, however, the characteristic note is not the mere disposition of niches or of supports in cross form, but the formation of *independent* cross arms that radiate freely from the ambulatory. The niches of *frigidaria,* of sepulchral monuments, and of round halls as we find them in earlier times, are *dependent* elements that are not put into relief but remain subordinate to the central space and are oppressed by its vault. They tend to disappear and do not detach themselves clearly. Their arrangement in the form of a cross may be felt but it is not visible.[51] Only after they have become independent is the cross shape put into visible relief. To arrive at this independence, two factors above all were necessary: in the first place, the secondary spaces must be clearly marked both toward the interior and toward the exterior of the structure. In the second place, they must have a notable depth in order to produce the effect of independent spaces—to assume, that is, the appearance of chapels. Only in this way does the cross-shaped form become evident.

Two distinct types of cross-shaped plans appear from the fourth century onward: the type of the Greek cross with a simple square center, and a more complicated type in which the arms radiate from a round or octagonal center. Guyer [52] has studied the two types, locating their origin in Asia Minor and tracing the later development in the West: among many examples, he cites the church of the Panaghia at Tomarza [53] and the Mausoleum of Galla Placidia at Ravenna. The complex type he considers a local fusion of the simple cross plan with the great octagonal churches of the Holy Land. Within this fusion type he distinguishes again between a richer form with an inner order of supports and an ambulatory, and a simpler form without inner supports and without an ambulatory. However, both these variants are provided with chapels projecting in the form of a cross. In regard to Santo Stefano the more developed form obviously is of greater interest. We find it for the first time in the church which Gregory of Nyssa (379–394) planned and described in a letter to Amphilochios of Iconium.[54] His description is in part unclear, but it seems certain that the church was laid out in the form of an octagon and covered by a cone-shaped cupola supported by an inner circle of supports. It is immaterial whether the supports were piers as Strzygowski believed, or columns as was Guyer's view. In any event, the church had an octagonal ambulatory with four shallow, semicircular niches in the diagonal axes, and four deep rectangular chapels projecting in the major axes. This represents the type in its pure form as it appeared at the end of the fourth century and as it reappears once again in grandiose form in the octagon of Wiranshehir. Here again four arms radiating in the form of a cross extend from the ambulatory of an octagon, preceded by a large atrium at the west and by two smaller rectangular porticoes toward the north and south.[55] The type reappears in simpler form, that is, without an ambulatory, in a small chapel at Binbirkilisse [56] and in different form with a notable enlargement of the cross arms in the great *martyria* of the τύπος σταυροειδής, also discussed by Guyer: [57] in the church of Jacob at Sichem, known only from a drawing of the seventh century; [58] in the first church of Saint John the Evangelist at Ephesus, at St. Elia at Esra and at Seqra.[59]

Thus numerous variations of the type are found in the Near East. They are restricted to a relatively limited area that is confined on the north by Ephesus, on the south by Kalat Siman, and range from simple to very complicated cross plans. On the other hand, the complex type is rarely found in the West, while the simple cross type was imported from the East into northern Italy and into Gaul. Monneret de Villard [60] has published two examples in Piedmont, both simple, central buildings with a round nucleus and radiating cross arms. It is not surprising, however, that also the more developed form with ambulatory, with an inner order of supports and with arms radiating in cross form should penetrate into the West. This is the historical setting of Sant' Angelo in Perugia as well as of another Italian church of similar plan and likewise undated, namely the Baptistery in Sanseverino [61] in Calabria. The overall form as well as the details of these two buildings, such as the horseshoe apses at Perugia, confirm that the type derives from the Near East. It is from this source also that the motif must have come to Santo Stefano Rotondo.

It is difficult to judge correctly the importance of the East for the Western architecture of the first Christian centuries. Doubtless the eastern part of the Empire had a decisive influence on the formation of certain types in the West. However, the Eastern motifs found in Western Christian architecture often comprise classical forms that have Roman or Hellenistic origins. We are, then, dealing more often than not with forms that are the fruit of Greco-Roman civilization as such and not the fruit of some undefined eastern culture. In the second place, we cannot trace the formation of well-defined types in the eastern part of the Empire until after Constantinian times. And in the third place we must always investigate the extent to which earlier Western examples influenced the formation of these Constantinian or post-Constantinian buildings in the East. The third motif underlying the plan of Santo Stefano, that of a central building with an inner order of supports and ambulatory, underscores the difficulties of the problem and the complexity of the relations between the eastern and the western parts of the Empire.

Central Buildings with Inner Supports. Central plan buildings with inner supports and an ambulatory are not frequent in Roman architecture prior to Constantine. The norm is rather the simple central building with niches. These niches may be contained within the thickness of the outer wall and in this case the central space remains unlit except for a possible opening in the vault; or they radiate outward from the central space, either projecting from the wall or more frequently concentrated in a ring that encircles the central space but is lower in elevation and in these two cases the central space frequently has its own clerestorey. These different types of central buildings were in use from the first century onward, and were still employed in the fourth and fifth centuries throughout the Empire. As an example of the first type, we might cite the Pantheon in Rome (Figs. 34, 36); of the second type, the so-called Temple of Minerva Medica; and of the third type, the mausoleum of the Honorian dynasty at St. Peter's in Rome or that of Galerius, now the church of St. George in Salonica.

In the second and third of these variants, the wall piers separating the encircling niches have their ends sometimes detached and replaced by columns. Thus a passage is created between wall and column: a form, then, resembling an ambulatory separated by means of an order of columns from the central space proper. Such a pseudo-ambulatory is found at a relatively late date, in the fourth century, in the Baptistery at Miletus. The relationship between this pseudo-type and the authentic type with a freestanding inner order of supports and thus unrelated to the tradition of the rotunda with niches remains uncertain. In any event, we already find the authentic type with an independent ring of supports as early as 360 B.C. in the Tholos of Epidauros. This type, however, remained rare in Roman architecture of the late Republican and early Imperial period and no examples are actually preserved;[62] they are known only from sixteenth-century drawings from the hands of Bramantino,[63] Ligorio,[64] and others. The evidence however, must be used cautiously; a true rendering of actual buildings and arbitrary reconstructions frequently were fused in archaeological drawings of the Renaissance. We may assume, however, in agreement with Dehio[65] and with Wulff[66] that the type was known within Roman architecture of the pre-Constantinian period.[67]

The Type in the West. In examining the surviving examples of the type in Rome in the Christian period a characteristic development of the proportions can be observed. In the earlier, presumably pre-Constantinian examples which we know only from drawings, the supports frequently stand so close to the wall as to raise doubts whether they represent the authentic type with ambulatory or the pseudo-type with a mere passageway behind the columns. On the other hand, Sta. Costanza (Figs. 27, 29) as well as the Lateran Baptistery are provided with genuine ambulatories. The central space no longer fills the entire building but is coordinated with the spatial volume of the ambulatory; and this latter, which in the pseudo-type is but a narrow passage in front of the wall, a simple background for the colonnade, is transformed into an annular aisle. Covered with a barrel vault and encircling the domed central space, it is not illuminated, while on the other hand, full daylight flows through the windows under the dome into the central space. The relative size of the central space, whose diameter in the pseudo-type was sometimes as much as nine times larger than the ambulatory,[68] is reduced while the ambulatory becomes wider. In Santa Costanza the proportion is somewhat less than 3:1; in the Lateran Baptistery,[69] it sinks to exactly 2:1.[70] We have, then, a clear development of proportions that evidently around the year 430 terminates in the Lateran Baptistery, and Santo Stefano fits into this process of evolution. Here, too, the inner width of the ambulatory is almost equal to the radius of the central space. We apparently are confronted with a development that takes place in the west of the Empire, proceeds rapidly and energetically, and radically transforms or replaces the presumably pre-Constantinian type with a pseudo-ambulatory.

The Type in the East. In the eastern parts of the Empire, on the other hand, central buildings with an inner order of supports but with a pseudo-ambulatory and with proportions that correspond not yet with those of Sta. Costanza continued to be built for quite some time. A proportion between central space and ambulatory such as that in the Rotunda of the Anastasis at Jerusalem of about 4.2:1 (Text Fig. 11)[71] continues until the sixth century without much variation. The ambulatory always remains narrow. We may cite, for example, the octagon of Wiranshehir, where the proportion between central space and ambulatory is 4:1 or the church on Mount Garizim with a proportion of 3.9:1.[72] The relationship of central space to ambulatory is always that of a major space to a secondary and subordinate one. It would seem that the type with pseudo-ambulatory was adopted in the East—a part of the Empire in some respects more conservative than the West—and survived for a longer time than it did in the West.

Large Dimensions. On the basis of the proportions alone, we might therefore number Santo Stefano as an example of central building in the West. A consideration of other characteristics, however, might lead to different conclusions. The overall dimensions of early central buildings with an inner order of supports in the West were extraordinarily small. The Tholos of Epidauros, for example, has an inner diameter of 13.50 m. The "Temple of Serapis" as drawn by Ligorio has an inner diameter of 72 *palmi,* that is 16.25 m., while that of the Temple of Pluto is 100 *palmi* or 22.30 m. Among the buildings drawn by Bramantino, only one is provided with measurements, having an inner diameter of 64 *palmi* or 14.27 m. The diameters of the other two can be estimated at about 66 *palmi* or 14.0 m., and at 48 *palmi* or 10.70 m., respectively.

Since these measurements may not be wholly trustworthy, it might be better to cite two surviving examples from the fourth and fifth centuries: Santa Costanza has an inner diameter of 22.32 m. and the Lateran Baptistery of 20.80 m. Comparing the combined diameter of central nave and ambulatory of Santo Stefano with these buildings we find that instead of the roughly 20 m. of the two earlier buildings, the total width amounts to about 42 m. However, we are not dealing merely with enlarged dimensions but with a wholly different spatial conception: size is not a matter of chance; it is an essential element of architectural design. The size and extension of the space signifies more than a mere enlargement of a smaller type. And we must keep in mind that in the western part of the Empire vaulted central plan buildings remained as a rule comparatively small, even in Rome and as late as the fifth century: witness the Lateran Baptistery.

On the other hand, from the Constantinian period on, all of the most important buildings in the East tend to be huge central buildings with an inner order of supports and with an ambulatory. It cannot be decided with certainty if the idea of large dimensions within the eastern Empire is of Hellenistic derivation or a new Constantinian transformation of a type derived from Rome. The appearance and dimensions of the Marneion at Gaza of the second century are too little known to be cited as an example.[73] In the fourth century, however, we have relevant examples in the octagon of Antioch around the year 330 and of Nazianz before 374, that is, of central buildings with an ambulatory, perhaps with a double ambulatory, and with galleries. Unfortunately, we know these buildings, too, only through descriptions of the period; that of Antioch through the description of Eusebius,[74] that of Nazianz through the writings of Gregory of Nazianz; [75] and these descriptions are unclear and do not provide us with the dimensions. However, we know other buildings of this type in the East, for example, the timber-roofed hexagonal building erected over the forecourt of the Temple of Baalbek [76] in the fourth century. In this new form it becomes a perfect example of the new type of central building with an inner order of supports with a diameter larger than 70 m. The Rotunda of the Holy Sepulchre in Jerusalem with a diameter of 33.68 m., the church on the Mount of Olives with a diameter of 34.80 m., as well as the great octagon of Wiranshehir with a slightly oval central space with eight pilasters and surrounded by an ambulatory with the radiating arms of the cross, are other examples. The central space of Wiranshehir with its ambulatory has a diameter of about 32 m. The best-known examples come from the fifth through the seventh centuries: the church on Garizim with a diameter of 24.20 m.; and the Dome of the Rock with a diameter of almost 55 m. All of these buildings with their large dimensions and with the effect produced by their great size differ profoundly from Sta. Costanza and the Lateran Bapistery, but they do recall Santo Stefano Rotondo.

The Wooden Roof. However, the element of enlarged size alone may not be sufficient to demonstrate the relationship that exists between Santo Stefano and the East. We must add then that like Santo Stefano and in contrast to the tradition of central plan buildings in the West, the central buildings of the East nearly always are timber roofed, be it open truss work, flat ceilings, or conical roofs. The hexagon of Baalbek had a flat ceiling already before the Constantinian period; the timber roofing of the octagon of Antioch is known from literary sources, while documentary and visual sources make it probable that the Rotunda of the Holy Sepulchre in Jerusalem had a conical wooden roof. In the fifth and sixth centuries the central buildings of Wiranshehir, on Mount Garizim, and the Dome of the Rock carried wooden cupolas and flat ceilings. In the eastern parts of the Empire stone vaults are found rarely and only in rural buildings in central Asia Minor, for example in Soasa,[77] or in the octagon described by Gregory of Nyssa. But even Gregory's description says that the stone vault in Asia Minor was considered nothing else than a substitute in stone for a wooden ceiling.[78] In fact, he writes that "given the scarcity of wood suitable for building, I have had the idea of building a vault: for in this part of the country we lack the wood for beams." [79]

The great central buildings of the eastern provinces, then, avoided the stone vault of the central nave and the barrel vaults of the ambulatory, that is to say, the very elements that clearly define the space of central buildings in the West and give these edifices their clear and easily identifiable form regardless of their dimensions. Spaciousness, extent, width, and a less compact interpretation of in- terior space are, then, characteristics of central buildings with an ambulatory and an inner order of support in the East of the Empire; new concepts, in a word, which have transformed the traditional Western type. Hence Eastern concepts would seem to have exerted a considerable impact on the design of Santo Stefano. This holds despite the Western roots of the plan, such as the assimilation of the type to an Early Christian basilica, seen in transversal section; the use of an outer circular corridor, and the 1:2 proportions of ambulatory and central space. Not only are the chapels, laid out in cross shape, easily recognized as unusual within the Western tradition, but also the huge central nave and its ambulatory, both timber-roofed, appear to be inspired by architectural concepts customary in the eastern provinces. Indeed, this huge central nave differs radically from the circular buildings with comparatively narrow naves and wide ambulatories, both compactly vaulted, as we find them in the West. There is, in other words, no single direct line leading from Santa Costanza to Santo Stefano.

III. Santo Stefano Rotondo and the Holy Sepulchre

Analysis of the Monument. The Rotunda of the Holy Sepulchre in Jerusalem has been so altered as to be no longer recognizable (Figs. 30, 31; Text Fig. 11). Today the core of the building is formed by a nave that occupies three-quarters of a circle and is supported by sixteen crude piers; the nave is enriched by an ambula- tory, completely obstructed by partition walls and provided with three apses. To the east, occupying the fourth quarter of the circle, a wide opening leads toward a chancel that also has an ambulatory with radiating chapels. Recent research, particularly the accurate studies of Fathers Vincent and Abel [80] and of Schmaltz,[81] has revealed the original appearance of the building. Until the nineteenth century the Rotunda was carried not by the present piers but by groups of three columns in the diagonal axes alternating with groups of two piers in the main axes (Text Fig. 11; Fig. 30). A gallery surmounted the ambulatory and from this rose the high drum of the center room, crowned by a wooden conical roof. This was the building as it existed after the chancel to the east had been added in the twelfth century. According to Vincent and Abel only parts of the Rotunda, the ambulatory with its walls and with the three apses and the order of supports alternating between piers and columns date prior to the twelfth century. But even these older parts, according to Vincent and Abel, belong to different building periods. They pro- posed that the structure was originally fully round, and reduced by transforming it into three-quarters of a circle only at the time of Constantine Monomachos (1049). The patriarch Modestos (614) would have built the gallery, the two heavy piers to which the chancel of the twelfth century was later added, the pairs of piers in the main axes—thus creating the alternation of supports—and finally the apses adjoining the ambulatory. Only the wall of the ambulatory, then, was attributed to the original construction of the fourth century—leaving open the question whether this building goes back to Constantine himself or to his sons.[82] Also, Vincent and Abel reconstructed this original rotunda with a regular order of twenty columns in place of the later grouping of piers and columns and proposed that these columns supported a stone dome.

The Cross Form. We may be able to go further with this reconstruction in some points, the more so since Vincent and Abel themselves did not consider it definitive. Within the limits of our problem it is of secondary importance whether the transformation of the rotunda into three-quarters of a circle was already carried out in the year 614 or not until the eleventh century, and whether the wall of the gallery also dates from this period. Our concern is with the original construction of the fourth century, and it appears that the accentuation of the main axes by means of the pairs of piers and the alternation of supports between units of two and three was established already at that time. The centers of the piers in the main axes are at distances from each other considerably wider than those between the centers of the present piers in the diagonal axes which stand in place of the original columns (Text Fig. 11). While these latter measure 2.75 m.[83], the pairs of piers in the north-south axis are at a distance of 3.05 m., those in the east-west axis of 3.58 m. Thus the supports do not follow at regular intervals. The difference between stronger supports with larger intercolumniations in the main axes and weaker supports in the diagonal axes is clearly marked. Furthermore, the east-west axis is accentuated over the north-south axis. Hence the grouping of the supports by means of stronger elements in the major axes, their accentuation, and the prevalence of the east-west axis seem to belong to the same period as the columns.[84] That the columns themselves go back to the fourth century, on the other hand, is made clear by the accurate drawings made by Horn in the eighteenth century.[85] In these drawings all the columns are placed on high socles with finely profiled bases and cornices, which cannot possibly be attributed to the seventh century. Their Corinthian capitals also can hardly be later than the fourth century. The articulation of the building with its emphasis on the main axes, and the accentuation of the cross form within the Rotunda thus must be dated in the fourth century. It is also beyond question that the original building, with its diameter of 33.70 m., is one-and-one-half times the size of Santa Costanza. The roof in the form of a wooden truncated cone over the central space also may have existed from the very beginning. The destruction of the church by fire in the year 613 [86] is more easily explained if instead of a stone dome—suggested by Vincent and Abel—the original building was covered with easily inflammable wood, either a truncated cone or a wooden dome. The original Rotunda of the Holy Sepulchre was therefore a large central building with a relatively narrow ambulatory, with an inner order of supports, and perhaps with a wooden roof. Moreover, it was a central building in which the major axes were accentuated over the diagonal axes and further the north-south axis subordinated to the east-west axis.

The Outer Circular Corridor. Up to the eleventh century the Rotunda of the Holy Sepulchre also seems to have been encircled by an outer corridor such as is found in Roman mausolea and, in modified form, in the church of Santo Stefano.[87] Arculf, who visited Jerusalem in 670, has left a description and, even more important, a plan (Fig. 31), which gives a clear idea of the building.[88] The sketch shows the tomb of Christ in the center of the church and three circles of wall around the tomb—not two walls, as now. These circles seem to be connected by means of wedge-shaped passages or by means of doors.[89] The three apses with altars abut the second circle. Arculf's description confirms the sketch: according to it, the church rose with *three* walls, with passages between one wall and the other, and with altars in three points of the middle wall;[90] twelve columns supported the high building and toward the northeast as well as the southeast four portals opened, joined to each other. From this description it is clear that a second corridor encircled the nucleus of the structure, a corridor which must logically have been an outer corridor since the wall of the first ambulatory has been preserved intact.[91] Further proof of the existence of this outer ambulatory is provided by a description of Jerusalem dating from the beginning of the ninth century,[92] the *Commemoratorium de casis Dei.* It fixes the total circumference of the Rotunda at 107 *dexteri,* that is 158.90 m.,[93] corresponding to a radius of 25.30 m.; the circumference of the inner circle is given as 54 *dexteri,* 80.20 m., with a resulting radius of 12.76 m. The information provided by the *Commemoratorium* seems generally credible. The circumference of the central space and its radius of 12.76 m. agrees entirely with the present radius as measured by Vincent Abel at 12.73 m., including the thickness of the piers.[94] Hence we may also trust the measurements of the total circumference of the building as given in the *Commemoratorium*[95] and of the corresponding radius, 25.30 m. Since the total radius of the present building including the thickness of the ambulatory wall is only 18.26 m., there remains an excess of roughly 7 m.; and this may be attributed justifiably to the external corridor as described and drawn by Arculf.

The existence of an outer corridor thus seems well established. Since we have found these corridors to be common in Roman mausolea of the first, second, and third centuries, but very rare after the middle of the fourth century (Sta. Costanza), it is likely that the exterior corridor at Jerusalem should also be attributed to the original fourth-century building. It would be more difficult to make any precise statements concerning the details of its appearance. From Arculf's description it appears only that there were groups of portals or passages on the southeast and the northeast connecting the outer ambulatory with the rotunda, and the courtyard with the outer ambulatory. Each group numbered four portals or passageways,[96] and these were divided by screens, walls, or piers.[97]

However we interpret this feature, it appears from the plan that through these passageways the outer ambulatory opened both towards the outside and towards the inner ambulatory. Furthermore the outer ambulatory could not have had the same height in its entire circumference. The rock to the west of the building rises to a height of about 5 m. above the interior, leaving no room for an outer ambulatory on the ground floor level. The shape of this outer corridor is hard to determine. It may have surrounded the building only on the east as a semicircle as De Voguë believed,[98] or it may have been two-storied on the eastern side, its groundfloor level with the interior, while on the west it was one-storied and level with the gallery. In this case its outer wall would have been the same height all around. Since according to the *Commemoratorium* the circumference was measurable in its entirety, the latter solution seems more probable.

The Holy Sepulchre and Santa Costanza. In its original form, then, the Rotunda of the Holy Sepulchre comprised not only a vast central space with an inner order of supports, probably with a wooden roof and an inner ambulatory, but also an outer corridor encircling this central nucleus and communicating with the inner ambulatory. Thus, a definite relationship seems to exist between the church of the Holy Sepulchre, Santa Costanza, and Santo Stefano (Figs. 26, 28, 30; Text Figs. 9, 11).[99] The resemblance to Santa Costanza is not surprising. Santa Costanza was a mausoleum of the house of Constantine, while the Rotunda of the Holy Sepulchre was the mausoleum erected by the house of Constantine for Christ. They share the annular outer corridor, the inner ambulatory, the order of supports, the high central space, and the form of a cross marked through the pairs of piers in the main axes. However, it remains questionable whether a direct connection exists. Both the Rotunda of the Holy Sepulchre and Santa Costanza, as mausolea, are derived from the tradition of Roman funerary monuments. The two buildings are members of the same family, stemming from the same root but the result of a different development. While Santa Costanza stands with the western Roman tradition, the Rotunda of the Holy Sepulchre represents an eastern type. While in the Rotunda at Jerusalem the ambulatory surrounding the center room is relatively narrow, as it is at Santa Costanza and as it remains in the east also later, the center room has expanded. A vault is lacking over the center space, and with it that concentration of the spatial volumes that remains so characteristic for central plan buildings in the West of the Empire. The clear and firm circular form that distinguishes Santa Costanza is missing from the Rotunda of the Holy Sepulchre.

The Holy Sepulchre and Santo Stefano Rotondo. The very elements, however, that distinguish the church of the Holy Sepulchre from Santa Costanza relate it to Santo Stefano. Here we have the large center room, covered by a timber roof, not a dome of masonry. Here we have also the outer corridor, generously open toward the inner ambulatory instead of being cut off. And while at Santa

Costanza as well as at the Holy Sepulchre the cross shape is merely hinted at, in the former by the wider arcades and the four larger niches, in the latter by the pairs of piers, at Santo Stefano the motif decisively dominates the whole arrangement. It breaks through the limits of the inner circle of supports and continues in the circle of the outer rooms and courtyards. The four main chapels radiate from the inner nucleus, as we find it in Asia Minor, where this same vigorous cross plan was already developed prior to Santo Stefano. The emphasis on the east-west axis over the north-south axis observed in Santo Stefano immediately recalls the same motif in the Rotunda of the Holy Sepulchre. In both churches the longitudinal axis is emphasized within the central space by larger intercolumniations in the inner circle of supports.

But beyond this general definition of an eastern Roman artistic ambience in which both Santo Stefano and the Holy Sepulchre find their place, a closer link between the two churches results from the comparison of their measurements (Text Figs. 9 and 11). The radius of the circle of supports in the Holy Sepulchre is 10.45 m. in the clear. The columns that touched the periphery of this circle with the front edges of their bases [100] had a diameter of roughly 1.57 m.[101] The radius of the circle, then, comprising the diameter of the columns was 12.02 m. In Santo Stefano the radius of the circular space including the columns is 12.06 m. Calculation by radii, however, is the modern method: the circumference was the fifth-century standard, and in this case the measurements of the church of the Holy Sepulchre and Santo Stefano are even closer. Indeed, at Jerusalem the circumference of the central space including the columns and the piers (which are thicker than the columns) is 75.80 m. and thus slightly larger than the theoretically calculated circumference based on the radius including only the columns. Calculated this way, it is extremely close to the circumference of 75.76 m. which is that of the circular nave of Santo Stefano, including the supports. Transposed into antique measurements and disregarding minor differences, we arrive at a round figure of 170 cubits (or 250 feet at 30.3 cm.) for both buildings.[102] The width of the inner ambulatory of the two buildings, however, differs notably. That of the church of the Holy Sepulchre has an inner width of 4.80 m.; if the columns and the thickness of the wall are included, the total is 7.81 m. The dimension of the first ambulatory (Text Fig. 8, a) at Santo Stefano is 9.10 m., and 11 m. comprising the inner and outer circles of supports. On the other hand, the measurements of the outer corridor in the Rotunda of the Holy Sepulchre and those of the sections of corridors in the diagonal axes of Santo Stefano (c) coincide perfectly. The corridor at the Holy Sepulchre, including its outer wall, was 7 m. wide, according to the *Commemoratorium* (we have seen how trustworthy the measurements of the *Commemoratorium* are), while the corresponding parts in Santo Stefano, including their outer supports are exactly 6.96 m.[103] One might possibly also compare the respective measurements of the heights of the center room in the two buildings: for the original building of the Holy Sepulchre this has been calculated by Mauss [104] and by Vincent and

Abel [105] at 20.90 m., that is to say, equal to the diameter of the inner circle; at Santo Stefano, similarly, the height of the central space is equal to its width; that is, 20 m.

All these similarities combined cannot be explained as simple coincidence. A relationship would seem to have existed between the church of Santo Stefano and that of the Holy Sepulchre and it is natural to explain it by assuming that the architect of Santo Stefano was in possession of a general description of the Rotunda of the Holy Sepulchre including the relevant dimensions. It is well known from the various pilgrim reports how spare such descriptions of visual aspects of the Rotunda in Jerusalem were and how much importance was attached in them to precise dimensions in terms of late antique and medieval practice. In measuring a circle the practice was to take the circumference because this was the dimension most easily measurable. The circumference was obtained by means of a string stretched around the support or around the wall. Thus it becomes understandable why the dimensions of the inner circles including the supports agree in both instances, while the inner dimensions taken without the supports do not agree. The architect of Santo Stefano simply used smaller supports within a circle of the same overall diameter. Thus he obtained a larger inner diameter without the supports in spite of the fact that he was dealing with the same overall diameter including the width of the supports.

The only difference of real importance between the dimensions of the two buildings is that of the width of the inner ambulatory. While the ambulatory of the Rotunda of the Holy Sepulchre including the circle of supports and including the outer wall is 7.80 m., that of Santo Stefano, including the inner and the outer circle of supports, is 11 m. We might even consider the possibility of an error, because at Jerusalem the ambulatory together with the outer corridor has a dimension of 14.85 m., that is 50 *feet,* while in Rome we have a dimension of 22 m., that is 50 *cubits.* There may, in other words, have been a confusion in the system of measurements. It is much more likely, however, that the architect of Santo Stefano took only the general plan and some of the measurements of his model into account, while for the rest he interpreted the few facts at hand arbitrarily, guided by his own intentions and his own architectural inventiveness. These architectural ideas differed from those of the fourth century, when the Rotunda of the Holy Sepulchre was designed. A comparison of the plans makes this clear. Mauss and De Vogüé [106] tried to demonstrate that the circumference of the outer wall of the ambulatory of the Rotunda of the Holy Sepulchre was obtained from the inner radius of the circle by constructing an equilateral triangle: a secant of the same length as the radius, doubled in both directions, cuts the periphery of the outer circle in two points. This construction, according to these authors, is frequently encountered in pre-Christian central building and it is also found in central buildings of Christian times.[107] But, whether correct or not, no complicated construction was employed at Santo Stefano. Indeed, the point of departure in laying out its plan was twofold: on one hand, the dimensions transferred from the Rotunda of the Holy Sepulchre; on the other, a geometrical construction based on the inner radius of the central nave, which, given the lesser width of the columns, was only eleven meters, that is, 25 cubits. No triangle, however, was constructed on these dimensions. Instead the radius was simply doubled to 50 cubits and a second circle of columns was placed on the new circle. Then the radius of this second circle was increased another 11 m., and thus the architect found by a simple procedure the third circle with a radius of 75 cubits, meaning the outer wall which delimits both the chapels (Text Fig. 8, *b*) and the vestibules (*d*). By placing into the third circle corridors of the same width as the external corridors of the Rotunda of the Holy Sepulchre, he was left with—and one wonders if it was a simple coincidence—4 m. or 9 cubits for the courtyards (*d*); the total measure of $5,^2$ hence, is divided into the proportions of 4^2 and 3^2.

The architect of Santo Stefano, hence, used the Rotunda of the Holy Sepulchre as a model in a way highly significant for the relations between model and copy in the Early Christian period and in the early Middle Ages. From our modern point of view, the decisive factor in the comparison between any two buildings is the formal relationships between the overall plans, the single parts, and the number and arrangement of articulating elements. The type as a type remains preserved, and a modification of the dimensions would not interfere with our recognition of this relationship. Just the opposite is true of the connections between Santo Stefano and the Rotunda of the Holy Sepulchre. Only the overall design of a central building with an inner ambulatory and an outer corridor is preserved. But it is altered by the new motif of chapels arranged in the form of a cross and interpenetrating the outer corridors and their courtyards. Likewise the rhythm of the supports has been modified: the alternation of piers and columns of the Holy Sepulchre has been abandoned in the inner circle of columns at Santo Stefano; on the other hand, a rhythmic arrangement is introduced in the circle of supports which separate the ambulatory from the chapels and corridors. What is preserved, however, are some of the principal *dimensions* of the model and they assume major importance: the new design is based on them rather than on the spatial proportions of the prototype. Man of the early Middle Ages was mainly interested in the general arrangement and in *measurable parts,* the *arithmetic dimensions* of the model.

Vincent and Abel and Creswell [108] have made similar observations in other buildings which use the Holy Sepulchre as a model; for example, the church of the Ascension on the Mount of Olives and the Dome of the Rock. The form of these buildings may vary. In place of the circular shape we find the octagon; the outer corridor, witness the Dome of the Rock, may be included within the building as a second ambulatory; and the rhythmic arrangement of the supports may be radically modified. Only the dimensions are equal.[109] In early medieval buildings similar relations based on a concordance of numbers frequently may be observed. This question requires further study. Within the present context it will be sufficient to have noted the relationship existing between Santo Stefano and the church of the Holy Sepulchre and to have observed the specific character of this relationship.

This leads to the question of the historical and the thematic background of these relationships and their significance for Santo Stefano. Dehio has suggested that the model of the church of the Holy Sepulchre was transferred to Santo Stefano by way of the church of Saint Stephen erected by Eudokia I in Jerusalem,[110] on the assumption that this church was a central plan building derived from the Rotunda of the Holy Sepulchre. However, the church of Saint Stephen in Jerusalem was a basilica.[111] Thematically, on the other hand, Santo Stefano in Rome and the Rotunda of the Holy Sepulchre are related. The church of the Holy Sepulchre stands at precisely that point within the history of architecture— and this is its significance for the story of architectural typology—where the central type mausoleum of Roman tradition was transformed into a type of commemorative monument which initiates an eastern Christian tradition. The Rotunda of the Holy Sepulchre, too, shelters a tomb, but it is an empty tomb honoring merely the *memory* of Christ, and with the passage of time it came to be considered a purely commemorative church,[112] without specific implications as a mausoleum. Thus the central plan type was transferred to other commemorative buildings such as the church of the Ascension, the church of the Death of the Virgin, etc. The central building, then, assumed a new significance; it became the type of commemorative building as such. Thus, when it was decided to erect a church to the memory of the protomartyr Stephen in Rome at a time in which the cult of this saint was already much diffused, the Palestinian type of commemorative building was chosen as the model. The *prototype,* however, of the commemorative monument was precisely the Rotunda of the Holy Sepulchre, and this explains the relation between it and the church of Santo Stefano in Rome from the thematic point of view.

If the Rotunda of the Holy Sepulchre was adopted as the model for Santo Stefano, the question arises of how the architectural problem in this latter church was resolved and what new conception resulted from the Roman ambience within which it was erected. Indeed, the independent stylistic character of the Roman milieu is evident, despite the dependence of Santo Stefano on the Holy Sepulchre and despite the collateral influence exerted by the cross churches of the Near East and perhaps by other East Roman buildings. The different basic principle of Santo Stefano is emphasized already in the subdivision of its plan into three concentric circles instead of the more complicated triangular construction of the Rotunda of the Holy Sepulchre. Thus Santo Stefano has lost that classical concentration which is still noticeable in the Rotunda at Jerusalem. The ambulatory is wider and transformed into an annular aisle which encircles the central nave. This feature in particular points up the differences between the Roman church of Santo Stefano and the central plan buildings of the East, where the ambulatory was comparatively narrow and a foil for the supports rather than an independent space. At Santo Stefano the bonds that tie the single parts of the whole together are loosened. Likewise, the articulation of the inner circle of supports is missing. Its columns are not grouped as in the church of the Holy Sepulchre; they are placed in a simple sequence. The supports are slimmer and occupy less space in the whole than they do in the church of the Holy Sepulchre, or, for that matter, at Santa Costanza. The wall that encircles the building, too, has only half the thickness of the walls in the Rotunda of the Holy Sepulchre. In this loosening of interrelationships, in the lesser emphasis on the particular importance of the individual elements, in the absence of rhythmic articulation and in the substitution of such earlier characteristics by means of thinner, smooth walls, by a simple order of columns, by means of a succession of vast spaces, we see the decisive transformation which made Santo Stefano into an Early Christian-Roman building. It presents the characteristic new aspect of the Roman basilicas of the fifth century, that of Sta. Sabina, of Sant' Agata dei Goti, of S. Pietro in Vincoli. It is within this framework that we must set the church of Santo Stefano Rotondo and must recognize its significance within the overall stylistic development: it is a building inspired in its essential typology by the Roman East, but transformed according to the Early Christian tradition of the city of Rome. From the historical point of view, Santo Stefano stands at the intersection of two lines: one of these lines derives from the eastern provinces of the Empire and may in itself represent a transformation of the Roman tradition that took place within the conceptions of the Hellenistic East, while the other is strictly Roman, that is, the Early Christian transformation of the classical Roman tradition.

Notes

1. The bibliography on Santo Stefano is considerable. Among the more important studies, we may cite the following: H. Hübsch, *Die altchristlichen Kirchen* (Karlsruhe, 1862), pp. 35 ff.; E. Isabelle, *Les édifices circulaires* (Paris, 1855), pp. 85 ff.; G. B. De Rossi, *I musaici cristiani* (Rome, 1872 ff.), *PL*, XVII; C. Dehio and G. V. Bezold, *Die kirchliche Baukunst des Abendlandes,* I (Stuttgart, 1892), 40 ff.; O. Wulff, *Altchristliche und byzantinische Kunst,* (Handbuch der Kunstwissenschaft [Berlin, 1914–24]) pp. 248 ff.; herein Wulff, *Altchr. Kunst.* Among special studies dealing with Santo Stefano, we cite G. B. De Rossi, "La basilica di Sto. Stefano ed il monastero di S. Erasmo sul Celio. Saggio unico dell'opera di G. Terribilini," *Studi e documenti di storia e diritto,* VII (1885), 217 ff. (herein De Rossi, *Studi*); R. Lanciani, "L'itinerario di Einsiedeln e l'ordine di Benedetto Canonico," in *Monumenti antichi pubblicati per cura della Reale Accademia dei Lincei,* I (Milan, 1891), 437 ff.; I. Just and A. Bardon, "A Római Magyar templom, a Santo Stefano Rotondo," *Magyar Müveszet,* VI (1930), 221 ff.

Of the numerous surveys published during the past century, we cite those of Hübsch, *Altchr. Kirchen,* Pls. 16, 17. Among those done by architects of the Renaissance we refer only to the most important ones published in A. Bartoli,

Monumenti antichi di Roma nei disegni degli Uffizi di Firenze (Rome, 1914–22), in particular those of Francesco di Giorgio Martini (Bartoli, I, Fig. 16), of Cronaca (Bartoli, I, Fig. 31), and of Sansovino (Bartoli, IV, Fig. 616). In addition we mention the plan in the so-called Bramantino sketchbook, *Le rovine di Roma,* ed. Mongeri (Milan, 1879), Pl. XXXIX; the one of Ligorio in the Oxford Codex, *Archaeologia,* LI, 2 (1888), 497; and one from the Palladio workshop in London (R.I.B.A., VIII, f. 3; our Fig. 28) as well as the views published by Egger, *Römische Veduten,* I (Vienna-Leipzig, 1911–1931), Pls. 87 and 90. Still more important is the survey of Desgodetz, *Les édifices antiques de Rome* (Paris, 1682), Pls. 29 and 30, and the additional survey drawings prepared by Valadier and Canina in their *Supplemento all'opera sugli edifici antichi di Roma dell'architetto Desgodetz* (Rome, 1843), Ch. III, Pls. 10–12 (herein cited as Canina-Valadier-Desgodetz).

The plan reproduced as Text Fig. 8, executed by Mr. Wolfgang Frankl, is based on a survey kindly put at our disposal by the Soprintendenza ai monumenti medievali del Lazio. However, our plan includes some corrections based on our own observations and measurements as well as on the plans prepared by Hübsch and by Bardon.

2. Hülsen, *Le Chiese di Roma nel medioevo* (Florence, 1925), p. 474.

3. De Rossi, *Inscriptiones Christianae Urbis Romae,* II (Rome, 1857–88), 152; it is uncertain whether the phrase "forum basilicae" in the inscription of Pope Felix IV should be translated as "atrium" or as "interior," or possibly as "outside" (*fuori*).

4. De Rossi, *Inscr. Chr.,* II, 152. We do not know when the consecration of an altar dedicated to Saint John by an otherwise unknown bishop whom Palumbus mentioned in an inscription (De Rossi, *Insc. Chr.,* II, 152–53) took place. It was certainly before the eighth century, because the compiler of the Sylloge of Lorsch had read it at that time. Concerning the translation of the relics and the construction of an altar dedicated to SS. Primus and Felicianus in 1736 in the eastern chapel, cf. also Marangoni, *De inventione cor-*

porum SS. Primi et Feliciani (1736), cod. Vat. lat. 9456, fols. 2 ff.

5. *LP,* I, 510 and II, 384.

6. Bramantino, as above, note 1: "raffaciollo papa Nichola ma molto più la guasto."

7. E. Müntz, *Les arts à la cour des papes,* I (Paris, 1898), 141 ff., 293.

8. The date 1580 is inscribed over the lefthand sacristy door.

9. Paper delivered by P. Antonelli, O.F.M., on April 15, 1934, at the Pontifical Institute of Christian Archaeology.

10. I would like to express my gratitude to His Eminence the Cardinal Vicar of Rome for allowing me access to the convent garden in order to examine the existing remains. My thanks go also to Msgr. G. Belvederi and Dr. J. Kollwitz, who kindly interceded with His Eminence in order to obtain this permission. (As of 1967, the garden is no longer *in clausura.*)

11. Müntz, *op. cit.,* 141 ff.

12. The small, smooth bricks, wholly different from the crude masonry generally used in Rome in the fifteenth century, as well as the round windows of this wall, demonstrate that this masonry dates from the twelfth century. The description of Giovanni Rucellai (G. Marcotti, "Il giubileo dell'anno 1450 secondo una relazione di Giovanni Rucellai," *Archivio della Società romana di storia patria,* IV, 4 [1881], 563 ff., esp. 573), who saw the building in 1450 before the restorations undertaken by Nicholas V, apparently already in the present state, is further evidence for this suggestion. He saw the nave enveloped by only one ambulatory, which was entirely walled up and flanked only by the choir chapel (". . . tondo, in su 20 colonne con architravi, aperto per tutto, et da torno uno andito con tetto serrato di mattoni, con una cappella antica dallato . . ."). There is further negative evidence for this assumption in the list of building expenses; they accurately note all of the construction carried out under Nicholas V, but the closing up of the ambulatory is not mentioned.

13. But see H. Glück, *Der Wölbungsbau* (Vienna, 1933), Pl. 133, and Isabelle, *Edifices,* pp. 85 ff., who erroneously as-

sume that the upper parts of the cross wall bond with the circular wall of the drum.

14. Concerning this problem, see De Rossi, *Studi* (1886), pp. 217 ff., and *Musaici cristiani*, Pl. XVII, text.

15. Isabelle, *Edifices*, Pl. 38.

16. R. Lanciani, pp. 437 ff., and *Forma Urbis Romae* (Milan, 1896), fol. 36.

17. Chr. Hülsen, "Dritter Jahresbericht über neue Funde und Forschungen zur Topographie der Stadt Rom 1891," *RM*, VII (1892), 297 ff.

18. L. Homo, *Léxique de topographie romaine* (Paris, 1900), p. 331.

19. K. Wulzinger, "Die Macellum-Dupondien des Nero," *Numismatik, II* (1933), 83 ff.; esp. 116 ff.

20. Canina-Valadier-Desgodetz, *op. cit.*, Pl. 12; see also our Text Fig. 8.

21. Not the western chapel, as Wulzinger states ("Macellum-Dupondien," p. 136).

22. The walls discovered at the time of the construction of the English hospital and published by Hülsen ("La pianta di Roma dell'Anonimo Einsidlense," *DissPontAcc*, 8–9 [1907], 379 ff., esp. 411) and by T. Ashby and P. K. B. Reynolds ("The Castra Peregrinorum," *JRS*, XIII [1923], 152 ff., esp. 154) seem to prove the opposite. These walls run at an oblique angle toward the church of Santo Stefano and, since corresponding walls were found next to the Piazza della Navicella (cf. Ashby and Reynolds, *op. cit.*, p. 157), it may be assumed that all of these remains as well as the walls found by Canina under Santo Stefano were part of a large building complex, which Ashby believed to have been the Castra Peregrinorum; in that case, however, there would have been no room on the site of Santo Stefano for a Macellum of Nero, the more so since the Castra Peregrinorum were in use at least until 350 (Ashby and Reynolds, "*op. cit.*, p. 162).

23. H. Hübsch, *Altchr. Kirchen.*

24. Dehio and Bezold, *Kirchl. Baukunst*, I.

25. De Rossi, *Studi* (1886).

26. Cf. Hübsch, *op. cit.*, pp. 37 ff.

27. Canina-Valadier-Desgodetz, II, 12,

have reproduced this wall in detail. It seems that they saw it without the plaster (our Fig. 25).

28. However cf. Isabelle, *Edifices*, p. 86. He claims to have seen horizontal traces over the arches of the outer circle of columns and on the upper wall at the point where the roof of the anteportico abuts the drum.

29. Cf. F. Mazzanti, "La scultura nei bassi tempi," *Archivio storico dell'arte*, II (1896), 33 ff.

30. Uffizi, Coll. Santarelli, 161 r (Bartoli, *Monumenti*, I, Pl. XV, Fig. 31).

31. Flavius Blondus, *De Roma instaurata* (Turin, 1527), Ch. LXXX, c. 13 v; Giovanni Rucellai, in Marcotti, as quoted above, n. 12, p. 573.

32. Canina-Valadier-Desgodetz, *op. cit.*, Pl. 12, and our Fig. 25.

33. Canina-Valadier-Desgodetz, *loc. cit.*

34. Mr. Peter Marx observed that the group of five columns in the northeast sector is somewhat higher than the columns in the other diagonal sectors.

35. Dehio and Bezold, *op. cit.*, I, 31 ff.

36. Dehio and Bezold, *ibid.*

37. Dehio and Bezold, *ibid.*

38. Bartoli, *Monumenti*, Figs. 597, 598, 627, 647, 648, 652, 662 (L. Donati, J. Sansovino, G. Vignola, S. Peruzzi).

39. L. Donati (Bartoli, *Monumenti*, Figs. 597, 598; H. Egger, *Kritisches Verzeichnis der stadtrömischen Architekturzeichnungen der Albertina* [Vienna, 1907] II, no. 101).

40. Compare the two drawings by Donati, cited above, n. 39.

41. Canina-Valadier-Desgodetz, Pl. IV, 9.

42. B. de Montfaucon, *L'antiquité expliquée* (Paris, 1722), V, I, Pl. XVIII.

43. De Montfaucon, *ibid.*, Pl. CXVIII.

44. De Montfaucon, *ibid.*, Pl. CXIII.

45. De Montfaucon, *ibid.*, Pl. CVIII.

46. *C.R.A.I.* (1922), pp. 380 ff.

47. D. Viviani, "Tempio di S. Angelo in Perugia," *BdA*, V (1911), 28 ff.

48. G. Lugli, *La zona archeologica di Roma* (Rome, 1924), p. 211.

49. G. T. Rivoira, *Le origini dell'archi-*

tettura lombarda (Milan, 2nd ed., 1908), Figs. 32–33.

50. D. Krencker, *Die trierer Kaiserthermen* (Augsburg, 1929), p. 224.

51. As far as I can see, there is only one exception. The "Istudio di Marcho Varone a San Germano" as drawn by Giuliano Sangallo (Hülsen, *Il libro di Giuliano da Sangallo* [Leipzig, 1910], fol. 8) shows the arms of the cross extending freely. But since the building is not preserved, it is impossible to check on the correctness of the drawing.

52. S. Guyer, "Die Bedeutung der christlichen Baukunst des inneren Kleinasiens für die allgemeine Kunstgeschichte," *BZ*, XXXIII (1933), 78 ff.

53. H. Rott, *Kleinasiatische Denkmäler* (Leipzig, 1908), pp. 180 ff.

54. J. Strzygowski, *Kleinasien* (Leipzig, 1903), 77 ff.; K. Friedenthal, *Das kreuzförmige Oktogon* (Carlsruhe, 1908), pp. 33 ff.; A. Birnbaum, "Die Oktogone von Antiochia, Nazianz und Nyssa," *RepKunstW*, XXXVI (1913), 181 ff.; *Gregorii Nysseni Epistulae,* ed. G. Pasquali (Berlin, 1925), pp. 76 ff.

55. J. Strzygowski, *Kleinasien*, pp. 96 ff.

56. S. Guyer, *op. cit.,* pp. 88 ff.; W. M. Ramsay and G. L. Bell, *The Thousand and One Churches* (London, 1909), pp. 428 ff.

57. S. Guyer, "Der Dom von Pisa und das Rätsel seiner Entstehung," *MünchJb* IX (1932), 351 ff.

58. Drawing after Arculf (our Fig. 31), in Adamuanus, *De locis sanctis* (*Itinera Hierosolymitana,* ed. P. Geyer, *CSEL,* 39 [Vienna, 1898]), p. 231.

59. J. Lassus, "Deux églises cruciformes du Hauran," *Bulletin d'études orientales de l'Institut français,* I (1931), 13 ff.

60. U. Monneret de Villard, "Note di archeologia lombarda," *Archivio storico lombardo,* XLI (1914), 37 ff. (Chieti, S. Ponzo Canavese).

61. P. Loiacono, "Sul restauro compiuto al Battistero di Santa Severina," *BdA,* XXVIII (1934), 182 ff.

62. Concerning this entire question, cf. W. Altmann, *Die italischen Rundbauten* (Berlin, 1906); for Epidauros, see P. Kavvadias, "Die Tholos von Epidauros," *Sit-*

zungsberichte der Preussischen Akademie der Wissenschaften, Phil.-hist. Klasse (1909), pp. 536 ff.; for Miletus, Th. Wiegand, *Sitzungsberichte der Preussischen Akademie der Wissenschaften, Phil.-hist. Klasse* (1904), pp. 87 ff.

63. Bramantino, as cited above, n. 1, Pls. XLVII, XLIX, LV.

64. Cod. Vat. lat. 3439 (Templum Plutonis et Proserpinae; Templum Isidis et Serapidis).

65. Dehio and Bezold, *Kirchl. Baukunst,* I, 32.

66. O. Wulff, *Altchr. Kunst,* p. 246.

67. But see the all too limited viewpoint of Pluto (70 *palmi*: 11 *palmi*) 15.62 m.:

68. Ligorio, as above, n. 1: Temple of Pluto (70 *palmi*: 11 *palmi*) 15.62 m.: 2.43 m.; Temple of Serapis (56 *palmi*: 8 *palmi*) 12:50 m.: 1.80 m. Bramantino, as above, n. 1, Pl. XLVII (36 *palmi*: 9 *palmi*) 8 m.: 2 m.; Pl. LI (38 *palmi*: 10 *palmi*) 8.50 m.: 2.23 m.; Pl. LV (36 *palmi*: 4 *palmi*) 8 m.: 0.89 m.

69. For the reconstruction of the Baptistery, cf. G. B. Giovenale, *Il Battistero lateranense* (Rome, 1929).

70. Sta. Costanza: 11.52 m.: 4.06 m.; Lateran Baptistery: 8.50 m.: 4.25 m.

71. 20.90 m.: 4.80 m.

72. For Bosra, see H C. Butler, *Ancient Architecture in Syria* (Leyden, 1910 ff.), II A, 281 ff.; for Garizim, see A. M. Schneider, in *Deutsche Ausgrabungen,* ed. G. Rodenwaldt (Berlin, 1930), p. 835.

73. Dehio and Bezold, *Kirchl. Baukunst,* p. 36, and recently Glück, *Der Wölbungsbau,* p. 133. Glück objects to the reconstruction of the Marneion with an inner order of supports, ambulatory, and galleries. He may be right. It should be noted, however, that the reconstruction of an oculus in the cupola is based on an erroneous Latin translation of the decisive passage in Marcus Diaconus, in the old edition of the Bollandists (*Life of Porphyry of Gaza, AASS, Feb.,* III, 649 ff. [*PL* LXV, col. 1249]). The original Greek text states only that there was a high cupola.

74. Eusebius, *Vita Constantini,* III, 50, ed. Heikel, *Über das Leben Konstantins* (Berlin, 1902), p. 99; cf. trans. H. Wace

and P. Schaff, *A Select Library of Nicene and Post-Nicene Fathers, The Nicene Fathers,* I (New York-Oxford-London 1890), 532 ff.

75. *PG,* XXXV, col. 1038; J. Strzygowski, *Kleinasien,* p. 94.

76. Th. Weigand, *Baalbek* (Berlin-Leipzig, 1921–25), p. 129.

77. Rott, *Denkmäler,* pp. 249 ff.

78. Guyer, *op. cit.,* 1933, p. 101.

79. In the East, too, the vault is used only rarely for central buildings *without* ambulatory (Hierapolis, Brussa).

80. H. Vincent and V. Abel, *Jérusalem nouvelle,* II (Paris, 1925), 89 ff.

81. K. Schmaltz, *Mater ecclesiarum* (Strassburg, 1918).

82. Vincent and Abel (*Jérusalem nouvelle*), among others, support the first hypothesis while Schmaltz favors the second.

83. This would hold true even if the pilasters as such were only put in place of older columns in 614; a passage from B. Amico, *Trattato delle piante . . . di Terra Santa* (Rome, 1609), p. 11 (". . . i pilastri sono palmi 7 per quadro dalla parte esteriore; ma di dentro sono sferici . . .") admits this alternative; but after 614 there were certainly pilasters according to Arculf's description.

84. Vincent and Abel, *Jérusalem nouvelle,* p. 252.

85. G. Horn, *Ichnographia Terrae Sanctae,* ed. Golubovitch (Paris, 1901), p. 48, and Vincent and Abel, *Jérusalem nouvelle,* p. 177. Should the observation made by Martini (according to C. J. M. de Voguë, *Les églises de la Terre Sainte* [Paris, 1860]), be factual, namely that some of the pediments of the columns were carved out of the rock itself, we would have the decisive evidence for the original form of this arrangement.

86 Cf. Antiochos Strategios, as quoted by Vincent and Abel, *Jérusalem nouvelle,* p. 217.

87. See also the excellent analysis of Wulff, *Altchr. Kunst,* pp. 247 ff., and Schmaltz, *op. cit.,* p. 268.

88. Cf. Vincent and Abel, *Jérusalem nouvelle,* p. 233.

89. Arculf's plan in its various manuscript versions is illustrated in Heisenberg, *Grabeskirche und Apostelkirche* (Leipzig, 1908), I, Pl. X, Figs. 1–4. The alternating white and black rings in some of the drawings have purely ornamental significance.

90. ". . . in tribus parietibus . . . inter unum quemque parietem et alterum latum habens spatium viae . . . tria quoque altaria in tribus locis parietis medii habens . . ."

91. See also the arrangement of the altars and their apses in the drawings of Arculf.

92. Vincent and Abel, *Jérusalem nouvelle,* pp. 234 ff. An Armenian description of the seventh century cited by Vincent and Abel, p. 235, has lesser significance; its importance lies in the reference to an upper gallery as existing already in the seventh-century building. But the recorded dimensions (100 *braccia* width and 100 *braccia* length) seem to be only approximations.

93. The *dexter* has been calculated by Vincent and Abel (*Béthléem* [Paris, 1913], p. 130) as 1.485 m., and by Schmaltz (*Mater ecclesiarum,* p. 81) as 1.51 m. Papias, the encyclopedist of the eleventh century, makes it equivalent to the Roman *passus* (according to Ducange, *Glossarium, sub voce*). This would accord with the opinion of Vincent and Abel, and a check with the dimensions recorded in the *Commemoratorium* confirms it.

94. The credibility of the *Commemoratorium* also is confirmed by a check of other dimensions: from the Holy Sepulchre to Golgotha, 28 *dexteri* or 41.58 m. (in actuality 41 m.); from Golgotha to the place of the invention of the cross, 17 *dexteri* or 28.73 m. (actually 28.70 m.); the overall length of the buildings at the Holy Sepulchre, 96 *dexteri* or 142.50 m. (actually 137.50 m.); the Church of the Nativity in Bethlehem, length, 38 *dexteri* or 56.43 m. (actually 56.65 m.), façade, 17 *dexteri* or 25.25 m. (actually 25.20 m.), length of the transept (greatest discrepancy), 23 *dexteri* or 34.15 m. (actually 35.82 m.). Cf. also Schmaltz, *Mater ecclesiarum,* pp. 81 ff.

95. Schmaltz, *Mater ecclesiarum,* pp. 81 ff., wanted to refer the dimensions of 54 *dexteri* recorded by the *Commemoratorium*

for the central nave to the height of the central nave. However, the resulting height of 81.14 m. is obviously impossible for the central space. The maximum height possible is equal to the diameter of the central space, or 21.25 m., as Vincent and Abel rightly assumed. Indeed, it is clear from the text of the *Commemoratorium* that the dimension of 54 *dexteri* refers to the circumference of the structure.

96. ". . . bis quaternales portas habet, hoc est quattuor introitus per tres e regione interiectis viarum spatiis stabilitos parietes . . ."

97. The arrangement is not wholly clear either from Arculf's drawing or from his description. Indeed, as we can see from other entrances drawn by him (Church at Golgotha, for example), the lines of his drawings may indicate either longitudinal dividing walls or the jambs of a door in the vertical sense; also the word "parietes" used in his description might mean either walls or pilasters.

98. De Vogüé, *op. cit.* (n. 85), Pl. VII.

99. Rivoira, "La Chiesa del S. Sepolchro in Gerusalemme," *DissPontAccad.*, ser. II, XIII (1918), 183, already has drawn attention to the relationship between the church of the Holy Sepulchre and Sta. Costanza. However, he wanted to make Sta. Costanza the model for the church of the Holy Sepulchre. The relationships between Santo Stefano and the church of the Holy Sepulchre also have been mentioned frequently, most clearly and fully by Wulff, *Altchr. Kunst*, I, 247 ff., whose studies have suggested the main lines I have followed in discussing this problem.

100. Calculated on the basis of the center of the lesser pilasters in the diagonal axes, which enclose the original columns; this also appears from the description of Amico, *Trattato*, p. 11, who records 21 *palmi* or 4.70 m. for the width of the ambulatory.

101. Amico, *Trattato*, p. 11, reports 7 *palmi* or 1.568 m.; Horn, *Ichnographia*, p. 48, reports 5 feet. The dimension of the foot used by Horn is 0.305 m., as deduced from all of the dimensions recorded by both Horn and Amico. Hence, according to Horn the diameter of the columns was 1.525 m.

102. That the cubit was the unit of measurement employed in the construction of the church of the Holy Sepulchre appears from a comparison of the dimensions of the church with, among others, the height of the stone blocks. According to Vincent and Abel, *Jérusalem nouvelle*, II, 109, Fig. 60, the height of the stone blocks varies from 42.15 to 44.5 cm. The cubit equals 44.35 cm.

103. Canina-Valadier-Desgodetz, *op. cit.*, Pl. 11.

104. C. Mauss, "Note sur la méthode employée pour tracer la plan de la mosque d'Omar et la Rotonde du Saint-Sépulchre à Jérusalem," *RA*, ser. 3, XII (1888), 20.

105. The height measured by Mauss, *loc. cit.*, however, is certain only for the building of the twelfth century.

106. Mauss, *ibid.*, and De Vogüé, *Eglises, loc. cit.*

107. For example, Santa Maria Maggiore in Nocera, or Sant' Angelo in Perugia.

108. K. A. C. Creswell, *Early Muslim Architecture* (Oxford, 1932), p. 75; Vincent and Abel, *Jérusalem nouvelle*, II, 370.

109.	Church of the Holy Sepulchre	Dome of the Rock	Church of of the Ascension
Inner circle, up to the center of the columns	11.40	11.40	(destroyed)
Inner circle, including the first ambulatory	18.26	18.20 (measured to the outer circumference)	18.40 (outer circumference)
Inner circle, including the two ambulatories	25.20	25.20	(destroyed)

110. Dehio and Bezold, *Kirchl. Baukunst*, p. 40.

111. Vincent and Abel, *Jérusalem nouvelle*, II, 743 ff.

112. Wulff, *Altchr. Kunst*, p. 247.

Postscript

In reading this early paper my feelings are mixed. It requires a thorough autocritique, both pro and con. On three points I am today highly critical, and I shall start with these.

1) The writing in the original Italian version is involved and often repetitious. In part this was due to my having mentally composed it in the yet more involved German of the 1920's and 1930's. It was equally due, I suppose, to the natural exuberance of the Italian language, which likes repetitions for emphasis. In the present English version, both translator and editor, whom I cannot sufficiently thank, with some assistance from myself, have pruned the text as much as possible.

2) As to method, I am struck today by the dogmatism of my approach in parts of the paper. Nobody today would attempt to interpret any historical development as a logical sequence and counterplay of types. Thinking in the abstract terms of a "typological history" was characteristic of German art history of the period, as in the work of Heinrich Wölfflin, Samuel Guyer, and my teacher, Paul Frankl. The method, despite its obvious drawbacks, is valuable when counterbalanced by well-controlled historical and archaeological data. After all, to quote Wölfflin, "The chaos of history can be stabilized only by applying a few principles." It certainly impressed me, perhaps unduly at the time, and I found the necessary balance only through the detailed research required by work on the *Corpus Basilicarum* and through encountering in the United States the eminently Anglo-Saxon concept of "history as it was," as different as can be from history as it ought to have been.

3) I probably relied too much on secondary sources published in German—Dehio and Bezold, Guyer, Strzygowski, Wulff; and I was unacquainted with most of the work done by such English or American scholars as Ramsay and Bell or H. C. Butler. Even had I known them, it would have contributed little to the problem at hand. After all, Early Christian archaeology all over the world was still a weak little plant.

Research in the Early Christian field over the past thirty-odd years has accumulated a vast amount of detailed archaeological evidence that changes the dating, description, and interpretation of some of the building types and individual monuments discussed. Among the large cross-shaped *martyria* such as the first church of St. John at Ephesus, the churches at Sichem and Kalat Siman, the *martyrium* of Saint Babylas at Antioch-Kaoussié, first published in 1938 (*Antioch*, II, 5 ff.), would now have to be mentioned. But as I see it today, there is no connection between these large, timber-roofed structures and the small vaulted cross chapels of the type of Tomarza. I was not aware, however, though I should have been, of the Baptistery of Canosa (of unknown date), where four chapels project from an octagonal center room and interpenetrate with an exterior ambulatory, comparable to Santo Stefano (Nachod, 1914). Regarding individual buildings, too, revisions are in order: Sant' Angelo in Perugia, contrary to what I thought in 1935, probably dates from the sixth rather than the fifth century, and thus after Santo Stefano Rotondo. The Church of the Ascension was circular rather than octagonal (Corbo, 1961–62). References to the cathedral of Bosra, not an octagon either (Crowfoot, 1937), have been dropped from this English version. The descriptions of Santo Stefano and of the Rotunda of the Holy Sepulchre require some revisions. In preparing the *Corpus*, Wolfgang Frankl, Spencer Corbett, and I have established that the diaphragm wall across the center room was inserted in the twelfth, not in the eighth century (*Corpus*, IV, in press); that the marble paneling and stucco decoration extended to the outer areas as well as the center room (*ibid.*); and that the Roman walls below the church, first seen by Valadier, were not those of a circular building, the *Macellum Neronis*, but straight walls belonging to the *Castra Peregrina* (Text Fig. 8; Fig. 25; Colini, 1944, pp. 240 ff.). Furthermore Deichmann (1954–1955) has suggested the convincing hypothesis that for the center room a dome of light material, possibly cane, was projected; even so, it remains true that the covering as executed consisted of an open timber roof construction. For the Rotunda of the Holy Sepulchre, Corbo has ascertained that the three apses abutting the ambulatory belong to the original structure. Indeed, doubts have arisen regarding even the reconstructions proposed. For Santo Stefano, Spencer Corbett (1960) has suggested reversing the arrangement of corridors and courtyards in the diagonal axes, but as to this I remain hesitant (Text Figs. 12, 13). For the Rotunda of the Holy Sepulchre, Corbo proposes a reconstruction in the form of a cylindrical freestanding nave within a lower ambience, semicircular in the rear and rectangular in front; but this reconstruction is so contrary to the descriptions beginning with Egeria's in the late fourth century and continuing with Arculf's that I should like to await the results of further examination of the structures.

This criticism of my youthful effort presented in this paper is tempered, however, by a few considerations. I still feel it was necessary at the time for somebody to prove by means of the architectural data that Santo Stefano was a fifth-century building from the foundations up and to present a stylistic analysis of the design. Likewise I still feel that the resemblances of Santo Stefano Rotondo to the Rotunda of the Holy Sepulchre as represented for instance by Arculf are so close as to indicate a direct link. Had I paid attention in 1935 to Santo Stefano in Bologna and its Holy Sepulchre as I did in 1942 (see below, p. 129; Fig. 46), I could have stressed the links more forcefully. In any event, not only have I never been able to find a better explanation for certain similarities in type and for the almost identical measurements of the two buildings, but nothing more convincing has come forth from any quarter. Certainly I was right in interpreting Santo Stefano as a member of the large family of Early Christian commemorative buildings of central type and thus explaining the uniqueness of the church in Roman Early Christian architecture. I also saw, correctly, I think, the link between these commemorative buildings in the eastern part of the Roman Empire and Roman mausolea. Indeed, I am quite proud that both these points, merely sketched in my early paper, are basic elements in André Grabar's splendid book *Martyrium*. Finally I am amused that some ideas of the "Iconography of Medieval Architecture" (below, pp. 115 ff.) are present in embryonic form in this paper.

Additional Bibliography

Antioch-on-the-Orontes, II, *The Excavations of 1933–1936*. Ed. R. Stillwell (The Hague, Princeton, and London, 1938), pp. 5ff.

Armellini, M. *Le chiese di Roma dal secolo IV al XIV*. Ed. C. Cecchelli (Rome, 1942), pp. 157ff.

Bandmann, G. "Die Vorbilder der aachener Pfalzkapells," *Karl der Grosse*, III, ed. W. Braunfels (Düsseldorf, 1967), 424ff.

Bernhard, H., and Hubert, J. "Les fouilles de Saint Riquier," *Bull. Soc. Antiqu. de France* (1962), pp. 203 ff.

Colini, A. M. "Storia e topografia del Celio nell' antichità," *Memorie della Pont. Accad. Rom. di archaeologia*, VII (1944), 245 ff.

Corbett, S. "Santo Stefano Rotondo," *RACrist*, XXXVI (1960), 249 ff.

Corbo, P. "Gli edifici della Santa Anastasis," *Liber Annuus*, XII (1961–62), 221 ff.

Crowfoot, J. W. *Churches at Bosra and Samaria-Sebaste.* (British School of Archaeology in Jerusalem, Suppl. Paper 4, London, 1937).

Deichmann, F. W. "Die Eindeckung von S. Stefano Rotondo," *Miscellanea Giulio Belvederi* (Vatican City, 1954–55), pp. 437 ff.

Forschungen in Ephesos, ed. Österreichisches archäologisches Institut, III (Vienna, 1923) IV, Die Johanneskirche (Vienna, 1951).

Giovanni Rucellai ed il suo Zibaldone, ed. A. Perosa ("Studies of the Warburg Institute," XXIV, London, 1960), pp. 73, 161 n. 7.

Grabar, A. *Martyrium* (Paris, 1946), *passim,* esp. pp. 311 ff.

Guyer, S. *Grundlagen mittelalterlicher abendländischer Baukunst* (Einsiedeln, 1950).

Krautheimer, R. and Corbett, S. *Corpus,* IV, in press.

————, *Early Christian and Byzantine Architecture* ("Pelican History of Art," Harmondsworth, 1965), *passim.*

Mâle, 9. *Rome et ses vieilles églises* (Paris, 1942), pp. 88 ff.

Moreno Cassano, R. "Il battistero di S. Giovanni a Canosa," *Vetera Christianorum,* 5 (1968), 163 ff.

Nachod, H. "Das Baptisterium von Canosa," *RM*, XXX (1915), 116 ff.

Tomei, P. *L'architettura a Roma nel quattrocento* (Rome, 1942), p. 103.

Verzone, P. "Le chiese cimiteriali . . . a struttura molteplice," *Arte del primo millennio,* ed. E. Arslan (Turin, 1953), pp. 28 ff.

7

SANCTA MARIA ROTUNDA*

THIS PAPER is a preliminary summary of a more comprehensive study and I apologize for offering only the outlines of a problem. It is a problem within the field of the iconography of architecture, the hardly explored discipline which deals with the relation between the form of a building and its use beyond the realm of mere practicability, specifically between the form of a church and its dedication to a given saint.

Among round churches, during the early Middle Ages a great number are dedicated to the Virgin. Needless to say, not *all* churches dedicated to her are round, nor are all round churches dedicated to her. *Memoriae* or *martyria* of central shape, as pointed out by Grabar,[1] were erected in commemoration of many holy sites or even of saints. But among them, sanctuaries of the Virgin appear to stand out as a large separate group. Within this group, it seems, specific prototypes and filiations thereof can be traced.

You may recall a group of round chapels of St. Mary erected in Carolingian times: a chapel at Centula, 790-99 (Fig. 32); one at Würzburg on the Marienburg, 780 (Fig. 33); one at Altötting near Munich, 877; finally, one at Ludwigstadt, likewise ninth-century. All are small; all are domed; all are round with eight or twelve niches arranged either within the thickness of the wall or slightly projecting; and all are dedicated jointly to the Virgin and to one or more of the apostles. The type survived in Southern Germany for centuries, and a late example on the Lechfeld (1603), dedicated to Our Lady's Succor, helps us in establishing the prototype of the entire group: for, according to a document, it was built in the image of Sancta Maria Rotunda in Rome.[2]

Sancta Maria Rotunda, of course, is the Pantheon (Figs. 34, 36). Possibly designed as a heroon of the Imperial family and its divine ancestors, it had been rededicated on May 10, 609 or 610 by Pope Boniface IV in honor of Mary Ever Virgin and of all martyrs, *sancta Maria ad Martyres*.[3] Legend quickly elaborated on the dedication: the Venerable Bede already explained the Christian patronage as intended to replace the alleged dedication to all the gods by one to all the martyrs of Christ; in the twelfth century the *Mirabilia* suggest even that the building originally had been consecrated to Cybele the mother of all the gods who had been replaced by the Virgin.

For modern architectural historians it is perhaps not too easy to see how

*From *Arte del primo millennio* (Atti del II° convegno per lo studio dell' arte dell' alto medioevo, Pavia, 1950) (Turin, 1953), pp. 23–27.

any of the small Carolingian chapels could be considered by the contemporaries as copies of the enormous structure the Pantheon was. We expect the resemblance between two buildings to be expressed in terms of mathematical similarities. But to medieval men this visual and mathematical correspondence was not the essential point. As long as the copy shared with the prototype some outstanding features; as long as it was round; as long as it was domed; as long as it was encircled by niches; and as long as it was dedicated to the Virgin, the copy could stand for the Pantheon.[4] In a way, these common properties are summed up in the latter's medieval name: Sancta Maria Rotunda, a round church dedicated to the Virgin.

Churches of the type of Sancta Maria Rotunda continued to be built throughout the Middle Ages, the Renaissance and the Baroque. The Mausoleum of Theodoric at Ravenna (Figs. 35, 37) was made into a church and named Sancta Maria Rotunda before and perhaps quite some time before 858. In a document of 1057 it is called expressly "the basilica of St. Mary which is shaped in the likeness (*ad similitudinem*) of the Roman Pantheon . . . "[5] In Rome itself, one of the round mausolea near old St. Peter's became popularly known as Sta. Maria della Febbre. When in 1434 Brunelleschi designed the church of Sta. Maria degli Angeli in Florence, he laid it out as an octagon with eight niches, surmounted by a dome. Other octagonal churches dedicated to the Virgin follow in a first project for Sta. Maria delle Grazie at Prato (1485), at Sta. Maria di fuori at Empoli (1522), and elsewhere throughout the fifteenth and sixteenth centuries. Still, Bernini's church of the Madonna at Ariccia (1661) is obviously linked to the Pantheon, with its pronaos, its two small towers, its domed interior and its eight niches; the architrave bears the dedication to Mary, the Mother of God, assumed to Heaven. A type had been established for churches of the Virgin and the link to the prototype of Sancta Maria Rotunda was intelligible to any educated person as late as the seventeenth and eighteenth centuries.

However, if the Pantheon really became the fountainhead of this group of early medieval round churches with niches, the question arises why had the Pantheon been dedicated just to the Virgin? Why was it considered appropriate for that specific patronage?

In this connection it must be recalled that the Pantheon and its derivatives are in no way the *only* group of round churches dedicated to the Mother of God. To begin with, nearly a century before the Pantheon, another central building had been consecrated to her in the West, the Daurade in Toulouse. Possibly a late Roman mausoleum with niches in its wall and with an opaion in its vault, it was decorated in the course or possibly at the end of the sixth century with mosaics whose subject matter has been reliably reconstructed by Miss Woodruff: the Virgin leading prophets, apostles, evangelists, archangels, patriarchs, the tribes of Israel and martyrs towards the Savior.[6] Another, perhaps more important group, quite different in plan, would appear to be exemplified by Charlemagne's palatine chapel at Aix-la-Chapelle: an eight-sided domed center room is surrounded by an ambulatory on its lower, by a gallery on its upper floor and surmounted by an eight-sided dome. Dedicated to the Savior and the Virgin, its principal relic during the Middle Ages—but since when? —was a dress of the Virgin. Greatly admired by the contemporaries and by later generations, the structure was reflected in derivatives all over Charles' Empire from the ninth through the eleventh century: at Compiègne, at Nymwegen, at Ottmarsheim and Mettlach, all close to the prototype in shape and in the dedication to Mary.[7]

Recent studies have stressed emphatically that Aix-la-Chapelle is not necessarily a copy of S. Vitale at Ravenna, but that both structures are members of a large family of *memoriae* (*martyria*) which frequently occur in the Near East from the fourth century on. Churches dedicated to the Virgin are anything but rare within this group: an octagonal church of St. Mary, it seems from literary sources, existed at Tyre in the fifth century; [8] another one, extant in ruins, was erected on Mount Garizim between 484 and 491 (Fig. 38), by the emperor Zeno on the site of the Samaritan mountain sanctuary and in commemoration of the quelling of an anti-Christian riot of the Samaritans: an octagonal center room was surrounded by an ambulatory and by outer porticoes and chapels with an apse and chancel piercing through the ambulatory opposite the entrance, not too different from Aix-la-Chapelle.[9]

The fifth-century buildings in Tyre and on Mount Garizim probably were *martyria* dedicated to the Virgin: their octagonal shape is due to the fact that they belong to the vast family of *martyria* and their dedication appears to be simply to the Theotokos without focusing on any specific aspect of or on any specific event in her life. But it is different with another building, outstanding in holiness among the *martyria* dedicated to the Virgin in the Eastern provinces of the Christian world: the chapel of the Hagia Soros, adjoining the Great Church consecrated in her honor in the Palace of the Blachernae in Constantinople. The Great Church, perhaps erected first by Pulcheria (450-457) or Leo I (457-474) after the mid-fifth century, was either altered or entirely rebuilt under Justin I (518-526).[10] When Procopius described the church the chapel does not seem to have been in existence as yet, later legendary reports to the contrary. But beginning in the seventh century it is mentioned frequently as one of the great sanctuaries of the capital, for at that time it sheltered the kerchief of the Virgin (*omophorion*) or else her belt, her dress or her shroud; whatever the relic was, it was kept in the Hagia Soros, the Holy Coffin.[11] The structures have disappeared, and the existing descriptions are anything but clear; still, it is certain that the chapel was round (*strongylos*) and probably surmounted by a dome (*sphairoeides*); that it was entered from the aisle of the main church through a narthex; that it terminated, opposite the narthex, with an apse; that the Soros, possibly a small chamber, rose free-standing in its center with an opening on one of its sides; and that a *parakyptikon,* a box for the Emperor, opened on the second floor, probably above the narthex and connected with the neighboring palace.[12] Its dedication, its principal relic and its function as a palace chapel would seem to be reminiscent of Aix-la-Chapelle.

Despite the obvious differences, the chapel of the Hagia Soros appears to share a number of features also with the group of churches which centered on the Pantheon and were dedicated to the Virgin: the round or polygonal plan; the vaulted construction; and the dedication to the Virgin focused on a specific aspect of her personality. For none of these structures is dedicated to the Virgin alone. They are all dedicated to her jointly with the Savior or with the apostles, or the entire celestial hierarchy and (for the two elements go together) the dedication is linked to her death and assumption. The Pantheon, one remembers, was consecrated to the Virgin and all the martyrs, that is the Just assembled in Paradise; the chapel at Centula to the Virgin *and* the Apostles; at the Daurade she was the leader, in the mosaics, of the Heavenly Host; at Aix-la-Chapelle she shared the dedication with the Savior whose second coming for the Final Judgement was represented in the dome; her coffin and the dress she had left in her tomb were venerated at Constantinople. She appears, then, in the dedications of the majority of these round churches as the one assumed to Heaven and as the leader of the Heavenly Host.

All this leads obviously into the complex problem of the Virgin's place in the celestial hierarchy.[13] To the fathers assembled at Ephesos in 431, she had been almost exclusively the spotless maid, ever virgin, whose womb had been chosen by the Lord for His incarnation. Yet, simultaneously, and specifically in the Eastern theological schools, a second concept placed itself alongside the first, that of Mary as Queen of Heaven and Intercessor. In that role nobody has depicted her more gloriously than Ephrem of Nisibis, about 370. To him she is "more to be honored than the cherubim, more clear-sighted than the many-eyed spirits, more holy than the seraphim and incomparably more glorious than all the rest of the heavenly host." She is "the only help of the sinners, the solace of the world, the redemption of captives, the salvation of all." [14] And while the bishops assembled at Ephesos did not take any special notice of the Virgin's part as intercessor at the throne of the Lord, the concept appears to have spread in the course of the fifth century in part to the West and wholly to Byzantium, and to have been further enlarged. Since Mary was "the protector of the whole universe," it was only natural to entrust to her intercession both the physical and the spiritual well-being of the Empire. In Constantinople as well as along the frontiers Justinian dedicated to her a number of churches "to be a guardian of the safety of the cities and of the true faith." [15] Within Justinian's policy such a concept was only natural: both throne and altar were threatened by the Arians, Goths and Vandals, and invoking the Virgin as protectress of the Empire meant concomitantly defeating the Arian refusal to recognize Christ as an essential and eternal part of the Trinity. With the Byzantine armies and diplomats, this concept of the Virgin's function conquered the West in the sixth century: the hymn *De laudibus Mariae* sums up the beliefs of Western Europe at that time; [16] so do the mosaics of the Daurade; so does finally the dedication of the Pantheon to the Virgin *and* all the martyrs.

Since she was enthroned as the Queen of Heaven, theological thought turned towards the death of the Virgin and her tomb. Her body, the pure vessel chosen for the Lord's incarnation, could not have decayed; it must have been bodily assumed to Paradise. Beginning with the fourth and elaborated upon more and more during the late fifth and sixth centuries, apocryphal writings tell the story of her dormition and burial, how her tomb in the valley of Josaphat was found empty except for her dress and how Christ carried her in the body to Heaven. The place of her death was originally uncertain; but since the middle of the sixth century her tomb was shown in the valley of Josaphat outside Jerusalem and a church arose over the place, built or enlarged by the Emperor Maurikios (582–602). In commemoration of this structure, the chapel of the Hagia Soros may have been set up in Constantinople.

The church over the Tomb of the Virgin, as it stands today in the valley of Josaphat, seems to be practically a construction of the twelfth century.[17] Yet the form of the building as it presented itself to visitors as early as the seventh century is suggested in its main lines by their descriptions of the structure. Here is what Arculphus, the Frankish pilgrim who visited Jerusalem about 670, has to say: "The church of St. Mary is double-storied; its lower part is round with a wonderful stone ceiling (*tabulatum*); in the eastern part is an altar and to its right the empty tomb of the Virgin hewn in the rock. The upper story is likewise round; it contains four altars . . . ." About 870, the monk Bernard confirmed that the church was round and added that the tomb, though it had no roof over it, was as he had been told, never touched by the rain. The Russian Igumenos Daniel, in 1106, still saw a wooden roof, obviously over the upper story.[18]

Clearly then, the church was round (or possibly polygonal; to the Middle Ages anything with more than four sides was round) and it had two stories. The lower story had a stone ceiling and this ceiling must have necessarily rested on supports. The upper floor was covered by a wooden roof, possibly with an *opaion* in its center as suggested by the description of the monk Bernard. His description seems to suggest also that the two stories were connected by an opening; but whether the upper story formed a semi-independent structure or simply a gallery (the architectural terminology of the early Middle Ages would allow for both interpretations) must remain an open question. In any case, the structure presents itself as a typical *martyrium,* the *mneme tes koimeseos tes theotokou.*

This round, double-storied church over the tomb of the Virgin, with its *opaion* in the roof and with her tomb on the ground floor, appears to have occupied an outstanding place within the ecclesiastical architecture of both the East and the West. Its immediate derivatives in the East, such as the chapel of the Hagia Soros in Constantinople, may seem to have differed widely from the archetype in Jerusalem, but they shared certain features: the roundness, the two stories and the dedication to the Virgin's assumption and implicitly to Mary as Queen of the Heavenly Host. Together with the *martyrium* in the valley of Josaphat they appear to have become the fountainhead of later filiations. In the West, Roman central structures such as the Daurade (Fig. 39) and the Pantheon, through their roundness, and through the *opaion* in their vaults, were reminiscent to early medieval eyes of the *martyrium* in the valley of Josaphat. Through being dedicated to the Virgin as Queen of Heaven, they became a likeness of the venerated prototype. From the Pantheon in turn descended the Carolingian chapels of the Virgin such as Centula or Würzburg. On the other hand, the palatine chapel at Aix-la-Chapelle, with its two stories, might well have recalled to medieval eyes the archetype of Jerusalem, either directly or by way of the Hagia Soros in Constantinople. Again, the derivatives and relatives of Aix would spread over the West. Diversified as the picture is, it reflects the complexity of ideas which to early medieval man would seem to have been summed up in the large group of round churches dedicated to the Virgin and her assumption.

Notes

1. A. Grabar, *Martyrium* (Paris, 1946), *passim*.

2. For illustrations, see P. Frankl, *Frühmittelalterliche und romanische Baukunst* (Potsdam, 1918), pp. 1 ff.; G. T. Rivoira, *Architettura lombarda* (Milan, 1908), p. 397; A. W. Clapham, *English Romanesque Architecture before the Conquest* (Oxford, 1930), pp. 79 ff.; M. Hauttmann, *Geschichte der kirchlichen Baukunst . . . 1550-1780* (Munich, 1928), p. 115.

3. *LP*, I (Paris, 1886–1892), 317 ". . . templum qui appellatur Pantheum, in quo fecit ecclesiam beatae Mariae semper virginis et omnium martyrum . . ."

4. See below, pp. 115 ff.

5. ". . . foras muros Ravennatis urbis in basilica S. Mariae ad similitudinem Romanae Pantheon formata . . ." (O. Lehmann-Brockhaus, *Schriftquellen zur Kunstgeschichte des 11. und 12. Jahrhunderts*, [Berlin, 1938], p. 503, no. 2372).

6. H. Woodruff, "The Iconography and Date of the Mosaics of La Daurade," *AB*, XIII (1931), 80 ff., suggests as a possible date the fifth or sixth century but appears to incline towards the latter.

7. Grabar, *op. cit., passim*.

8. Quoted by Birnbaum, "Die Oktogone von Antiochia, Nazianz und Nyssa," *RepKunstW*, XXXVI (1913), 181 ff., esp. 192.

9. A. M. Schneider, "Römische und byzantinische Bauten auf dem Garizim," *Zeitschrift d. dtsch. Palästina Vereins*, LXVIII (1944-1951), 211 ff.

10. J. Ebersolt, *Sanctuaires de Byzance* (Paris, 1920), pp. 44 ff.; J. B. Papadopoulous, *Le palais et les églises des Blachernes* (Saloniki, 1928), *passim*. M. Jugié, *La mort et l'assomption de la Vierge* (*Studi e Testi*, 114 [Vatican City, 1944]), 688 ff., inclines towards a later date.

11. Nikephoros Kallistos, *Historia Ecclesiastica*, XV, Ch. 24 (*PG*, CXLVII, col. 69).

12. Constantinos Porphyrogenetos, *De Caerimoniis*, Lib. II, cap. 12, ed. J. Reiske (Bonn, 1829), 551 ff.; Jugié, *op. cit.*,

p. 699, thinks of a chamber rising inside the nave of the Great Church.

13. Jugié, *op. cit., passim.*

14. L. Hammersberger, *Die Mariologie der ephremschen Schriften* (Innsbruck, 1938), *passim.*

15. Procopius, *De aedificiis,* III, IV, 12 (ed. H. B. Dewing and G. Downey, "Loeb Classical Library" [Cambridge, Mass. and London, 1954], 369). See also I, III (*ibid.*, p. 41): "in order that [two churches of the Virgin in Constantinople] may serve as invincible defenses of the circuit-wall of the city."

16. Venantius Fortunatus, *Miscellanea,*

Lib. VIII, cap. 7 (*PL,* LXXXVIII, cols. 276 ff.).

17. H. Vincent and F. M. Abel, *Jérusalem nouvelle,* II (Paris, 1914), 805 ff., offers a careful analysis both of the monument and the sources, but a somewhat free reconstruction.

18. Arculf, from Adamnanus, *De locis sanctis* (*Itinera Hierosolymitana,* ed. P. Geyer, *CSEL,* XXXIX [Vienna, 1898], 240 ff.); Bernardus monachus, *Itinerarium,* quoted in *PL,* CXXI, cols. 572 ff.; Daniel Igumenos, from B. de Khitrovo, *Pélerinages russes en Orient,* I, 1 (Geneva, 1889), 23.

Postscript

As presented to the Meeting for the Study of the Early Middle Ages at Pavia in 1950 and as printed in its *Acts,* the paper was the condensed version of a more ambitious study on round and polygonal churches consecrated to the Virgin assumed to Heaven, Queen of the Heavenly Host and intercessor.

The study was never quite finished for a number of reasons. It would have had to discuss in detail the plans and the specific original dedications of a large number of "round" churches bearing the name of the Virgin, beginning with the sixth century: the decagon, dated 534, which terminates the nave of Sta. Maria Maggiore in Ravenna; the rededication in 558 of the Arian Baptistery in Ravenna to the Virgin; the church at Hexham, built prior to 709 "in honore beatissimae Virginis Mariae opere rotundo quam quatuor porticus quatuor respicientes mundi climata ambiebant . . ." (Lehmann-Brockhaus, 1956, I, 562, no. 2109); the church of Sta. Maria alle Pertiche outside Pavia, dating from the mid-seventh century; the sanctuary adjoining the church of the Chalkopratiai in Constantinople and sheltering, at least since the early eighth century, a relic of the belt of the Virgin like the Soros in the Blachernae church; and dozens of later churches, in the West continuing through the entire Middle Ages, known in their majority only by name from the literary sources as collected in the invaluable volumes of E. Knögel and Lehmann-Brockhaus, and to a lesser degree in Schlosser's *Schriftquellen.* However, it turned out to be next to impossible to pin down precisely the dedications, whether to Mary as Mother of God or as Assumed to Heaven. Clear cases are exceptional, such as the Hagia Soros of the Chalkopratiai with its relic; the round church at Hexham, which by the ninth century, if not from the outset, sheltered altars dedicated to Saint Michael, the Baptist, the Apostles, Martyrs, Confessors and Virgin; or Sta. Maria della Tosse at Tivoli, the round vestibule of a Roman villa, dedicated as a church and decorated with a fresco of the Assumption. In most cases, the dedication to the Virgin is not further specified, probably because the founders and their ecclesiastical advisors themselves did not draw any sharp distinctions regarding her respective roles as God Bearer and as the One Assumed to Heaven. Concomitantly a more detailed study would have required discussing and eliminating the round churches of Bohemia, Moravia and Poland, dedicated in their majority to Saints Peter, George,

Adalbert or Vitus rather than to the Virgin. Caution, then, being the better part of bravery, counselled limiting the paper to a few examples definitely established in plan and in their consecration to *Maria Assumpta et Regina Coeli*. Kept within these limits, the argument, I feel, holds.

A second major difficulty rested and still rests obviously with the structure sheltering the tomb of the Virgin in the valley of Josaphat. As to its design, round and double-storied, the sources seem clear to me. I was puzzled for a while by the passage in the *Commemoratorium de casis Dei* which in 806 indicates for the church a length of nearly 75 m. and a width of nearly 50 m. and thus a longitudinal plan. However, the solution seems simply that this church and the structure over the tomb stood side by side, more or less the way the Hagia Soros at the Blachernae and the one in the Chalko-pratiai rose alongside their basilicas; and indeed, the monk Bernard in 870 saw side by side in "villa Gethsemani" an "ecclesia permaxima . . . sanctae Mariae" and "in ipsa quoque villa" the "ecclesia sanctae Mariae rotunda ubi est sepulcrum ipsius" (*PL*, CXXI, col. 572 ff.). The dates of construction of both the round church over the tomb and the large church nearby remain obviously uncertain. But it seems to me at present possible that as early as 550 the *Breviarius de Hierosolyma* (*Itinera Hierosolymitana*, ed. P. Geyer [*CSEL*, XXXIX] [Vienna, 1898], p. 155) referred to two distinct structures, the "basilica sanctae Mariae" and—introduced by a new "ibi"—her tomb, "sepulchrum eius." New studies and—quite unlikely at present—excavations may clarify the situation.

In any event, I feel safe in letting stand the condensed version as written in 1950; but I thought it useful to expand the footnotes, both in number and in content.

Additional Bibliography

Kleiss, W. "Neue Befunde zur Chalcopratenkirche . . . ," *Istanbuler Mitt.*, XV (1965), 149 ff.

Knögel, E. "Schriftquellen zur Kunstgeschichte der Merowingerzeit," *Bonner Jahrbücher*, CXL–CXLI (1936), 1 ff.

Lehmann-Brockhaus, O. *Die Kunst des X. Jahrhunderts im Lichte der Schriftquellen* (Strassburg, 1935).

———. *Lateinische Schriftquellen zur Kunst in England, Wales und Schottland vom Jahre 901 bis zum Jahre 1307* (Munich, 1956).

———. *Schriftquellen zur Kunstgeschichte des 11. und 12. Jahrhunderts für Deutschland* (Berlin, 1938).

Schlosser, J. *Schriftquellen zur Geschichte der karolingischen Kunst* (Vienna, 1896).

8

INTRODUCTION TO AN
"ICONOGRAPHY OF MEDIEVAL ARCHITECTURE"

SINCE THE RENAISSANCE it has become customary to consider architecture as being determined by "commodity, firmness and delight" or, to use a less Wottonian terminology, by function, construction, and design. To view architectural problems from these angles and from them alone has become something like a fundamental tenet of architectural history. Yet the validity of such a view appears rather doubtful where medieval architecture is concerned.[1] Obviously there can be no doubt that problems of construction, design and function, and of the integration of these elements, were of fundamental importance to medieval as well as to later architects. Yet it would seem that these essentials of architecture as laid down by Sir Henry Wotton, and before him by Alberti and Vitruvius, were differently emphasized and that in addition to them other elements played a vital part in the medieval conception of architecture. As a matter of fact, no medieval source ever stresses the design of an edifice or its construction, apart from generalities regarding plan, size or material. On the other hand the practical or liturgical functions are always taken into consideration; they lead on to questions of the religious significance of an edifice and these two groups together seem to stand in the center of medieval architectural thought. Not once, it will be remembered, does Suger refer to the revolutionary problems of vaulting and design in his new building at St-Denis. Evidently the design of an edifice or for that matter the construction were not within the realm of theoretical discussion. On the other hand the religious implications of a building were uppermost in the minds of its contemporaries. Time and again Suger discusses the dedications of altars to certain saints. Questions of the symbolical significance of the layout or of the parts of a structure are prominent: questions of its dedication to a particular saint, and of the relation of its shape to a specific dedication or to a specific religious—not necessarily liturgical—purpose. The 'content' of architecture seems to have been among the more important problems of medieval architectural theory; perhaps it was indeed its most important problem. The total of these questions would form the subject of an iconography of architecture. Such an approach would merely return to an old tradition which as recently

*This article, from the *Journal of the Warburg and Courtauld Institutes,* V (1942), 1–33, is based on a brief paper read to the meeting of the College Art Association held in Chicago in January 1941. I want to thank my wife, Mrs. Trude Krautheimer-Hess for her continuous collaboration in preparing and writing this essay.

as a century ago was still present in the minds of ecclesiastical archeologists; [2] it is during the last fifty years only that this has apparently been superseded by a purely formalistic approach. The following remarks are not intended to be complete; they are meant merely to form contributions towards a future iconography of medieval architecture.

Copies in Medieval Architecture

An approach toward the discovery of those elements which in the view of the medieval men were outstanding in an edifice is offered by the numerous architectural copies which were erected throughout the Middle Ages. Obviously the relations between these copies and their originals are bound to reveal some of these elements. Often when two buildings are compared with one another in medieval writings the modern reader may wonder how the author came to see any resemblance between the two. The tenth-century *Miracula S. Maximini*, for instance, records that the church at Germigny-des-Près was built like the palatine chapel at Aix-la-Chapelle, ". . . instar eius . . . . quae Aquis est constituta . . .;" [3] two hundred years later, William of Malmesbury makes a similar statement with reference to the chapel of Bishop Robert of Lorraine at Hereford, " . . . ecclesiam tereti edificavit scemate Aquensem basilicam pro modo imitatus suo." [4] Since two of these edifices, Aix-la-Chapelle and Germigny-des-Près, still exist and Hereford is recorded in an eighteenth-century drawing [5] it is easy to check these examples; yet it is hard for a modern beholder to see anything comparable in them. The chapel of Aix, with its domical-vaulted octagonal center room surrounded by a sixteen-sided ambulatory and by galleries, seems quite different from the square church of Germigny with its open central tower, its barrel-vaulted cross arms and its domed corner bays; nor does it seem to resemble the square double-storied chapel at Hereford in which of the nine bays the middle one is open in order to connect the two stories and the remaining eight are covered with groin vaults. One might at first be inclined to say that these statements are based simply on mistakes; but they are made so frequently and with such precision that this explanation seems too easy an escape. For instance Sta. Sofia at Beneventum, a hexagonal structure with two ambulatories, is compared to the Hagia Sophia at Constantinople; [6] the small tenth-century church of Petershausen is likened to St. Peter's in Rome, ". . . secundum . . . formam basilicae principis apostolorum Romae constructa . . . ; [7] the eleventh-century cathedral at Bremen to those of Cologne and Beneventum.[8] This list could be enlarged considerably, yet time and again the validity of the comparison would be questioned. The only justifiable conclusion seems to be that the medieval conception of what made one edifice comparable to another was different from our own. Medieval men must have had *tertia comparationis* utterly at variance with those to which we are accustomed.

In order to understand these different principles it may be advisable to turn to buildings which were definitely copied from clearly established prototypes.

Among the great number of edifices erected throughout the Middle Ages with the intention of imitating a highly venerated prototype, one group is particularly suitable for establishing the nature of a medieval copy: the imitations of the Holy Sepulchre at Jerusalem. They exist not only in great numbers but also depend on a model which is still relatively well preserved and can easily be reconstructed in its original aspect. These copies were built all over Europe from the fifth to as late as the seventeenth century.[9] Yet although the intention of imitating the Rotunda of the Holy Sepulchre is expressly stated in many instances, the buildings vary surprisingly from each other; they are also astonishingly different from the prototype which they mean to follow.

There is, for instance, the small church of St. Michael at Fulda (Figs. 40, 41). It was erected by Abbot Eigil, possibly with the advice of Hrabanus Maurus, between 820 and 822. Although in its present state the structure is largely eleventh-century, the few extant original parts the contemporary descriptions and recent excavations are sufficient to give a fairly accurate idea of the aspect of the ninth-century edifice.[10] A small center room is surrounded by an ambulatory; a crypt, covered with an annular barrel vault on a single short Ionic column extends under the center room and is surrounded by a ring-shaped corridor beneath the ambulatory. Eight columns—they were replaced in the eleventh century [11]—carried what appears to have been a dome or an eight-sided domical vault over the center room.[12] It is not known whether this original structure had a gallery over the ambulatory. Certainly it had not the three chapels which now radiate from the ambulatory but only one to the east; the north and south chapels as well as the gallery, the clerestory, the roof and the long nave were all added in a restoration of 1092. The "titulus" of the main altar leaves no doubt that the original structure was already linked to the Holy Sepulchre [13] and in fact as late as 1715 a Tomb of the Lord, conical in shape, rose in the center of the edifice.[14]

Two hundred years after Eigil and Hrabanus had erected the chapel at Fulda, Bishop Meinwerk of Paderborn wanted to build a church "ad similitudinem s. Jerosolimitane ecclesie" and dispatched Abbot Wino of Helmershausen to Jerusalem to bring from there the required measurements "mensuras eiusdem ecclesie et s. sepulcri. Reverso autem Winone abbate . . . et mensuras eiusdem ecclesie et sepulchri sancti reliquas referente . . . ," [15] the church was built and consecrated in 1036 (Fig. 42). It was situated in what is at present the Busdorf convent. Excavations have shown that the original edifice was an octagonal structure rising from circular foundation walls. Three large rectangular chapels radiated from this central room in the main axes; a fourth chapel, possibly flanked by two round towers, may have served as an entrance structure. No supports divided the interior. Whether the building was vaulted or had a wooden roof remains unknown.

The Rotunda at Lanleff, not far from Caen (Fig. 44), was erected late in the eleventh century.[16] It is again a round structure with center room and ambulatory; the ambulatory was covered by groin vaults carried by twelve supports, each a square pier with four engaged columns. Three small absidioles radiated from the ambulatory. Although, in contrast to Fulda or Paderborn, the dedication of Lanleff is not certain, the very motive of these absidioles and their position off-center leaves no doubt that this structure also is derived from the Holy Sepulchre at Jerusalem.

A fourth building, the church of the Holy Sepulchre at Cambridge, would seem to date from the first quarter of the twelfth century (Figs. 43, 45). It was badly restored in 1841, but earlier reproductions give a good idea of the original state.[17] Eight sturdy columns separated the rib-vaulted ambulatory from a center room which until 1841 was surmounted by a tall tower. The first story of this tower was obviously the clerestory of the center room. Evidently the original structure had no choir (the present one was added in 1313) and no radiating chapels. Eight twin openings, supported by sturdy piers and slender intermediary columns, were arranged above the arcades of the ground floor, forming a sham gallery.

All four of these structures were intended to represent the Holy Sepulchre at Jerusalem. But all four are quite different from one another: they are round or octagonal, with a single nave or surrounded by an ambulatory, vaulted or possibly with timber roofs, with one or more absidioles, and eight or twelve supports. The differences seem considerably to outweigh the similarities.

These differences become even more striking when the four edifices are compared with their common prototype at Jerusalem (Figs. 30, 31). This is not the place to enter into the complicated history of the Anastasis Rotunda.[18] Yet it is certain that from 628, when the Rotunda was restored,[19] and in all likelihood from the very outset, it was a round structure with an ambulatory, surmounted by a gallery. Three small absidioles projected from this ambulatory. An outer ambulatory apparently encircled the whole building.[20] The central room was surrounded by twenty supports, eight piers in the main axes and three columns in each of the diagonal axes. In the gallery two columns and one pier rose in the diagonal axes above the three columns on the ground floor, while in the main axes two piers corresponded to those below. The arches of the gallery openings were as wide as those of the lower arcades. It remains uncertain whether the center room was vaulted or had a conical roof similar to that which existed from the twelfth to the early nineteenth century.

Doubtless there are some general similarities between the copies of the Holy Sepulchre at Fulda, Paderborn, Lanleff and Cambridge, and their Early Christian prototype. Yet these similarities seem to be rather vague to the modern eye. Three of the copies are round, whereas the fourth, Paderborn, was octagonal. Indeed there are more examples of Holy Sepulchres with polygonal rather than round plans. The twelfth-century Rotunda of the Holy Sepulchre at Sto. Stefano at Bologna [21] forms an irregular dodecagon (Figs. 46, 47) whereas the church of the S. Sepolcro at Pisa, built in the middle of the twelfth century,[22] is a perfect octagon with a very wide ambulatory and unusually tall piers. In the church of the Holy Sepulchre at Northampton, dated circa 1120,[23] the ambulatory is round although divided into eight square and eight triangular bays, whereas the center room, which was rebuilt at a later period, is octagonal. It seems as though circle and polygon were interchangeable throughout the Middle Ages. Indeed as early as the fourth century Gregory of Nyssa described the plan of an octagonal church as forming "a circle with eight angles" although he apologized for his somewhat loose terminology.[24] From then on distinctions of this kind lost their precision more and more. To Arculf, who visited the Near East late in the seventh century, the octagonal church of the Ascension on the Mount of Olives, the Imbomon, was "rotunda" and so was the complicated plan of the Hagia Sophia in Constantinople.[25] Even as late as 1322 Sir John Mandeville called the octagonal Dome of the Rock "a circular edifice." [26] It could almost be said that to medieval eyes anything which had more than four sides was approximately a circle. Nor were semi-circle, square and rectangle clearly differentiated: the semi-circular apses of the Anastasis were transformed into squares in Meinwerk's chapel at Paderborn, while in the Arculf-Adamnanus plans of the Rotunda they were given unmistakably as rectangles.[27] An approximate similarity of the geometrical pattern evidently satisfied the minds of medieval men as to the identity of the two forms; survivals of such an attitude could probably be found to this day.

This "indifference" towards precise imitation of given architectural shapes prevails throughout these "copies" of the Holy Sepulchre. The ambulatory around the center room is one of their usual characteristics but it is not by any means indispensable. It is missing not only at Paderborn but also in the round single-naved chapel of St. Maurice at Constance, which was erected between 934 and 976 to contain a "sepulchrum Domini in similitudine illius Jerusolimitani. . . . " [28] The three apses off the ambulatory of the Anastasis, if they are repeated at all, are sometimes not only square instead of semi-circular as at Paderborn and perhaps also in the closely related eleventh-century chapel at the Krukenburg; [29] they are also frequently arranged in a position different from that in the Anastasis. In the church of Lanleff alone they keep the off-center position of the Holy Sepulchre at Jerusalem. In the chapel of the Holy Sepulchre at St. Léonard a fourth chapel was added [30] with the result that the four chapels occupy the main axes of the structure forming a cross. In the churches of Paderborn and of the Krukenburg the place of this fourth chapel was taken by a longish entrance wing and the same arrangement was used when the chapel of St. Michael at Fulda was rebuilt in 1092 (Figs. 40, 41). In all probability the fact that, in addition to the three already existing chapels, a chancel was added to the Anastasis in 1017 by the Emperor Monomachus, inspired this four-chapel plan of the copies, although other types may have exerted a collateral influence. The interpenetration of circular shapes and cross types is frequently found in Early Christian memorial churches as Wiranshehir or the octagon church projected and described by Gregory of Nyssa; in the Occident Sto. Stefano Rotondo in Rome, S. Angelo in Perugia and the Baptisteries of Santa Severina and Canosa in Southern Italy may be cited.[31]

The internal supports are sometimes exclusively columns, as for instance at Fulda, at St. Léonard, at Cambridge, at Northampton and in the church of S. Giovanni del Sepolcro at Brindisi; at S. Sepolcro at Pisa they are hook-shaped piers with responds, and at Lanleff composite piers with engaged columns. An alternating rhythm of piers and columns, though different from the particular pattern of the Anastasis, is found only once, in the Pisa Baptistery (Figs. 48, 49), which in its original form of 1153 ff. was clearly copied from the Holy Sepulchre at Jerusalem.[32] Nor is the gallery of the Anastasis always repeated even in those copies which have ambulatories surrounding the center room. Frequently, at St-Léonard, for instance, and possibly in the ninth-century chapel at Fulda, it is omitted altogether; the clerestory also is frequently wanting, so that the whole edifice is reduced to a one-storied structure and thus quite different from the three-storied original. If on the other hand a gallery does surmount the ambulatory, its arrangement differs entirely from that in the Anastasis. Instead of its complicated rhythm of supports, small twin openings are sometimes arranged above each arch of the ground floor; this is the case at Cambridge (Fig. 45), at Bologna, and in the present edifice of St. Michael at Fulda (Figs. 40, 41) as rebuilt in 1092. Elsewhere, for example at Neuvy-St. Sépulchre, all the gallery openings form a continuous band, supported by sturdy plain columns.[33] Finally, in the vaulting patterns of center room and ambulatory all these churches are as different as possible from one another as well as from the original.

This inexactness in reproducing the particular shape of a definite architectural form, in plan as well as in elevation, seems to be one of the outstanding elements in the relation of copy and original in medieval architecture. Indeed it recalls a well-known phenomenon, the peculiar lack of precision in medieval descriptions not only of architectural patterns but of all geometrical forms. When discussing the elements of geometry, a somewhat pedestrian but usually precise scholar such as Isidore of Seville becomes completely vague. A sphere is, in his words, a round figure which is alike in all its parts; a cylinder is a square figure which has a semi-circle on top; a pyramid—since its name is derived from πῦρμη—is a figure which tapers like a flame.[34] Even such an outstanding authority on geometry as Gerbert is quite unprecise as far as the description of geometrical shapes is concerned.[35] On the other hand the number of parts that make up a geometrical pattern is always strongly stressed. A square, for instance, is described as being contained within four straight lines: the number four is decisive while the relation of the four lines to one another (which we would qualify by indicating their length and by saying that they stand at right angles to one another) is simply omitted. The geometrical form is, as it were, translated into arithmetical figures.[36]

This particular attitude suggests a quite different approach as compared with that of the modern mind to the whole question of copying. Indeed the lack of geometrical precision is as characteristic as the "indifference" towards precise imitation of architectural shapes and patterns. In lieu of this, other intentions seem to be at the basis of copying architecture in the Middle Ages. It would seem as though a given shape were imitated not so much for its own sake as for something else it implied: the connotations of the cross-shaped ground plan are stressed time and again in medieval sources, as has been frequently pointed out.[37] St. Ambrose in 382 was among the first to emphasize that the cross plan of the church of the Holy Apostles at Milan (Fig. 19), which he laid out, was meant to symbolize the victory of Christ and His cross. The same interpretation was given as late as 1122, when the church at Kappenberg was built.[38] Over and over it is emphasized that such and such a church was laid out "instar crucis"[39] or, as at St. Gall in 898 "in honore et modum s. Crucis. . . ."[40] Yet it does not seem to matter greatly which particular cross shape was meant, whether it was a basilica plan in the pattern of the Latin *crux capitata,* as at Déas;[41] whether it was the pattern of the T-cross as at Bamberg cathedral (1117);[42] or whether a Greek cross plan was referred to as in Arculf's description of the church at the well of Jacob "quae quadrifida in quatuor mundi cardines formata extenditur quasi in similitudinem crucis."[43] The term may possibly have been applied even to round edifices with cross chapels, such as Meinwerk's Holy Sepulchre in Paderborn; a chapel which in 1064 was erected at Schaffhausen is described as having "capellas . . . in modum crucis per gyrum constructas . . ."[44] Occasionally the cross shape refers even to the pattern in which five churches are laid out within or around a city.[45]

Similarly the round (or polygonal) shape of a church evidently had some symbolical significance and again it did not make any great difference whether the ground plan of an edifice formed a regular circle or an octagon or a dodecagon or any related pattern. The circle according to St. Augustine[46] was a symbol of virtue, an interpretation which he based on Horace, "fortis et in se ipse totus teres atque rotundus."[47] It is preeminent among all other geometrical figures and comparable to virtue because of the conformity and concordance of its essentials, its "congruentia rationum atque concordia." According to Candidus the circle is a symbol of the Church, never ending and containing the sacraments; also it signifies to him the reign of eternal majesty, the hope of future life and the "praemia mansura quibus justi merito coronantur in aevum."[48] Other interpretations of the circle continue throughout the Middle Ages down to Dante; the *Divina Commedia* is full of such references. Whatever the particular interpretation, however, it is unquestionably not so much the precise geometrical shape of a form as its general pattern and its implications which count in the opinion of the medieval beholder.

On the other hand it would certainly be a mistake to assume that symbolical interpretations of this kind were always the preponderant reason for giving a structure a certain shape, to make it for instance round or cross-shaped. Sometimes this may have been so—as in the case of St. Ambrose's cross church at

Milan; at other times an existing plan may have been interpreted *post festum* as having some symbolical meaning.[49] Usually, however, the interrelations between the symbolical significance of a geometrical pattern and the ground plan of a building are not so plain. The process is of a much more intricate nature; probably the relation between pattern and symbolical meaning could be better described as being determined by a network of reciprocal half-distinct connotations. Rather than being either the starting point or else a *post festum* interpretation, the symbolical significance is something which merely accompanied the particular form which was chosen for the structure. It accompanied it as a more or less uncertain connotation which was only dimly visible and whose specific interpretation was not necessarily agreed upon. Yet as a connotation it was nearly always coupled with the pattern which had been chosen. Its very vagueness explains the variety of interpretations given to one and the same form either by one or by different authors. The situation can hardly be better expressed than it was by Johannes Scotus Erigena.[50] He speaks about the symbolism of the number eight, of its relation to Sunday and Easter, to resurrection and regeneration, to spring and new life. All these different connotations—he says—are ever present and "vibrate" in him whenever he thinks of eight:

> Haec sunt quae tacite nostris in cordibus intus
> Octoni numeri modulatur nabla sonorum
> Spiritus interior clamat nec desinit unquam
> Semper concrepitans, quicquid semel intonat annus
> Haec scriptura docet cui rerum concinit ordo.

This brings us to the symbolical meaning of figures and numbers throughout medieval architecture in general and their importance in architectural copies in particular. Indeed they appear to be prominent among the elements which determine the relation between copy and original. At St. Michael at Fulda, it will be remembered, the center room was carried by eight columns, at Lanleff by twelve. In fact the number of eight or twelve supports almost seems to be a constituent of all imitations of the Holy Sepulchre throughout the Middle Ages.[51] The chapel at St. Léonard, the Holy Sepulchre at Cambridge, the one at Northampton, the one at Pisa and S. Giovanni del Sepolcro at Brindisi all have eight supports; twelve are found, in addition to Lanleff, at Bologna and at the Holy Sepulchre at Augsburg.[52] This seems hard to explain, except on the grounds that after all in any circular building a number of supports divisible by four is easiest to arrange. While this is undeniably the case, it might be pointed out, first, that divisions of central edifices into seven (Ste. Marie at Rieux Minervois),[53] ten (S. Lorenzo at Mantua) or eleven (Neuvy-St. Sépulchre) bays do occur. An arrangement of six supports is even quite frequent; it seems to prevail in most Templar churches.[54] Second, within the group of the Holy Sepulchres eight and twelve appear to be the only multiples of four chosen for the number of supports. The real explanation may be found in the very fact that they were actually intended to reproduce an important feature of the Rotunda at Jerusalem: for it will be recalled that this Rotunda was carried by twenty supports, viz. eight piers and twelve columns. Evidently in the "copies" either the number of the piers or that of the columns was chosen and "imitated" regardless of the particular shape of the supports. Definite proof of this procedure is found in medieval descriptions of the Rotunda at Jerusalem. Arculf in describing it mentions only the twelve columns and completely omits the eight piers in the main axes. They simply did not exist in his account.[55]

Obviously the choice of the numbers eight and twelve from the twenty supports which were present in the prototype is again linked to the symbolical associations of these numbers within medieval numerology. The existence of these numbers in the Anastasis and their numerological meaning stand in a reciprocal interrelation to one another. The importance of number symbolism in medieval thought is too well known to need any emphasis.[56] Obviously the number twelve was bound to remind any medieval beholder of the number of the Apostles, particularly when connected with the Tomb of the Lord; composed as it is of four times three, it linked the number of the four regions of the world with that of the Trinity whose gospel was spread by the Apostles throughout the world.[57] As early as the fourth century the twelve columns supporting the hemisphere of the Constantinian basilica opposite the Anastasis reminded Eusebius of the Disciples.[58] In the seventh century Arculf compared to their number the twelve lamps which hung inside the Tomb of the Lord, divided into three groups of four.[59] Likewise the number eight was bound to have a particular meaning in association with the Anastasis. It was a perfect number, which generally referred to Sunday, Easter and Pentecost, to circumcision and baptism, to regeneration and immortality [60] and—most important of all—to resurrection;[61] indeed it symbolized Christ Himself. With such connotations in mind it must have been quite a natural solution to single out the number of eight supports which actually was given by the number of piers in the Anastasis. If this number was emphasized in a structure which copied the building over the spot where the resurrection of the Lord had taken place, it was bound to hold out hope for future resurrection to the faithful.

Of course, the actual number of elements in the prototype may frequently have stimulated subsequent and divergent interpretations; thus the monk Candidus in describing the church of St. Michael at Fulda saw in the eight columns not a symbol of resurrection but of the eight Beatitudes.[62] The same Candidus likened both the one base of the column in the crypt of St. Michael and the one keystone of the vault to Him who is the Beginning and the End,[63] and one may recall that to the Early Christian period and to the Middle Ages eight was nothing but a return of one, a symbol of regeneration.[64] Candidus incidentally made it quite clear that his interpretations were an afterthought when he stated that he *thought* the chapel of St. Michael *could* represent Christ and the Church

"... Christi et ecclesiae puto praesignari posse figuram." [65] In the *Vita* of Benedict of Aniane it is mentioned that the three altars of the eighth-century church of S. Salvator signify the Trinity, and that the church of St. John contained seven altars and seven candelabras consisting of seven lamps or seven branches each, which had to be understood as the seven gifts of the Holy Spirit.[66] The symbolical value of numerology (and the instances given are merely a small selection) and the preponderance of certain numbers in architectural copies seem to be interlinked.

This number consciousness is likewise evident in the importance of measurements in architectural copies. Measurements are several times referred to as having been brought from Jerusalem for the specific purpose of laying out a copy of the Anastasis or of the Tomb of Christ. Meinwerk's chapel at Paderborn was not by any means an isolated case. At Cambray a Holy Sepulchre was erected in 1063-64 "rotundo schemate in modum scilicet sepulchri quod est Jerosolimis. Unde et marmor superpositum sepulchro Cameracensi habet longitudinem 7 pedum quoniam et locus, ubi positum fuit corpus Domini eiusdem longitudinis existit." [67] Sometimes a mere linear indication sufficed to give the measurements of the Tomb of the Lord: such is the case at Bebenhausen where as late as 1492 the sarcophagus of Christ was represented by three intersecting lines on the wall of the cloister, accompanied by inscriptions describing them as representing its length, depth and width.[68] This particular emphasis given to measurements is clearly shown in some of the medieval descriptions of the Holy Sites in Jerusalem. Arculf's report mentions expressly the length of seven feet for the Tomb of Christ and adds that he measured it with his own hand, "propria mensus est manu." [69] He gives also the approximate height and width of the tomb chamber by stating it had room for nine people—he says "ter terni" and one thinks again of the symbolical value of the number three—and that it was one and a half feet higher than a rather tall man. About 806 the *Commemoratorium de casis Dei* gives the circumference both of the outer ambulatory of the Anastasis and of its center room.[70]

These descriptions make it quite clear that as in the case of other elements the measurements were not by any means reported *in toto*. In the same way in which only one group of supports or only one of the three stories of the Anastasis was chosen for reproduction in its copies, only one or two measurements were selected from a much greater number. The writer of the *Commemoratorium* does not report to his correspondent the measurements of the inner ambulatory nor does he indicate the height of any part of the building. This selective transfer explains also the strange use of measurements in a building such as the chapel of the Holy Sepulchre at Paderborn. Despite the elaborate statement of the chronicler that the exact measurements of the Anastasis were dispatched by special messenger from Jerusalem to Paderborn,[71] to a modern beholder not only the plan but also the measurements of the chapel look *totaliter aliter*. Some measurements however do appear to have been transferred from the Holy Land and used in Meinwerk's structure: the interior length of each side of its octagon is

5.80 m. and this corresponds roughly to the distance of 5.70 m., measured between the outer corners of the pairs of main piers in the east-west axis of the Anastasis.[72] The eight piers at Jerusalem would seem to have suggested to Meinwerk's messenger an octagon and the measurements taken between two of those piers were used as a basis for the construction of the whole plan.

This selective transfer of measurements finds its exact parallel in the way in which prototypes are generally copied in the Middle Ages. It has been pointed out before that the model is never imitated *in toto*. A selective transfer also of the architectural elements takes place. In the chapel at Constance it is only the roundness of the Anastasis which is transferred; at Paderborn the roundness and the radiating chapels are taken over. In the S. Sepolcro at Pisa and likewise in the chapel at Brindisi the roundness, the ambulatory, the clerestory and eight supports are reproduced. In addition to these elements the chapels of the Holy Sepulchre at Cambridge and Northampton also took over the gallery above the ambulatory. Evidently the medieval beholder expected to find in a copy only some parts of the prototype but not by any means all of them.

Another point will have become apparent in this connection. The parts which have been selected in these "copies" stand in a relation to one another which in no way recalls their former association in the model. Their original coherence has been discarded. The original unity has been disintegrated and the elements have been reshuffled, as it were. To take just one instance, the twin openings of the galleries in the chapels of the Holy Sepulchre at Cambridge (Fig. 45) and in Sto. Stefano at Bologna (Fig. 47) seem to reproduce in an abbreviated form the gallery in the Anastasis. In the gallery at Jerusalem two piers always seemed to flank one column, but it evidently appeared quite natural in these later churches to reduce the more complicated rhythm to the usual form of a Romanesque twin opening and to arrange one of these twin openings above every intercolumniation of the ground floor. It is significant to observe that, as late as the seventeenth century, engravings of the Anastasis occasionally transform the rhythm of the gallery into twin openings, although the original pattern was preserved until 1819.[73] Obviously all the proportions are entirely changed; the ambulatory, which in the Anastasis has hardly one-fourth the width of the center room, is in the medieval copies usually more than one-third and sometimes more than half of its width (Cambridge, Northampton, Fulda, St. Léonard). Thus in these copies center room and ambulatory stand in an entirely different relation to one another. Needless to say the relative vertical proportions of arcade zone, gallery and clerestory are correspondingly re-arranged.

This procedure of breaking up the original into its single parts and of reshuffling these also made it possible to enrich the copy by adding to it elements quite foreign to the original. Buildings which bear a general resemblance to the prototype seem to have exerted a collateral influence on the copy: at St. Michael at Fulda a crypt extends underneath the structure; a similar crypt, also surrounded by a corridor, appeared in the fourth or fifth century at SS. Karpos and Papylas at Constantinople, an edifice which was likewise laid out ". . . εἰς μίμησιν τοῦ ναοῦ τοῦ τάφου τοῦ Χριστοῦ . . ." [74] In both instances the crypt seems to have been derived ultimately from late antique mausolea and merged with the prototype of the Holy Sepulchre.

Representations of buildings in medieval sculpture and painting appear to confirm the peculiar relation between copy and original in medieval architecture. The methods used in these medieval depictions have frequently been discussed.[75] Like the "copies" they show the disintegration of the prototype into its single elements, the selective transfer of these parts, and their reshuffling in the copy. When in 1017 the Anastasis was represented in the Sacramentary of Henry II (Fig. 50), one sees at the bottom of the page the lower part and the interior of the Tomb of the Lord.[76] Immediately above this a series of four openings with four windows in the background indicates the gallery of the Rotunda; four windows of the inside clerestory are seen higher up. Then the illustration shifts from the interior to the exterior and above these clerestory windows shows the roof of the gallery, the clerestory from the outside with nine windows, the dome and the opaion in it; from there the representation moves back to the interior and to the ground floor of the edifice, and *above* the dome of the Rotunda shows the upper part of the Tomb flanked by the sleeping soldiers. The disintegration of the "model" into its single elements and the reshuffling of these elements correspond exactly to the procedure which prevails in the relation of copy and prototype in actual architecture. Most of the elements of the prototype are present, but they have been entirely re-grouped.

Representations of such completeness, however, are rare. Most reproductions are limited to a few elements essential for identifying the Anastasis. The wooden casket of the Sancta Sanctorum, for example, gives the tomb as a simple *tegurium* and floating above it the clerestory and the dome of the Rotunda (Fig. 51).[77] The same holds true, *mutatis mutandis,* for the numerous representations on ampullae, on ivories and in manuscripts.[78] Evidently the tomb, the circular shape of the whole and the uncommon construction of the vault were prominent characteristics and therefore sufficient to distinguish the Anastasis from any other structure.

Indeed it is these same few conspicuous features which also seem indispensable for identifying an actual architectural copy of the Anastasis; to be recognizable it has to be "round" and it has either to contain a reproduction of the tomb or to be dedicated to it. These essential outstanding elements might be elaborated by adding to them other features such as the ambulatory, the chapels, the gallery, the clerestory, the vault, a certain number of supports and some measurements. These also are typical features of the prototype and therefore might be carried over into the copies. The model contains, as it were, a repertory of uncommon elements from which very few have to be chosen whereas others might or might not be selected.

These considerations also give an answer to the question with which we started. Apparently medieval writers felt perfectly justified in comparing buildings with one another as long as some of the outstanding elements seemed to be comparable. The church at Petershausen, for example, despite its entirely different plan, had some features in common with Old St. Peter's in Rome; it was turned towards the west and the convent of which it formed part bore the name of St. Peter.[79] Germigny-des-Prés, in spite of all differences, shared with Aix-la-Chapelle the central plan, arranged around a dominating central "tower," and the dedication to the Saviour and His Mother.[80] Lastly Sta. Sofia at Beneventum had nothing in common with its prototype in Constantinople but the central plan and the dedication.[81]

But to medieval men the dedication of an edifice was one of its outstanding characteristics. Of course, the dedication was sometimes accompanied by a more tangible feature, for example by a reproduction of the Tomb of the Lord if the church was dedicated to the Holy Sepulchre. Such reproductions were quite frequent. It is sufficient to mention those at St. Michael at Fulda, at Constance,[82] at Neuvy-St. Sépulchre;[83] others are still preserved at Aquileia [84] and at Bologna. Similarly S. Sepolcro, now S. Lanfranco, at Pavia, founded in 1090, a single-naved cruciform church, contained a copy of the Holy Sepulchre "secundum longitudinem latitudinem et altitudinem;"[85] and the church of the Trinity at Milan built in 1036, was reconsecrated in 1099 to the Holy Sepulchre in memory of the re-conquest of the Holy City, and a *similitudo* of the Tomb of the Lord was erected in it.[86]

At times, however, the name alone seems to have stood for all other features: the church of S. Sepolcro at Barletta had, as far as we know, nothing in common with the Anastasis but the name.[87] The dedication—sometimes supplemented by the existence of a relic from the Holy Site or by a *similitudo,* a *forma* of the venerated original—was evidently considered a sufficient stimulus to arouse all the religious associations which were connected with the prototype. Sometimes the particular manner of laying out an edifice may have formed the *tertium comparationis.* When Vratislav II in the fourth quarter of the eleventh century laid the foundations of SS. Peter and Paul on the Vysehrad at Prague, he carried on his own shoulders twelve hods of stones "ad modum quondam Constantini imperatoris" and thus built the church "ad similitudinem ecclesie Romanae s. Petri . . ."[88] The common element between a church which shared with its prototype only the name or the particular manner of its dedication and an architectural copy proper was evidently the fact that both were mementos of a venerated site. The difference is rather between a more or less elaborate reproduction; and one might say that the more elaborate ones only add some visual elements to the "immaterial" features, that is to the name and dedication. Both immaterial and visual elements were intended to be echoes of the original capable of reminding the faithful of the venerated site, of evoking his devotion and of giving him a share at least in the reflections of the blessings which he would have enjoyed if he had been able to visit the Holy Site in reality.[89] When in 1076 at St. Hubert an oratory was consecrated under the name of "Jerusalem" it was made quite clear that the chapel was meant to reproduce the Sepulchre of the Lord, and thus to represent it for the devotion of the faithful: "dedicavit oratorium unum quod dicitur ad sanctam Jerusalem, eo quod ad modum dominici sepulchri conditum, ipsam quoque eius formam repraesentet devotioni fidelium." [90] With this in mind, it is easy to understand why these copies of the Holy Sepulchre are sometimes situated in cemeteries, such as St. Michael in Fulda or the Holy Sepulchre at Cambray; obviously a copy of the Church of the Resurrection of the Lord was particularly fit to hold out to the visitor the hope of his own future resurrection. The architect of a medieval copy did not intend to imitate the prototype as it looked in reality; he intended to reproduce it *typice* and *figuraliter,* as a memento of a venerated site and simultaneously as a symbol of promised salvation.

Indeed *"typice"* and *"figuraliter"* are the terms used by a twelfth-century chronicler when describing the structures of Sto. Stefano at Bologna as a reflection of Jerusalem.[91] There a whole complex of churches was laid out with the particular aim of reminding the pilgrim of a number of venerated sites in the Holy Land, and throughout the centuries, despite many changes of dedication and pattern, the memento character of these edifices has remained clearly preserved.[92]

The present structures (Fig. 46) date mainly from the eleventh and twelfth centuries, but their foundation certainly goes back to a much earlier period. At present two churches, SS. Peter and Paul to the north, and to the south the Crocefisso flank an irregular dodecagonal church, consecrated to Sto. Stefano; east of these churches is a courtyard surrounded by arcaded porticoes—the so-called Atrium of Pilate—which extends towards a fourth edifice, the church of the Trinity, a shallow structure ending in a series of small chapels.

Today only the twelfth-century polygon of Sto. Stefano (Fig. 47) with its twelve supports and its galleries above the ambulatory, points clearly towards Jerusalem. Its shape as well as the fourteenth-century Tomb of Christ in the center of it leave no doubt as to its significance.[93] Indeed as early as the twelfth century a copy of the tomb is mentioned in this church which at that time bore the name of the Holy Sepulchre as well as that of Sto. Stefano. The hall opposite, now the church of the Trinity, was then called Calvary, or Golgotha or the Holy Cross; one or perhaps two crosses were venerated in this hall. Although the Atrium of Pilate was then without a name, the church to the south, the present Crocefisso, was dedicated from 1019 onwards to St. John the Baptist, like the chapel which at Jerusalem was joined to the right flank of the Anastasis. The twelfth-century dedications all point not to the Holy Land in general but to the buildings around the Anastasis in particular.

The group itself was called "Jerusalem" long before the twelfth century, indeed as early as 887 and again in 973 and in 1017.[94] Moreover older architectural remains found on the site prove the existence of ecclesiastical forerunners of the present twelfth-century buildings; a series of chapels, the one in the center cross-shaped, have been excavated below the twelfth-century ones which terminated the Hall of Calvary before the present series of chapels was built.[95]

Whatever may be the exact date at which the layout at Bologna was first designed, it is obvious that it reproduces the pattern which existed at the Holy Sepulchre in Jerusalem between 628, when the Constantinian buildings were remodelled, and the beginning of the twelfth century when the now existing large choir with its ambulatory and its radiating chapels was added to the Anastasis by the Crusaders.[96] Before this transformation, the Rotunda to the west, the chapel of Golgotha to the South-east, and the church of the Invention of the Holy Cross to the South were linked by an open courtyard, the focus of the layout, with porticoes on its north and possibly also on its south side (Fig. 31). It is this pattern which is clearly reproduced in the plan of the buildings at Bologna, and it is not particularly relevant whether Bologna was based on the actual layout of Jerusalem prior to the first Crusade or whether it depended on plans or maps which reproduced this earlier state.

Of course the layout of the complex at Sto. Stefano departs from the original like any copy of the Middle Ages. Only a few prominent parts are selected: the Rotunda, the courtyard and the hall opposite the Rotunda; in this latter the sites of Calvary and of the Invention of the Cross—which in Jerusalem were separate sanctuaries—seem to have been merged. In addition to these elements a measurement seems to have been transferred: the distance which at Jerusalem separates the Tomb of Christ from Mount Calvary corresponds approximately to that between the copy at Bologna of the Tomb in the Rotunda and the center of the cross-shaped main chapel at the end of Golgotha Hall.[97] These few selected elements enabled the pilgrim to visit the holy places in effigy and in the very sequence which they have in the prototype. He could come and venerate here the Tomb of Christ, there His Cross or the site where the Cross was found. The emphasis is on the commemorative character of the copy.

This "Jerusalem" at Bologna also seems to illustrate the practice which was followed in laying out a "copy." Obviously the builder of a "reproduction" of a Holy Site would try to get the needed data about the original either by travelling himself or by sending correspondents to the site; or he would rely on plans, and study descriptions of the prototype. As a matter of fact, plans, such as the one by Arculf which was copied throughout the Middle Ages, were evidently of considerable importance, and it is most likely that it was this or a similar plan which formed the basis from which the general arrangement of the edifices at Bologna was taken. The wide use made of such plans throughout the Middle Ages becomes evident time and again. Bede, for instance, who had never been in the Holy Land, when describing Jerusalem must have drawn upon a map of the Holy City. He speaks of right and left, above and below, evidently with a map on his desk.[98]

It is significant that these plans and descriptions stress the very points which prevail in actual architectural copies. Based on Arculf's notes, Adamnanus mentions first the general layout of the Anastasis, its roundness (its "mira rotunditas"), the three walls which enclose the center room and the ambulatory, the three altars in the inner aisle, the twelve columns "mirae magnitudinis" and the four doors on either side. He strongly emphasizes and carefully describes the Tomb of the Lord in all its details. In the plan which accompanies the description (Fig. 31) the tomb is so oversized that it almost fills the entire center room. All the contiguous buildings are only sketched in, in his description as well as in his plan. He emphasizes what was important from the pilgrim's point of view, the Tomb of the Lord. In his conclusion he makes it quite clear that he is able to give merely a feeble reflection of what he has seen: "Has itaque quaternalium figuras ecclesiarum iuxta exemplar quod mihi, ut superius dictum est, sanctus Arculfus in paginula figuravit cerata, dipinximus, non quod possit earum similitudo formari in pictura, sed ut dominicum monumentum, licet tali vili figuratione, in medietate rotundae ecclesiae constitutum monstretur aut quae huic propior ecclesia vel quae eminus posita declaretur." [99]

The difference between such an attitude and a modern approach to architecture is obvious. From Early Christian times and throughout the Middle Ages descriptions, depictions or architectural copies were nothing but a *vilis figuratio,* limited to a selected number of outstanding elements; their selection was determined by and their visual aspect subordinated to the hierarchic order of their religious importance.[100] This attitude seems to change gradually after the beginning of the thirteenth century. From then on (and the association with the analytical methods used in the natural sciences is apparent) copies, depictions and descriptions strive more and more towards giving a reproduction of the original in its visible aspects. From the fifteenth century on this process becomes quite obvious: although scale and material may be changed in a copy or the original elaborated upon or curtailed in details, the relation between the constituent elements and their relative proportion remains essentially unaltered. At the same time, however, a gradual process of draining the edifice of its "content" seems to begin. It is by no means a continuous development and is constantly interrupted by counter-movements, but it grows stronger and reaches its peak in the late nineteenth and early twentieth centuries. Architectural patterns are then used regardless of their original significance: a Greek temple for a customs house (New York, Customs House, now Subtreasury); a Gothic cathedral for an office building (New York, Woolworth Building); a thermal room for a railway station (New York, Main Concourse of Pennsylvania Station). The modern copy with all its exactness in reproducing the whole building and with its striving towards absolute faithfulness definitely omits the elements which were important to the Middle Ages: the content and the significance of the building.

Baptisteries and Mausolea

The previous discussions have led far beyond the problem of architectural copies as such. They reveal by implication that a number of elements were evidently considered essential to any edifice during the Middle Ages and that these characteristic features were different from what a modern beholder would consider of fundamental importance. Foremost among these elements is the principle that any medieval structure was meant to convey a meaning which transcends the visual pattern of the structure. This is so obvious and it has been so often analyzed that no further discussion seems warranted. Nor does it seem necessary to elaborate the importance of the repetition of types in medieval architecture.

Although the existence of such architectural series is well established, other questions remain to be answered. Time and again it becomes evident that certain architectural patterns are related to specific dedications. Churches dedicated to the Holy Cross are frequently cross-shaped; sanctuaries of St. Michael are situated on heights, in towers or on hills, and they are frequently of circular shape; Templar churches are round and their roofs are often supported by six piers; churches of the Virgin also are frequently centrally planned.[101] In every case the pattern of the structure is linked to the commemoration of a particular saint or of a specific object; or it is related to the use of the edifice by a specific group such as a religious order. Some kind of affinity seems to connect architectural patterns and their "content." Once established, the different patterns continue to follow traditional lines. Yet the question remains as to how these patterns were first associated with the particular content with which they are subsequently identified. In other words, in what way and for what reasons did these iconographical types originate?

It is proposed here to investigate one question only: why are baptisteries round? The reason which has generally been given for their circular plan is their alleged derivation from round, vaulted rooms of Roman baths. These rooms seemed to offer a clear prototype; they appeared to have the same shape and to be laid out for a similar use. Despite the difference between an act of simple cleanliness and a ritual immersion, the similarities have always been considered strong enough to warrant such a derivation of the baptisteries from Roman baths.

But the question arises whether this explanation is actually sufficient for explaining the origin and the survival of the central type in baptisteries, or whether additional prototypes could have exerted any influence. Of course the connection between baptisteries and thermal rooms is undeniable although it is hardly as plain as has been sometimes assumed. Round rooms *do* occur frequently in Roman *thermae,* cold water rooms, *frigidaria,* such as at Badenweiler and in the Stabian Baths at Pompei, and hot water rooms, *calidaria,* such as those in the Thermae of Caracalla and Constantine in Rome.[102] Circular *calidaria* or *frigidaria* are, however, relatively rare; the majority of the round rooms in thermal establishments are either *apodyteria,* wardrobes and cloak rooms, or *laconica,* steam baths.[103] As such they neither contained water basins nor were they used for ablutions of any kind.

The problem is made even more complicated by the fact that the earliest baptisteries of the third and fourth centuries were never round or octagonal. They were square or rectangular with or without an apse at one end, though the piscina itself was sometimes round; it is sufficient to mention the Baptistery at Dura-Europos about 231 A.D. (Fig. 1),[104] the first Baptistery of the Lateran of the early fourth century,[105] and the fourth-century Baptisteries of Aquileia,[106] Nesactium and Salona.[107] The same type is found in the fourth-century (?) structure underneath the Baptistery of St. Jean at Poitiers.[108] Even as late as the middle of the fifth century baptisteries of Roman churches are frequently square rooms,[109] and this type seems to have survived in North Africa,[110] Greece,[111] and throughout the Near East up to the seventh century.[112] One is almost tempted to say that the kinship of these early rectangular baptisteries with Roman thermae rooms is much more evident than that of their later round successors. Like the early baptisteries the Roman *frigidarium* was often a square or rectangular room, sometimes with an apse; a basin for cold water occupied either the centre of the room or stood at one end, an arrangement which seems to be repeated literally in the Baptistery of Dura.

It is only from the middle of the fourth century onwards that this rectangular type seems to be gradually superseded by baptisteries of circular or octagonal shape. While these differ widely in their particular pattern, they are all of one of these two forms or combine a circular shape with eight supports. The second Baptistery of the Lateran, which replaced the first rectangular one about 350 A.D., was a round building with eight engaged columns along its interior walls (Fig. 52 a, b).[113] Similarly at Salona, between 404 and 420, a polygonal structure with seven columns close to the wall replaced its rectangular fourth-century predecessor.[114] Occasionally, for instance at S. Giovanni in Fonte at Naples (about 400) and possibly in the Baptistery of Gül-bagtsche near Izmir, the room is square but covered with an octagonal vault supported by squinches.

The most frequent type, however, is that with four niches arranged in the corners of an octagon, the lower part of which is sometimes enclosed within a square. This type is found all over the Christian world from the fifth century and throughout the early Middle Ages: in Syria (Kalat Siman),[115] in Egypt (Menas Sanctuary),[116] in Constantinople (Baptistery of the Hagia Sophia),[117] in Ravenna (Baptistery of the Orthodox; Baptistery of the Arians),[118] and in the Alpine countries (Riva S. Vitale; Novara; Lomello).[119] At times the pattern is slightly more elaborate: in the Baptistery of St. Mary at Ephesus,[120] at S. Aquilino at Milan and in those of Albenga, Fréjus and Mélas [121] rectangular niches occupy the main axes, semicircular niches the diagonals. Frequently this scheme is enriched by columns in front of the piers which separate the niches. At other times the pattern is reduced to a plain polygonal plan. A simple octagonal pattern appears before the middle of the fifth century at Hemmaberg [122] and some decades later at Grado cathedral; it survives for centuries in upper Italy in baptisteries such as those at Lenno and Oggione, both of the late eleventh century.

Generally speaking it would seem that round or octagonal baptisteries were introduced into Christian architecture only after the middle of the fourth century and that they did not become common until the fifth century. Despite the differences in use which were mentioned above, these central patterns may have had some connection with thermal rooms. Octagonal plans with or without corner niches are not unusual in thermae, although regular round types occur much more often; but after all, some baptisteries were round, such as that of 350 at the Lateran. On the other hand, neither octagonal nor round rooms are in any way limited to thermal architecture; indeed vaulted centralized patterns with or without niches and engaged columns were widespread in antiquity. They occur throughout secular architecture, for example as vestibules in palaces and villas such as the Domus Aurea or the Villa of Hadrian at Tivoli.[123] They are also frequently found in the so-called "nymphaea" such as the Minerva Medica in Rome. Although it has been proved recently that most of them were really *diaetae,* garden pavilions, flanked by fountain rooms, but not containing any water basins,[124] their plan belongs into the same family as the vestibules and the thermal rooms. Evidently the round baptisteries form part of a large interrelated group of late antique buildings, and while the central rooms of thermal architecture are among their ancestors, other types may and, indeed, are likely to have exerted a collateral influence.

This is extremely probable in view of the fact that baptisteries display a number of peculiar features which certainly do not occur in *thermae.* Often they are surrounded by a low outer ambulatory with which the center room communicates by one or more doors. Such ambulatories are at times square in plan, a type which occurs in the Baptistery adjoining St. Mary at Ephesus and in those at Gül-bagtsche, Riva S. Vitale and Kalat Siman (Fig. 53).[125] At other times they are polygonal, as in the Baptistery of the Arians at Ravenna and in the sixth-century Baptistery of Parenzo.[126] The fifth-century Baptistery of Djémila (Fig. 54) was encircled by an annular corridor covered with a barrel vault; its walls are articulated by niches and pilasters.[127] A similar ambulatory, interrupted by four cross chapels and half open towards the center room, surrounded the dodecagonal Baptistery of Canosa; here too the ambulatory was covered by a barrel vault, the center room possibly by a dome. The date of the structure is apparently sixth century.[128] The purpose of these corridors is uncertain, although their shape seems to suggest that they were used for regulating the access of the faithful to the interior of the baptistery and the font.

Interior ambulatories were developed at about the same time as these exterior corridors. Indeed, the Baptistery of Canosa, though relatively late, may be considered as representing an intermediary type between the patterns with outer and inner ambulatory. The best known among these latter is the Baptistery of the Lateran, the third one on the site (Fig. 55), which was laid out in 432–40 and which still forms the nucleus of the present structure.[129] The center room is supported by eight columns; until 1632 it was covered by an eight-sided domical vault, surmounting a clerestory with eight large windows. An octagonal inner ambulatory originally covered with a barrel vault with interpenetrations surrounds the center room, which is completely filled by the piscina. A similar interior ambulatory is found in the Baptistery of Sta. Maria Maggiore at Nocera (fifth century), where it is separated from the domed center room by a circle of 14 pairs of columns (Fig. 56).[130] Another instance of this type occurs at Butrinto in Albania;[131] there the center room was surrounded by two rings of eight columns each, whose wide spacing makes it rather unlikely that the building was vaulted. In a number of baptisteries in Southern France, for instance at Marseilles, at Riez and at Aix-en-Provence, niches are arranged in the four corners of the ambulatory.[132] At Santa Severina in Southern Italy four short chapels arranged in cross shape radiate from the annular interior ambulatory; its date may be eighth or ninth century.[133]

None of the round rooms in thermal establishments shows the combination of a vaulted center room with either an outer or an inner ambulatory.[134] As a matter of fact the outer ambulatory is quite rare in Roman secular architecture. The outer portico on columns in round temples, which at first glance might look similar, is really entirely different. Its openness, the lack of a vault and especially its height, which normally equals the height of the cella, make the dissimilarity quite clear. Indeed the combination of a vaulted center room with either an inner or a closed and relatively low outer ambulatory seems to be found in only one group of Roman buildings: that is, in sepulchral architecture. Roman mausolea of the third and fourth centuries use all the different patterns which occur in the baptisteries, from the simple round or octagonal plan with or without niches to the complicated forms with inner or outer ambulatories. Round mausolea with niches in the thickness of the walls or enclosed in a surrounding ring of masonry are found for instance in the tomb in the Villa de' Gordiani (Figs. 57, 58), the so-called Tor de' Schiavi; in the Mausoleum of St. Helena near Rome; in that of the West Roman dynasty near St. Peter's; in H. Georgios at Salonica and perhaps in the Mausoleum of Constantine at Constantinople.[135] In the monument of the Turcia family the niches in the four main axes protrude so as to merge circular and cross plans, with a result similar to that of the Baptistery of Canosa.[136] In the Mausoleum of Diocletian at Spalato columns are arranged in a double order between the wall niches and though the interior is round, the exterior is octagonal. Another octagonal tomb with a round inner chamber with eight supports along its walls was situated near Frascati.[137] Similar patterns must have been quite frequent. Often the tomb chamber is situated below ground and surrounded by an outer ambulatory which may be square or semicircular or round in plan; it communicates with the inner chamber through only one or two doors. Such ambulatories are found, for instance, in the tomb of the Furii family near Tivoli, in the Mausoleum of the Vigna Cavalieri (Fig. 59), in that of the Servilii on the Via Appia and in one of the tombs on the Via Latina.[138] As late as the fourth century exactly the same type occurs in the necropolis of Tarragona.[139] The octagonal mausoleum at Blad Guitoun in Algeria is possibly even later; its round inner tomb chamber has an octagonal exterior, encircled by an annular corridor.[140]

This originally subterranean barrel-vaulted corridor survives, although slightly transformed, as late as the fourth century in one of the most famous Christian mausolea, Sta. Costanza in Rome (Figs. 7, 27, 29).[141] From remains and from numerous fifteenth- and sixteenth-century drawings, it becomes evident that the building was surrounded above ground by a barrel-vaulted low outer portico on columns. The motive of an encircling colonnade may have been influenced by the circular peristyles of round temples; occasionally, though rarely, such peristyles were used for mausolea, for example in the Mausoleum of Diocletian at Spalato. But the outer portico of Sta. Costanza amalgamates the peristyle motive with that of the Roman tomb corridor; its barrel vault points clearly to the subterranean origin of the ambulatory. At the same time an inner ambulatory covered by a barrel vault and separated from the domed center room by twelve pairs of columns makes its appearance at Sta. Costanza. Thus this fourth-century mausoleum unites all the different elements which distinguish the group of central baptisteries from all Roman secular architecture.

Sta. Costanza was in no way unique in the development of fourth-century sepulchral architecture. Another Christian mausoleum with an inner ambulatory supported by eight columns, possibly not vaulted, existed at Tipasa.[142] Obviously there is no way of telling how many, if any, of the "temples" and "tombs" with inner or outer ambulatory or with both, which are recorded in sixteenth-century drawings,[143] were of the fourth or fifth century. Round or octagonal memorial churches closely akin to late Roman mausolea continue to use the device of the inner ambulatory from the fourth through the sixth century, particularly in the Near East.[144] The combination of a center room with an inner and outer ambulatory characterizes the most famous among these memorial churches: the Anastasis at Jerusalem.

Thus it seems that the baptisteries share a great number of features with these Roman mausolea and particularly with their Christian variations, features which they do not share with any other Roman monuments. The third Baptistery of the Lateran can be explained only as a close relative, if not a derivative, of the mausoleum of Sta. Costanza. Strange as it appears at first glance, the links between baptisteries and mausolea are quite close both in content as well as in pattern. Undoubtedly baptism was a ritual intended symbolically to cleanse the catechumen from his sins. But this was not its only aspect: other connotations associated it with burial and death.[145] St. Paul's letter to the Romans started Christian thought on one of the fundamental tenets of baptismal mysticism: "An ignoratis quia quicumque baptizati sumus in Christo Jesu, in morte ipsius baptizati sumus? Consepulti enim sumus cum illo per baptismum in mortem: ut quomodo Christus surrexit a mortuis per gloriam Patris, ita et nos in novitate vitae ambulemus." [146] A mystical equation seems to be established between baptism, death and resurrection, death meaning the dying of the old Adam and at the same time a mystical imitation of the death of Christ. This two-fold equation is made perfectly clear by St. Basil in his Book on the Spirit, when discussing St. Paul's letters: "How then are we made in the likeness of His death? In that we were buried with Him by baptism. What then is the manner of the burial? And what is the advantage resulting from the imitation? First of all, it is necessary that the continuity of the old life is cut. And this is impossible unless a man be born again, according to the Lord's word; for the regeneration, . . . is a beginning of a second life. So before beginning the second . . . it seemed necessary for death to come as mediator between the two . . . How then do we achieve the descent into hell? By imitating through baptism the burial of Christ. For the bodies of the baptized are, as it were, buried in water. . . . For there the death on behalf of the world is one, and one the resurrection of the dead, whereof baptism is a type." [147]

Obviously this mystical death in baptism holds out the hope of future resurrection and is at the same time regeneration and resurrection in itself. It is also a symbol of the resurrection of the Lord through whose death Christian resurrection in and through baptism becomes possible. The same idea recurs in other Patristic writers. To St. Augustine baptism is nothing but a *"similitudo"* of the death of the Lord and at the same time a death of the old Adam "since we have been baptized in the death of Christ." [148] According to Hilarius of Poitiers baptism is a sacrament of regeneration and of resurrection; [149] it is a symbol of the future resurrection of man as well as of the resurrection of the Lord, a promise of rebirth in eternity, of eternal life.[150] Consequently, the *symbolum fidei,* professed at the occasion of baptism, strongly emphasized Christ's resurrection, His return to judge over the quick and the dead and their entering into eternal life. Leo the Great discusses the same idea in similar terms; baptism is a mystical imitation of Christ's death, of his burial and of his resurrection, "ut . . . per similitudinem formamque mysterii ea quae geruntur in membris his quae in ipso sunt capite gesta, congruerent; dum in baptismatis regula et mors intervenit interfectione peccati, et sepulturam triduanam imitatur trina demersio, et ab aquis elevatio resurgentis instar est de sepulcro." [151] As late as the twelfth century, Anselm of Canterbury repeats literally St. Paul's classical formula that baptism is a symbol: "figura cuiusdam mortis et sepulturae." [152] From the fifth century throughout most of the Middle Ages, Easter, the day of the Lord's resurrection, was the traditional day when baptism could be lawfully administered; an alternative occasion was Pentecost, the day when the Holy Spirit was poured out and when for the first time the people were baptized. Baptism on Epiphany, the day of Christ's baptism (and originally of His nativity) was expressly forbidden by Leo the Great.[153]

Evidently baptism and resurrection and therefore symbolical death and burial were closely linked in the minds of Early Christians. Thus it is not surprising to find baptisteries and sepulchral architecture related to one another. Occasionally baptismal fonts were placed in catacombs; the existence of a baptistery in the catacombs of Sta. Priscilla is suggested by remains of walls and conduit pipes and on the testimony of a possibly related late fourth-century inscription.[154] Although the connection of these remains with baptism has been contested,[155] a baptistery certainly existed in the catacombs of S. Pontianus. It was evidently laid out in the fifth or sixth century inside an older tomb chamber; the *piscina* and the steps leading down to it are preserved, as well as a sixth-century fresco which represents the baptism of Christ and the stag drinking from the fountain of life.[156] A baptistery connected with a cemetery basilica was erected possibly as early as the fourth century in a necropolis near Tarragona.[157]

Occasionally tombs were placed in the baptistery proper. In one of the hymns of Prudentius, a baptistery is mentioned which commemorated the death of two martyrs who were either buried or slain on the site.[158] Tombs are known to have existed in the Baptistery of the Arians at Ravenna and at least one of them was contemporary with the structure.[159] The prohibition of burials in baptisteries issued in 578 by the Council of Auxerre only proves the existence of the habit; it reveals at least that burials in baptisteries were not uncommon.[160] Still another link in this chain should be mentioned. It has been pointed out that the pictorial decorations of catacombs time and again depict baptism as a symbol of resurrection; on the other hand the mosaic decorations of fifth-century baptisteries allude frequently to death and resurrection, for example at S. Giovanni in Fonte at Naples and in the Baptistery of the Orthodox at Ravenna.

These links may help to support the thesis that the centralized plans of baptisteries as they appear from the late fourth century onwards had at least one of their roots, and quite an important one, in sepulchral architecture. It must have seemed perfectly natural to any Early Christian believer to use the pattern of a mausoleum for an edifice in which his old sinful Adam was to die and where he was to be buried with Christ so that he might be resurrected with Him. In the mausolea he would find a type similar enough to thermal rooms to be merged with their pattern and thus to carry over the concept of cleansing from the thermae into the round baptisteries; on the other hand the mausoleum type would transfer to the baptistery all the implications of burial and resurrection which Early Christianity connected with baptism. Indeed Roman mausolea would contain an element which in connection with a sepulchral monument was bound to hint specifically at resurrection: an octagonal pattern which was in itself a symbol of resurrection and regeneration.[161] An inscription attributed to St. Ambrose which decorated the Baptistery of Milan cathedral and which has been conserved in the *Sylloge Laureshamensis* III carefully elaborated this symbolism. In eight distichs it is pointed out that the edifice is octagonal and that its shape and that of the octagonal *piscina* correspond to the significance of that number; for eight is the number of salvation and regeneration, of the death of the old Adam, and of the beginning of new life. As Doelger [162] has pointed out, these verses conform completely to the symbolism of numbers in the writings of St. Ambrose and of other Early Christian authors. Time and again they emphasize the character of baptism as a spiritual regeneration which is symbolized by the number eight. Baptism is a "creation from the womb of the water," a rebirth into the "spiritual octave." [163] This explains the predilection for octagonal patterns which prevails throughout Early Christian baptisteries.[164]

These patterns which connect the baptistery with the mausoleum and thus with the idea of resurrection continued throughout the Middle Ages. Examples are numerous, particularly in Northern Italy, and they occur even north of the Alps, although there baptisteries were rare after the twelfth century. The circular shape with eight engaged columns (Agrate Conturbia), the structure with an octagonal inside and round outside plan (Baptistery of Bari cathedral), the octagon with alternating semi-circular and rectangular niches (Como, S. Giovanni in Atrio), the plain octagon (Lenno), the center room with eight columns and with octagonal ambulatory (Asti, Baptistery near S. Pietro)—these do not depart essentially from the Early Christian patterns.[165] The octagonal shape or the design with eight supports, with their implications of regeneration and resurrection remain present in all these buildings. The same holds true, of course, for shrines which were dedicated to the Baptist, without necessarily containing a baptismal font. They are not infrequently situated in cemeteries, thus emphasizing the mystical equation between baptism, burial and resurrection. As early as the late eighth century a chapel in the cemetery of the convent of Aniane was dedicated to the Precursor of the Lord; [166] in the eleventh century a chapel "in hon. s. Johannis baptiste et s. Nicolai et aliorum sanctorum . . ." was erected in the cemetery of Petershausen; [167] perhaps somewhat earlier, a new baptistery in front of the church and surrounded by tombs was built at Aquileia. Shortly before 1200 St. John in Worms was erected in the early medieval cemetery south of the cathedral itself, possibly on the site of an older baptistery. Also the Baptistery of S. Giovanni at Florence was constructed on an early medieval necropolis; it is as little known whether the present eleventh-century structure had an early forerunner of similar size and shape as whether the site around the church was used for burial in the high Middle Ages. Yet at least three persons of particular eminence were buried inside the baptistery: Bishop Rainerius (d. 1113), who evidently completed the main part of the structure, Bishop Johannes of Velletri and finally Pope John XXII (d. 1419).[168]

The question arises whether medieval baptisteries always continued those early patterns whose origin can be linked to late antique mausolea in general. At times it seems they went further and actually copied the model of the Anastasis in

Jerusalem, where Christ had risen from His tomb, setting the prototype of resurrection and symbolically of baptism.[169] Millet has suggested such a connection, not for baptisteries proper but for a group of round buildings at Constantinople, of which at least two were dedicated to the Baptist.[170] Unfortunately the identification of these Rotundas of St. John and their reconstruction from older descriptions is rather doubtful. However, such an influence of the Anastasis on baptisteries or on churches of St. John seems the more natural since as early as the end of the fourth century the Anastasis played an important role in the baptismal rites at Easter in Jerusalem. Etheria describes the rites in detail; [171] the catechumens had been catechized for seven weeks in the basilica and had been instructed in the literal meaning of the Scriptures. On Palm Sunday they professed the Creed and thus became neophytes. Then during Easter week they were led every day into the Anastasis to hear "the teachings of the deeper mystery, that is of Baptism itself. . . . There the bishop stands, leaning against the inner rails which are in the cave . . . and explains all things that are done in Baptism. In that hour no catechumen approaches the Anastasis, but only the neophytes and the faithful, who wish to hear concerning the mysteries, enter there, and the doors are shut lest any catechumen should draw near . . . And truly the mysteries are unfolded that there is no one unmoved at the things that he hears to be so explained." Nothing could stress more strongly the link between resurrection and baptism than this scene: the bishop's voice coming out of the tomb whence the Lord had risen and explaining to the neophytes the mystical meaning of baptism, the mystical death and the spiritual resurrection which they were to undergo during the last hours of the week. At Jerusalem at least, the significance of the Anastasis within the baptismal ceremonies is quite evident. By the later Middle Ages this connection of the Anastasis with baptism had evidently become so close that at least in popular usage St. John the Baptist was sometimes linked as co-patron to churches dedicated to the Holy Sepulchre; a thirteenth-century chronicler reports that after the first Crusade a church had been built at Huy "in hon. s. sepulchri Domini et b. Johannis Baptiste ob venerationem et recordationem ecclesie Ierosolimitane, que ecclesia in hon. predictorum patronorum dicitur esse fundata." [172] The same combination occurs about the middle of the twelfth century in the dedication of S. Giovanni del Sepolcro in Brindisi. In the same way the eleventh-century church at the Krukenburg, copied from the Holy Sepulchre at Paderborn, was dedicated to the Baptist.[173] In each case the combined name may be influenced by the importance of the Order of St. John of Jerusalem to which was entrusted the care of the pilgrims who came to visit the Holy Sepulchre; indeed, the churches of this order were traditionally round and "copied" from the Anastasis.

All these examples are somewhat tenuous proof for the connection between baptisteries and the Anastasis in Jerusalem. Yet there exists at least one medieval baptistery which is an actual copy after the Rotunda of the Anastasis: the Baptistery of Pisa (Figs. 48, 49). The structure begun in 1153 [174] is characterized by a number of elements which clearly are "copied" from the Anastasis. It is circular in shape and its center room is surrounded by an ambulatory and by an upper gallery. Four cross-shaped piers alternate with eight columns so that twelve supports carry the arcade on the ground floor; on the upper floor, four stronger alternating with eight weaker piers repeat exactly the rhythm of the lower arcade. The uncommon vault of the center room, a steep conical roof, originally truncated and open at the top, is still preserved beneath the fourteenth-century dome. As Rohault de Fleury has already pointed out, this roof in itself clearly proves the architect's intention of copying the Rotunda at Jerusalem; so does the interior arrangement with its groin-vaulted ambulatory and gallery, and its two-times-twelve supports. The departure from the number eight which had been traditional in baptisteries, and the replacement by twelve supports points clearly to the influence of a new prototype. Even the alternation of piers and columns in the Anastasis is repeated though it is accomplished by changing the original rhythm of two piers and three columns for each quarter circle into the simpler one of one pier and two columns. As in any medieval copy, the model has been broken up into its single elements; a selection of them has been made and the selected parts have been rearranged, possibly under the collateral influence of related structures. The rhythm of supports at Pisa might have been coinspired by the more refined pattern of pilasters and columns on the ground floor of the Baptistery of Florence.

There cannot be any doubt that the Baptistery of Pisa was intended to be a copy of the Anastasis at Jerusalem. The question is whether such an "imitation" of the Anastasis in a baptistery is an isolated case. It may be well-nigh impossible to give a definite answer to this question. Still, there is at least one element to be found in a great number of eleventh- and twelfth-century baptisteries which looks suspiciously as though it had been inherited from the Anastasis: from the eleventh century onwards galleries make their appearance in baptisteries, starting with the small village baptistery of Galliano di Cantù early in the eleventh century. Half a century later at S. Giovanni in Florence, the grandest of all the buildings of this type, narrow dwarf galleries are arranged above the rhythmical orders of pilasters and columns on the ground floor which would seem to have been inspired by the Pantheon.[175] The same motive is taken up in the baptisteries of Cremona (1176) and of Parma (1196), the latter being obviously a more distant derivative of Florence. Fully developed dwarf galleries appear late in the eleventh century at St. Martin in Bonn, which was laid out behind the cathedral, possibly in place of an older baptistery, and about 1130 in the baptistery of Arsago. Obviously galleries had no liturgical meaning and could be of no practical use in baptisteries; and since the motive of galleries becomes general throughout ecclesiastical architecture in Lombardy as well as in the Rhineland during the late eleventh and the twelfth century it may well have been introduced into copies of the Holy Sepulchre, such as St. Michael at Fulda, Sto. Stefano at Bologna and the Holy Sepulchre at Cambridge. Thus these baptisteries take up their "unfunctional" galleries and dwarf galleries at the very time when the Anastasis exerted more and more of an impact on the imagination of laymen and architects throughout the Occident.[176] We do not intend to give any definite answer to this question. But it may be well to remember that many of the "approved" copies of the Anastasis which were erected "instar dominici sepulchri Ierosolimitani" resembled their prototype no more than did the Baptistery at Florence.

Notes

1. Throughout this paper the term "Middle Ages" will be used so as to cover the whole period from the fourth to the end of the twelfth century.

2. J. Ciampini, *Vetera monimenta* . . . (Rome, 1690-99); J. Bingham, *The Antiquities of the Christian Church* (London, 1708-22); J. Britton, *Architectural Antiquities* (London, 1807); J. Kreuser, *Der christliche Kirchenbau* (Regensburg, 1860-61); Otte, *Handbuch der kirchlichen Kunstarchäologie des deutschen Mittalalters* (Leipzig, 1883-85). A very few ecclesiastical archaeologists have continued this century-old tradition to the present day; the most prominent among them are: J. Sauer, *Symbolik des Kirchengebäudes* (Freiburg, 1924), and F. J. Doelger, *Antike und Christentum* (Münster, 1929 ff.).

3. J. v. Schlosser, *Schriftquellen zur Geschichte der karolingischen Kunst* ("Quellenschriften für Kunstgeschichte . . . herausgegeben von R. Eitelberger," N.F., IV [Vienna, 1896]; henceforth quoted as Schlosser, *Karol. Kunst*), no. 682.

4. Willelmi Malmesberiensis, *Gesta Pontificum Anglorum*, ed. N.E.S.A. Hamilton (Rolls Series) (London, 1870), p. 300.

5. A. W. Clapham, *English Romanesque Architecture after the Conquest* (Oxford, 1934), p. 112, from Society of Antiquaries, *Vetusta monumenta*, I (London, 1747), Pl. XLIX.

6. *Translatio Sancti Mercurii, MGH, SS., Rer. Langob.*, pp. 576 ff., particularly p. 577: ". . . sancte Sophie basilica, quam exemplar illius condidit Justinianae;" cf.

Carmen de translatione duodecim martyrum, ibid., p. 575.

7. *Vita Gebhardi Episcopi Constantiensis, MGH, SS.* X, 582, particularly 587; cf. J. Gantner, *Kunstgeschichte der Schweiz*, I (Frauenfeld, 1936), 134 ff.

8. *Adami gesta Hammaburgensis eccl. pont.*, Lib. II, cap. 77; Lib. III, cap. 3 (ca. 1075), in O. Lehmann-Brockhaus, *Schriftquellen zur Kunstgeschichte des 11. und 12. Jahrhunderts* (Berlin, 1938), nos. 230, 232.

9. The subject of these copies has been treated in a more or less general way by G. Dalman, *Das Grab Christi in Deutschland* ("Studien über Christliche Denkmäler," XIV) (Leipzig, 1922); N. C. Brooks, *The Sepulchre of Christ in Art and Liturgy* ("University of Illinois Studies in Language and Literature," VII, 2) (Urbana, Ill., 1921); Anonymous, "Das Grab des Welterlösers in seinen mittelalterlichen Nachbildungen," *Der Kirchenschmuck*, XXVI (1895), 125 ff., 141 ff., 153 ff.; XXVII (1896), 10 ff., 33 ff. The latest copy of the Anastasis which has come to my knowledge was erected at Innichen in 1653; it was copied after 1888 at Potsdam to serve as a mausoleum for the Emperor Frederick III; see *Kirchenschmuck*, XXVII (1896), 12.

10. Candidus, *Vita Eigilis, M.G.H., SS.* XV, I, 221 ff., particularly 230 ff.; J. Schalkenbach, "Die Wiederherstellung der Michaelskirche zu Fulda," *Deutsche Kunst und Denkmalpflege* (1938), pp. 34 ff. Only the crypt and the ground plan of the main floor are ninth-century.

11. The old bases have been found underneath the eleventh-century ones; four of the Carolingian capitals have been reused; see Schalkenbach, *loc. cit.*

12. Candidus, *Vita Eigilis, op. cit.*, p. 231: ". . . in summo uno lapide istius aedificii perfectio consummatur . . ."

13. Hrabanus Maurus, *Carmina*, 42, *MGH, Poet. L.*, II, 209; "In primo Altare: Hoc altare deo dedicatum est maxime Christo cuius hic tumulus nostra sepulcra juvat . . ."

14. Dalman, *op. cit.*, pp. 27 ff.

15. *Vita Meinwerci episc. Patherbrunensis*, cap. 209 ff. (second half of twelfth century), Lehmann-Brockhaus, *op. cit.*, nos. 1046-1050. The excavations have been discussed by W. Rave, "Die Entdeckung der ursprünglichen Busdorfkirche zu Paderborn," *Deutsche Kunst und Denkmalpflege* (1936), pp. 221 ff.

16. A. Rhein, "Le Temple de Lanleff," *Congrès archéol.*, LXXXI (1914), 542 ff.; E. Viollet-le-Duc, *Dictionnaire raisonné de l'architecture française*, VIII (Paris, 1866), 287 ff. The church is at present a ruin; one of the radiating chapels is preserved, the others have been restored on the basis of reliable traces; see Rhein, *loc. cit.*

17. J. Essex, "Observations on the Origin and Antiquity of Round Churches," *Archaeologia*, VII (1787), 163 ff.; Ch. Clarke, "An Essay towards an History of Temples and round Churches," in J. Britton, *Architectural Antiquities*, I, 1 (1807); Clapham, *op. cit.*, 109 ff.

18. H. Vincent and V. Abel, *Jérusalem nouvelle*, II, I (Paris, 1944), 89 ff.

19. J. W. Crowfoot, *Early Churches in Palestine* (London, 1937), pp. 9 ff. The restoration of 628 has sometimes been assumed to have been a complete rebuilding. Vincent and Abel's findings have definitely disproved this hypothesis.

20. R. Krautheimer, above, pp. 69 ff. particularly pp. 90 and postscript, p. 104.

21. See below, pp. 128 ff.

22. M. Salmi, *L'architettura romanica in Toscana* (Rome, n. d.), p. 16, Fig. 26, Pl. 105; G. Rohault de Fleury, *Les monuments de Pise* (Paris, 1866), pp. 55 ff., Pl. XVII.

23. Clapham, *op. cit*, pp. 109 ff., Pl. 23, Fig. 35.

24. *Gregorii Nysseni opera*, VIII, 2 (*Epistulae*, ed. G. Pasquali [Berlin, 1925]), pp. 76 ff. ". . . κύκλος ὀκτώ γωνίαις διειλήμμενος . . . κύκλον δὲ διὰ τὸ περιφερὲς ὠνόμασα τὸ ὀκταγώνον σχῆμα . . ."

25. Arculf, in Adamnanus, *De locis sanctis* (*Itinera Hierosolymitana*, ed. P. Geyer, *CSEL*, XXXIX [Vienna, 1898], 219 ff.; hereafter quoted as "Arculf").

26. *The travels of Sir John Mandeville, The version of the Cotton MSS.* ed. by A. W. Pollard (London, 1915), p. 54.

27. Arculf, *op. cit.*, Lib. I, cap. 2, p. 231.

28. *Vita Chuonradi Constantiensis Episcopi, MGH, SS.* IV, 429 ff., especially 432.

29. H. Hartung, "Die Kapelle auf der Krukenburg," *Die Denkmalpflege* (1920), 27 ff.; R. Schultze, "Eine mittelalterliche Rundkirche im Wesergebiet," *Bonner Jahrbücher*, CXXVII (1922), 237 ff. The church was evidently dedicated to St. John the Baptist, but was never a baptistery.

30. R. Fagé, "L'église de Saint Léonard et la chapelle du Sépulchre, *BMon*, LXXVII (1913), 41 ff. The fourth chapel is a modern restoration based on old remnants.

31. Krautheimer, *op. cit.*, pp. 77 ff.

32. Salmi, *op. cit.*, p. 16, Figs. 27-29, Pls. 106-109; Rohault de Fleury, *op. cit.*, pp. 56 ff., Pls. XVIII-XXI; see below, pp. 139 ff.

33. R. Michel-Dansac, "Neuvy-Saint Sépulchre," *Congrès archéol.*, 94 (1937), 523 ff. The building was founded in 1042 or 45 "ad formam sancti Sepulchri Ierosolimitani." According to Michel-Dansac the lower part of the Rotunda was built about the middle of the eleventh century, the nave c. 1087, the upper parts of the Rotunda, including the gallery, between 1120 and 30. J. Hubert, "Le Saint-Sépulcre de Neuvy," *BMon*, XC (1931), 91 ff., dates the whole Rotunda twelfth century without giving any convincing reasons.

34. Isidore of Seville, *Etymologiarum sive originum Libri xx*, Lib. III, cap. XII, ed. W. M. Lindsay (Oxford, 1911); *PL*, LXXXII, col. 162.

35. *PL*, CXXXIX, cols. 93 ff.

36. Isidore, *loc. cit.*

37. H. Graf, *Opus Francigenum* (Stuttgart, 1878), "Die Entstehung der kreuzförmigen Basilika," pp. 42 ff.; Sauer, *op. cit.*, pp. 110 ff., 291 ff., 431.

38. *Origo monasterii Cappenbergensis,* Lehmann-Brockhaus, *op. cit.*, no. 669: "constructa surgit ecclesia instar crucis erecta . . . deinceps quoque victoriosissimae crucis ac reliquorum visuntur miracula."

39. Lehmann-Brockhaus, *op. cit., passim;* J. von Schlosser, *Quellenbuch zur Kunstgeschichte des abendländischen Mittelalters* (Vienna, 1896), *passim;* Schlosser, *Karol. Kunst, passim, Cas.*

40. *Ekkehardi* IV. *Casus s. Galli, MGH, SS,* II, 79 (Schlosser, *Karol. Kunst,* no. 455).

41. *Translatio s. Filiberti,* cap. 29, Schlosser, *Karol. Kunst,* no. 666.

42. *Ebbonis vita Ottonis Bambergensis,* Lib. I, cap. 22, Lehmann-Brockhaus, *op. cit.*, no. 115.

43. Arculf, *op. cit.*, Lib. II, cap. 21, p. 270.

44. *Notae s. Salvatoris Scafhusensis, MGH, SS.,* XIII, 727; Lehmann-Brockhaus, *op. cit.*, no. 1292.

45. Such a scheme is mentioned in Bamberg by Adalbertus, *Vita Heinrici,* II, (mid-twelfth century), Lib. I, cap. 6, Lehmann-Brockhaus, *op. cit.*, no. 99.

46. Augustine, *De quantitate animae,* cap. XVI, *PL,* XXXII, cols. 1051 ff.

47. *Satirarum Lib. II,* sat. 7, v. 86.

48. *Vita Eigilis, MGH, SS.* XV, I, 231. Candidus' interpretation precedes by three hundred years the similar one of Honorius of Autun, *Gemmae animae,* Lib. I, cap. 147, *PL,* CLXXII, col. 590; see Sauer, *op. cit.*, p. 110, n. 1.

49. Sauer, *op. cit.*, pp. 289 ff.

50. *Versus Iohannis Scotti ad Karolum Regem, MGH, Poet. L.,* III, cols. 550 ff., particularly v. 45 ff.

51. The 11 columns in the church of Neuvy St. Sépulchre are probably due to a lax execution of the plan which can also be observed in other parts of the edifice: half of the vaults are out of shape and the niches are almost all different in size. It is likely that the plan originally was intended to have 12 supports; see Michel-Dansac, *op. cit.*

52. The chapel is known through a number of seventeenth-century drawings; see Dalman, *op. cit.*, pp. 44 ff.

53. The church at Rieux Minervois, rather than being a Holy Sepulchre, as has been assumed, was always dedicated to the Virgin; see J. de Lahondes, "Rieux Minervois," *Congrès archéol.,* LXXIII (1906), 54 ff.; M. Young de Veye, *Congrès archéol.,* XXXVII (1870), 117 ff.

54. We quote only a few instances, such as the Temple in London and the one which existed in Paris until the eighteenth century; see *Royal Commission on Historical Monuments* (England *London,* IV (London, 1929), 137 ff.; Viollet-le-Duc, *op. cit.*, IX, 14 ff.

55. Arculf, *op. cit.*, Lib. I, cap. 2, p. 227: "duodecim mirae magnitudinis lapideae sustentant columnae."

56. V. F. Hopper, *Medieval Number Symbolism* (New York, 1938), *passim;* Sauer, *op. cit.*, pp. 61 ff.; J. F. Doelger, "Zur Symbolik des altchristlichen Taufhauses," *Antike und Christentum,* IV (1934), 153 ff.

57. Augustine, *In Johannis Evangelium,* XXVII, 14, *PL,* XXXV, cols. 1619 ff.: ". . . per quatuor cardines mundi Trinitatem fuerant annunciaturi. Ideo ter quaterni . . ."

58. Eusebius, *Vita Constantini* III, 37, ed. I. Heikel (Berlin, 1902), p. 94; *Nicene and Post-Nicene Fathers,* I (Oxford and New York, 1890), 530.

59. Arculf, *op. cit.*, Lib. I, cap. 2, p. 229: "in quo utique sepulchro duodenae lampades iuxta numerum XII sanctorum apostolorum . . . lucent, ex quibus quattuor in imo illius lectuli sepulchralis loco inferius positae, aliae vero bis quaternales super marginem eius superius conlocatae ad latus dexterum oleo nutriente praefulgent." According to the *Testamentum Domini Nostri Jesu Christi,* I, 19, ed. I. E. Rahmani (Mainz, 1899), 23, a baptistery should be 21 cubits long "ad praefigurandum numerum . . . prophetarum" and 12 cubits wide "pro adumbrandis iis

qui constituti fuerunt ad praedicandum evangelium."

60. Augustine, *De Sermone Domini in monte*, Lib. I, cap. IV, 12, *PL*, XXXIV, col. 1235; *idem*, *Epist*. LV, cap. 7, 32, *PL*, XXXIII, col. 220; see also Hopper, *op.. cit*, p. 85; Sauer, *op. cit.*, pp. 78 ff. and Doelger, *op. cit., passim*, based on numerous quotations from Early Christian and medieval writers, have discussed at length the symbolism of numbers in general and of the number eight in particular.

61. Augustine, *De Civitate Dei*, Lib. XV, cap. 20, *PL*, XLI, cols. 462 ff.

62. Candidus, *op. cit.*, p. 231.

63. Candidus, *op. cit.*, p. 230: "Cuius tecturae princeps et conditor est Christus Jesus, fundamentum scilicet columnaque manens semper immobilis . . . in quo omnis aedificatio constructa crescit. . . . Quid vero significet hoc, quod in summo uno lapide istius aedificii perfectio consummatur idem Doctor insinuat . . . , ut ille qui coepit in nobis opus bonum, perficiat usque in diem Christi Jesu, quatenus cuncta operatio nostra a Deo semper incipiat, et per eum coepta finiatur."

64. Augustine, *Epist*. LV, cap. 27, 32, *PL*, XXXIII, col. 220: ". . . ut octavus primo concinat."

65. Candidus, *op. cit.*, p. 231.

66. *Vita s. Benedicti Anianensis*, cap. 26, Schlosser, *Karol. Kunst*, no. 574: "tres aras censuit subponi, ut in his personalitas trinitatis typice videatur significari. . . . In septem item altaria, in septem candelabria et in septem lampades septiformis gratia spiritus sancti intelligitur."

67. *De Sanctis Ecclesiae Cameracensis Relatio, auctore Monacho Valcelleni* (twelfth century), Lehmann-Brockhaus, *op. cit.*, no. 1670.

68. Dalman, *op. cit.*, pp. 90 ff.

69. Arculf, *op. cit.*, Lib. I, cap. 2, p. 229.

70. *Commemoratorium de casis Dei vel monasteris*, T. Tobler and M. Molinier, *Itinera Hierosolymitana et Descriptiones Terrae Sanctae* (Geneva, 1879), pp. 299 ff., especially p. 305.

71. See above, p. 117 and note 15.

72. Rave, *op. cit.*, Fig. 232 and Vincent-Abel, *op. cit.*, II, 1, Pl. XIII and Fig. 59.

73. See for instance C. Lebruyne, *Voyage au Levant*, II (Paris, 1728), 242.

74. A. M. Schneider, *Byzanz, Vorarbeiten zur Topographie und Archäologie der Stadt* ("Istanbuler Forschungen herausgegeben von der Abteilung Istanbul des archäologischen Institutes des deutschen Reiches," VIII [1936]), 1 ff., Pls. 1-3.

75. A. Goldschmidt, "Mittelstücke fünfteiliger Elfenbeintafeln des vi-vii. Jahrhunderts," *JKunstW*, I (1923), 30 ff. D. Frey, *Gotik und Renaissance* (Augsburg, 1929), pp. xxix and 38, while discussing the problem, extends the principles of medieval representations of architecture into the Gothic period which to this writer seems to be dominated by entirely different rules. On this one point I agree as fully with the brief remarks in the pamphlet of H. Rosenau, *Design and Medieval Architecture* (London, 1934), "Planning and architectural Design," pp. 12 ff., as I disagree with the author's confused interpretation of earlier medieval representations of architecture.

76. Munich, Staatsbibliothek, Clm. 4456, cim. 60; see Brooks, *op. cit.*, Fig. 15.

77. C. R. Morey, "The painted panel from the Sancta Sanctorum," *Festschrift Paul Clemen* (1926), pp. 151 ff.; Parker Lesley, "An Echo of Early Christianity," *Art Quarterly*, II (1939), 215 ff.

78. E. B. Smith, "A Source of Medieval Style in France," *Art Studies*, II (1924), 58 ff.

79. See above, n. 75.

80. P. Clemen, *Romanische Monumentalmalerei in den Rheinlanden* (Düsseldorf, 1916), 55, n. 111.

81. See above, p. 116.

82. See above, p. 119, n. 28.

83. Hubert, *op. cit.*, see above, n. 33.

84. *La basilica di Aquileia, a cura del comitale del . . . IX centenario* (Bologna, 1933), pp. 55 ff.

85. A. Kingsley Porter, *Lombard Architecture*, III (New Haven, 1917), 180, n. 4: "Ecclesia S. Sepulchri in qua est forma Sepulchri Dominici secundum longitudinem, latitudinem et altitudinem. . . ." Porter's translation, *loc. cit.*, text: "The church of S. Sepolcro has the same length,

width and height as the sepulchre of our Lord" is erroneous; see also, *loc. cit.*, n. 4: "Ecclesia S. Sepulchri ubi est similitudo et forma Sepulchri Domini."

86. Porter, *op. cit.*, II, 648. Neither the documents nor the plan of the edifice suggest in any way that bishop Anselm's "rebuilding" of 1099 was intended to imitate the pattern of the Anastasis.

87. J. Supino, *L' Arte nelle chiese di Bologna, secoli* VIII-XIV (Bologna, 1932), pp. 43 ff. and p. 104, n. 29, gives a list of buildings which according to him shared only the name with the Holy Site of Jerusalem; see J. Hubert, "Notes sur l' histoire de l' abbaye de Ferrières," *Annales de la Societé hist. et archéol. du Gâtinais*, XLII (1934), 95 ff., where it is shown that as early as the ninth century the seventh-century convent of Ferrières was called "Bethlehem." Whether the "copy" was merely a "copy in name" remains to be carefully checked in every single case.

88. *Chronicon Bohemicorum auctore anonymo* (before 1380), Lehmann-Brockhaus, *op. cit.*, no. 1147.

89. The indulgences to be acquired, however, were rarely as extensive as those connected with the original; cf. Dalman, *op. cit.*, p. 23.

90. *Chronicon s. Huberti Andaginensis*, cap. 23 (early twelfth century), Lehmann-Brockhaus, *op. cit.*, no. 1776.

91. The documents and the descriptions of the buildings have been amply discussed by Porter, *op. cit.*, II, 124 ff. The only major point on which I find myself in disagreement with Porter is the date of the church of the Crocefisso; quite apart from its Romanesque capitals, it contains, in my opinion, large parts of a twelfth-century structure in its south flank. A more recent but also more arbitrary discussion of the building complex, accompanied by excellent illustrations, will be found in Supino, *op. cit.*, pp. 26 ff. Supino's main thesis is that when founded in the fifth (?) century, the complex of Sto. Stefano shared with the Holy Sepulchre only the name Jerusalem. Both the fifth- and eighth-century buildings which, according to Supino, preceded the twelfth-century Rotunda at Bologna, would have been baptisteries belonging to the adjoining "cathedral" of

SS. Vitale and Agricola, now SS. Pietro e Paolo; the whole present layout of the structures would be twelfth-century and only this late layout would imitate Jerusalem. This whole thesis is based on two erroneous assumptions; first that the original layout of the buildings of the Holy Sepulchre at Jerusalem corresponded to Heisenberg's reconstruction rather than to the one of Vincent and Abel which, in its general features at least, is the only one possible; and second, that SS. Pietro e Paolo was the "cathedral" (and thus could have a baptistery), an assumption which has been disproved by Testi-Raponi (see below, n. 93).

92. Since the structures were completely altered by a thoroughgoing restoration some 50 years ago, it will be preferable to base the description on older plans, such as the one in F. Osten, *Die Bauwerke in der Lombardei* (Darmstadt 1846-54), and the sixteenth-century plans, published by Supino, *op. cit.*

93. The present names are relatively modern. Apart from Sto. Stefano with its reproduction of the Holy Sepulchre, only the names of two buildings, the Atrium of Pilate and the Crocefisso have now some connection with either Jerusalem or the Passion of Christ. Yet these present dedications are only residuals from a large and widely-varied array of names of devotional stations which in the sixteenth and seventeenth centuries referred to all kinds of venerated sites scattered all over the Holy City and indeed over the Holy Land. Within the complex of buildings, the Valley of Josaphat (the present Atrium of Pilate), the place of the denial of St. Peter (S. Pietro in Gallicantu) and a chapel of the Annunciation were represented; a *Scala Santa* and a window, called the *Ecce Homo*, were shown inside the present church of the Crocefisso. On the other hand the twelfth-century titles were quite simple. There were only a few and they all referred to the buildings of and around the Holy Sepulchre at Jerusalem. The church of SS. Peter and Paul did not form part of the convent of Sto. Stefano before 1200 (Testi-Rasponi, "Note marginali al Liber Pontificalis di Ravenna," *Atti e memorie della R. Deputazione di Storia Patria per le provincie di Romagna* [1911],

pp. 391 ff.). This explains why it is the only building within the group whose name had no connection with the sites near the Holy Sepulchre. See Porter, *op. cit.*, particularly p. 129, n. 21; p. 136, n. 51; pp. 138 ff., n. 59; pp. 141 ff., n. 61 and 63.

94. Porter, *op. cit.*, pp. 134 ff., nn. 47 and 49: "Sanctum Stephanum quod dicitur Hierusalem;" "ecclesia sancti Stephani q.v. Jerusalem."

95. Porter, *op. cit.*, p. 130, n. 29.

96. This addition was made between 1105 (?) and 1149 when a consecration took place; but building went on until 1169. As a whole the architectural history of the Crusaders' choir is far from clear; see C. Enlart, *Les monuments des Croisés, II* (Paris, 1928), 136 ff., and Vincent and Abel, *op. cit.*

97. The *Commemoratorium de Casis Dei*, Tobler-Molinier, *op. cit.*, p. 305, gives the distance at Jerusalem as 28 *dexteri*, i.e., 41.58 m. In reality the measurement is 41 m.; the distance at Bologna measures 42 m.

98. *Bedae Liber de locis sanctis*, I-V, Geyer, *op. cit.*, pp. 301 ff., for instance, p. 306: "In inferiore . . . parte urbis, ubi templum . . . ;" p. 309: "In hac (sc. valle Josaphat) turris est regis Josaphat . . . cuius ad dexteram de rupe. . . . excisa. . . . domus."

99. Arculf, *op. cit.*, Lib. I, cap. 2, pp. 227 ff., esp. p. 230.

100. In reviewing Lehmann-Brockhaus' book, W. Haftmann, *ZfK,* VIII (1939), 285 ff., particularly 289, has made some interesting remarks about copies which lead towards similar conclusions.

101. Compare the lists of dedications which are given in: H. Otte, *op. cit.*; J. L. Petit, "Notes on circular churches," *Archaeological Journal,* XVIII (1861), 101 ff.; H. Bogner, *Die Grundrissdispositionen der zweischiffigen Zentralbauten* (Strassburg, 1906); F. Bond, *The Consecration. . . . of Churches* (London, 1914). No far-reaching conclusions have been drawn from these lists. See, however, pp. 107 ff. above.

102. The most recent and complete collection of ground plans of Roman thermae is found in D. Krenker and others, *Die trierer Kaiserthermen* ("Trierer Grabungen und Forschungen," I, I) (Augsburg, 1929).

103. See for instance the *laconica* at El-Djem, Khamissa, Lambaesis and in the two thermae of the Villa of Hadrian at Tivoli, and the *apodyteria* at Marienfels and Vieil-Evreux; illustrations in Krenker, *op. cit., passim.*

104. C. Hopkins, *The Christian Church at Dura-Europos. Preliminary Report of Fifth Season* (New Haven, 1934), pp. 249 ff.

105. G. Giovenale, *Il Battistero lateranense* ("Studi di antichità cristiana" I) (Rome, 1929), pp. 72 ff.

106. *La basilica di Aquileia, op. cit.*, pp. 109 ff., Fig. 10; pp. 165 ff., Fig. 18; p. 280.

107. R. Egger, *Frühchristliche Kirchenbauten im südlichen Norikum* ("Sonderschriften des Österreichischen Archäol. Inst.," IX) (Vienna, 1916), p. 117, Fig. 105.

108. C. de la Croix, "Poitiers," *Congrès archeol.,* 70 (1903), 7 ff.

109. S. Crisogono, second phase, see *Corpus,* I, 152; L. Fortunati, *Relazione degli scavi . . . lungo la Via Latina* (Rome, 1859).

110. S. Gsell, *Les monuments antiques de l'Algérie,* II (Paris, 1900-01), 12 ff.

111. G. Soteriu, *Hai Christianikai Thebai kai hai palaio-christianikai Basilikai tes ellados* (Athens, 1931).

112. H. C. Butler, *Early Churches in Syria* (Princeton, 1929), *passim;* J. W. Crowfoot, *Early Churches in Palestine* (London, 1941).

113. Giovenale, *op. cit.*

114. E. Dyggve, "Salona Christiana," *Atti del III Congresso internazionale di archeologia cristiana* ("Studi di antichità cristiana," VIII) (Rome, 1934), pp. 237 ff.

115. Butler, *op. cit.*, p. 156.

116. C. M. Kaufmann, *Die Menasstadt,* I (Leipzig, 1910), Figs. 22, 23.

117. E. Swift, *Hagia Sophia in Constantinople* (New York, 1940), pp. 147 ff.

118. C. Ricci, *Tavole storiche dei mosaici di Ravenna* (Rome, 1932); G. Gerola, "Il restauro del battistero Ariano di Ravenna," *Studien zur Kunst des Ostens* (Vienna, 1923), pp. 112 ff.

119. F. Reggiori, *Dieci battisteri lombardi minori* ("I monumenti italiani," IV) (Rome, 1935). See also S. Steinmann-

Brodtbeck, "Das Baptisterium von Riva San Vitale," *Zeitschrift für scheweizerische Archaeologie und Kunstgeschichte*, III (1941), 193 ff.; the issue arrived in U.S.A. only while I was revising the galley proof of this paper.

120. Österreichisches Archäologisches Institut, *Die Marienkirche in Ephesos* ("Forschungen in Ephesos," IV, I) (Vienna, 1932), p. 43 ff.

121. C. Chierici, "Di alcuni risultati sui recenti lavori intorno alla basilica di San Lorenzo a Milano . . ." *RACrist*, XVI (1939), 51 ff.; I. Reggiori, *op. cit.*; J. Hubert, *L'art pré-roman* (Paris, 1938), pp. 2 ff. G. De Angelis d' Ossat, "Sugli edifici ottagonali a cupola nell'Antichità e nel Medioevo," *Atti del I° Congresso nazionale di storia dell' architettura* (Florence, 1938), pp. 13 ff. enumerates a great number of octagonal baptisteries and other structures.

122. Egger, *op. cit.*, p. 68.

123. See the list in De Angelis d' Ossat, *op. cit.*, pp. 17 ff.

124. K. Lehmann-Hartleben and J. Lindros, "Il palazzo degli Orti Sallustiani," *Opuscula archeologica*, I (1935), 196 ff.

125. Steinmann-Brodtbeck, *op. cit.*, enumerates a great number of these square ambulatories.

126. D. Frey, "Neue Untersuchungen und Grabungen in Parenzo," *Mitteilungen der K. K. Zentral-Kommission*, 3. Folge, XIII (1914), 144 ff., 179 ff., especially Fig. 31.

127. E. Albertini, "L' archéologie chrétienne en Algérie," *Atti del III° Congresso*, *op. cit.*, pp. 411 ff.

128. H. Nachod, "Das Baptisterium von Canosa," *RM*, XXX (1915), 116 ff.

129. Giovenale, *op. cit., passim.*

130. M. Stettler, "Das Baptisterium zu Nocera Superiore," *RACrist*, XVII (1940), 82 ff.

131. L. M. Ugolini, "Il Battistero di Butrinto," *RACrist*, XI (1934), 265 ff.

132. H. Koethe, *Frühchristliche Nischen-Rundbauten* (Diss. Marburg, 1928). The date of Marseilles is certainly fifth-century; the Baptisteries of Riez and Aix may be somewhat later.

133. P. Laicono, "Sul restauro compiuto al battistero di Santa Severina," *BdA*, XXVIII (1934), 174 ff.

134. On plans of Roman thermae, what sometimes looks like such an outer corridor is really nothing but a furnace passage.

135. H. Koethe, "Zum Mausoleum der weströmischen Dynastie," *RM*, XLVI (1931) 9 ff.; *idem*, "Das Konstantins-mausoleum und verwandte Denkmäler," *JdI*, 48 (1934), 185 ff.; R. Egger, "Die Begräbnisstätte des Kaisers Konstantin," *JÖAI*, XVI (1913), 212 ff.

136. L. Canina, *Gli edifizi di Roma . . . antica e sua Campagna*, VI (Rome, 1848-56), II, Pl. CXXIII; the monument which now goes by the name of Sta. Maria della Tosse seems to have been erected in the middle of the fourth century.

137. Canina, *op. cit.*, VI, I, Pl. LXXXII. Similar patterns, sometimes of a more complicated type, are frequent among the Roman monuments drawn in the sixteenth century, for instance, by Bramantino, *Le rovine di Roma. . . .*, ed. Mongeri (Turin, 1879), or by G. B. Montano, *I cinque libri di architettura* (Rome, 1621). Yet these drawings seem to be frequently "variations on Roman themes" rather than actual surveys. Thus it seems inadvisable to depend on them too much.

138. B. de Montfaucon, *L' antiquité expliquée*, V, I (Paris, 1719), Pls. 18, 108, 111, 118. The history and the significance of these subterranean tomb corridors in pre-Roman and Roman times have been discussed by G. Welter, "Zwei vorrömische Grabbauten in Nordafrika," *RM*, XLII (1927), 84 ff.

139. E. Junyent, "I monumenti cristiani di Spagna," *Atti del III° Congresso, op. cit.*, pp. 255 ff.

140. Gsell, *op. cit.*, II, 421 ff.

141. C. Cecchelli, *S. Agnese fuori le mura e S. Costanza* (Le chiese di Roma illustrate, 10) (Rome, n.d.); see also my remarks in "Santo Stefano Rotondo and the Church of the Holy Sepulchre," above, pp. 69 ff.

142. Gsell, *op. cit.*, II, 410 ff.

143. Ligorio, *cod. Vat. lat.* 3439, f. 70, "*Templum Platonis et Proserpinae;*" f. 25, "*Templum Isidis et Serapis.*" See, however, above, n. 137.

144. H. Koethe, *op. cit., JdI,* 48 (1934), 185 ff., especially 198 ff.

145. P. Styger, "Nymphäen, Mausoleen, Baptisterien," *Architectura,* I (1933), 50 ff. has taken a strong stand against the thesis that baptisteries had any connection with thermal rooms or with nymphaea. He suggests the possibility that a great number of baptisteries were in reality originally mausolea—for example, the Baptisteries at Naples, at Ravenna and at Agliate. No proof is given to support these suggestions. On the other hand he vehemently objects to the possibility that the type of the baptistery as such should be derived from mausolea types. Yet, the resemblance of the niche over the baptismal font at Dura with Eastern Roman tomb types has been pointed out by Hopkins, *op. cit.,* p. 249.

146. Paulus, *Epistola ad Romanos,* VI, 3, 4; cf. also *Epistola ad Colossenses,* II, 12 ff.

147. Basil, περὶ τοῦ ἁδίου πνεύματος, cap. XV, 35; *PG,* XXXII, col. 129; *Nicene and Post-Nicene Fathers* VIII, (Oxford and New York, 1895), 21 ff. Cf. R. Reitzenstein, "Heilige Handlung," *VorWarb,* 1928-29 (Leipzig, 1930), 21 ff.

148. Augustine, *Enchiridion,* cap. LII, *PL,* XL, cols. 256 ff.; *idem, Contra Julianum Pelàgium,* cap. V, 14, *PL,* XLV, col. 683.

149. Hilarius of Poitiers, *De Trinitate,* Lib. IX, cap. 9, *PL,* X, col. 288.

150. Pseudo-Augustine (possibly Faustus), *Sermo clxviii,* 2, *PL,* XXXIX, col. 2070.

151. Leo Magnus, *Epist. xvi,* cap. 3, 3, *PL,* LIV, col. 698.

152. Anselm of Canterbury, *De azymo et fermentato,* cap. IV, *PL,* CLVIII, col. 544.

153. Leo Magnus, *op. cit.,* col. 696.

154. O. Marucchi, "La basilica papale del Cimiterio di S. Priscilla," *Nuovo BACrist,* XIV (1908), 5 ff., especially 48 ff.

155. G. P. Kirsch, *Le catacombe romane* (Rome, 1933), pp. 93 ff.

156. Kirsch, *op. cit.,* p. 229.

157. Junyent, *op. cit., Atti del III° Congresso,* pp. 283 ff.

158. Prudentius, *Peristephanion,* VIII, V, 1 ff., *PL,* LX, cols. 430 ff.

159. Gerola, *op. cit., passim.*

160. F. W. Unger, "Über die christlichen Rund- und Octogon-Bauten," *Bonner Jahrbücher,* XLI (1866), 52, n. 2. As late as the ninth century, the Baptistery of Santa Severina was crowded with tombs; see above p. 147, n. 133.

161. F. J. Doelger, *op. cit., Antike und Christentum,* IV (1934), 153 ff.; *idem,* "Die Inschrift im Baptisterium S. Giovanni in fonte . . . ," *Antike und Christentum,* II (1932), 252 ff. While Doelger strongly emphasizes the symbolical link between baptism and resurrection he derives the plan of the baptistery from thermal rooms only; see also Sauer, *op. cit.,* p. 78.

162. Doelger, *op. cit.* (1934), pp. 153 ff.

163. Clemens of Alexandria, *Stromata,* IV, 25; *PG,* VIII, col. 1372, pp. 179 ff.

164. Doelger, *op. cit.* (1934), 182 ff. On p. 187 Doelger points out that sometimes a hexagonal piscina is arranged inside an octagonal baptistery; he interprets the hexagon as symbolizing Mother Church. The pattern seems to be particularly frequent along the Dalmatian Coast and in North Africa. I should be inclined to interpret it rather as symbolizing the "Old Adam." Adam, since he was created on the sixth day, is represented by the number six; see Hrabanus Maurus, *De Universo,* Lib. II, cap. I, *PL,* III, col. 31; and A. Goldschmidt, "Frühmittelalterliche illustrierte Enzyklopädien," *VorWarb,* 1923–1924 (Leipzig-Berlin, 1926), pp. 218 ff.

165. Porter, *op. cit., passim;* Reggiori, *op. cit.*

166. Schlosser, *Karol. Kunst,* no. 578.

167. *Casus monasterii Petrishusensis,* Lib. II, cap. 16, Lehmann-Brockhaus, *op. cit.,* no. 1095.

168. The tomb of Guccio de' Medici which is now inside the Baptistery was transferred there from the piazza. The burials inside the Baptistery of Florence prove, by the way, that the prohibition of the Council of Auxerre was not of much effect.

169. Unger, *op. cit.,* pp. 25 ff. has strongly emphasized the possibility of such a link between the medieval baptisteries and the Anastasis. In his opinion all baptisteries were laid out on an octagonal plan from the seventh century onwards,

because they all were derived from the Holy Sepulchre; this, in his reconstruction, combined from 628 on an octagonal exterior with a round interior. Unger's reconstruction is, of course, mistaken, and consequently also his conclusions are erroneous. Yet his fundamental assumption seems to be quite correct; he is wrong in his reasoning but right in the ultimate reasons for his reasoning.

170. G. Millet, "L'église ronde de Preslav," *Comptes rendus de l'Académie des inscriptions et belles-lettres* (1933), pp. 169 ff.

171. *S. Silviae . . . peregrinatio ad loca sancta*, Geyer, *op. cit.*, pp. 35 ff., particularly pp. 98 ff. We are quoting from the English translation by M. L. McClure and C. L. Feltoe, *The Pilgrimage of Etheria* (Translations of Christian Literature, ser. III, Liturgical Texts) (London and New York, n.d.), 90 ff., particularly p. 94.

172. *Chronica Albrici monachi Trium Fontium, MGH, SS.*, XXIII, 815, Lehmann-Brockhaus, *op. cit.*, no. 1787.

173. See above, p. 117.

174. Rohault de Fleury, *op. cit.*, pp. 56 ff., Pls. XVIII-XXI; Salmi, *op. cit.*, p. 16.

175. W. Horn, "Das florentiner Baptisterium," *Mitteilungen des kunsthistorischen Instituts in Florenz*, V (1938), 99 ff.

176. *Idem*, as quoted above, n. 33.

Postscript

This paper at an early moment staked out the outlines of a new field. The idea, though, must have been "in the air": Grabar's *Martyrium*, touching upon similar problems, was in preparation, unbeknown to me; and Bandmann's *Mittelalterliche Architektur als Bedeutungsträger* appeared a few years later. Were I to rewrite my paper today, I would obviously have to take into account these major works, not to mention the numerous contributions to the problem published since (Bandmann, 1962, 1967; Heitz, 1963; Belting, 1962). But I doubt that I should attack the problem differently after these twenty-five years or that I could improve on formulating the essential question. Perhaps —and in part with a wary eye on some quite recent publications—I would stress even more strongly than I did then the medieval pattern of "double-think" or, better, "multithink." Indeed, what counts in medieval thought, in the context of any given theme, as reflected in the verses I quoted from John Scotus Erigena, is the multitude of its connotations, fleeting, only dimly visible, and therefore interchangeable. Hence I have no quarrel with Paul Underwood's interpretation of baptism and baptisteries, slightly different from mine: obviously, Romans 6:3 ff. and John 3:3, the image of the tomb and the *fons vitae*, the concepts of death, resurrection, rebirth and regeneration, all "vibrated" simultaneously in the mind of educated Early Christian and medieval men. At the same time I would today point more emphatically to the seemingly opposed, yet complementary, need to look for specific *tertia comparationis* between copies and originals in architecture as well as between building types and their meaning.

As to details, I would have to make a few corrections. The building history of the Anastasis Rotunda is less clear today than it seemed in 1942, but the division of its supports into four groups of three columns and four pairs of two piers certainly existed by the seventh century, and the three niches in the ambulatory belong to the original structure. On the other hand, it appears possible that the restoration of the Lateran Baptistery, at present under way, may result in the discovery that the circular wall below the octagonal outer wall (Fig. 52, a), rather than representing the remains of an early Constantinian baptistery, is but the foundation of that wall, and that this latter is indeed the enclosing wall of the Constantinian baptistery. In that case, the octagon as the characteristic form of baptisteries (and perhaps even its connection with mausolea and its symbolism) goes back to the early fourth century rather than to its second half.

Likewise, the discovery of the fourth-century baptistery of Milan cathedral (Mirabella, 1963) establishes an early date for the origin of the octagon plan with niches and suggests Milan as the center from which the type spread to both Provence and the Alpine regions. Concomitantly, the likelihood of S. Aquilino's being a mausoleum rather than a baptistery reaffirms the close links between the two types in both form and function. The catalogue of Khatchatrian (1962) supplies a wealth of material on baptisteries, unknown in 1942.

Additional Bibliography

Bandmann, G. *Mittelalterliche Architektur als Bedeutungsträger* (Berlin, 1951).

———— "Die Bischofskapelle in Hereford," *Festschrift Herbert von Einem,* ed. G. v. d. Osten (Bonn, 1965), pp. 9 ff.

———— "Früh- und hochmittelalterliche Altaranordnung als Darstellung," *Das erste Jahrtausend,* ed. V. H. Elbern, I (Düsseldorf, 1962), 371 ff.

Bauerreiss, R., O.S.B. *Fons Sacer* (Munich, 1949).

Belting, H. "Studien zum Beneventanischen Hof," *DOPapers,* XVI (1962), 141 ff.

Corbo, P. "Gli edifici della Santa Anastasis," *Liber Annuus,* XII (1961-1962), 221 ff.

Daniélou, J., S.J. *The Bible and the Liturgy* (Notre Dame, Indiana, 1956).

Grabar, A. *Martyrium* (Paris, 1946).

Heitz, C. *Architecture et liturgie* (Paris, 1963).

Kraeling, C. H. *The Christian Building* (*The Excavations at Dura-Europos, Final Report,* VIII, 2) (New Haven, 1967).

Khatchatrian, A. *Les Baptistères paléochrétiens* (Paris, 1962).

Klauser, Th. "Taufe in lebendigem Wasser," *Pisciculi . . . F. J. Doelger* (Münster, 1939), pp. 157 ff.

Mirabella Roberti, M. "La cattedrale antica di Milano e il suo Battistero," *Arte Lombarda,* VIII (1963), 77 ff.

Stommel, E. "Christliche Taufriten und antike Badesitten," *Jahrbuch für Antike und Christentum,* II, (1959), 5 ff.

———— "Begraben mit Christus . . . ," *RQuSchr,* XLIX (1954), 1 ff.

———— "Das Abbild seines Todes . . ." *RQuSchr,* L (1955), 1 ff.

Underwood, P. "The Fountain of Life," *DOPapers,* V (1950), 41 ff.

9

REVIEW OF ANDRE GRABAR,
MARTYRIUM. RECHERCHES SUR LE CULTE DES RELIQUES ET L'ART CHRETIEN ANTIQUE, 2 VOLS., PARIS, 1943–1946 *

M. GRABAR'S VOLUMES are among the most outstanding contributions to the interpretation of Early Christian and Byzantine art made anywhere during the past fifty years. The wealth of material, the stimulating ideas and penetrating insights presented by M. Grabar will explain to some degree why it has taken this reviewer nearly five years to digest and think through the most significant of these ideas. On the same grounds, he asks to be forgiven for limiting his remarks to the field of architecture, and primarily of Western architecture: *ultra posse nemo obligatur.*

The basis of M. Grabar's research is the conviction that no work of sacred art, pagan or Christian, ancient or medieval, can be understood unless its religious implications are given due consideration. Always recognized in the realm of representational art, this principle had been lost sight of during the last century where architecture was concerned: the symbolic significance of a building, its "content," the ties existing between its shape and its dedication or function had been forgotten and replaced, under the impact of nineteenth-century architectural concepts, by a formalistic and technical approach. Firmness and Delight, to use Vitruvian terms, were considered all-important, and Commodity, deprived of its late antique and medieval figurative connotation, became literally usefulness. That the iconography of architecture should have been rediscovered quite independently during the war years by a number of scholars and in continents far apart is one of the strange quirks not infrequent in the historiography of art.[1]

M. Grabar's starting point, as explained by himself both in the preface of his book and in a splendid summary of his thesis,[2] was determined by a number of premises: first, an awareness of the bonds linking pagan and Christian sacred art; second, the recognition of basic differences separating, from the outset, the ecclesiastical architecture of East and West, and the refusal to take these differences for granted without explanation; third, the need to explain the rise, since the fifth century, of a new iconography in place of that of the catacombs, and its intimate connection with the cult of relics.

*From *AB*, XXXV (1953), 57–61.

On this basis, M. Grabar divides Christian cult buildings from their very beginnings into two classes, distinct both in form and function: meeting places for the regular Eucharistic assemblies of the congregations; and shrines, that is, martyria or memoriae, marking a site which had witnessed the presence of Christ or of the Virgin, or the tomb of a witness to Christ in the blood, a martyr. Meeting places as a rule are longitudinal and covered by open timber roofs. Martyria, on the other hand, as the author points out in Chapter I, started out as areas *sub divo,* with benches surrounding the tomb; but as early as the third century (Chapter II) they turned into more monumental forms: two-storied structures, as M. Grabar sees them reproduced, for instance, in the Alexandria tapestry formerly in the Kaiser-Friedrich Museum and in the Menologium of Basil II; *exedrae* added to open areas or to transverse oblong halls; triconchs, as at S. Callisto in Rome. Finally, still in the second century, M. Grabar sees these primitive types superseded by central plan buildings on a large scale and with a wide variety of rooms, but always vaulted, whether in stone or in wood. Rich and varied as their plans are, these central plan martyria all derive, in both type and function, from Roman mausolea and *heroa,* and these prototypes are represented, according to Grabar, by extant ruins as well as by fifteenth- and sixteenth-century drawings of Roman "sepolchri" and "tempietti."

Evolving from these third-century forms, the great martyria of the Constantinian period (Chapter III) begin to demonstrate the fundamental distinction between Christian architecture of the East and West. In the East, large martyria of central type rise in commemoration of holy sites and of relics: the Octagon of Antioch, the Apostoleion of Constantinople, the Rotunda of the Anastasis over the Sepulchre of Christ, and the Imbomon over the site of the Ascension. Only occasionally, as in the Sanctuary of the Nativity at Bethlehem, an oblong basilica is joined to the polygonal martyrium, which shelters the Grotto of the Nativity. In the West, on the other hand, the basilica, designed for regular Eucharistic gatherings, would seem to have been the dominant type. Only occasionally is the nave of a basilica followed by a martyrium-like structure, as a rule a rectangular transverse hall terminated by an apse. Hence, the transept would seem to be a substitute for the martyrium. It thus appears in churches that sheltered the tomb of a saint or some other great relic, such as St. Peter's in Rome.

In the course of the fourth and fifth centuries, centralized martyria spread throughout the East. They no longer commemorate primarily Christ, but the Virgin or the tombs or relics of martyrs as well, and vary in plan from round and octagonal to quatrefoil and cruciform structures. At this time, as M. Grabar brings out (Chapter IV), the boundaries between martyria and assembly halls begin to blur in the eastern provinces: most of the great Eastern martyria were also regular churches dedicated to Christ and designed for regular Mass. By virtue of their regular liturgical function, these central plan martyria were apt to supersede the basilican type. Centralized plans became the hallmark of

ecclesiastical architecture throughout the East, both of large independent structures such as Justinian's Hagia Sophia and of small chapels sheltering relics and
attached to large regular churches. The relic, then, was kept outside the church
proper, in a separate mausoleum, and as the cult of relics increased in the
East, these mausolea grew larger and gained in importance. Finally, since "all
churches . . . possessing relics were and at the same time were not sepulchral
shrines . . . , the sanctuary which contained the . . . tomb of the saint was no
longer distinguished from the other churches dedicated to the saint which possessed
a tiny fragment of his relic. . . ."[3] In consequence, regular churches since the
early sixth century adopted the vaults and domes of martyria chapels. The complete assimilation throughout the East of regular churches to the martyrium
type was promoted since the seventh century by the renascence of a Neo-Platonic
mysticism which interpreted the domed structure as a symbol of the Universe,
surmounted by the Dome of Heaven.[4]

In contrast to this development of Eastern, i.e., Byzantine, church architecture,
the West (Chapter 5) continued to erect basilicas over the tombs of martyrs.
According to Grabar, the reason for this different approach lies in the demand,
raised in the West since the fourth century, for the presence of relics under
every altar, based on Revelation VI: 9. Hence, in the West the martyrium is
incorporated into the basilica, and the cult of relics is concentrated around the
High Altar. The chancel becomes the nucleus of future architectural development, including a crypt underneath, an ambulatory with radiating chapels, and
a crossing tower over the altar. In brief, the Romanesque chevet is basically
the martyrium of Western medieval architecture.

With this thesis M. Grabar strikes to the very heart of the problem of the
origins of church architecture in the East and the West. In contrast to earlier
and current interpretations, he opposes any attempt to explain this development
on technical grounds. How indeed could the origin of Byzantine church types be
explained as a "development" from longitudinal structures? We should have to
assume (as has been done) that the basilica was first covered with barrel vaults;
that a dome was then inserted into the vault of the nave in front of the chancel;
that this dome was further expanded by deep arches into the area of the
aisles; and that this domed area was isolated and elaborated until it turned
into a domed building. History does not work on a drafting board, and M.
Grabar is undoubtedly right in basing his thesis on the premise that form and
content in late antique and early medieval architecture are but two facets of
the same phenomenon. The application of this thesis to Early Christian and
Byzantine church architecture has led M. Grabar to what may well be the first
consistent interpretation of the origin of these forms and of the basic differences
that separate Eastern and Western medieval architecture.

The wide perspectives envisaged by M. Grabar make us gratefully aware of
how much he has contributed to our understanding of the period under discussion; they also emphasize how much remains to be done if we are to broaden

and consolidate our knowledge of this area. It is with such possibilities of further study in mind that I venture to present here for discussion a few points of a factual and methodological nature.

The limitations of our factual knowledge of Early Christian architecture become evident in any attempt to establish chronological sequences, to ascertain the precise plan and elevation of a given structure, to determine its function, or to evaluate the links between East and West. I am inclined at times to a more cautious attitude regarding the material on which M. Grabar bases his discussion. Very little is certain in the period prior to Constantine; all the primitive martyria analyzed by the author, in the Rhineland (Bonn, Xanten), in Africa (Tipasa), in Dalmatia (Salona-Kapljuc), date from between the third and fifth centuries, but none bears a precise date. Nor is it possible to assign all (or indeed any) of the martyria in the Holy Land visited by Etheria in the later fourth century to the pre-Constantinian era with any degree of certainty. We are hardly on safer ground with regard to the sanctuaries assigned to the age of Constantine and to the following century; true, the date of the church of the Nativity seems to be established, and Grabar rightly questions the Constantinian character of the transept of St. John Lateran,[5] but the Rotunda of the Anastasis has also been assigned to the period of Constantine's sons, and not on bad grounds, I feel. Regarding St. Peter's in Rome, the recent excavations suggest that the building, while begun under Constantine, was but little advanced at the time of the Emperor's death. On the other hand, the relation of the *hemisphairion* to the basilica of the Holy Sepulchre could perhaps be clarified somewhat more precisely: why should it not have risen from the outset at the very end of the nave, supported by twelve columns and sheltering the site of the Invention of the Cross, a solution once suggested by Kenneth J. Conant, just as at Bethlehem the octagon rose at the end of the nave over the Grotto of the Nativity?

Contestable points are unavoidable in a work of the scope of M. Grabar's, just as it is difficult to keep factual mistakes from creeping in with the material culled from more specialized researches. To begin with one caused by an error of my own (1934), the assumption that there was an original transept at S. Lorenzo fuori le mura must be discarded. Likewise, Sta. Maria Maggiore (I am limiting myself to my Roman bailiwick) need not even by implication be assigned a date prior to the fifth century, nor was its transept added in the fifth century "at the time the relic of the Manger was installed here" (Grabar, I, 298, 316): the nave is definitely fifth century, the transept dates from 1290, and the relic of the Manger turns up for the first time in the seventh century. S. Pancrazio, founded in the fifth (not the fourth) century, in its present state dates from the seventh century, the martyrium-basilica of SS. Nereo, Achilleo, and Petronilla from the mid-sixth century. The plan of SS. Apostoli was not that of an inscribed Greek cross; S. Martino ai Monti received its present *patrocinium* not in the fifth, but only in the ninth century.

Such secondary errors can easily be eliminated in a revised edition. In any case, methodological questions are of greater importance in the evaluation of M. Grabar's work, and I am going to select a few such questions, all of them incidental, but pertinent to the main problem.

The first concerns the use of reproductions or descriptions as a basis for the visual reconstruction of buildings, late antique (both pagan and Christian) or medieval. Clearly, prior to the Renaissance, such representations must not be interpreted as true-to-life renditions of the model in the modern sense of the term. Rather, the prototype is dissected into its constituent elements and these are reassembled in a new order, determined more often than not by factors quite extraneous to the architectural organism. Hence, the martyria on the Alexandrian carpet formerly in the Kaiser-Friedrich Museum may or may not have been two-storied structures above ground; the flights of steps leading to what seem to be upper stories may have been on the outside, as indeed they were at the Anastasius Mausoleum at Salona-Marusinac and in the mausolea of Pecs and La Alberca; but they may as well stand for inside stairs descending to subterranean tomb chambers. For the same reason, I feel that the reconstruction of martyria based on representations in the Menologium of Basil II or in the ninth-century manuscript, Milan, *Ambros.* 49-50 (Grabar, I, 263, fig. 20), must necessarily remain hypothetical.

Architectural representations of the sixteenth century, on the other hand, are indeed intended to reproduce the model faithfully. But it seems to me that more often than not the architects and archaeologists of the Renaissance were inclined to intersperse their surveys of extant structures with plans and elevations which are at best free variations on Roman themes. M. Grabar appears to be certain that Montano's plans are not in this category; that therefore the types transmitted in his *Scelta di varij tempietti* can be taken to represent Roman funerary monuments and thus prove the general derivation of Christian martyria from pagan mausolea. Still, one cannot help feeling a bit uneasy about a number of M. Grabar's examples: of the two "tempietti" reproduced in his figs. 30 and 31, the first looks like a free reproduction of SS. Cosma e Damiano, the second like a cross between the temple of Venus and Roma, and the entrance rotunda of SS. Cosma e Damiano, the so-called Temple of Romulus. Thus it seems difficult to see them as forecasting Christian structures of the type of the Nativity at Bethlehem; the less so since only in the second of these plans is the rotunda placed behind the longitudinal hall. Again, the combination of a circular aisle with a series of triconch chapels (Grabar, I, fig. 69) would seem to be a free combination of a structure resembling Sta. Costanza and of Brunelleschi's S. Maria degli Angeli in Florence. It should therefore not be enumerated among the possible late antique prototypes of Early Christian martyria and Byzantine and Armenian churches. And while one of Montano's plans (Grabar, I, fig. 99) is no doubt close to the crypt of St. Peter's as it appears on Drei's plan of 1608 (I, p. 475), it should perhaps be made clear that this plan represents the crypt as remodelled in the sixteenth century, so that Montano's plan again arouses some suspicion. M. Grabar, in a footnote (I, 100 ff.), promises a critical edition of Montano's work, and until then we shall want to reserve judgment. This much, however, can be said even now: in none among the controllable Roman monuments have such weird combinations survived, and one cannot escape the suspicion that Montano often dealt somewhat arbitrarily with the existing remains.

The perhaps somewhat exaggerated skepticism of this reviewer applies equally to literary descriptions as a basis of reconstruction. Every excavation of a building "known" from descriptions has been a warning in that respect, from Paulinus' basilicas at Cimitile to S. Lorenzo in Rome. In my opinion, this holds even more for descriptive formulas, such as *instar* (or *in modum*) *crucis*. The terms were apparently applied to all kinds of cross-shapes alike: witness the indices of Schlosser's *Schriftquellen* and of Mortet's *Recueil de textes* or, for that matter, the group of fourth-century churches in Milan as listed by M. Grabar (I, 423). Investigation in the years since the war has shown S. Simpliciano to have had a T-cross plan; the others, S. Eufemia and S. Eustorgio, remain to be investigated. In any case, it seems hazardous to conclude from the mere formula that every structure laid out *in modum crucis* was necessarily a martyrium.

Regarding the fundamental issues of M. Grabar's thesis, the reader will occasionally be left with one or another unanswered question. For the pre-Constantinian and Constantinian periods, the distinction between church buildings of basilican type, designed for the regular Eucharistic synaxes of the congregation, and commemorative martyria of central plan is fundamentally sound. Also, it is no doubt true that by and large these types were gradually adapted to their opposite functions only in the centuries to follow, centralized structures absorbing regular Eucharistic services and the martyr cult absorbing basilican elements. But one wonders whether in M. Grabar's deductions the boundaries are not somewhat sharply drawn at times, particularly for the Constantinian period, and whether these elements did not frequently intermingle even then. M. Grabar would not deny this regarding, for example, St. Peter's in Rome, where the transept has martyrium character, yet served from the outset as the site for the regular celebration of the Mass. Yet, it would seem that the basilica near the Holy Sepulchre is another case in point and that for this very reason it offers much resistance to any explanation on a single plane. After all, Eusebius designated just this basilica as the martyrium. True, this designation was due in all likelihood to the fact that under the *hemisphairion* the building sheltered the site of the Invention of the Cross; but at the same time this very martyrium served, certainly in the days of Etheria and possibly from the outset, the regular synaxes of the congregation as the local cathedral. M. Lassus has similarly pointed out, though as a probable exception, that Constantine's church of the Holy Apostles in Constantinople was designed for the regular celebration of the Mass.[6] It would then appear that in a number of cases regular services were held as early as the fourth century in structures designated and laid out as martyria.

Starting from the distinctly separate functions of regular synaxes and martyr cult, M. Grabar is at times forced to contrast the corresponding architectural types with some sharpness. This introduces a danger which certainly is not great with a master like M. Grabar, but might become perilous in over-zealous disciples: that of concluding all too freely from the known plan as to the unknown function of the building. M. Grabar would be the first to acknowledge the fact that in the great majority of cases the original function of the early structure is in the dark, and at times this reviewer would be inclined to even greater skepticism than the author. The attempt to present the Golden Octagon of Antioch, because of its centralized plan, as the successor to the pagan city-*heroon* and hence as a martyrium has not convinced me; no document ever mentions it as anything but the cathedral designed for the regular services of the congregation.[7] Likewise S. Lorenzo in Milan (fourth century), despite its tetraconch shape and despite the frequency of the plan among sixth-century martyria in the East, need not have been a martyrium to begin with: the *patrocinium* of the Roman martyr is of late date, and no relic seems to be connected with the building.[8] Would it not seem that, in the fourth century at any rate centralized types were used not only for martyria but under other specific circumstances as well? In this connection, M. Grabar himself refers time and again to the baptisteries, which like the martyria were evolved since the fourth century from funeral architecture, both pagan and Chistian. This is no doubt correct, regardless of whether the reasons for this transfer lie in the meaning of the baptistery as an image of Heaven (Grabar), as the Fountain of Life (Underwood), or as the tomb of the old Adam and the symbol of his rebirth in Christ (Krautheimer). But is it not possible that other currents of Roman architecture also contributed to the formation of Christian centralized edifices? At least as a working hypothesis, it might be kept in mind that in the fourth century both the Octagon of Antioch and S. Lorenzo in Milan were founded (the first certainly, the second possibly) under the auspices of the Imperial court. On the other hand, centralized throne rooms had apparently not been uncommon in the Imperial palaces of the third and fourth centuries,[9] and their survival, if nothing else, is demonstrated by the *Chrysotriklinos* in the Sacred Palace in Constantinople. It has been maintained that this specific throne room exerted a considerable influence, particularly on Aix-la-Chapelle, and on Western church architecture generally.[10] In any case, it seems worthwhile to explore the possible impact of such palace halls on centralized churches erected by the courts, from the Antioch Octagon to the Palatine Chapel at Aix-la-Chapelle, and to combine such a study with an investigation of their character as martyria plain and simple (Grabar, I, 559 ff.).

A measure of simplification is essential in any book dealing with fundamental problems, and the intelligent reader will keep this factor in mind. Fundamental as the cult of relics, and hence the martyrium, is for the formation of ecclesiastical architecture in the East and West, it is not always easy to identify those elements of Western church architecture that can claim direct descent from the early martyria and their forerunners in pagan funeral architecture. The annular crypts, beginning with the late sixth-century crypt of Old St. Peter's in Rome, are a case in point. M. Grabar tends to derive them straight from Roman sepulchral structures with closed and vaulted exterior ambulatories. But is it really true that such independent martyria were introduced directly into the interior of the basilica, thus imparting to the latter the character of a "martyrium basilica"? To be specific, was a mausoleum such as the one presented by Montano (Grabar, I, fig. 99) the model for the very crypt of St. Peter's (I, 475)? Is it not rather the result of a longer and more complex development in which many an element intermingles, including not only such preliminary forms as the "high crypt" of Stobi (I, 453 ff., 476), but also the corridors embedded in the foundations of the amphitheatrical *synthronoi* in the apses of St. John at Ephesos and St. John of the Studion at Constantinople? While the former are no doubt directly linked to the cult of relics, the latter would seem to have the additional, or even the sole, purpose of regulating the processions of the congregation during regular services, rather than just the flow of pilgrims. Hence, the martyrium would appear to form at best one of several roots from which spring the annular crypts of Western Europe. In any case, by the time these latter spread from St. Peter's in Rome to the rest of the Occident in the course of the seventh, eighth, and ninth centuries, the link with the Early Christian martyria had become somewhat tenuous. On the other hand, it seems to me that a secondary source, the crypt of St. Peter's in Rome, had become the mainspring of this development.

The same may be said of the towers, square or round, that rise above the transepts of Carolingian churches, surmounting the High Altar. True, the idea of marking the site of the relic by a towerlike structure may have originated in martyria and ultimately in Roman tomb structures. But by the time the motif penetrated into Western architecture, it had passed through centuries of development in the East which may have obliterated the original source even further than M. Grabar's careful words (I, 414) appear to suggest. The two tall towers of the large church of Saint-Riquier, one rising from the transept, the other from the *Westwerk*, are in our opinion at best distantly related to the rotunda of Hexham and to the Mary Chapel at Saint-Riquier (I, 413 ff.); nor do the wings of transept and *Westwerk* compare to the porticus of Hexham. The entire arrangement at the east end of the large church of Saint-Riquier (tower, transept wings, chancel, and galleries) forms a complex unit and its ancestry includes, it would seem, a number of diversified elements: the dome or tower above the High Altar (witness Koja Kalessi or the Ilissos church); towered cross churches as reflected in Tomarza in Asia Minor; cross transept churches with galleries such as Hagios Demetrios in Salonica; and even the column screens that cut off the ends of the transept of Old St. Peter's in Rome. In brief, the original source, the martyrium, is hardly sufficient to explain the crossing tower of Saint-Riquier as a historical phenomenon. M. Grabar is fully cognizant of the complexity of the historical process. But since misunderstandings might arise, it seems important to rely on further research to clear up the specific family ties of a motif such as the crossing tower or the annular crypt and to establish, beyond their general origin within the realm of the cult of relics, their direct sources within Eastern or Western architecture. At the same time, it seems to me, some emphasis might be placed on the fact that in the course of time such elements as the crossing tower tend to lose most or all of their links with the *ambiente* from which they may have sprung. The ties between form and significance, indissoluble as they are at the beginning of the development, become tenuous in the end, and at times the reader might want to sever them before M. Grabar is ready for that operation.

To establish such family trees within the broad framework outlined by M. Grabar appears to be a task of prime importance. Within the large circle of martyria and structures linked to the cult of relics and venerated sites, specific groups can be worked out and possibly traced to their direct sources. The annular crypts appear to be one such group. Another is represented by the martyria dedicated to the Virgin: one group in the West, among them the Mary Chapel at Saint-Riquier, seems to me to derive not just from the martyrium type in general, but specifically from the Pantheon in Rome, *Sancta Maria Rotunda*. Another group, in the East, may go back to the Tomb of the Virgin in the Valley of Josaphat and may have penetrated the West either directly or by way of an intermediary secondary source, perhaps in Constantinople. Other family trees would clarify the relationship of the various transept types, a crucial element within M. Grabar's picture of the origins of Western church architecture under the impact of the cult of relics.

Only a work of fundamental importance can form the starting point for fruitful discussions and M. Grabar's, needless to say, is such a book. It comes at the end of a half-century during which new material has been accumulating in the field of Early Christian and Byzantine scholarship. M. Grabar's work is manifest proof that the time has come for attempts to synthesize this material and to reappraise our approach to the art of the first millennium of our era, while continuing to collect material and to sift and check carefully what has been found so far. This reappraisal will eventually lead to a better understanding of Early Christian and early medieval architecture, both in the East and in the West. The great lines as laid down by M. Grabar will form a key pattern in this reappraisal and are bound to have a decisive influence on our approach. It is a rare pleasure for a reviewer to deal with a work of such importance to the fundamental problems of his own field. I should like therefore to express to M. Grabar both my admiration and my gratitude.

Notes

1. R. Krautheimer, "Introduction to an Iconography of Medieval Architecture," above, pp. 115 ff.; K. Lehmann, "The Dome of Heaven," *AB,* XXVIII (1945), 1 ff.; J. Lassus, *Les sanctuaries chrétiens de la Syrie* (Paris, 1947); G. Bandmann, *Mittelalterliche Architektur als Bedeutungsträger* (Berlin, 1951).

2. A. Grabar, "Christian Architecture, East and West," *Archaeology,* II (1949), 95 ff.

3. *Ibid.,* p. 101.

4. Cf. Lehmann, *op. cit.*

5. In the latter church, the original foundation walls across the transept open-ings, uncovered in the 1930's by E. Josi, suggest the idea either of continued aisles or of a tripartite transept. But see now R. Krautheimer and S. Corbett, "The Constantinian Basilica of the Lateran," above, pp. 21 ff.

6. Lassus, *op. cit.,* pp. 101ff.

7. *Ibid.,* p. 109.

8. See A. Calderini, G. Chierici, and C. Cecchelli, *La basilica di S. Lorenzo Maggiore in Milano* (Milan, 1951).

9. Cf. Lehmann, *op. cit.*

10. H. Fichtenau, *Byzanz und die Pfalz zu Aachen* (Vienna, 1951).

THE TWIN CATHEDRAL AT PAVIA*

FOLIO 2 of the Opicinus manuscript in the Vatican (Pal. lat. 1993) represents, as Salomon has shown, the bell tower and the two churches of the twin cathedral at Pavia: to the left the summer church Sto. Stefano, to the right the winter church Sta. Maria Maggiore, or del Popolo (Fig. 60).[1] Both are aisled basilicas; both carry in the east a strong octagonal tower, encircled by a dwarf gallery and crowned by a peaked, pyramidal roof; and both terminate in a slender semi-circular apse. The larger church to the left faces the square with a simple high sham-façade. Articulated by two buttresses, it opens in three portals, one in the center and a smaller one in each side bay. The center bay, moreover, has two pairs of rectangular windows surmounted by two oculi and a cruciform opening in the gable. Another oculus can be recognized in the clerestory to the right. The façade of the smaller church is basilican and has only one portal, surmounted by two arched windows, two oculi and a cruciform opening; its right side aisle, articulated by robust buttresses, shows two arched windows below and three in the clerestory. The center window is placed in a curious projection of the wall which rises somewhat above the roof. At the end of the nave, the right arm of a transept protrudes; the crossing tower rises above it, behind is the apse. Like the campanile, both buildings are articulated by simple corbel-table friezes. Lion figures emerge from the façades below; sheds with lean-to roofs surround the whole complex; in the open square stands on a column the equestrian statue of the Regisole.

This depiction of the cathedral of Pavia generally agrees with other representations of the building (or rather, buildings) which have come down to us in old city maps such as the map of L. Curtius and J. Maius of 1600,[2] or the somewhat later one of Mattheus Florinus,[3] or the map of 1654.[4] It also tallies with the description of Opicinus.[5] Furthermore, remains of both buildings are still preserved. On the southwest corner of the campanile remains of the façade of Sto. Stefano are still seen. Likewise, in a court south of the present cathedral (which in 1487 replaced Sto. Stefano) remains of the right aisle, transept and crypt of Sta. Maria Maggiore have survived. Much larger parts of both edifices stood until the end of the nineteenth century. They are known from short descrip-

---

*Translated by Joachim Gaehde from Appendix to *Opicinus de Canistris; Weltbild und Bekenntnisse eines avignonischen Klerikers des 14. Jhs.*, by R. Salomon (*Studies of the Warburg Institute*, I, 1936), pp. 325–37.

tions [6] and above all from the excellent account given by Camillo Brambilla and accompanied by a plan (Fig. 61).[7] As these remains and the drawing point clearly to the first half of the twelfth century for the time of construction of both churches, it may seem that the above short description has exhausted the importance of the drawing for the history of architecture.

However, one need not be satisfied that easily. On closer view, the drawing shows several curious features. There is first the remarkable width of the larger church, particularly conspicuous in its contrast to the narrowness of the smaller one. The reason for this extraordinary width becomes clear when one draws on the accounts and the preserved groundplan of the old cathedral of Sto. Stefano. They show that the old building was five-aisled,[8] and it is this that the draftsman of the leaf seems to have wanted to express by the exceptional width he gave to its façade. Few other details are given in this drawing. Only in the clerestory is an oculus indicated, a detail that cannot be verified; but the draftsman showed neither the decorative arcades of the façade which are firmly documented by the descriptions, nor the pilaster strips which are still preserved, nor the dwarf galleries.[9] And, of course, the drawing does not say anything about the interior of the building. But from the older accounts and the ground plan of Brambilla we learn that the aisles had responds on the walls and that the free-standing piers between the first and the second aisle had engaged half-columns in the arcade openings; these latter were converted into rectangular piers with rectangular responds only in the sixteenth century. From these piers and the wall responds one can infer that the aisles were covered by groin vaults, and this is also evident from the description of Opicinus.[10] The aisle wall of Sto. Stefano communicated through large arcades with the neighboring church of Sta. Maria del Popolo. As to Sta. Maria, as it appears in Opicinus' drawing, one is particularly struck by the strange projection which rises high and interrupts the roof line of the nave near its middle. At first glance it looks as if the draftsman had merely let his pen wander. But this seeming playfulness has sound reasons. Indeed, in trying to reconstruct Sta. Maria Maggiore in accordance with the well-preserved remains, one quickly comes to the conclusion that the rising projection is a feature in an exceptional and complex whole which the draftsman wished to record as curious and extraordinary. Indeed, already Dartein and Kingsley Porter have seen from the remains of the building that the nave bays of Sta. Maria del Popolo were not arranged in an even sequence as is usual in Romanesque churches: a first, broad bay covered by a cross-ribbed vault was followed by two narrower ones; the fourth bay was broad again, and finally the fifth, narrow one preceded the square bay of the crossing with its transept wings, and the apse.[11] The rhythm in the ground plan produced an elevation in which the broad and high nave bays opened onto raised barrel-vaulted aisle bays, while the narrow nave bays corresponded to groin-vaulted aisle bays of normal height. Further, while all the nave bays were rib vaulted, the springing of the vaults in the broad bays was placed somewhat higher. Thus the spatial volumes were laid out in a complex rhythm and their masses imparted to the exterior the aspect of a rich grouping (Fig. 62). The transverse gables of the high barrel-vaulted aisle bays rose far above the sloping roofs of the groin-vaulted bays. Touching with their ridges almost the eaves of the nave, the high aisle bays became pseudotransepts, as it were, inserted between the lower bays of the aisles and holding an intermediate position between these latter, the nave and the transept proper. This complicated silhouette was further enhanced by a slight rise in the upper wall and roof of the nave at the points where the pseudotransepts abutted. The motif of the transept with its crossing tower was echoed in the nave's progression toward the façade. Of this multiform and rich grouping, the author of the Opicinus drawing noted only the elevation of the nave roof in the broader bays above that in the narrower bays; also this feature he marked only once, while actually two of the nave bays were broad and high. Thus he reduced the complex rhythm of the grouping to a simple formula. He was concerned less with copying something seen than with a short-hand notation of a few peculiar features.

We do not know the origin of the pseudotransept motif, until now the only known instance in Lombardy. A similar concept is hinted at earlier in the third building of Cluny.[12] The growing cities of Lombardy had become a focus of artistic life since the late eleventh century. Impulses from everywhere met here: above all, of course from France, and they were transmitted, enriched and transformed in every direction. Thus it seems not impossible that the idea of the pseudotransept could have come from Cluny to Pavia. The migration of the motif from Lombardy to the North can be followed more easily: it appears between 1143 and 1153 in the church of Klosterrath[13] and, at about the same time in especially clear form, in the destroyed church of St. Mary's at Utrecht, which is known from countless drawings and pictures by Pieter Saenredam,[14] and in the church of Our Lady at Maestricht. The connection between Rhenish and Lombard architecture, one of the most manifold and fruitful among the many reciprocal movements between artistic centers of the high Middle Ages, becomes once more evident in an unusual motif, and the hitherto obscure report that Klosterrath was designed "scemate langobardino"[15] assumes new meaning.

More important than these facts of pure architectural history may be considerations—suggested rather than represented by our sheet—that belong to an "iconography of architecture": an urgently wanted and still unwritten study of architectural monuments according to their meaning. It is, after all, most unusual for two buildings to stand side by side on the cathedral square of Pavia, to be known jointly as "the Cathedral,"[16] and of which one, Sto. Stefano, is recorded as *basilica aestivalis*, the other, Sta. Maria Maggiore, as *basilica hiemalis*. Now, this coupling of two churches which together form the cathedral, and their designation as summer and winter churches is not infrequent in Lombardy. Kingsley Porter has pointed this out briefly,[17] and Monneret de Villard has compiled the instances hitherto known, listing Milan, Brescia and Como.[18] In all these cases, two churches jointly form the cathedral,[19] a *basilica aestivalis,* and a *basilica hiemalis.* Como has to be excluded as an obviously late descendant, its winter-summer cathedral being recorded only since the thirteenth century.[20] For the other three places, however, the bipartition of the cathedral into a summer and winter church is mentioned far earlier. In Pavia itself it is found for the first time between 912 and 924,[21] long before the edifice depicted on the Opicinus drawing was built; in Milan in 879; [22] in Brescia as early as 838.[23] It is self-evident that the winter services were held in the *basilica hiemalis* and the summer services in the *basilica aestivalis.* In Milan the move into the *basilica aestivalis* took place on Whitsaturday, the move into the *basilica hiemalis* on the day of its consecration, the third Sunday in October.[24] We do not know when the move occurred in the other places nor do we have literary evidence about the purpose and origin of this arrangement.

Concerning the origin of the bipartition of the cathedral, the designation of the buildings as *basilica hiemalis* and the *basilica aestivalis* thus appears in documents of the late ninth century; and this very much as a matter of course and not at all as if it were a reference to a new and remarkable arrangement. In fact, earlier sources occasionally refer to the cathedral in these Lombard cities as to two neighboring and associated buildings. They are consequently not new foundations of the ninth century. The two Milanese churches Sta. Maria Maior, later named *basilica hiemalis,* and Sta. Tecla, later known as *basilica aestivalis,* are certainly treated as two connected parts of the cathedral by 803–813.[25] The two churches of Brescia, the *ecclesia maior Sancti Petri,* later called *basilica aestivalis,* and the *ecclesia maior Sanctae Dei Genetricis,* the later *basilica hiemalis,* must also precede their first mention as winter and summer church. The church dedicated to Mary is recorded in 774 and by 838 had been the see of the bishops of Brescia already for centuries.[26] In Pavia, finally, the case is similar. Sto. Stefano must have existed before 680 when a baptistery was built nearby,[27] and Sta. Maria del Popolo was erected between 712 and 736 at the latest, as is indicated by an inscription found in 1709 and since lost. The church may even be earlier: the tenor of the inscription is ambiguous in this respect.[28] In any case, it is certain that the building of twin cathedrals, whether or not designated as *basilica hiemalis* and *aestivalis,* was usual in Lombardy. Supporting this conclusion is the fact that, besides the four mentioned buildings which are specified as winter and summer churches since the ninth century, other twin cathedrals are to be found which are not linked to the designation *basilica hiemalis* and *aestivalis.* How common the construction of twin cathedrals was is particularly clear at Bergamo. In 774 two cathedrals are mentioned: S. Alessandro with the sister edifice S. Pietro, both situated outside town; and, within the city, the twin churches of S. Vincenzo (originally S. Agnese) and Sta. Maria.[29] The quarrel for primacy between the competing twin cathedrals was resolved in 1189 by a union of both in a "double twin cathedral" despite their location at two distant points of the enlarged twelfth-century city.[30] In Verona, excavations next to the present cathedral have unearthed two associated buildings which are precursors of the existing cathedral.[31] Documents, however, are lacking.

All these edifices, no matter whether recorded as *basilica hiemalis* and *aestivalis* or not, are therefore twin buildings which form the cathedral only in unison. If one follows the architectural type of the twin building, one finds that it belongs to concepts of planning current since the first centuries of Early Christian building. Twin churches are but one example from the rich treasury of types which Early Christian architecture since its beginnings dispersed over the *Orbis Christianus*. They are but one special instance of late antique architectural thought which, since the first century, readily manifested itself in building complexes, not single buildings in isolation. Characteristic of the manifold possibilities of such late antique and Early Christian group formation is the grouping around the body of the church proper of subordinate structures: consistories and consignatories, baptisteries and mausolea, atria and side courts, martyria and chapels, sometimes placed along axes, sometimes spreading to all sides. Out of the abundance of monuments one may name at random the Syrian Kalat Siman or the North African Tebessa, the Dalmatian Salona (Fig. 64), the Transjordanian Gerasa and the Roman Old St. Peter's (Fig. 79); or, as a last offshoot of these late antique architectural concepts, the Carolingian building group of Ingelheim or the Minster at Aix-la-Chapelle with its flanking subsidiary churches. The duplication of edifices is only one of the possibilities within this rich diversity.

Twin churches could hitherto be localized only in Istria, Dalmatia and Carinthia. But the circle is extended when one looks closer: the Lombard examples can be added [32] and other regions as well; in Africa the twin basilica of Djémila has become known in recent years,[33] in Bosnia, in the Dalmatian hinterland, one finds the type at Zenica; [34] and, finally, a number of twin churches are found in Constantinople and Greece since the sixth century. With this enlargement of the material a sharper differentiation of the type will become possible and an attempt can be made to establish its development. At the outset we have to exclude two types which are only peripherally connected with the genuine twin church: the type which arranges two or more buildings on an axis behind one another (Menas basilica [Fig. 16],[35] Gerasa Cathedral [36]) and the type which places a small central or longitudinal chapel next to the large basilica (Dermech,[37] Alaja Jaila,[38] S. Giusto in Trieste [39]). Essential to the genuine twin church is the arrangement of two approximately equivalent structures parallel or almost parallel to each other and separated only by a narrow passage-like court into which a baptistery or chapel was sometimes inserted. If possible, a common narthex or common atrium is placed before the buildings. As far as can be seen at present, the type seems to have originated in Istria.[40] There, since the earliest fourth century, we find double buildings in Aquileia (Fig. 63),[41] Parenzo,[42] Nesactium,[43] and, later in the Carinthian and Hungarian hinterland, in Hemmaberg,[44] Virunum [45] and Kekkút.[46] These early double buildings show all the formal characteristics of the type: two nearly equal structures placed parallel side by side, separated by a narrow court and provided with a common atrium. In function, however, the two buildings seem not entirely equal; only one appears to have been reserved for the service of the Eucharist. Indeed, if one can trust the archaeological findings and their interpretation, only one seems to have contained an altar. The other is generally thought to have been a consignatorium, an assembly room for confirmation.[47] The dedications of these first twin cathedrals have not come down to us. Thus only the formal twin character can be ascertained for these early buildings of the fourth century and the question of their function cannot be solved with finality. However, with the spread of the type since the early fifth century it becomes evident that the two buildings also have sacral equivalence. Next to the Basilica Urbana at Salona (ca. 350, Fig. 64) there was built in the first years of the fifth century the Basilica Episcopalis, which has the character of a proper and equally important church.[48] At Djémila a grandiose new church was placed in 411 alongside a smaller one which had been there already in the fourth century. To be sure, the second building is later than the first, and in this instance one can say only that the image of the double edifice was familiar and readily adopted. But since the early fifth century, twin buildings were also erected in one campaign, both structures similar in form, and both with the unequivocal characteristics of a church.[49] In this context belong the Anastasius complex at Salona (Fig. 11),[50] the churches of SS. Sergius and Bacchus and SS. Peter and Paul in Constantinople (ca. 530),[51] the two basilicas at Grado, i.e., the Cathedral and Sta. Maria delle Grazie (571–586),[52] the double church at Zenica, probably S. Michele in Monte near Pola,[53] and perhaps the Cathedral and S. Tommaso at Pola.[54] All these are genuine twin churches. One is the bishop's or community church and dedicated to Mary or to another great saint, the other carries preferably the title of a martyr. This is the case with the double structure of SS. Sergius and Bacchus and SS. Peter and Paul in Constantinople, with Sta. Eufemia and Sta. Maria delle Grazie in Grado, with the Anastasius complex at Salona, and with the churches of Sta. Maria and S. Tommaso in Pola. The chapel of S. Mauro in Parenzo lies still today next to the cathedral of Sta. Maria which, by its situation and therefore probably also historically, replaced the northern hall of the twin structures of the fourth and fifth centuries excavated below. This type of genuine twin structure normally consisting of two basilican buildings, of which one is dedicated to a martyr, appears at least since the fifth century.

Beside it is found an older type in which the large basilica proper is accompanied by a smaller, usually centralized, mausoleum or martyrium. This older type was formed already since the beginning of Christian architecture and the prototype of the combination of the basilica with a small mausoleum or martyrium is in all likelihood the building group at the Holy Sepulchre in Jerusalem.[55] This type appears further in Milan where at the end of the fifth century the martyrium S. Vittore is placed next to the older basilica S. Ambrogio; in Verona where Sta. Teuteria stands behind SS. Apostoli;[56] in Dere-Ashy,[57] in Alaja Jaila,[58] in

Miletus, Trieste, Zara, Hippo;[59] and it survives into the high Middle Ages (S. Satiro near S. Celso in Milan, Sta. Fosca near the Cathedral of Torcello). Considering this development, one comes to the conclusion that the genuine twin churches of the fifth and sixth centuries represent a fusion of two traditions: in regions where twin structures were already a common form (and that seems to have been not only in Istria but in the Byzantine orbit in general), the small martyrium was readily exchanged for a second basilican structure which took over the title of the martyr. This is the type of genuine twin church that spread into different regions of the *Orbis Christianus* in the fifth and sixth centuries and remained current in the Byzantine sphere of influence into the fourteenth century,[60] although not always realized with equal strictness in function and form.

To this group of twin churches of the fifth and sixth centuries belong also the Lombard monuments. Of course, only traces of this connection are found in the extant churches at Brescia, Milan, Bergamo and Verona. For Pavia, the drawing of the Opicinus manuscript transmits only the state of the twelfth-century, not of any earlier, buildings. While thus only a medieval or even Baroque reconstruction is preserved, there is, as has already been shown, documentary proof for predecessors to all these buildings already from the earliest Middle Ages. In Brescia, Verona and Pavia, remains of these earlier structures are also tangible, known through excavations or through transmission of accounts and ground plans. For instance, in the medieval structure of Sto. Stefano, depicted on the Opicinus drawing, remains of a pre-medieval columnar basilica were discovered about the middle of the past century.[61] Brambilla records two of the columns in his plan (Fig. 61) and he mentions that two others had been found earlier. One of the two which he saw is still incorporated in the western pier between the two southern aisles of the medieval structure; the other remains to the west of this pier in the wall of a Baroque corridor. A corresponding column walled into the western pier between the two northern aisles was uncovered in 1894.[62] Thus three columns of the oldest structure are preserved, and from their position between the two outer aisles, it is clear that this oldest building already must have been a five-aisled columnar basilica. Little is known of the details of this oldest basilica of Sto. Stefano. One capital is described by Brambilla and this description allows one to identify it still today in the Museo Civico of Pavia.[63] It is to be dated into the late sixth century and the high impost block that Brambilla saw above it points to the same date.[64] The five-aisled plan of the church would favor a still earlier date because five-aisled buildings are not known in Italy after the end of the fourth century. After St. Peter's, S. Giovanni in Laterano, S. Paolo f.l.m. in Rome, and after the Cathedral of Ravenna, no five-aisled buildings can be found there. Only in Africa do they survive into the sixth century. In the Occident the idea reemerges only in the eleventh century, probably in connection with the renaissance concepts of the Cluniac reform, in Cluny III, S. Abbondio in Como and Novara.

While the outlines of the martyr basilica of the original double structure of Pavia can thus still be established, no pre-medieval remains of the sister edifice of Sta. Maria Maggiore have been preserved—except for the account of the inscription of 712-736. However, one important feature of its layout can yet be ascertained: the left side aisle of .Sta. Maria cannot originally have been connected with the right side aisle of Sto. Stefano through large arcades as it has been since the twelfth century.[65] As shown by Brambilla's plan, the left side aisle was unusually wide, more than two meters wider than the right side aisle, and nearly as wide as the nave. This can mean only that it was widened so unusually in the rebuilding of the twelfth century to effect an immediate connection with Sto. Stefano. In other words, the early medieval structure of Sta. Maria —to which the inscription of 712–736 belongs (as either a foundation or furnishing account)—must be assumed to have had side aisles of equal width, and a narrow pasage of about two meters width separating it from Sto. Stefano. The two original structures thus stood parallel alongside each other, separated by a narrow alley and they still had a common atrium, sixty meters wide, in the fourteenth century.[66] The Cathedral of Pavia in its first state was therefore a genuine twin cathedral, and at least one of its churches goes back to the Early Christian period.

The same layout can be established for Brescia and, while the date of the first building of Pavia must necessarily remain insecure, one is on firmer ground for the dating of Brescia. In the seventeenth century the present Duomo Nuovo in Brescia, S. Pietro (beg. 1604), was built to replace a three-aisled columnar basilica of the same name, known throughout the Middle Ages as S. Pietro in Dom or as *basilica aestivalis*. This older cathedral, while smaller than the present one, had the same orientation, and in its nave it had thirteen arcades carried by columns.[67] The time of its origin is unknown. But below it was an older building, remnants of whose floor mosaics were found during the construction of the new cathedral in the seventeenth century.[68] The older building was evidently the original cathedral. Next to the new cathedral, and therefore also to its two antecedents, the so-called Duomo Vecchio still stands today, a rotunda built in the twelfth century. Excavations of the seventeenth and nineteenth centuries [69] have disclosed below its pavement a single-naved edifice,[70] the old *basilica hiemalis Sanctae Mariae*. This church stands parallel to the new cathedral and its two precursors, and it lies definitely on the same level as the remains of the oldest three-aisled building of S. Pietro. From the position of the buildings, approximately established for S. Pietro and securely for Sta. Maria, one can conclude that both were separated by a narrow court. Documentary sources testify to the existence, also in the medieval successors of the two churches, of this court which contained, as in the Istrian and Dalmatian twin structures, a small chapel, SS. Crisanto e Daria.[71] Also, the two churches certainly had always had a common atrium. Thus Brescia, like Pavia, had a genuine twin cathedral, and one may recall that the literary sources testify to this since 838. But the building must in fact have been much older. Of the mosaics found in both churches in 1625,[72] those below the rotunda were finally uncovered in 1896.[73] Their style points to a fifth- or sixth-century date, as do the dedicatory inscriptions of the mosaics which record donations of certain parts of the floor. Another dedicatory inscription, entirely identical in content and form, was found during the excavations of the seventeenth century in the floor of the oldest structure of S. Pietro.[74] Furthermore, all these inscriptions agree exactly with corresponding ones in Parenzo, Cilli, Pola and Aquileia, that is, in fourth- to sixth-century Istrian twin churches.[75] The names of the donors also point to an early, at least pre-Langobard period: they are Greek, Latin and Oriental; none is Germanic. Brescia is therefore an old, and Early Christian example of the genuine double basilica on Lombard soil, a clear parallel to the Istrian and Dalmatian twin churches.

The same is true of the building group excavated below the cloisters of the Cathedral of Verona. One is a basilican structure, more than 47 m. long and 28.20 m. wide, with 7 m. wide side aisles and a 10 m. wide nave; the other has a single nave of about 30 m. length. Their axes are not quite parallel.[76] In both buildings extensive remains of floor mosaics have been uncovered. Ornament and coloration seem to indicate that they still belong in the early fifth century [77] and there are again dedicatory inscriptions, as in the double cathedral of Brescia. Thus Verona also offers an example of an Early Christian twin structure.

The Early Christian buildings of Milan and Bergamo have disappeared without trace. But of Milan at least one can say with certainty that Sta. Tecla was a regular basilica of almost 90 m. length, that it was situated at the north side of the present Cathedral square, and that the building already existed before 451–462.[78] Nothing definite is known of the time of the foundation of the church of Sta. Maria below the western bays of the present Cathedral except that it stood there by 803–813,[79] and was mentioned long before in missals of the fifth century. The formation of a proper twin cathedral at Milan must thus antedate the ninth century. Indeed, the aforementioned Milanese missal of the fifth century [80] prescribes in its rubrics two Masses to be read in all churches of the city after the example of the Cathedral. Milan must therefore already have had a twin cathedral in the fifth century.

Twin churches thus were known in the entire region of Lombardy by the fifth and sixth centuries, and the connection with contemporary twin churches in Dalmatia and Istria, and with earlier twin cathedrals in and near Aquileia is evident. The fact that one of the paired structures in Verona and Brescia was single-naved, as were both halls in the early twin cathedrals of Pola, Nesactium and Parenzo, brings the connections into even clearer focus.[81] The Lombard twin churches were thus not essentially different from the Dalmatian-Istrian sister structures, either as a whole or in detail. Closest to these in general layout are Brescia and Pavia. Here, the buildings are placed parallel to one another, are separated by a narrow court and have a common atrium in front. The layout in Verona and Milan differs somewhat. But at least the floor mosaic in Verona, with its dedicatory inscriptions, points distinctly to the orbit of the Istrian twin churches. In Lombardy as in Istria and Dalmatia as well as in Constantinople, in the twin churches of SS. Sergius and Bacchus and SS. Peter and Paul, one of the two churches is usually dedicated to a martyr: in Pavia to St. Stephen, in Milan to Sta. Tecla, in Bergamo to St. Alexander and St. Agnes. S. Pietro in Brescia is an exception, unless the original dedication was to one of the numerous martyrs named Peter and not to the prince of Apostles whose name is first attached to the church in the eleventh century. The dedications of the twin cathedral in Verona have not come down to us. The other church of the Lombard twin cathedrals always bears the title of the Virgin as is the case in Istria, in Parenzo, Grado, Pola, Trieste and S. Michele in Monte.

The use of one building as summer church and the other as winter church can so far only be traced to Lombardy. But the provision of a warmer, that is, smaller and more protected, winter church is quite usual even in the Catholic Church of today. In the monastery of Maria Wörth in Carinthia, there is still a summer church on the mountainside and a protected winter church at its foot.[82] Similar arrangements are found in a number of Benedictine monasteries; in Montecassino, for example, or in S. Paolo f.l.m. in Rome, where in winter the choir service is held in a special smaller winter choir. The reasons for this arrangement are quite obvious, and it has parallels everywhere in the secular architecture of late antiquity and the early Middle Ages. No matter whether they are the summer or winter triclinia of antiquity [83] or the monastic or palatial *zetae hiemales* and *aestivales* [84] or the winter and summer refectories of the Middle Ages [85]—the rooms for summer and winter use are always clearly distinguished. It is a matter of course that the room for winter use is always the smaller one. This disposition, entirely based on practical needs, is transferred already in late antiquity to a sacred (or at least semi-sacred) building type in at least one instance: a passage in the Talmud distinguishes between winter and summer synagogues.[86] For Christian architecture outside Lombardy there is to my knowledge only one testimony to such an arrangement. The Life of Sta. Matrona of Perge mentions that the saint established two churches in the nunnery built by her in 470, one on the second floor suitable for winter time, and another on the third floor which was fitted for the summer services.[87] This particular instance makes it quite clear that the distinction between the two buildings is based solely on practical requirements. It is expressly said that the second-floor church was more suitable for the winter (it would presumably be warmer) and that the third-floor church was more agreeable in the warm season.

As the designation *basilica aestivalis* and *hiemalis* for the Lombard churches can be traced only from the ninth century onward, it is conceivable that the already existing twin churches were adapted to the new function only then. However, it is more likely that the use of the buildings as summer and winter churches was customary in Lombardy already since the fifth and sixth centuries (perhaps still without specific designation as such). This is indicated by one fact. The winter churches of Milan, Pavia and Brescia are smaller than the summer churches, and both in Pavia and Brescia they lie to the south. While an already existing southern church could possibly have been adapted as a winter church, it cannot be accidental that it was also the smaller one, and therefore more suitable for the winter services. Everything indicates that the southern church was kept smaller with regard for the winter service already in the planning of the entire complex. Practical considerations must have been decisive. Opicinus is quite clear in this respect when he points out that, at Pavia, the winter church lies toward the south and the summer church toward the north [88] —and this at least represents the opinion current in the fourteenth century. Adding this note to the passage from the Life of Sta. Matrona, it appears that in Lombardy a consideration for the climate of North Italy lent to the twin church type, as customary in Istria and farther off in Byzantium, a second function which was current in Christian antiquity without relinquishing the more common designation and separation as martyrium and community church.

No liturgical reasons of any kind can be found for such a distinction between winter and summer churches either in present or earlier liturgy. But even if the arrangement is surely based on practical requirements, such demands of daily life were naturally integrated into the religious life and the liturgy of the Early Christian world. After all, the winter churches of the Lombard twin cathedrals are not only the smaller of the two buildings and situated to the south, but in all the instances where a dedication is preserved they are consecrated to Mary.[89] The consecration of one of the twin buildings to Mary is usual also in Istria and Dalmatia. But here Mary's name might be borne by either of the buildings and it is rarely the southern one. We may say with some confidence that the dedications in Istria must have occurred about the middle of the fifth century [90] because the title of Mary is disseminated in the Occident since 431, as are, roughly about the same time, the dedications to oriental martyrs—and the patrons of the other building in the Istrian and Lombard twin cathedrals are all oriental martyrs. The Lombard custom of dedicating one of the double churches to Mary thus has its parallel and its model in the Istrian sister structures. But there must have been a special reason in Lombardy for regularly giving to Mary the title of the smaller and southern church intended for winter service. There is, in the fifth century, only one great feast celebrated in the Occident which is connected with Mary, and that is Christmas, the sole major feast of the winter. The ecclesiastical winter term begins with its celebration.[91] At Christmas, according to the Roman Church calendar, takes place the first station of the year. One may recall that in Rome this first station of the year is read in Sta. Maria Maggiore, the city's church of Mary *kat' exochen,* and the church which since the fifth century is particularly closely attached to the memory of Bethlehem, to the manger of Christ.[92] Thus it seems that in Lombardy also the link between the winter church and the title of Mary is more than merely accidental. The building which is appointed as winter church to meet practical needs, and in which the major feast of the winter is celebrated, must have a correlation for its practical purpose also in the cult. And this correlation finds expression in the consecration to Mary, the mayor saint of the winter. The ambivalence of Christian antiquity to the worlds of the practical and the spiritual is here evident once more.

Notes

1. R. Salomon, *op. cit.*, pp. 152 ff.

2. London, B.M., map 21470 (7).

3. London, B.M., map 21470 (1).

4. London, B.M., map 21470 (2).

5. Cf. the summary in R. Salomon, *op. cit.*, pp. 152 ff. Particularly important to this context is the passage *De laudibus* (L. A. Muratori, *Rerum Italicarum Scriptores,* ed. Maiocchi and Quintavalle [Città di Castello and Bologna, 1903]), 18: "ecclesia cathedralis eo quod ex duabus ecclesiis perficitur, sine media pariete contiguis, quemdam magnum pretendunt in latitudine cursum, id est terciam fere partem stadii, habens nichilominus testitudines undique cum columpnis. Ante cuius frontem est platea, que dicitur atrium, eque longitudinis ecclesie latitudini et amplius . . ." One may perhaps also point to *ibid.*, p. 20: "Habent autem omnes. . . . ecclesie in medio murum cancellorum, quibus separantur a mulieribus viri, totum solidum sine foraminibus, vel fenestris, unde non possunt mulieres altare videre nisi per unum ostium in medio in parvis ecclesiis, in maioribus vero per tria ostia . . ." This last curious arrangement remains entirely unexplained. The spreading of curtains to separate the sexes is more frequent. It occurs occasionally still today.

6. D. and G. Sacchi, *Antichità romantiche,* (Milan, 1828/29); G. Bosisio, *Notizie storiche del tempio . . . di Pavia* (Pavia, 1858); F. de Dartein, *Etude sur l'architecture lombarde* (Paris, 1865). Among modern studies see in particular A. Kingsley Porter, *Lombard Architecture,* III (New Haven, 1915-17), 185 ff., 231 ff. Here also the report on the demolition of the remains in 1894 according to *Bolletino storico pavese,* I (1893), 190 and *Archivio storico lombardo,* 23, 2 (1896), 421 ff.

7. C. Brambilla, *La basilica di Sta. Maria del Popolo in Pavia ed il suo mosaico* (Pavia, 1876).

8. The brothers Sacchi had still seen a complete groundplan of the church, dated 1705, but now unfortunately lost, and give the following description: "era a cinque navi . . . aveva . . . la cupola . . . la facciata era formata di sette archi, tre corrispondenti alla nave di mezzo . . . aveva tre porte negli archi secondo, quarto e sesto." That the church was claimed to have had galleries is based on the Sacchis' erroneous translation of the word "cancelli" (in Opicinus) as galleries.

9. *Archivio storico lombardo, loc. cit.*

10. See above, note 5.

11. Porter, *loc. cit.* errs in one detail; he supposes elevated aisle bays for the first, third, and fifth bay instead of only for the first and fourth as is shown by examination of what remains of the building.

12. R. de Lasteyrie, *L'Architecture religieuse en France à l'époque romane* (Paris, 1912), pp. 238 ff.; P. Frankl, *Die frühmittelalterliche und romanische Baukunst* (Wildpark-Potsdam, 1926), p. 164.

13. H. A. Van Diepen, *Die romanische Bauplastik in Klosterrath* (The Hague, 1931), Pl. 14,3.

14. E. Gall, "Die Marienkirche in Utrecht und Klosterneuburg," *JKunstW,* I (1923), 34 ff.

15. Frankl., *op. cit.*, p. 196.

16. See above, note 5.

17. Porter, *op. cit.*, I, 85.

18. Monneret de Villard, "L'antica basilica di Sta. Tecla in Milano," *Archivio storico lombardo,* series 5, 44 (1917), 1 ff.

19. For Brescia see: B. C. Zamboni, *Memorie intorno alle pubbliche fabbriche di Brescia* (Brescia, 1778), p. 103: "Queste due chiese . . . constituivano la Cattedrale di Brescia, perchè tutte e due servivano agli usi del Vescovo, e del Capitolo . . ."

20. S. Monti, *La Cattedrale di Como* (Como, 1897).

21. Document of bishop John III (912-924); after Bosisio, *op. cit.*, p. 54.

22. Second testament of archbishop Anspert: ". . . casas . . . non longe ab ecclesia estiva . . ." (after G. Giulini, *Memorie spettante alla storia . . . de Milano*, I [Milan, 1760], ad an. 879, 394, 471 f.).

23. Document of bishop Rampertus on occasion of the translation of St. Philasterius: "in matrem ecclesiam hiemalem nostram Brixiensem penes altare Sanctae Dei Genetricis Mariae . . ." (Zamboni, *op. cit.*, p. 106 and Porter, *op. cit.*, II, 203).

24. Cabrol and Leclerq, *DACL* I, cols. 1396 ff.

25. The *Rogationes* of Milan, processions lasting for three days, emerge in their later form first in 803-813 but the institution may have been older and only reformed at that time. On the first day the processions went from Sta. Maria through several churches of the city and ended at Sta. Tecla; on the second day they began and ended at Sta. Maria; on the third day Sta. Tecla was the point of departure and return. Cf. Cabrol and Leclerq, *op. cit.*, cols. 1396 ff.; G. P. Puricelli, *De Sanctis Martyribus Nazario et Celso* (Milan, 1656), 64 ff.; G. Giulini, *op. cit.*, ad an. 813, pp. 100 ff. By the ninth century, then, and perhaps earlier, both churches together must have formed the cathedral and Sta. Tecla is the second patroness of the cathedral of Sta. Maria still today.

26. Document of bishop Rampertus: "Triginta Brixienses . . . episcopi . . . in matrem ecclesiam hiemalem nostram . . . ubi prescriptorum pontificum erat sedes . . ." (Zamboni, *op. cit.*, p. 106 and Porter, *op. cit.*, II, 203).

27. Bosisio, *op. cit.*, p. 32.

28. Most easily accessible in Porter, *op. cit.*, III, 189: "Nomine quod vocitans ornavit marmore pulcro/intima cum varii templi fulgore metalli/templum domino devotus condedit Anso/tempore paecelsi Liutprandi denique regis/aedibus in propriis Mariae virginis almae/orntes penitrent hinc coelos, vota god (gaudeant)."

I believe that we have here a reference to a renovation of the church ("ornavit marmore pulcro . . .," "condedit fulgore varii metalli") rather than to the foundation. In the latter case it should read "condidit" instead of "condedit." For a different opinion see Porter and the entire older literature.

29. Donation document of May 744; Porter, *op. cit.*, II, 162, n. 10.

30. P. F. Kehr, *Italia pontificia*, VI (Berlin, 1935), 364 ff.

31. A cathedral is mentioned in 780. It is immaterial in our context whether it was only then that the bishop's see was transferred from Sto. Stefano to this church or whether there existed in Verona as in Bergamo a cathedral "extra moenia" (Sto. Stefano) and one "intra moenia."

32. Monneret de Villard, *op. cit.*, has touched upon the connection between the buildings at Pavia and Milan with the Istrian double churches.

33. E. Albertini in: *Atti del III° Congresso internazionale di archeologia cristiana* (1934), pp. 411 ff.

34. C. Truhelka, "Zenica und Stolac," *Wissenschaftliche Mittheilungen aus Bosnien und der Herzegovina*, I (1893), 273 ff.

35. C. M. Kaufmann, *Die Menasstadt* (Leipzig, 1910).

36. J. W. Crowfoot, *Churches at Jerash* (London, 1931).

37. P. Gauckler, *Basiliques chrétiennes de Tunisie* (Paris, 1913).

38. H. Rott, *Kleinasiatische Denkmäler* (Leipzig, 1908), p. 318.

39. G. Gärtner, *S. Giusto a Trieste* (Trieste, 1928).

40. R. Egger and W. Gerber, *Forschungen in Salona*, I (Vienna, 1917), 97 ff.

41. K. Lanckoronski and G. Niemann, *Der Dom von Aquileia* (Vienna, 1906); C. Cecchelli, *La Basilica di Aquileia* (Bologna, 1933); A. Gnirs, "Zur Frage der christlichen Kultanlagen aus der ersten Hälfte des vierten Jahrhunderts im öster-

reichischen Küstenlande," JÖAI, XX (1919), *Beiblatt,* pp. 181 ff.

42. Gnirs, *op. cit.,* pp. 165 ff.

43. Gnirs, *op. cit.,* and R. Egger, "Frühchristliche Kirchenbauten im südlichen Noricum," *JÖAI, Sonderhefte,* IX. (Vienna, 1916), 115-117.

44. Egger, *op. cit.,* p. 73 ff.

45. Egger, *op. cit.,* pp. 73 ff.

46. L. Nagy in: *Atti del III° Congresso internazionale di archeologia cristiana* (1934), pp. 293 ff.

47. This function in particular is advocated by Gnirs, *op. cit.* (see above n. 41), based on the fact that in all buildings mentioned at least one room was found without the marks that an altar would leave. One must, however, remember that wooden altars without fixed location were current in this early period and that, still in the twelfth century during Mass in S. Giovanni in Laterano, the Cardinals carried each time a wooden altar into the church. According to P. Battifol (*Leçons sur la Messe* [Paris, 1923], pp. 51 ff.), fixed altars occur only since the fourth century, and then in the East. Also: D. Bartolini, *Sopra l'* . . . *altare di legno della* . . . *Arcibasilica Lateranense* (Rome, 1952).

48. Egger and Gerber, *op. cit.,* I.

49. Cecchelli, *op. cit.,* p. 246, n. 1, believes that all double structures were created by addition. However, the findings made in almost all the buildings mentioned above are contrary to this opinion.

50. I owe a ground plan to the kindness of E. Dyggve whose publication of the complex of Marusinac is quoted in the Postscript. According to a kind communication of R. Egger the Anastasius basilica was not a twin church proper but a funerary basilica.

51. The basilica of SS. Peter and Paul—now destroyed, though traces are still visible on the north wall of SS. Sergius and Bacchus—is described by Procopius, *The Buildings,* I, IV ("Loeb Classical Library," VII, 44 ff.; translation slightly revised): "There too he (Justinian) built another shrine to the famous Saints Sergius and Bacchus, and then also another shrine which stood at the flank of this one. These two churches do not face each other, but they stand side by side to one another, being at the same time joined to each other and rivalling each other; and they share the same entrances (*eisodoi*) and are like each other in all respects, even to the open spaces (*kraspeda*) by which they are surrounded. . . . In one respect, however, they do differ. For the long axis (*mêkos*) of one of them is built straight, while in the other church the columns stand for the most part in a semi-circle (*hêmikyklos*). But whereas they possess a single colonnaded stoa, called a narthex because of its great length, for each of their porches (*prothyra*), they have their propylaea (*propylaia*) entirely in common, and they share a single court (*aulê*), and the same doors leading in from the court (*metauloi thyrai*), and they are alike in that they belong to the Palace."

52. Egger, *op. cit.*

53. W. Gerber, *Altchristliche Kultbauten Istriens und Dalmatiens* (Dresden, 1912), p. 61.

54. A. Gnirs, *op. cit.* (n. 41), pp. 185 ff.

55. L. H. Vincent and F. M. Abel, *Jérusalem nouvelle,* II, 1 (Paris, 1925), 154 ff.

56. A. Da Lisca, *Madonna Verona* (1913), pp. 161 ff.; 1914, pp. 17 ff.

57. Rott, *op. cit.,* p. 303.

58. Rott, *op. cit.,* p. 318.

59. Augustinus, *De Civitate Dei,* XXII, 766 (*PL,* XLI, col. 10) refers to the "memoria gloriosiissimi Stephani" which he had added to the large basilica and to its enclosing "cancelli." I owe the reference to the passage in Augustine and to the corresponding passage in Possidius, *Vita Aug.,* III, 5, 1 (*PL,* XXXII, col. 36) to the kindness of Father Kuno Mohlberg, O.S.B.

60. Hosios Lucas in Phocis; Zeirek-Cami (Pantocrator church); Fenari Isa Cami (Constantine Lips church); Kahrie Cami, all in Constantinople. Traces of a twin church of the eleventh century seem to have been preserved in the cathedral of Amalfi.

61. Dartein, *op. cit.;* and in particular Brambilla, *op. cit.*

62. Porter, *op. cit.,* III, 231 ff. (after *Boll. stor. pavese,* 1893).

63. Museo Civico, no. 95 under the signature "da Sta. Maria di Popolo." The measurements given by Brambilla for the capital from Sto. Stefano (0.35 m. high and 0.67 m. wide) coincide exactly with the measurements of the capital in the museum. Furthermore, this capital is completely different from all the other capitals actually belonging to Sta. Maria.

64. The impost block carried an arch which led across the side aisle.

65. Opicinus, *loc. cit.*, see above, p. 161, n. 5.

66. *Ibid.*

67. Zamboni, *op. cit.*, p. 114.

68. Zamboni, *op. cit.*, p. 129, n. 106, after the diary of G. B. Bianchi (Ms.) and O. Rossi, *Memorie bresciane* (Brescia, ed. 1693), p. 16. Both authors were contemporaries of the excavation: ". . . ritrovansi giù nel fondo alcune muraglie antiche con tre colonnate a filo . . ."; ". . . sotto al piano di S. Pietro e sotto a quello della Rotonda . . . v'era un lastricato di mosaico antico, ben lavorato . . .". The "tre colonnate" might be interpreted as referring either to a multi-aisled (five-aisled?) building or to a continuation of the columns into a narrow side of the church.

69. See, aside from note 68, *Archivio storico lombardo*, 22, 2 (1895), 245 ff.; 1896, 446 ff.; and *Emporium*, VII (1898), 198 ff.

70. It is possible that the building was transformed into a basilica with nave and aisles when in the ninth century a tripartite choir and its crypt were added. Cf. Porter, *op. cit.*, II, 197 ff.

71. Zamboni, *op. cit.*, p. 117, n 60.

72. See above, note 68; also F. Odorici, *Antichità cristiane di Brescia*, II (Brescia, 1848), 25 ff.

73. *Archivio storico lombardo*, *loc. cit.* and *Emporium*, *loc. cit.* (n. 69).

74. The inscription found during the baroque rebuilding of S. Pietro reads MAXIMIANUS ET LEONTIUS CUM SUIS PC. Another: SYRUS DIACONUS H.L.T.C.S. Already published in the seventeenth century it was retrieved with other similar fragments during the excavations below the Rotunda in 1895. Cf.

Archivio storico lombardo (1895), *loc. cit.; Emporium, loc. cit.;* and *C.I.L.*, V, I, nos. 4841 and 4842.

75. Cf. Monneret de Villard, "I dati storici relativi ai musaici pavimentali," *Archivio storico lombardo,* series 5, 43 (1916), 341 ff.

76. *Notizie degli scavi* (Verona, 1884), pp. 401 ff.; 1885, p. 307; 1886, p. 213; 1888, p. 215; also Porter, *op. cit.*, III, 466 ff.

77. F. S. Maffei, *Museum veronese* (Verona, 1749), p. 208.

78. Compare the excellent reconstruction of Monneret de Villard, *loc. cit.*

79, See above, p. 164, n. 25.

80. Cabrol and Leclerq, *op. cit.*, I cols. 1396 ff.

81. Whether or not one of the two churches in these earliest Lombard buildings served as consignatorium remains an open question as long as the problem of the Dalmatian consignatories is unresolved.

82. I owe this reference to the kindness of Prelate Rainer of Maria Wörth.

83. See R. Lantier ("Les grands champs des fouilles de l'Afrique du Nord," *JdI,* XLVI [1931], 543-44) regarding the summer and winter thermae in Thuburbo Maius. Literary documentation in Apollinaris Sidonius (ed. Baret, Paris, 1899), lib. I, XIX, p. 71: "Porticus ad gelidos patet hinc aestiva triones/hinc calor innocuus thermis hyemalibus exit/atque locum tempus mollit . . ." For winter and summer triclinia, *idem,* lib. II, I, *op. cit.,* p. 213: "ex cryptoporticus in hyemale triclinium venitur." I owe thanks to Prof. Karl Lehmann-Hartleben for pointing out these passages.

84. J. v. Schlosser, *Beiträge zur Kunstgeschichte aus den Schriftquellen des frühen Mittelalters* (Vienna, 1891), p. 46: *Descriptio Farfensis* of 814, *Passio S. Thomae* (4th c.) *et al.*

85. J. v. Schlosser, *Schriftquellen zur karolingischen Kunst* (Vienna, 1896), p. 86 (with references to Freckenhorst).

86. Talmud Babli, Baba Bathra, fol. 3 b (after the German translation of Goldschmidt, VII, p. 9): ". . . (a dilapidated synagogue is to be demolished only) if there exists another prayer house. Meremar

and Mar Zutra tore down and built one destined for summer in the winter and one destined for winter in the summer . . ." The distinction between summer and winter synagogue (the summer synagogue is a court) is still to be found among the Jewish peasants of Kurdistan (W. Schwarz in *Jüdische Rundschau*, 12, VII [1935], 3).

87. *Vita Sanctae Matronae Pergensis, PG* CXVI, cols. 951 ff. (see also *AA. SS.,* Nov., III, 821); cited by Schlosser, *Beiträge zur Kunstgeschichte aus den Schriftquellen des frühen Mittelalters*, p. 46: "Monasterium muro circumdedit, tres autem tabulatorum habitaculum extruxit. Primum quidem et terrae propinquum, quod est ad sepulcrum definitum, secundum autem et medium quod est aptum ad hyemandum et habet templum, quod in ea tempore aptum, ad quo conveniatur, tertium vero ed postremum, quod ipsum quoque templo ornatur pulcherimo et est pulchre accomodatum ad ver illic agendum."

88. *De Laudibus*, p. 4: "in basilica enim estivali, que est Sancti Stephani in aquilone, celebrant in estate canonici; in basilica vero yemali Sanctae Marie in meridie celebrant in yeme."

89. With exception of the cathedral *extra muros* in Bergamo which is dedicated to Saint Peter.

90. Church dedications to specific saints do not occur before the fifth century except for funerary churches. The Istrian twin structures which date in part from the earliest fourth century must therefore be older than their titles. For Rome see the *Liber Pontificalis* where titles for other than funerary churches are not found until the fifth century.

91. L. Eisenhöfer, *Handbuch der katholischen Liturgik* (Freiburg i. Br., 1927), pp. 473 ff.

92. Cf.: H. Grisar, "S. Maria ad Praesepe," *Civiltà cattolica* (1895), IV, 467 ff.

Postscript

Since 1936 a great deal of material has accumulated concerning twin cathedrals in Early Christian times, and some modifications and additions have been possible.

To start with, two self-corrections, the date and circumstances under which the twin cathedral at Pavia was established can now be clarified. Professor Giovanni Panazza in two studies, supported by Professor Donald Bullough, contends with good reasons that the first cathedral at Pavia was situated *extra moenia* where remains of a fifth-century (?) church survive; that the see, not before 680–710, was transferred *intra moenia* to the five-aisled basilica of Sto. Stefano which Bullough dates in the first half of the sixth century; and that the adjacent church of Sta. Maria became the winter cathedral not long after its foundation as a private church (this part does not quite convince me) in the reign of King Liutprand, 712–744. Hence my tentative suggestions of a fifth-century date for Sto. Stefano, both in this essay and still in *Early Christian and Byzantine Architecture*, p. 131, must be revised. Further, one of the building complexes enumerated by me in 1936 as a twin cathedral should be struck from the list: the Anastasius group at Marusinac-Salona, rather than forming a twin cathedral, consisted of but a funerary basilica accompanied by a memoria courtyard enveloped by porticoes and chapels ("basilica discoperta").

On the other hand, a large number of finds and studies concerned with twin cathedrals have tended over these past thirty years to confirm the main thesis of this my old paper. In Verona the north church of the early twin cathedral, to the north of the twelfth-century church, has been excavated (Tamaro-Forlati, 1959); it was a columnar basilica of fifth-century date, with floor mosaics and a chancel and obviously intended for the service of the Eucharist. Hence it was not a ninth-century foundation as suggested by the late De Capitani d'Arzago in his polemic against my essay (1952, pp. 48 ff.). Nor can I agree with his contention (*ibid.*, pp. 45 ff.) that the double cathedral at Milan was not established prior to 836. Excavations undertaken in 1943–1962 to the west of the Gothic cathedral and started by Capitani d'Arzago himself, have brought to light the huge basilica of S. Tecla, dating perhaps as early as 350 and in no case after 370, and its baptistery (Mirabella, 1963). In the Middle Ages S. Tecla, jointly with S. Maria Maggiore, formed the twin cathedral of the city. To be sure, S. Maria, as it existed into the fifteenth century, has turned out to have been a twelfth-century building, and of its predecessor no remains are known except its separate baptistery, Sto. Stefano. In my opinion, however, S. Maria Maggiore was founded long before the twelfth or, indeed, the ninth century. Granted, the references to a summer and winter church contained in the Ambrosian Missal are far less certain than I thought, since that reference—which Cabrol-Leclerq (and hence I in 1936) placed in the fifth century—appears only much later; on this point, then, I deserved to be and was rapped over the knuckles (De Capitani d'Arzago, *op. cit.*, p. 50). On the other hand, I think my critic was wrong in assigning to S. Maria Maggiore and hence to the formation of a double cathedral at Milan a ninth-century date. The date 836 given for the foundation of S. Maria Maggiore comes from a late source and may well refer to a rebuilding. On the contrary, the existence of a fifth-century baptistery, Sto. Stefano, attached to S. Maria Maggiore (*op. cit.*, p. 40 ff.) seems to me to constitute incontrovertible evidence that this latter was either contemporary with or indeed older than its baptistery. Finally, both Saint Ambrose (Epist. I, 20; *PL* XVI, col. 1036) and Paulinus (*Vita Sancti Ambrosii*, cap. 48; *PL* XIV, col. 46) refer along with S. Tecla, the "basilica nova quae maior," to the "basilica vetus" or "minor" nearby—and this latter structure which obviously antedated S. Tecla, I propose to identify with S. Maria. Hence I submit that the twin formation of the Milan Cathedral originated in the fourth century. The two basilicas of Djémila-Cuicul, rather than succeeding each other, appear to be contemporary and hence founded in 411 as a genuine twin cathedral (Février, 1964). Finally, at Trier a huge twin cathedral has come to light consisting of two basilicas running parallel to each other, joined by a baptistery and other halls and safely dated 326, with a *terminus ante* of 340 (Kempf, 1958, 1965). In our context the most important features are the existence, in the south church, from the outset of chancel screens, apparently an altar, and certainly a heating system below the chancel; and the traces in the north church—as early as 340 or 350, though not from the outset—of a small *memoria* structure sheltering presumably a relic; finally, the dedication at an early yet indefinite time of the south church to Mary (our Fig. 65).

These discoveries have both clarified and complicated the problem of the twin cathedrals. They have confirmed that the type was not confined to Istria and Dalmatia. Milan had a twin cathedral, it seems to me, as early as the third quarter of the fourth century; and while the other twin cathedrals of Lombardy are undated, certainly Verona and Brescia go back at least to the fifth century. North of the Alps, the twin cathedral at Trier is a Constantinian foundation and, beyond the seas, Constantinople may have had a twin cathedral to start with, since still in the early fifth century H. Sophia and H. Irene "the Old," were "enclosed in one precinct and bear the name of one church" (Socrates, *HE* II.16 [*PG* LXVII, col. 217]). Similarly, the new finds have made it clear that the two halls joined in a twin cathedral were not necessarily established or built at the same time. While Aquileia and the majority of the related Istrian and Carinthian structures as well as Trier were planned from the outset with parallel double buildings, in Milan and presumably in Constantinople the twin formation of the cathedral resulted from the construction of a new next to an older church.

Likewise the differing functions assigned to the twin halls of a double cathedral have become more clearly separated than was possible thirty years ago. At that time only that much was clear that one of the halls, provided with an altar, was assigned to the celebration of the Eucharist and thus served the faithful proper; the other hall was vaguely termed a *consignatorium*, the place for the confirmation of the catechumens. Concomitantly, the hall of the faithful was taken to have been dedicated to the Virgin, the hall of the catechumens to a martyr whose relics it sheltered; and while the former served as winter cathedral, the latter was the summer cathedral. All these functions were understood as more or less coterminous and to have been assigned to the two halls regardless of their time of foundation or geographical location. From this decidedly unclear concept which prevails in my own essay, two opposing views have evolved. One view (Lehmann, 1962) interprets the hall of the faithful as the church of the congregation, that of the catechumens as the bishop's church, stresses the contrasting dedications to the Virgin and a martyr and traces this latter motif down to medieval churches with doubled apses or with a *Westwerk* and with doubled *patrocinia*. The opposite view (Jean Hubert, 1951; Menis, 1964) considers the problem of dedication of the twin halls irrelevant, since they were nonexistent before the fifth century. Instead, it emphasizes the contrast between the hall of the faithful and that of the catechumens and the functions performed: in the former, the celebration of the Eucharist; in the latter, instruction, withdrawal during the Eucharistic celebration, possibly, celebration of the Mass of the Catechumens in the presence of the full congregation, salution by the bishop at the termination of the service. (The term *consignatorium* [used by myself in 1936 and still by Menis] I should today avoid). These, it seems to me at present, are indeed the principal functions of the twin halls in fourth-century double cathedrals. Had I, in 1936, paid due attention to Paulinus of Nola's letter to Sulpicius Severus (Ep. 32; *PL* LXI, 330 ff.; Kempf, 1953), I could have brought out these functions as they ought to be stressed: two halls, one for the faithful, the other for the catechumens, parallel to each other and linked by a baptistery.

However, any rigid position fails to do justice to the historical picture. Separated places of worship for faithful and catechumens respectively make little sense in twin cathedrals either existing or built anew or formed by joining a new structure to one already existing, once the institution of the catechumenate was no longer of major significance. Hence, beginning in the early fifth century, one of the twin halls or both, may have added new to their old or, indeed, they may have changed functions entirely. Either the hall of the catechumens or that of the faithful as early as 403, witness Paulinus' letter 32 (Kempf, 1953), was provided with relics and possibly dedicated to a martyr. Other changes of that kind are readily listed from Istria and Carinthia (Menis, 1958, 1964). Similarly, the use and designation of the twin halls as summer and winter church respectively, may well be due to such a later addition to or change of functions, in Lombardy possibly as late as the eighth century. Moreover, the change may have been limited geographically as well.

Yet, caution is indicated and the functions at an early time may have differed regionally, while some functions may have been coterminous to start with. The finds in the twin cathedral of Trier would appear to indicate that as early as the middle of the fourth century, when the twelve-sided *memoria* was installed in the north church (Kempf, 1965), one of the twin halls could serve both as *catechumeneum* and martyrium-basilica or only as the latter, while the south hall, containing an altar, served the celebration of the Eucharist. Moreover, the south church at Trier was particularly provided for services during the winter—witness the heating system in its chancel area. This does not mean, obviously, that at Trier, as early as 326 or 350, the south church was consecrated to the Virgin; or that the seasonal liturgical partition into summer and winter church was anticipated. But one wonders whether this seasonal partition common in Lombardy since at least the eighth century was not rooted in earlier custom elsewhere. In short, as recently pointed out by Menis and Zovatto (1964), the two structures paired in twin cathedrals may well have served varying functions in different regions of the Christian world and at different times.

To conclude with two minor points: S. Maria Maggiore at Pavia as rebuilt in the twelfth century was not the only Romanesque church in Lombardy to have had pseudo-transepts; I had overlooked the cathedral of Novara, demolished in 1863, but known from earlier surveys (Verdier, 1953). Also, the relic of the manger appears at Sta. Maria Maggiore in Rome not in the fifth, but presumably only in the seventh century.

Additional Bibliography

Bullough, D. "Urban change in early medieval Italy," *BSR*, XXXIV (1966), 82 ff.

De Capitani d'Arzago, A. La *"Chiesa Maggiore" di Milano* (Milan, 1952).

Dyggve, E. and Egger, R. *Der altchristliche Friedhof Marusinac (Forschungen in Salona,* III [Vienna, 1939]).

Février, P. A. "Le dévelopment urbain en Afrique du Nord," *CahArch,* XIV (1964), 1 ff., esp. 15 ff.

Hubert, J. "Les Cathédrales doubles de la Gaule," *Genava,* n.s. II (1963), 105 ff.

———, "Les cathédrales doubles et l'histoire de la liturgie," *Atti I° Congresso internazionale di Studi Longobardi* (Spoleto, 1951), 167 ff.

Kempf, Th. K. *Frühchristliche Zeugnisse im Einzugsgebiet von Rhein und Mosel* (Trier, 1965), pp. 209 ff., esp. 223 ff., 271 ff.

———, "Trier Domgrabungen 1943–1954," *Neue Ausgrabungen in Deutschland* (Berlin, 1958), pp. 368 ff.

———, "Ecclesia Cathedralis eo quod ex duabus ecclesiis perficitur," *Arte del I° Millennio* (Turin, 1953), pp. 3 ff.

Kraeling, C. H., ed. *Gerasa* (New Haven, 1938).

Lehmann, E. "Die frühchristlichen Kirchenfamilien der Bischofssitze im deutschen Raum und ihre Wandlung während des Frühmittelalters," *Beiträge zur Kunstgeschichte und Archäologie des Frühmittelalters. Akten zum VII. Intern. Kongr. für Frühmittelalterforschung,* 21–28. Sept. 1958 (Graz-Köln, 1962), 88 ff.

Menis, G. C. "La 'Basilica doppia' in un recente volume di 'Atti,'" *RACrist,* XL (1964), 123 ff., with considerable bibliography.

———. La *basilica paleocristiana nelle diocesi settentrionali della metropoli d'Aquileia (Studi di antichità cristiana,* XXIV [Vatican City, 1958]).

Mirabella Roberti, M. "La cattedrale antica di Milano e il suo battistero," *Arte Lombarda,* 8 (1963), 77 ff.

Panazza, G. "Le basiliche di Santo Stefano e di S. Maria del Popolo di Pavia," *Pavia,* (September–December, 1964), pp. 4 ff.

Sonje, A. "Contributo alla . . . Basilica Eufrasiana di Parenzo," *Felix Ravenna,* Ser. 3, 46 (97) (1968) 27 ff.

Tamaro-Forlati, B. "La basilica paleocristiana di Verona," *Rendic. Pont. Accad.,* XXX–XXXI (1949), 117 ff.

Verdier, Ph. "L'origine . . . des transepts de nef . . . ," *Arte del I° Millennio* (Turin, 1953), pp. 354 ff.

Verzone, P. *L'architettura romanica nel Novarese,* I (1935), 60 ff.

Zovatto, P. L. "Il significato della basilica doppia. L'esempio di Aquileia," *Rivista di storia della Chiesa in Italia,* XVIII (1964), 357 ff.

11

THE ARCHITECTURE OF SIXTUS III:
A FIFTH-CENTURY RENASCENCE? *

THE AUTHOR OF "Renaissance and Renascences" [1] will be the first to agree that not everything that looks like a renascence need be one, properly speaking. He will also understand why I turn to an aspect of Early Christian architecture long fascinating to me. Finally, he will forgive me if I sketch the picture as I see it with rather broad strokes.

Sta. Maria Maggiore in Rome has been for some time a bothersome Early Christian church. Weakened, rather than strengthened, by restorations in the sixteenth and seventeenth centuries, its design to this day is dominated by a classical note (Figs. 66, 67). The pristine aspect of the building is easily visualized: the nave terminated by an apse right behind the triumphal arch; a complete set of marble columns separating nave and aisles (Figs. 68, 69); Ionic capitals, presumably less schematic and academically correct than their eighteenth-century replacements; an entablature, surmounted in the clerestory zone by a Corinthian order of huge fluted pilasters, their brick core bonded to the walls; between them in each bay an aedicula, flanked by small pilasters or columns (?) and surmounted by alternating triangular and segmental gables, to shelter the mosaic panels from the Hexateuch; leaning against the pilasters, two superimposed orders of colonnettes, twisted clockwise and counterclockwise and supporting a profiled band around the windows; finally, below the open timber roof, a tendril frieze of the purest design *all'antica,* worked in stucco like the rest of the decor (Fig. 70). [2]

Art historians and archaeologists have been perplexed by the classical purity of the design (Fig. 71), seemingly incompatible with the fifth-century date of foundation assigned to Sta. Maria Maggiore by the dedicatory inscription of Sixtus III (432–440). Efforts were made to fit the structure into supposedly more classical periods of late antiquity, pagan or Christian: an early fourth-century date [3] and a date about 360 [4] were proposed; it was even suggested that the structure was a private basilica of the second century, rededicated as a church with an apse added, but otherwise without essential changes. [5] Yet every brick and stone throughout the original structure—in *opus listatum* for the foundations, in brick for the rising walls—the building technique, the mortar, and whatever is left of the decoration confirm the date given by the *Liber Pontificalis* [6] and by the inscriptions placed by Sixtus III in the newly built church when dedicating

*From *De Artibus Opuscula XL, Essays in Honor of Erwin Panofsky* (New York, 1961), pp. 291–302.

it, a few years after the Council of Ephesus, to the Theotokos. A redating is just not possible.

Nor was it necessary, for the classical features of Sta. Maria Maggiore are not that exceptional in the architecture of Rome during the second third of the fifth century. The Lateran Baptistery, built *de novo* by Sixtus III over the foundation walls of a fourth-century, possibly Constantinian, baptistery, resembled the basilica of Saint Mary in the classical conservatism of its vocabulary and its over-all design. Its present form, with two superimposed orders of freestanding columns carrying a wooden center dome and coffered ceilings in the ambulatory, goes back to a series of sixteenth- and seventeenth-century remodelings.[7] Only the octagonal outer wall, the two orders of eight columns enclosing the octagonal center room, and high above, hidden behind the seventeenth-century paintings, the eight huge windows of the old clerestory date from the time of Sixtus III. The front may go back to the fourth-century structure. But the building as it stood until the 1520's and 1530's is easily visualized, best from an engraving published by Lafréri after 1544 and before 1570 but apparently done prior to 1534 or based on an early drawing (Fig. 55). The eight windows, set off by what seem to be stucco profiles and marble revetment, were capped by an eight-sided gored dome.[8] The ambulatory was surmounted by a barrel vault with mosaic decoration; its walls were lined with a many-colored marble revetment, divided into tiers and panels by a sequence of cornices and pilasters (Fig. 73, right). The decoration, extant in part in the porch, gives an idea of this variegated yet articulate decor. In its entire design, its proportion, and its vocabulary, then, the small elegant structure of the Lateran Baptistery prior to the sixteenth century breathed the same classical spirit as the contemporary basilica of Sta. Maria Maggiore.

This classical view continued in Roman church design for some decades after the death of the third Sixtus. The decoration of S. Paolo fuori le mura prior to its destruction in 1823 dated from the time of Leo I (440–461) and it showed the very characteristics which marked the Sistine buildings: stucco tendrils rising from tondi in the spandrel zone; coffered rosettes and garlands alternating in the soffits of the arcades; colonnettes with spiral flutings, clockwise and counterclockwise in two tiers separating the fresco panels of the triforium zone; finally a laurel strip below the window zone.[9] During the pontificate of Hilarus (461–468) the Oratory of Sta. Croce in the Lateran, possibly part of a second-century thermae building, was sheathed with a new marble revetment and mosaic decor much like that in the ambulatory of the neighboring Baptistery (Fig. 73, left). In front of the new oratory an atrium was laid out, with *jeux d'eau,* a nymphaeum enclosed by three porticoes supported by "columns of wonderful size which are called *exatonpentaicae.*" [10] On either side water spouted from a porphyry column into a shell. In the center under the open sky rose a porphyry basin, enclosed by bronze grills and surmounted by a canopy resting on black, *giallo antico,* and porphyry columns, trabeated and decorated with mosaic.

Perhaps the chronicler did exaggerate the beauty of the design, but the tenor of this description and the very choice of words bring out the intention of resuscitating the spirit of classical antiquity. The last of all this glamor was destroyed in 1588, but the plan and the decoration of the oratory are known from a number of drawings and from a few descriptions.[11]

Sto. Stefano Rotondo, built under Simplicius I (468–483), still reflected this classical spirit, though as the last echo of the movement started under Sixtus III.[12] The spatial design is well preserved: the wide and tall center room, the broad ambulatory, the four projecting chapels, the connecting vaulted elements and their courtyards (Figs. 22–26, 28; Text Figs. 10, 12, 13). The columns of the center room with their awkward Ionic capitals and their entablature were surmounted by a marble revetment articulated by pilasters and panels, witness a drawing of Cronaca's (Fig. 26), that covered the walls of the chapels and corridors (the holes for fastening its plaques are everywhere visible). Finally, elegant stucco profiles with egg-and-dart motifs of the purest classical design have survived along the edges of the arches of these chapels. The original plan may have been to raise a dome built of cane over the center room.[14] Had it been carried out, the classical tenor of the structure would have been more strikingly evident. As it is, the classical vocabulary, even prior to the sixteenth-century denudation, presumably looked somewhat lost in the vastness of the flat covered space.

The four buildings from Sta. Maria Maggiore to Sto. Stefano Rotondo form a homogeneous group. The new style starts fully developed under Sixtus III, seemingly without preparation. Perhaps Sta. Sabina forecasts some of the features of the new style: uniform rows of splendid Corinthian columns and capitals, obviously Roman spoils carefully selected, and marble revetment in the arcade zone. Begun prior to, but completed under, Sixtus' pontificate, Sta. Sabina may thus anticipate scattered elements of the new style, just as Sto. Stefano Rotondo echoes it as a late, somewhat crude offshoot. But the group as a whole is clearly set apart from concepts of church building in Rome either after 470 or, what is more important, during the century preceding the year 430. No structure, from late Constantinian times through the reign of the Theodosian house, is comparable in the consistent use of a pure and conservative classical vocabulary, in the lavishness of the materials employed—marble, *opus tessellatum,* mosaic, stucco— or in the careful selection of homogeneous sets of pilfered columns. No doubt the great churches founded by the Emperors of the fourth century are far larger in size: Constantine's basilica of St. Peter's,[15] his *basilica maior* on the Verano,[16] the basilica near the tomb of his mother, Helena,[17] or, in 386, S. Paolo fuori le mura.[18] But all, including S. Paolo before it received (around 450) its stucco decor, lacked the clear articulation of the walls, be it the clerestory, the triforium zone, or the aisle, by orders of single or doubled pilasters; aediculae, twisted stucco colonnettes, the stucco profiles of arches with or without egg-and-dart design are unknown to them. None have Ionic capitals, or after Constantine's first basilicas, straight entablatures. Column shafts and capitals are heterogeneous in form and material. The sculptural molding of a wall, as at Sta. Maria Maggiore, is entirely foreign to fourth-century church building in Rome, as is, finally, the clear interlocking of vaulted spaces in the Lateran Baptistery or of vaulted and unvaulted spaces at Sto. Stefano Rotondo.

The church buildings of Sixtus III do recall structures from the second through the fourth centuries, but these are structures of a secular, at least of a non-ecclesiastical nature. The double order of Sta. Maria Maggiore and its quiet, majestic space evoke the image of Roman forensic or palace basilicas with superimposed orders of columns, such as Trajan's Basilica Ulpia (Fig. 72), the Basilica of Septimius Severus at Lepcis Magna, or Domitian's audience hall on the Palatine. The marble revetment of the Oratory of Sta. Croce and of the Lateran Baptistery recalls the fourth-century Basilica of Junius Bassus, a secular reception hall.[19] The fusion of marble revetment, mosaic, and stucco finds its parallel in the thermae buildings of imperial times or in the Basilica of Maxentius. Details such as the aediculae of Sta. Maria Maggiore flanked by engaged supports recall nothing so much as the design of imperial thermae, be they those of Trajan, of Caracalla, or of Diocletian (Fig. 74). Or else they call to mind the curved fourth-century façade of the vestibule of the so-called Templum Romuli—if not the Templum Urbis, in any event a public building—whose interior shows also the typical marble revetment of the walls.[20] Finally, nothing is closer to the Lateran Baptistery than the Mausoleum of Constantina, now Sta. Costanza (Fig. 27).

It goes without saying that this Sistine architecture in fifth-century Rome seems at first glance to be a renascence of classical antiquity, short-lived, intense, and focused on a few aspects rather than on the totality of the prototype to which it aspires. But like any good renascence, this Sistine renascence, if renascence it is, builds up in a number of layers.

In the first place, all the buildings in the group, save Sta. Sabina which stands on the fringe, are papal foundations in a very special sense, the pope's own, as it were. Sta. Maria Maggiore, as his dedicatory inscription attests, was Sixtus III's ex-voto gift to the Virgin after the Council of Ephesus, at which the legates of the Roman See battled for the dogma of the Theotokos. The list of gifts presented to the new church [21] reveals Sixtus' intention to let his church compete with those of the princes of the Apostles, and as a papal donation to rival Constantine's St. Peter's, and the still unfinished St. Paul, founded by the three Emperors of the past generation. S. Giovanni in Fonte, within the precinct of the papal residence in the Lateran, was the baptistery where the pope, as bishop of Rome, would officiate; since it took the place of a presumably Constantinian structure, it again competed with an imperial foundation. The Oratory of Sta. Croce likewise was a papal palace chapel and sheltered part of a relic supposedly brought to Rome by Constantine's mother, Helena. Sto. Stefano, apparently a martyrium, was laid out close to the papal palace and certainly within the papal quarter, the *borgo,* as it were, of fifth-century Rome. If, as I believe, it was a "copy" of the Anastasis in Jerusalem,[22] it was again designed to rival one of the great church buildings of the Constantinian House. But whatever Sto. Stefano was, like all its sister buildings within the Sistine group it was not a parish church. Indeed, the parish churches erected under the pontificate of Sixtus and his immediate successors, from all we know, were not particularly lavish in design and apparently employed the ordinary vocabulary of fifth-century architecture. Granted that our knowledge of their original decoration is far from perfect, on the basis of present information we can surmise that Sistine parish churches, such as S. Lorenzo in Lucina and S. Sisto Vecchio, were simple in design and decor; the splendid set of Tuscan columns—Roman spoils—at S. Pietro in Vincoli may have been used already in a first church on the site, of early Sistine date or slightly earlier.[23] The intention of Sixtus III and perhaps of his successors was, no doubt, to outdistance in their own papal foundations the run-of-the-mill parish churches and to compete with imperial church buildings of the fourth century. This intention, however, explains only the lavishness of the design. To understand the striving for what appears at first to be a renascence of classical antiquity, other layers must be explored.

The imperial court in Constantinople, and, after 430, the satellite court in Ravenna had possibly clung throughout to a classical tradition. But this tradition in the imperial capitals was different in kind from the classicism of the Sistine buildings. As it happens, no fourth-century building has survived in Constantinople. Not until the fifth century are we on safe ground regarding the appearance of churches and palaces in the orbit of the imperial courts: in Constantinople, the propylaeum of the second Hagia Sophia (415),[24] the church of St. John of the Studion (463),[25] the palace north of the Hippodrome (ca. 410), uncovered and published during recent years;[26] in Salonika, by then closely tied to Constantinople, the church of the Acheiropoietos (prior to 470);[27] in Ravenna, perhaps the original parts of the Baptistery of Neon (ca. 450)[28] and S. Giovanni Evangelista (425–440),[29] the present structure different in proportions from the fifth-century church but retaining the original set of columns and capitals. In most, if not in all of these buildings, elements of a classical vocabulary come to the fore: in Constantinople in the propylaeum of Hagia Sophia, the fastigium façade, its splendid entablature with an egg-and-dart design and Lesbian cyma frieze curving around the center arch; in the Studion church, the entablature with its deeply undercut tendril frieze above the ground-floor colonnade and the elegant profiles of the window frames; in Ravenna, the Ionic capitals, the stucco decor, and the marble revetment inside the Baptistery. But no building within the ambient of the imperial courts, whether of Constantinople or Ravenna, during the fifth century, is as conservatively classical in decor as the contemporary Sistine buildings in Rome. (The difficulty, outside Rome, of procuring large sets of spoils may also have had its effect.) In Constantinople and Ravenna the classical vocabulary lacks the conservatively monumental, though slightly monotonous consistency of Sta. Maria Maggiore and S. Giovanni in Fonte. The classical elements are scattered over the buildings, rather than consistently applied. Nor is the classical vocabulary as complete as in Rome, where it includes pilaster orders bonded to the walls, three-dimensional aediculae, acanthus friezes which look as if they had been designed and executed in the second century. The effect of dispersed classical elements—and this is striking in the Ravenna Baptistery—at times recalls more closely than the early instances of Sistine architecture its late reflections, such as Sto. Stefano Rotondo. But as a rule the classical forms in Constantinople and Ravenna are full of life and immensely rich. The purely classical elements stand amidst sets of profiles, friezes, and capitals which, starting from a classical tradition, evolve a new style of their own. Constantinople and the allied centers in the fifth century are more progressive than contemporary Rome. Hence they do not cling as slavishly to classical models. Conversely, they do not equal the homogeneous but conservative classical design of Sta. Maria Maggiore or the Lateran Baptistery, with their strong sense of orders super-imposed or juxtaposed, their sculptural handling of the wall, their addition of quietly closed spatial units.

Despite these basic differences, the persistence of a live classical tradition at the court of Constantinople may have been a contributing factor in shaping the Sistine architecture in Rome. So was, no doubt, the intention of the papal court to create buildings of unheard-of lavishness, worthy to compete with the older churches founded by the Christian Emperors. But the real roots of this Sistine style descend into yet another layer.

As pointed out over these last twenty years, Roman architecture, starting per-haps as early as the first century B.C., evolved in a number of separate yet interdependent modes.[30] At one pole extends the vast realm of utilitarian build-ing—farmhouses, tenement and shop-houses (*insulae*), barracks, fortifications, warehouses and other commercial structures, workshops and factories. Based on new building techniques, both vaulting in concrete or cane and a concrete masonry faced with reticulate, brick, or a combination of the two, or with alternating courses of brick and tufa stones (*opus listatum*), these structures employ a minimum of classical decorative forms or none at all. The grandiose starkness of such Roman *machines à vivre* has quite naturally made a powerful im-pression on a generation of architects, scholars, and laymen schooled in the tradition of the Bauhaus and of Le Corbusier. At times they have focused their eyes on this utilitarian architecture of Rome to a degree which, it seems to me, has distracted their attention from other equally or more important facets of Roman imperial architecture of the same time. Indeed, from the first century B.C. through the fourth A.D., Roman religious architecture, far from being moribund, stood at the pole opposite utilitarian building. Temples, whether the traditional Italic triad type or the Roman-Hellenistic cella plan, and *heroa*, circular or otherwise, certainly might, and frequently did employ the masonry and vaulting techniques first evolved in utilitarian constructions, but they were preceded by pronaoi or surrounded by peristyles; their walls were covered on the outside by stone masonry, genuine or stucco imitation; on the inside they were sheathed by marble revetment, and articulated by orders of pilasters, half columns, or projecting colonnades; their vaults were molded by cofferings. In short, Roman religious architecture displayed the entire rich vocabulary of the classical Roman-Hellenistic tradition.

Between the two poles, utilitarian and religious architecture, extended the huge province of what might broadly be called public architecture: civic buildings proper, basilicas, town halls (*curiae*), thermae, market halls; triumphal arches; imperial residences; mausolea, increasingly adapted to *heroa* and temples. These structures, it seems to me, ranged from the utilitarian or nearly utilitarian to the religious or nearly religious in design. One might almost distinguish in all these categories a lower and a higher order of "official" design. Basilicas, town and market halls, or baths in an out-of-the-way small town may be indistinguishable from any utilitarian building. On the other hand, in the large cities of the Empire and above all in the capital, these same building types were pronounced with a high-class accent, and were provided with all the trimmings retained by religious architecture—colonnades, marble revetments, coffered vaults, imitation masonry, and so forth. Examples are easily quoted: in Rome, the Basilicas of Trajan and Maxentius, the Thermae of Diocletian, the Curia Senatus. Imperial palaces and villas, including their audience halls, more than any other public buildings employed the vocabulary of religious architecture. Used as we are to post offices with Grecian fronts and Gothic town halls, we tend to interpret the display of a religious vocabulary in Roman public architecture as a mere expression of a governmental spending spree. No doubt the desire to impress the multitudes played a very considerable part in such lavish designs. But is there not more to it? After all, the entire public architecture of the Empire, as time went on, became increasingly permeated by religious connotations, largely linked to the Emperor's Divine Majesty. The palace where the God-Emperor resided was plainly a religious building. (To call it semi-religious conveys not quite the right idea.) The curia where he resided in effigy and where an altar rose dedicated to Victory—his victory, obviously—had numerous religious connotations; so had the basilica, where his effigy stood on the tribunal, presiding over the law court in session, and where his portrait was exhibited upon his accession to the throne.[31] Even the thermae building, where a shrine was set up for the Emperor's genius or for some other divinity, absorbed an odor of sanctity.[32] From the outset, mausolea, obviously, were surrounded by the atmosphere of religious thought and assimilated at an early time the plans and vocabulary of temples and *heroa*. But even among mausolea, those of the imperial house more than those of ordinary mortals took up the full panoply of religious architecture. In short, public architecture in its top layers had been invested with religious connotations and therefore was clothed in the regalia of temple architecture. By the end of the third century, then, a complex hierarchy of architectural types and modes had evolved, with many interweaving social layers, and it continued unchanged after the imperial house had turned to Christianity.

The Christian communities, when designing places of public worship during the fourth century, were thus confronted with a baffling situation. The religious architecture of paganism, for reasons both practical and spiritual, could not be adapted to the needs of the new cult, except perhaps in the borderland of *heroa* and martyria. Utilitarian tenements, heretofore the milieu of Christian worship, did not correspond any longer to the position, requirements, and demands of the "Established Church." The natural ambience in and from which to evolve the new architectural forms, both in plan and design, was the vast realm of public architecture and, within it, forensic and palace basilicas [33] and funerary structures.[34] Yet official architecture of the highest class in these very categories was permeated by pagan religious connotations, largely connected with the Emperor cult. As a result, architects and patrons of Christian building in the first decades after the Edict of Milan were confronted with a dilemma.

In the orbit of the imperial court, whether it resided in Constantinople, Milan, Trier, or Ravenna, Christian builders and church leaders had apparently no difficulty in adapting to their needs and demands the types and the lavish classical vocabulary of official architecture of the highest level. The concept of the Emperor's Divine Majesty lived on, Christianity or not, and as has been pointed out, classical culture remained "the one cornerstone of the rule of the Emperor." [35] Hence it seemed only natural that the buildings of Christian worship erected under his eye or with his personal backing would incorporate the entire panoply of Hellenistic-Roman official architecture, as it had evolved since Augustan and Flavian times and lived on in the fourth and fifth centuries. The transfer from imperial palace to imperial-sponsored church architecture can be traced in the churches erected in the Holy Land by the imperial house: Constantine's martyrium at the Holy Sepulchre in Jerusalem—as far as Eusebius' description allows any judgment—and the Anastasis Rotunda with its set of beautiful Corinthian columns known from seventeenth- and eighteenth-century illustrations (Fig. 30), whether a work of Constantine or his son. It can be seen likewise in Milan, in a late fourth-century church such as the tetraconch of S. Lorenzo. In Constantinople the propylaeum of the second Hagia Sophia and the Studios church possibly reflected a fourth-century classical tradition, otherwise lost.

In Rome as in the rest of the Empire the situation was apparently different. Ordinary parish churches as late as 400 still evolved their plans and vocabulary more often than not from tenement houses or from the milieu of low-brow public architecture, the simplest near-utilitarian assembly halls. This is only natural. Even imperial foundations in Rome, however, for the greater part of the fourth century seem to have shunned, far more than their sister buildings in the East or in Milan, the elegant vocabulary of high-class official architecture. Of the Lateran Basilica, to be sure, little is known (Text Fig. 5). It may have displayed homogeneous sets of precious marble columns, if the few remnants are indicative. In any case, built as it was in the first years of Constantine's reign, with the patronage of the imperial court in residence, it showed the characteristic lavishness of a structure erected under the Emperor's very eyes. On the other hand, St. Peter's, built in Constantine's later years, probably after his removal to Constantinople, was haphazardly thrown together, intermingling columns and capitals of disparate materials and sizes; the wall decoration, apparently murals, lacked the sculptural emphasis and the marble revetment of contemporary secular basilicas and palaces (Fig. 80). Likewise in the huge *coemeterium-basilica* on the Verano (Text Figs. 6, 7), the helter-skelter of columns, heterogeneous in size and material, is as marked as the crude profiling of the entablatures. But it was hardly lack of funds or of imperial backing and interest that caused this remarkable spurning of the classical tradition, for, to judge from the imperial donation lists in the *Liber Pontificalis,* these same buildings gleamed with silver and golden lamps, with altar furnishings and canopies, with gilded roof beams and roof tiles.

Two possible explanations come to mind. For one thing, the greater number of the Constantinian churches in Rome were completed only after the court's removal to Constantinople: hence both the funds and the mainstay of classical culture within the Christian community had gone from Rome. This ties up with another and perhaps more important factor. Classical culture and art throughout the fourth century remained alive among Christians wherever it was carried by the Christian court, by a predominantly Christian aristocracy, and by large numbers of Christian scholars and theologians.[36] This combination of forces prevailed in the Eastern capitals, Constantinople and perhaps Antioch, and in Milan as long as the court resided there in the last third of the century. Judging from the classicist tenor of Christian sculpture and architecture in Milan around 380, in Constantinople around 400, one tends to assume that a classical current in art, whether Christian, secular, or pagan, survived in the atmosphere of the imperial court throughout the fourth century,[37] just as it survived in literature. In this atmosphere of a classically minded Christian court, the continued teaching of a few of the greatest pagan scholars and rhetoricians created no serious trouble; the reign of Julian the Apostate turned out to be an episode quickly forgotten. Christian theologians in the East never saw any difficulty in clothing Christian thoughts in beautiful Greek, and the greatest of them—Basil, Gregory of Nazianzus, John Chrysostom—were students of the profoundly pagan Libanius, the rhetorician and comrade-in-arms, the ἑταῖρος of Jullian.[38] There was no reason why Christian themes should not be clad in classical forms, Christian church buildings not employ a traditional vocabulary of the highest class of official architecture.

In Rome on the other hand, and throughout the Latin West except for Milan, classical culture was carried largely by an aristocracy which was intensely pagan and thus remained linked to a pagan heritage.[39] Christian leaders during the first half of the fourth century remained aloof from the world of the classics; by and large not highly educated, they could afford such indifference. Within this late Constantinian and post-Constantinian Christian milieu of Rome, surrounded as it was by powerful pagan families trained in the classical tradition, there was obviously no room for a church architecture clad in the regalia of official architecture with its religious connotations. Nor was there any room for Christian sculpture with classical features. When, after the middle of the century, an educated Christian group came to the fore in Rome, the situation changed for a short time. A few aristocratic families, at last converted to Christianity but obviously continuing to cultivate a classical tradition, would demand a Christian art with classical overtones. Hence workshops of sculptors trained along such lines penetrated into Rome. They are said to have come from the East, possibly by way of Milan.[40] I, for one, would rather tend to say that they came from the imperial court, which just about that time had transferred itself from Constantinople to Milan. In any event, the sarcophagi of Junius Bassus, of the Two Brothers, and Lat. 174 reflect this classical Christian art of the sixties and seventies in Rome as clearly as the contemporary Philocalian lettering and the facile classicizing verses of the poetaster on the See of Saint Peter, Pope Damasus (366–384). This brief interlude of a classical art sponsored by Christian aristocrats was cut short about 380 by the recrudescence of paganism in Rome. Anew the classical tradition was vigorously taken up by the great pagan families, such as the Nicomachi and Symmachi. It was they who commissioned the ivories, silver vessels, and presumably the manuscripts of emphatically classical design during the last two decades of the century, when Christian sarcophagi or ivories in Rome are practically unknown.

As the fourth century ended, Christians in the West, indeed, were confronted with a conflict between their anti-pagan religious convictions and their classical cultural tastes, a conflict unknown to their forefathers in Constantinian times. "Quid facit cum psalterio Horatius? cum evangeliis Maro? cum apostolo Cicero?"[41] The conflict, to be sure, was not always as violently stressed as by Jerome. Not everyone vowed not to read any more pagan writings;[42] not everyone would look upon the "songs of the poets, or worldly wisdom, or the pomp of verbiage of the orators" as a feast prepared by the demons.[43] Occasionally the writings of a Christian leader seem to belie the existence of any dilemma. Saint Ambrose, trained as an administrator and living in an aulic ambience, was not faced with the conflict. But Jerome and many of his contemporaries were troubled by it, just because they were so thoroughly imbued with the classical tradition, because "their ears had been captivated by the sweet melody of fluent verses which penetrate the soul and conquer the innermost heart."[44] In his late writings the solution for Jerome was the flight into the *rustica simplicitas* of an intentionally inelegant and highly powerful language. Shaped after the Latin translations of the Scriptures, both his own and earlier versions, this *sermo humilis* was defended both by Jerome and Augustine as being more sublime than any traditional style of writing.[45] Certainly it forms the strongest possible contrast to the rhymes of Damasus and the "official" Latin of Ambrose. Only with the final defeat of paganism in the West in 395 was the dilemma resolved. The bond between classical culture and paganism was severed. Without fear of pollution Christians could attempt to write elegant Latin prose—it never became as powerful as Jerome's language—and poetry, from Augustine to Prudentius.

The "renascence" of classical architecture in Rome under Sixtus III must be placed, it seems to me, against the backdrop of the final defeat of paganism in the West. It stands out even more clearly when it is viewed as a reaction against the shock suffered by every educated Latin, whether pagan or Christian, through the conquest of Rome by Alaric in 410. The depth of the trauma can be measured in Augustine's writings,[46] in the pagan Claudius Rutilius Namatianus' lines to the city that is still "Golden Rome," [47] in Jerome's "Capitur urbs quae totum cepit orbem." [48] The consequences were obvious to the mind of any educated man in the West. The Empire in the West had collapsed. The Emperor in Ravenna was a mere shadow. The Eastern Emperor, powerful though he was, was distant and uninterested. The Roman aristocracy, pagan to the last, was gone as a political force. The only power left in Rome was the papacy. Its aspirations to be recognized not only as the spiritual center of the West but also as *the* Apostolic See, apparent for some time, grew infinitely stronger after the fall of Rome, under Innocent I and further under Sixtus III.[49] Quite naturally, with the continuous weakening of the Empire these claims carried, for the city of Rome at least, political overtones. Sixtus' archdeacon Leo, later Leo I, may well have been a leading figure in this political movement. A sermon of his sums up the claim of Rome to be the new capital of the West: Peter and Paul, so he says, have led Rome "to such glory that she has become a priestly and royal city, the head of the World through this holy see of Peter. Wars, indeed, have made fewer conquests for you than the Christian Peace." [50] Such political claims became linked with cultural aspirations, the more so since the pagan aristocracy, thus far the principal carrier of classical culture in Rome, had disappeared. The papacy, in short, had reached a point at which it could not but accept the heritage of Rome, both political and cultural. Art and literature of classical antiquity, no longer tied to paganism, had become a language to be used freely and without religious compunctions by educated Christians. In the realm of architecture the Hellenistic-Roman vocabulary of official building, no longer permeated by pagan religious connotations, could be freely used for the design of churches.

The continuance and disappearance of classical currents in Christian and pagan art of the fourth century, the defeat of paganism in Rome, the shock of the fall of *the* city, finally, the resurgence of the papacy as heir to the Roman Western legacy: this is the background against which the classicism of the Sistine buildings must be seen. Much in contrast to the classical currents in fourth-century sculpture, Sta. Maria Maggiore and the Lateran Baptistery do not depend—or do not depend exclusively—on the art of the imperial courts in Constantinople or Ravenna. Nor do they represent a renascence proper; they do not hark back to second- or third-century Hellenistic-Roman architecture. They represent a shift in ecclesiastical building in Rome, a shift from an architecture rooted in utilitarian and near-utilitarian public building to designs stemming frankly from high-class official architecture. Now the Lateran Baptistery could freely use as a prototype an imperial mausoleum, Sta. Costanza, while Sta. Maria Maggiore could work with the vocabulary of secular forensic or palace basilicas. The traditions, the plans, and the vocabulary of official civic architecture, alive throughout the fourth century but unusable for Christian building in the West because of their pagan religious overtones, could be employed by Sixtus III in the church buildings close to his heart because these overtones had become meaningless. Indeed, he *had* to seek models in official civic architecture since his buildings were designed to reflect the new claims of the papacy to the cultural and to some degree the political heritage of Rome.

Notes

1. Erwin Panofsky, in *Kenyon Review*, VI (Spring 1944), 201 ff.

2. A. Schuchert, *S. Maria Maggiore zu Rom*, ("Studi di antichità cristiana," XV) (Rome, 1939); R. Krautheimer, "Recent Publications on S. Maria Maggiore in Rome," *AJA*, XLVI (1942), 373 ff.; *idem*, "Some Drawings of Early Christian Basilicas in Rome," *AB*, XXXI (1949), 211 ff.; C. Cecchelli, *I mosaici . . . di S. Maria Maggiore* (Rome, 1956).

3. J. Wilpert, *Die römischen Mosaiken und Malereien*, I (Freiburg, 1917), 415, quoting an opinion of Ashby's.

4. G. B. De Rossi, *Musaici cristiani* (Rome, 1899).

5. P. Crostarosa, "Inventario dei sigilli . . . di S. Maria Maggiore," *Nuovo bollettino di archeologia cristiana*, II (1896), 52 ff., esp. 84; J. P. Richter and C. Taylor, *The Golden Age of Classical Christian Art* (London, 1904), pp. 26 ff.

6. *Le Liber Pontificalis*, ed. L. Duchesne, I (Paris, 1886), 232. The information that the church of Sixtus III "of old was called Basilica of Liberius" (presumably Pope Liberius, 352–366), has been recognized as a sixth-century interpolation; see Schuchert, *op. cit.*, pp. 43 ff., also for the older bibliography.

7. G. B. Giovenale, *Il battistero lateranense* ("Studi di antichità cristiana," I) (Rome, 1929), pp. 89 ff.

8. The reliability of the Lafréri engraving need not be doubted. On all points which can be checked it is in accord with the findings of Giovenale, with other drawings of fifteenth- and sixteenth-century date, such as Barb. lat. 4424, f. 31 (Chr. Huelsen, *Il libro di Giuliano de Sangallo*) [Leipzig, 1919], p. 46 and Pl. 33) and Barb. lat. 4333, f. 69v (unpublished), and with the descriptions of ca. 1560 given by Panvinio (*De praecipuis . . . basilicis* [Rome, 1570], pp. 154 ff.), and Vat. lat. 6110 (published by Ph. Lauer, *Le palais de Latran* [Paris, 1911], pp. 464 ff.). Singly and combined, they confirm elements shown in the engraving which are no longer visible, or are hard to recognize after the early sixteenth-century remodeling, such as the plan of the font, the placing and width of the clerestory windows, the design of the barrel vault in the ambulatory, and the marble revetment of its wall. Hence other elements of the engraving should also be trusted. Dr. Tilmann Buddensieg, in a recent study which he was good enough to communicate to me in summary form, has arrived at essentially the same conclusion; the engraver is trust-

worthy—except that in one major point he has placed at the same level the architrave above the inner columns and the top of the marble revetment on the ambulatory wall. I would add that the lantern too would seem to be of sixteenth-century date. The contention that the clerestory windows are no longer those of Sixtus III (A. Tschira, "Die ursprüngliche Gestalt des Baptisteriums in der Lateransbasilika," *RM*, LVII [1942], 116 ff.) is contradicted by their fifth-century brickwork (see Giovenale, *op. cit.*, pp. 41, 100).

9. An impression of the fifth-century decoration is gained best from the engravings of Piranesi, of L. Rossini (*Le antichità romane* [Rome, 1829], Pls. 98-101) and N. M. Nicolai (*Della basilica di S. Paolo* [Rome, 1815], Pl. III).

10. *LP*, I, 236.

11. A short list of drawings was given by H. Egger, *Kritisches Verzeichnis der stadtrömischen Architekturzeichnungen der Albertina* (Vienna, 1903), p. 36, and supplemented by Huelsen, *loc. cit.* It can be further enlarged by drawings in the Uffizi (A. Bartoli, *I Monumenti antichi di Roma nei disegni degli Uffizi* [Florence, 1914 ff.], Figs. 4, 193, 679, 689) and in Turin (G. Mongeri, *Le rovine di Roma* [Milan, 1880], Pl. 30, with the draftsman's remarks regarding the hollow tube construction of the vault). Lafréri's engraving of 1568 seems reliable and tallies with Panvinio's description, *op. cit.* (1570), p. 164, and Vat. lat. 6110 (Lauer, *op. cit.*, pp. 467 ff.).

12. See above, 69 ff.; A. M. Colini, *Storia e topografia del Celio* (*AttiPontAcc,* ser. III, *Memorie,* VII) (Vatican City, 1944), 245 ff.

13. Florence, Uffizi, dis. Santarelli, 161 (Bartoli, *op. cit.*, Fig. 37); Colini, *op. cit.*, p. 245, where the quotation from Rucellai is also to be found (n. 49).

14. F. W. Deichmann, "Die Eindeckung von S. Stefano Rotondo," *Miscellanea Giulio Belvederi* (Rome, 1955), pp. 437 ff.

15. See below, pp. 211 f.

16. R. Krautheimer, W. Frankl, G. Gatti, "Excavations at San Lorenzo fuori le Mura, in Rome, 1917," *AJA,* LXII (1958), 379 ff.; R. Krautheimer, *Corpus,* II (1959), 93 ff., 116 ff.

17. F. W. Deichmann, A. Tschira, "Das Mausoleum der Kaiserin Helena . . . ," *JdI,* LXXII (1957), 44 ff.

18. N. M. Nicolai, *Della basilica di S. Paolo* (Rome, 1815), *passim;* F. W. Deichmann, "Die frühchristlichen Basen and Kapitelle von S. Paolo," *RM,* LIV (1939), 99 ff.

19. G. Lugli and Thos. Ashby, "La Basilica di Giunio Basso," *RACrist,* IX (1932), 221 ff.; Krautheimer, *Corpus,* I (1937), 62 ff., with bibliography.

20. Krautheimer, *op. cit.*, pp. 137 ff.

21. *Le Liber Pontificalis,* I, 232.

22. See above, p. 69 ff.

23. R. Krautheimer, "S. Pietro in Vincoli and the Tripartite Transept," *Proceedings of the American Philosophical Society,* LXXXIV (1941), 353 ff. The remnants of the first church, then unsuspected, were uncovered in 1957–58; see below, Additional Bibliography (Colini, 1966; *Corpus,* III).

24. A. M. Schneider, *Die Grabung im Westhof der Sophienkirche* ("Istanbuler Forschungen," XII) (Berlin, 1941); F. W. Deichmann, *Studien zur Architektur Konstantinopels* ("Deutsche Beiträge zur Altertumswissenschaft," 4) (Baden-Baden, 1956), 57 ff., 70 ff.

25. A. Van Millingen, *Byzantine Churches in Constantinople* (London, 1912), pp. 35 ff.

26. R. Duyuran, "First report on Excavations on the site of the new Palace of Justice at Istanbul" (in Turkish with English summary), *Istanbul Arkeoloji Müzeleri Yilligi,* V (1952), 23 ff.; idem, "Second report . . . ," *ibid.,* VI (1953), 21 ff., 74 ff.

27. A. K. Orlandos, Ἡ Ξυλοστέγος Βασίλικὴ (Athens, 1952 ff.), *passim.*

28. S. Bettini, "Il battistero della Cattedrale di Ravenna," *Felix Ravenna,* LII (1950), 41 ff.

29. C. Ricci, *Tavole storiche dei musaici di Ravenna* I (Rome, 1937), 43 ff.

30. A. Boëthius, "Roman Architecture from its classicistic to its late imperial phase," *Göteborg Högskolas Arsskrift,*

XLVII (1941), 8; *idem*, "Three Roman Contributions to World Architecture," *Festskrift J. Arvid Hedvall* (Goteborg, 1948), pp. 59 ff.; *idem*, "The Reception Halls of the Roman Emperors," *BSA*, XLVI (1941), 25 ff.

31. See above, pp. 12 f.; J. Ward Perkins, "Constantine and the Origins of the Christian Basilica," *BSR*, XXII (1954), 69 ff.

32. The Talmud consequently enjoins Jewish masons to cease work on a thermae building "once they reach the arch (scil. apse) where they [meaning the pagans] place an idol" (H. L. Gordon, "The Basilica and the Stoa in Early Rabbinical Literature," *AB*, XIII [1931], 363). Similarly Saint Augustine is once questioned regarding the use by Christians of a thermae building "where incense is offered to the gods" (quoted without reference by P. de Labriolle, *La réaction païenne*, 2nd ed. [Paris, 1948], p. 491. Dom Anselm Strittmatter, O.S.B., has been good enough to suggest as the probable source a passage in Ep. XLVI, Quaestio XV (*PL XXXIII*, col. 184): "Si Christianus debet in balneis lavare, vel in thermis, in quibus sacrificatur simulacris . . .").

33. See above, n. 31.

34. A. Grabar, *Martyrium* (Paris, 1946), *passim*.

35. A. Alföldi, *A Conflict of Ideas in the Late Roman Empire* (Oxford, 1952), p. 117.

36. P. de Labriolle, *op. cit., passim*.

37. J. Kollwitz, *Die Lipsanothek von Brescia* (Berlin-Leipzig, 1934), p. 54; *idem, Oströmische Plastik* (Berlin-Leipzig,

1935), *passim*; H. U. von Schoenebeck, *Der mailänder Sarkophag* ("Studi di antichità cristiana," X) (Vatican City, 1935), 116 ff.

38. P. de Labriolle, *op. cit.*, pp. 424 ff.

39. A. Alföldi, *op. cit., passim*.

40. Kollwitz, *Lipsanothek*, pp. 53 ff., and *idem*, review of Schoenebeck, *op. cit.*, in *Gnomon*, XII (1936), 601 ff.

41. Saint Jerome, Ep. XXII, 29 (*CSEL*, LIV, ed. A. Hilberg, 189); see also R. Eiswirth, *Hieronymus' Stellung zur Literatur und Kunst* ("Klassisch-philologische Studien," no. 16) (Wiesbaden, 1955).

42. Jerome, Ep. XXII, 30 (*op. cit.*, p. 191).

43. *Idem*, Ep. XXI, 13 (*ibid.*, p. 122).

44. *Ibid.*

45. E. Auerbach, "Sermo humilis," *Romanische Forschungen*, LXIV (1952), 304 ff., esp. 320 ff.

46. *De Civitate Dei*, Lib. I, cap. I (*CSEL*, XL, 4 ff.); *Retractationes*, Lib. II, cap. 43 (*PL XXXII*, cols. 647 ff.) *De excidio Urbis* (*ibid.*, XL, cols. 715 ff.).

47. *De reditu suo*, ed. D. Ruhnken, in *Elogium Tiberii Heinsterbusii* (Leipzig, 1875), pp. 1 ff., esp. p. 4.

48. *Selected Letters of Saint Jerome*, ed. F. A. Wright ("Loeb Classical Library") (London and New York, 1933), p. 462, Epistle 127.

49. E. Caspar, *Geschichte des Papsttums*, I (Tübingen, 1930), 296 ff., 416 ff.

50. Sermo LXXXII (*PL* LIV, cols. 422 ff.).

Postscript

I have no qualms regarding the main points I was trying to make in this essay: the prevalence in Roman church design between 350 and 410 of an indifferent if not hostile attitude toward classical tradition as marked, for instance, by the nave of Old St. Peter's, which may date anytime between 330 and 360; the emphatic renascence of a classical design, particularly in churches built under the aegis of the papal court, between 425 and 470; and the impact exerted on this renascence by secular public monumental architecture erected from the second through the early fourth century. Likewise, I still suspect that the beginnings of this renascence were sparked by the final defeat of paganism and by the deep impression made on the civilized world by the sack of Rome, and that it was related to the subsequent social, cultural, and political ascendancy of the papacy. Nor am I greatly disturbed by my growing conviction that this renascence movement starts in the twenties rather than under Sixtus III. Indeed Sta. Maria Maggiore, including its classical orders, was probably begun and possibly built (though not decorated) prior to 432. The outer wall of the Lateran baptistery may be Constantinian (see above, p. 149), leaving to Sixtus only the inside upper and lower colonnades, the drum, and the barrel vault of the ambulatory. Still, the movement reaches its peak under Sixtus, and the term "Sistine Renaissance" remains valid. This reading has been confirmed, I think, by recent research on the architecture of both Imperial and Christian Rome (Brown, 1961; MacDonald, 1965; Krautheimer, 1965 and 1967), as well as on individual buildings in Rome, Ravenna and Constantinople: at the Lateran Baptistery (where, incidentally, Lafréri's engraving turns out to be less reliable than I used to think above, note 8); at Sta. Maria Maggiore (*Corpus,* III 1 ff.), S. Lorenzo in Lucina (*ibid.,* II, 159 ff.), S. Pietro in Vincoli (*ibid.,* III, 178 ff., and Matthiae and Colini, 1966), S. Sisto Vecchio (*Corpus,* IV, in press), Sto. Stefano Rotondo (*ibid.*); at S. Giovanni in Laterano (Krautheimer-Corbett, 1965); at the Orthodox Baptistery in Ravenna (Kostof, 1965; Herrmann, 1964); in Constantinople, in the palace north of the Hippodrome (Naumann, 1965; Naumann-Belting, 1965).

However, I think I should have gone more fully into what appears to be a dichotomous situation in the Christian art of Rome after 350: an aclassical (or anticlassical) church architecture contrasted with a highly classical approach in at least one and possibly more groups of Christian sarcophagi produced in Rome at that time, such as the sarcophagus of Junius Bassus and its relatives. The explanation I think rests with a number of factors. Classical concepts continue to survive outside Rome at the imperial court throughout the fourth century and beyond and are strengthened just after 350 by a renascence movement (wrongly termed the "Theodosian Renaissance"). Simultaneously, since the middle of the fourth century, a Christian civil service aristocracy comes to the fore in Rome, linked closely to the imperial court, especially during the latter's residence in Milan. On the other hand and at the same time, the Christian middle class in Rome maintains its everpresent conservative tendencies and remains distrustful of the penetration of a classical tradition into religious art. Thus the contrast between classical sarcophagi and precious silver work, produced within the renascence movement for Christian aristocrats in Rome, and the contemporary aclassical or anticlassical sarcophagi likewise originating in that city may be one of social stratification. Similarly the social position of the church in Rome during the fourth century and the basis of its leadership in the middle classes may well be at the root of the prevalence of an aclassical design in church building. Unlike sarcophagi or silver caskets, churches are, after all, produced not by private initiative and for personal use but for and as a rule by the anonymous, predominately middle class and hence conservative mass of the faithful.

These factors might have thrown light also on the development of church design in Rome prior to Sixtus III. The highly classical element in Constantinian church and funerary buildings—for example, Sta. Costanza and presumably the Lateran basilica—rooted in the tradition of secular monumental architecture, contrasts with later fourth-century building in Rome, indifferent or indeed hostile as it was to classical concepts; and the renascence movement in sculpture and silver work is felt sooner than that in architecture. Already the construction of S. Paolo f.l.m. after 386 by the three ruling emperors parts ways with the indifferent attitude prevailing in church design not under the protection of the highest classes. But the aclassical approach to church design in Rome is really overcome only in the early fifth century with the rise to prominence within the church of a cultured class bred in the civil service or that of the church and represented by figures such as Leo I, the archdeacon of Sixtus.

Additional Bibliography

Brown, F. E. *Roman Architecture* (New York, 1961).

Herrmann, J. *Studies in Ravenna impost blocks* (M.A. Thesis, Institute of Fine Arts, New York University, 1964, unpublished).

Kostof, S. *The Orthodox Baptistery of Ravenna* (New Haven, 1965).

Krautheimer, R., Frankl, W., Corbett, S. *Corpus,* II (New York and Vatican City, 1959); III (New York and Vatican City, 1967); IV (in press).

Krautheimer, R. *Early Christian and Byzantine Architecture* (Pelican History of Art) (Harmondsworth, 1965).

———— "The Constantinian Basilica," *DOPapers,* XXI (1967), 115 ff.

Krautheimer, R. and Corbett, S. "La Basilica Costantiniana al Laterano," *RACrist,* XLIII (1965) (*Miscellanea Enrico Josi,* II), 125 ff.

MacDonald, William Lloyd, *The Architecture of the Roman Empire* (New Haven, 1965).

Matthiae, G. and Colini, A. M. *Ricerche intorno a S. Pietro in Vincoli* (*MemPontAcc,* IX, 1966).

Naumann, R. "Ausgrabungen zwischen Mese und Antiochus-Palast . . . ," *Istanbuler Mitteilungen,* XV (1965), 135 ff.

Naumann, R. and Belting, H. *Die Euphemia Kirch . . . ,* ("Istanbuler Forschungen," XXV) (Berlin, 1965).

12

A NOTE ON JUSTINIAN'S CHURCH
OF THE HOLY APOSTLES
IN CONSTANTINOPLE *

JUSTINIAN'S CHURCH of the Holy Apostles in Constantinople has long disappeared. Begun ca. 540 in place of the sanctuary erected by Constantine in honor of the Disciples, it was dedicated in 548.[1] In 1461, it was razed to the ground by Mehmed the conqueror, and a mosque, the Fatih, was built on the site. Two centuries later, between 1767 and 1771, this first Fatih gave way to the present Fatih mosque, Selim III's grandiose monument.[2]

Still, a large number of sources would appear to give a fairly clear idea of Justinian's church, and ever since Heisenberg collected them, these sources—literary descriptions, architectural filiations and depictions in illuminated manuscripts—have been well known.[3]

Procopius, writing shortly after construction had been completed, noted the main features of the plan: a cross with arms of equal length, the five resulting bays surmounted by domes, of which only the one in the center was lit through a circle of windows "much like the dome of the H. Sophia." [4] He neither elaborates on details of the plan nor mentions any decoration of the interior; but then, the walls may well have been bare when Procopius wrote. Nearly four hundred years later when Constantine the Rhodian composed his lengthy poem on Constantinople, he filled in some of the missing elements [5]: the colonnaded aisles and the galleries which accompanied each of the four cross arms whether flanking its domed squares or enveloping them on three sides, and the interior decoration, marble revetment and mosaics in the vaulting zone. But the building itself was apparently in all respects the one described by Procopius. Indeed, the Rhodian stresses again the lighting of only the main dome over the center bay. Finally, Nikolaos Mesarites' prose ekphrasis, written shortly before 1200, describes in great detail the mosaic decoration which he saw on the domes, the barrel vaults and the upper walls of the Apostle Church.[6] But he says little about plan, elevation and lighting of the structure, except for the obvious elements implied in his description: the cross plan, the five domes, and the connecting barrel vaults.

Architectural filiations of Justinian's Apostle Church seem to be as rare as those of its Constantinian predecessor are frequent. Among the earliest is the church of St. John at Ephesus, built by Justinian only a few years after his

*From *Mélanges Eugène Tisserant*, II (Vatican City, 1964), 265–70.

Apostle Church had been completed. Procopius considered it a close copy of the Constantinopolitan sanctuary despite one obvious deviation.[7] The west arm was longer than the other three, and therefore vaulted with two domes, both slightly oval. Since only the lower parts of the building—piers, aisle colonnades and the colonnades of the galleries—survive, the lighting of the domes—whether of all, of none, or of only the center dome—cannot be determined.[8] On the other hand, St. Mark's in Venice, begun ca. 1070 and thus a late filiation of the Holy Apostles in Constantinople, preserves not only the cross plan, the five main bays, the colonnaded aisles and, originally, the surmounting galleries, but also the five domes raised on drums, the one in the center slightly higher, but all five lit by large windows.[9]

Finally, four depictions in illuminated manuscripts apparently show the Holy Apostles in Constantinople as the building presented itself in the early eleventh and the late twelfth centuries respectively. Three are contained in the Menologium of Basil II (Vat. gr. 1613) under the dates of January 22 (fol. 341), January 27 (fol. 353), and October 18 (fol. 121) (Figs. 75, 76, 77). The first forms the backdrop for the martyrdom of St. Timothy and the translation of his relics; the second for the reception by Patriarch and Emperor of the relics of St. John Chrysostomus; the third, for the burial of the Evangelist St. Luke. All three events are closely linked to the Church of the Holy Apostles at Constantinople. Since 359 it had sheltered the relics of St. Luke and St. Timothy, and since 438 those of St. John Chrysostomus, whose life had been so closely linked to the church.[10] Thus, the building in the background of all three scenes is no doubt the Apostle Church as it presented itself between 979 and 989 or slightly later when the Menologium was presumably illustrated.[11] The five domes are unmistakable. Also unmistakably, all five are raised on drums pierced by windows, the center drum and dome rising higher than the others. A fourth representation is contained in two manuscripts of the sermons of the monk James Kokkinobaphos, both dating from the twelfth century (Vat. gr. 1162, fol. 2; Paris, B.N. gr. 1208, fol. 2ᵛ) (Fig. 78).[12] Again one recognizes the five domes, the center dome higher, all raised on tall drums and all lit by windows. Exterior and interior features of the building are intermingled in the illumination, and the Mission of the Apostles shown in one of the vaults is the very scene which Nikolaos Mesarites describes as the mosaic contained in the west dome of the Apostle Church.[13]

Since the minor domes of the structure represented in the Kokkinobaphos manuscripts seem to occupy the diagonal rather than the main axes, it has been doubted that the structure is intended to represent the Apostle Church.[14] But depictions of buildings, beginning with Late Antiquity and continuing for a thousand years East and West, must not be interpreted literally. The medieval or Middle Byzantine painter does not represent a building analytically as would, beginning with the sixteenth century, a painter or architect in the West. Nor does he arbitrarily invent. On the contrary, he selects wholly or in fragments a few features he considers essential in the structure to be represented, and he reshuffles them so as to fit narrative and composition.[15] The five domes, their drums of different height, and their windows were apparently essential to the painters both of the Menologium and of the Kokkinobaphos manuscripts. But their position could be shifted from the cross axes to the diagonals. Or else, one of the minor domes which would have disappeared behind the main dome could be displaced to the far right, deceiving the modern viewer into interpreting it as an apse (Vat. gr. 1613, fol. 353); or again, two of the five domes in conflict with the composition of the scene might be omitted (Vat. gr. 1613, fol. 341). Other elements appear in abbreviated form: the wall which since Constantine's time enclosed the precinct of the Apostle Church seems to be indicated in the Transfer of the relics of St. John Chrysostomus (Vat. gr. 1613, fol. 353) by the stretch of wall to the right, and in the Burial of St. Luke (*ibid.,* fol. 121), by the corner of a wall to the left. One even wonders whether the lone tree shown inside the enclosure stands for a grove within the actual precinct. In a correspondingly fragmentary and abbreviated manner, interior features are reshuffled and interwoven with the exterior elements. A portal appears to the far left of the domes and is surmounted by a barrel vault, presumably one of the vaults which linked the domes to one another (Vat. gr. 1613, fol. 341). The interior of a dome turns into what seems to the modern eye a semicircular barrel vault (Vat. gr. 1162, fol. 2, and Paris, B.N. gr. 1208, fol. 3). The marble revetment of the end wall of one of the cross arms is shown below the arch of a barrel vault surmounted by a dome—its drum omitted because it would cover the main drum and dome (Vat. gr. 1613, fol. 121), and in the same miniature, the colonnade to the right and the wall behind with its marble revetment and barred windows would seem to represent one of the aisles of the church. No such reshuffling of elements mattered as long as the identification of the structure was guaranteed by the presence of one or more elements considered essential by the painter and his contemporaries: be it one or two outstanding physical features—such as the five domes and drums, the precinct wall, or the principal mosaic of the interior; or an abstract characteristic, such as the dedication; or in Vat. gr. 1613 an allusion (as provided by the foreground scenes) to the main relics sheltered in the Holy Apostles.

The physical features of the Apostle Church most outstanding in the eyes of Middle Byzantine visitors were, then, apparently the cross plan; the five domes, all raised on drums, the one in the center higher; and the windows in these drums which admit light into the five main bays. These are the elements which stand out in the depictions of the church in our manuscripts and they equally stand out at St. Mark's in Venice, the one architectural filiation of the Apostle Church dating from Middle Byzantine times. However, the drums and the lighting of all five bays of the cross plan are the very features which were not present in the church as laid out and completed under Justinian. Procopius leaves no doubt that the domes over the four cross arms remained dark—and presumably low—and that the center dome, while higher than the others and lit by windows, resembled that of the H. Sophia. Given the date of Procopius' writing, the reference is to the first dome which collapsed in 558: a dome twenty feet lower than the present one and thus certainly not raised on a drum.[16] The conclusion seems inevitable that some time between the late sixth and the late tenth century, when the drums first appear in depictions and architectural filiations, the church was remodelled. Its entire vaulting zone was rebuilt and Justinian's low domes were replaced by domes mounted on high, well-lit drums.

No documentary evidence speaks of such an incisive alteration.[17] The work undertaken by Basil I between 868 and 881 was no doubt limited to repairs; but since it included buttressing, the old building was apparently in bad shape.[18] The building of an Apostle Church attributed to Constantine Porphyrogenetos [19] refers to a church at Hieria, not to a rebuilding of Justinian's Holy Apostles.[20] Also, it seems clear that about 940, Constantine the Rhodian still saw Justinian's church unaltered, with only the center dome lit. On the other hand, when the Menologium of Basil II was illustrated, the rebuilding had apparently taken place. It is relevant to point to the tentative suggestion recently proferred that the mosaic decoration was significantly altered between the time it was described by Constantine the Rhodian and Nikolaos Mesarites' ekphrasis.[21] The exact date at which the Justinianic vaults were replaced by the drums and domes must be left open between the *termini* 940 and ca. 989. It may have occurred under Romanos II, under Nikephoros Phokas, under John Tsimiskes or in the first decade of the reign of Basil II. This is a hypothesis. But the fact of an incisive rebuilding of Justinian's Apostle Church at some time in the second third of the tenth century seems to me evident.

Notes

1. The sources are most conveniently collected in: R. Janin, *La géographie ecclésiastique de l'empire byzantin, première partie, Le siège de Constantinople et le patriarcat aecuménique, tome III, Les églises et les monastères* (Paris, 1953), pp. 46 ff.

2. K. Wulzinger, "Apostelkirche und Mehmedije . . . ," *Byzantion,* VII (1932), 7 ff. has attempted to reconstruct the plan of Justinian's church based on that of the present mosque, but his proposal carries little conviction.

3. A. Heisenberg, *Grabeskirche und Apostelkirche* (Leipzig, 1910), II, *passim.*

4. Procopius, *De aedificiis* I, iv. 9 ff.;

Procopius, VII, *Buildings* ("Loeb Classical Library") (London and Cambridge, Mass., 1954), 48 ff.

5. Legrand, E. "Description . . . des Saints Apotres à Constantinople." *Revue des études grecques,* IX (1896), 32 ff.; Reinach, "Commentaire sur le poème de Constantin le Rhodien," *ibid.,* 66 ff.; Heisenberg, *op. cit.,* II, 120 ff.

6. Heisenberg, *op. cit.,* II, 10 ff.; G. Downey, "Nikolaos Mesarites: Description of the Church of the Holy Apostles . . . ," *Transactions of the American Philosophical Society,* n.s. 47 (1947), 859 ff.

7. Procopius, *Buildings,* V, i. 4 ff., in *ed. cit.* (n. 4), 316 ff.

8. *Forschungen in Ephesus,* IV, 3 (Österr. Arch. Inst. [Vienna, 1951]), H. Hormann.

9. O. Demus, "The Church of San Marco in Venice," *DOPapers,* 14 (1960), pp. 88 ff.

10. C. Stornajolo, *Il Menologio di Basilio II (Cod. Vat. grec 1613),* 2 vols., ("Codices Vaticanis Selecti") . . . VIII (Rome, 1907). Heisenberg, *op. cit.,* II, 133 and Pls. III, a, b, c, and S. Bettini, *L'architettura di San Marco* (Venice, 1946), pp. 74 ff. have previously identified as the Apostle Church the building shown in the Menologium.

11. S. Der Nersessian, "Remarks on the Date of the Menologium of Basil II," *Byzantion,* XV (1940–41), 104 ff. See also I. Sevcenko, "The Illuminators of the Menologium of Basil II," *DOPapers,* 16 (1962), 243 ff., esp. p. 245, note 2.

12. Heisenberg, *op. cit.,* II, 200 and Pl. I.

13. Downey, *op. cit.*

14. Bettini, *op. cit.,* pp. 74 ff., n. 2.

15. See above, p. 125 f.

16. Procopius, *Buildings,* I, i, 41 (Loeb Classical Library, as quoted, p. 20); Johannes Malalas, *Chronographia* XVIII, ann. 558 (*PG,* XCVII, cols. 708 ff.); Agathias, *Historiarum libri quinque,* v, 9 (*PG,* LXXXVIII, col. 1555); finally K. J. Conant, "The first dome of St. Sophia . . . ," *Bull. Byz. Institute,* I, 1946, 71 ff. Regarding the date of Procopius' writing, the year 558/559 (G. Downey, in Procopius, *Buildings,* as quoted, p. ix) represents at best a *terminus ante.*

17. Demus, *op. cit.,* p. 91, n. 129.

18. Theophanes Continuatus, *Chronographia,* V, 80 (*PG,* CIX, cols. 338 ff.).

19. Bettini, *op. cit.,* pp. 60 ff., based on *Theophanes Continuatus,* VI, 27 (*PG,* CIX, cols. 469 ff.).

20. Demus, *loc. cit.*

21. E. Kitzinger, in *Enciclopedia universale dell' arte,* VIII (1963), 690. I know the quotation from the galley proofs which Mr. Kitzinger kindly showed me.

13

THE CAROLINGIAN REVIVAL OF
EARLY CHRISTIAN ARCHITECTURE *

SOME THIRTY YEARS AGO the development of ecclesiastical architecture from late Antiquity to the Romanesque period seemed fairly well established. The consensus of opinion was that it had evolved according to the following pattern: in the beginning there was the Early Christian basilica, and this was of the type represented in Rome by Old St. Peter's or St. Paul's—an atrium, surrounded by porticoes, was followed by a colonnaded nave with four side aisles; this led to a long narrow transept which in turn was terminated by a semicircular apse. This T-type basilica was thought to have survived in Italy from the fourth to the twelfth century; the lack of the transept and of two of the four aisles was considered merely a reduction of the basic type. From Italy the scheme was supposed to have spread all over Europe from the fifth century on, and to have undergone continuous transformation until in the eleventh century, Romanesque architecture evolved from it.[1]

This historical conception was based on a point of view which considered Early Christian architecture merely an occidental development and nothing but a forerunner of Romanesque architecture. Looking backward from the organized system of the Romanesque church, one saw in the Roman T-shaped basilica its still unorganized precursor. Early Christian and early medieval types which did not fit the picture were unconsciously disregarded.

This pattern has been shattered during the last decades: the rich Early Christian architecture along the shores of the Mediterranean was discovered, reaching from North Africa to Asia Minor and Dalmatia and, in the hinterlands of the Near East, from Syria to Armenia. The plain basilica of the T-type revealed itself as only one among numerous other quite different Early Christian solutions: the basilicas without transepts but with three apses, or with dwarf transepts, with twin towers and pastophories, with galleries above the aisles, with piers instead of columns, with triconch endings and east towers.[2] It became evident that Early Christian architecture presented an array of complex and unexpected features many of which had previously been considered to be innovations of the high Middle Ages. On the basis of this new knowledge of Early Christian architecture outside of Rome, the older conception of western architecture before the Romanesque period had to be revised. The "Orient or Rome" question arose.

*From *AB*, XXIV, 1942.

The *"premier art roman,"* [3] Asturian and Mozarabic architecture, and their relations with the Near East and with North Africa were traced.[4] Likewise it was realized that African and Asiatic elements had found their way into France, England, and Lombardy [5] throughout the pre-Romanesque period.

On the other hand these discoveries did not necessarily clarify the problem of early medieval architecture in the Occident as a whole. That the origin of its various types in different regions of the Near East was never clarified is after all only too understandable, given our fragmentary knowledge of the eastern as well as the occidental material. It is perhaps less understandable that more definite stress has not been laid upon the fact that the Near Eastern elements in early medieval architecture were not just accidental infiltrations, but that they formed the basis of this entire architecture.[6] Nor—with rare exceptions—has any attempt been made to define the position which the Roman Early Christian basilica occupied in this development.[7] The Roman plan on the one hand, and the different Near Eastern types on the other, seemed to stand side by side within European church architecture far into the beginning of the second millennium, and the choice of the prototypes—Roman or Near Eastern—appeared to be more or less arbitrary.[8]

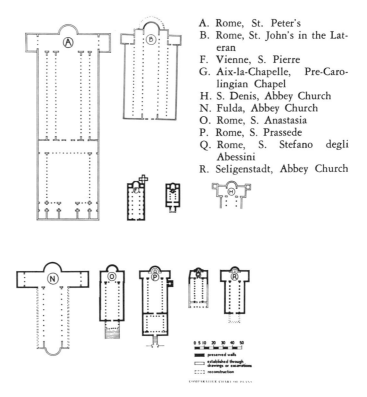

A. Rome, St. Peter's
B. Rome, St. John's in the Lateran
F. Vienne, S. Pierre
G. Aix-la-Chapelle, Pre-Carolingian Chapel
H. S. Denis, Abbey Church
N. Fulda, Abbey Church
O. Rome, S. Anastasia
P. Rome, S. Prassede
Q. Rome, S. Stefano degli Abessini
R. Seligenstadt, Abbey Church

Text fig. 14a. Comparative chart of plans. Sketches, not exact in details, drawn to the same scale (Hoffmann)

Among the numerous questions involved we propose to deal with one limited and definite problem: the part which the Early Christian basilica of the Roman type played during the early Middle Ages up to around 900 A.D. To this end we must discard all types which share only those factors, such as the basilica layout, common to most Early Christian provinces throughout the Mediterranean world, but which combine this pattern with elements foreign to the Roman type, such as polygonal apses, galleries, pastophories, or triconchs.

This process of elimination discloses the surprising fact that actually in Early Christian times, i.e. up to the fifth century, the T-shaped basilica with one apse hardly ever appeared outside Rome, and that even in Rome itself it was anything but frequent. Throughout this period in the whole of Europe it seems to be represented by only three, or possibly four, edifices: old St. Peter's, and in Rome, St. Paul's, and perhaps S. Eusebio in Vercelli (Text Fig. 14A, a, 14B, c; Figs. 12, 79, 81, 82, 83).[9] Certainly it did not survive anywhere for any length of time, let alone for centuries, beyond the Early Christian period in the most limited sense of the word. Whenever it appears after 400 A.D., and wherever it appears in Central Europe, it represents not a survival but a revival of some kind. Such a revival of the Roman Early Christian T-basilica can be noted several times during the high Middle Ages;[10] in the early Middle Ages only one can be ascertained, which takes place during the end of the eighth and the greater part of the ninth

C. Rome, St. Paul's
D. Rome, S. Maria Maggiore
E. Rome, S. Sabina
L. Rome, S. Maria in Cosmedin
M. Rome, SS. Nereo ed Achilleo
S. Hersfeld, Abbey Church
T. Rome, S. Martino ai Monti
U. Rome, S. Cecilia
V. Rome, SS. Quattro Coronati

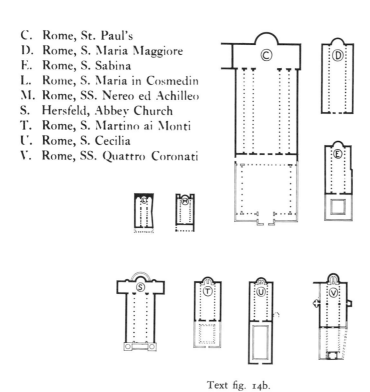

Text fig. 14b.

century. For convenience we will call these decades the Carolingian period.[11]

The revival in this period of the Early Christian architecture of Rome is the subject of our investigation. We shall also consider the ideological reasons for this revival, and the rôle which it played within the phenomenon which is generally known under the name of the "Carolingian Renaissance."

I

The Carolingian church of St. Denis would seem to represent one of the milestones within the development of Carolingian architecture. It is known mainly from literary references and from the sketch and the short article in which Viollet-le-Duc summarized the results of his rather rough excavations (Text Fig. 14A, h). Sources and excavations have both recently been re-interpreted and abundantly supplemented by Crosby.[12] What Viollet-le-Duc had found were not, as he believed, the remains of a church of 638 but those of an edifice which had been begun under Pepin, probably after 754,[13] and which was consecrated under Charlemagne in 775.[14] At the west end of the present twelfth-century chancel and corresponding to it in width were found the remnants of a semicircular apse. According to Viollet-le-Duc's plan, a transept extended in front of the apse, a long and narrow structure with a proportion of 1:4; if his plan can actually be relied upon, the transept was continuous and uninterrupted by any divisions. The nave, as we know from literary sources, was bounded by colonnaded arcades and was roofed with a flat ceiling. A (wooden?) tower rose from the transept. There was possibly an atrium in front of the church.[15] A porch with two low towers was added to the building by Charlemagne.

Despite a number of deviations, such as the relatively narrow proportion of the nave and the slightly later west façade with its twin towers, St. Denis has always been considered a direct continuation of the Roman T-basilicas of the fourth century. Indeed, quite apart from its colonnaded arcades and its single apse, the existence of an atrium and of a continuous transept would recall the ground plan of an Early Christian basilica in Rome such as St. Peter's or late fourth-century St. Paul's outside-the-walls. Of course much of this comparison rests on the reliability of Viollet-le-Duc's transept plan: if we can really depend on it, the importance of St. Denis can hardly be overemphasized. Indeed the surprising thing about this plan is that nobody has ever shown any surprise about it. It was simply taken for granted that a building of the late eighth century should have continued the plan of the fourth-century Early Christian Roman basilica. This assumption is one of the common errors made in discussing the history of European architecture. In reality neither in France nor anywhere else is such a basilican plan with a continuous transept and a single apse known to have been used after the end of the fifth century. We know today at least a few things about the type of churches on French soil which preceded the abbey church of St. Denis; [16] and while it is possible (though by no means certain) that the very early ones of the fifth century [17] had something in common with the Roman Early Christian basilicas, not one among the churches erected in the following centuries shows the pattern of St. Denis. The sixth- or seventh-century church of St. Etienne at Paris was a relatively large edifice with a complicated narthex and possibly with lateral porches; the known parts, at least, have nothing in common with the Roman type.[18] The contemporaneous oratory of Glanfeuil was a small three-naved building with three apses, covered with barrel vaults [19] like the small churches at Binbirkilisse in Anatolia.[20] St. Pierre in Vienne (fifth century) seems to have had pastophories flanking its main apse, a well-known eastern motive (Text 14A, f, Fig. 86); galleries were arranged over the aisles as in the churches of Byzantium and its vicinity.[21] St. Martin at Autun (589–600),[22] a large building with a tripartite transept and with an apse, resembles a group of churches in Greece.[23] In the cathedral of St. Pierre at Geneva (sixth century),[24] the apse was flanked by two long protruding pastophories with apses, a pattern found in North African churches.[25] The trefoil and quatrefoil chapels of St. Laurent at Grenoble (sixth century) and of Venasque (about 600),[26] with their colonnaded screens along the walls, seem to indicate Palestinian, Egyptian, and North African models.[27] Nor do the plain rectangular box-churches of the period, such as St. Paul at Jouarre or Ste. Reine at Alésa [28] have any connection with Roman Early Christian architecture in particular: they represent a type which was commonly used throughout the Christian world up to the middle of the fourth century and which frequently seems to have survived as late as the eighth century. Not Rome but the eastern and southern coastlands of the Mediterranean from Dalmatia to North Africa inspired all this architecture. This is true not only for France but for practically the whole of Europe. In South England a single-naved plan, with chambers all along the nave and in place of the narthex, dominates the Kentish group from St. Peter and Paul in Canterbury (602–604) to St. Pancras (late seventh century) and Reculver (after 669); [29] frequently two of the chambers, evidently pastophories, protrude right in front of the apse like the wings of a dwarf transept. The type finds its closest parallels in the southern Alps [30] and in the hinterlands of the Adria.[31] Its origin is obscure but it is certainly not Roman. Occasionally from the late seventh century on, a church type with a long nave, a square choir, and sometimes a west tower, possibly of Irish origin, is found in Northumbria.[32] This Northumbrian type prevails among a few examples of pre-Carolingian ecclesiastical architecture in Germany [33] such as Büraberg or Fritzlar (732).[34] Yet alongside the Anglo-Irish plans, Near Eastern types appear also in Germany: at Aix-la-Chapelle, a small basilica with pastophories, resembling Syrian prototypes, preceded Charlemagne's Palatine Chapel to the north (Text Fig. 14A, g). Its date is doubtful; it may be seventh century.[35] The same layout is found in a church at Dompierre in Alsace.[36]

Nor are any instances of the Roman type to be found in early medieval architecture of either northern Italy or Spain. Spain follows prototypes in the Near East, evidently Asia Minor,[37] from San Juan de Baños (661) through the ninth and tenth centuries. Upper Italy as early as the fourth century works with types which are closely akin to, though not necessarily derived from, Near Eastern church plans. The first church of Sant' Ambrogio in Milan was a basilica without a transept but with three apses;[38] S. Lorenzo in Milan, likewise of the fourth century, is a central edifice with four protruding apses surrounded by a correspondingly shaped ambulatory,[39] like the cathedral at Bosra in Syria and the similar martyria at Antioch and Apamea; [40] the first church of Sant' Abbondio in Como (fifth century), with transept-like sacristies and with chambers all along the single nave, belonged to the same group as the Kentish and the related Dalmatian buildings.[41] Of later churches some show definitely Byzantine features, for instance S. Prosdocimo near Sta. Giustina at Padua, or SS. Tosca e Teuteria at Verona (eighth or ninth century).[42] S. Pietro in Marina at Sirmione follows a type of box-church [43] with three apses which is well known in the Grisons [44] and which possibly originated in Egypt.[45] The churches of the Veneto and of the Romagna, finally, follow the Near Eastern type which from the fifth century on had prevailed in Ravenna. Thus Sant' Apollinare in Classe with its polygonal apse flanked by pastophories, and with its narthex flanked by west towers, finds its closest parallels in a church such as the Thecla basilica of Meriamlik in Cilicia.[46]

It may be possible (and I feel it will be possible some day) to distinguish between the different stages within this "Near Eastern architecture in the West" which covered the whole of Europe from the fourth and fifth through the eighth century: an earlier stage before 600 which is actually Near Eastern, and a later one which works with and transforms the Near Eastern prototypes into a new style of its own. Perhaps this importation of eastern and other Mediterranean prototypes into Central Europe did not always take the most direct route. While it seems reasonably certain that some patterns were carried directly from Egypt into southern France,[47] Near Eastern motives seem to have been imported to England via North Italy and Dalmatia,[48] to western France via Spain.[49] It is not even impossible that some eastern prototypes reached northern Europe by way of Rome.[50] For, remarkably enough, Rome too ceases to use the T-shaped Early Christian basilica after 400. S. Paolo f.l.m. (386ff.) is the last basilica with four aisles accompanying the nave and with a regular continuous transept; in the early fifth century S. Vitale (401–417),[51] Sta. Sabina (417–32), Sta. Maria Maggiore (ca. 420–40)[52] (Figs. 66, 71, 85), and SS. Giovanni e Paolo (410ff.)[53] reduce this type by omitting the transept. On the other hand, even in Rome, Near Eastern elements had made their appearance as early as the late fourth century: Sant' Anastasia [54] was laid out as a cross-shaped church between 366 and 384, perhaps similar to buildings in Asia Minor; S. Lorenzo in Lucina (432–40)[55] had a long fore-choir in front of the apse and at least one pastophory adjoining the fore-choir like many churches in North Africa.[56] Contemporaneously Sto. Stefano in Via Latina [57] shows a similar arrangement. The tripartite transept of S. Pietro in Vincoli (440–50) points to Greece,[58] the polygonal apse and the fore-choir flanked by pastophories as seen at S. Giovanni a Porta Latina (ca. 500) to Constantinople and Asia Minor.[59] The trefoil choir of SS. Apostoli parallels that of the Church of the Nativity at Bethlehem.[60] Sta. Petronilla, S. Lorenzo f.l.m., and Sant' Agnese with their galleries readapt a Byzantine-Greek type, while Sta. Sinforosa on the Via Tiburtina, with its oblong piers and barrel-vaulted fore-choir, recalls a plan common in Asia Minor.[61]

To sum up, in not one single instance can the Roman type of the Early Christian basilica be traced anywhere in Europe from the middle of the fifth through the first half of the eighth century, either in Rome or outside.[62] Occidental architecture of this period depends on Near Eastern, and perhaps on North African and Irish, but certainly not on Roman Early Christian prototypes.

Seen within this whole development the plan of the abbey church of St. Denis as reconstructed by Viollet-le-Duc would seem to mark a turning-point in occidental architecture, a break with the Near Eastern tradition and a revival of a Roman Early Christian type. Even if we hesitate to accept without reservations Viollet-le-Duc's plan, the break would merely be postponed a few decades. For, thirty years after the consecration of St. Denis, the abbey church at Fulda shows with full clarity all the elements which at St. Denis may still be considered somewhat doubtful (Text Fig. 14A, n; Figs. 87, 88). The present church—it is now the cathedral of Fulda—is an early eighteenth-century construction; yet the aspect of the Carolingian structure and of a few tenth-century additions have been established beyond doubt through excavations. Moreover several seventeenth-century reproductions and a number of ninth-century descriptions give the clearest possible picture of the original aspect of the structure.[63] At the same time the descriptions present an unusually exhaustive and remarkably vivid account of the history of the building, of its interior layout, and of the intentions of the builders, of the architects as well as of the abbots who commissioned the work.

The first large church on the site had been completed in 751 by Sturmi, the disciple and friend of St. Boniface, who had founded the convent in 744. To replace this older church, a three-naved or single-naved building with quite a large semicircular apse to the east,[64] a new structure was begun some time between 790 and 792 under abbot Baugulf.[65] In 802, when only the eastern parts of the building were completed,[66] Baugulf resigned, perhaps not voluntarily, and the monk Ratger succeeded him as abbot,[67] not quite to everybody's satisfaction. Ratger was possibly an experienced architect [68] and certainly he was bitten by the building bug. Indeed, things became so bad that in 812 the monks of the convent petitioned Charlemagne to stop the abbot from continuing the "enormous and superfluous buildings and all that other nonsense (*inutilia opera*) by which the brethren are unduly tired and the serfs are ruined." After all "everything should be done within limits (*iuxta mensuram et discretionem*) and the brethren should be allowed, according to the rule, to read at times and to work at other times." [69] This revolt, while not immediately successful, led in 817 to the forced resignation of Ratger and to his replacement by Eigil, who apparently had been one of the leaders of the opposition. In accordance with the platform on which he had been elected Eigil speedily brought the construction to a close: [70] the decoration was completed, and in 819 the relics of St. Boniface were transferred into the western apse and the whole structure was consecrated.[71]

209

This information combined with the results of the excavations and of the investigation of the present baroque edifice gives a clear picture of the process of construction. Baugulf's new church, while certainly designed to be larger than Sturmi's earlier one, was still planned on a scale and on lines that did not radically depart from the existing building. Like the earlier church it had a semicircular apse, though this was 15 instead of 11.10 m. wide. Yet it certainly had a nave and two aisles; no transept separated the nave from the apse.[72] Aside from these few established facts, no further details are known; it is not even known whether columns or piers were intended to separate the nave from the aisles. When Ratger took over, radical changes were undertaken. In his project the nave was bounded by columns; remnants of their bases have been found. What is more important, he added a "western church and united it with the eastern one which already existed." [73] This allows for only one interpretation: he constructed the transept to the west, large remnants of which are still preserved. The decoration of the edifice may also have been begun under Ratger.[74] It is not certain whether he had also planned two hall-crypts, each with nine groin vaults carried by four columns, which were constructed and vaulted under the east and west apses under his successor Eigil by the new architect Racholph.[75] The pavement was laid and the altars were erected under Abbot Eigil.[76] For the main parts of the edifice, and for its plan as a whole, Ratger is responsible.

The building as it stands today, while seemingly a completely baroque structure, still contains considerable remnants of the ninth-century church. The eighteenth-century cathedral is directed westward like the old one instead of being oriented; it retains the length and width of the Carolingian basilica and has preserved the proportion of nave to aisles; the two towers enclose the core of the two turrets, which in the tenth century were added to flank the east apse; and, most important, the three-storied structures which flank the baroque choir on either side contain the original west transept almost in its entirety.

Thus a fairly clear picture can be gained of the original edifice as laid out between 790 and 819. The nave, 63.30 m. long and 16.70 m. wide, was accompanied by two aisles; the total width was 33.40 m. Nave and aisles were separated by presumably ten columns on either side.[77] Some remnants of composite capitals postulate the considerable diameter of about 0.78 m. for the columns. A number of indications seem to suggest that they carried an architrave rather than an arcade.[78] The seventeenth-century reproductions show four (or five) rather large windows in the walls of the aisles in contrast to seemingly eleven in each clerestory wall of the nave (Figs. 87, 88). While to the east the nave ended in a semicircular apse,[79] to the west it terminated in a huge continuous transept. The wings of this transept protruded far beyond the lateral walls of the aisles; its ends were shut off from the rest of the transept by colonnades. Three tall windows opened in the short walls and in the east walls of each wing.[80] A second semicircular apse finally terminated the building to the west.

The specific character of the plan of Fulda and its kinship with that proposed for St. Denis can be clearly defined. Peculiar to it is not so much the arrangement of two apses as the way in which the west apse is related to a transept. The presence of two apses can be explained on liturgical grounds, for since Baugulf's project took over from Sturmi's church its site and its dedication to the Savior, the east apse could not be used for the relics of St. Boniface, which in the older church rested in the center of the nave under the cross altar.[81] Consequently to accommodate the body of the saint in a more dignified way, some kind of a structure had to be added by Ratger to the western end of the nave after 802. This does not, however, account for the particular form which was actually chosen for this western structure, a semicircular apse with a long transept in front of it and a continuous one at that, like the one on Viollet-le-Duc's plan of St. Denis. The addition in this particular form shows the revolutionary character of Ratger's project: by adding this long continuous transept he transformed the church of Fulda into a regular basilica of the "Roman" type.

The same Roman character appears in the structure as a whole. The enormous size of the edifice with a nave 63 m. long and a transept length of 77 m.; the wide openings of the apses, each 15 m.; the columns with composite capitals; the architrave (if indeed there was one); the bare, plain walls of the exterior, the long flow of the nave roof which is intersected by the transverse roof of the transept—everything points clearly to one prototype, the great Roman Christian basilicas of the fourth century. Thus if St. Denis was a basilica of the Roman type, it need no longer be regarded as an isolated instance; Fulda shows the very same characteristics, and it shows them on quite a different scale. The very size of the building evidences the difference between Fulda and St. Denis. St. Denis was quite a small building; it was not much larger than the contemporaneous "Near Eastern" types in occidental architecture, such as Sta. Maria in Cosmedin or SS. Nereo ed Achilleo (Text Fig. 14A, B, 14B, L, M), and it was a great deal smaller than the Roman fourth-century basilicas. At Fulda the scale has undergone a decisive change: Ratger's new church was as large as St. John's in the Lateran and not much smaller than old St. Peter's in Rome (Text Fig. 14A, n, a, b). Moreover, the implications of the appearance of the "Roman" Early Christian basilica in the North became much more clearly evident at Fulda than they could be at St. Denis.

For not only is the church of Fulda related in a more or less general way to the prototype of the Roman fourth-century basilicas; the relation to one particular model can be definitely established, at least for those parts of the structure that were laid out by Ratger—the transept and the elevation of the nave. Not only is the transept continuous like that of St. Paul's and St. Peter's, it is at the same time a western transept, and it is extremely narrow in comparison to its length, its proportion being exactly 1:5. Another peculiar element is the use of colonnades to shut off the outer ends of the transept. All these characteristics appear in the transept of one particular basilica in Rome and only there, namely in St. Peter's (Figs. 12, 13, 79). The proportions of the transept in St. Paul's are different— 1:3; and not only was St. Peter's equipped with a western transept (the one at St. Paul's being laid out at the east end), it also had the colonnaded partition across the ends of the wings (Text Fig. 14A, a, 14B, c). This feautre in itself is so very exceptional that wherever it occurs it is a clear indication of the use of St. Peter's as a prototype. Likewise the architrave over the colonnades of the nave would point only to St. Peter's among all the Roman basilicas with transept. The two other early basilicas in Rome with an architrave, the Lateran and Sta. Maria Maggiore, had no transept (Figs. 66, 71, 80; Text Fig. 14A, b, 14B, d).[82] Even the measurements and proportions of Fulda would seem to correspond to St. Peter's in Rome.[83] There can be no doubt that the architect who designed the transept at Fulda wanted it to be a real "Roman" structure even to the scale employed. As a matter of fact it is not only the plan of the transept which proves that the monks at Fulda wanted to be as Roman as the Romans or even more so. There is other, documentary, evidence for this. The martyr's altar had been erected in the western apse "according to Roman custom"; [84] there his tomb is still preserved at the former boundary line of transept and apse. Thus it corresponds exactly to the place where St. Peter's altar rose over his tomb, and the specific kinship between the Fulda abbey church and St. Peter's in Rome manifests itself again: in contrast to St. Peter's, the tomb of the saint at St. Paul's is in the transept close to the nave (Figs. 83 and 81). In 822 the cloister was laid out at Fulda; it was arranged not to the south, where the old one had been, but *Romano more* to the west, because "thus it was closer to the body of the saint." [85] Taken by themselves, all these allusions to Rome may seem of minor consequence; yet when taken collectively, no doubt is left as to the intentions of the builders of Fulda: they wanted to create north of the Alps an effigy of the great basilica of St. Peter's in Rome. They sought to establish an equation between St. Boniface and his church in Fulda and St. Peter and his sanctuary on the Vatican Hill. In the fifty years following his death, St. Boniface had become the protomartyr of the German part of the Frankish kingdom. He was considered the Apostle of the Germans in much the same way in which St. Peter and St. Paul had been considered for centuries the Apostles of the Romans.[86] Although it is by no means certain, a similar situation may have prevailed at St. Denis, where the Apostle of the Gauls was buried.[87] This analogy of St. Boniface—and perhaps of St. Denis—with St. Peter and St. Paul may help to explain why possibly the church of the Apostle of the Gauls, and certainly that of the Apostle of the Germans, were the first in the North to take up the plan of the great proto-basilicas of Christianity in Rome.

II

These considerations lead to a more general problem. The veneration of St. Peter had grown constantly throughout the Frankish kingdom during the eighth century. Only Christ and the Virgin take precedence over him in the number of dedications of altars and churches.[88] This is only natural: the Roman Church was symbolized by St. Peter. Time and again his name was used to mean Rome and the papacy in particular.[89] Thus it is not surprising to see that, with the growing supremacy of Rome north of the Alps, the veneration of St. Peter and of his sepulchre in Rome also increased all over Central Europe. The rising importance of St. Peter, of his basilica, and of Rome were indissolubly linked together.

This veneration of St. Peter is but one element within a progressive Romanization of Christian Europe: from the early eighth century on the Gallican Church and the Irish monasteries within the Frankish kingdom, both strongly Near Eastern, were gradually eliminated, largely under Boniface's leadership, in favor of Roman institutions. This tendency increased during the second half of the century. Shortly after 754 the Roman mass was introduced into Metz and somewhat later into the whole kingdom to replace the Gallican liturgy.[90] Simultaneously, and in connection with the Roman liturgy, the Roman chant was transplanted to the North by members of the papal choir and by monks sent to Rome to study with the pontifical *schola cantorum*.[91] Through a decree of 789 all monastic orders were forced to submit to rules shaped after those of the Benedictines, one of the main points being the immediate jurisdiction of the Curia over all monasteries.[92] Foremost among the Benedictine monasteries were Fulda and St. Denis. At the same time Roman relics began to be transferred in large numbers to churches north of the Alps: as early as 765 Fulrad, the abbot of St. Denis, and later on his successors, brought Roman relics to St. Denis and then to convents in Alsace-Lorraine; simultaneously Roman relics were transferred to Bavaria.[93] Among the relics deposited at Fulda between 790 and 819, at least half came from Rome; the rest were a collection of local, Frankish, Dalmatian, and Near Eastern relics.[94] Roman saints competed more and more with the Frankish, Irish, and Near Eastern saints, who until then had been venerated almost exclusively throughout Gaul and the Rhineland.

This ecclesiastical policy of the Curia was paralleled by the general policy of the papal court as well as of the Frankish kings.[95] From 750 on, Rome asserted not only its spiritual but also its political influence north of the Alps, while Frankish policy gravitated more and more towards Italy and Rome. The Frankish court, impelled by ecclesiastical as well as by political reasons, became the foremost champion of ecclesiastical Romanization north of the Alps.[96] Through quite different interests a partnership developed between the Frankish and the papal courts, beginning with the visit of Pope Stephen II to Paris in 753, when Pepin and his sons were anointed as kings and undertook to protect the Roman Church and its possessions, and culminating in the coronation of Charlemagne as emperor on Christmas Eve in the year 800.[97]

In its effects, however, the coronation of 800 was more than a mere seal on the fifty-year-old collaboration between the Frankish kings and the popes. With the spread of Carolingian power over almost all the Christian parts of Europe there had arisen a new conception of rulership.[98] Charlemagne by his coronation laid claim to succession to the Roman emperors of Antiquity; since he dominated large parts of what had been their domain, he considered himself and his successors their legitimate heirs. From the coronation on, his official titles were those of the Roman rulers, Caesar and Augustus; one of his bulls shows a symbolic representation of Rome and the inscription *Renovatio Romani Imperii;* [99] Alcuin addressed him as "Flavius Anicius Carlus" with the names used officially by the Roman emperors; [100] time and again contemporaries alluded to the Carolingian house as legitimate successor to the Roman emperors.[101] This conception clearly reveals an attempt to revive certain aspects of the Roman past; it formed the backbone of medieval policy for half a millennium to come.

A similar desire to revive a state of affairs which had supposedly existed in ancient times underlay the political philosophy of the papal court. Throughout the eighth century one of the aims of papal policy had been to create moral and legal justification for the claims of the Church to a secular territory in Italy and to a leading position in occidental politics. To this end a fiction was created which found its foremost expression in the famous spurious document of the Constantinian Donation. Its main thesis was that Constantine entrusted to Pope Sylvester as the successor to St. Peter the spiritual leadership of the world, and when transferring the capital of the Empire to Constantinople, and indeed because of this transfer, bestowed on the pope the territorial rule over Rome, Italy, and the West. On the basis of this fiction the pope could consider himself the *de iure* ruler of Europe; he had the power to delegate this right to those who were to govern—in other words to crown the emperors who were to practice these powers in his place.[102]

Obviously this fiction, like Charlemagne's conception of his empire, implied the ideal of re-creating a situation of the historical past. It involved the conception of cancelling half a millennium, during which the papacy had been dependent on Byzantium. It pretended to re-establish a state of affairs which had existed in late Antiquity, under Constantine, at the very moment when Rome and Christianity had been merged.

This revival of the past necessarily entailed a new interest in the city of Rome and its ancient institutions. In both the papal and Carolingian camp, there was a manifest desire to restore some of its ancient importance to Rome, the burial place of St. Peter, the former capital of the world, the imperial city.[103] In Rome itself something like a feeling for the Roman national past was revived with the support of the aristocracy of the city. Returning to ancient Roman terminologies which had ceased around 600, the Senate and people of Rome became again elements of importance, and again the term *Res Publica Romanorum* was used, now to signify the Roman element within the Empire.[104]

The same return to Roman customs took place in the Church; the Near Eastern element was eliminated, not so much because it was objected to but because new emphasis was given to Roman elements as such. While from 640 to 752 thirteen among twenty popes had been Dalmatians, Sicilians, Greeks, or Syrians, from the mid eighth century on the pontiffs were chosen with one exception from the families of the Roman aristocracy.[105] Greek churches and monasteries which had been so frequent in Rome during the previous centuries became quite rare.[106]

Greek saints and festivals which had entered into the Roman missal during the seventh century[107] were replaced by Roman martyrs; Eastern relics which had occupied an important place in Rome during the sixth and seventh centuries [108] were superseded by Roman ones. Beginning with the middle of the eighth century and continuing through the first half of the ninth, Roman relics were brought in increasing numbers from the catacombs into the city.[109] A depository seems to have been formed for them, a depository from which relics were distributed all over Europe.[110] Consequently the cult of Roman martyrs gained a new importance; most of the churches erected in Rome during the period were dedicated to one or another of these Roman saints who, while sometimes Greek by birth and name, were considered Roman by right of their provenance from the Roman catacombs.

The goal of all these currents within the later eighth century was clearly a return to a period in Roman history which preceded the Byzantine domination. The idea was to renew the great Roman tradition of the Church, to create a *renovatio* of Rome as of old. Obviously the idea of a *renovatio* was bound to include the most heterogeneous concepts: a "Golden Age" of undetermined Antiquity; a pre-Byzantine Rome in which the Church had been more independent; a fictitious Constantinian Rome in which imperial power had been conferred on the pope; the Rome of the emperors which had been the capital of the world up to Constantine, the first Christian emperor; and last but not least the Rome of the first Christian centuries where so many thousands of martyrs had died, among them the Princes of the Apostles, and where Christ had built His Church on the rock of St. Peter.[111] All these different images of a Rome of the past were blended into one; and the ardent desire to revive the past was vital and compelling in the philosophy and policy of the eighth and ninth centuries. It is only natural that this idea of a return to the past should manifest itself in architecture as well.

III

Up to the very end of the eighth century, however, not one of the Roman churches reflects this new trend. Near Eastern types which had dominated the sixth and seventh centuries were still prevalent.[112] Indeed it seems at first glance a strange phenomenon that the very popes who were the champions of the process of Romanization in Central Europe and of the re-Romanization in Rome did not apply these ideas to architecture. The church of Sant' Angelo in Pescheria, laid out by one of the leading popes of the Roman *renovatio*, shows a characteristic Near Eastern plan with three parallel apses.[113] Hadrian I (772-75) transformed Sta. Maria in Cosmedin (Text Fig. 14B, 1), into a typical Near Eastern basilica, terminating in three apses with a long fore-choir flanked by pastophories and with sham galleries above the aisles.[114] Even Leo III (795-816) still followed the Near Eastern tradition in almost all his buildings: Sta. Susanna, evidently one of the first churches he erected, is again a basilica with galleries—this time, however, with only one apse [115]—while the church of SS. Nereo et Achilleo assumes a definitely Syrian type: its apse is flanked by two pastophories which are surmounted by upper stories (Text Fig. 14B, m).[116]

It was under the same Leo II, however, that a reaction against this predominance of Near Eastern elements took place in Roman ecclesiastical architecture, contemporaneously with the completion, north of the Alps, of the abbey church of Fulda as a basilica of the "Roman" type.

The transformation of the church of Sant' Anastasia seems to have been the first step within this architectural reaction in Rome (Fig 89).[117] The present baroque edifice—it is one of the most beautiful and one of the least known examples of an early eighteenth-century church interior in Rome—contains a great number of older remnants. Evidently within the first years of Leo's pontificate (795-815),[118] a fourth-century cross-shaped church was transformed into a typical basilica. Its nave was separated from the aisles by colonnades which carried either an architrave or a series of arches. The cross arms of the older edifice were adapted to form a normal continuous transept between the new nave and the old semicircular apse, and consequently the new plan took on an appearance that closely resembled the Roman basilicas of the fourth century (Text Fig. 14A, o). A wide flight of steps in front of the façade led to what seems to have been a narthex with two openings on either side and, originally, with a row of supports along its front: a monumental approach was created corresponding to the monumental size which the whole building had acquired in the course of the alterations and which, while much smaller than the fourth-century basilicas, strongly differed from the miniature eighth-century buildings in Rome and elsewhere (see Text Figs. 14 A, B). The eleven windows of the clerestory corresponded to the axes of the intercolumniations below and, although small in comparison to the windows of fourth- and fifth-century basilicas, were considerably larger than any windows found in the immediately preceding period, for instance at Sta. Maria in Cosmedin.[119] Their arches are formed of two rows of bricks—an old Roman device used frequently in the fourth and fifth centuries in Rome, but which had disappeared during the sixth century.

At Sant' Anastasia the relation to Roman fourth-century architecture, though obvious, is necessarily somewhat obscured by the fact that large parts of an older structure had to be incorporated into the new building. While the general kinship to early Roman ecclesiastical edifices is manifest, it would be hard to point out any specific Constantinian or Theodosian basilica which the architect of Leo III might have taken as his model. In another building of Leo III, however, such a specific relation becomes quite striking: Sto. Stefano degli Abessini, situated behind St. Peter's, seems to have been laid out in the later years of Leo's pontificate.[120] It was a normal basilica, quite small, with a continuous transept and with one semicircular apse; in front of the façade extended a narthex, supported by a series of columns and with lateral openings resembling those at Sant'

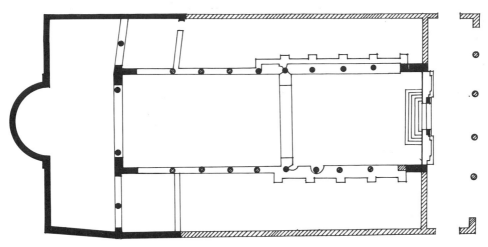

Text fig. 15. Rome, Sto. Stefano degli Abessini, plan (Giovannoni)

Anastasia (Fig. 90 and Text Fig. 15).[121] Only eight columns on either side separated the nave from the aisles. This time it is certain that these columns carried an architrave: remnants of it are still *in situ* (Fig. 90). The transept communicated with the aisles by twin openings. The triumphal arch leading from the nave into the transept was supported by T-piers with large columns next to them. A semicircular apse terminated the transept; underneath it extended an annular crypt, consisting of a semicircular corridor along the curve of the apse wall and of a straight corridor which led from the apex of the apse to the square *confessio* under the high altar.[122]

The model from which the plan of Sto. Stefano is derived can be established in quite a definite way. The continuous transept, it will be remembered, had appeared only in two of the great proto-basilicas of the fourth century: St. Peter's and St. Paul's.[123] The twin openings between aisles and transept wings point to these same basilicas: the column in the center of the twin openings at Sto. Stefano is evidently nothing but a reminiscence of the pier, which in these proto-types with their four aisles had marked the end of the colonnades between the inner and outer aisles. The transept of Sto. Stefano does not protrude beyond the aisle walls and is rather wide in proportion to its length, exactly 1:3. This is the very proportion of the transept of S. Paolo *f.l.m.,* quite different from the strongly protruding, extremely narrow transept of St. Peter's (Text Fig. 14A, a, o, 14B, c). On the other hand, the use of the architrave at Sto. Stefano indicates St. Peter's as a model, for of all the great basilicas in Rome only St. Peter's combines the architrave and the transept. While taking over the general layout of S. Paolo, the architect at Sto. Stefano fused it with elements carried over from St. Peter's.

One can hardly overemphasize the significance that these new edifices must have had in the Rome of Leo III. Up to his time and even during his own

pontificate, the rich variety of Near Eastern motives had dominated the architectural production of the city. Evidently no architect had used the models
established by the great imperial foundations of the fourth century, despite the
fact that they had always been extant, in good state and highly venerated. With
Sant' Anastasia and Sto. Stefano degli Abessini the spell seems to be broken.
The more complicated Near Eastern types with their pastophories and galleries
are abandoned, and the simple beauty of the contrast between nave and transept,
the opposition of clear horizontals and verticals in the architrave and the colonnade, seem to have come back to life. Paralleling the *renovatio* in the political
field, and the revival of the cult of Roman saints and Roman martyrs, the
architecture of the city of Rome likewise returned to its own past.

This revival of the Roman Early Christian basilica continued and gathered
momentum under the pontificate of Paschal I (817-24). One can hardly help
feeling that the beginnings of this architecture were closely tied up with his
personal influence. Among the churches erected under his pontificate only the
diaconia of Sta. Maria in Domnica still followed the older Near Eastern scheme
of a basilica with three apses. He probably had been *praepositus* of Sto. Stefano
degli Abessini when the new church was designed under Leo III,[124] and the
two main churches erected under his own pontificate, Sta. Prassede and Sta.
Cecilia, definitely belong to the new current.

With the church of Sta. Prassede, the architects of Paschal created a perfect
example of this new style, an example which fortunately is also perfectly preserved, much better than either Sant' Anastasia or Sto. Stefano degli Abessini,
its next of kin. Only the sixteenth-century murals of the nave and the three
thirteenth-century diaphragm arches spanning it are later additions (Figs. 91 and
92).[125]

In plan the edifice again shows a nave, two aisles, a semicircular apse, and a
continuous transept which opens toward the aisles with twin apertures. An annular crypt extends underneath the apse (Text Fig. 14A, p, a). The nave is bounded
by columns which are surmounted by an architrave; windows with double arches
pierce the clerestory, each corresponding to the axis of one intercolumniation. All
this resembles Sto. Stefano degli Abessini. The architect of Sta. Prassede, like
the designer of Sto. Stefano, strove for the neat purity of the simple basilican
plan with its clear contrasts. Sta. Prassede has also preserved at least a large
part of its original decoration, which in its sister church has been lost. The apse
still shows its resplendent mosaics: so do the "east" wall of the transept next to
the apse, and the triumphal arch between transept and nave. A rich mural decoration, parts of which are preserved in the north transept, supplemented this
array of colors. What is irretrievably lost—the marble incrustation of the apse
wall [126]—can be reconstructed from the chapel of S. Zeno adjacent to the right
aisle, where the blending of the rich colors of the mosaics in the vaults and
of the marble incrustation on the walls is still preserved. If one adds to these
remnants the marble paneling and the stucco decoration of the crypt and the
ornamented portal leading to the chapel of S. Zeno, one understands the delighted

enthusiasm with which the writer of the *Liber Pontificalis* described the splendor of the edifice and of its furniture: [127] the ciborium, the altar, the textiles. The aim of this architecture was evidently to create a contrast between the plainness of the structure, the bareness of the exterior, and the sumptuous wealth of the interior decoration.

At the same time, one should realize that Sta. Prassede was built on a scale much more monumental than anything in the previous period (see Text Figs. 14A, B). Even Sto. Stefano, while larger than most churches of the seventh and eighth centuries, is small in comparison with Sta. Prassede, where nave and aisles communicate through twelve instead of nine intercolumniations and the absolute measurements have also increased.[128] Only Sant' Anastasia is similar in size, but there the length of the nave was conditioned by the Roman structures which has been re-used. The size of Sta. Prassede, the plan with its T-transept and its single apse, the tall, narrow structure of the transept which is opposed to the nave in direction and in proportion; the colonnades with their architraves, the comparatively wide windows of the clerestory; the lavish mosaic and marble decoration of the interior and the sobriety of the exterior; the clear contrast of the parts in plan and elevation—the whole lay-out and style find their exact prototype in the great basilicas of the fourth century. Only as a revival of the architecture of the great Christian century can Sta. Prassede be explained.

And not only these general features but the details of the plan and even the building technique also point in the same direction. The small chapel of S. Zeno which is joined to the right aisle of the church (Fig. 91), a cross-shaped structure with a groin-vaulted center bay and barrel-vaulted wings, is one of the elements which would seem to hark back to the Early Christian period. It evidently represents a combination of mausoleum and memorial chapel.[129] Thus it recalls the mausolea of central plan which surrounded the *basilicae ad corpus* of the fourth century, S. Sebastiano [130] as well as St. Peter's or St. Paul's (Figs. 9, 12, 79, 81). Likewise it recalls the memorial chapels constructed for relics, which had grown up around these basilicas and around other ecclesiastical buildings at least during the fifth century. The custom seems to have disappeared after the late sixth century. The chapel of S. Zeno obviously revives the type in general as well as the particular cross pattern which had existed in the fourth century at St. Paul's outside-the-walls, and in the fifth century in the two chapels of St. John the Baptist and St. John the Evangelist adjoining the Lateran Baptistery.[131]

Even the technique of brickwork in this whole group of churches, from Sant' Anastasia on, seems to have reverted to that of the Early Christian period proper. Of course, brickmasonry had remained a common technique in Roman building throughout the sixth, seventh, and eighth centuries. It had been somewhat displaced by the use of *opus listatum,* but it had never completely disappeared. However, the technical standards of the fourth and fifth centuries had not been maintained. Old, pilfered, broken bricks were used; the courses were exceedingly irregular, at times closely packed, at others separated by very wide joints. The arches consisted of only one row of short voussoirs, and these voussoirs took on a radial position only far above the springing of the arch. The brickwork was interspersed with numerous bits of stone: Sta. Maria in Cosmedin provides a good instance of this technique. From the late eighth century on, however, the masonry becomes more regular, resembling that of the Early Christian period proper; the courses, while still undulating and not quite as regular as those of the old parts of St. John's in the Lateran or of Sta. Maria Maggiore, for example, are separated by joints of approximately even thickness; the arches are surmounted by double rows of voussoirs which assume a radial position right at the springings of the arches. Tufa stones disappear completely from the masonry. It is this building technique which characterizes the new parts of Sant' Anastasia, the contemporary parts of Sta. Susanna, and the basilicas of Sto. Stefano and Sta. Prassede. Comparison with the preceding period leaves no doubt that this change of technique finds its explanation in a conscious attempt to imitate the technique of the early centuries of Christian architecture in Rome.

These general features which link Sta. Prassede to the prototypes of fourth- and fifth-century architecture in Rome in general, are supplemented by a number of details which point specifically to St. Peter's as its model. The combination of an architrave in the nave with a transept, as will be remembered, is found only there. Moreover the particular shape of the transept of Sta. Prassede points to the same source. It is a long and tall structure, extremely narrow. While quite different in scale,[132] its unique proportion of 1:5 corresponds exactly to that of the transept of St. Peter's, and to this transept only, among all the basilicas of the fourth century, and consequently to the transepts of later filiations of St. Peter's such as the abbey church of Fulda.

The atrium of Sta. Prassede is preserved only in remnants, but these remnants allow for a reconstruction. A square center courtyard was surrounded on at least three sides by porticoes, each consisting of five arches carried by columns; a fourth portico ran in all likelihood along the façade of the church.[133] A flight of steps leads and always led from the Via S. Martino, the ancient *Clivus Suburanus*, up to the atrium.[134] Such an atrium (especially one with a flight of steps leading to its entrance), familiar though it may seem, is not a common feature in the late centuries of Early Christian architecture in Rome. While it occurred, of course, in the fourth century, in St. Peter's and in St. Paul's and throughout the first half of the fifth century,[135] during the following period the atrium was apparently replaced by a plain arcaded portico along the façade, equivalent to the exonarthex of Near Eastern churches.[136] Sto. Stefano degli Abessini and Sant' Anastasia were still entered through a plain narthex of this sort. After three and a half centuries, Sta. Prassede is the first church to take up the more pretentious form of the complete atrium. It may even be no mere chance that the twenty-five steps which led to the atrium of Sta. Prassede corresponded in number to those by which one ascended to the atrium of St. Peter's.[137]

Sto. Stefano and Sta. Prassede are the most complete examples of this renascence of fourth century types which in the decades between 800 and 820 manifests itself in Roman ecclesiastical architecture. Yet not all the elements, atrium, transept, and so forth need correspond to the great fourth-century basilicas in order to relate a building to this revival of Early Christian architecture; nor need it be St. Peter's or St. Paul's which the Roman architects of the early ninth century had in mind. Only the early edifices follow the fourth-century pattern completely; later churches erected between 820 and 850 prefer other Early Christian models. There are three churches in this later group, Sta. Cecilia, S. Marco, and S. Martino ai Monti, and all of them are patterned after basilicas of the early fifth century. Sta. Cecilia, the earliest among them (Fig. 93), erected under Paschal I (817–24), already omits the transept.[138] Its nave was originally separated from the aisles by plain colonnades with arches rather than an architrave. While these elements differ, other features conform to the practice of the earlier ninth-century basilicas: like Sta. Prassede, Sta. Cecilia shows traces of a large atrium; the nave terminates in a single semicircular apse with an annular crypt underneath; the windows of the apse as well as those of the clerestory wall are topped by the characteristic double arches. As at Sta. Prassede, a memorial chapel was attached to the right aisle above the so-called "Bath of Sta. Cecilia," of circular rather than of cross shape (Text 14B, u). S. Marco (827–44), though slightly later, seems to have been almost identical with Sta. Cecilia before it was transformed in the fifteenth and eighteenth centuries. It shows the by now familiar type (Fig. 94) with arcades bounding the nave, semicircular apse, annular crypt, and possibly an atrium in front.[139] Both S. Marco and Sta. Cecilia resemble the great early fifth-century basilicas without transept: at Sta. Sabina (Fig. 86), at S. Vitale, at S. Lorenzo in Lucina, at SS. Giovanni e Paolo,[140] we find the arcades bounding the nave, the plain circular apse, and—at least at Sta. Sabina and SS. Giovanni e Paolo—also the atrium. Significantly enough the number of columns in the arcade which divides nave and aisle at Sta. Cecilia is twelve, exactly the same number as in the naves of Sta. Sabina, SS. Giovanni e Paolo, and S. Lorenzo in Lucina.

The latest church of the group, S. Martino ai Monti (844–47), clearly recognizable under the splendid seventeenth-century decoration of its interior (Fig. 95), differs somewhat from this pattern: [141] while its plan with nave, aisles, apse and —originally—atrium, resembles Sta. Cecilia, even in the use of twelve columns on either side of the nave and in its measurements,[142] the colonnades of its nave carry an architrave instead of arches. Thus the elevation seems to have been inspired not so much by Sta. Sabina and the related basilicas, but by Sta. Maria Maggiore with its architraved colonnades (Fig. 71).

The close of the "Renaissance of the Early Christian Basilica" in Roman architecture of the ninth century seems to be represented by two churches, both erected under the pontificate of Leo IV (847–55): Sta. Maria Nova, now S. Francesca Romana, and the church of the Quattro Coronati. While the two clerestory walls of Sta. Maria Nova [143] with their double-arched windows, the walls of the aisles, and one fragment of an architrave show that the nave of the small basilica was linked to S. Martino ai Monti, it cannot be established whether the church ended like Sta. Prassede in a transept and an apse with annular crypt, or whether as at S. Martino the transept was omitted. The porch, which instead of an atrium ran along the façade and along the front part of the right flank, clearly represents a departure from the "classical" type with atrium which had been re-established in Rome from 810 on, and a retrogression to the narthex type which had prevailed up to the end of the eighth century. The church of the Quattro Coronati (Text Fig. 14B, v), in its original state would also seem to be closely akin to S. Martino or even more to Sta. Cecilia.[144] The atrium, the nave with twelve intercolumnia on either side, the semicircular apse, the annular crypt, the absence of the transept, the windows with double arches, everything seems to tally: there is even a square chapel adjacent to the left aisle with four columns in the corners, with a groined vault, and with three apses forming a kind of trefoil (Text Fig. 14B, u), in position and function resembling those at Sta. Prassede and Sta. Cecilia.[145] Yet while all these features seem to coincide with the earlier churches, a number of elements at SS. Quattro Coronati depart from the norm: instead of continuing from the façade to the beginning of the apse, the series of columns was broken by a pier in the middle of the nave, on either side; a respond in front of the pier rose to the open timber roof. Thus the nave was divided into two large bays; a rhythmical element was introduced, quite foreign to the quiet flow of the colonnades in the other buildings of the renaissance movement of the ninth century. Likewise the atrium is surmounted by a clumsy square tower with a passage (Fig. 96). Its upper story exhibits four openings on each side, supported by small baluster-like piers.[146] The tower created a strong accent at the entrance to the atrium; it conforms perfectly to the rhythm created in the interior. Both rhythm and accentuation are foreign not only to Roman ninth-century architecture, but to Early Christian and medieval ecclesiastical architecture in Rome in general.

Thus the development of Roman architecture during the first half of the ninth century becomes apparent. During the last years of the pontificate of Leo III and during the pontificate of Paschal I, roughly speaking within the first two decades of the ninth century, the Near Eastern church types were superseded by a renaissance of Roman Early Christian models, more specifically of the great fourth-century basilicas, primarily St. Peter's and secondarily St. Paul's. The first renaissance group, which includes the transformation of Sant' Anastasia and the building of Sto. Stefano degli Abessini and Sta. Prassede, is characterized in its technique of construction by the constant use of columns, by the improvement of the brick masonry, and by the use of double arches over the windows; in plan and elevation it is marked by the re-introduction of the atrium, by the re-establishment of a continuous transept, and by the re-appearance of an architrave over the columns. This first group is followed from 820 to 850 by a second one, which includes Sta. Cecilia, S. Marco, and S. Martino ai Monti. In contrast to the first, their main feature is the omission of the transept which points to a derivation of this type from fifth- rather than from fourth-century Early Christian models. More specifically the absence of a transept, together with the occurrence of an architrave over the colonnades, tends to establish Sta. Maria Maggiore as the prototype of S. Martino ai Monti, while the arcaded colonnades of Sta. Cecilia and S. Marco suggest inspiration from such prototypes as Sta. Sabina or SS. Giovanni e Paolo. The use of the smaller fifth-century basilicas as prototypes instead of the large fourth-century ones is evident. Possibly this change represents at the same time a shift from the shrines of the great Roman saints to those of lesser martyrs. Throughout the first half of the ninth century this whole movement is characterized by the plain beauty of the basilican plan, by the uncomplicated contrast of nave and transept or nave and apse, and the simplicity of the elevation. Emphasis is laid upon the quiet flow of the colonnades, the wide windows, the bare outer walls, the straight inner walls with their mosaics and marble incrustations, and the flood of light that fills the nave in contrast to the windowless dark aisles.

Shortly after the middle of the century the church of the Quattro Coronati introduced a number of quite unusual elements which cannot be explained through the Roman tradition. Yet SS. Quattro Coronati remained an exception; at the same time smaller churches such as Sta. Maria Nova more or less continued the "Renaissance" types without changing them decisively. After 860 ecclesiastical architecture in Rome seems to come to a standstill. Nothing worth mentioning was built in Rome from this date up to the end of the millennium.

IV

It is evident that the architectural revival conforms to the political and ecclesiastical *renovatio* movement which from the middle of the eighth century on had formed the backbone of the policy of the papal court. While the architectural renaissance in Rome follows about half a century in the wake of the political *renovatio,* the intimate connection between the two movements is obvious. Likewise it is evident that it parallels the acceptance of Roman Early Christian types north of the Alps. Fulda, and possibly St. Denis, revert to the identical Early Christian proto-basilicas from which Roman ninth-century architecture was derived, and stand against a similar ideological background. But, while this background is similar it is by no means identical; it has obviously different connotations north and south of the Alps and thus leads to a somewhat different course of architectural development. South of the Alps, in Rome, the movement was that of a *renovatio;* it was an attempt to revive the city's own glorious past by eliminating the "foreign" Near Eastern influence in architecture as well as in any other field. In the North, the basic element was not so much a *renovatio* in the proper sense; it was rather a movement towards Rome, an outgrowth of the general process of Romanization in the Frankish kingdom. The renascence of the Early Christian basilica has in the North a more specific, in Rome a more general character; while in the North it is limited to the emulation of the great proto-basilicas, in Rome after an initial period it is inspired by the totality of Early Christian architecture of the fourth and fifth centuries.

Whether the two architectural trends, the one in the Frankish kingdom and the other in Rome, are merely parallel to each other or whether they are more directly related is another question.

If it could be definitely established that the Roman Christian type existed at St. Denis before 775, no doubt would be admissible as to the priority of the revival of the Roman Christian basilicas in the Frankish kingdom to the parallel development in Rome which took place after 800. On the other hand, Ratger's "Roman" project of 802 for Fulda would be exactly contemporary with the very first "Renaissance" basilicas in Rome: Sant' Anastasia was probably designed between 795 and 800, Sto. Stefano after 806. Theoretically an influence exerted by Roman ninth-century architecture on that of the North would be as possible as an influence in the reverse direction, moving from the North to Rome. *A priori* one might be inclined to assume that architecture north of the Alps must have depended of necessity on a previous architectural revolution in Rome; an impact coming from Rome always seems more natural than one exerted upon it. Still there is no need to deny offhand the possibility that the Roman architectural movement might have been inspired by an earlier development north of the Alps. Frankish workmen were used in Rome; they evidently even enjoyed a high reputation as carpenters and builders. Pope Hadrian I in two letters asked Charlemagne not only for beams for the repair of the roof of St. Peter's but also for a *magister* to supervise the work; Wilcharius, Bishop of Sens, was to direct the restoration, probably as a consulting engineer.[147] Works of art were also imported from France: after Hadrian's death Charlemagne had the Pope's epitaph sent to Rome, a slab of black marble from Port-Etroit, decorated with an elegant rinceaux ornament *à l'antique* and an inscription in beautiful lettering.[148] One wonders whether architectural elements were not also imported from north of the Alps: the wooden tower which Stephen II erected over the nave of St. Peter's is an element which remained as unique in Rome as it was common in the North from the late eighth century on.[149] Thus it may be safe to conclude that during the second half of the eighth century, Rome was at least as willing to receive from the North as the North was eager to emulate earlier, and possibly contemporary, Roman prototypes.

While these possibilities remain open, it would seem that actually the churches at Fulda (and St. Denis) and the contemporary churches in Rome do not depend on each other. In none of the Roman churches of the ninth century are the ends of the transept wings shut off by colonnades as was done at Fulda in direct imitation of St. Peter's; none of them competes in size with the fourth-century proto-basilicas as did Fulda. It would seem that Ratger at Fulda and Leo III's architects in Rome had simultaneously yet independently reached similar solutions on the basis of a related historical ideology.

This situation changes when after 830 the plan which had appeared early in the century in Rome and in Fulda was taken up more generally north of the Alps.

The first church in Germany after Fulda to adopt the new style is the church of Sts. Peter and Marcellinus at Seligenstadt (Text Fig. 14A, r). In 827 the relics of the saints had been transferred by Einhard, Charlemagne's ex-chancellor, to his country estate at Steinbach. Evidently irritated by the removal from Rome without their volition and dissatisfied with their new abode, the saints insisted on being transferred again and thus caused the construction of the new church at Seligenstadt between 831 and 840.[150] Nave and aisles communicated by nine brick arches on either side, supported by slightly rectangular brick piers; the upper walls of the nave, like those of the aisles and of the transept wings consist of ashlar masonry. A triumphal arch supported by T-piers opens onto a continuous transept, rather wide in plan and based on a proportion of 1:4. The single semicircular apse had an annular crypt underneath.[151] While this plan certainly shows all the elements of the ninth-century revival, it is not derived from Fulda (or from St. Denis), nor does it depend directly on the fourth-century basilicas of Rome. The proportion of the transept, however, is identical with that of Sto. Stefano degli Abessini (Text Figs. 14A, r; 15; Fig. 90) and so is the number of nine intercolumniations per arcade, a number which among all the ninth-century churches of this type is found only at Seligenstadt and at Sto. Stefano.[152]

Thus it is hardly doubtful that Einhard's architect drew on the contemporary Roman churches. Nevertheless he combined with the Roman elements some features of quite different character: the oblong piers of the nave which he used instead of columns are more massive and solid than anything found in Rome, and still belong to the Near Eastern tradition; a towerlike structure seems to have risen from the west façade,[153] creating a strong vertical accent quite at variance with the long-drawn horizontal lines of Roman ninth-century architecture. The revived plan of the Early Christian basilica is fused with different elements, and this fusion dominates the subsequent development of the type north and south of the Alps from 830 to 870. In the Benedictine abbey church at Hersfeld (831–50),[154] a long nave bounded by eleven arches on columns and terminated by a huge continuous transept (Text Fig. 14B, s; Fig. 97), quite "Roman" in aspect,[155] was flanked by two vertical accents; a group of three apses, not a single one as in the churches of the Roman type, rose to the east, while the west façade was surmounted by some tall towerlike structure. Rival architectural masses with vertical accents balance one another at either end of the building; they manifest a conception of architecture which is diametrically opposed to the continuous flow and the simple contrast of masses which dominated the Early Christian basilicas in Rome as well as their eighth- and ninth-century derivatives in Rome and in the North, and which in Hersfeld still survives in the nave and in the transept.

A number of smaller buildings erected after the middle of the ninth century in the eastern parts of the Frankish Empire show a similar fusion of Roman-Christian with new architectural elements: the Frankfurt Stiftskirche, the Regensburg Alte Kappelle (both 840–47), the abbey church at Heiligenberg (873), the Frauenmünster at Zürich (874) [156]—all combine a small basilican nave and a continuous transept with rather elaborate structures at the west end, and with a group of three apses or a main apse flanked by sacristies, or with a longish fore-choir.[157] A comparable fusion seems to take place during the ninth century in a group of structures south of the Alps: even in Rome the entrance of the atrium of the Quattro Coronati, while not a regular west-work, is reminiscent of the arrangements at Hersfeld and possibly Seligenstadt. A similar isolated tower opposite the church, possibly as early as 797–818, surmounted the entrance side of the atrium of S. Salvatore at Cassino.[158] The plan of its transept with three semicircular apses perhaps depended on the supposedly contemporaneous analogous solution at the neighboring pre-Desiderian basilica of Monte Cassino.[159] At Farfa a west-work may have been added to the earlier church between 830 and 840.[160]

The place of the new fusion-types north and south of the Alps within the general development of medieval architecture can be sketched in a summary fashion. The conception of the building as a group composed of structural masses of diverse shape, size, and height had already played a considerable part in what we called "Near Eastern architecture in the West" from the sixth through the eighth century. This Near Eastern tradition survived throughout the first half of the ninth century: Einhard's church at Steinbach (815–20) with its dwarf transepts, the quincunx central building at Germigny-des-Près (ca. 800), St. Philibert-de-Grandlieu (819–36; 836–53) with its dwarf transepts and its exterior corridor crypt, are a few instances selected at random.[161] Likewise the Northumbrian (?) western tower survived: the church on the Petersberg near Fulda (779/802–836) represents a late though not by any means the latest instance.[162] Out of a fusion of these older motives with one another and with certain Roman Early Christian elements a new style grew up late in the eighth century. At Centula (190–99)[163] the short basilican colonnaded nave of the church of St. Riquier seems to be almost crushed between the two enormous architectural groups at opposite ends of the building, the tower over the monks' choir with its dwarf transept wings (in all likelihood with inner galleries), and its long low fore-choir to the east and the similar tower-like west-work. The eye is led up from the aisles to the radiating wings of the east and west structures, from there to the turrets in the corners, to the nave, and finally to the spires which dominate the whole edifice. The single motives, the dwarf transepts, the western tower, the enormous spires may have been derived from the Near Eastern and Celto-Northumbrian foundations of early European architecture; yet they have been transformed into elaborate structures, each of which is composed of a number of units of different height and mass; they constitute multiform groups of diversified shape and outline which balance each other at opposite ends of the building. A new style develops which transforms the pre-Carolingian inspirations into something quite different and which, on the other hand, has little to do with the contemporary revival of the Early Christian basilica in Rome and in the Frankish kingdom. Only a very few Roman Christian elements have been incorporated into the church at Centula, such as the colonnaded nave and the atrium, albeit with towers over the entrances. This new style becomes increasingly important throughout the Carolingian Empire during the ninth century; at Corvey, at St. Germain at Auxerre, at Cologne, at St. Gall, ponderous yet clearly organized west-works are balanced by equally dominating groups over the eastern ends of the edifice. Hersfeld and the related structures in the North as well as in Italy are nothing but a collateral of these trends: in them certain elements of the "Centula" type have been merged with others from the Roman Christian revival, yet without submerging these Roman Christian elements completely in the new style which was to dominate the future. It is this style with its counterbalancing masses at either end of the basilican nave which forms the basis of post-Carolingian and Romanesque architecture in Burgundy, in the Rhineland, in England—in all the regions which were dominated neither by the architecture of the *premier art roman* (which itself would seem to depend on the Near Eastern art in Europe) nor by the numerous post-Carolingian renascences of the Roman Early Christian basilica. For the Carolingian Renaissance of Early Christian architecture is only the first in a long series of attempts to follow Roman Christian prototypes. New renaissances follow one another from the late tenth through the twelfth century all over Europe, from southern Germany to Spain, from the Upper Rhine valley to Holland, and to southern Italy. Yet these revivals are not by necessity directly inspired by the Early Christian prototypes proper; frequently they depend less on them than on the Carolingian imitations of Early Christian architecture. Of course northern Spain and northern France early in the eleventh century experienced a genuine Roman Christian renaissance directly dependent upon the Roman proto-basilicas: Ripoll, the cathedral of Orléans and St. Remy in Reims, with their four aisles and with the numerous chapels along the transept, can be explained only by a direct inspiration from St. Peter's. On the other hand there exists a contemporary movement in southern Germany and North Italy which would seem to depend rather on churches of the Carolingian Christian renaissance type such as Fulda or Hersfeld: the cathedrals at Augsburg, Mainz,[164] or Aquileia[165] with two aisles, with an overlong transept and with hall crypts are indicative of this. Similarly an Early Romanesque revival which takes place in the Upper Rhine valley during the second quarter of the eleventh century, e.g., at Strassburg, Einsiedeln, and Muri,[166] while seemingly inspired by Early Christian models, proves really to be influenced by the Carolingian basilicas of St. Gall and possibly by Fulda. Likewise in the third quarter of the century the Desiderian basilica of Monte Cassino with its three apses may have depended on its Carolingian fore runner[167] which would thus form an important link between the Early Christian period and the eleventh and twelfth centuries. The Monte Cassino type spread during the last quarter of the century to Campania and Apulia,[168] and early in the twelfth century to Rome. Strange as it may seem the Roman churches of the twelfth century, Sta. Maria in Trastevere, the upper church of S. Crisogono, or Sant' Eusebio do not depend directly either on the fourth- or on the ninth-century basilicas of the city; their transepts, which hardly protrude beyond the aisles, and their three apses give evidence that they depend on the great Benedictine abbey of Monte Cassino. A comparable situation prevails in later "Early Christian Renaissances." Indeed Carolingian buildings and their twelfth-century filiations rather than Early Christian originals determined the conception of Early

Christian architecture throughout the Renaissance and up to our own day: Brunellesco's "Early Christian" churches of S. Lorenzo and Sto. Spirito in Florence,[169] or the slightly later ones in Rome,[170] all follow churches like SS. Apostoli in Florence or Sta. Maria in Trastevere in Rome, not St. Peter's or St. Paul's. Far beyond the Carolingian period the development of medieval architecture was largely shaped by the architecture of the ninth-century revival.

Even this brief outline may help to indicate the decisive place which the Carolingian Renaissance holds within the development of medieval architecture in Europe. To state it explicitly: it marks the point at which European architecture turns from its Near Eastern background to the West and looks there, and more particularly to Rome, for new prototypes. From the fifth century up to the end of the eighth century Europe had been, one might almost say, a provincial country which depended almost wholly on the culture and the architecture of the littorals and the hinterlands of the Eastern Mediterranean. It was in no way connected with the tradition of Christian architecture in the West which in the fourth century had accepted the eminently sober and simple type of the Roman Early Christian basilica, and which through the following hundred years maintained it without changing it essentially. The Near East had entered upon the inheritance of late Antiquity with quite a different spirit: Kalât Simân, Hagia Sophia at Constantinople, the centralized churches of Antioch and Ephesos, the Menas basilica, had taken up and developed the types and the architectural conceptions of late Antiquity with a richness and an inventiveness which continually led to new forms and new solutions. While the Islamic conquest from the second quarter of the seventh century on arrested this lively and rich development in Syria, Egypt, and North Africa, this style continued unabated in the Byzantine Empire. But church architecture in the Occident up to the end of the eighth century is merely a reflection of this post-antique Near Eastern art which continually changed form and which was extraordinarily alive. The achievement of the Carolingian Renaissance was to cut off the dependence of occidental architecture upon that of the Near East; this means at the same time that it brought to an end the reverberations of Near Eastern late antique architecture in the Occident.

By introducing for the first time the type of the Roman Christian basilica into general European architecture, and by re-introducing it into Roman architecture, the Carolingian Renaissance replaced this living development of late-antique art with the revival of a form of the fourth and fifth centuries. The sobriety and simplicity of this obsolete form together with its monumental scale and its conception of plain surfaces and walls form a new element within western architecture. From the time of its revival at the end of the eighth and early in the ninth century, this new element becomes one of the essential constituents of medieval and post-medieval architecture in Europe: throughout the Romanesque and the Gothic period and deep into the Renaissance, the basilican plan remains basic to Christian church building; the same holds for the monumental size of the edifice, and for the proportions of its parts to each other. The fact that the cathedral of Amiens has nave, aisles, and a transept; that in its elevation arcades, triforium, and clerestory succeed each other; that the walls seem to consist of transparent screens: all this would seem to be rooted in the tradition of the fourth-century basilicas, which was revived and made known to the Occident by the architects of the Carolingian Renaissance. Obviously the fourth-century type was changed and this transformation took place largely during the Carolingian period. Near Eastern and possibly Irish elements persisted, for instance transept forms that separated the transept into a number of units; the façade, to which no emphasis was given in the Roman Christian basilica, becomes emphasized by westworks and sometimes by twin towers; the eastern parts are developed by the addition of the three-apse group or the forechoir, both elements of Near Eastern derivation. These features, which are foreign to the Roman Christian basilica, are of utmost importance in evolving the styles of the Middle Ages. The stress laid on façades and choir parts leads to the complicated articulation of the exterior in Romanesque and still later in Gothic architecture; the partition of the transept is linked to the evolution of the segregated crossing, and through it to the articulation of the interior into the clearly segregated bays of the Romanesque and the Gothic systems. Both the Near Eastern and the Roman Christian tradition concur in creating medieval architecture: one terminates in, the other is introduced during, the Carolingian period, and both are merged into something new. The decisive rôle of the Carolingian Renaissance within this whole development of medieval architecture thus becomes evident.

V

Conversely, the dominant part which the renascence of Early Christian prototypes plays within Carolingian architecture may also have a bearing in redefining the meaning of the Carolingian Renaissance as such. Indeed the Early Christian revival apparently forms one of the basic and even indispensable constituents of this renaissance of Antiquity. This realization would seem to conflict somewhat with the view frequently held on the problem; for generally speaking it has been taken for granted time and again that the architects, painters, sculptors, and writers of the ninth century, when going back to Antiquity, would indiscriminately take anything for a model so long as it was antique and just because it was antique. It was assumed that they would do so since to them antique art as a whole was an idea to be emulated, because of what they considered its "superiority," in which concept technical skill, precious material, illusionistic naturalism, and so forth were indissolubly interlinked. In architecture this thesis of an indiscriminate imitation of Antiquity may be valid as far as the elements of architectural decoration are concerned: Carolingian capitals north of the Alps, whether composite, Corinthian, or Ionic, seem with rare exceptions to be copied from Roman capitals in the Rhineland, and so also are mouldings and bases (Fig. 100). The models were evidently used because by their "superiority" they were recognized as antique, and because they were at hand; [171] they could be taken over wholesale since architectural decoration was void of specific content.

Similarly Carolingian writers would use isolated phrases and terms chosen at random from any Roman author at their disposal. Yet what is true of the decorative elements does not necessarily pertain to the whole edifice within which these elements were used: the evidence seems to show that in the design of a church, preference among the prototypes of Antiquity was given to buildings of Christian Antiquity of the fourth or fifth century.

Of course one might say that this is no more than self-evident. Obviously the architect who in the ninth century was to design a church *à l' antique* would try to find a homogeneous model and—since it was churches he was looking for—he would be able to find this prototype nowhere but in the Christian art of Antiquity. Yet it was in no way self-evident that he would look for his model to the Christian art of Rome and would select his prototypes exclusively within the period from *ca.* 325 to 450. Why should he discard—or largely discard—the art of the eastern coastlands of the Mediterranean, where antique patterns had been kept alive without interruption, and which in a somewhat diluted form had constituted the very basis of pre-Carolingian art throughout the Occident, including Rome itself? Why should he so rarely use central plan types [172] or the basilicas with or without galleries which were still being erected in his own time throughout the Balkans? After all, they had inspired the whole pre-Carolingian period and were to inspire to a large degree occidental architecture of the early eleventh century. Why this complete about-face, which meant no less than abandoning the tradition of late antique art as manifested in the Near East and its western dependencies, and replacing it by a "rebirth" of the art of Rome? And in Rome itself, why should the architect confine himself to the architecture erected before the middle of the fifth century? Considerations of an archaeological character could hardly have impelled him to do so, since such a point of view did not exist in the Middle Ages. Only one answer is possible: the aim of the Carolingian Renaissance was not so much a revival of Antiquity in general as a revival of Rome, or specifically of one facet of the Roman past: the Golden Age of Christianity in that city.

While this fact easily explains why the Carolingian architect should look for his prototypes to the churches of pre-Byzantine Rome, it has more far-reaching implications. For whatever Rome was in the eyes of the Carolingian period—the Golden, the Imperial City, the mother of Europe, the capital of the world [173]— it invariably included this Christian element. Thus the question arises whether the Carolingian artist, when looking at the complex image under which Rome presented itself, would not quite as a matter of course and unconsciously always prefer such prototypes as either had, or else were apt to be loaded with, Christian connotations. Would that mean that he would always do so, even if the character of the prototype were not, as in the case of a church, necessarily implied by the "theme" of the copy? Would the Carolingian artist, even when thematically free, still be inclined to give preference to Christian, or what he thought to be Christian, prototypes of Roman Antiquity?

Such a question is the more legitimate since this Christian interpretation of

Antiquity seems to be clearly dominant in Carolingian literature. Here the problem can be more easily discerned since a greater amount of relevant source material has been preserved. As has frequently been pointed out, the intelligentsia at Charlemagne's court liked to play with nicknames and allusions drawn from pagan Roman literature;[174] the libraries of the Carolingian monasteries owned and copied many pagan writings, and the Carolingian authors frequently formed their entire style on these models.[175] Yet the fact is often overlooked that this knowledge of antique literature was far outweighed by the knowledge of and the preoccupation with Christian literature. Alongside the pagan nicknames, biblical ones were used in Charles's circle; and while hardly more than a dozen pagan writers were actually known and used by the Carolingian *literati,* Christian antique literature formed the real basis of their literary production: Prudentius, Augustine, Ambrose, Fortunatus, Orosius, Isidore were far more frequently drawn upon than Virgil, Horace, or Suetonius.[176] This is a clear analogy to the revival of the Early Christian types in architecture. Like the Early Christian basilicas, the Early Christian writings were selected because, while speaking the language of Antiquity, they express themes which were Christian and therefore entirely congenial to the Carolingian writer. What is far more relevant, however, is the particular way in which pagan authors were actually used as prototypes: unless they were studied merely for purposes of philology, grammar, syntax, or rhetoric (that is to say "void of content," and comparable to the way antique capitals or mouldings were used in Carolingian architecture)[177] either their writings or their personalities were frequently re-interpreted so as to make them acceptable to the mind of the ninth century which could see the universe only from a Christian point of view. The pagan elements were either expurgated[178] or transformed to impart a Christian meaning, or were taken to mean mere forces of nature; or else they were interpreted allegorically as "hidden truths" referring under the guise of pagan gods or pagan events to vices or virtues, to human life, or to Christ.[179] A similar *reinterpretatio christiana* is not infrequent with reference to the character of pagan authors: that Virgil, among all the classical poets, is the one most frequently used in Carolingian times, is of course due to the interpretation of his Eclogue IV as a reference to Christ, an interpretation which from the early fourth century throughout the Middle Ages made him a harbinger of the Lord, a *Christianus sine Christo.*[180] Similarly Pliny, Seneca, Cato, and possibly even Cicero[181] were considered forerunners of Christianity; Statius was even supposed to have been a Christian. Whenever, on the other hand, such an interpretation was clearly not possible, either because of the specific character of the ancient author or else because of the attitude of the Carolingian interpreter, his work was as a rule not accepted. Alcuin in his old age or Paschasius Ratbert or Walafrid Strabo refused to have anything to do with the "liar poets" of Antiquity: they recognized the incompatibility of the pagan writers with the Christian world of the ninth century. Indeed, the ninth-century literary renaissance of Antiquity can best be understood, it seems, if one realizes the basic relevance of the question whether a model of Antiquity was Christian or pagan, and if pagan, whether it was susceptible of Christian re-interpretation, or whether at least it could be made void of content. The choice did not lie simply between acceptance or refusal of pagan elements; it lay between either rejection or re-interpretation.[182]

To illustrate the parallel problem in architecture we choose as an instance a well-known edifice, the Torhalle at Lorsch (Figs. 99, 100).[183] While the church of this famous monastery was a characteristic pre-Carolingian structure of 767, the gate-house may be slightly later. It is a small rectangular building, which stands isolated in the middle of a plaza on the axis of the atrium and the church, but at some distance from them. Three wide arches on both its long sides lead into an open hall on the ground floor; staircase towers on either end of the short sides ascend to a similar, though closed, room on the upper floor, with a painted Ionic order along its walls. The arches rest on four square piers with engaged columns; high above the arches the composite capitals of the columns carry a floating palmetto band in place of an architrave. Corresponding to this tripartite division of the lower section, the upper one is articulated by nine triangular gables which are carried by slender Ionic pilasters. This whole thin and unstable order is set against the background of a tapestry-like wall incrustation of red and white squares, diamonds, and hexagons.

The purpose of the structure has never been determined. The general assumption used to be that the whole edifice was nothing but a chapel. Indeed, the upper story may have contained from the very outset a chapel of St. Michael; however, this is not quite certain,[184] and it may have served any other ecclesiastical or even secular purpose. The lower story on the other hand was always open in front and rear and can have served only one purpose: to be walked through. The structure was always isolated between the entrance of the monastery and the atrium of the church. Thus, while not an entrance gate, it can have been nothing but a sumptuous arch across the road to the church, in function reminiscent of a Roman triumphal arch.[185] In its form, also, the structure strongly recalls Roman triumphal arches. While the series of pilasters which articulate the upper story of the Torhalle may have been inspired by the series of pilasters along the dwarf galleries of such Roman city gates as the Porte d'Arroux at Autun, city gates can hardly have served as models for the whole structure.[186] Their constituent factor is the connection with a continuous wall. The isolation of the Lorsch gate-house, on the other hand, its freestanding position in the center of a plaza, the triple entrances, the piers with engaged columns in the lower section, the architrave-like band, all emphasize the resemblance to Roman triumphal arches. The separate upper story of the Torhalle with its large inner chamber, its architectural murals, and its exterior decoration of unsubstantial gables on slender pilasters would at first glance seem to contradict this comparison. Yet one must recall that Roman triumphal arches often had attics above the archways, attics that were always vaulted, and in some instances even made accessible by stairs. Thus they would form regular stories above the thoroughfare on the ground floor. While no general explanation seems to have been agreed upon for the function of these upper stories in Antiquity, in at least one case the use of the vaulted attic as a tomb chamber or a cenotaph has been suggested.[187]

Thus from its form the Lorsch Torhalle would seem related to those Roman triumphal arches with a chamber in their attic. Still the question remains whether the Carolingian architect had in mind just a vague idea of such an antique prototype or whether he thought of some specific monument. Of course the whole of the Roman Empire was full of triumphal arches. Yet triumphal arches of the particular form found at Lorsch, raised on a platform, with a triple passage, with columns in front of the piers, and with an accessible upper story in the attic, are not numerous.[188] Only very few examples existed throughout the former Roman Empire, and the number becomes even smaller when one excludes the regions that had become practically inaccessible to the architects of the Carolingian period, such as the Islamic territories in North Africa or the hinterlands of Hither Asia. Admittedly, all the single constituent elements of the Lorsch gate-house, or even several together, occur in different Roman triumphal arches; but the peculiar combination of all these elements in one single monument is extremely rare. Indeed triple arches with upper stories in the attic, and even more so those with upper stories which are accessible by stairs, seem to be limited to only two monuments: the Arches of Septimius Severus and of Constantine in Rome.[189] One of these two would seem to offer itself as the prototype of the strange Carolingian structure at Lorsch.

In a merely formal way the Torhalle might depend on either of the two arches; from an iconographical point of view the Arch of Constantine is more likely to have been the actual model.[190] It dominated medieval imagination much more than the Arch of Septimius Severus which, after all, for the Middle Ages held no significance at all. The pre-eminent position of the Constantinian monument shows even in ninth-century terminology: it has been pointed out that the term *arcus triumphalis* is used for ecclesiastical architecture for the first time in the biographies of Paschal I and Gregory IV in the *Liber Pontificalis;* as is well known, it designates the arch which leads from the nave to the transept and which prior to this time had been known as *arcus maior*.[191] It has also been shown that the new expression seems to have a twofold root: while it is linked with the image of the triumphant Christ which decorated the arch in Constantine's basilica of St. Peter, it is also meant to refer to the triumphal arches of Roman Antiquity. Yet the term *arcus triumphalis* which we use quite as a matter of course, heretofore had been very unusual in Antiquity.[192] In Rome a similar term, *arcu(s) triumph(is) insign(is)*, occurs only once, and this precisely in the inscription on the Arch of Constantine. From there the expression could most easily have entered the architectural glossary of the papal biographers of the ninth century.[193] One may thus conclude that among all the arches in Rome, this one made a particularly strong impression on the imagination of the Carolingian period. One may assume that the authors of the biographies of Paschal I and Gregory IV, when using the term "triumphal arch" for ecclesiastical architecture, thought of the inscription on the Arch of Constantine; and that the architect of the Lorsch Torhalle, when designing his structure after the pattern of a Roman triumphal arch, chose the Arch of Constantine, a monument of Christian Antiquity, as his prototype.

To the Middle Ages, indeed, the Arch of Constantine was a monument of Christian Antiquity. It was known that the arch had been erected for the first Christian emperor in memory of the victory at the Milvian Bridge, the victory which, according to legend, had been foretold by the apparition of the Cross which led to the Emperor's conversion. The inscription on the Arch would quite naturally tend to corroborate such a Christian interpretation; for it stated that the victory had been won *instinctu divinitatis,* through the help of the Godhead,[194] and while this term actually reflects only the late antique belief in an impersonal deity, it was susceptible of the interpretation (and indeed was interpreted as late as the nineteenth century) as meaning the Christian God. Consequently this particular arch, which apparently recorded the victory of Christianity over Paganism and the battle which was linked to the conversion of Constantine, was bound to become in the conception of the Middle Ages a Christian monument and simultaneously the triumphal arch κατ' ἐξοχήν. Thus between the Arch of Septimius Severus, which could have no particular significance to the Carolingian period, or the Arch of Constantine which was full of Christian meaning, it seems rather likely that the designer of the Lorsch Torhalle would prefer the latter as a model.

The pre-eminence of the Christian element among the Roman models of the Carolingian Renaissance manifests itself with greater clarity in the Palace of Aix-la-Chapelle. The architectural prototype of the Palace has not been established, and it would be premature to attempt its definition before the plan of the building is better known.[195] Thus, while the *material* model remains obscure, it nevertheless seems certain, that the *ideal* model, or at least one of the ideal models which Charlemagne and his advisors had in mind, was the Lateran in Rome: not the palaces of the Roman emperors on the Palatine which were preserved only in ruins, nor those of the Byzantine emperors at Constantinople which were extant, but the edifice which according to tradition as laid down in the Constantinian Donation had been Constantine's own palace, which the Emperor had given to the Church and which consequently had become the residence of the popes.[196] A considerable number of elements point in this direction and the concurrence of these indications leaves no doubt that to his contemporaries Charlemagne's Palace at Aix-la-Chapelle represented the Lateran and represented it in the medieval way, in which the presence of some outstanding features was sufficient, despite any formal dissimilarities, to make the original recognizable in a copy. To enumerate some of this evidence: in a number of documents the Palace at Aix is actually called "the Lateran" and while this term once refers only to part of the Palace, no doubt is left that in at least one case reference is made to the whole complex of buildings.[197] This latter reference is particularly revealing: for after having stated that Charlemagne built the Palace and that he called it the Lateran, the chronicler goes on to say that the Emperor assembled treasures from all his kingdoms in his Palace. Now we happen to know from other sources what some of the treasures were which had been carried to Aix-la-Chapelle, and while they differ widely in origin and in quality they all have one thing in common: they all seem to "represent" similar treasures which were kept at the Lateran in Rome. There was the bronze figure of a she-wolf or a she-bear which may have been brought from southern Gaul, and which throughout the Middle Ages stood in the vestibule of the chapel at Aix; it would seem to form a parallel to the Roman *Lupa* which throughout the Middle Ages was preserved at the Lateran.[198] Within the complex of the Palace rose the equestrian statue which had been brought from Ravenna to Aix-la-Chapelle immediately after Charlemagne's coronation in 800.[199] Whether the monument was originally meant to represent Theoderic, King of the Goths, or the Byzantine Emperor Zeno is rather irrelevant in this connection; for whomever it actually represented and whomever contemporaries thought it represented, it impersonated for them a ruler of Antiquity. Again this equestrian statue at Aix-la-Chapelle forms an obvious parallel to a Roman monument which up to the sixteenth century was one of the landmarks of the Lateran Palace,[200] the equestrian statue of Marcus Aurelius which played such a great rôle in the medieval interpretation of Roman monuments. Its medieval name, *Caballus Constantini,* was evidently derived from the neighboring Lateran Palace and its church, both of which bore the name of the great Christian Emperor throughout the Middle Ages. Could it be said that the collateral dedication of the Palatine Chapel at Aix-la-Chapelle to the Savior [201] was also intended to parallel the dedication of the Constantinian church in the Lateran? [202] All these indications concur; more obviously than the Lorsch Torhalle, the Palace at Aix attempted to emulate not just any Roman monument but a monument of Christian Antiquity in Rome—or what was supposed to be such a monument.

All these lines of evidence appear to lead in one direction: indeed one sometimes wonders whether they not only lead in the same direction but actually converge towards one point. Already the revival of the Roman proto-basilicas in the first decades of the ninth century north and south of the Alps, seems to give a hint: St. John's in the Lateran, St. Peter's, and St. Paul's are the three churches which the Constantinian Donation had credited to Constantine. In view of this tradition, the inscription at St. Paul's which clearly stated that the church had been rebuilt half a century after Constantine's death, was evidently disregarded. Like the imitation of St. Peter's and St. Paul's from Fulda to Sta. Prassede, the emulation of the Arch of Constantine and of Constantine's palace at the Lateran seems to center around Constantine and his period.

After all, the figure of Constantine formed a pivotal point in the whole philosophy of the Carolingian period. All Charlemagne's political ideas, his conception of a new Empire, and of his own status were based upon the image of the first Christian emperor. Numerous documents testify to the parallel which time and again was drawn between the Carolingian house and Constantine: the scribes of the papal chancellery, as well as other contemporaries throughout the last decades of the eighth century, addressed Charlemagne and referred to him as the "New Constantine"; [203] the crown which Constantine was supposed to have given to Pope Sylvester was allegedly used in 816 by Stephen V for the coronation of Charlemagne's son, Louis the Pious; [204] Aix-la-Chapelle was in Carolingian terminology a *Nova Roma,* like Constantinople in the phraseology of the fourth century. Aside from these documents, visible proof of the equation between the Frankish emperor and Constantine was given by the famous mosaics in the triconch triclinium of Leo III in the Lateran (Fig. 101). The apse of the building contained a mosaic with the Mission of the Apostles, the triumphal arch a group of three figures on either side. In its original state the group to the right represented St. Peter giving the pallium to Leo III and a standard to Charlemagne; in the group to the left Christ conferred the keys on a pope, probably Sylvester, and the labarum on Constantine. [205] Nothing could better illustrate the intended parallelism between the two emperors, both defenders of the Church: the Roman who was the first Christian upon the throne of the Caesars, and the Frank who succeeded him after half a millennium; nothing could show better the parallelism between the two popes, the one who received the rule over Rome and the West from the first Christian emperor, the other who bestowed this rule on a new emperor. As visualized in Rome, at the papal court, the parallelism is a characteristic example of medieval typology intended to illustrate the papal and the imperial policies. Beyond that it illuminates the conception which the Carolingian period had of Roman Antiquity: it seems as though Antiquity were epitomized in the Christian Rome of Constantine and Sylvester.

In this form, however, the point seems overstated. For while Charlemagne and his contemporaries paralleled the new Empire with that of Constantine, this comparison was seen against a larger background, against the idea of Charlemagne's legitimate succession to the Roman emperors *in toto.* One could perhaps say that the figure of Constantine was only selected because it was best suited to represent what the Carolingian period considered the true essence of a Roman emperor. For in the ninth century the conception of the Empire was necessarily limited by two qualifications, both of which were based on the general concept of history which had found its foremost expression in the Donation of Constantine: first, Charlemagne, while sometimes claiming in theory the whole former Roman world, as a rule limited himself to the Occident—and not only for practical reasons. The Occident, with Rome as its capital, was the part of the Empire which according to the Constantinian Donation had been bestowed by Constantine on the pope. Consequently it was only the rule over the Occident which could be conferred by the pope on the new emperor. Byzantium, as well as the Islamic world, was not only outside the material power of Charlemagne but foreign to his philosophy. Second, and this is of greater importance in this discussion, the new Carolingian Empire could be Christian only, and only the Christians among the Roman emperors could be the legitimate forerunners of a medieval Christian ruler. Thus it was not the person of Constantine on whom the Carolingian concept of an emperor was focused; he merely symbolized the Christian ruler of the Empire. Consequently other representatives might be selected in his place. Yet the Christian connotation seems indispensable in order that a Roman emperor be eligible as a legitimate forerunner of the Carolingian house. Based on Orosius and ultimately on Augustine, a Christian interpretation of history had developed from the fifth century on: since history's function was to discuss the relation of mankind to God, only those among the Roman emperors were worthy of mention whose rule was marked either by some important Christian event or by the "Christian" virtues with which they had been endowed, or who were believed to have adhered secretly to Christianity. Further elimination then led to those who had actually been Christians; yet the selective principle permitted the inclusion only of those who had been "good Catholics," that is, who had fought Arianism.[206] Thus the list as a rule included Augustus, Trajan, Marcus Aurelius, Constantine, and Theodosius. Frequently, and especially in the Carolingian period, this list was contracted even more: all the great rulers were omitted or placed on the "bad" side of the ledger; only the two Christian, "Catholic" emperors, Constantine and Theodosius, were enumerated and were followed by the members of the Carolingian house, Charles Martel, Pepin, and Charlemagne. These are the "good" rulers, who were depicted in the frescoes of Ingelheim Palace about 820 and who were contrasted by the Poeta Saxo with all pagan heroes.[207] To the mind of the ninth century, Constantine and Theodosius were the only really lawful predecessors on the Roman throne of the new Carolingian emperors—the two who had linked true Christianity to sovereignty over the Roman world.

This fusion of Rome and Christianity underlies the whole of Carolingian policy; it corresponds perfectly with the conception which the Carolingian Renaissance had of Roman art, a conception in which Christian and Roman elements are linked to one another. While antique monuments without Christian connotations were not excluded *a limine,* the fact remains that antique buildings which had, or could have, such a Christian connotation—and thus pre-eminently the great Christian basilicas which had been founded by the imperial house, and what were believed to be the palaces and the triumphal arches of the Christian emperors —formed the real basis of the Carolingian revival.

Notes

1. This view dominated practically every history of architecture written between 1880 and 1925. See, e.g.: G. Dehio, *Geschichte der deutschen Kunst*, I (Berlin and Leipzig 1921), 33.

2. This is not the place to give a complete bibliography of the discovery of Near Eastern Early Christian architecture. Suffice it to mention Strzygowski's numerous publications, and the writings of G. L. Bell, S. Gsell, S. Guyer, H. C. Butler, U. Monneret de Villard, etc.

3. J. Puig y Cadafalch, *La géographie et les origines du premier art roman* (Paris, 1935); cf. also his earlier publications.

4. G. G. King, *Pre-Romanesque Churches in Spain (Bryn Mawr Notes and Monographs)* (Bryn Mawr College, 1924).

5. J. Hubert, *L'art pré-roman (Les monuments datés de la France)* (Paris, 1938); A. W. Clapham, *English Romanesque Architecture before the Conquest*, (Oxford, 1930); A. Kingsley Porter, *Lombard Architecture* (New Haven, 1917).

6. Both Hubert, *op. cit.*, pp. 167 ff. and O. Müller, *Die Einhartsbasilika zu Steinbach* (Diss. Leipzig, 1936), Seligenstadt, n.d., pp. 76 ff., stress this point, although neither attempts to distinguish the different origins of these infiltrations.

7. G. Weise, *Untersuchungen zur Geschichte der Architektur und Plastik des früheren Mittelalters* (Leipzig and Berlin, 1916), pp. 151 ff.; *idem., Studien zur Entwicklungsgeschichte des abendländischen Basilikengrundrisses . . . (Sitzungsberichte der Heidelberger Akademie . . . , Philos. histor. Klasse,* 21. Abh.) (Heidelberg, 1919), pp. 63 ff. While all too strict in his attempt to construe a development of pre-Carolingian architecture in Europe, Weise was quite right in determining the general position of the T-basilica in early medieval architecture. E. Weigand's objections on this particular point in *Byzantinische Zeitschrift,* XXIV (1923–24), 476 are hardly justified: the references to cross plans made in Early Christian and early Medieval sources need not and probably do not refer to transepts of the Roman T-type; they may refer to anything from dwarf transepts to Greek cross plans.

8. This opinion still characterizes E. Lehmann, *Der frühe deutsche Kirchenbau (Forschungen zur deutschen Kunstgeschichte,* 27) (Berlin, 1938). If our interpretation of his text is correct (and even with a quite thorough knowledge of pre-1933 German it is not always easy to interpret his involved style) Lehmann realizes the existence of the Roman influence in German architecture throughout the Carolingian and early Romanesque period. Yet he interprets it as a continuous "undercurrent" or "counter-current" which opposes the "*bodenständig* German" centralizing elements. Since Lehmann's book has been splendidly published and is evidently widely used, I feel it ought to be added that the reconstructions as well as the plans are frequently unreliable and should be used with great caution. The catalogue is the really useful part of the book.

9. Reliable reproductions of the original state of these basilicas are rare. The principal ones are, for Old St. Peter's: plan, Tiberius Alpharanus, *De basilicae Vaticanae antiquissima et nova structura*, ed. M. Ceratti (*Studi e testi,* 26) (Rome, 1914), Pl. I (our Fig. 79); interiors and exteriors: Jehan Fouquet, *Grandes Chroniques de Saint Denis* (P. Durrieu, "Une vue intérieure de l'ancien St. Pierre de Rome . . . ," *Mélanges G. B. De Rossi, Ecole Française de Rome, Mémoires,* XII, 1892, Supplément, pp. 221 ff.), Marten van Heemskerk (H. Egger and Ch. Huelsen, *Die Skizzenbücher des Marten van Heemskerk,* I [Berlin, 1910], Pls. 14, 15; II [1916], Pls. 67, 69, 70, 72), Jacopo Grimaldi, Barb. lat. 4410 and Barb. lat. 2733, *passim;* for St. Paul's: N. M. Nicolai, *Della basilica di S. Paolo . . .* (Rome, 1815), and L. Rossini, *Le antichità romane* (Rome, 1829), Pls. 98-101.

10. See below, pp. 227 f.

11. We shall use this term to embrace the whole or practically the whole of the territories dominated by Charlemagne and by his successors. On the other hand, we will restrict the use of the term chronologically to the period up to the end of the ninth century, in spite of the fact that in France the Carolingian house continued through almost the whole of the tenth century.

12. The discussion of St. Denis is based on Viollet-le-Duc's plan and description (*Dictionnaire raisonné d'architecture*, IX, [Paris, 1868], 228 and *idem*, "L'église impériale de Saint-Denis," *Revue archéologique*, n.s. III [1861], 301 ff., 345 ff.); these have to be revised following Mr. Sumner McK. Crosby's studies which will be published in his forthcoming book. I want to express my warm thanks to Mr. Crosby who kindly discussed with me the results of his excavations and his reconstruction of the Carolingian edifice. Mr. Crosby's excavations of the Carolingian structure will furnish for the first time a solid basis for reconstructing the building and for clarifying and revising Viollet-le-Duc's plan. Mr. Crosby has not yet been able to excavate within the transept and thus to verify Viollet-le-Duc's drawings on this point. [See now, however, Crosby, 1942 and 1953; Formigé 1960, in *Additional Bibliography*, p. 256 below].

13. J. von Schlosser, *Schriftquellen zur Geschichte der karolingischen Kunst* ("*Quellenschriften für Kunstgeschichte und Kunsttechnik*," N.F. IV) (Vienna, 1896), pp. 209 ff.; Suger, *De consecratione ecclesiae sancti Dionysii*, and *De administratione*, both in *Oeuvres complètes de Suger*, ed. A. Lecoy de la Marche (Paris, 1867).

14. The sources have been interpreted in different papers of L. Levillain: "L'église carolingienne de Saint Denis," *BMon*, LXXI (1907), 211 ff.; *idem*, "Les plus anciennes églises abbatiales de Saint Denis," *Mémoires de la Société de l'histoire de Paris et de l'Isle de France*, XXXVI (1909), 143 ff.; *idem*, "Etudes sur l'abbaye de Saint Denis à l'époque mérovingienne," *Bibliothèque de l'Ecole des Chartes*, LXXXII (1921), 5 ff.; LXXXVI (1925), 5 ff., 44 ff. While Levillain clarified the history of the abbey and proved that no church of 638 had ever existed on the site of the present St. Denis, his reconstruction of the Carolingian church (*BMon, loc. cit.*) has not been quite so fortunate. For the date after 754 at which the Carolingian church was begun, see M. Buchner, *Das Vizepapsttum des Abtes von St. Denis* (Paderborn, 1928), pp. 80 ff.

15. Mr. Crosby, on the basis of literary sources, assumes the existence of an atrium with colonnades.

16. Hubert, *L'art pré-roman, passim*, and the bibliography quoted by him.

17. The reconstruction of the fifth-century church of St. Martin at Tours is quite uncertain, but it may possibly have shown this plan.

18. A. Lenoir, *Statistique monumentale de Paris* (Paris, 1867), pp. 20 ff., Pls. XVII-XXI. For the date see P. Batiffol, *Etudes de liturgie et d'archéologie chrétienne* (Paris, 1919), pp. 288 ff.; a comparison with the similar ground plans of the Merovingian church of St. Martin at Angers and of the Kentish churches of the seventh century may help to determine the date more exactly. See below, note 29, and G. H. Forsyth, Jr., "The Church of St. Martin at Angers," *Antiquity*, X (1937), 400 ff; Hubert, *op. cit.*, pp. 39 ff.

19. C. de la Croix, *Fouilles archéologiques . . . de Saint Maur de Glanfeuil . . .* (Paris 1899); Hubert, *op. cit.*, pp. 10 ff.

20. W. R. Ramsay and G L. Bell, *The Thousand and One Churches* (London, 1909), *passim*.

21. J. Formigé, "Vienne. Abbaye de Saint Pierre," *Congrès archéol.*, LXXXVI (1923), 77 ff. and Hubert, *op. cit.*, p. 46, date the niches and columns along the aisle walls, and consequently the galleries, in the ninth century. From my own observations on the site I am quite sure that the niches and columns bond into the walls and that the galleries were original. See also R. de Lasteyrie, *L'architecture réligieuse en France à l'époque romane* (Paris, 1912), p. 43.

22. Hubert, *op. cit.*, pp. 11 ff., Pl. I a.

23. Γ. Α. Σωτηρίου, Αἱ παλαιοχριστιανικαὶ βασιλικαὶ τῆς Ἑλλάδος (Athens, 1931): Corinth, Nikopolis B.

24. L. Blondel, "Les premiers édifices chrétiens de Genève," (*Genava* X, 1933), 77 ff. has a good plan, yet with a slightly incorrect interpretation.

25. One might compare the large basilicas at Timgad and at Morsott; see S. Gsell, *Les monuments antiques de l'Algérie* II (Paris, 1900), 231 ff., 309 ff.

26. M. Reymond and Ch. Giraud, "La Chapelle Saint Laurent à Grenoble," *Bull. archéol.* (1893), pp. 1 ff.; Hubert, *op. cit.*, p. 103 assumes a later date without specifying his reasons. L. H. Labande, "Venasque. Baptistère," *Congrès archéol.*, LXXVI (1909), I, 282 ff.

27. Jerusalem, St. John the Baptist: H. Vincent and F. Abel, *Jérusalem nouvelle*, pt. 3 (Paris, 1923), pp. 642 ff.; Der-el-Abiad and Der-el-Akhmar near Sohag: U. Monneret de Villard, *Les couvents de Sohag* (Milan, 1925–26), *passim*. For the North African instances, see Gsell, *op. cit.*, II, 140 ff.

28. Hubert, *op. cit.*, pp. 18 ff.

29. Clapham, *op. cit.*, pp. 17 ff.

30. SS. Peter and Paul (below S. Abbondio, Como, fifth century); C. Boito, *Architettura del medioevo* (Milan, 1880), pp. 14 ff. and Kingsley Porter, *op. cit.*, II, 301 ff., whose doubts do not seem justified in view of Boito's careful description of the remnants; Romainmotier I and II (630 and 750 respectively); see J. Zemp, "Die Kirche von Romainmotier," *Zeitschrift für Geschichte der Architektur*, I (1907–1908), 89 ff. Contrary to Clapham's thesis, *op. cit.*, p. 13, the square rooms in front of the apse are not the wings of a regular transept; see Zemp, *op. cit.*, p. 90.

31. St. Peter im Holz-Teurnia (Carinthia): R. Egger, *Frühchristliche Kirchenbauten im südlichen Norikum* ("Sonderhefte des Oesterr. archäol. Inst.," IX) (Vienna, 1916), pp. 12 ff.; Mokropolje (Dalmatia), unpublished (I am indebted to Mr. E. Dyggve for a plan of the church); Majdan (Bosnia): W. Radinsky, "Die römische Ansiedlung von Majdan bei Varcar Vakuf," *Wissenschaftliche Mitteil. Aus Bosnien und Herzegovina*, III (1895), 248 ff.

32. Clapham, *op. cit.*, pp. 38 ff.

33. Lehmann, *op. cit.*, pp. 10 ff. and *passim*; see also Erich J. Schmidt, *Kirchliche Bauten des frühen Mittelalters in Südwestdeutschland* ("Kataloge des Römisch-Germanischen Zentralmuseums zu Mainz," II) (Mainz, 1932), to be used, however, with great caution.

34. Lehmann, *op. cit.*, pp. 109, 113, where previous bibliography is indicated.

35. P. Clemen. "Die mittelalterlichen Profanbauten. Die Kaiserpfalzen," *Deutscher Verein f. Kunstwissenschaft, Zweiter Bericht über die Denkmäler deutscher Kunst* (Berlin, 1912), p. 27; Lehmann, *op. cit.*, p. 106 where the date is suggested. There is no reason on earth to assume (as has been done by Schmidt, *op. cit.*, p. 42) that this north chapel was contemporaneous with the similar south chapel and like this later than the Minster, The results of the excavations make it quite clear that the north chapel was the first post-Roman structure on the site, that it was followed by the Minster proper, and that still later the south chapel was laid out as a pendant to the older structure to the north.

36. Weise, *op. cit.* (1916), pp. 142 ff.

37. King, *op. cit.*, *passim*.

38. Kingsley Porter, *op. cit.*, II, 582 ff.

39. G. Chierici, "Di alcuni risultati sui recenti lavori intorno alla Basilica di S. Lorenzo a Milano . . . ," *RACrist*, XVI, (1939), 51 ff.

40. J. W. Crowfoot, "Churches at Bosra and Samaria-Sebaste" (*Brit. School of Archaeology in Jerusalem, Suppl. Report 4,* 1937); W. A. Campbell, in *Antioch-on-the-Orontes*, III, ed. R. Sillwell, Princeton, 1941, 35 ff., where also a bibliography for the related churches will be found.

41. See above, n. 30.

42. Kingsley Porter, *op. cit.*, III, 511 ff.

43. *Ibid.*, III, 427 ff.

44. Disentis, St. Mary and St. Martin, see J. R. Rahn, "Die Ausgrabungen im Kloster Disentis," *Anzeiger für schweizerische Altertumskunde*, X (1908), 35 ff.; Müstail, St. Peter, see E. Poeschel, *Die Kunstdenkmäler des Kantons Graubünden*, II (Basel, 1937), 266 ff.; S. Steinmann-Brodtbeck, "Herkunft und Verbreitung des Dreiapsidenchors . . ." *Zeitschr. Schweiz. Arch. und Kunstgesch.*, I (1939), 65 ff.

45. Menas City, so-called consignatorium of the cemeterial basilica, see C. M. Kauf-

mann, *Die Menasstadt* (Leipzig, 1910), pp. 101 ff., fig. 46.

46. E. Herzfeld and S. Guyer, *Meriamlik and Korykos* (Manchester, 1930) pp. 4 ff.

47. A. Kingsley Porter, *The Crosses and Culture of Ireland* (New Haven, 1931), p. 79.

48. See above, notes 29, 30, 31.

49. King, *op. cit.*, pp. 61 ff.

50. Thus an iconostasis, a clearly eastern element, is enumerated among the objects which are expressly mentioned as having been imported by Benedict Biscop from Rome to England; see Beda Venerabilis, *Vitae sanctorum abbatum monasterii in Wiramuth et Girvum* (*PL.* XCIV, cols. 713 ff., especially 717 f.).

51. E. Junyent, "Le recenti scoperte . . . di S. Vitale," *RACrist,* XII (1939), 129 ff.

52. J. Berthier, *L'église de Sainte Sabine à Rome* (Rome, 1910); A. Schuchert, *S. Maria Maggiore zu Rom* ("*Studi di antichità cristiana,*" XIV) (Vatican City, 1939).

53. P. Germano di S. Stanislao, *La casa Celimontana* (Rome, 1894).

54. R. Krautheimer, *Corpus,* I (1937), 42 ff.

55. R. Krautheimer and W. Frankl, "Recent Discoveries in Churches in Rome," *AJA,* XLIII (1939), 388 ff.

56. Gsell, *op. cit.*, II, 137, n. 4; 141 ff.

57. L. Fortunati, *Relazione . . . degli scavi . . . lungo la Via Latina* (Rome, 1859).

58. R. Krautheimer, "S. Pietro in Vincoli and the Tripartite Transept," *Proceedings of the American Philosophical Society,* LXXXIV (1941), 353 ff.

59. R. Krautheimer, "An Oriental Basilica in Rome," *AJA,* XL (1936), 485 ff.

60. Krautheimer, *Corpus,* I, 77 ff.

61. E. Stevenson, "La basilica doppia di Sta. Sinforosa," *BACrist,* III (1878), 75 ff.

62. Only a few edifices seem at first glance to contradict this statement, such as S. Pancrazio in Rome, the remnants of the pre-Carolingian cathedral at Chur (E. Poeschel, "Zur Baugeschichte der Kathedrale und der Kirche S. Lucius in Chur," *Anzeiger für schweizerische Altertumskunde,* N.F., XXXII [1930], 99 ff.) and those of St. Andrew in Hexham (Clapham, *op. cit.*, pp. 43 ff.). All three are reconstructed as basilicas with nave and aisles and with a continuous transept.

At S. Pancrazio—it is dated 625–38—a regular continuous transept would seem to be well preserved and one would suppose the edifice to have been an unusually early copy after St. Peter's. Yet in its present state the transept is really not continuous; it is separated into three parts by colonnades and upper walls which intervene between the center bay and the transept wings, and while the walls above the colonnades are (as I know from personal examination) twelfth-century, the colonnades themselves may be original. Thus the transept plan may have been not of the continuous type (as was suggested in *Proceedings of the Amer. Philos. Society,* LXXXIV [1941], 413), but of the tripartite type, similar to that of S. Pietro in Vincoli.

The date of the cathedral at Chur, which is given as fifth century, is quite uncertain. Only very few remnants of the structure have been excavated south of the apse, and these were taken by Poeschel (*op. cit.*) and by Hubert, (*op. cit.*, p. 49) to suggest a regular "Roman" transept. The scanty remains may as well belong to the transversal arms of a cross church like Sant'Anastasia in Rome, or to dwarf transept wings which would have been much lower than the nave. More likely they belong just to a protruding sacristy like those which characterize the fifth-century churches of Sant' Abbondio at Como and of Romainmotier. J. Gantner (*Kunstgeschichte der Schweiz,* I, Frauenfeld [1936], p. 44), seems also to doubt Poeschel's reconstruction of Chur as having a continuous transept. Similarly the reconstruction of St. Andrew at Hexham as a basilica with transept has no basis whatsoever in the remnants excavated.

This quite unjustified preference given to the plan with continuous transept has resulted in erroneous reconstructions for buildings of the late eighth or the early ninth century also. The Palatine Chapel at Ingelheim, for instance, has been generally reconstructed as a basilica of the T-type with continuous transept (C. Rauch, in G. Rodenwaldt, *Neue deutsche Ausgrabungen* [Berlin, 1930], pp. 266 ff.; Lehmann, *op. cit.*, p. 118; Schmidt, *op. cit.*, pp. 132

ff.). The Palace at Ingelheim has been assigned various dates, either 774–78 (Lehmann, *loc. cit.*) or 807–817 (P. Clemen, "Der karolingische Kaiserpalast zu Ingelheim," *Westdeutsche Zeitschrift*, IX [1890], 54 ff., 97 ff.). Since the church is mentioned as early as the middle of the eighth century on the site of the palace, neither of the two dates needs refer to the present Palatine Chapel which might easily be older. Yet regardless of the date, the structure was neither a basilica nor did it have a continuous transept (Lehmann, *op. cit.*, fig. 85) or a transept with a segregated crossing (Rauch, *op. cit.*). Both these reconstructions neglect in an astounding way the results of the excavations as shown in Rauch's own plan (reproduced by Schmidt, *op. cit.*, Fig. 29). This plan shows that: 1) The "aisles" of the basilica were not aisles, but formed a series of chambers along either side of the single nave; two rectangular corridors and one square chamber are clearly marked to the south, one square and one very long rectangular chamber to the north. Narrow chambers (or could they have been closets? See C. de la Croix, "Poitiers. Monuments réligieux. Le Temple Saint Jean," *Congrès archéol.*, LXX [1903], 7 ff.) accompanied these chambers north and south respectively; they in turn were followed by one more rectangular room further outside. 2): the row of chambers seems to have continued along the west façade where in spite of the remnants of at least five north-south walls, the reconstructions give a continuous narthex. 3): the transept was certainly not continuous; the remnants of an L-shaped pier are clearly marked at the southeast end of the nave. On the other hand a regular segregated crossing is likewise out of the question: the stem of the L between the central bay and the south wing of the "transept" is considerably longer (2.20 m.) than that between central bay and nave (1.70 m.). Moreover the nave is considerably wider than the transept wing. Thus the opening of the "central bay" towards the nave was *ca.* 3.20 m. wider than its openings towards the transept wings and consequently probably also higher than those. *Ergo* the transept was neither continuous nor did it have a segregated crossing; but it consisted of a center part and two dwarf transept wings. That these were

shut off from the central bay is also proved by the solid buttress which flank the apse. The relatively weak walls between the openings of the central bay to the west, north, and south might be interpreted as having been "span walls" for a central tower. More likely, however, they were merely the foundation walls for a choir screen. With its single nave, its lateral chambers, and its dwarf transept, the plan of Ingelheim recalls that of Sant' Abbondio in Como, which is only about ten percent smaller, and that of St. Peter and Paul at Canterbury. To sum up: the Palatine Chapel at Ingelheim was not in any way related to the "Roman" type.

63. Interpretation of literary and visual sources: G. Richter, *Die ersten Anfänge der Bau- und Kunsttätigkeit des Klosters Fulda (Zweite Veröffentlichung des Fuldaer Geschichtsvereins)* (Fulda, 1900); *idem, Beiträge zur Geschichte des Heiligen Bonifatius (Festgabe zum Bonifatius-Jubiläum,* 1905), I (1905). Excavations: J. Vonderau, *Die Ausgrabungen am Dom zu Fulda, 1908–1913 (Sechzehnte Veröffentlichung des Fuldaer Geschichtsvereins),* Fulda (1919); *idem, Die Ausgrabungen am Dom zu Fulda . . . 1919–1924 (Siebzehnte Veröffentlichung des Fuldaer Geschichtsvereins),* Fulda (1924). Since I am unable to find a copy of the latter publication, I cannot check on a few notes which I made from it some ten years ago. Extensive and reliable excerpts are given, however, in G. von Bezold, "Zur Geschichte der romanischen Baukunst in der Erzdiözese Mainz," *Marburger Jahrbuch für Kunstwissenschaft,* VIII/IX (1933), 1 ff.

64. A small chapel may have belonged to the first monastery of 744, remnants of which have been found on an axis diagonal to that of the present cathedral and therefore of the ninth-century church. Convent and chapel were destroyed to make room for Sturmi's church of 751. Of this structure nothing is known aside from the width of the nave and of the apse. Both had the same width, that is to say the apse did not recede. Whether the wall south of the nave wall was that of an aisle or of a building belonging to the monastery must remain an open question. Thus it cannot be established either whether this church was single naved (von Bezold, *op. cit.,* 10)

or whether it was a basilica. In the latter case there is no reason for reconstructing it with columns rather than piers; nor is the length of its nave or the number of bays known. These points should be kept in mind with regard to reconstructions which make the edifice look like an Early Christian church of the type of Sta. Sabina (Lehmann, *op. cit.*, p. 11 and Fig. 76).

65. *Annales Fuldenses antiqui, MGH, SS.*, III, 117 * *Annales Sancti Bonifacii, MGH, SS.*, III, 117; *Annales breves Fuldenses, MGH, SS.*, II, 237. The date is given with slight variations as 790, 791, or 792.

66. *Catalogus abbatum Fuldensium, MGH, SS.*, XIII, 272.

67. *Annales Fuldenses, MGM, SS.*, I, 353.

68. *Catalogus abbatum Fuldensium, MGH, SS.*, XIII, 272, calls him *"sapiens architectus"* but this source is of the tenth century and therefore not quite dependable as to events 150 years earlier. Likewise another notice of the same source cannot be relied upon, according to which Ratger was already the architect of the building when under Baugulf the eastern parts of the nave were laid out. On the contrary the stylistic differences between nave and transept are evidence that the two structures could hardly have been designed by one and the same architect.

69. *MGH, Epist.*, IV, 548 ff., see Richter, *op. cit.* (1900), p. 10; Candidus, *Vita Eigilis, MGH, S.S.*, XV, 1, 221 ff.

70. Candidus, *Vita Eigilis, MGH, SS.*, XV, 1, 228 ff.

71. *Annales Fuldenses antiqui, MGH, SS.*, III, 117 *; Candidus, *Vita Eigilis, MGH, SS.*, XV, 1, 230; Candidus, *De vita Aeigili (vita metrica), MGH, Poet. L.*, 11, 96 ff., particularly 111.

72. The projecting walls which in the reconstructions of Vonderau, *op. cit.*, 1925 and Lehmann, *op. cit.*, Fig. 87 separate the eastern bays of nave and aisles would seem to represent an interesting example of a Near Eastern fore-choir with flanking side rooms comparable to Near Eastern churches in Rome, such as S. Giovanni a Porta Latina. Unfortunately I cannot discover on what the assumption of these walls is based.

73. *Catalogus abbatum Fuldensium, MGH, SS.*, XIII, 272.

74. *Ibid.*

75. Candidus, *Vita Eigilis, MGH, SS.*, XV, 1, 229; Candidus, *De vita Aegili (vita metrica), MGH, Poet L.*, II, 96 ff., particularly III. Compare also *SS.*, XV, 1, 137.

76. Candidus, *Vita Eigilis, MGH, SS.*, XV, 1, 229; Candidus, *De vita Aeigili (vita metrica), MGH, Poet L.*, II, 96 ff.

77. The number of intercolumnia can be concluded from the number of windows as shown in the seventeenth-century reproductions of the old church (Richter, *op. cit.*, 1905, Figs. 3 and 4); they are unfortunately not very clear. Still, von Bezold's assumption (*op. cit.*, p. 12) of eighteen intercolumnia does not seem necessary. The distance of about 4.90 m. from column to column, resulting from eleven intercolumnia less ten shafts, is rather wide; yet as von Bezold himself points out, it would be easily spanned by an architrave with relieving arches above.

78. First of all, early in the seventeenth century, Brower (*Antiquitates Fuldenses*, [Fulda, 1612]; after him Richter, *op. cit.*, [1905], XXXV) saw a long continuous inscription (which referred to a reconsecration of 948) *"super epistylia columnarum."* *Epistylia* has been interpreted to mean architrave (von Bezold, *op. cit.*, pp. 6 ff.), which is undoubtedly incorrect; it means capitals (Lehmann, *op. cit.*, p. 113). Yet in spite of this incorrect translation of the term *epistylia*, von Bezold's reconstruction of an architrave seems to be more likely than Lehmann's reconstruction of arcades (*op. cit.*, p. 113). The inscription as read by Brower could not have been on the capitals of the columns (J. F. Schannat, *Diocesis Fuldensis, Frankfurt a.M.* [1727], p. 58 quotes Brower incorrectly ". . . *Epistyliis columnarum per totum Basilicae circuitum insculptum . . ."*); there is no room for any long continuous inscription on the capitals of a building. It was *"super epistylia,"* above the capitals; thus it could only have been on an architrave; if it had been above the apex of an arcade it could hardly have been termed *"super epistylia."* Secondly, the reconstruction of the edifice really requires an architrave. The height of the nave is known to have been 21.10 m.;

the original height of the aisles is given as 9.55 m. by a door which still exists, and which led from one of the tenth-century turrets to the roof of the aisles. If there had been arches above the columns the height of these arches, approximately 2.45 m. (see note 77), would leave only about 6.55 m. for the height of the column, including base and capital. This seems very low in proportion to the height of the aisle (1:1.45) and the nave (1:3.10). If, on the other hand, an architrave is assumed the height of the columns would have been *ca.* 9 m. Thus their proportion in relation to the height of the nave would have been 1:2.34 and would have corresponded much better to the proportion normally found in Carolingian structures.

	columns	total height	
STEINBACH	2.95 m. :	8.20 m.	= 1:2.66
HOCHST	4.60	: 12.40	= 1:2.7
WERDEN II	5.00	: 14.80	= 1:2.96
	arch	total height	
STEINBACH	3.60 m. :	8.20 m.	= 1:2.28
HOCHST	6.00	: 12.40	= 1:2.066
WERDEN II	6.40	: 14.80	= 1:2.3

79. The turrets shown in the seventeenth-century reproductions were added to the east apse after 937 (Vonderau, *op. cit.*, 1924), *passim*.

80. It seems somewhat doubtful whether the windows in the clerestory and those in the short walls of the transept as shown in these reproductions are of the ninth century. After all, the church was altered in 937–48; possibly, then, the upper parts of the whole structure, including the windows, were changed at that time. The windows in the east walls of the transept wings as shown in Münster's woodcut (Fig. 87), would seem to be original. There is obviously no reason to assume the existence of a segregated crossing in the western transept (Richter, *op. cit.*, Fig. 6).

81. Hrabanus Maurus, *Tituli ecclesiae Fuldensis*, v, *Ad crucem*, MGH, Poet. L., II, 206.

82. The present transept at Sta. Maria Maggiore is an addition of the thirteenth century; see A. Schuchert, *S. Maria Maggiore zu Rom* ("Studi di antichità cristiana," XV) (Vatican City, 1939), pp. 83 ff.

83. At St. Peter's the transept in the clear (according to Alpharanus, *op. cit.*, p. 7)

was 390 palmi = 86.97 m. long and 78 palmi = 17.39 m. wide (one palmo being 0.223 m.). The walls were, as a rule, 6½ palmi (1.45 m.) and exceptionally 7 or 8 palmi (1.56 and 1.78 m. respectively) thick (*ibid.*, p. 12). Transposed into Carolingian scale, these measurements correspond to 256, 51, and 4½ Carolingian feet respectively (see chart, Schmidt, *op. cit.*, p. 36). The corresponding measurements at Fulda are 74.36 m. length, and 1.32 m. thickness of walls; thus the length taken from wall axis to wall axis is 75.68 m. If these figures are translated into Carolingian feet, the comparison does not work; but it *does* work if the change is made into Roman feet (one Roman foot = 0.2956 m.); then the length is 256 feet. In other words, the same figures were used in Fulda as in Rome; but while in Rome they had been taken in Carolingian feet, at Fulda they were translated into Roman feet. Also at Fulda they refer to the distances between the centers of the walls, while in Rome they are measurements taken in the clear. This latter difference is easily understandable: Ratger's agent in Rome could only report the clear measurements of St. Peter's, while the architect at Fulda would quite naturally use these same figures to lay out his plan from wall-center to wall-center according to the usage of the period. As to the strange difference of the foot scale employed, viz. the Carolingian in Rome and the Roman in Fulda, it seems at first glance quite topsy-turvy. Yet what happened is probably that the correspondent in Rome took the measurements correctly on the scale he knew to be in use north of the Alps. The architect in Fulda, on the other hand, on receiving the letter, evidently assumed them to have been taken in Roman feet, and contrary to local habit he preserved this Roman scale in his building.

84. The sources are not quite clear. The relevant verses (Candidus, *De vita Aeigili* [*vita metrica*], MGH, Poet. L., II, III), referring to the dedication of the church by the archbishop of Mainz in 819, run: *Martyris exhibuit ostra peplumque rigentem Insuper accumulans auxit pro seque suisque His ita perceptis gressum porrexit ad aram Pontificalis apex magno comitatus honore In parte occidua Romano more peractum Elevat interea populari voce repente*

Advena plebs kyrie eleison fit clamor ad astra. "Peractum" is meaningless within the context; thus Richter, *op. cit.* (1905), XIII, and note 1, assumed it to read *"peractam."* Then the meaning is clearly that, following Roman custom, an altar had been set up in the western apse of the church for the relics of St. Boniface.

85. Candidus, *Vita Eigilis, MGH, SS.,* XV, 1, 231. Which Roman models the monks at Fulda had in mind cannot be established; possibly they thought of the Lateran, where a courtyard extended behind its western apse, possibly of atria, such as that of St. Peter's.

86. For the life and the importance of St. Boniface see the biography written by his disciple Willibald of Eichstätt, *MGH, SS.,* II, 331 ff.; cf. also *Allgemeine deutsche Biographie,* III (Leipzig, 1876), 123 ff.

87. Weise, *op. cit.* (1919), pp. 66 ff. Still, quite apart from the question whether St. Denis actually had the plan of a Roman Christian basilica, it is rather doubtful whether St. Denis was already considered the Apostle of the Gauls when his church was erected between 761 and 775. The conscious analogizing of the Parisian saint and the Princes of the Apostles has been proved to be due to the policy of Abbot Hilduin of St. Denis (Buchner, *op. cit., passim*). Between 830 and 835 Hilduin had a number of documents fabricated which purported to refer to the coronation of Pippin and the visit of Stephen II, and in which Saint Denis is continuously compared with Saint Peter and Saint Paul (Hilduinus, *Liber de sancto Dionysio* [excerpt], *MGH, SS.,* XV, 1, 2 ff.). Simultaneously the *Vita Dionysii* was written at St. Denis. in it the saint is for the first time identified with Dionysius the Areopagite from Corinth and reported to have been a disciple of St. Paul's; after St. Paul's death, St. Denis was supposed to have been sent by Pope Clement, St. Peter's third successor, to Paris and to have become the Apostle of Gaul. Yet this whole legend was created between 830 and 835, and it is questionable whether a parallel between him and St. Peter would have been drawn as early as 760–775. Cf. Buchner, *loc. cit.;* but see J. Havet, *Oeuvres,* I, Paris (1896), "Les origines de Saint Denis," 191 ff.

88. Schlosser, *op. cit.,* 1896, index.

89. For this and the following, cf. E. Caspar, *Geschichte des Papsttums,* II (Tübingen, 1933), 669 ff.

90. L. Duchesne, *Christian Worship* (transl. M. L. McClure), London, 1904, p. 102, was the first to point out that this change took place before 768. Th. Klauser, "Die liturgischen Austauschbeziehungen zwischen der römischen und fränkisch-deutschen Kirche vom 8. bis zum 11. Jahrhundert," *Hist. Jahrbuch der Görresgesellschaft,* LIII (1933), 169 ff., assumes a date between 754 and 760.

91. See preceding note.

92. *MGH, LL.,* Section II, 1, 62 ff. (789); cf. also *LL.,* Section III, II, 464 ff. (817).

93. W. Hotzelt, "Translation von Martyrerleibern aus Rom ins westliche Frankenreich," *Archiv für elsässische Kirchengeschichte,* XIII (1938); *idem,* "Translationen von Martyrerreliquien aus Rom nach Bayern im 8. Jahrhundert," *Studien und Mitteilungen zur Geschichte des Benediktinerordens,* LIII (1935), 286 ff. We are referring to translations of actual relics rather than of *brandea* such as had been transferred previously.

94. Hrabanus Maurus, *op. cit., MGH, Poet. L.,* II, 205 ff.

95. Caspar, *op. cit.,* II, 669 ff.

96. Klauser, *op. cit.,* p. 169.

97. Whole libraries have been written about the question whether the Curia or Charlemagne or else some faction at the imperial court was the motivating force behind the policy that led to the coronation, and what the coronation was actually intended to mean. Probably it was a combination of forces in different camps, and the motives as well as the intentions of the various factions differed considerably: possibly, as Brackmann has suggested, the papal diplomats thought rather of a shadow *Imperium* created for and by "the Romans," that is, the papal court, while the Frankish diplomats had in mind a more universal *Imperium* of Roman antique character. See A. Brackmann, "Die Erneuerung der Kaiserwürde im Jahre 800," *Geschichtliche Studien Albert Hauck . . . dargebracht* (Leipzig, 1916), pp. 121 ff.; G. Laehr, *Die konstantinische Schenkung in der abendländischen Literatur des Mit-*

telalters ("Historische Studien, 166," Berlin, 1926); K. Heldmann, *Das Kaisertum Karls des Grossen* (Weimar, 1928), *passim;* A. Kleinclausz, *Charlemagne* (Paris, 1934), pp. 287 ff.

98. Heldmann, *op. cit.,* pp. 5 ff. probably goes much too far in alleging the purely spiritual character of Charlemagne's empire; both Brackmann and Kleinclausz, *op. cit.,* seem to come closer to the truth.

99. Kleinclausz, *op. cit.,* p. 307.

100. *Carmina, MGH, Poet. L.,* I, 226 ff.

101. Ermoldus, Nigellus, *In honorem Hludovici, MGH, Poet. L.,* II, 5 ff., particularly lib. II, vv. 67–68; lib. IV, vv, 268–269.

102. C. B. Coleman, *Constantine the Great and Christianity* (New York, 1914; text of Donation, pp. 228 ff.); Laehr, *op. cit.* It seems to be beyond doubt that the forgery originated in the chancellery of Paul I (757–67); see Coleman, *op. cit.,* pp. 209 ff.

103. See a list of quotations in P. Schramm, *Kaiser, Rom und Renovatio* ("Studien der Bibliothek Warburg," Leipzig, 1929) I, 37 f. Cf. also Einhard, *Vita Caroli Magni,* cap. 27 (ed. O. Holder-Egger, *Scriptores Rerum Germanicarum in usum scholarum* [Hanover and Leipzig, 1911], pp. 31 ff.).

104. F. Schneider, *Rom und Romgedanke im Mittelalter* (Munich, 1926), pp. 42 ff.

105. The *Liber Pontificalis* mentions the nationality of each pope at the beginning of the biography (*L.P.* I, *passim*). If those from Campania also can be considered to have been Greek in their education, the number rises to sixteen among twenty-three popes in the period from 619 to 752. The only non-Roman pope in the second half of the eighth century is Stephen III (768–772), a Sicilian who was educated in the (possibly Greek) monastery of S. Crisogono (*L.P.* I, 468).

106. Among the Greek monasteries are S. Giorgio in Velabro, Sta. Saba, Sant' Anastasia, Sta. Maria in Cosmedin, Sant' Anastasius ad Aquas Salvias (M. Mesnard, *La basilique de Saint Chrysogone à Rome* ["Studi di antichità cristiana," Vatican City, 1935], pp. 54 ff.). The number and size of these Eastern monasteries was evi-

dently strongly reinforced by refugees from the East during the first iconoclastic movement, 724/26–787. A new wave of Greeks entered Rome with the second flare-up of iconoclasm in the East, after 813, inferior to the first in size and importance: in that period the monastery of Sta. Prassede (817–24; *L.P.* II, 54) and the church of SS. Stefano e Cassiano near S. Lorenzo f.l.m. (847–55; *L.P.* II, 113) were given to Greek monks. See F. Schneider, *op. cit.,* pp. 113 ff.

107. See Klauser, *op. cit.,* p. 181, n. 42.

108. The relics of the Maccabeans were brought from Antioch to S. Pietro in Vincoli between 579 and 590; a relic of the manger of Christ was transferred to S. Maria Maggiore before 642; the martyrs from Salona were brought to S. Venanzio in 642; the head of Saint George was "rediscovered" between 741 and 752 and brought to his church in the Velabrum.

109. The translation of Sts. Primus and Felicianus to Sto. Stefano Rotondo, 642–49, is an isolated forerunner. The great translations commence in 752 (or 770) with the transfer of St. Sinforosa and her sons to Sant'Angelo in Pescheria. Under Hadrian I (772–95) the number of translations grew steadily; he transported large numbers of relics to Sta. Maria in Cosmedin, where he erected a special crypt for them. Leo III continued in the same line and Paschal I (817–24) was the most active pope in this direction. In the seven short years of his pontificate he transferred hundreds of relics into the city: Caecilia, Tiburtius, Valerianus, Praxedis, Zeno and their numerous companions took possession of their churches and altars in Rome. His successors kept on with this policy: the relics of a number of martyrs from the catacombs on the Via Latina were brought to Sta. Maria Nova, others to S. Martino ai Monti and to the Quattro Coronati.

110. P. Franchi de Cavalieri, "Le reliquie dei martiri Greci nella chiesa di S. Agata alla Suburra," *RACrist,* X (1933), 235 ff., especially 256; see also Hotzelt, *op. cit.* (1935), pp. 301 ff.

111. Scramm, *op. cit.,* I (1929), 3 ff.; Kleinclausz, *op. cit.,* pp. 289 ff.

112. See above, p. 208.

113. The church was built by either

Stephen II in 755 or by Stephen III in 770; see Krautheimer, *Corpus,* I, 73 ff.

114. G. B. Giovenale, *La basilica di S. Maria in Cosmedin* (Rome, 1927).

115. Krautheimer, *AJA,* XLIII (1939), 398 ff. The approximate date of a building within the pontificate of a pope can frequently be concluded from the place it occupies within his biography in the *Liber Pontificalis.*

116. *Ibid.,* p. 392.

117. Krautheimer, *Corpus,* I, 42 ff.

118. It is the first church mentioned in Leo's biography, *L.P.* II, 1.

119. Giovenale, *op. cit.,* Pl. VII b.

120. G. Giovannoni, *La chiesa vaticana di San Stefano Maggiore, Atti della Pont. Accad., ser.* III, *Memorie,* IV (Vatican City, 1934), reports on the previous state and on his reconstruction of the edifice. The foundation of the church in Leo's biography in the *Liber Pontificalis* (*L.P.* II, 28) follows the long list of gifts made to Roman churches in 806.

The present façade was erected in 1706; in the fourteenth century the aisles were destroyed and the present clerestory with its small windows was constructed, and simultaneously a diaphragm arch was built across the nave (Giovannoni, *op. cit.,* pp. 3, 10, 24).

121. *Ibid.,* pp. 3 ff.

122. Giovannoni, *op. cit.,* p. 13, who dates this crypt in the pontificate of Leo IV (847–55).

123. See above, note 9.

124. *L.P.,* II, 52.

125. The old *titulus* of Sta. Prassede which is first mentioned in 491 (G. B. De Rossi, "Scoperta della cripta di S. Ippolito," *BACrist* [1882], pp. 56 ff., particularly pp. 64 ff.) had been repaired by Hadrian I (772–95), (*L.P.* I, 509). This restoration, however, was evidently insufficient, and a new church was started at some distance from the old building. Paschal's official biography (*LP* II, 54) and an inscription at the foot of the mosaic in the apse (G. B. De Rossi, *Musaici cristiani . . . delle chiese di Roma* [Rome, 1899], plate 25) attribute the new structure without any qualification to Paschal, and thus to the period between 817 and

824. The place of the report within the biography would suggest an early date within this period. On the other hand an inscription by the triumphal arch commemorates a mass transfer of relics from the catacombs into the church which was undertaken by Paschal (*LP* II, 63, n. 12); there the date is given as July 20, 817, which would be only six months after the Pope's election late in January. However, this inscription has been proved to be a copy made in 1730 from a thirteenth-century original which pretends to be ninth-century but contains a number of chronological and other errors (F. Grossi-Gondi, "La celebre iscrizione agiografica della basilica di Sta. Prassede," *Civiltà cattolica* [1916], I, 443; see also, *Idem,* "Excursus sulla paleografia medioevale epigrafica del secolo* IX," *Diss. Pont. Accad.,* ser. II, XIII [1918]; see especially p. 173). If in spite of this rather dubious pedigree there were any truth in the date mentioned by this inscription, the brief lapse of time between it and Paschal's election would suggest the possibility that the church had actually been begun before Paschal attained the pontificate.

The edifice as it presents itself today has never been properly studied. The present decoration of the interior was executed around 1600 (G. D. Franzini, *Roma antica e moderna,* Rome, 1653, pp. 357 f.). A. Muñoz ("Studii sulle basiliche romane di S. Sabina e di S. Prassede," *Diss. Pont. Accad.,* ser. II, XIII [1918], 117 ff., fig. 5) was the first to point out that the diaphragm arches were not an original part of the building; indeed he found the original columns well preserved within the piers that carry the arches and was able to point out that the arches obstructed some of the original windows; possibly the piers consist of two parts, of the thirteenth and sixteenth century respectively. For the rest the following remarks are based on my own survey of the building made in connection with the preparation of the *Corpus Basilicarum,* in collaboration with Messrs. A. Todini, W. Frankl, and (since 1956) S. Corbett.

126. P. Ugonio, *Historia delle stationi di Roma* (Rome, 1588), c. 299.

127. *LP* II, 54.

128. The total interior length of the

edifice is about 46 m. (156 R. ft.), its width 26 m. (about 87 R. ft.); this is almost one and a half times the measurements of Sto. Stefano which is 33 m. by 19.50 m.

129. It was erected as a mausoleum for Paschal's mother Theodora Episcopa, and as a chapel for the relics of St. Zeno and two other saints. See *L.P.* II, 55 and 56, n. 14; De Rossi, *Musaici, op. cit.,* text for Pl. 23. The inscription referring to Theodora Episcopa is mostly modern (Grossi-Gondi, "Excursus," p. 173).

130. F. Fornari, "Il rilievo del complesso monumentale di San Sebastiano," *Atti del IIIº Congresso di archeologia cristiana* (Rome, 1934), pp. 315 ff. (see our fig. 9).

131. At St. Paul's, a cross-shaped structure, possibly contemporaneous with the basilica, adjoined the south wing of the transept (Fig. 80). It presented the pattern of the chapel of S. Zeno: the square bay in the center was covered by a groined vault and supported by four columns in the corners, and the four shallow wings were surmounted by barrel vaults. Whether this structure was a mausoleum proper is not quite clear; it may have been a memorial chapel erected in honor of some relic which had been deposited within. The anonymous guide *La basilica di S. Paolo sulla Via Ostiense* (Rome, 1933), p. 93 mentions that when in 1930 the chapel was transformed into a baptistery, bones and fragments of fourth- and fifth-century frescoes were found. For the similar chapels at S. Giovanni in Fonte near the Lateran see Ph. Lauer, *op. cit.,* p. 54; for those at St. Peter's, the Alpharanus plan (Fig. 79).

132. It is about 30 m. (100 R. ft.) long and 6.25 m. (21 R. ft.) wide.

133. Remnants of the porticoes along the flanks and on the entrance side of the atrium are preserved in the walls of the courtyard in front of the church and in the houses of the neighborhood. The existence of the fourth portico in front of the façade of the basilica can be deduced from the traces of a roof across the façade of the basilica, and from the distance which the last support would have had from the façade, which is considerably greater than the usual intercolumnium of the porticoes.

134. The level of the atrium corresponds to that of the nave. The level of the street is 3.30 m. lower; since the level of the ancient street was somewhat lower even than that of the present one (R. Lanciani, *Forma urbis Romae* [Milan, 1893], Pl. 23), a flight of steps must always have led up to the entrance of the atrium.

135. Whether the third great fourth-century basilica, St. John's in the Lateran, had one is undetermined. Atria can be proved to have existed at S. Clemente late in the fourth century (E. Junyent, *Il titolo di S. Clemente* ["*Studi di antichità classica,*" VI, Rome, 1932]); and at SS. Giovanni e Paolo, *ca.* 450 (Krautheimer, *Corpus,* I, 267 ff.). At Sant'Agata dei Goti, *ca.* 470, an atrium of reduced form is still preserved.

136. A narthex without an atrium is found as early as 440–61 at Sto. Stefano in Via Latina; a similar one may have existed *ca.* 500 at S. Giovanni a Porta Latina. In the third quarter of the eighth century the Roman portico in front of Sant' Angelo in Pescheria was used as a narthex for that church, and as late as the early ninth century a narthex existed at SS. Nereo ed Achilleo.

137. Ugonio, *op. cit.,* c. 298*v*, mentions the number of steps at Sta. Prassede. As to St. Peter's, see Alpharanus' plan (Fig. 79).

138. Krautheimer, *Corpus,* I, 94 ff.; in Paschal's biography (*LP* II, 57) the foundation of Sta. Cecilia follows that of Sta. Prassede at some distance.

139. S. Marco has never been properly dealt with from the point of view of its architectural history. Because it is located within the Palazzo Venezia, Premier Mussolini's official residence, any thorough investigation has been practically impossible for the past fifteen years. Thus we have to rely on notes made after frequent brief visits and a few insufficient plans. The *titulus* is mentioned from the fourth century on (*LP* I, 202); it was repaired by Hadrian I (*LP* I, 500) and completely rebuilt by Gregory IV (827–44), (*LP* II, 74 ff.). Later restorations took place under Paul II (1464–71) and Cardinal Quirini (1728–38): see Ph. Dengel, H. Egger and others, *Palast und Basilika San Marco in Rom* (Rome, 1913); D. Bartolini, *La sotterranea confessione di*

S. Marco (Rome, 1844). A well-head with an inscription of the ninth century now in the portico came possibly from the atrium (G. B. De Rossi, "Secchia di piombo trovata nella Reggenza di Tunisi, § II, Simbolismo cristiano dell'aqua," *BACrist*, ser. I, an. 5 [1867], 78).

140. See above, p. 208.

141. R. Vielliard, *Les origines du titre de Saint-Martin aux Monts à Rome* ("*Studi di antichità cristiana,*" IV [Rome, 1931]).

142. Sta. Cecilia is 44 m. long and 23.60 m. wide, S. Martino 45 m. long and 23.28 m. wide.

143. A. Prandi, "Vicende edilizie della basilica di Sta. Maria Nova," *Rendiconti della Pont. Accademia* (1937), pp. 197 ff., where some results of my investigations of the year 1935 are published.

144. A. Muñoz, *Il restauro della chiesa . . . dei SS. Quattro Coronati* (Rome, 1914); H. Thümmler, "Die Baukunst des 11. Jahrhunderts in Italien," *Römisches Jahrbuch für Kunstgeschichte*, III (1939), 149 ff. The *titulus* of the Quattro Coronati is first mentioned in 595 and goes back possibly to the fourth century (*LP* I, 326, n. 13). It was completely rebuilt by Leo IV (*LP* II, 115). In 1144/45 a restoration cut off the first six bays of the original nave and transformed this part into a second atrium; the aisles of the ninth-century church were eliminated, and the six eastern bays of the former nave subdivided so as to form a considerably smaller church, consisting of a nave and two aisles with galleries above, a transept, and the (original and therefore incongruously large) apse; see Muñoz, *op. cit.*, *passim*.

145. Possibly also the chapel contiguous to the right aisle belonged to the original building.

146. Muñoz, *op. cit.*, pp. 7 ff., has dated this tower in the high Middle Ages; still the shape of the balusters, the character of the masonry, and the double arches of the openings leave no doubt that as a whole this tower forms part of the original ninth-century plan. Only the pointed entrance arches on the ground floor are a high-medieval transformation of the original ninth-century entrance.

147. *MGH, Epist.*, III, 592 ff. (799–80); 609 f. (781–86).

148. G. B. De Rossi, "L'inscription du tombeau d'Hadrien Ier," *Ecole française de Rome, Mélanges d'archéologie et d'histoire*, VIII (1888), 478 ff.; Hubert, *op. cit.*, p. 99.

149. *LP* I, 454. The transfer of the relics of Sts. Denis, Rusticus, and Eleutherius from St. Denis to S. Silvestro in Rome has been occasionally cited as proving the existence of Frankish influence in Rome in the eighth century; see Kingsley Porter, *op. cit.*, I, 67, n. 3 (the reference made there to the seventh century is, of course, a mere *lapsus calami*). Since however the whole story of the transfer belongs to the group of spurious documents fabricated at St. Denis under Abbot Hilduin (see above, note 87) and is taken up in Roman sources only after 850 (*LP* II, 145, 152 ff.), no conclusions can be drawn from it.

150. Einhardus, *Translatio . . . , MGH, SS.*, XV, I, 239. The original structure of the church at Seligenstadt was uncovered a few years ago and the results published by O. Müller. Neither his final report nor the one by A. Schuchert, *Die Gruftanlage der Märtyrer Marcellinus und Petrus zu Rom und Seligenstadt* (Mainz, 1938), are available to me at this time. I have to rely on the preliminary reports: O. Müller, "Die Einhartsbasilika zu Seligenstadt," *Deutsche Kunst und Denkmalpflege*, XXXVIII (1936), 254 ff.; *idem,* "Die Einhartsbasilika zu Seligenstadt," *Forschungen und Fortschritte*, XII (1936), 254 ff.; XIII, 1937, 373 ff., and A. Schuchert, "La basilica dei SS. Marcellino e Pietro a Seligenstadt sul Meno," *RACrist*, XV (1938), 141 ff.

151. The results of the excavations as published by Müller and Schuchert, *op. cit.*, are contrary to a reconstruction of the transept with a segregated crossing such as is indicated in their plans. This has already been corrected by Lehmann, *op. cit.*, Fig. 106 and p. 140. The details of the crypt do not seem to be quite definitely established.

152. No rule can be established for the number of intercolumniations in the large fourth-century basilicas; St. Peter's has

twenty-three, St. Paul's and Sta. Maria Maggiore twenty-one intercolumniations. On the other hand in the smaller basilicas of the fifth century, and likewise in the "pseudo-Early Christian" basilicas of the ninth century, the number of intercolumniations seems anything but arbitrary. The occurrence of thirteen intercolumniations seems to be particularly frequent: that number is found in the fifth century at Sta. Sabina, at S. Lorenzo in Lucina, at SS. Giovanni e Paolo, and possibly at Sta. Prisca; in the ninth century at Sta. Cecilia, S. Martino ai Monti, and Sta. Susanna. Evidently their twelve supports were meant to suggest the number of the apostles. Sometimes only ten of these twelve supports are free-standing, while the remaining two are formed by the pilasters at either end of the row of supports; thus the number of intercolumniations results in eleven, as is the case in the fifth century at S. Pietro in Vincoli, in the ninth century at Sant'Anastasia, at Fulda, and at Hersfeld. In smaller churches twelve supports are occasionally achieved by arranging seven arches in each of the two arcades (Sant'Agata dei Goti). Eight supports— the figure corresponding to Resurrection and to the Beatitudes (Candidus, *Vita Eigilis, MGH, SS.,* XV, 1, 231)—occur only rarely: at S. Clemente late in the fourth century, at Sto. Stefano degli Abessini, and at Seligenstadt in the ninth. While in every one of these cases it is evidently the solids which represent the symbolical number, twelve or eight, in the ninth century it is also frequently the number of intervals that counts. Sta. Prassede and SS. Nereo ed Achilleo in Rome, and the church of S. Salvatore (near Monte Cassino), have their naves bounded by twelve intercolumniations on either side; the small churches at Höchst, Steinbach, Heiligenberg, and possibly that of Frankfurt by six. This change from the number of solids, i.e., columns, to the number of voids, i.e., distances, may be of far greater importance for the history of architecture than one might be inclined to think at first: it may mean that the edifice is no longer considered as consisting of solids only, but that the intervals between the solids enter into the conception of the architect and of the spectator.

153. Weise, *Untersuchungen,* pp. 104 ff.

154. For the results of the excavations which uncovered the ninth-century basilica and its small eighth-century predecessors inside the present south transept, see J. Vonderau, *Die Ausgrabungen der Stiftskirche zu Hersfeld in den Jahren 1921 und 1922* ("Achtzehnte Veröffentlichung des Fuldaer Geschichtsvereins" [Fulda, 1925]), and von Bezold, *op. cit.,* p. 18. What is preserved today are the magnificent ruins of an eleventh-century construction (1038– 1144); yet this edifice departs only slightly from the ninth-century structure. The nave was two bays longer than it is at present, and the main apse, instead of being preceded by a long fore-choir, was joined directly to the transept. The structure which terminated the nave at the west end was perhaps not too different from the eleventh-century arrangement in which an entrance hall on the ground floor is topped by a western apse, the whole being flanked by two tall turrets. Vonderau, *op. cit.,* was inclined towards reconstructing a twin tower façade; H. Reinhardt, "Das erste Münster zu Schaffhausen," *Anzeiger für schweizerische Altertumskunde,* XXXVII (1935), 241 ff., thought of a regular westwork.

155. The proportion of the transept, 1:4, is never found among churches of the Early Christian period or the eighth- and ninth-century revival in Rome. The still unexplained remnants around the main apse at Hersfeld resemble the beginning of an ambulatory-like crypt and certainly look different from the outside crypts which extend behind the apses of Centula and of St. Philibert-de-Grandlieu.

156. G. Schönberger, *Beiträge zur Baugeschichte des Frankfurter Doms* ("Schriften des historischen Museums," 3 [Frankfurt, 1927]), 7 ff.; *Die Kunstdenkmäler von Bayern, Oberpfalz,* XXII, ed. F. Mader (Munich, 1933), 13 ff.; Schmidt, *op. cit.,* p. 115; J. Zemp, "Baugeschichte des Frauenmünsters in Zürich," *Mitteilungen der Antiquarischen Gesellschaft in Zürich,* XXV (1914), 5 ff.

157. There is no reason for reconstructing the main apse at Heiligenberg as rectangular (Schmidt, *loc. cit.;* but see Lehmann, *op. cit.,* p. 115). The existence

of square sacristies at either side of the apse at Frankfurt is possible (Schönberger, *op. cit.*, pp. 9 ff.).

158. A. Pantaloni, "Problemi archeologici Cassinesi," *RACrist*, XVI (1939), 271 ff., particularly 277 ff. and 283, n. 4.

159. *Ibid.*, 272 ff.

160. *Ibid.*, 279, and G. Croquison, "I problemi archeologici Farfensi," *RACrist*, XV (1938), 37 ff., particularly 56 ff.; see also H. Thümmler, *op. cit.*, pp. 141 ff., particularly p. 211 and p. 224. The date of the Farfa west-work seems, however, somewhat doubtful; possibly it is as late as the eleventh century.

161. O. Müller, *Die Einhartsbasilika zu Steinbach* (Diss. Leipzig, 1936), Seligenstadt (n.d.); J. Hubert, "Germigny-des-Près," *Congrès archéol.*, XCIII (1930), 534 ff.; R. de Lasteyrie, "L'Eglise de St. Philibert-de-Grandlieu," *Mémoires de l' Académie des inscriptions et belles lettres*, XXVIII (1911), 1 ff.

162. Weise, *Untersuchungen*, pp. 78 ff.

163. The reconstruction of the abbey church of St. Riquier at Centula is based on some descriptions and *tituli* (Schlosser, *op. cit.*, 253 ff., no. 782 ff.) and one seventeenth-century engraving after a (lost) eleventh-century reproduction of the church. They have been carefully used by W. Effmann, *Centula-St. Riquier, Forschungen und Funde*, Bd. 2, Heft 5 (Münster, 1912); see, however, the important corrections in H. Beenken, "Die ausgeschiedene Vierung," *RepKunstW*, LI (1930), 207 ff., particularly 211 ff. Hubert's suggestion (*op. cit.*, 79 ff.) to reconstruct the crossing as a kind of central edifice added to the nave is hardly acceptable.

164. Von Bezold, *op. cit.*, pp. 21 ff.; R. Kautzsch, *Der Mainzer Dom* (Frankfurt, 1925).

165. *La basilica di Aquileia, a cura del comitato per le ceremonie del IX centenario* (Bologna, 1933).

166. Gantner, *op. cit.*, 132 ff.

167. See above, p. 226.

168. When previously discussing this particular revival ('San Nicola in Bari und die apulische Architektur des 12. Jahrhunderts," *Wiener Jahrbuch für Kunstgeschichte*, IX [1934], 5 ff.), I was of course quite mistaken in assuming (p. 18 f.) that Cluny had exerted any influence on the building of Monte Cassino. K. J. Conant's excavation (reproduced in J. Evans, *The Romanesque Architecture of the Order of Cluny*, Cambridge, Mass. [1938], p. 64) has proved that Cluny had nothing to do with this Early Christian groundplan. On the other hand the importance of Monte Cassino for Apulia (Bari, S. Nicola, first stage; Trani, S. Nicola; Otranto Cathedral and others) and Campania (Salerno Cathedral, Amalfi Cathedral, Ravello Cathedral, and S. Giovanni del Torre, etc.) has been proved correct. See also Thümmler, *op. cit.*, pp. 216 ff.

169. In this connection it is interesting to see that Vasari actually thought Brunellesco's Romanesque prototypes to have been of Carolingian origin; see G. Vasari, *Vite de' pittori . . . ,* "Proemio," (ed. G. Milanesi, I [Florence, 1906]), 235.

170. Krautheimer, "S. Pietro in Vincoli," *Proceedings Amer. Philos. Soc.*, 84 (1941), 364 ff.

171. W. Meyer-Barkhausen, "Karolingische Kapitelle in Hersfeld, Höchst a.M. und Fulda," *Zeitschrift für bildende Kunst*, LIII (1929/30), 126; *idem*, "Die Kapitelle der Justinuskirche in Höchst a.M.," *JPKS*, LIV (1933), 69 ff.; H. Kähler, *Die römischen Kapitelle des Rheingebietes* ("Römisch-germanische Forschungen," 13 [Berlin and Leipzig, 1939]). The capitals with full leaves may form an exception; as Meyer-Barkhausen (*op. cit.*, 1933) has pointed out, they may be derived from Rome. There they are frequently found from the first century on; best-known examples are those at the Colosseum. Still, one can possibly go even further: St. Paul's was filled with capitals of this type (F. W. Deichmann and A. Tschira, "Die frühchristlichen Basen und Kapitelle von S. Paolo fuori le mura," *Mitteilungen des Deutschen archäologischen Instituts, Römische Abteilung*, LIV [1939], 99 ff.) and it may be legitimate to ask whether the preference given to such capitals in Carolingian architecture north and south of the Alps was not due to their occurrence in one of the proto-basilicas.

172. The Palatine Chapel at Aix-la-Chapelle would seem to be the outstanding exception to this statement. While I am

inclined to link it up with other central edifices rather than with S. Vitale, there can be no doubt of its derivation from Near Eastern prototypes.

173. See above, p. 214 f.

174. H. Dümmler, *s.v.* "Alcuin," in: *Allgemeine deutsche Biographie*, I (Leipzig, 1875), 343 ff.

175. G. Becker, *Catalogi bibliothecarum antiqui* (Bonn, 1885); J. W. Thompson, *The Medieval Library* (Chicago, 1939), pp. 54 ff.

176. A. Ebert, *Allgemeine Geschichte der Literatur des Mittelalters*, II, (Leipzig, 1880); M. Manitius, *Geschichte der lateinischen Literatur des Mittelalters*, I (I. von Müller, *Handbuch der klassischen Altertumswissenschaften*, IX, pt. 2, 1 [Munich, 1911]).

177. Aside from the grammarians and rhetoricians, Terence would have to be included in this group.

178. As early as the fourth century, this procedure is recommended by St. Jerome, *Ep.* 70 (*PL*, XXII, cols. 664 ff.). For Christian additions made to pagan writers in the Carolingian period see, e.g., Ebert, *op. cit.*, p. 19.

179. Ebert, *op. cit.*, pp. 70 ff.; see Theodulf, *De libris quos legere solebam et qualiter fabulae poetarum a philosophis mystice pertractentur*, *MGH*, *Poet. L.*, I, 543 ff.

180. D. Comparetti, *Vergil in the Middle Ages*, transl. E. F. M. Benecke, (London, 1895), *passim;* see also T. W. Valentine, "The Medieval Church and Vergil," *Classical Weekly*, XXV (1931-1932), 65 ff.

181. Comparetti, *op. cit.*, pp. 98 ff. Seneca was known not so much by his genuine writings but by the spurious letters he was supposed to have addressed to St. Paul, see *MGH Poet. L.*, I, 300.

182. Lupus de Ferrières would seem to be an outstanding exception; see C. H. Beeson, *Lupus of Ferrières* (Cambridge, Mass., 1930).

183. F. Behn, *Die karolingische Klosterkirche von Lorsch* (Berlin and Leipzig, 1934), pp. 70 ff.

184. The fresco of St. Michael on the upper floor is of the fourteenth century; see Behn, *loc. cit.*

185. While F. Schneider, "Der karolingische Thorbau zu Lorsch," *Korrespondenzblatt des Gesammtvereins der deutschen Geschichts- und Altertumsvereine*, XXVI (1878), 1 ff., certainly went too far in assuming that the Lorsch gatehouse was a regular triumphal arch erected possibly for the victory of Louis the German over the Arabs, he was the first to suggest the comparison with triumphal arches as such.

186. R. Schultze, "Das römische Stadttor in der kirchlichen Baukunst des Mittelalters," *Bonner Jahrbücher*, CXXIV (1917), 41. Of course it must be borne in mind that any medieval copy in architecture would tend to mix the principal prototype with details borrowed from other models (see "Introduction to an 'Iconography of Medieval Architecture,'" above, pp. 115 ff.).

187. K. Lehmann-Hartleben, "L'arco di Tito," *Bulletino communale*, LXII (1934), 89 ff. K. Grube, *Die Attika an römischen Triumphbögen* (Diss. Karlsruhe, 1931), assumes the function of the attic to have been merely structural, a statement which does not seem quite convincing.

188. H. Kähler, *s.v.* "Triumphbögen," in A. F. Pauly and G. Wissowa, *Realencyclopädie des klassischen Altertumswissenschaft*, 2. Reihe, XIII. Halbband (1939), cols. 373 ff., gives a fine survey of the problems and good lists of the monuments which are either preserved or else known through literary or illustrative sources. For our particular problem one would need a list indicating which arches were still preserved in the ninth century. Only for Rome can such a list be compiled from the late eighth-century itinerary of the Anonymous of Einsiedeln (R. Lanciani, "L'itinerario d'Einsiedeln," *Monumenti antichi . . . della R. Accademia dei Lincei*, I [1891], 437 ff.), and from the twelfth-century *Mirabilia* (P. Schramm, *Kaiser, Rom und Renovatio* [Leipzig and Berlin, 1929], II 76).

189. Lehmann-Hartleben, *op. cit.*, p. 114, n. 80. It might be objected that both the Arch of Septimius Severus and that of Constantine have full—not engaged—col-

umns in front of the piers, contrary to the arrangement at the *Torhalle*. Yet considering the peculiar character of medieval copies, the engaged columns of Lorsch may be derived either from misinterpreted drawings of the Roman arches, or else from arches with engaged columns like those at Mainz, Reims, or Orange, which are different in other respects but may have exerted a collateral influence; see above, note 186.

190. For the history and the architecture of the Arch of Constantine, see H. P. L'Orange, *Der spätantike Bildschmuck des Konstantinsbogens* ("*Studien zur spätantiken Kunstgeschichte,*" X [Berlin, 1938]), 1 ff. with bibliography.

That, as at Lorsch, a chapel was connected with the Arch of Constantine is certain, and this would seem to have considerable bearing on the matter; unfortunately it cannot be proved that this chapel already existed in the ninth century, nor can it be established whether it occupied the upper story of the arch as did that at Lorsch. It is first mentioned in 1230 as *S. Salvatore de arcu Trasi.* C. Huelsen, *Le chiese di Roma nel Medio Evo* (Florence, 1925), p. 431, locates the chapel near the Arch; indeed a small building, possibly the chapel, appears east of the monument in drawings up to the early seventeenth century. On the other hand, these same drawings frequently show the remnants of a medieval tower surmounting the east corner of the arch; it cannot be established whether this belonged to a fortification or whether it had any connection with a chapel in the attic.

191. For this and the following see C. Huelsen, "Zu den römischen Ehrenbögen," *Festschrift zu Otto Hirschfelds sechzigstem Geburtstage* (Berlin, 1903), pp. 423 ff.

192. According to Huelsen, *op. cit.*, pp. 424 ff., it occurs in only four inscriptions on North African arches of the third and fourth centuries, and in one passage in fourth-century literature (Ammianus Marcellinus, *Libri gestarum qui supersunt,* XXI, 15, ed. C. U. Clark [Berlin, 1910], I, 249). St. Jerome's translation of the Vulgate, I Kings 15: 12, uses the kindred term *fornix triumphalis.*

193. It may possibly have entered by way

of eighth-century glossaries; see Huelsen, *op. cit.*, p. 424, n. 4. Huelsen, *op. cit.*, p. 425, n. 1, also points out "dass es bemerkenswerter Weise gerade zwei constantinische Denkmäler (i.e., the Arch of Constantine and the arch at the end of the nave of St. Peter's with its inscription referring to the triumph of Christ) gewesen zu sein scheinen, denen der Ausdruck Triumphbogen seine weite Verbreitung verdankt."

194. The former assumption that these words represent an alteration of an original inscription referring to Jupiter has long been proved wrong (*CIL,* VI [Berlin, 1876], 236 ff., no. 1139; De Rossi, *BACrist,* I (1863), 58.

195. P. Clemen, *Die romanische Monumentalmalerei in den Rheinlanden* ("*Publikationen der Gesellschaft für rheinische Geschichtskunde,*" 32 [Dusseldorf, 1916]).

196. Coleman, *op. cit.*, p. 324.

197. B. Simson, *Jahrbücher des fränkischen Reiches unter Ludwig dem Frommen,* I (1874), 83, n. 3; *MGH, LL.,* Sectio III, II, 464, n. 1, "*in domo Aquisgrani palatii quae Lateranis dicitur,*" seems to use the name Lateran only for the archchaplain's apartment within the palace, where a synod was held in 817. Yet another mention of a synod held in 836 (*MGH, LL., Section* III, II 705) "*. . . Aquisgrani palatii in secretario basilicae sanctae genetricis Dei Mariae quod dicitur Lateranis . . .*" refers possibly, and a remark in the *Chronicon Moissiacense* (*MGH, SS.,* I, 303) certainly, to the whole palace: "*Fecit autem ibi et palatium quod nominavit Lateranis et collectis thesauris suis de regnis singulis, in Aquis adduci praecepit . . .*" Simson, *loc. cit.*, has intimated but not proved that this reference was made erroneously by the chronicler.

198. The parallel has been pointed out by St. Beissel, "Die Wölfin des Aachener Münsters," *Zeitschrift des Aachener Geschichtsvereins,* XIII (1890), 317 ff.; it has been contended by P. Clemen, *Romanische Monumentalmalerei,* p. 700, n. 5, but Clemen's reasoning to the effect that the bronze at Aix represented a bear and not a wolf is hardly valid. The more refined details of zoölogy did not mean so much to the Middle Ages and certainly not in

this case where any animal which looked somewhat like a wolf would suffice to stand for the Roman *Lupa*. Southern Gaul as the country of origin for the Aix bronze has been suggested by A. C. Kisa, "Die römischen Antiken in Aachen," *Westdeutsche Zeitschrift für Geschichte und Kunst*, XXV (1906), 38 ff. The Roman *Lupa* is first mentioned as being preserved at the Lateran in the tenth century (*MGH, SS.,* III, 720), yet there is reason to assume that the figure was always there from Antiquity on; see R. Lanciani, *Ancient Rome in the Light of Recent Excavations* (New York, 1890), pp. 21 and 285. Unfortunately I can find no proof for Lanciani's assertion (p. 285) that as early as the ninth century the *Lupa* is mentioned as standing at the Lateran.

199. Agnellus, *Liber Pontificalis Ravennatis* (*MGH, SS., Rer. Langob.,* p. 338); see also Walafrid Strabo, *Versus . . . de imagine Tetrici* (*MGH, Poet. L.,* II, 370 ff).

200. H. Jordan, *Topographie der Stadt Rom,* I, 2 (ed. C. Huelsen) (Berlin, 1907), 245.

201. Poeta Saxo, *De gestis Caroli Magni,* V, *vv.* 431 ff. (*MGH, SS.,* I, 274).

202. The name of St. John instead of that of the Savior appears first in 870; see *Itinerarium Bernardi monachi*, in T. Tobler and A. Molinier, *Itinera Hierosolymitana* (Geneva, 1879), p. 318. The date "shortly before the year 1000" as given by C. Huelsen, *Le chiese di Roma* (Florence, 1925), p. 272 should be corrected accordingly.

203. *MGH, Epist.,* III, 586 ff.; IV, 203 ff.

204. Ermoldus Nigellus, *In honorem*

Hludovici, II, 1, *vv.* 424 ff. *MGH, Poet. L.,* II, 36.

205. The present mosaic was made between 1736 and 1744 from an older one which was destroyed at that time (G. Rohault de Fleury, *Le Latran au moyen âge* [Paris, 1877], pp. 539 ff.). This older one in turn was a copy executed in 1625 from the badly damaged original; while the group to the right was well enough preserved to leave no doubt as to the identity of those represented, the group to the left had completely disappeared before 1564. The restorers of 1625, however, worked from a drawing evidently made before 1564, on which this group was still preserved. Thus the copy made between 1736 and 1744 from their restoration seems to be a reasonably reliable reproduction of the original. The date of the original can be established by the title *rex* given to Charlemagne in the inscription; it must precede the coronation as emperor, and thus can be dated between the election of Leo III (795) and the coronation (800). See N. Alemanni, *De Lateranensibus parietibus* (Rome, 1625); P. Schramm, *Zeitgenössische Bildnisse Karls des Grossen* (Leipzig, 1928), pp. 4 ff.; G. Ladner, "Mosaici . . . nell' antico palazzo Lateranense" *RACrist*, XII (1935), 265 ff.

206. For the Christian interpretation of Roman history see Fredegarius, *Chronicae,* Lib. II (*MGH, SS., Rer. Merov* II, especially 55 ff.).

207. Ermoldus Nigellus, *op. cit.,* IV, *vv.* 245 ff. (*MGH, Poet L.,* II, 65; Poeta Saxo, *op. cit.,* V, *vv.* 645 ff.:; *MGH, SS,* I, 278 ff.).

Postscript

Some details in this paper need supplementation in the light of recent discoveries.

1) In 1942 I shared, of course, the common opinion which saw in the existing transept of St. John's in the Lateran a feature taken over from the Constantinian structure. Excavations undertaken by myself and Mr. Spencer Corbett (see above, pp. 21 ff.) have proved this to be wrong. The place of the transept in Constantine's Lateran basilica was taken by low projecting sacristies, and the present continuous transept is a medieval addition in imitation presumably of St. Paul's, St. Peter's, or their Carolingian progeny (Fig. 5). In this reprint I have therefore removed from the original text references to the transept of St. John's in the Lateran.

2) My suspicions regarding the existence of a continuous transept in the Carolingian church at S. Denis have been justified by the excavations undertaken by Jules Formigé (*L'abbaye royale*, pp. 50 ff., though with the erroneous date of *ca.* 636). The center bay of the transept was segregated and its wings projected but slightly beyond the aisles; but it remains undetermined, whether they were as high as the nave or lower.

3) Research over these past twenty-five years has also clarified the history of some of the churches mentioned by me in passing references. The tripartite transept of S. Tecla at Milan, rather than later churches in Greece (see above, pp. 59 ff.), is the source of that at S. Pietro in Vincoli. S. Ambrogio in Milan was terminated by one single apse (Reggiori, *La basilica ambrosiana,* p. 28; Krautheimer, *Early Christian and Byzantine Architecture,* p. 131). The basilicas adjoining the palatine chapel at Aix-la-Chapelle have turned out both to be later additions to the main building (*Vorromanische Kirchenbauten,* p. 16). Also, contrary to what I thought, the recent finds at Ingelheim (*ibid.,* p. 129) preclude a segregated crossing as definitely as I postulated; nor is it quite certain that the colonnades at Fulda carried an architrave (*ibid.,* pp. 85 ff.). In Rome, Wolfgang Frankl, Spencer Corbett and I jointly have been able to confirm the earlier findings on the Carolingian basilicas, such as S. Maria Nova, S. Marco, S. Martino, S. Prassede, SS. Quattro Coronati and Sto. Stefano degli Abessini. But we have also established that SS. Nereo ed Achilleo was provided with galleries as well as with end towers; that the core of Sta. Susanna, including the galleries, apparently belonged to a fourth-century private basilica which was remodeled and decorated by Leo III; that—a point of some importance in the present context—the arcaded nave of the Quattro Coronati, including the dividing cross pier and diaphragm arch, replaced in the early twelfth century the trabeated unbroken colonnades of the Carolingian nave; and that Sto. Stefano degli Abessini was possibly built by Leo IV about 850 rather than fifty years before. (*Corpus Basilicarum* I, 220 ff.; II, 216 ff.; III, 87 ff., 135 ff., 232 ff.; IV, in press). G. Ferrari (*Early Monasteries, passim*), has brought out that contrary to previous assumptions the Greek monasteries of Rome in their majority were founded in the late eighth and early ninth centuries after the recrudescence of iconoclasm in the East. Falkenstein (1966) has called into question my interpretation of the palace at Aix-la-Chapelle as a "copy" of the Lateran, without convincing me, though. Finally, the studies of Crosby (1942 and 1953), Fisher (1962), Formigé (1960), Forsyth (1953), Grossmann (1955), Schlunk (1947), Verzone (1942) and of the Munich Zentralinstitut (1966 ff.), among others, have clarified many a problem of pre-Carolingian and Carolingian building, while Panofsky (1960) has thrown new light on the question of the Carolingian and other Renascences.

None of this affects the argument as presented. (Schafer Williams' suggestion of a mid ninth century date for the fabrication of the Constantinian Donation, in two articles published in 1964, leaves me unconvinced.) Were I to write the paper today, I would change very little. I might tone down the statement that the revival of the Golden age of Christianity in Rome was the aim of the Carolingian Renaissance by saying that it was a major aim; and I would say that the reverberations of Near Eastern architecture in the Occident, rather than being ended by the Carolingian Renaissance, were forced into the limbo of undercurrents. Otherwise I stick to my guns.

Additional Bibliography

Crosby, McK. S. *The Abbey of St. Denis,* I (New Haven, 1942).

———— *L'abbaye Royale de Saint Denis* (Paris, 1953).

Falkenstein, L. *Der 'Lateran' der karolingischen Pfalz zu Aachen* (Cologne, 1966).

Ferrari, G. *Early Monasteries in Rome* (Vatican City, 1957).

Fisher, E. A. *The Greater Anglo-Saxon Churches* (London, 1962).

Formigé, J. *L'abbaye royale de Saint-Denis* (Paris, 1960).

Forsyth, G. H. *The Church of St. Martin at Angers* (Princeton, 1953).

Grossmann, D. *Die Abteikirche zu Hersfeld* (Kassel, 1955).

Krautheimer, R. *Early Christian and Byzantine Architecture* (Pelican History of Art, Harmondsworth, 1965).

Krautheimer, R., Frankl, W., and Corbett, S. *Corpus basilicarum christianarum Romae,* II (Vatican City and New York, 1959); III (Vatican City and New York, 1967); IV, in press.

————. "La Basilica Costantiniana al Laterano," *RACrist.,* XLIII (1967); "Miscellanea E. Josi," II), 125 ff.

Panofsky, E. *Renaissance and Renascences in Western Art* (Stockholm, 1960).

Reggiori, F. *La basilica di Sant' Ambrogio a Milano* (Florence, 1945).

Schlunk, H. in: *Ars Hispaniae,* II (Madrid, 1947), 225 ff.

Verzone, P. *L'architettura religiosa dell' alto medioevo nell' Italia settentrionale* (Milan, 1942).

Williams, S. "Le Ms. Saint-Omer 189 des fausses décrétales d'Isidore Mercator," *Bull. Soc. acad. des Antiquaires de la Morinie,* fasc. 381 (1964), 1 ff.

————. "The Oldest Text of the 'Constitutum Constantini,'" *Traditio,* XX (1964), 448 ff.

Vorromanische Kirchenbauten, ed. Zentralinstitut für Kunstgeschichte, I, II (Munich, 1966, 1968).

14

THE BEGINNINGS OF
ART HISTORICAL WRITING IN ITALY *

A HISTORY of the pictorial arts becomes possible only within a special cultural and intellectual milieu.[1] Its writing presupposes that art be recognized as an autonomous phenomenon and that hence the activity of the artist be viewed as set apart from ordinary activities; an attitude moreover which presupposes for art a special relation to reality different from but on a level with other higher activities such as scholarship, religion or politics. As long as the pictorial arts were included among the *artes mechanicae,* as they were in the early and high Middle Ages, and thus subordinate to such higher activities, they were not nor could they be an object of the historian's preoccupation. They were understood only as an accompaniment, a side-effect, at best a verification of one of the higher activities. Hence they could not be recognized as worthy of the historian's consideration. Indeed, in order to recognize a theme as worthy of such consideration, that is as an historical datum, it must be seen as an entity continuing through time. And in order to be seen as such an entity, the object may not be dependent upon other entities. Accordingly, the primary premises are both the existence and the recognition of an autonomous artistic sphere, distinct from the areas of religion, scholarship, science, politics. Only when this autonomy has been established can the past be examined with an eye to the emergence of artistic phenomena and to the history of the arts. This then is the *conditio sine qua non* of a history of art as a literary form.

This new intellectual and cultural atmosphere arose slowly in the course of the period we call the high and late Middle Ages. As early as the beginning of the thirteenth century, literature came to be considered in its own right. At that time the history of one of its branches was committed to paper in the form of the biographies of the Provençal troubadours:[2] Ughes de St. Cir, himself a troubadour, recounted the lives of his predecessors and his contemporaries, including his own, and he did so in the clear awareness of an historical sequence, a succession of events not based on mere chronology. True, in his biographical sketches the evaluation of the literary element is shot through with anecdotal features, as indeed being a troubadour was more a mode of life than a purely literary phenomenon. The point of the matter is that Ughes carried the concept

*Translated by Cecil L. Striker from *RepKunstW*, L (1929), 49–63.

of the literary achievements of his "sitters" through all of the biographies; that he represented these achievements as a common factor linking two centuries of troubadours; and that within this their common literary activity, he set off an earlier from a later stage, not simply in terms of a chronological succession, but as an irreversible sequence of events. In other words, Ughes' presentation is pervaded by the awareness that the earlier was necessarily different from the later, that certain literary qualities developed only in the course of time. Witness the passage in the biography of Peire d'Auvergne that no chansons were written by him since this form was first created by Guirautz de Borneilh, but that in Peire's own time he was regarded as the best troubadour in the world down to the time of Guirautz. In short, the biographer notes that in the sphere of literature a series of qualities follow one another; that a more primitive is succeeded by a more fully developed stage; that this succession is irreversibly tied to the chronological sequence and that finally in each successive stage a high point is reached which can be measured only in terms of its own age. This then is the first occurrence in post-antique times of a consciously historical outlook on one of the arts.

It is by no means accidental that this new outlook on one of the arts as an historical entity opens up in the history of literature long before it does in the history of the pictorial arts. Quite understandably literature could come to be viewed relatively early as an entity in its own right. It was unsoiled by association with the mechanical arts and with matter, those inherent properties of the pictorial arts always regarded as degrading by the Middle Ages.[3] Literature is free from matter; it is linked both to rhetoric and to music, two of the liberal arts; hence while it does not actually belong to the *artes liberales,* it is close to that sphere of pure knowledge. The pre-established hierarchy of the arts which thus ranks literature near the liberal and high above the mechanical arts explains why the history of a literary movement could be composed by Ughes de St. Cir as early as the first years of the thirteenth century.

The beginnings of a history of the pictorial arts emerge gradually, but a century and a half later. Only slowly does the awareness prevail that the pictorial arts embody values of an order higher than the sheer manual ability needed for their creation. Yet through large parts of the fourteenth century the awareness of the pictorial arts as an object of historical consideration remains limited. As a rule they are viewed as exempla of political or moral phenomena. Artistic events serve in Dante to substantiate ethical sentences.[4] In Giovanni Villani they are used to support the status of Florence as a major political power.[5] The first of these functions is revealed in the purely exemplifying manner in which Dante uses an art historical observation, the replacement of Cimabue by Giotto, as a premise from which to draw a moral conclusion.[6] The latter is clear from Giovanni Villani's only passing mention of an artistic datum—Giotto's building of the Campanile—among a host of political events; and likewise from his repeated insistence upon the close relation between Giotto and the commonwealth of Florence on this occasion, from his emphasis on the fact that the commune not only employed this greatest artist of his time, but sent him abroad as a good will ambassador, as it were, *ad majorem gloriam* of Florence.[7]

Such scattered remarks do not yet constitute a history of the pictorial arts. The premise for writing such a history is the full awareness of their autonomy as an entity, of their disengagement from external bonds, political or moral, and of their place in a category higher than ordinary life. The premises for such awareness took root slowly among the humanists of the Italian Trecento, and their growth may be followed in Petrarch and Boccaccio. More indicative than anything else, is the new demand for the expert approach to art; a demand expressed in the distinction now introduced between the outlook on art of connoisseurs and laymen. Accordingly, Boccaccio speaks of the artists prior to Giotto who painted ". . . più a dilettar gli occhi degli ignoranti che a compiacere allo intelletto de' savi . . ." [8] And Petrarch in his testament of 1370 wills to Jacopo di Carrara a picture by Giotto ". . . cuius pulchritudinem ignorantes non intelligunt: magistri autem artis stupent . . ." [9] Artistic achievement becomes something accessible not to everyone, something removed from the commonplace, something distinct, autonomous, superior and reserved for the understanding of the expert.

In terms of a history of the pictorial arts this new attitude is reflected for the first time in the book written about 1404 by Filippo Villani on the famous citizens of his native city, Florence.[10] Here is to be found among many others devoted to statesmen, scholars, theologians and poets a brief chapter on the artists of the city. This in itself is of significance; for it is a separate and complete chapter and neither the figures of the artists nor the historical data are submerged into or subordinated to extraneous factors. In this Filippo differs decidedly from Giovanni Villani, from Boccaccio and from Petrarch, where artistic events still take second place although they are no longer mentioned as by Dante as merely supporting examples. Moreover, Filippo emphatically views artists and their achievements in an irreversible historical sequence. He recounts how Cimabue introduced a new art and how Giotto then followed him. This Giotto, so he continues, was experienced in many fields besides his perfection as a painter; he had great historical and poetical knowledge and sought fame rather than wealth. A whole school developed around him and they perfected further the new "naturalistic" painting he had started.

One senses how a clever mind has conceived of the possibility of a history of the pictorial arts, but at the same time must grapple with this new awareness. Time and again he apologizes for focusing his attention on painters, and invokes the example of antiquity where after all artists had also been written about.[11] Still, in the end he does compose his chapter on the artists. Indeed, he reports that in the opinion of many and not wrongly either, painters are the peers of masters of the *artes liberales;* the latter acquire their knowledge through industry and study, the former through their high genius and their retentive memory.[12] Here as well, the apologetic note is quite clear: in general opinion, so Villani implies, knowledge ranks higher, but at the same time he stresses that in the opinion of what appears to be a significant minority (presumably of connoisseurs) the pictorial arts can lay claim to equal evaluation. Equally telling is the way in which Villani, entirely in the framework of humanist thought, pushes into the background the dirty quest for money and brings to the fore the desire for fame.[13] The artist is placed within the framework of humanism.

A beginning, in any case, has been made. Pictorial art has made its first claim to be worthy of the historian's consideration. The first complete chapter devoted to an art historical theme has been written. A new literary form, art history, has begun to emerge just as a history of literature had made its first appearance in the biographies of the troubadours in the thirteenth century.

Probably these biographies of the troubadours had exerted some influence on Villani's thinking. They were known in Italy and a number of anecdotes had found their way from them into the Italian *novelle* of the Trecento. There is of course no need to suppose direct borrowings from them by Villani. The basic ideas are identical but they seem to have been generally known in Italy in the fourteenth century. The growth of the idea of an autonomy of the artistic sphere and therewith implicitly of its being raised to the rank of a theme worthy of the historian's attention may be followed from the Lives of the Troubadours through Ristoro d'Arezzo, Boccaccio and Petrarch.[14] And likewise the other idea so important both for the biographies of the troubadours—that of the irreversibility of the historical sequence—may have entered Italy from Provence by way of Petrarch and Boccaccio.

In particular, this idea of irreversibility and the related concept of the sequence of an immature earlier stage to be supplanted by a mature later one is evident in Villani's chapter. Before Cimabue, he writes, art was empty and dead. He was the first to bring it closer to Nature, and following this new path, Giotto and his school brought it to true imitation of Nature.[15] The idea of progress is clear: the idea of the constant development toward something better, the progressive approach to an ideal which, with few exceptions, has dominated art historical writing to our own day.

Moreover, strictly from the standpoint of content, the thesis of the beginning of the new art by Cimabue and Giotto is for the first time committed to paper and it becomes of unexpected importance for all later art historical writing. Indeed, practically every history of the art of the Renaissance still begins with these two. This is strange, for Villani's statement rested on a premise which could and should have been valid only for him and his time. Indeed, Cimabue appears to have been placed by Villani at the beginning of the new art history only because he was mentioned by Dante—with totally unhistorical intentions—in the same breath as and preceding Giotto; [16] and because the αὐτὸς ἔφα of the hero of Italian literature must possess unquestioned value. For Villani, however, Giotto with his new apparent naturalism was the evangelist of the modern art from France, the Gothic; and it is this Gothic of Giotto which Villani contrasts with the Romanesque anti-naturalism of Cimabue. This is the sense of his formulation, and it has nothing to do with the Renaissance. The fact that it was later misinterpreted is evidence enough for the persistence of traditional concepts and prejudices.

But in our context the content is less relevant than the principles and the premises that underlie Villani's outlook on the history of art. They are the new ideas of the autonomy of the sphere of art which makes a history of art possible at all; of the irreversibility of the historical process which necessitates the separation of earlier from later events; finally, of progress which identifies the later with the better. They are ideas already fundamental to the biographies of the troubadours. The significance of Villani lies in his having applied them to the history of the pictorial arts. In this lies the foundation of any history of art, and through this the pictorial arts become possible as a historical subject.

The same ideas determine the art historical parts of Ghiberti's *Commentaries*.[17] But the difference from Villani is that now an artist is speaking, not a humanist. For Ghiberti the idea of the independence of the artistic sphere has become self-evident; he sees this, his own area of activity standing fully on equal footing alongside the areas of humanist scholarship, science, theology and literature; and he correspondingly seeks to determine the area by basing it on theoretical and historical principles of its own. The idea of the autonomy of art, with which Villani still had to grapple, for Ghiberti has become an axiom.

Lorenzo Ghiberti wrote his memoirs about 1450, shortly before his death. Following a brief introduction about the auxiliary disciplines necessary for the artist, the first *Commentary* gives a survey of the history of art in antiquity based on Pliny and Vitruvius.[18] The second *Commentary* deals with the artists of the Trecento in Florence and Siena; it terminates with an extensive autobiography of himself as an artist in the form of an exact account of his life work. The third *Commentary,* in size the largest by far, deals with questions of optics and proportions, matters which to a modern artist like Ghiberti should serve as auxiliary disciplines. It appears that Ghiberti died while busy with this third *Commentary*.

However, art historical questions are not the primary issue for Ghiberti. They are only part of his whole scheme. Clearly they are not incorporated, as in Villani, into a *elogium Florentiae*. The autonomy of art is preserved. Nonetheless, the history of art is not written for its own sake, but for the education of the growing artist. Consequently the intention of Ghiberti's entire work is to give direction to the would-be artist (similar to Dürer's intention in composing his *Speis der Malerknaben*). For this reason, the first *Commentary* begins with a basic exposition of the auxiliary disciplines needed; [19] for the same reason the third *Commentary* treats in detail the special auxiliary disciplines wanted by the sculptor. The role played by the art historical parts of the *Commentaries* becomes clear only in the context of the general scheme. The setting down of premises and the explanation of the auxiliary disciplines are intended to guide the would-be artist; so likewise is the same function assigned to the account given of the art of antiquity, of the Trecento, and of Ghiberti himself. Indeed, the art of antiquity, like contemporary art—the art of the Trecento was for Ghiberti only preparation for his own—is intended paradigmatically to inform the younger artist of the historical basis on which his own art is to rest. Ghiberti's *Commentaries* are the memoirs of an old man. They represent the essence of his life and experience, put down in writing for the education of younger men— and education here is meant in the broadest sense as education for life—comparable to the conversations of the old Goethe with Eckermann, which were similarly written down with his knowledge and upon his express wish in order to serve mankind as an example of a true man.

Within this framework any criticism of Ghiberti's "unhistorical" or "dilettante" method loses its meaning.[20] To Ghiberti, the writing of a history of art for its own sake would have been beside the point; in fact he could not have done so. The autonomy of the sphere of art, to be sure, had been recognized already by Villani and therewith the theoretical basis for a history of art was laid. To Ghiberti it was self-evident. But it would be a long time before a history of art could be written for its own sake: the first one being Vasari's.

The art historical parts in Ghiberti's *Commentaries* are intended as a model. They give an account of his life's work and of his art. They present the historical premises of this art both in the Trecento and in antiquity, the latter to him being the image of great art as such. He views history from the vantage point of his own art and the past is to him a premise of his own development. Antiquity is the paramount height to which everything present and past must be compared. The Trecento is preparatory for his own achievement. His existence and his achievement as an artist enable Ghiberti to write a highly personal history of art. They enable him also to formulate criteria by which to view history and to select from the amorphous past what to him is worthy of historical presentation. This selection he makes as an artist from his very own point of view; and this most of all distinguishes him from Villani whose criteria for ordering the past of art are far more commonplace and less clearly enunciated.

Villani's foremost criterion was that of the "naturale."[21] But what in Villani was halting, or simply taken over from tradition, or limited by the compulsion to see the artist also as a man, not just as an artist, in Ghiberti is developed and secured by theoretical reflection. For him, the whole point of the matter was how the new criteria—which for him were necessary for art to exist—developed in the slow passage from generation to generation. The effect of this on his art historical writing was the complete elimination of biographical detail from his artists' biographies, and his effort to represent an artist in terms of, and only in terms of, his achievement. It is most indicative that he gives the life of Buffalmacco, the "buffoon of Florentine *novella* literature," stripped of all its anecdotal trappings, and renders it only in terms of his artistic achievement.[22]

Thus we have arrived at the biography of the artist on the basis of his work, and hence, at the isolation of the artist from the man. The focus of the history of art has changed: in place of a history of artists stands a history of artistic achievement.

The basis of this is clear. In Ghiberti, an artist is writing, one who knows the issue to be that of visual problems and of pictorial achievements, who knows these issues to be decisive. The *Commentaries* are not the work of a *littérateur* who approaches the objects from his desk, who does not trouble to look at them. They are not the work of a humanist who bases himself exclusively on the literary tradition, a tradition in which life is at least as important as achievement. It is this in particular which makes the art historical chapters of Ghiberti so important: the recognition that art history can be made only with the eye (even if not with the eye alone).

This is the reason why Ghiberti did not simply adopt the older conception of the artistic course of events. To be sure, Villani worked with criteria, and on the basis of these criteria tried to organize the historical data; but he used these criteria neither effectively nor fully consciously, since his concept was affected by literary influences which compelled him, for example, to hold up antiquity (without even knowing it) as a model, or to bring in the figure of Cimabue, despite the fact that he did not fit into his historical sequence of events. Ghiberti's is a different outlook. He is clear as to the criteria which qualify the style of his own work, and he seeks their origin in history. He inquires as to the theoretical principles which make possible the recreation of reality in a rational order (*misure, abbreviare, prospectiva*), or those necessary to create the impression of mass (*rilievo*) and which in turn will convince the beholder of the veracity of the content (*naturale*). It is according to their significance for the realization of this end that Ghiberti arranges the artistic accomplishments of the past.

Thus Ghiberti corrects the prior conception of the art historical course of events. For him Cimabue no longer stands—on the basis of a literary tradition, as he did with Villani—as the fountainhead of a sequence of artists who successively led art in a new direction. Ghiberti sees that this is not the case, that Giotto is fundamentally different from Cimabue, who, we are told, still belonged to the period of the *maniera greca* or, as we would say, the Romanesque style.[23] He sees that Duccio or Cavallini were excellent painters, but that they were still painting in the Romanesque style.[24] For him the art of antiquity was not simply a schema: it takes on a reality and becomes a model for the very reason that its theoretical bases—those bases to which all true art should aspire—are now recognized.

But by this visual grasp of events, by this vital criticism of tradition, a blow is struck at the idea of progress, an idea which dominated Villani without qualification. Villani would never have thought to describe an artist whom he recognized as representing the *maniera greca* as an excellent painter. Ghiberti on the other hand, less through knowledge than through his instinctive feeling, realizes that quality does not depend on stylistic development. Above all, however, the subject matter of the history of the pictorial arts was changed. The artistic accomplishment alone was decisive, and the artist was depicted only *qua* artist, not *qua* human being.

It is indicative that in the course of the fifteenth and early sixteenth centuries no history of art was composed that takes the premises of Ghiberti's *Commentaries* as its point of departure, and which is worthy of serious consideration. Neither the *Libro di Antonio Billi* [25] nor Manetti's *Uomini famosi* [26] nor the work of the Anonymous Magliabecchiano [27] even approach Ghiberti. This is not simply because of the quality of their writing or their lack of freshness. More important is the fact that in their work the body of historical events was not made subordinate to a set of normative criteria. It was Ghiberti's achievement to have recognized the need for such criteria in any writing of history. In this he had no successor. The art historians of the late fifteenth and the sixteenth centuries all picked up from Villani. They took over his antiquated criterion of the illusionistic imitation of nature, the *naturale;* or, having become uncertain of this, they either chose not to or were not in a position to formulate new normative criteria, valid for their own time.

What resulted was a stringing out of biographies, written always from a different historical point of view, mostly in the manner of the *Uomini famosi* or the praise of Florence, entirely like that of Villani.[28] Or there would be a series of *oeuvre* catalogs in which no history, in the sense of a development of artistic events, is to be found. Anecdotal elements and biographical details again assume pre-eminence; no attempt is made to distinguish the artist from the human being, and studio gossip abounds. Moreover, exactly as in Villani, the literary *concetto* prevails, the blind, turbid repetition of tradition in total ignorance of the material. Now the dogma of Cimabue's position as progenitor of the new art becomes entrenched, as does the dogma that the art of Giotto and the Trecento is the true beginning of the Renaissance. With respect to Ghiberti, this is a regression: by no means progress, it is the simple imitation of Villani, the attempt to make do, well into the mature Cinquecento, with the methods and mentality of the end of the Trecento.

But there emerged alongside the leading Florentine local historiographers of second and third rank, and alongside Ghiberti, yet another figure. About 1450, contemporaneously with Ghiberti's *Commentaries,* L. B. Alberti wrote his *De re aedificatoria,*[29] into which is injected a chapter [30] on the history of architecture in antiquity. Alberti sees events as follows: out of purely utilitarian architecture in prehistoric times there arose under the great kings in Asia a magnificent, rough, monumental architecture. This made its way then to Greece, where sheer size was replaced by gracefulness through the genius of the Greeks. Through continuous effort to harmonize the building as a whole originated the orders. These Greek orders were then combined by the Romans with their own utilitarian outlook, and through this the acme of architecture was achieved. For Alberti, the essential purpose of the new century was to achieve this once again with the help of deductive contemplation of the theoretical basis of Roman antiquity—universal *bellezza*—and by means of inductive understanding of their individual forms—*ornamenti.*

It is evident that ideas of Vitruvius stand behind this proposition, but ideas that Vitruvius only suggested.[31] From him comes the conception of the primitive architecture of primeval man, and from him likewise the idea of the conscious harmonization of architectural orders by the Greeks.[32] But apart from the fact that Alberti develops the ideas of Vitruvius and that he enlarges upon his historical conception—he includes both Asiatic and Roman architecture—an essential point is that he conceives of the successive stages of antique architecture as a self-contained development, much in the manner that Ghiberti had represented it in his first *Commentary.*

If one wishes to understand fully the new historical conception of Alberti, one must clarify his personality. Alberti was not an artist like Ghiberti; at least he was not predominantly an artist. He was a jurist and a diplomat, a mathematician and an architect, a painter and a sculptor, a moral philosopher and a sociologist. He was among the first to create a scientific Italian prose,[33] and was an athlete and sportsman, horseman and traveler. He has been termed an "eternal dilettante," [34] but this misses his true nature. Throughout his writings he is never interested in that which is sensually perceptible in an object, but rather in the theoretical basis of that object. He is less jurist than legal philosopher, less painter and architect than theoretician of art. It is thus that he comes to mark out the theoretical basis of painting in his book on painting; and it is thus that he is concerned in his architectural writings with the theoretical basis of architecture. And the history of architecture is for him but a verification of these theoretical principles. As he saw it, the architecture of antiquity proceeded in a series of steps, each representing one of the fundamental elements on which all architecture must rest. As these elements had fused in the end to form the basis of architecture in Roman antiquity, so they must be reinstated as the basis of modern architecture of the fifteenth century. History for Alberti was but the proof of his program.

From this starting point he developed the new boundaries of the historical realm. He measured the past in terms of the new criteria which he thought to reinstate as the formulation of a new architecture. The traditional concept of ancient architecture—whether Greek or Roman—as a unit, unbroken and always perfect, held no meaning for Alberti. To him the architecture of antiquity, too, had a past and a development, before reaching what it ultimately was in Rome: the model and paragon of all true art. Likewise, from this picture of history, the entire Middle Ages must be eliminated—including the Trecento which Ghiberti had recognized to be an essential component of his own art. Alberti had the tough ingratitude of the grand programmer toward that which had come before. What his own art and his own theories owed to the Trecento was consciously suppressed. He saw no direct ancestor. Into the realm of history he admitted only Roman antiquity and his own times, as long as they yielded to the program set down by him. Everything else was eliminated. For the first time an art history was written consciously from the vantage point of the Renaissance.

In this lies the difference from Ghiberti. Ghiberti likewise was blind to the early Middle Ages. But for him that period was devoid of art, and he believed quite naively in the nonexistence of artistic manifestations in the early Middle Ages. Alberti on the contrary knew very well that the Middle Ages had an art, and an art of its own. But he suppressed this knowledge, and did so because medieval art did not fulfill the demands he made of "good" art. He knew Gothic architecture—this is clear in a number of places, for example where he discusses the construction of the pointed arch. And this knowledge is even more evident in his successors, in the anonymous biographer of Brunelleschi [35] which supposedly originated in his immediate circle, and in the so-called Raphael letter,[36] from the same intellectual milieu, though dating from the early sixteenth century. Although it is elaborated upon only by his successors, Alberti's theory must have already contained the idea of the intrusion of barbarian art to form the art of the Middle Ages, even though he did not elaborate on it in writing. According to this theory, reflected in his successors, the Germanic conquerors intruded with their art—for Alberti and his circle an anti-art—and without making any improvements, dominated the entire Middle Ages (including the renascence of an architecture *all' antica* in the Carolingian Renaissance) up to the time that the new architecture of the fifteenth century came to restore and fulfill those requirements that once had been fundamental to Roman art. Alberti and his circle—and this is decisive—did not see, like Ghiberti, the simple unfolding of a single principle of plain progression, but rather the confrontation of two diametrically opposed principles in the history of art. That he termed one bad, the other good, adds little to the matter. The negative recognition alone is sufficient.

With this, the compass of the historical past is immensely widened, even though this widening is based on rejection. The continuity of the total course of events in the history of art is recognized; and within this continuity an ordered, clear, symmetric-harmonic principle alternates with an unordered, unclear, unharmonic one. Alberti the programmer recognizes at least by implication the antithesis between his program and the historical data.

This is the one side of Alberti: the comprehension of the total course of the history of art in terms of two opposed principles—totally different from the naive retrospection of the artist Ghiberti. But it is only one side. Quite as important is the other which concerns the subject matter of art history.

For Ghiberti, the subject was the artistic achievement as reflected in the work of the individual artist. In following its course, he could follow the development of art. The carrier of this development was for him the artist. Alberti approaches the process from another side. For him, the essential events are not the achievements of the artists, but rather the sum of their works, separated from the personalities that created them. The sequence of these works alone is the decisive factor and it is they which are the carriers of history; it is less the individual than the community which lies behind him, the community limited by its time and place: the Asian despotisms; Greece; the Roman republic; the barbarians of the Middle Ages; the Italians of his own time.

The creative act, the gifted accomplishment, is thus toned down. Alberti of course also saw the individual, and this is reflected in the writings of his successors such as the anonymous biographer of Brunelleschi. But at the same time he saw that the individual always provided but the impulse, and that a host of individuals must cooperate and follow one another in order to slowly bring about something new. Even genius is capable only of creating a new idea; its development rests with succeeding generations.

Both the carrier and the object of history have thus shifted in Alberti's philosophy of history. The carrier of the development is no longer the individual artist, but the community in which he stands, be it the despotisms of the ancient East or Greece or contemporary Italy—and therewith the door is opened to concepts unknown heretofore: national styles, the political determinants of a style, whether despotism or a republic, ethnic characteristics. Explicitly stated or by implication, such concepts underlie Alberti's presentation of Roman architecture, or of his theory that the architecture of the barbarians supplanted that of Rome. Concomitantly the subject of history is no longer the artist, as it was with Villani, nor his personal achievement, but the body of works created by such a community and their common style.

Therewith a principle is elucidated, bluntly opposed to all those which had come before. The suprapersonal style is the only element under consideration; the principle of objectivity which Ghiberti had first applied in separating out the artistic achievement from the complex of the personality is now carried to its ultimate. The body of the works is now arranged in a causal series according to criteria gleaned from a program. The chronological sequence is treated at least secondarily to that which is logically necessary. The reality of events is subordinated to a historical system, a reality of the necessary, as it were. The principle of an ultimate objectivism determines the carrier of history as well as its object and its course.

The principles of a systematic art history, an "art history without names," can be no more clearly stated than it is here by Alberti. To the position of the "pure" art historian Ghiberti, a new position is now sharply counterposed. In its formulation lies the significance of Alberti for all future art history up to now.

This is the historical situation into which Vasari is born. On the one side are the Billis and Magliabecchianos who follow in the steps of the old Villani, the representatives of a history of art presented as a sequence of artists' biographies. Alongside this stands Ghiberti who synthesizes the historical data in conformity with criteria drawn from his own time and his own art, and who thus attempts to render the history of art in terms of artistic achievement, not of artists. On still another side, Alberti and his successors are the representatives of a history of art in terms of large stylistic concepts, who tone down the artistic achievement, seeking to master or, one might even say, to do violence to the reality of history.

What is important and truly new in Vasari's work is that for the first time he writes a history of art as such. All that had come before was art history included in some extraneous context, not art history for its own sake alone. Ghiberti had subordinated his art historical chapters to the idea of instructing the young artist; Alberti wrote his in support of his program for a new architecture *all' antica;* not even to mention Villani or Landini, where explicitly, or Billi and the Magliabecchiano, where implicitly, it was subordinated to the idea of an *elogium Florentiae.* With Vasari, a history of art is written for the first time without being a side-program. And if a practical consideration is emphasized from time to time—the consideration of instructing other artists [37]—it is at the same time clear that this takes second place. In Vasari we are truly dealing with a history of art. The beginnings of art historical writing have been surmounted.

Within this new revolutionary train of thought,[38] Vasari fuses, as it were, the positions of Alberti and Ghiberti. He writes artists' biographies the subject of which is the accomplishment of the individual artist. This separates him from his immediate predecessors, from the epigones of Villani; and it brings him close to Ghiberti. But he arranges these biographies—and this separates him from Ghiberti—according to specific, periodic, sequential categories in which the particular is absolutely subordinated. He is more concerned with the history of style than with the history of the artists.[39] The carrier of history, as in Alberti, is not so much artistic genius as it is the artist in his temporal and national context. The result is—and this is the practical effect—that the Middle Ages is no longer recognized only in negative terms, as with Alberti; the way is paved for its recognition in positive terms; or, at least the basis is laid for this recognition.

Two further considerations underlie Vasari's approach. Ghiberti and Alberti had one thing in common: the ordering of history in the sense of continuous progress; a progress which with Ghiberti moved from Cimabue to Giotto and himself; with Alberti, from the buildings of Asia, by way of the Greeks, to the Romans. Only forcible intrusion—such as the barbarian invasion—could interrupt this progress. The idea is given up by Vasari. Instead, he takes over—perhaps from late-antique literature [40]—the idea of a biological development in history. Just as man is born and matures, so also art; but in logic must follow the further idea that as with men, also with art death is certain by necessity.[41] The optimistic concept of progress is abandoned and the opposite concept of biological development is applied to the history of art.

This is one side of the situation. The other, perhaps even more important, is that Vasari sees a parallel course of this biological development in antiquity and in the Renaissance.[42] Alberti had put an end to the unhistorical idea of an unbroken perfection pervading the entire art of antiquity, an idea which had dominated Ghiberti; and had as well introduced the idea of progress. To this, Vasari adds the idea of the mortality of antiquity, the idea of death by natural causes,[43] rather than by the violence of the Migrations. Also, he transfers the same idea to the course of modern art. Just as in antiquity, where the imperfect archaic sculpture of early times is followed by that of Myron and the Golden Age until this is once again supplanted by the "crude" art of the late Empire; so in modern times, following upon Giotto and his successors who slowly overcame the Middle Ages, the artists of the fifteenth century built upon that which Giotto had struggled for; and following upon them came the artists of the High Renaissance who reached perfection. This is where Vasari sees the sitation still to be in his own time; but already he writes that one must fear that art has risen to such a height that it must now surely decline.[44] One sees here how moral elements are used to justify the biological concept. What is more important, however, is that the idea of rise and fall, regardless of whether intended in a purely biological or half-moral sense, is seen in conscious parallelism in two epochs of history as the necessary scheme of things. The concept of periodicity, of a cycle, is introducted into the history of art.[45] And it has remained as an inherent component ever since.

This is where Vasari goes beyond Ghiberti, Alberti and all prior art history. The idea of the biological development and that of periodic cycles were new. But they could not have been conceived were it not for the idea coined by Alberti of the necessary development of every art—even the greatest—out of conditions determined by the character of a community at a given time. Nor, for that matter, could they have been formulated without Ghiberti's conception of separating artistic achievement from the personality of the artist. On the other hand, both Ghiberti and Alberti built upon the concept first enunciated by Villani, who transferred the ideas of the autonomy of art, of the irreversibility of its course, and of progress, from the history of literature to the history of art. The development of the new history of art becomes perfected in a logical sequence —and so it was to continue, almost without qualification, from the sixteenth through the nineteenth centuries.

Notes

1. The basis of this article is my inaugural lecture at the University of Marburg an der Lahn. Essential for all pertinent questions is J. v. Schlosser, *Die Kunstliteratur* (Vienna, 1924), and Panofsky, *Idea* (Hamburg, 1927). See further Kallab, *Vasaristudien* (Vienna, 1908); Karl Frey, *Il Codice Magliabecchiano* (Berlin, 1892), introduction; Lionello Venturi, "La critica dell'arte in Italia," *L'Arte,* XX (1917), 305 ff.; XXV (1922), 237 ff.; XXVIII (1925), 233 ff.; S. Ortolani, "La critica dell'arte a Venezia," *L'Arte,* XXVI (1923), 1-17.

2. Chabaneau, *Les biographies des troubadours* (Toulouse, 1885).

3. See the relevant passages in Schlosser, *op. cit.*, pp. 64 ff.

4. See Schlosser, *op. cit.*, pp. 67 ff.; K. Vossler, *Die göttliche Komödie* (Heidelberg, 1907), *passim*.

5. Giov. Villani, *Storie fiorentine* (Milan, 1802/3) XI, 12; VII, 50.

6. See below, n. 16; also *Purgatorio*, XI, 100, ". . . non è il mondan rumore altro che un fiato. . . ," or *Purg.*, XXXII, 67, ". . . come pittor che con esemplo pinga. . . ." The only apparent exception is given in *Purg.*, X, 32 ff., where the example itself, however, has a moral meaning.

7. ". . . e proveditore della detta opera (of the Campanile) fu fatto per lo comune maestro Giotto nostro cittadino, il più sovrano maestro, che si trovasse . . . al suo tempo . . . e fu gli dato salario per lo comune per remunerazione . . . Il quale maestro Giotto, tornato da Milano, dove il nostro comune l' avea mandato al servizio del signore di Milano. . . ."

8. Boccaccio, *Decamerone*, Giorno VI, nov. 5.

9. *Le rime di M. Francesco Petrarca* (Padova, 1722), p. LII. One finds the same idea of the separation of the connoisseur from the layman prior to this already in Ristoro d'Arezzo, ca. 1285; see Schlosser, "Über einige Antiken Ghibertis," *JKSK*, XXIV (1903), 125 ff.

10. Filippo Villani, *De famosis civibus*; most conveniently accessible in Schlosser, *Quellenbuch zur Kunstgeschichte des abendländischen Mittelalters*, "Wiener Quellenschr.," VII (Vienna, 1896), 370 ff.

11. ". . . . michi quoque fas fit (sit?) hoc loco, irridentium pace dixerim, egregios pictores florentinos inserere. . . ."

12. "Extimantibus multis, nec stulte quidem, pictores non inferioris ingenii his quos liberales artes fecere magistros, cum illi artium precepta scriptis demandata studio et doctrina percipiant, hii solum ab alto ingenio tenacique memoria que in arte sentiant mutuentur."

13. "(Giotto). . . . fuit etiam, ut virum decuit prudentissimum, fame potius quam lucri cupidus."

14. Cf. notes 2, 8, 9.

15. "Huius enim figurate radio ymagines ita liniamentis nature conveniunt ut vivere et anhelitum spirare . . . viderentur. . . ."

16. This is the oft-cited passage in *Purg.*, XI, 91 ff.:
O vanagloria dell' umane posse
Com' poco verde in sulla cima dura,
Se non è giunta dall' etati grosse!
Credette Cimabue nella pittura
Tener lo campo ed ora ha Giotto il grido,
Si che la fama di colui è oscura.
That this is meant in a purely moral, exemplary, un-historical sense, has already been emphasized by Schlosser, *Kunstliteratur*, p. 39, and by Vossler, *op. cit.*, p. 1118. Rintelen, "Dante über Cimabue," *Monatshefte für Kunstwissenschaft*, VI (1913), 200 ff. and E. Benkard, *Das literarische Porträt des Cimabue* (Munich, 1915), are certainly incorrect in their contrary opinion. It is impossible to draw any conclusions as to the art historical significance of Cimabue from this passage in Dante.

17. Fundamental for this is the edition of Schlosser, *Lorenzo Ghibertis Denkwürdigkeiten* (*I Commentarii*) 2 vols. (Berlin, 1912).

18. Cf. the evidence for this in the edition of Schlosser, *passim*.

19. ". . . . in questo primo volume o explicato delle cose le quali bisognj essere ammaestrato lo scultore . . . e 'l pictore . . . (e) . . . quale fù el primo origine . . . dell' arte statuaria et della pictura. . . ." *Commentarii*, ed. Schlosser, I, 31.

20. Olschki, *Geschichte der neusprachlichen wissenschaftlichen Literatur* (Heidelberg, 1919), pp. 91 ff.

21. On the extremely difficult and ambiguous term "naturale" see especially Schlosser, "Lorenzo Ghibertis Denkwürdigkeiten, Prolegomena zu einer künftigen Ausgabe," *Jahrbuch der K. K. Zentralkomm.*, IV (1910), 105 ff.

22. *Commentarii*, ed. Schlosser, II, 130 ff.

23. "Cimabue . . tenea la maniera greca . . . Giotto . . . lascio la roçezza de' Greci. . . ." For the contrary, cf. Benkard, *loc. cit.*

24. "(The figures of Cavallino). . . . sono excellentemente fatte et di grandis-

simo rilievo. . . . ma tiene un poco della maniera anticha cioè greca. Fù nobilissimo maestro. . . . (ed. Schlosser, I, 39). "Duccio . . . fù nobilissimo, tenne la maniera greca . . . questa tavola . . . è magnifica cosa" (ed. Schlosser, I, 43).

25. Karl Frey, *Il libro di Antonio Billi* (Berlin, 1892).

26. Printed by Karl Frey, *Ausgewählte Viten Vasaris, Vita di Filippo Brunellesco* (Berlin, 1887).

27. Cf. note 1.

28. Cf. the introduction to Cristoforo Landini's commentary on Dante, Florence, 1485, p. 9, where among Florentines who have distinguished themselves as philosophers, theologians, doctors, jurists, etc., is to be found a chapter "Florentini eccellenti in pictura et sculptura" just as in Filippo Villani. See Schlosser, *Kunstliteratur*, pp. 92 ff.

29. L. B. Alberti, *De re aedificatoria libri decem* (Florence, 1485).

30. Lib. VI, cap. 3.

31. *De Architectura*, Lib. II, cap. 1 and Lib. IV, cap. 1.

32. ". . . . ex incertis ad certas symmetriarum rationes perduxerunt" (*ibid.*, Lib. II, cap. 1).

33. Olschki, *op. cit.*, pp. 45 ff.

34. Schlosser, *Kunstliteratur*, p. 100.

35. Frey, *Ausgewählte Viten Vasaris, Vita di Filippo Brunellesco* (Berlin, 1887); the biography, attributed to Manetti, was written about 1485.

36. Most conveniently accessible in Venturi, IX, 2, pp. 45 ff. Venturi wishes to attribute the letter once again to Raphael (with the assistance of Castiglione).

37. Such as in the *Proemio* I, in the final passage where Vasari says he has said much about medieval art ". . . . non tanto trasportato dall' affezione. . . . quanto mosso dal beneficio ed utile comune degli artefici nostri; i quali . . . potranno ora . . . cono-

scere il progresso . . . di quella perfezione, dove ella è risalita ne' tempi nostri . . . ed a cagione che se mai acadesse ella incorresse di nuovo nel medesimo ordine di rovina, possano quelle fatiche mie . . . mantenerla in vita. . . ." But such a sentence is obscured by the great mass of others, and by the frequently expressed pleasure in the art historical object itself.

38. The extent to which Vasari is influenced here by the little noticed Gelli G. Mancini, "Vite d' artisti di Giovanni Battista Gelli," (*Archivio storico italiano*, ser. V, XVII [1896], 32 ff.) (or whether the relationship is the other way around, namely Gelli dependent upon Vasari, as Schlosser, *Kunstliteratur*, p. 171, based on Kallab, *loc. cit.* assumed, remains to be clarified.

39. Cf. *Proemio* I, ". . . . l' ordine delle maniere loro più che del tempo. . . ." and *Proemio* II, ". . . . far conoscere le cause e le radici delle maniere. . . ." and ". . . . ragionero . . . più presto della qualità dei tempi, che delle persone. . . ."

40. Schlosser, *Kunstliteratur*, p. 277; Waetzoldt, "Die Anfänge deutscher Kunstliteratur," *Monatshefte für Kunstwissenschaft* (1920), pp. 147 ff.

41. *Proemio* I, toward the end ". . . . la natura di quest' arte simile a quella dell' altre, che come i corpi umani hanno il nascere, il crescere, lo invecchiare ed il morire. . . ."; cf. also Gelli using almost the same words.

42. *Proemio* I and II.

43. Cf. the passage on Constantinian art, *Proemio* I, ". . . . e nondimeno non erano ancora venuti i Goti. . . ."

44. *Proemio* II, ". . . che ella sia salita tanto alto, che più presto si abbia a temere il calare a basso che sperare oggimai più augmento. . . ."

45. Cf. the passage in Schlosser, *Kunstliteratur*, pp. 277 ff.

Postscript

I had quite forgotten this essay until reminded of its existence some ten years ago by Erwin Panofsky. It is a very early paper of mine, but perhaps the editors were right in selecting it for republication in English. In any event, I had great fun rediscovering it.

True, the style of writing was impossibly involved and I admire the translator who was able to transpose it into intelligible English. Even so, I took it upon myself to elucidate the text by occasional inserts. They might help to clarify what I had in mind when drafting my inaugural lecture in 1928. Nevertheless, there remains a good deal of youthful exaggeration in the essay. The contrast between Ghiberti and Alberti and their opposing concepts of history seems to me today somewhat overstressed. Presented as "history as it was" against "history as it must have been," it was, I suppose strongly influenced by my experiences as a student of, successively, Adolph Goldschmidt and Paul Frankl. Likewise, the characterization of both Ghiberti and Alberti as writers of history is probably exaggerated. Today, I would no longer imply that Ghiberti was entirely free of an outlook on art characteristic of the theoretician and *littérateur*. Only in the Second Book and in a few passages of the Third Book of the *Commentarii* did he base himself entirely on his visual contact with and understanding of works of art. But this does not hold true for the better part of Book Three or indeed for Book One, which is but a compilation from Pliny, Vitruvius and other ancient writers. He would have liked to be a theoretician, but he had neither the humanistic preparation nor the talent. On the other hand I would probably not discuss Alberti either today without bringing out more strongly the *littérateur* in him. These questions I have discussed meanwhile in *Lorenzo Ghiberti* in 1956. There I have also revised some factual errors not yet recognized as such at the time of the early essay: the *Commentarii* were written not about 1450 but over a long period, beginning perhaps in the twenties, with Book Two not completed until 1447–48; Book Three is not a finished book but a collection of reading notes, as established by Doesschate; Manetti's *Vita di Brunellesco*, while influenced by Alberti's concept, was not written in his closest circle; and, in contrast to Manetti, Alberti saw the decline of ancient art caused not by the barbarian invasions but by the collapse of Roman *virtù*. Lastly, in reading over the essay I must plead guilty to another sin characteristic of youth—ingratitude. I wish I had brought out more strongly that material used in the essay was drawn from Schlosser's *Kunstliteratur*, published five years before, and that without Schlosser's painstaking labor my little essay could never have been conceived. Its writing, of course, implied a critique of Schlosser's approach and I doubt that he could have liked it.

All the same, I still feel it was worthwhile and even necessary to have a try at this little sketch of a history of the history of art in the fifteenth century—a history seen in terms of opposing and successive interpretations of the past, as represented by Filippo Villani, Ghiberti, Alberti and Vasari. Also, it gave me the first occasion to busy myself with Leone Battista Alberti, whom Schlosser in 1929 treated as an "anemic" theorist and eternal dilettante. Three essays (pp. 323 ff., 333 ff). written thirty-odd years later continue this effort to understand him not so much as a historian and theoretician of architecture, or for that matter as an artist, but as a "counsellor-at-antiquity." Like some of the chapters in *Lorenzo Ghiberti*, they are installments of a small book on Alberti—a book which may never be written.

Additional Bibliography

Krautheimer, R., and Krautheimer-Hess, T. *Lorenzo Ghiberti* (Princeton, 1956).

Panofsky, E. *Renaissance and Renascences in Western Art* (Stockholm, 1960).

Schlosser, J. *Ein Künstlerproblem der Renaissance: Leone Battista Alberti.* Akademie der Wissenschaften in Wien, Philosophisch-historische Klasse, Sitzungsberichte, 210, 2 (Vienna and Leipzig, 1929).

———, *La Letteratura artistica* (Florence, 1935; 2nd revised ed., Florence, 1964).

ten Doesschate, G. *De deerde commentaar van Lorenzo Ghiberti* (Dissertation, Utrecht, 1940).

15

GHIBERTI AND MASTER GUSMIN *

LORENZO GHIBERTI in the second book of his *Commentaries* gives a history of the art of the Trecento, introductory, as it were, to his autobiography.[1] Beginning with Cimabue, he discusses in brief biographical sketches the *oeuvre* of what he would probably have called his ancestors in the realm of art. He deals first with Florentine painters, beginning with Giotto and his disciples, Stefano, Taddeo Gaddi, and Maso; these are followed by Bonamico-Buffalmacco and, after the interpolation of a chapter on the Roman school as represented by Pietro Cavallino, by the brothers Orcagna. The second part is given over to the Sienese masters; to the two Lorenzetti, Simone Martini, Barna da Siena, and Duccio. In a third, very short chapter, the sculptors are discussed, represented by Giovanni Pisano, Giotto, and Andrea Pisano. The choice of this ancestry, the great emphasis given to Sienese artists and among them, in contrast to the general consensus, to Ambrogio Lorenzetti, the stress laid upon painters, the omission of any artist of the second half of the fourteenth century, aside from Orcagna—all this is obviously highly subjective, a personal confession and account of Ghiberti's indebtedness to a group of masters of his own choice.[2] Thus it is of no minor importance to find at the very end of the chapter, right before Ghiberti's autobiography, the life story of a mysterious foreigner: Master Gusmin from Cologne.[3] The following is Ghiberti's strange tale.

"In Germany,[4] in the city of Cologne, lived (*fu*) a master much experienced in the art of sculpture; he was of the highest genius (his name was Gusmin)[5]; he lived with the Duke of Anjou who caused him to make very many works in gold; among other works he made a golden altar (*tavola d'oro*) and, with all solicitude and care, he executed this altar very wonderfully. He was perfect in his works, he was equal to the ancient Greek sculptors; he did the heads marvellously well and all the nude parts. There was no fault in him save that his statues were somewhat short. He was very outstanding and skilled and excellent in this art. I have seen many figures cast after his.[6] He had the most gentle air in his works, he was very skilled. He saw his *oeuvre* destroyed, which he had

* From *AB*, XXIX (1947), 25-35. For advice and helpful suggestions I wish to thank my friends and colleagues, Dorothy Miner, Erwin Panofsky, Hanns Swarzenski, Martin Weinberger. I am especially indebted to Mr. Clarence Kennedy for supplying some of his beautiful photographs of Ghiberti's competition relief, to M. Pierre Verlet of the Musée du Louvre for providing new photographs of the scepter of Charles V and to M. Jean Adhémar of the Bibliothèque Nationale for a photograph of the bust of "Constantine."

made with so much love and art, for the public needs of the duke; he saw that his labor had been in vain, and he fell on his knees and raised his eyes and his hands to heaven and spoke as follows: O Lord, Thou who governest heaven and earth and has created all things: my ignorance be not so great that I follow anything but Thee, have pity on me. Forthwith he undertook to give away whatever he owned for the love of the creator of all. He went up to a mountain where there was a great hermitage; he entered and did penance as long as he lived; he grew old (*fu nella età*)[7]; he died at the time of Pope Martin. Some young men who tried to gain knowledge in the art of sculpture told me how skilled he was in one art and in the other and how where he lived he painted; skilled he was and he died in the 438th Olympiad. He was a very great designer and very gentle (*docile*). The young men who had the desire to learn went to see him and when they asked him he used to receive them most humbly and gave them skilled advice and many examples; he was most perfect, with great humility did he die in this hermitage. Altogether he was very excellent and of a most saintly life."

Ghiberti's tale is corroborated and it can possibly be enlarged by the account of Gusmin's life in the manuscript of the Anonymous Magliabecchiano;[8] writing about 1450, he appears to have used Ghiberti's original manuscript together with an enlarged copy. Possibly from these sources he added some details to the story as preserved in the one imperfect manuscript in which the *Commentarii* have come down to us: he gives the master's name, Gusmin; and he adds that Gusmin lived for many years in his hermitage. Of course, these additions need not reflect Ghiberti's original; they may have been drawn from the enlarged copy, or they may even be the Magliabecchiano's own interpretations. But the master's name at least is hardly a free invention.

What then do we learn from Ghiberti's tale about the mysterious Master Gusmin?

To begin with, the master was a goldsmith. Ghiberti leaves no doubt on this point. He speaks of the numerous works in gold done by the master, among them the golden altar; he mentions that these works were destroyed to produce cash for the needs of Gusmin's patron; he points to the many casts he had seen with his own eyes which would be best explained as made from existing molds of metalwork.[9]

Second: the master hailed from Cologne. This may be literally true, though to an Italian of the fifteenth century, the term Cologne need not mean more than the region of the lower Rhine; just as the reiteration that the master came from Germany means only that he was born beyond the Alps but neither in France nor in England. His name may have been Gusmin, as rendered by the Anonymous Magliabecchiano; or it may have been something similar, Goswin[10] or Gossyn for example, or Guissin (or even Gossman or Huysman, the latter in view of the assimilation of G and H in Dutch, Flemish, and Lower Rhenish usage). He died in the 438th Olympiad, at the time of Pope Martin, obviously Martin V who occupied the Holy See from 1417 to 1431. If our calculation of Olympiads is correct the date of Gusmin's death would correspond to 1415–1420.[11] Before his death and, if we are to trust the Anonymous Magliabecchiano, many years before, he had retired to a hermitage: Ghiberti expressly uses the term *romitorio* twice, not *convento* or *monastero,* thus suggesting that Gusmin at the end of his life was a member of the Carthusian or some other hermit order, rather than a monk in a regular monastery. He was an old man when he died; this is evident not only from Ghiberti's terminology (if our interpretation of *fu nella età* is accepted) but from the entire context of his narrative: the aged master lived in the hermitage to which he had retired, occasionally painting (frescoes? miniatures? easel paintings?—we do not know), giving advice to young students of art, making sketches for them, instructing them in the knowledge of proportions, and above all leading a saintly life. All this gives the impression that he dwelt in his hermitage for a considerable time, even if one were to disregard the explicit statement of the Magliabecchiano.

Third: the tenor of Ghiberti's tale has frequently been termed legendary, starting with Chamisso's poem on the Cologne master,[12] written about 1830 in the spirit of the early Pre-Raphaelites, and ending with Schlosser's metaphor of "a painting on a golden background." [13] Yet the legendary elements in the narrative, the prayer of the unhappy master, composed in the spirit of Ecclesiastes, and the repeated emphasis on his saintliness, merely represent elements of "human interest" in an otherwise quite factual report. Of course, Ghiberti had never seen the master or any of his original works. But he had heard stories about Gusmin, studio gossip, which had grown into a tale, but which nevertheless was based on sober facts. He knew more or less in detail about Gusmin's activity before his retirement; he had seen casts of his metal works; possibly he had seen sketches made by the master in his hermitage; and he knew when the master had died. He had spoken to "some young men" who had gone to see Gusmin in his hermitage but there is obviously no way of telling whether Ghiberti knew these "youngsters" when he was their age or at a later time or when he was a boy. On the other hand, the tenor of Ghiberti's story makes it unlikely that Gusmin was his own or nearly his own age. It makes it just as unlikely that Gusmin lived where Ghiberti's and his paths might have crossed, in other words anywhere in Italy. The whole story as told by Ghiberti about 1450 sounds as if Gusmin had been a goldsmith of renown, active quite some years before and who had lived and died in what was to Ghiberti a faraway country.

Fourth: Master Gusmin had been for a considerable time in the service of one of the dukes of Anjou; the length of his service is indicated by the use of the term *stette.* Indeed, in view of his having made *moltissimi lavorij d'oro* for his duke, he must have been one of the court goldsmiths. To understand fully the implications of this relationship, we will have to sketch briefly the sad and sudden rise and decline of the Anjou family.[14]

The ducal title was revived in 1360 when Jean le Bon, the father of Charles V, appointed his second son, Louis, to be Duke of Anjou, while the third son Jean became Duke of Berry; in 1363 the fourth son, Philip, was made Duke of Burgundy. Louis I, born in 1339, resided in style at Angers until the death of his brother, King Charles V, in 1380 made him regent of France. As early as 1375 he had begun to claim a throne in Italy, first the kingdom of Lombardy, then the even more nebulous kingdom of Adria. In 1380, he finally won a claim to the kingdom of Naples through being adopted as heir presumptive by Queen Joan I. This doubtful present proved to be the undoing of the Anjou family. Louis I spent his own, and then embezzled part of his late brother Charles' fortune on equipping an expedition and financing allies. In 1382 he marched into Italy with a large army but failed to wrest Naples from his competitor Charles III of Durazzo. While preparing a new campaign he died in September 1384 at Bisceglie, at the age of forty-five. His son, Louis II of Anjou, was then but seven years old. He was brought up in France, was recognized as King of Naples by his uncles, the dukes of Burgundy and Berry, was crowned in 1389, and with the help of his father-in-law, the king of Aragon, he sailed against Naples in 1391. He entered the city and lived there, supported by the armies and subsidies of his relatives, for eight precarious years, under constant pressure from his competitors.[15] He was expelled permanently in 1399. Unable ever to return, despite repeated attempts, he died in 1417. His son, Louis III (born in 1403, crowned pretender in 1420, and adopted in 1423 by Joan II of Naples as Duke of Calabria and heir presumptive), continued to fight for Naples and for his French possessions, in the meantime lost to the British, until his early death in 1434. Occasionally he was able to enter the lost capital of his Neapolitan kingdom and lived there intermittently between 1420 and 1430. His brothers, *le bon roi René,* king of Provence and titular king of Naples, and Charles, Duke of Maine and Guise, were more fortunate; but they no longer bore the ducal title of Anjou. Only one of the three Louis can have been the Duke of Anjou for whom, as Ghiberti tells us, Gusmin produced his splendid masterpieces.

Indeed, the Duke of Anjou remains the pivotal figure in the story, the villain of the play who destroyed Master Gusmin's work and ruined his life because he was in need of money for his political chimeras. Among the various dukes, however, only Louis I seems to fit the part. Certainly his grandson Louis III cannot have been Gusmin's patron.[16] He lived too late to have employed the master who, if we follow Ghiberti, had retired years earlier to his hermitage or was even already dead when Louis III came to Naples in 1420. Moreover Louis III never had a penny to start with. He borrowed money right and left.[17] He could hardly have afforded any precious goldsmiths' work on a large scale. The same is true of his father. Like his son, Louis II wandered from place to place most of his life, supported by his relatives and in-laws[18] and trying forever to reconquer a lost crown. He cannot be the right duke either. Of course, he owned a few manuscripts [19] but no record exists that either Louis II or his son

Louis boasted the fabulous treasures alluded to in Ghiberti's tale, including the altar of massive gold.[20]

The outlook changes when we turn to Louis I of Anjou. Like his brothers, Charles V of France, Jean of Berry, and Philip of Burgundy, Louis I was one of the great art patrons and collectors of the fourteenth century. The inventories of his collections, which he dictated himself alone (a fragment, in 1364 and 1365; another in 1369; the last in 1379 and 1380),[21] reflect some faint idea of his treasures. The first list enumerates nearly 800, the third one over 3,600 items, including goldsmiths' work, table plate, tapestries and jewelry, gold and silver tabernacles covered with pearls, rubies and emeralds, reliquaries by the dozen. Nearly all these fabulous riches were sold, pawned [22] or sent to the mint [23] when the Duke needed money for the conquest of Naples in 1381 and 1382, the ill-starred adventure which broke his fortune and that of his son and grandson. He may still have owned some treasures when starting for Naples; but only a paltry few pieces were left to his widow.[24] Yet, in his time, Louis, the first Duke of Anjou, must have been known all over Europe as *the* Duke of Anjou whose fairytale-like collections of precious metalwork and jewelry were rivalled only by the treasures owned by his three brothers. His bankruptcy must have been as notorious as his riches among men who appreciated goldsmiths' work and knew about its makers and collectors. As late as the 1430's Poggio's anecdote of the encounter between the duke and Rodolfo da Camerino testifies to Louis' posthumous fame,[25] just as the praise given by Filarete between 1451 and 1464 still glorifies the collections of the Duke of Berry and his enthusiasm as a collector, forty years after his death and the dispersal of his treasures.[26] If Ghiberti, himself a goldsmith by profession and a goldsmith's son (or rather step- and foster-son), speaks of a Duke of Anjou in connection with goldsmiths' work, it makes sense only if he refers to the first duke, the only Anjou, who was a famous collector. Louis I of Anjou is the logical and the only possible figure to connect with Ghiberti's account of Master Gusmin. His whole story fits the part of Master Gusmin's patron, and the melting down of his collection for political enterprises, his *publici bisogni*, which caused Master Gusmin so much grief, is again not legendary but a stark historical fact.

If our interpretation is correct, four principal facts must be kept in mind in any attempt to identify or, if this should prove impossible, to reconstruct the figure of the master: his name was Gusmin and he was a goldsmith; he came from the Lower Rhine and died at a ripe age after many years of retirement, probably between 1417 and 1420 and certainly between 1417 and 1431; he had been in the service of the first Duke of Anjou who sent his work to the mint in 1381; and he evidently did not live or work in Italy. Attempts to identify Master Gusmin have often started from the reverse premise, in suggesting that he was one of the sculptors from North of the Alps who, during the first half of the fifteenth century, descended upon Italy. This is hardly compatible with the tenor of Ghiberti's tale, and obviously all the pertinent facts must be taken into account if the *locus geographicus* of the master is to be delimited. Consequently Gusmin should not be identified with a sculptor from North of the Alps, Piero di Giovanni Tedesco,[27] who worked at Florence Cathedral and whom Ghiberti in his early years must have seen every day around the *opera del duomo*. He cannot well be identified with an anonymous alabaster sculptor of German origin, the master of Rimini,[28] who worked in Italy between 1430 and 1440, after Pope Martin's death, and thus after Gusmin's. Nor can Gusmin have been an artist at the court of Louis III of Anjou [29] who ruled at Naples at the time of Pope Martin from 1420 on, probably after Gusmin's death and certainly after his withdrawal to a hermitage. Much closer to the facts as presented by Ghiberti is Courajod's suggestion that Gusmin be identified with a Flemish artist of the school of Claus Sluter.[30] In general terms this thesis seems most convincing, but it is perhaps not specific enough; true, Sluter's school flourished in Burgundy, in a faraway country; the sculptures of that school are somewhat squat, *un poco corte*. Yet they are enormous in size and feeling; nobody would call them gentle and sweet. And the capital point is that Sluter's school, as far as we know, did not produce any goldsmiths.

None of these hypotheses appears to tally with the data of Ghiberti's tale: Gusmin cannot be identified with any artist known by any other name and it is unlikely that we ever shall find any appreciable amount of his *oeuvre*. We know the bulk of his work made for the Duke of Anjou has been destroyed; what could be expected at best is either a record of his name in some document or perhaps some identifiable work which perchance might have survived the holocaust of the ducal treasures; but the records are hopelessly incomplete and the chance of ever finding any work of Gusmin's is minimal at best, in view of the nearly wholesale destruction of all French goldsmiths' work of the fourteenth century. On the other hand, one thing has been gained: we can attempt to determine the *locus historicus* of Gusmin and perhaps to reconstruct a rough outline of his life, based on the data given by Ghiberti and on the known facts about the Duke of Anjou's life; such a hypothetical reconstruction might run as follows.

We know that Gusmin died as an old man between 1417 and 1431, or more precisely between 1417 and 1420. We assume with good reason that the master worked for Louis I of Anjou who formed his collections between 1360 and 1380 and sent them to the mint in 1381–1382. This would suggest that Gusmin was born before 1345. Let us suppose he was born as early as or slightly before 1340 and was thus a contemporary of his patron. In that case he would have been in the service of the duke between 1360 and 1380 and he would have created his masterpieces during that period. The crisis in his life then falling in 1381–1382, he would have retired into monastic solitude at the age of slightly over forty. Young men of Ghiberti's acquaintance might well have visited him in his hermitage between 1390 and 1420, roughly between Ghiberti's tenth and fortieth year. And he would have died at the ripe age of eighty between 1417 and 1420, as a saintly old man.

Also Gusmin's lower Rhenish origin, possibly in Cologne, would tally with such a reconstruction. Between 1360 and 1400 Flemish, Dutch, and German names are frequent enough in the inventories and accounts of the royal court and of the courts of Anjou, Burgundy, and Berry, as far as they contain any names at all. We might mention just a few, such as Claus Sluter, Jacques Broederlam, Jacquemart de Hesdin, the goldsmiths Claus de Fribourg, Franchequin and Hennequin de Vivier, Hans Karast, Hennequin de Hacht; there even appears a *Wynant de Cologne, orfevre à Paris*.[31] It has not yet been possible to trace the name of our master in these account books and inventories, but the name Gusmin and similar ones are frequent in the Flemish and Lower Rhenish milieu of the later Middle Ages: among several Goswins, Gussins and Gossuyns [32] there even occurs in the early fifteenth century a goldsmith, Gossuyn de Bomel; the toponym shows that he came from Gelderland, near the Lower Rhine; moreover he worked first in Paris and then in Chambéry, in the immediate vicinity of the Grande Chartreuse, certainly a *grande romitorio su uno monte*.[33] Everything seems to fit Ghiberti's description of Gusmin like a glove. But the identification (it is tempting indeed) does not stand up to further investigation; for Gossuyn de Bomel can be traced only after 1415, and he was still active in 1429 when he was removed as master of the mint for the Duke of Savoy. Also he was a layman and the minutes of an arbitration between him and his brother Alard, likewise a goldsmith, seem to suggest that he was not too saintly a man. Still, this much is certain: Gusmin is a Rhenish name, and artists from these parts were frequent in the services of the French royal and princely courts of the later fourteenth century.

Should one go a step further? The inventories of Charles V and his brothers mention fairly frequently golden altars (*tableaux d'or*) with figures or scenes inside and decorated on the outside with precious stones and pearls. These pieces, as a rule, weigh from two to six ounces (40 to 120 grams); only rarely do they amount to as much as one mark of gold, corresponding to approximately 233 grams.[34] In brief, all of them were quite small. Only once, one of the inventories mentions *une très grande table d'autel d'or* and this is, of all things, the opening item in the last inventory (1379/80) of the Duke of Anjou's collection. The item does not yet appear in the inventory of 1369 and the altar must therefore have entered the collection between that date and 1379. It did not pass from the Anjou collection into the hands of Louis' widow or of his brothers. In all likelihood it went to the mint in 1381–1382. Could this by any chance have been Gusmin's *tavola d'oro,* which Ghiberti mentions? The question must be answered with a *non liquet,* for this one piece which opens the inventory and which therefore appears to have been the most important items in the Duke's collection of ecclesiastical objects is recorded merely in a fragmentary remark; the description which was to accompany the entry (and which indeed accompanies other entries) is missing, and with it, perhaps, the name of the artist, which sometimes occurs in descriptions of major objects. Even so, the uniqueness of the piece, its obviously short life, and the similar wording of the inventory and of Ghiberti's account are worth noticing in an attempt to reconstruct Gusmin's life.

Of course, one would still like to know approximately what Gusmin's *oeuvre* looked like and what caused Ghiberti to wax so enthusiastic over the casts of Gusmin's figures. Obviously this can be done only in very general terms, by substituting the style of French goldsmiths' work of the late fourteenth century for the personal style of Master Gusmin. Even then it is anything but easy, for of the precious pieces whose descriptions fill the inventories of the Duke of Anjou and of his royal brothers, only a few have survived; yet these few pieces of goldsmiths' work and jewelry are superb in quality. Outstanding is the scepter of Charles V topped by the figure of the enthroned Charlemagne [35] from St.-Denis, now in the Louvre (Figs. 102, 103). The *"Libretto"* reliquary in the Baptistery of Florence, a gift made to Louis I of Anjou by his brother Charles V, is another product of the royal ateliers,[36] and so is the Royal Gold Cup of the Kings of France and England at the British Museum,[37] dated certainly before 1391 and possibly in 1380. Remnants of decorative jewelry from these workshops are preserved in the magnificent though slightly restored mounting of the cameo with Jupiter and the Eagle in the Bibliothèque Nationale, offered by Charles V to Chartres cathedral,[38] and in the mounting of the Lothar Crystal in the British Museum.[39] The bookcovers of four manuscripts in the Bibliotheque Nationale, gifts of Charles V to the Sainte Chapelle, show how the royal goldsmiths re-used, copied, and restored relics and models of earlier centuries.[40] A cross at La Boissière, with jewelled decoration at the end of the cross and a figure (possibly later) of Christ was allegedly a gift of Louis I of Anjou, presented in 1364 to the Abbey.[41] Until the middle of the eighteenth century a somewhat greater number of such pieces had survived, some in the very treasure of St. Denis: most important, a representation of Charles V and his wife and son kneeling before the Virgin.[42] A slightly later group of French goldsmiths' works of about 1400 and after appears to be somewhat, though not much, better preserved. Suffice it to enumerate the more prominent early items: a small half-figure of Saint Catherine in the Morgan Collection at the Metropolitan Museum; [43] a morse with the Trinity from the Widener Collection, now at the National Gallery in Washington (Figs. 104, 105); [44] the Madonna on the folding chair in the cathedral of Toledo; [45] the reliquary of the Holy Spirit at the Louvre; [46] and last but not least, the Little Golden Horse of 1404 of Altoetting.[47] There are a few dozen more larger or smaller items scattered throughout provincial museums, church treasures, and private collections.[48] But whatever has survived today has done so by mere chance. The bulk of the treasures of the fourteenth century in France, among them Master Gusmin's work for the Duke of Anjou, is irretrievably lost.

The superb quality of what little is preserved of the goldsmiths' work of these treasures justifies and explains Ghiberti's enthusiasm for Gusmin. Obviously Gusmin was to him the representative of a great art of the recent past. As a rule Ghiberti is not apt to be over-enthusiastic; on the contrary, he is somewhat critical and matter-of-fact. The only two artists by whose work he is fascinated are Ambrogio Lorenzetti and Gusmin. His reticence about Florentine artists, in contrast to the preferences of his countrymen, may be justified or not; but in any case, individualist and independent of mind as he is, Ghiberti hardly discusses Florentine Trecento sculpture aside from a few lines, cool at that, on Orcagna and Andrea Pisano; not one word does he waste on the local silversmiths' tradition as represented by parts of the silver altars at Pistoia and of St. John the Baptist in Florence (Fig. 106). Rightly or wrongly they did not impress Ghiberti. But he was evidently greatly struck by French goldsmiths' work. Indeed, it would be hard to deny that the scepter of Charles V, and most of this French jewelry, are among the greatest works of art the fourteenth century had to offer; and Ghiberti knew, if anything, a great work of art when he saw one.

It would be strange if this French goldsmiths' work had not left some trace in Ghiberti's early *oeuvre*. Obviously no one would suggest that Ghiberti derived his early style from French goldsmiths' work or for that matter from any other style. In its fundamentals Ghiberti's style remains highly personalized, from the competition relief of the twenty-three-year-old beginner to the tabernacle door of S. Egidio of the seventy-two year-old master; nevertheless, it is obvious that in successive stages he works more or less under the impact of local and foreign experiences which are woven into the fabric of his background.

His early style (and within the scope of this study we are interested only in this phase) is marked by the competition relief (Figs. 107, 108, 109, 110) and by some plaques on the first door, such as the Nativity, or Christ on the Mount of Olives (Fig. 111); [49] the composition, as a rule, develops in two complementary triangles, separated by a diagonal across the quatrefoil; each triangle is occupied by one group of figures enclosed by a "space cave" of its own creation; every corner of the plaque is filled, and yet all elements are clearly outlined against carefully balanced stretches of blank ground; the figures within each group move against each other in swinging curves, accompanied, but not continued, by the complementary group across the barrier of the diagonal; the ground is rocky, the trees dwarfed and knotty; "realistic" details are merged with antique reminiscences such as the torso of Isaac or the young shepherd's head in the Nativity. This early style, first evident in the competition relief of 1401-1403, seems to disappear around 1407.

The general assumption is that the basis for this earliest phase of Ghiberti's style lies in the tradition of Florentine Trecento sculpture or, to be more precise, Florentine metalwork of the Trecento.[50] No doubt this is true with regard to the pattern of the door with its twenty-eight quatrefoils set into square panels, the two rows at the bottom filled with seated figures, the five upper rows with scenes.

Obviously enough the scheme follows Andrea Pisano's bronze door of 1330; but this resemblance of the general layout was in all likelihood demanded by the Arte di Calimala which was in charge of decorating the Baptistery. Florentine, to be sure, are some of the individual features which characterize the early reliefs. The antique reminiscences, for example, which crop up time and again, appear to be part of a general Florentine fashion around the turn of the century. Witness the jambs of the Porta della Mandorla, dated 1396–98, with its well-known antique motifs among the tendrils of jambs and lintel, such as the standing Hercules; the "Apollo"; the Abundantia; the Muses, putti, and Sirens. They vary in quality but all are *all' antica* in both iconography and form. Yet, if one comes down to the essentials of Ghiberti's early reliefs, if one actually compares trait by trait the *Sacrifice of Isaac* (Fig. 107) with the reliefs from the silver altar of the Baptist in the Opera del Duomo (Fig. 106),[51] one is astonished to discover differences rather than similarities. On the front of the silver altar, in the plaques which were designed between 1367 and 1387 (later work on the altar frontal until 1400 seems to have centered on the small statuettes rather than the reliefs), the compositions are strictly axial. The ground is all filled with "stage props," trees, rocks and buildings. The figures are bulky, their draperies organized by a few straight folds. The heads are formed by large simple planes without furrows and bumps; little attention is paid to the bone structure. The faces are framed by the big ornamental masses of large wigs. The whole composition, both figures and "props," runs strictly parallel to the front plane; the figures do not create space, they move ponderously and with dignity on a previously prepared narrow stage.

All this is best explained as the upshot and echo of the art of the first and second Trecento generations in Florence, different in quality and detail, yet in principle closely related to Andrea Pisano's bronze door and his Campanile sculptures, to Orcagna's reliefs in Or San Michele, and ultimately to Giotto's frescoes. The silver altar of the Baptist represents the style that dominates the metal workshops of the last third of the fourteenth century in Florence. Indeed, Brunelleschi's competition relief of 1401 (Fig. 112) is in a number of ways still linked to this style. The scene develops in two superimposed tiers parallel to the front plane, without much attempt at recession. In both tiers the figures move on a narrow stage. The horizon is pushed up high. In the head of Abraham the angular planes and the long coils of the hair still reflect the head of Herod, for instance, from the silver altar. The drapery of Abraham envelops the figure. Of course Brunelleschi in many decisive ways transforms the tradition of Florentine Trecento metalwork. Not only is his relief crowded with elements *all' antica:* the thornpicker, the servant to the right, the figure of Isaac; it is likewise saturated with "realistic" elements and concepts: the donkey with its shabby, worn-out saddle, and the ram scratching its ear. Merged with all these elements are the new dramatic approach, the jaunty angular movements, the quest for out-of-the-way motions and tricky positions of the figures, for violent action. Despite all these revolutionary elements, however, Brunelleschi's relief emphasizes how decisively the young Ghiberti—but one year his junior—departs from this or from any earlier Florentine work. The composition is unified, the figures stand against the deep rocks, which hover like shells about them, the blank stretches of the background form part of the design. The heads are finely chiseled, the curls are short and crisp, the foreheads and cheeks are strongly modelled. All this differs from the Florentine tradition to which Brunellesco's relief was linked by strong ties.

To analyze all the elements that went into the making of Ghiberti's style goes well beyond the scope of this paper. Alongside Florentine components, the iconographic schemes of Siena may have exerted no small influence. On the other hand, the free compositional patterns, their eccentric arrangements, the bony, well-modelled heads can hardly be linked to any Tuscan tradition. To some degree they are reminiscent of a new current which in the late fourteenth century replaces the earlier one-sided, south-north movement from Siena, Modena and Verona to Avignon and Prague [52] by a network of exchanges of artists, works of art, and ideas. This exchange more often than not leads from Central Europe to Northern Italy. There, the workshop of Milan cathedral from 1389 on forms one of the centers, that of the Masegne in Venice, shortly after 1380, another; a third one, dependent on these two, assembles at S. Petronio in Bologna. In the last analysis all three are closely linked to the centers of the "new realism" north of the Alps, at Paris, Dijon, Vienna, and Prague. From there the Italian centers receive not only their basic philosophy of art, types, and models, but also part of their personnel: witness the activity of *oltramontani* in Upper Italy, such as Hans Fernach at Milan and Hans Ferabech at Bologna.[53] One need not overrate the importance of these foreigners: but at Milan, where the account books of the *fabbrica del duomo* are preserved, one in ten sculptors between 1390 and 1410 is French, Flemish, Dutch, German or Austrian by birth and training.[54]

This is the general background against which the early *oeuvre* of Ghiberti must be placed. Florentine and antique elements are fused with Sienese and with other factors from north of the Alps. Indeed, at first glance one might believe a general vague and indirect link with the *arte oltramontana* to be sufficient explanation for the un-Tuscan elements in his style. One might pick, for example, the relief of Christ among the Doctors (Fig. 113)—it is not even from Ghiberti's earliest period—and look at the crouching, turbaned gentleman to the right: both pose and headdress are reminiscent of French parallels such as the little figure of a crouching prophet in the Louvre (Fig. 114). On the other hand, these resemblances offer no definite proof for assuming that Ghiberti necessarily knew such French works of art; crouching figures occur also in Northern Italy. At Milan Cathedral, as early as 1393–97, they fill the lintel of the portal which leads to the south sacristy, a work in which Hans Fernach took a hand, and similar figures appear in drawings of the milieu of Giovanni de' Grassi.[55]

Another motif of Ghiberti's first door may help to establish more clearly his position within this network of relations reaching across the Apennines and possibly across the Alps to Florence. Indeed, how does it come about that on his door the moldings of the large square panels are interspersed with tiny animals, spiders, grasshoppers, bugs, frogs, and snails, and occasionally with small human heads (Fig. 115)? On Andrea Pisano's door, otherwise in its pattern the prototype for Ghiberti's, these border moldings were articulated by diamonds and rosettes, a geometric type of decoration which in Florence continued to persist throughout the Trecento.[56] Nor is Ghiberti's border ornament linked to the acanthus scrolls of the Porta della Mandorla or to the undulating tendrils with vine or oak leaves that occur in Italy from the early Trecento on, wherever French influence makes itself felt.[57] Only in the last two decades of the Trecento, and obviously under a new impulse from France, does a richer kind of foliage infest the architectural decoration of the Upper Italian centers. Lively and irregular clusters of leaves surround Hans Fernach's sacristy door, irregular singular leaves frame Hans Ferabech's *Madonna* at S. Petronio and two of the quatrefoils on the façade of that church.[58] More regular foliage, ironed out, as it were, and interspersed with putti, stags, rabbits, and hounds accompanies the borders of some of the ivory caskets of the Embriachi workshop.[59]

Only this latter kind of foliage shows a vague similarity to the border decoration of Ghiberti's first door. Never, however, is it quite so free and rich; never are the leaves quite so closely heaped, creeping along the grooves of the molding, rolling over and covering each other; never are they interspersed with a tiny hopping and crawling fauna. To quote only one splendid example and moreover an example in metalwork: just this kind of foliage (though oak rather than ivy) fills the groove along the rim of the enameled morse with the Trinity in the Widener Collection in Washington (Fig. 104). The small bits of branches and the six large pearls take the place which in Ghiberti's door is occupied by small interspersed animals. But it is again in France, in the illuminated manuscripts of the 1370's and 1380's, that the flora of such decorative borders is invaded by hosts of tiny butterflies, birds, snails, and bugs, just as on Ghiberti's door: witness for example the *Cité de Dieu* of the Bibliothèque Nationale, *ca.* 1376.[60] In Italy this type of marginal decoration is not only extremely rare, but when it occurs, it is much cruder: in a Genovese manuscript the border is filled with big insects set against a background of thin regular foliage, clearly under French influence, clearly inferior, and clearly different from Ghiberti's design.[61] Consequently it is, to say the least, possible that Ghiberti was acquainted with French miniatures of the last quarter of the fourteenth century.[62] More likely this type of foliage with small animals and thick luscious leaves was not limited to the margins of illuminated manuscripts: it may well have occurred in some of the lost goldsmiths' work of the royal ateliers of France under Charles V and Charles VI. Thus around 1400 it may have come to the attention of Florentine goldsmiths such as Bartolomeo di Cione and his foster-son Lorenzo Ghiberti.

The question remains whether Ghiberti's sculptural style in his early years in any way reflects the impact of French fourteenth-century goldsmiths' work. Certainly none of Ghiberti's works show any longer the facial types that had been common to all later Trecento art, to the art of Florence, and with only slight variations to that of Siena, Milan, and Venice. The heads in the competition relief—that of Abraham or those of the servants—are not developed simply by superimposing on a traditional pattern a few or more "realistic" elements, tense facial expressions and ferocious miens. On the contrary, Ghiberti appears to avoid this vogue, dominant in the leading workshops of Milan and Venice in the late fourteenth century. He introduces a different fundamental concept and a different technique. Throughout, the modelling is built up from the bone structure, the cheekbones protrude strongly, the brows and the forehead overshadow the deep-set eyes (Figs. 107, 108). The entire face is modelled in small nervous planes, the hair is chiselled in short curls, the nose is thin, the nostrils appear to vibrate. Light and shade flicker over the surface in sharp contrasts. Abraham fixes his glance on his son; Isaac turns his eye quickly and firmly to Heaven; of the servants the younger one looks at the scene of the sacrifice, the older one toward his companion (Fig. 110). The play of light and dark, the emphasis on brows, cheekbones, and frowns underscore Ghiberti's attempt to create a network of relationships in general and of psychological interplay in particular. Every detail is clearly marked and, nevertheless, blended into the grandiose and momentous entity of the head; the heads dominate the bodies; and the movements and glances of the figures replace dramatic action. Each detail, as of heads, hands, and garments, is modelled with the utmost sharpness and precision. Body and drapery are clearly differentiated and so are the single pieces of apparel, dress and cloak. The folds swing in elegant curves, they are twisted atop the ridges, interspersed with short broken cavities and supplemented by rich cascades of thin and fine drapery.

All this is quite different from the tradition of Florentine goldsmiths' work with its clear-cut, simple types, its undifferentiated, rigid and monotonous, though monumental draperies, its unsophisticated if impressive interplay of actors (Fig. 106). It differs just as much from Brunelleschi's figures with their angular movements, their solid heads, deep-cut, massive draperies (Fig. 112). On the other hand French goldsmiths' work of the later fourteenth century shows a similar handling of the draperies and features, a similar emphasis on modelling and chiselling the surface in small planes, a similar precision of craftsmanship. The head of Charlemagne from the scepter of Charles V (Fig. 102) with its high, strong cheekbones, its furrowed, deeply modelled forehead, its finely shaped nose, its deep-set eyes, its bushy brows, is based on a sculptural concept similar to that of Ghiberti's in the competition relief. Like Ghiberti's, the French head merges the detailed and precise modelling of the face into a monumental pattern. In fact there is no need to limit the comparison to the scepter of Charles V, that masterpiece of French metalwork: in the Widener morse, God the Father shows the same concentrated glance, the same minute execution of detail, the same sharpness of modelling (Fig. 105). In a similar way, in the handling of the draperies, Abraham's mantle with its fine cascades, the crumpled folds on his dress and on that of Isaac in front of the altar (Fig. 108) are reminiscent of French metalwork, the mantle of Charlemagne such as on the scepter (Fig. 102). To insist on details, one may compare the triangular drapery over Charlemagne's right knee with the same motif on the crouching figure in Ghiberti's panel of Christ among the Doctors (Fig. 113). At the same time, the draperies in Ghiberti's reliefs are not important in themselves. They conform to the whole pattern, to the light swaying curves which swing from one part of the composition to the next and lead the eye all over the panel: Abraham bends over Isaac and his motion is continued above by the Angel and below by the cloak before the altar; the motion is accompanied by the curves of the boy's body and by the contour of the rock (Fig. 107). Nothing could be more different from the relief style of the late Trecento in Florence. Rather Ghiberti's composition seems to hark back to a "truly Gothic" tradition, the French tradition of the late thirteenth and early fourteenth centuries, only rarely reflected in Italian sculpture, in Lorenzo Maitani's or Nino Pisano's *oeuvre,* and relatively early in the Trecento at that. However, it differs insofar as in Ghiberti's work the sway of the figures is purposely used to conquer the space of the relief by moving in contrasting curves. A very similar variation of the earlier melodious Gothic style seems to occur in the midst of the "new realism" in France under Charles V. In the relief of Charlemagne's vision of Saint James on the pummel of the scepter of Charles V, the emperor, to the left, sits crouched on the ground, the sword in his right, the globe in his left hand (Fig. 103). His left shoulder pushes forward, his right shoulder is sharply thrust back. A tree bends its branches over him; its trunk carries Charlemagne's shield. His beard flows in a wide curve to the left, following, as it were, the folds of the garment over his chest. From the right, the figure of Saint James approaches out of the depth of the relief, floating on a cloud, his body hidden by the pilgrim's cloak. A scroll leads in a wide S-curve from the apostle's left hand towards the emperor. The background is covered with large oak leaves set against an irregularly hatched pattern. The other two reliefs of the pummel, the emperor with his *preux* and Charlemagne's death, are beyond any doubt inferior in quality, but even in them all the elements of the composition complement each other in wide swaying curves which hint at space and depth.

The very comparison of Ghiberti's early style with French art of the late fourteenth century leads right into the core of the problem. Indeed, despite all resemblance, Ghiberti's work remains different from the French masterpieces produced in the period of Charles V. His figures are more slender, less squat; they stand more firmly on their feet and they glide more freely through a space created by their own movements and by the shell-like caves of the rocks. Both Ghiberti's and the French figures express the individual in typical patterns. But the differences between these patterns are considerable: the French sculptors think in terms of fundamentally Gothic figures, of a geometrical scheme into which the precise modelling and the realistic details are incorporated. Ghiberti, the representative of a new generation, starts with a different heritage, blends these same elements into a pattern imbued more often than not with antique reminiscences and classical concepts. The impact of French goldsmiths' work is but one of numerous factors which we feel have gone into the making of Ghiberti's style. And whatever the impact of this French goldsmiths' work on him, it has become completely merged into his art, complex as it appears already in the competition relief of the young goldsmith.

Indeed all these elements of French goldsmiths' work, composition, figures, heads, may or may not have left their stamp on the young Ghiberti. What certainly impressed him was the quality of workmanship in these tiny objects, their precision and delicacy. His admiration for precise and subtle craftsmanship, for *perfezione* runs as a leitmotif all through the *Commentarii*. It comes to the fore when he describes works of antiquity, the chalcedon of Niccolo Niccoli, the Roman hermaphrodite, the Marsyas gem of the Medici collection; and when he discusses his own handiwork, the "diligent and loving modelling" of the first door or the tiny details of the mounting of the Medici gem and its diligent lettering. At great length, comparable in emphasis to the account he gives of the first door, he depicts minutely and in detail the mitre for Eugene IV, metalwork, precious stones and pearls, with the affectionate devotion of a goldsmith to his work and to his material.[63]

In sum, what interested him in French metalwork of the latter part of the fourteenth century, as exemplified by Master "Gusmin" was probably not so much details, or motifs, or individual traits, as a fundamental approach. This fundamental approach, as well as the part it played in the formation of Ghiberti's art, becomes, so we feel, quite transparent both in his early *oeuvre* and in his description of Gusmin's works. What characterizes all details, the heads, the hands, the draperies, down to the very embroideries on these draperies in both Ghiberti's early work and that of the French goldsmiths of the fourteenth century, is first the precision and neatness of workmanship, their "perfection." Second, it is the emphasis on the "marvelous make of heads and nude parts"; a face is convincing in appearance and expression, a hand grips the object it holds, knife or imperial globe, a body is modelled in small planes. And it is, third, the "gentle air of these works" their sweetness and unsentimental melodiousness. It must have been this very combination of precise workmanship, minute detail, and melodious monumentality, which fascinated Ghiberti in the *oeuvre* of Master Gusmin.

Notes

1. Lorenzo Ghiberti, *Lorenzo Ghibertis Denkwürdigkeiten* (*I Commentarii*), 2 vols., ed. J. von Schlosser (Berlin, 1912), I, 35 ff.; II, 17 ff.

22. Schlosser, *op. cit.*, II 18 ff.

3. Schlosser, *op. cit.*, II, 164 ff.

4. "In Germania nella città di Colonia fu uno maestro nell' arte statuaria molto perito, fu di excellentissimo ingegno (nominato Gusmin), stette col duca d' Angio, fecegli fare moltissimi lauorij d'oro; fra gl' altrij lauorij fè una tauola d'oro la quale con ogni sollicitudine et disciplina questa tauola condussela molto egregiamente. Era perfecto nelle sue opere, era al pari degli statuarij antichi greci, fece le teste marauiglosamente bene et ogni parte ignuda; non era altro manchamento in lui se non ch'elle sue statue erano un poco corte. Fu molto egregio et dotto et excellente in detta arte. Vidi moltissime figure formate delle sue. Aueua gentilissima aria nell' opere sue, fu doctissimo. Vide di(s) fare l'opera la quale aueua fatta con tanto amore e arte pe' publici bisogni del duca, uide essere stata uana la sua fatica, gittosi in terra ginocchioni alzando gli ochi al cielo e' lle mani parlo dicendo: 'o signore il quale gouerni el cielo et la terra et costituisti tutte le cose: non sia la mia tanta ignorantia ch' io seghui altro che te, abbi misericordia di me.' Di subito cio che aueua ciercho di dispensare per amore del creatore di tutte le cose. Ando in su uno monte oue era uno grande romitorio, entro et iui fece penitentia mentre che uisse; fu nella età, finì al tempo di papa Martino. Certi giouani e quali cercauano essere periti nell' arte statuaria mi dissono come esso era dotto nell' uno genere et nell' altro et come esso doue abitaua aueua picto, era docto et finì nella olimpia 438. Fu grandissimo disegnatore et molto docile. Andauano i giouani che aueuano uolontà d' aparare a uisitarlo pregandolo, esso humilissimamente gli riceueua dando loro docti amaestramenti et mostrando loro moltissime misure et faccendo loro molti exempli; fu perfectissimo, con grande humiltà fini in quello romitorio. Concio sia cosa e excellentissimo fu nell' arte et di santissima uita." Ghiberti, ed. Schlosser, *op. cit.*, I, 43 f.

5. See below, note 8.

6. This is the meaning of "formate delle sue"; see *Vocabolario degli Accademici della Crusca*, 5th ed. (Florence, 1863 ff.), VI, 336, sections XXXI, XXXII. Another possible though less usual translation would be "drawn after his figures," *ibid.*, 333, section III. Should, incidentally, "delle" read "dalle"?

7. The *Vocabolario . . . della Crusca,* V, 417, Section XXVI, explains the term *essere d' età* to mean among others "to be advanced in years." However, the sense of Ghiberti's text is not quite clear; it might be interpreted to mean "he lived in the time, he died at the time of Pope Martin." The passage occasionally has been translated as "All this occurred before the time of Pope Martin" (Charles Perkins, *Ghiberti et son école,* 2nd ed. [Paris, n.d.], p. 125, and others). This is plainly incorrect.

8. K. Frey, *Il codice Magliabecchiano* (Berlin, 1892), pp. 87 f., 328 ff.

9. See also Cennino d'Andrea Cennini, *Il libro dell'arte,* ed. D. V. Thompson (New Haven, 1932), I, 117 ff.

10. J. v. Gaye, "Zur Kunstgeschichte, I, Über den unbekannten Meister aus Cöln bei Ghiberti," *Schorn's Kunstblatt,* No. 21. (Supplement to *Cotta's Morgenblatt* [March 12, 1839]).

11. The date 1437 for the time of Gusmin's death, as calculated by Schlosser (*op. cit.,* II, 108 ff. and 165 ff.) and accepted by G. Swarzenski, "Der Kölner Meister bei Ghiberti," *VorWarb, 1926-1927* (Leipzig, 1930), pp. 22 ff., falls at least six years after Pope Martin's death. This is obviously not the place to discuss

in detail Ghiberti's queer calendar of Olympiads and the reasons which led him to build it up. I can only indicate my position. I agree with Schlosser's hypothesis that Ghiberti calculated his Olympiads at five years each, but I am inclined to think that (contrary to his own statement) he started his calendar not with the date of the foundation of Rome (753 B.C.), but with 776, the starting point of the Greek calendar of olympiads (or possibly with 775). Only on this basis does the date of Gusmin's death coincide with the pontificate of Martin V, the activity of Andrea Pisano (Ol. 420) with the date on his door, 1330. I hope to have an opportunity to present this thesis in full at some later time.

12. Adalbert von Chamisso, "Ein Kölner Meister zum Ende des XIV. Jahrhunderts (Nach Ghiberti)," *Sämtliche Werke*, I (Leipzig, n.d.), 334 ff.

13. Schlosser, *op. cit.*, II, 165.

14. Sir John Froissart, *Chronicle of England, France and Spain*, translated by Th. Johnes (London, 1839), *passim; Nouvelle biographie générale*, XXXI (Paris, 1862), cols. 1016 ff.; J. Balteau, M. Barroux, M. Prévost, *Dictionnaire de biographie française*, II (Paris, 1936), cols. 1277 ff.

15. *Chronicon Siculum*, ed. Josephus de Blasiis, Naples, 1887 (Società Napoletana di Storia Patria, *Monumenti storici*, ser. I, Cronache), pp. 68 ff.; Jean Le Fèvre, seigneur de Saint-Remy, *Chronique*, ed. F. Morand, I (Paris, 1876), *passim;* see also preceding note.

16. Against Schlosser, *op. cit.*, II, 165 f.

17. *Dictionnaire de biographie française*, II, cols. 1292 ff.

18. *Ibid.*, cols. 1286 ff.

19. F. Baldinucci, *Notizie dei professori del disegno*, I (Florence, 1681 [ed. Florence 1845]), 303 ff., reports on manuscripts written for Louis II of Anjou by a monk from Lérins who died in 1408 at the age of eighty-two.

20. In his *Facetiae* written down between 1430 and 1440, but composed earlier, Poggio Bracciolini relates an anecdote (LXXV) which is often referred to Louis II and which if it did refer to him,

would prove that this unfortunate duke owned enough jewelry to show off and to be rebuked for it. Poggio tells of a visit paid by the condottiere Rodolfo Varano II of Camerino to the Duke of Anjou when the latter was on his march towards the kingdom of Naples: the duke boasts of his precious plate (*supellectilis*) and stones, and Rodolfo rejoins that he owns two stones of no value but which will bring him a good income—to wit, two millstones. Yet, the anecdote is referred to Louis II and to his march towards Naples in 1409 (or 1410) only by the commentators of Poggio, e.g. (Lenfant), *Poggiana*, II (Amsterdam, 1720), 187 f. and W. Shepherd, *The life of Poggio Bracciolini* (Liverpool, 1837), p. 144, note. Poggio's original text (*The Facetiae or Jocose Tales of Poggio*, English and Latin edition [Paris, 1879]) speaks simply of the Duke of Anjou. This can refer only to Louis I and his campaign of 1382, since the famous wit Rodolfo Varano II of Camerino died in 1384, long before Louis II's campaign of 1409.

21. M. de Laborde, *Notice des émaux . . . du Louvre* (Paris, 1852), 2ième partie, pp. 1 ff.; G. Ledos, "Fragment de l'inventaire des Joyaux de Louis I, duc d'Anjou," *Bibliothèque de l'Ecole des Chartes*, L (1889), 168 ff.; H. Moranville, *Inventaire de l'orfèvrerie et des joyaux de Louis I, duc d'Anjou* (Paris, 1906).

22. *Journal de Jean le Fèvre, évêque de Chartres*, publié par H. Moranville, I (Paris, 1887), 6, 62.

23. Moranville, *Inventaire*, pp. xi ff.

24. *Journal de Jean le Fèvre*, p. 84.

25. See above, n. 20.

26. J. von Schlosser, *Die Kunst-und Wunderkammern der Spätrenaissance* (Leipzig, 1908), pp. 24 ff.

27. K. Rathe, *Der figurale Schmuck der alten Domfassade in Florenz* (Vienna and Leipzig, 1910), pp. 121 ff. See, however, L. Courajod, *Leçons professées à l'Ecole du Louvre*, II (Paris, 1901), 285.

28. Swarzenski, *op. cit., passim*.

29. Schlosser, *Commentarii*, II, 165. For a while Schlosser toyed with the idea of linking Gusmin to the abbot Babboccio, but later relinquished this notion.

30. Courajod, *op. cit.*, II, 282 f. Courajod's words are "un autre artiste flamand de l'école de Sluter." He never identified Gusmin with Sluter himself (Schlosser, *op. cit.*, I, 165).

31. J. Labarte, *Histoire des arts industriels au moyen age et à l'époque de la Renaissance*, II (Paris, 1864–66), 388 f.; H. Havard, *Histoire de l'orfèvrerie* (Paris, 1896), pp. 237 ff.

32. Between 1299 and 1306 a sculptor, goldsmith, and engineer by the name of Guissin worked at Hesdin (E. Marchal, *La sculpture et les chefs d'oeuvre de l'orfèvrerie belges* [Brussels, 1898], pp. 148 ff.); a Cistercian Goswinus died in 1228 in Villa in Brabant; another namesake lived in Mainz in the late eleventh century (J. A. Fabricius, *Bibliotheca mediae et infimae latinitatis*, III [Hamburg, 1734 f.], p. 228). A Ghoswin Coudrudère is mentioned in 1385–1386 in Bruges; a "maistre de verrerie . . ." Gossuyn de Bos-le-Duc (probably s'Hertogensbosch in Holland) 1388–1389 in the services of the Duke of Burgundy in Paris (Deshaisne, *Documents . . . concernant l'histoire de l'art dans la Flandre . . .*, [Lille, 1886], pp. 626, 657). Goswinus de Beka, in the early fifteenth century, was prior of the Carthusian convent of Val Royal near Ghent; Goswinus de Hex, a Brabantian Carmelite died in 1475 as suffragan bishop of Utrecht (Fabricius, *op. cit.*, pp. 228 ff., 235 ff.).

33. I want to thank my old friend Henry Kahane of the University of Illinois for having established the acquaintance between myself and Gossuyn de Bomel. Details on Gossuyn's life are found in: A. Dufour and F. Rabut, "Les orfèvres . . . en Savoie," *Mémoires et documents publiés par la société savoisienne d'histoire et d'archéologie*, XXIV (1886), 329 ff., especially 373 ff.

34. M. de Laborde, *op. cit.*, *passim*.

35. A. Darcel, *Musée National du Louvre, Notice des émaux et de l'orfèvrerie* (Paris, 1891), *Supplément* (ed. E. Molinier), p. 570, D. 943, gives a careful description of the scepter: top and pummel are authentic; the staff, probably from a cantor's baton from St.-Denis, dated 1394, was added in 1804 in preparation for the coronation of Napoleon I. The scepter is mentioned in the inventory of 1379 (J. Labarte, *Inventaire de Charles V, Collection de documents inédits sur l'histoire de France*, III ser., XVI [Paris, 1879], no. 3449) and later in that of the objects entrusted to the monks of St.-Denis on May 7, 1380, among the "nouveaux habiz royaulx et joyaulx ordonnez pour le fait du sacre des roys de France." See also Sir M. Conway, "The Abbey of Saint-Denis and its Ancient Treasures," *Archaeologia*, LXVI (1914–1915), 103 ff., especially 155 ff.; J. J. Marquet de Vasselot, *Musée National du Louvre, Catalogue sommaire de l'orfèvrerie . . .*, (n.d. [about 1914]), p. 30, n. 149.

36. G. Poggi, "Il reliquario 'del libretto' nel battistero fiorentino" *RivdA*, IX (1916), 238 ff. I am greatly indebted to Professor Ulrich Middeldorf for calling my attention to this paper and providing me with a reprint.

37. O. M. Dalton, *The Royal Gold Cup in the British Museum* (London, 1924).

38. E. B(abelon), *Le Cabinet des Medailles et Antiques de la Bibliothèque Nationale, Notice historique et guide de visiteur*, I, *Les antiques et les objets d'arts* (Paris, 1924), p. 137.

39. (O. M. Dalton), *British Museum, A Guide to the Medieval Antiquities* (London, 1924), pp. 103 ff., Fig. 58. The Lothar Crystal evidently was never owned by the French crown; but it comes from the Belgian monastery of Waulsort, in the very neighborhood whence many of the fourteenth-century goldsmiths of the French courts appear to have originated.

40. Labarte, *op. cit.*, pp. 340 ff.; H. Bouchot, *Les reliures d'art à la Bibliothèque Nationale* (Paris, 1888), *passim*. The covers in question are those of mss. lat. 8851, 8892, 9455 and 14497. The back cover of ms. lat. 8851 is a curious copy from the time of Charles V after an illuminated page of the eleventh-century ms. which it encloses. The other covers until recently have been assumed to belong to the period of Charles V. Lately the thirteenth-century date of at least one of these covers has been recognized (Bibliothèque Nationale, *Les plus belles reliures . . .* [Paris, 1929], n. 18, Pl. II). A detailed study seems to be called for; it

would probably reveal that the other two covers are also thirteenth-century work, in part restored and remounted under Charles V.

41. L. de Farcy, "Croix d'Anjou. La vraie croix de l'Abbaye de la Boissière," *Revue de l'art chrétien,* n.s. (XIV (1903), 93 ff. The reproduction is unfortunately a poor chromolithograph.

42. Conway, *op. cit.,* p. 155, n. 3 and Pl. III b. In addition to these pieces one might mention the undated reliquary of Mau-beuge; two similar lost reliquaries carried by two angels, one dated 1394, one at St.-Denis, the other from the Duc de Berry's collection, formerly at Ingolstadt in Bavaria (H. Havard, *Histoire de l'orfèv-rerie française,* I [Paris, 1896], Pl. XV; M. Frankenburger, "Zur Geschichte des ingolstadter und landshuter Herzogschat-zes," *RepKunstW,* XLIV [1923], 24 ff., esp. 32); and, poorer in quality, a cross in the Rothschild Collection in the Louvre (Marquet de Vasselot, *Catalogue som-maire,* p. 27, n. 129).

43. From a convent in Clermont-Ferrand; J. Breck and M. R. Rogers, *BMMA* (New York, 1929), pp. 127 ff., Fig. 72.

44. H. Kohlhausen, *Gotisches Kunst-gewerbe,* in: Th. Bossert, *Geschichte des Kunstgewerbes,* V (Berlin, 1932), 367 ff., Pl. XXI.

45. Kohlhausen, *op. cit.,* p. 387.

46. Labarte, *op. cit.,* II, 352 ff. Pl. L.

47. Havard, *op. cit.,* I, 249 ff.; Franken-burger, *op. cit.,* pp. 23 ff., especially pp. 37 ff.

48. A number of these are illustrated by H. Kohlhausen, "Niederländisches Schmelzwerk," *JPKS,* LII (1931), 153 ff., and in M. Rosenberg, "Studien über Goldschmiedekunst in der Sammlung Fig-dor," *Kunst und Kunsthandwerk,* XIV (1911), 329 ff. The splendid Calvary with Christ at the Column in the cathedral of Gran in Hungary, possibly from an early fifteenth-century Paris workshop, has been only insufficiently published by C. Pulsky, E. Radisics and S. Molinier, *Chefs d'oeuvre d'orfèvrerie ayant figures à l'ex-position de Budapest,* II (Paris, 1888), 123 ff.; Kohlhausen, *Kunstgewerbe,* p. 389. Some lost works of this group have been discussed partly on the basis of Baroque

reproductions by Frankenburger, *op. cit., passim.*

49. See also R. Krautheimer, "Ghiberti-ana," *BurlM,* LXXI (1937), 68 ff.

50. Courajod, *op. cit.,* II, 266 ff.

51. G. Poggi, *Catalogo del Museo dell' Opera del Duomo* (Florence, 1904), pp. 43 ff.

52. M. Dvorak, "Die Illuminatoren des Johann von Neumarkt," *Gesammelte Auf-sätze zur Kunstgeschichte* (Munich, 1929), pp. 74 ff.

53. The identity of these two names has been suggested by W. Körte, "Deutsche Vesperbilder in Italien," *Kunstgeschicht-liches Jahrbuch der Bibliotheca Hertziana,* I (Rome, 1937), 3 ff., n. 85.

54. I wonder whether it is still necessary to combat the nationalistic tendencies which cropped up in the 1930's and in which influences from north of the Alps were either tremendously exaggerated or else rebuked as an attack on the greatness of Italian art and as "una assurdità . . . del Courajod" (G. de Francovich, "Ap-punti su Donatello e Jacopo della Quercia," *BdA,* IX (1929), 145 ff., especially 150).

55. P. Toesca, *La Pittura e la minatura lombarda* (Milan, 1912), Fig. 26 (Rome, Bibl. Casanatense, ms. 459).

56. Diamonds decorate the horizontal bands of the Pistoia altar, roses those of the altar of St. John the Baptist in Flor-ence, ornamental shells Orcagna's taber-nacle at Or San Michele.

57. For example, the façade of Orvieto cathedral.

58. L. Planiscig, "Geschichte der ven-ezianischen Skulptur im XIV. Jahrhun-dert," *JKSK,* XXXIII (1916), 31 ff., espe-cially 182 ff.

59. J. von Schlosser, "Die Werkstatt der Embriachi," *JKSK,* XX (1899), 200 ff.

60. Other examples are: the *Beau brevi-aire de Charles V,* the *Petites heures* and the *Grandes heures du Duc de Berry,* be-fore 1390, the *Chronique des roys de France* of the Bibliothèque de l'Arsenal. Illustrations in H. M. R. Martin, *La mini-ature française du XIII au XV siècle* (Paris, 1923), Pls. 59, 69, 70, 71, 72, 76.

61. London, British Museum, Add. Mss. 28841, f. 6: "fragment of a . . . treatise on

the vices by a member of the Cicharelli family at Genoa . . . late XIV century . . . attributed to the Genoese miniaturist of the family of Cybo, known as the 'Monk of Hyeres' . . ." (British Museum, *Reproductions from Illuminated Manuscripts*, ser. IV [London, 1928], p. 13 and Pl. XXXI).

62. Ghiberti's reference to "verdure"

(*Commentarii*, I, 28) has been used by Schlosser (*ibid.*, II, 105, n. 74) to prove the master's acquaintance with Flemish and French tapestries to which the term is constantly applied. Schlosser also alludes to the foliage borders of *Livres d'Heures*.

63. Schlosser, *Commentarii*, I, 46, 47 ff., 61 ff., 64.

Postscript

While Master Gusmin's personality, dates, and links to Louis I of Anjou are neatly pinned down, the stylistic comparisons between Ghiberti's early *oeuvre* and French goldsmith work of the late fourteenth century appear to me on re-reading not nearly so tight as I should like them to be. But then, I do not see how they could be made tighter as long as our knowledge of precious jewelry wrought for the French courts shortly before and after 1400 is so woefully inadequate. Recent publications and exhibitions have enlarged our knowledge of the field, but they could not shed any further light on Gusmin's life and work.

Willibald Sauerländer has pointed out to me that the mounting of the "Constantine" bust (Paris, Bibl. Nat.) dates from the late thirteenth or the early fourteenth centuries and thus two or three generations prior to Gusmin's times. I have had a good look at the piece when last at the Bibliothèque Nationale, and I think he is right. Hence, I have removed from this reprint the passing reference I made to it in the original text.

Additional Bibliography

Europäische Kunst um 1400, Catalog, [Krautheimer-Hess] (Vienna, 1962).

Krautheimer, R., and Krautheimer-Hess, T., *Lorenzo Ghiberti* (Princeton, 1956).

Meiss, M., *French Painting in the Time of Jean de Berry,* pt. I-II (London and New York, 1967–1968).

Müller, K. Th., and Steingräber, E. "Die französische Goldemailplastik um 1400," *MünchJB,* ser. 3, 5 (1954), 29 ff.

Les trésors des églises de France, Catalogue, II (Paris, 1965).

16

HUMANISTS AND ARTISTS *
in collaboration with Trude Krautheimer-Hess

THE VISUAL IMAGE of antiquity, such as we hold at present, goes back to Winckelmann and Jefferson, to the Adam brothers and David, and beyond them to Bellori and Poussin, to the Carracci, Raphael, and Vasari. Through the continuous interplay of creative art and creative scholarship, a picture of antiquity had been formed, multiform but consistent. By and large this interplay came to an end around the middle of the nineteenth century. But the mutual impregnation of art and scholarship, extending over four centuries, has remained potent to this day. Indeed, it has led us to forget that when antiquity was rediscovered in the fourteenth and fifteenth centuries in Italy, such cross-fertilization did not necessarily exist. Throughout the fourteenth century, and far into the fifteenth, there stood on one side the literary set, the learned—poets, philosophers, historians, antiquarians—and on the other, in a separate camp, those whom contemporaries called the experts and connoisseurs. Though these latter may have been erudite, they were not so of necessity. While undoubtedly some were to be found among the humanists, the majority, it would seem, were either collectors or practitioners of art.

Petrarch's concept of antiquity established the approach of the learned.[1] Needless to say, his outlook was permeated with medieval thought: Rome and antiquity were synonymous; Rome and her monuments symbolized all that was worth remembering of antiquity, and memorable to Petrarch was only that which had living significance for the present. History to him, as to the entire Middle Ages, was part of politics, and the past, therefore, represented a political reality. Consequently, like many a medieval visitor in Rome, he expected to find the city a tangible symbol of the entire past in which Christian and pagan elements were inextricably interwoven.[2] But once arrived in Rome, the Christian memories, though essential to his philosophy, did not greatly affect his image of the city. It was the pre-Christian past (rather this than the pagan) that prevailed in his mind. From his reading of Virgil, Horace, and Ovid, he had conjured up a preordained idea of Rome and her past; hence in his wanderings around the city, he saw the dream image, not the reality.[3] Instead of monuments, he saw sites, meaningful to him only insofar as they were scenes of historic or pseudo-historic events: the "palace" of Evander, the youth of Romulus and Remus, the rape of the Sabines, the trysts of Numa and Egeria, the triumph of Pompey,

*From *Lorenzo Ghiberti* (Princeton, 1956), pp. 294–305.

the rule of Trajan. Sometimes these sites were marked by monuments: the *Lupa,* the Grotto of Egeria, the Column of Trajan. But to Petrarch it mattered little whether or not a site was commemorated by a monument, or merely haunted by memories. For his approach was entirely literary, almost emphatically non-visual. Monuments and sites alike stimulated his imagination, evoked a picture of Rome as a blend of political, historical, archeological and poetical factors, be it the Rome of the legendary heroes or, as in his late years, of the early emperors.[4] He visualized antiquity not only without much stress on the magic-legendary elements that had prevailed in the *Mirabilia* and still in Dante,[5] but with nearly exclusive emphasis—it need hardly be said of the days of Cola di Rienzo—on its political and moral character. Delving into antiquity was not a pastime for Petrarch; it was a serious and essential occupation. Rome was to become again the *caput mundi;* she was to be revived, and this rebirth would succeed through a revival of her ancient virtues. They had made possible her great deeds of the past, and by implication they promised a comparable future. Hence her monuments were mementos not so much of the past, and certainly not of the past alone, as of an exemplary and timeless way of life, of *virtus,* manliness with all its moral and pragmatic connotations. At the same time these monuments held out a promise of future greatness and were, besides, reminders of the passing of all earthly grandeur—a concept medieval in origin. Within this same intellectual framework, a collection of antiques was meant to incite the owner "to follow the ways of the ancients," which leads one to assume that such was the aim underlying Petrarch's own sporadic attempts to collect Roman coins and the like.[6]

Thus in the circle of Petrarch and his learned humanist followers, the deter-mining factors in their image of antiquity were moral and political by implica-tion, literary by character, and always comprised more a mood than a clear con-cept. Monuments, whether inscriptions or figurative, were, as their name implies, mementos: Cola di Rienzo, brooding all day over marble fragments scattered through Rome, read "li antichi pataffi; tutte scritture antiche volgarizzava, queste fiure di marmo justamente interpretava." [7] Rarely does this approach find clearer expression than in a letter written from Rome by Giovanni Dondi, Petrarch's learned medical friend from Padua. [8] As he saw them in 1375, Roman monu-ments and their inscriptions were mementos of Roman *virtù* and of great men: "the statues . . . of bronze or marble preserved to this day and the many scat-tered fragments of broken sculptures, the grandiose triumphal arches and the columns that show sculptured into them the histories of great deeds and many other similar ones erected publicly in honor of great men, because they established peace and saved the country from threatening danger or enlarged the empire by subjugating the barbarians; as I remember reading about, not without some remarkable excitement, wishing you also might see them [the monuments] some day, similarly strolling and stopping a little somewhere and perhaps saying to yourself: These are indeed the testimonies (*argumenta*) of great men." [9] The inscription on the Arch of Septimius Severus had moral and political meaning for Dondi, just as the writings of the ancients seemed to him testimony of their superiority in "justice, fortitude, temperance and prudence." [10] It would seem the realm of Roman *virtù* was in all innocence being invaded by the quadrivium of medieval virtues.

This nonvisual, evocative approach to antiquity among the learned has dominated nearly all humanist thought down to recent times. To this day the literary outlook survives among historians, philologists, and educated sightseers. Of all Coluccio Salutati's letters, none shows any concern over a work of art except for an occasional reference to subject matter. This is only natural, since literary men will follow literary lines, and humanism has reached us largely through its literature. The prevalence of the literary point of view has thus obliterated the fact that once a different, indeed, a diametrically opposed approach to antiquity existed among men who did not live by their pens, men who were for the most part artists. Their attitude is to be gleaned from occasional remarks, and has been made crystal clear in a passage from the same letter by Giovanni Dondi. The excerpt has been quoted several times,[11] but is worth repeating: the learned doctor deplores the small number preserved of "works by those geniuses of old," and tells how eagerly these relics were hunted and highly paid for "by those who have a feeling for the matter" (*ab iis qui in ea re sentiunt*); he remarks on how these remnants demonstrate the greater natural talent and the superior skill of the ancients as compared to those of today: "I am referring to the ancient buildings and statues and reliefs and other similar things. If our modern artists look at them carefully they are stunned (*obstupescunt*). I myself used to know a marble sculptor—a craftsman in this field, famous among those whom Italy then had, particularly in working figures. More than once I heard him discuss (*movere*) the statues and sculptures he had seen in Rome with such admiration and veneration that in this discourse he seemed to be all beyond himself, so full of wonder was the subject. It was said that once he came along with five friends [to a site] where some such images were to be seen; he looked and was so arrested by the wonder of the craftsmanship (*artificii*) that he forgot his company and stood there until his friends had gone on half a mile or more. He talked a great deal about the excellence (*bonitas*) of these figures and praised their makers and acclaimed their genius beyond all measure. He used to conclude —I quote his own words—that if such sculptures had only the spark of life, they would be better than nature; as if he wanted to say that by the genius of such great artists nature had not just been imitated but indeed excelled."

Dondi's story is illuminating from more than one point of view. We have no idea which sculptor he had in mind. It seems he had not known him in Rome and whether he knew him in Padua or elsewhere remains an open question. Whether or not the sculptor was Dondi's contemporary is not clear; but his statement that he was "the most famous artist among those whom Italy *then* had," gives the impression that he had died by 1375 when the letter was written. He may have been older than Dondi and active in the first half of the century. Whatever his name, age and origin, however, to Dondi the scholar, he was obviously an expert, and one who loved art. Nor was he unique, for he belonged to a wider circle of men with "a feeling for the matter" among whom were some willing to pay good money for works of ancient art—collectors who did not seek such objects solely for their literary value. In contrast to them, Dondi, despite all his learning, did not feel altogether at home with ancient art. He was purblind to the very qualities which others looked for. But he by no means felt inferior to these art lovers. He simply regarded them as artists and collectors who admired beyond comprehension achievements of antiquity to which his own criteria did not apply. Dondi felt himself at home when the hermeneutics of an ancient relief or statue were in question, especially when they were linked to an inscription. But obviously the sculptor and the collectors to whom he alludes did not look upon these works as illustrative of historic events, or as evocative of political dreams or of an elegiac mood. Their attitude was more direct and naïve. Just because they had not read their Virgil and Livy, or not in the way the humanists read them, they were free to discover other aspects of Roman art. Clearly it was the visual aspect that attracted them: for Dondi's sculptor staked his judgment on criteria of craftsmanship (*artificium*), excellence (*bonitas*) and lifelikeness—"if they had but the spark of life, they would be better than nature."

That artists and collectors should adopt a visual approach to antiquity was nothing new to the fourteenth century. New was the incomprehension with which the learned looked upon those queer ducks who admired fragments of the ancient world for reasons other than their literary overtones. But even this incomprehension was not quite new. As far back as the twelfth century, Henry of Winchester had exposed himself to the ridicule of serious scholars by scouring Rome for ancient statues,[12] "his beard unkempt." The collecting of antiques, along with other art objects, continued sporadically all through the Middle Ages. The purchase list of a collector from Treviso, Oliviero Forzetta, is well known. It was compiled in 1335, and among other works of art, antique as well as contemporary, there is mentioned for possible acquisition the Roman relief with Four Putti, which was then in S. Vitale in Ravenna and later in S. Maria de' Miracoli in Venice.[13] Aesthetic enjoyment, pride in owning the wondrous and precious, and admiration for ancient as well as modern art, were likewise inherent in the collecting activities of Charles V of France and his royal brothers. Mentioned in their inventories, among hundreds of medieval *objets d'art,* are a few antique cameos and other gems. Such collecting reflects a naïve and natural approach to the art of antiquity, one that was apparently widespread in the High Middle Ages. Against this background must be viewed the classical renascence movements which pervaded France, Germany, and Italy in the eleventh, twelfth, and thirteenth centuries:[14] the schools of Provence and Campania; Villard de Honnecourt; the Peter and Paul Master and the Visitation Master of Rheims; the Master of the Bamberg Visitation; Capuan and other South Italian workshops; Niccolo Pisano. These schools and masters readily transposed antique models into their own language. The art of antiquity was not alien to them or to their patrons. They saw no chasm between their own products and those of the faraway past. Their approach to antiquity was naïvely visual. Occasionally a scholar would look at the art of antiquity with the same naïve pleasure: for instance, early in the thirteenth century Magister Gregorius, a British jurist, visiting in Rome, felt constrained to return three times, each time walking two miles, to see a statue of Venus on the Quirinal, "executed with such marvelous and inexplicable skill that it bore its nudity like one blushing, the forms suffused with reddish color . . . on account of its wonderful beauty and some magical power. . . ." [15] Ristoro, an Italian scholar at the end of the thirteenth century, praised fragments of Aretine vases for their figures "so excellent and natural [that] . . . sculptors, draftsmen, and other connoisseurs (*cognoscenti*) go almost crazy with pleasure, [and] . . . preserve them like sacred relics and are stunned to see that human nature could rise so high in a craftsmanship." [16] One hundred years later this terminology was used almost verbatim by Dondi as he quoted the unknown sculptor.

During the course of the fourteenth century, this naïve, simple appreciation came to an end with the recognition of a fundamental difference between the late medieval present and the ancient past.[17] In the courtly *ambiente* of France and in North Italy this recognition led to picturing literary works of antiquity in contemporary settings, to transposing Greek and Roman history and legends into an atmosphere of chivalric romance. Certainly it was not by chance that the illustrated manuscripts from the circle of Petrarch conformed to the general tendency which, from the middle of the fourteenth century, especially north of the Alps, was to present antique themes with chivalric overtones. Personages and themes from antiquity were transcribed into contemporary costume, with just a detail *all'antica* added, a laurel wreath or the like. Simone Martini's illustrations for Petrarch's Virgil strikingly illuminate the approach: much like the French *grand-seigneurs* of his time, Petrarch, Italy's most learned antiquarian and most sensitive poet, approached his beloved world of antiquity as an experience of exclusively political and moral meaning; his visual image of it was fettered to traditional medieval forms,[18] and both he and his circle disregarded the visual aspects of ancient art. Naïve delight felt by artists and collectors was considered suspect, perhaps slightly ridiculous. Scholars and artists parted ways. The artists, in Tuscany at any rate, continued on their way undisturbed. At least, during the first half of the fourteenth century they absorbed and admired antique forms, at times assimilating the vocabulary into their own work. Andrea Pisano's reliefs of the *artes* on the Campanile include Hercules as representing the art of war, an antiquish ploughman as the symbol of agriculture and an antiquish horseman as the personification of horsemanship. Ambrogio Lorenzetti's *Pax* from the Palazzo Pubblico and the reclining *Eve* at Montesiepe, from the Lorenzetti workshop,[19] both *all'antica,* are proof of the impact of antique vocabulary on the art of Siena. Dondi's sculptor may well have been the contemporary of Pisano and Lorenzetti.

After the middle of the fourteenth century, however, antiquity no longer found an echo in either Florence or Siena. Circumstances did not favor the use of a vocabulary *all'antica* in public art. In the general mood of penitence and asceticism that followed the Black Death,[20] a Hercules or a Venus, even disguised as Eve, as a Christian Virtue, or as one of the *artes,* was none too acceptable. The destruction by the Sienese in 1357 of the statue of Venus for which Ambrogio Lorenzetti had still recorded his appreciation in a drawing, reflects the change of atmosphere. In any event, the demand for an art permeated with antique elements was small, almost nonexistent, among those who were in a position to commission extensive and expensive works. If some individual artists continued to admire ancient art, their admiration remained entirely passive, finding no expression in their works.

But in the last years of the Trecento a new and positive approach to the art of antiquity began to appear, both in northern Italy and in Florence. In Padua, from about 1390 on, the medals of the house of Carrara reproduced Roman imperial coins.[21] As might be expected in this milieu which, more than any other, lay beneath the spell of Petrarch and his work, antiquity was viewed in an evocative and erudite humanist spirit. In Florence the jambs of the Porta della Mandorla and, a few years later, both Brunelleschi's and Ghiberti's reliefs for the competition of 1401, reflect a fresh vogue for the antique. In fact, under the leadership of Petrarch's disciple, Coluccio Salutati, Florence, shortly before the turn of the century, was fast becoming the center of humanist endeavor south of the Apennines. It is doubtful, to say the least, whether all the leaders and scholars of the new generation, from Niccolò Niccoli to Palla Strozzi, appreciated or were indeed interested in the visual interpretation of antiquity manifested in the work of the Hercules Master and young Ghiberti. What scholars would obviously welcome was antique subject matter, a Hercules or an Abundantia, for its power to evoke the antique world and all it meant to a learned humanist. This renewed interest in antiquity was bound to reactivate among artists the fascination which ancient sculpture had held for their predecessors of the first half of the fourteenth century. Its lifelike quality, "better than nature," its relaxed movements and tactile values, while perhaps not attracting the run-of-the-mill sculptors, would and did attract the best, such as the Hercules Master from the workshop of the Porta della Mandorla and young Ghiberti.

Yet, the fresh visual attraction which antique art had for this generation was not limited to the artists' workshops. It would appear that by the end of the century, at least some humanists no longer felt the sense of superiority towards the visual aspects of art, either antique or reborn, that Giovanni Dondi had felt. They must have enjoyed the antique motifs hidden under the medieval overlay of Brunelleschi's design, and they could not have missed the tactile values of Ghiberti's Isaac, even though the underlying antique prototype was disguised as a

Biblical figure. The interest of learned humanists in subject matter, and that of artists spellbound by the aesthetic qualities of antique art, while not coincident, were slowly approaching one another. One wonders if it were not by more than mere chance that Palla di Nofri Strozzi, the eager and financially powerful champion of humanism, was assigned to the three-man committee appointed by the *Calimala* to supervise work on Ghiberti's first door.

The gradual rapprochement between artists and humanists continued during the next decades, reaching a peak of coincidence in the twenties and thirties. A number of contemporary phenomena concurred to make it apparent: the increasing desire on the part of humanists to build up collections of antiques; the new spirit in which these collections were assembled; the new approach of artists to the world of antiquity and to both its artistic and scholarly interpretation; and—a revolutionary phenomenon—the exchange of ideas between artists and humanists on ancient and modern art. Art became permeated with the concepts and vocabulary of humanism; it became a part of humanist endeavor. Concomitantly, the humanists turned art into a problem of their own.

Throughout the fourteenth century, if not earlier, the *grand-seigneurs,* from Oliviero Forzetta to Jean, Duc de Berry, had included in their collections antique gems, coins, bronzes, and occasional marble sculptures.[22] The collections of the Medici in the first half of the fifteenth century were hardly different in character. A few antique pieces were mixed in with hundreds of other precious objects. Lorenzo de' Medici the Elder upon his death in 1440 left "precious clothes and plate, statues (*signa*), paintings, wrought vessels, pearls and books"—a collection, in other words, in which antiques played a minor part, if any.[23] Neither was Cosimo's collection focused on antiques, despite the general assumption to the contrary. When Ciriaco d'Ancona visited it in 1433, he saw only precious table plate and no antiques whatsoever.[24] Timoteo Maffei, writing before 1450, vaguely mentions, together with "egregious paintings," some marble statues as being in Cosimo's collection.[25] The cornelian representing the Flaying of Marsyas, which Ghiberti mounted around 1430,[26] may well have been a unique item at the time. The large Medici collection of antiques, gems, coins, and medals seems to have been accumulated by Cosimo's son, Piero, in the fifties and sixties of the fifteenth century. His first inventory, dated 1456, lists nineteen cameos and hundreds of ancient coins. By 1464, when a second inventory was drawn up, the number of cameos had increased to twenty-nine.[27] He may have inherited the added ten from Cosimo's collection developed over the last twenty-five years of the old gentleman's life. Cosimo, in turn, may have acquired them in 1437 trom the estate of Niccolò Niccoli.

Indeed, prior to 1450, the scholars, rather than the *grand-seigneurs,* appear to have concentrated on collecting antiques. What is more important, they did so in a new spirit. Niccolo Niccoli was foremost among them. True, as scion of an old family and a gentleman through and through,[28] he had a good deal of the *grand-seigneur* about him, and like them, he collected medieval paintings as well.[29] But by and large his emphasis was on antiques. Friends and agents combed Italy and the Near East seeking Greek and Roman relics to send him.[30] He himself purchased whatever he could, sometimes paying up to the limits of his financial ability,[31] at other times making his buys dirt cheap. His best *trouvaille* was the chalcedony with the Rape of the Palladium which he bought right off the neck of a child playing in the street.[32] In his house he assembled innumerable coins dating "from the oldest times," statues (*signa*), portraits of the ancients (*veterum imagines*), "many ancient bronze figures, many marble heads," statues, ancient vessels and crystal cups, inscriptions and reliefs (*sculture*).[33] No doubt Niccolò's image of antiquity, like Petrarch's, was largely determined by his profound knowledge of Greek and Latin literature. His collection of antiques, much as he rejoiced in it, was mainly for the purpose of illustrating and evoking past history. He was even occasionally chided for using his numismatic collection as reliable philological material.[34] Still, his approach did differ from that of previous generations. For one thing, Niccolò's collection was enormous in comparison to the few paltry coins and potsherds which Petrarch had owned; second he lived amid his antique objects as everyday surroundings; he regarded them not only as objects of study, but used the drinking cups, table plate and so forth, as implements of his household. They were a part of his normal existence, the tools of his single purpose in life, to relive antiquity and thus to revive it. And while his approach was decidedly that of a learned man, he liked these works of art for their beauty as well—and this was the third new phenomenon. This attitude is reflected clearly in his correspondence. Traversari, in his letters to Niccolò, cannot limit himself to philological and historical statements. He feels impelled to include aesthetic evaluations: Ciriaco d'Ancona, he says, owns "a portrait in onyx of Scipio the Younger, of supreme elegance; never had I seen a more beautiful one." [35] Small wonder that Niccolo was considered an expert on art by his contemporaries and as one who had revived not only the ancient writers but "painting, sculpture and lettering [36] and other noble arts," including book illumination.[37] He advised not only scholars but artists as well "knowing much about painting, sculpture, and architecture and giving them great support in their profession: Pippo di Ser Brunellesco, Donatello, Luca della Robbia, Lorenzo di Bartoluccio—and with all of them he was on the most friendly terms." [38]

What remains unclear is Niccolò's exact relation to these artists. We know of his personality and behavior. We picture him as "dressed always in rose-colored stuffs . . . trailing on the ground" and as having meticulous table manners.[39] He was no doubt very courteous. But he was perhaps a bit awe-inspiring. Consequently, one would suspect that his attitude toward artists was slightly patronizing. Great scholar and gentleman that he was, he must have been only too happy to give advice from his enormous store of knowledge to artists who sought it; but he would have had to be the one to give, and they the ones to receive.

Nevertheless, Niccolò approached ancient art and contemporary artists in a new spirit. Although artists belonged to a different social category from his own, he did not look down on them as did Aurispa when speaking of "that sculptor," Ghiberti, or as did Leonardo Bruni. Bruni, in the preamble to his program for the Gates of Paradise, has no doubts whatever that not only should it be he, the scholar, who advises the artist, he who chooses the events worthy of memory; but also he who through his personal supervision will make sure that they will also "please the eye by the variety of their design." The scholar should not only lay down the program, he should also decide about the propriety and beauty of design. To Bruni, the artist was fundamentally the *vilis mechanicus,* a mere practitioner, and, accordingly, he attempted to appropriate for himself nearly all the functions which the commissioning bodies of Florence usually ascribed to three advisory committees, composed of scholars, artists, and "men with common sense." [40] Remarks reflecting a similar attitude occur in at least one of Bruni's letters: artists, he says, neither need to be possessed of theoretical knowledge (*scientia*), nor steeped in the natural sciences (*materiae rerum cognitio*).[41] It is doubtful if he ever collected antiques. The "little stone with a Narcissus" which he mentions in a letter to Niccolò Niccoli was intended for the latter's collection, and one wonders if it is by chance that the phrase, "you who are so keen on that kind of thing," should sound a bit critical of Niccolò's collecting mania.[42] In short, one suspects Bruni of being as purblind as had been Giovanni Dondi two generations earlier.

Poggio Bracciolini went much further than Niccolò Niccoli in his approach to artists and their works a few years later.[43] Niccolò's junior by twenty years, and —a point of some relevance—not a gentleman by birth, Poggio was a *littérateur.* When in 1429, in the company of Antonio Loschi, he looked at the ruins of Rome from the foot of the *rupe Tarpeia,* he was deeply imbued with the nostalgic, literary, moralizing mood of Petrarch and his circle. Poggio's interpretation of Rome, like theirs, was fundamentally literary: the importance of antique remnants lay in their inscriptions; the admonitory flavor of these inscriptions he stressed time and again; and his prevailing mood was one of sorrow over the decay of the ancient buildings listed in his treatise on the changes of fortune, *De Varietate Fortunae:* "few . . . are left and they are half destroyed and decayed." Still, Poggio represented also a new kind of humanist. His list of Roman ruins was not only a good deal longer than Petrarch's, it also excluded all Christian sites; most important, it was based on visual impressions, on observations of monuments, not on mere sites. His motives for collecting were different from Niccolò Niccoli's, and his choice of objects new. He focused exclusively on works of ancient art—probably he could not afford medieval *objets d'art;* he copied inscriptions and epitaphs but did not collect them. What he owned, however, he loved. Overtones of pride, often clad in bantering self-persiflage, permeate his letters to Niccolò whenever he mentions his treasures: "I have gone a bit crazy and do you want to know how. I have had my bedroom furnished with marble heads; one is elegant and intact, the others have had their noses broken off, but still they will delight a good artist. . . ." [44] "I have picked up (*expiscatus sum*) the marble bust of a woman, the breast well preserved—anyway, I like it. . . ." [45] [Francesco di Pistoia] . . . has written me from Chios that he holds for me three marble heads of Juno, Minerva, and Bacchus, by Polycletus and Praxiteles. As for the names of the sculptors I would not be sure: you know those little Greeks talk a lot and may have made up those names to raise the ante. I hope I am wrong. . . . The head of Minerva wears a marble wreath; that of Bacchus has two little horns. When they arrive I shall place them in my little study (*gymnasiolum*). Minerva will not be out of place. I shall put her among my books. Bacchus will fit even better. Also for Juno we shall find a place. She was once married to a philanderer; now she will be a concubine. I have here also [he writes from Rome] something I shall send home. Donatello has seen it and praised it greatly." [46] To more distant acquaintances he wrote more seriously about what he saw in ancient works of art and why he wanted to own them: "I am moved by the genius of the artist when I see how the very forces of nature are represented in marble. . . . Many suffer from other diseases; but mine is that I admire too much perhaps and more than a learned man should, those marbles carved by great artists. True, nature herself must be greater than those who work like her; but I am forced to admire the art of him who, in mute matter, expresses [her] as living so that often nothing but the spirit seems to be lacking." [47] Or else he says, "I am greatly delighted by sculptures and bronzes (*caelaturis*) made in memory of the excellent men of old. I am forced to admire their genius and art since they render a mute and lifeless thing as if it breathed and spoke; often indeed they represent even the emotions of the soul so that a thing which can feel neither pain nor joy looks to you as if it laughed or mourned." [48]

All this points to one simple fact: Poggio loved ancient art. He did so with a bad conscience. He tried to rationalize his feelings to himself and his correspondents in the traditional terms of an aesthetic inherited from the Trecento. He felt a learned man should not dote on these playthings quite so much, and he poked fun at his passion for a pastime which was perhaps not altogether shared by Niccolo; he jested about the broken noses of his marble heads, about the way he was going to distribute the gods over his study so they would fit in nicely; he possibly did not know the head of a faun from one of Bacchus; nor did he care—at least he pretended not to—who made the sculptures in his collection, whether Polycletus or Praxiteles; but then he retorts: "anyway, I like them"; "still they will delight a good artist"; or he insists that Donatello has seen it and says it's good. Doubtless Poggio was on the defensive against Niccoli and possibly others. He thought himself just as good a scholar as they, but he sought in ancient art not only its subject matter but its beauty.[49] To justify his stand he appeals to his own taste and to the judgment of contemporary artists, among them Donatello. Scholar though he was, he combined for the first time scholarly knowledge, not only with a highly developed taste, as did also Niccolò Niccoli, but also with a genuine love of ancient art and a deep respect for the artists of his time. The time had ended when Giovanni Dondi could only shake his learned head in amazement over the enthusiasm of an unlearned sculptor. Poggio called on Donatello to hear his judgment on the quality of a work of ancient art.

Humanist scholars and artists in the twenties and thirties groped for a new mutual understanding. An exchange of ideas began to take place. The group of artists and scholars involved was small—among the scholars, certainly Poggio and to some degree Niccolò Niccoli; among the artists, as witness Vespasiano da Bisticci, Brunelleschi, Donatello, Ghiberti, Luca della Robbia. It was obviously not by chance that in 1436 Alberti named these same four artists together with the late Masaccio as the leaders of the new style.[50] In the eyes of their learned contemporaries they represented a new type of artist who had grown beyond the stature of the traditional craftsman. They knew and cared about art by inclination and training. For years they had been enthusiastic about the art of antiquity, vaguely and emotionally, with intuitive understanding, but without what the humanists would have considered precise knowledge. They had attempted along scientific lines to solve problems of space representation, proportion, balance, and a credible rendering of reality. They had begun to build a vocabulary *all'antica* in architecture, sculpture and, to a lesser degree, in painting. Now the scholars would guide them toward an ever greater number of antique monuments and explain precisely matters large and small: the subject matter of these monuments, their meaning, the costume of antiquity, the new antique lettering, *veterum helementorum forma,* the scientific basis of perspective, the importance of collecting and thus living in daily contact with works of ancient art. Thus enlightened by humanist scholars, the artists would be able to help create the new world for which every humanist longed. They would be the artists of humanism.

Ghiberti holds a key position in this area of rapprochement between humanists and artists. Yet it is important to realize that only during the last twenty years of his life did he join the circle of the select. Only in the Gates of Paradise did he evolve a homogeneous and consistent style *all'antica.* Only in the late thirties and forties did he apparently develop into a collector of antiques on a large scale. When in 1434 Ciriaco d'Ancona visited his house, it contained but a few old and new bronze and marble statues (*simulachra*); at the time of Ghiberti's death in 1455, on the other hand, the collection was valued at the sizable sum of 1,500 florins.[51] Only in the thirties did he turn to the problems of scientific perspective, and only late in life did he try his hand at the eminently humanist task of writing. The *Commentarii* indeed are but one, though perhaps the most signal product, of Ghiberti's humanist endeavors.

Notes

1. E. Müntz and Prince d'Essling, *Pétrarque* (Paris, 1902), p. 32, note 2, and pp. 37, 38, note 1; G. B. De Rossi, "Sull'archeologia nel secolo decimo quarto," *Bulletino di corrispondenza archeologica* (1871), pp. 3 ff.

2. F. Petrarca, *Le familiari,* ed. V. Rossi I (Florence, 1933 ff.), 95 (*Ep. fam.* II, 9).

3. *Ibid.,* II, 56 ff. (*Ep. fam.* VI, 2).

4. T. Mommsen, "Petrarch's Conception of the Dark Ages," *Speculum,* XVII (1942), 226 ff.; C. C. Bailey, "Petrarch, Charles IV and the Renovatio Imperii," *Speculum,* XVII (1942), 323 ff.

5. De Rossi, *loc. cit.*

6. Petrarca, *op. cit.,* III, 289, 315, 337 (*Ep. fam.* XVIII, 8; XIX, 3, XIX, 12). See also Müntz-Essling, *op. cit.,* p. 37, notes 2 ff.

7. De Rossi, *loc. cit.*

8. J. Morelli, "De Joanne Dondio," *Operette,* II (1820), 285 ff., with excerpts from Dondi's letters (Venice, *Marc. lat.,* Cl. XIV, 223, fols. 47–68v).

9. Letter to Fra Guglielmo da Cremona, *ms. cit.,* fols. 56 ff.; Morelli, *op. cit.,* pp. 303 ff.

10. Letter to Paganino da Sala; Morelli, *op. cit.,* p. 302.

11. Letter to Fra Guglielmo da Cremona, *ms. cit.,* 56–59. It is quoted in Müntz-Essling, *op. cit.,* p. 45, note 3 and translated into German in J. von Schlosser, *Leben und Meinungen des florentinischen Bildners Lorenzo Ghiberti* (Basel, 1941), pp. 148 f.

12. John of Salisbury, *Joannis Sarisberiensis Historiae quae supersunt,* ed. R. L. Poole (Oxford, 1927), pp. 60 ff.

13. J. von Schlosser, "Die ältesten Medaillen und die Antike," *JKSK,* XVIII (1897), 104, note 1 and, the more complete version, E. Müntz, "Essai sur l'histoire des collections italiens d'antiquités . . . ," *RA,* LXIX (1879), 47 ff.

14. E. Panofsky, "Renaissance and Renascences," *Kenyon Review,* VI (1944), 201 ff. [See now, *idem, Renaissance and Renascences in Western Art* (Stockholm, 1960)].

15. G. McN. Rushforth, "Magister Gregorius De Mirabilibus Urbis Romae . . . ," *JRSK,* IX (1919), 49 f.

16. Ristoro d'Arezzo, *Mappa Mundi,* in: V. Nannucci, *Manuale della letteratura . . . italiana,* II (Florence, 1857), 201 ff., quoted in German translation also by J. von Schlosser, *Leben und Meinungen Ghiberti* (Basel, 1941), pp. 143 ff.

17. J. Adhémar, *Influences antiques dans l'art du moyen âge français* (London, 1937), pp. 270 ff.; E. Panofsky and F. Saxl, "Classical Mythology in Mediaeval Art" (*Metropolitan Museum Studies,* IV, 2 [1933]), 255 ff.; Panofsky, "Renaissance and Renascences" as above, n. 14.

18. Müntz-Essling, *op. cit.,* p. 37; L. Chiovenda, *Die Zeichnungen Petrarcas,* (Diss. Frankfurt a. Main, 1929); reprint from *Archivum Romanicum,* XVI (1933), 13 f.

19. R. van Marle, *The Development of the Italian Schools of Painting,* VI (The Hague, 1925), 6, with further references.

20. M. Meiss, *Painting in Florence and Siena after the Black Death* (Princeton, 1951), *passim.*

21. J. von Schlosser, *JKSK* XVIII (1897), 86 ff.

22. A history of collecting in the fifteenth century remains to be written, despite the splendid work Müntz and Schlosser have done: E. Müntz, *Les collections des Médicis au XV siècle . . .* (Paris, 1888) and "Essai sur l'histoire des collections italiennes d'antiquités . . . ," *RA,* LXIX (1879), 45 ff., 84 ff., Schlosser, *op. cit.,* and Über einige Antiken Ghiberti's," *JKSK,* XXIV (1903), 25 ff. The material is scattered through inventories of collections and through letters of humanists as

they were published two hundred years ago by the indefatigable Mehus. But despite his efforts and his meticulous precision, the epistolarium of Traversari, (Ambrosius Traversarius, *Latinae Epistolae . . .* , ed. P. Cannetus and L. Mehus [Florence, 1759]), is probably still incomplete (L. Bertalot, "Zwölf Briefe des Ambrogio Traversari," *RQuSchr,* XXIX [1915], 91 ff.; G. Mercati, *"Studi e Testi,"* 90, *Ultimi contributi alla storia degli umanisti* [Vatican City, 1939]. Poggio's letters have been edited only in part in the (extremely rare) edition of Tonellis: Poggio Bracciolini, *Epistolae,* ed. T. de Tonellis (Florence, 1831 ff.). Niccolo Niccoli's epistolarium seems to be lost. Among inventories the catalogue of the collection of antiques of Pietro Barbo, that is Pope Paul II, has been published *in extenso* (Ministero della Pubblica Istruzione, *Documenti inediti per servire alla storia dei musei d'Italia* [Rome, 1878 ff.]), those of the Medici collections incompletely (E. Müntz, *Les collections des Médicis au XV siècle* . . . [Paris, 1888]). Hence, any attempt to give an even partially complete survey of Florentine collections and collectors in the first half of the Quattrocento is impossible. Nor can any interpretation of the spirit in which these collections were built up be more than tentative at best.

23. Antonio Pavino, as quoted by Mehus in Traversari, *op. cit.,* I, xviii f.

24. Ciriaco d'Ancona, as quoted by Müntz, *Les collections des Médicis au XV siècle* . . . pp. 3 f.

25. Timoteo Maffei, *In Magnificentiae Cosmi Medicei Detractores,* in G. Lami, *Deliciae Eruditorum,* XII (1742), 155 limits himself to general terms: ". . . videritque . . . marmoreas statuas picturasque egregias . . ." Mr. Ernst Gombrich has been good enough to inform me that the account of the Medici collection of antiques as given by Alberto Avogadrio from Vercelli (Albertus Avogadrius), *De Religione et Magnificentia Cosimi Medices Florentini* (ca. 1455) in G. Lami, *op. cit.,* pp. 147 ff., must be discounted since Avogadrio probably wrote from hearsay. (See now, Gombrich, "The Early Medici as Patrons of Art," *Norm and Form* [London, 1966], pp. 35 ff.)

26. Lorenzo Ghiberti, *Lorenzo Ghiberti's*

Denkwürdigkeiten (I Commentarii), 2 vols., ed. J. von Schlosser, I (Berlin, 1912), 47.

27. Müntz, *Les collections des Médicis au XV siècle* . . . (Paris, 1888), pp. 11 ff., 38 f.

28. Vespasiano da Bisticci, *Vite di uomini illustri . . .* , ed. A. Mai and Z. Bartoli (Florence, 1859), p. 470.

29. Poggio's funeral oration for Niccoli as quoted in excerpts by Mehus, in Traversari, *op. cit.,* I, li.

30. Traversari, *op. cit.,* II, cols. 393 ff., 417 (Lib. VIII, ep. 35, 48).

31. Gianozzo Manetti, as quoted by Mehus in Traversari, *op. cit.,* I, li.

32. Bisticci, *op. cit.,* pp. 476 ff.

33. Poggio, as quoted by Mehus, in Traversari, *loc. cit.;* Bisticci, *op. cit.,* pp. 476, 480; Traversari *op. cit.* vol., II cols. 393 f. (Lib. VIII, ep. 35).

34. Guarino Veronese, *Epistolario di Guarino Veronese,* ed. R. Sabbadini, I-III (*"Miscellanea di storia veneta,"* ed. R. Deputazione veneta di storia patria, ser. 3, VIII, XI, XIV), I (Venice, 1915 ff.), 33 ff., esp. 38, letter to Biagio Guasconi, dated 1413.

35. Traversari, *op. cit.,* II, cols. 411 ff. (Lib. VIII, ep. 45).

36. This is the meaning of the term *veterum helementorum forma,* as witness Alberti's corresponding usage in *Della pittura,* ed. H. Janitschek (*Quellenschriften für Kunstgeschichte,* XI [Vienna, 1877]), 149: see below, note 50.

37. Bartolommeo Fazio (Bartolomeus Fazius), *De Viris Illustribus,* ed. L. Mehus (Florence, 1745), p. 11.

38. Bisticci, *op. cit.,* pp. 478 ff.

39. *Ibid.,* p. 480.

40. G. Poggi, *Il Duomo di Firenze* (Kunsthistorisches Institut in Florenz, *Italienische Forschungen,* II [Berlin, 1909]), doc. 905.

41. Leonardo Bruni, *Epistolarum Libri VIII,* ed. L. Mehus, II (Florence, 1741), 134 ff., esp. 143 (Lib. IX, ep. 2.).

42. "Pollicitus fuit mihi Romanus quidam civis lapillum cum Narcisso in aqua sese vidente, quem averat Ostiae dum foderetur inventum. Hunc ego laeto animo exspec-

tabam ut tibi qui harum rerum studiosus es gratificarer. Statueram enim illum ad te mittere quam primum essem assecutus. Verum mihi iste qui promiserat . . . fidem fregit . . ." (H. Baron, *Leonardo Bruni Aretino* ["*Quellen zur Geistesgeschichte des Mittelalters und der Renaissance*," I] [Leipzig, 1928], 105 ff., with the date March 1407). The letter is missing from Mehus' edition of Bruni's letters, *op. cit.;* but he quotes the above passage with slight variations in his introduction to Traversari, *op. cit.,* I, liii.

43. The passages referring to Poggio's collecting activities have been compiled from his letters by Mehus (Traversari, *op. cit.,* I, lii ff.) and by E. Walser, *Poggius Florentinus, Leben und Werke* ("*Beiträge zur Kulturgeschichte des Mittelalters und der Renaissance,*" XIV (Leipzig and Berlin, 1914), pp. 147 ff.

44. Poggio, *op. cit.,* I, 213 ff. (Lib. III, ep. 15).

45. *Ibid.,* p. 284 (Lib. III, ep. 37).

46. *Ibid.,* pp. 322 ff. (Lib. IV, ep. 12).

47. *Ibid.,* pp. 330 ff. (Lib. IV, ep. 15). In the last sentence I have emended the word *"ipsum"* to *"ipsam."*

48. *Ibid.,* pp. 374 ff. (Lib. IV, ep. 21).

49. I fail to see how Gutkind, an understanding scholar, could characterize Poggio's attitude as "the learned sentimentality of a recording antiquarian": C. S. Gutkind, "Poggio Bracciolini's geistige Entwicklung," *Deutsche Vierteljahrsschrift für Geistesgeschichte*, X (1932), 548 ff.

50. Bisticci, *op. cit.,* p. 476; L. B. Alberti, *Leone Battista Alberti's kleinere Kunsttheoretische Schriften*, ed. H. Janitschek ("*Quellenschriften für Kunst-*

geschichte," XI) (Vienna, 1877), p. 47 (*Della Pittura,* dedicatory preface).

51. Ciriaco d'Ancona, as quoted by Müntz, *Les Collections . . .* (Paris, 1888), p. 3. Baldinucci still saw among the papers of Cristofano Berardi the original list of antiques Ghiberti owned at the time of his death: F. Baldinucci, *Notizie dei professori del disegno . . .* (Florence, 1845 ff.) (first published 1681), p. 355.

In years of masterful research Schlosser (1903) has attempted to reconstruct the collection. Albertini in 1510 was shown "excellent pieces by the hand of Polyclitus in the house of the Ghibertis and a carved marble vase which Lorenzo caused to be brought from Greece": F. Albertini, *Memoriale di molte statue et picture sono nella inclyta cipta di Florentia* (Florence, 1510), p. 12 (facsimile ed. H. Horne, London, 1909); Vasari, in 1550, listed a bronze leg, lifesize, male and female heads, some torsi, finally the *letto di Policleto*, apparently a bronze relief with an erotic scene (or possibly a funeral meal; O. Siren, *Studier i florentinsk Renassansskulptur . . .* [Stockholm, 1909], pp. 109 ff.). These pieces were sold by Ghiberti's grandson to Monsignor Giovanni Gaddi. From Gaddi's collection Schlosser has traced the *letto di Policleto* further to Prague, a satyr torso to the Uffizi. An eighteenth-century commentator of Vasari mentions two *torsi* of Venus, one of the Medici type, a genius, a Narcissus and a Mercury. Yet, the fact that with increasing distance in time these reports become ever more specific, deprives them of much of their value. After all, a good number of the objects may have been acquired by his son, Vittorio, or by his grandson after Ghiberti's death. Others may have disappeared.

Postscript

This chapter from *Lorenzo Ghiberti* started from the contrasting approaches to ancient art obtaining during the fourteenth century among artists and collectors on one hand, humanist scholars on the other: that of the former naive and visual, of the latter cerebral and literary. The gradual rapprochement during the first third of the fifteenth century of these points of view and the establishment of personal contacts between small groups of scholars and artists in Florence seems to me decisive for the beginnings of the Renaissance right there. These contacts on the scholars' side lead to a new approach to collecting and to an acceptance both of visual and esthetic rather than literary standards and of artists' judgments on art, if not of their overall point of view. Concomitantly the artists bow to the humanists' learning in interpreting the content of ancient art. However, I did leave open the question of the scholars' immediate impact on the artists' understanding and reception of the language of ancient art.

In a recent paper Ernst Gombrich has set out to close this gap. He reasons that the humanists at the very beginning of the century, in the first place Niccoli, in a spirit of rebellious criticism start from a reform of Latin spelling and lettering with the aim to eliminate thoroughly "ingrained errors"; that Niccoli as early as 1413 busied himself likewise with the externals (the spelling, as it were) of Roman building; that Brunelleschi similarly eliminated "ingrained errors" by distilling from the pseudo-Roman buildings of Florence, such as the Baptistery, his vocabulary 'all'antica'; that in short, the same critical attitude led Niccoli to the reform of letters and Brunelleschi to the reform of architecture and perspective. Here, then, lies if not the answer, perhaps the basis for answers to the question I left open in my own chapter. What one wants to know is, after all, how this critical attitude was transmitted; whether Niccoli explained the problem to Brunelleschi; whether he called his attention to Roman building; and, if so, whether Brunelleschi really drew exclusively on the pseudo-Roman churches of eleventh century Florence; or whether it was not Brunelleschi who surveying the ruins of Rome "su striscie di pergamene . . . con numero d'abbaco e carattere . . ." pointed out in 1413 or before, their importance and character to Niccoli. But this means writing another chapter.

There are two notes to be added to the chapter as it stands. One concerns the last paragraph and its references to Lorenzo's collection. My wife and faithful collaborator has been able to track down a few documents which tell us a bit more about its history after Lorenzo's death (*AB*, 1964). Alas, the itemized list, still extant in 1682, has not yet turned up. Second, I forgot to include in the notes the charming study of my friend J. B. Ross (1938).

Additional Bibliography

Gombrich, Ernst. "From the Revival of Letters to the Reform of the Arts. Niccolo Niccoli and Filippo Brunelleschi," *Essays in the History of Art presented to Rudolf Wittkower* (London, 1967), pp. 71 ff.

Krautheimer-Hess, T. "More Ghibertiana," *AB*, XLIV (1964), 307 ff.

J. B. Ross, "A study of twelfth-century interest in the antiquities of Rome," *Medieval and historiographical essays in honor of James Westfall Thompson*, Chicago, 1938, pp. 302 ff.

17

A DRAWING BY JACOPO DELLA QUERCIA? *

SOME TIME AGO, a drawing measuring nine by twenty centimeters appeared on the art market (Fig. 116); Mr. E. Schilling, the curator of Prints and Drawings at the Staedel Institute of Frankfurt-am-Main, classified it as an Italian drawing of around 1400.[1] The drawing is executed with pen and brown ink, outlined in sanguine, on paper that is tinted yellow in the upper part and left white below. A saint is represented, young and beardless, who faces to the right and carries a book in his hands. His head, with its soft curling hair, is inclined slightly to the left; the left foot rests firmly on the ground and the right leg is bent and meets the base only at the tip of the foot. An ample cloak covers the figure; at its feet a plinth is indicated, sketched in with a few lines.

The pen stroke is short and very incisive; the modelling is suggested by means of cross-hatching and brief pen strokes, the highlights are accentuated by letting the white of the ground show through. Everything is directed towards the sculptural effect: to the spectator's right, the figure stands forth sharply from the ground; to the left, folds surround the leg, heightening the plastic values. The swelling movement of the cloak pushes forward the right arm of the saint. The artist obviously had no intention of spreading the parts of the body over the available surface; no intention, that is, of filling the page in calligraphic style. He aims instead at the compact corporeality of the figure, at its full relief, making a three-dimensional creation of it, and placing it in an immediate relationship with its surroundings. The limbs, gathered around an axis which passes through the left leg of the figure, turn in a rotary movement. The plinth strictly limits the figure isolating it in every direction. This is not a painterly concept; it is the concept of a sculptor.

Before the Quattrocento, the novel idea of developing a sculpture from every visual standpoint, of giving it real substance, was not imaginable; this idea was formulated only in the first decades of the fifteenth century and it developed slowly. It was then that in Italian sculpture the problems came to the fore that we mentioned above: to create a human body as a stereometric figure, to develop it in every dimension, to place it in relationship with its surroundings.

Throughout Italy, in every province, new ideas were formulated and developed in this period, but especially in Tuscany, in Florence and Siena. Whereas in Florence these new principles were already visible in the very first years of the

*Translated by Marjorie M. Licht from *La Diana,* III (1928), 276–79.

new century, in the first youthful works of Donatello and Nanni di Banco, creating a new stability of the figure and a clear and distinct articulation of the structure of the organism based on scientific knowledge of the laws of nature, in Siena they were still tied to the artistic ideals of the fourteenth century with remarkable firmness. Up to 1420, Sienese artists clung to the slender, spiritual figure—the delicate and tremulous hands, the limbs intertwined in serpentine patterns. The sweetness and delicacy of the fluid and ethereal body was brought together with the new notions of a sculptural control of movement in space. This singular confrontation of new and old concepts is characteristic also of the drawing which we have been discussing; only in Siena could a sculpture similar to this young saint have been conceived.

There is one sculptor whose work dominates Sienese sculpture in these first decades of the Quattrocento: Jacopo della Quercia. Our drawing, if it is not from his own hand, certainly came into being under his direct influence.

Naturally we must not consider his late style—the main portal of San Petronio in Bologna (1425–38), the baptismal font of San Giovanni in Siena (1419–31); after 1420, the work of Jacopo della Quercia demonstrates a fullness and monumentality lacking in our drawing. But one must keep in mind that Jacopo achieved this late style step by step. One can observe the evolution of it in the sculptures of the Fonte Gaia (1414–19);[2] in the *Giustizia,* for instance, which must have been one of the earliest figures executed, one can still see the slender delicacy of his youthful works. In the *Sapienza,* probably the latest figure for the fountain, the new impulse towards monumentality is already evident.

Before beginning work on the Fonte Gaia, during the years 1412–1413, Jacopo della Quercia was working on four figures of saints for the altar of the Trenta family in the church of San Frediano in Lucca (Fig. 117);[3] it is to these figures that the saint of our drawing should be compared. Here we find the same slender bodies, animated and serpentine, the same heads poised gracefully on the neck, the same hands slithering forth like snakes from the folds of the mantle. Here is the same manner of placing the figure hesitantly on the toes of feet which are too small, of turning the body at the waist; one sees the same emphasis on the solid parts of the body and the same manner of relating them to the surrounding space. There is, in the altar and in the drawing, the same mixture of the new sculptural problems with elements from the Trecento.

Let us compare the details of the drawing with the figures from the altar: the Saint Ursula has the same bodily structure as the saint in the drawing: the left leg is bent and turned to the rear; tube-like folds fall from the right thigh; the same pleat of the mantle, fluid and serpentine, defines the neck to the left. The gathered folds on the left leg of the saint in the drawing are so much like those of the Saint Lawrence on the altar that they would seem interchangeable; like his are the locks of hair, the long fluent neck, the tapered hands with the ends of the fingers bent. The carefully worked head of the saint in the drawing with its nervous outline and the fold of skin under the chin is very similar to the head of the Saint Jerome of the altar: the mouth, the eyes, the eyebrows, the structure of the cheekbones are nearly identical.

Surely the drawing represents a lost sculpture from the hand of Jacopo della Quercia, made during the period in which he was executing the earliest figures of the Trenta altar, that is, around 1411–13. One cannot say with absolute assurance that the drawing is from his own hand. There are no positively documented drawings by him; the project for the Fonte Gaia which has recently been discovered by Mr. Lanyi [4] was not attributed by him to the artist himself and there is therefore no possible comparison. Our drawing could have been made by a student after a work of the master or it could be one of Jacopo's sculptural projects, drawn by an assistant, as is probably the case with the project for the Fonte Gaia. Both are possibilities, but there are elements which make one think directly of the master himself: the drawing has a breath of liveliness (especially in the strokes of chalk sanguine which appear under the pen strokes), a quickness, a lightness, a deftness in delineating the contours of the head, a mixture of the sweet and the bitter in its mood, which tempt us to exclude a minor hand. It is a drawing of the first quality and it is this quality which is decisive.

Let us propose, then, that in the first years of the second decade of the fifteenth century, Jacopo della Quercia executed the sculpture that we see in our drawing. We cannot specify for which work the statue was destined, but one hypothesis, deserves discussion.

The stucco cast of the half figure of a female Saint in the Museo Industriale in Bologna (Fig. 118), so far unpublished, belongs apparently to the same years in which the altar of the Trenta family was executed; in this work, too, the fluid pleating of the mantle follows the curve of the neck—as in the Sant Ursula of the altar; the great folds fall from the thigh; the hands are elongated and slender. The same affinities, then, unite both the stucco cast and our drawing to the Trenta altar. On a stylistic basis the cast must, like the drawing, represent an original, now lost, from these same years. Since this hypothetical original and the sculpture represented in our drawing were so close in style, one might imagine both of them to have been once part of an altar, now lost, similar to that of the Trenta family. This, too, is conjecture; only one thing is absolutely certain: that the drawing which we publish here is the reflection of a work by the great Sienese master.

Notes

1. The drawing has passed to the Boymans Museum in Rotterdam from the Koenigs collection in Haarlem. It was published for the first time in the catalog of the Boerner sale (Leipzig, December 28, 1912), number 141, under the title "Gothic, around 1350."

2. Five years separate the project of 1409 from the beginning of work.

3. Cf. the new documents published by E. Lazzareschi in the *Bulletino senese di storia patria,* XXXII (1925), 63 ff. The Madonna must, for stylistic reasons, have been executed later than the four saints, perhaps in 1416, the year in which Quercia returned to Lucca. Later still, in 1422, the bas reliefs of the predella were executed.

4. F. Lanyi, "Der Entwurf zur Fonte Gaia in Siena," *Zeitschrift für bildende Kunst,* LXI (1927), 257 ff.

Postscript

I am as convinced as ever that the drawing discussed in this paper represents a lost statue by Jacopo della Quercia and that this statue was close to the saints he carved for the Trenta altar at S. Frediano in Lucca. I also maintain for this lost statue the date suggested here, about 1412. This I do despite the continued discussion regarding the date of these saints: a date of 1416–1422, as suggested by A. C. Hanson and James H. Beck, for the entire altar rather than for the predella only (and perhaps the Madonna?) does not yet convince me. On the other hand, the drawing is certainly not by Quercia himself; I was doubtful in 1929, but now I am certain.

When the essay was prepared for publication in *La Diana,* I had compared the figure reproduced in the drawing with the stucco of the half figure of a female saint in the Museo Industriale at Bologna (Fig. 118), which obviously reflects another lost work of Quercia from roughly the same time. In its place and without my knowledge (I was sent no proof sheets), in the printed version the mediocre statue of a Madonna was illustrated and my text correspondingly altered. It was just one of those things. I had never seen that Madonna before, thought it terrible, and believed the incident would end my career as an art historian. Well, it did not. A few years later to my great surprise, I saw the piece in the inner sanctum of an art dealer on the Via Sistina: it was just as poor and as far from Quercia as the reproduction had suggested. I am glad that in republishing the little essay I can restore text and illustrations to the original version.

Additional Bibliography

Beck, J. H. Review of Anne Coffin Hanson, *Jacopo della Quercia's Fonte Gaia,* in *AB,* XLVIII (1966), 114 ff.

Hanson, A. C. *Jacopo della Quercia's Fonte Gaia* ("Oxford-Warburg Series") (Oxford, 1965), with bibliography through 1962.

Krautheimer, R. "A Drawing for the Fonte Gaia in Siena," *BMMA,* n.s., X (1952), 265 ff.

Seymour, C., "Fatto di sua mano," *Festschrift Ulrich Middeldorf* (Berlin, 1968), pp. 93 ff.

18

TERRACOTTA MADONNAS *

THE ART OF THE ITALIAN RENAISSANCE is so well known in all of its details that it seems hardly possible to find any new and interesting aspect of it. The relation between the single Italian schools, for instance, or between that of Venice and that of Florence, the work of the leading artists, the genesis of Italian Renaissance art all seem entirely clarified. Nevertheless even such well known works of art as the Tuscan terracotta Madonnas, examples of which are to be found in every large collection in Europe and America, may, if seen from a new angle, sometimes open new vistas which, besides clarifying the relation between single artists and explaining the development of their style, go far beyond the limits of the Renaissance back into Byzantine art.

In the courtyard of the Cà d'oro in Venice behind the beautiful façade which looks onto the Canale Grande, stands a large marble well-head (Fig. 119). Rich late-Gothic foliage grows up from the socle, two stems on each of the four sides of the well; emerging from the foliage are four heads at the corners of the well and the figure of one of the cardinal virtues on each side. The work has always been known and its history has been clarified by Paoletti and Planiscig. It was done by Bartolommeo Buon, the leading Venetian sculptor of the first half of the fifteenth century, and it was his first independent work. He was paid for it in 1427 when he was probably in his early twenties. Likewise, its historical place in the development of Venetian sculpture has never been questioned. The style of the well-head itself, with the four heads at the corners and the cardinal virtues on the sides, is familiar in the tradition of Venice and the type of the work not only influenced quite a number of later works in Venice, but it also leads clearly to the later works of Bartolommeo Buon at the Porta della Carta.

But what strangely enough has never been mentioned is that this well-head of the Cà d'oro might take quite an important place also in the history of Florentine sculpture—to say it more precisely, in the history of Lorenzo Ghiberti and his atelier. The Caritas on one side of the well-head is recognizable by the blazing flame she holds in her right hand. This hand emerges from a bundle of folds that conceal, or better replace the arm which ought to be here, and thus form a strange contrast to the complicated and nevertheless logical

*From *Parnassus*, VIII (1936), 4–8.

arrangement of forms on the opposite side. The figure represents a familiar type: a seated virgin with the child sitting on her left hand. The back of the child is turned towards the spectator but its head is turned over its left shoulder so that it looks straight ahead while its forehead leans towards the cheek of the mother, a movement which seems to be interrupted. Its left arm skews towards its right shoulder between the head of the mother and its own head, while its right arm is pressed against its right side. While the right foot is visible only under the hand of the mother, the left leg, which is rather long, crosses over her breast. The foot seeks hold, without finding it, on the large fold which crosses from the right arm of the Caritas to her left knee. From there a rich pyramid of folds slants down, balanced by a shorter triangular fold over her right knee.

Now it is obvious (and it seems most strange that nobody has yet referred to it) that the upper part of this Caritas is actually identical with the type of a bust of the Madonna with child, examples of which are to be found in many churches in Italy and in most of the larger museums of Europe and America (Fig. 120) and which have been attributed by Bode and by others with some slight hesitation to Ghiberti and have been dated to his later period between 1430 and 1450. These busts are all similar in character and it is logical to assume that they all are derived from a common prototype. They consist either of terracotta or stucco, most of them being painted; and they all show the virgin and child in generally the same attitude as the Caritas of Bartolommeo Buon. It is the same twisted position of the child, the same characteristic design of the heads of mother and child, of the child's body and its left leg which all envelop the right side of the group in a large semicircular sweep. Only a few particulars in the terrocotta Madonnas are different from the Caritas of Bartolommeo Buon, and they are just such particulars which prove that the Caritas depends on these terracotta virgins—i.e., on their common prototype—and not vice versa. In the terracotta madonnas the child actually presses its head against the cheek of the Virgin; the movement, in the Caritas interrupted, is complete in the madonnas, where both heads together with the arm of the child form one coherent curve. The left leg of the child which in the Caritas is seeking in vain for a hold in the folds of her robe, rests firmly on the arm of the madonna. And this right arm with its hand which Bartolommeo Buon disengaged in such a clumsy way in order to transform the virgin into a Caritas, forms in the terracotta madonnas the basis for the whole group and connects itself with the complicated arrangement of forms on the right side. There can be no doubt that the Caritas of Bartolommeo Buon has drawn upon the prototype of these terracotta virgins.

Three questions arise: first whether there existed an earlier prototype (which is no longer preserved) on which not only the preserved busts but also the Caritas in Venice depend; second, whether or not the prototype and the preserved examples of these busts are related to Ghiberti; and third, whether these terracotta busts are earlier or later than 1430.

The first question is already answered by the Caritas in Venice: if Bartolommeo

Buon used the type in 1427, the model on which he drew must have been created before this date, and likewise all the preserved terracotta busts must depend on this same early prototype which unfortunately is lost. (Art history in this case has to use the methods of archaeology which almost always reconstructs the lost prototype after the copies preserved, and we should do it less hesitatingly than we usually do.) The second question, whether this prototype was created, not only before 1427, but by Ghiberti himself, allows only a hypothetical answer. But again the well-head in the Cà d'oro enables us to make this answer perhaps more affirmative, for the four heads at the corners of this well-head are certainly inspired by Ghiberti, more precisely by the heads on the frame of his first bronze door. The head on the right of the Caritas has the same broad, round and solid face, the same protruding cheekbones, the slanted eyes, the broad nose, the heavy flowing curls as have some of the heads on the first door, *e.g.* the head of the laughing girl (Fig. 121), or another head which is copied after a Hellenistic bust of Alexander. Also the way in which the heads in Venice emerge from the foliage recalls the much more logical way in which Ghiberti's heads emerge from their quatrefoil. Without being outright copies, Bartolommeo Buon's heads are so definitely inspired by the heads on Ghiberti's frame that a direct relation between his early style and Ghiberti's first door must be assumed. Thus it becomes likely also that the model of the Caritas, the virgin and child, was not just any Florentine model, but that this model also was connected with Ghiberti. And this is proved by the style of this Caritas: the folds over her knees are identical with Ghiberti's draperies on the first door, *e.g.* in the reclining figure of Mary in the Nativity; and they are very similar to the draperies in the figures of St. Luke, St. John, St. Matthew, and Christ among the Doctors (Fig. 113). Thus an immediate connection to Ghiberti in his earlier period, when he did the first door, becomes evident; not only for the Caritas of Bartolommeo Buon, but also for the prototype from which he drew his Caritas and from which the terracotta and stucco replicas took the busts of the virgin and child.

A connection between Bartolommeo and Ghiberti can even be assumed on a documentary basis: in 1424 or 1425 Ghiberti went for some time to Venice in order to escape the epidemic which at this time ravaged Florence. Now it may be that he brought with him wax models or drawings of the first door which he had completed the year before; or it may be that Bartolommeo Buon worked for some time in Ghiberti's atelier at Venice. It may also be that Bartolommeo accompanied him when he went back to Florence. The way in which Bartolommeo came in contact with Ghiberti and with his first door is finally irrelevant; it is pertinent only that he became so much impressed by Ghiberti that he drew upon him when two or three years later he did his first independent work—the well-head of the Cà d'oro in Venice.

As to the preserved terracotta busts of the virgin and child, one point has still to be made clear. The examples which are preserved certainly do not show the three phases of Ghiberti's earlier style as it manifests itself on the first door: a first realistic stage (Abraham, Nativity), a second stage that is characterized by a decorative lyricism of design and content (Last Supper, Christ Among the Doctors), and a third classical stage that develops gradually from the second style (Pentecost, Bearing of the Cross).

The preserved busts of the virgin and child (and here we come to the last of the three questions which we referred to above) do not fit into any of these periods of Ghiberti's style before 1424, the date of the termination of the first door. They present the definite characteristics of his later style, as manifested on the second door, 1425–45: the folds are thin and strand-like, the face, although it is square in its general contour, is composed of thin features, a straight forehead, a pointed chin, a thin nose, small rather distant eyes, and a little mouth. One may compare the busts with any of the heads of the figures of the second door. Thus the samples preserved, although they may be products of Ghiberti's atelier, are certainly late, not early, and, as Bode assumed, executed between 1430 and 1450.

The prototype, however, from which they as well as the Caritas are derived, must have been entirely different in style: the full, round faces of the Caritas of Bartolommeo Buon and of her boy, their heavy flowing locks, the soft and full lines of the drapery are much more similar to the heads and the draperies of Ghiberti's first door. If we transpose the preserved busts into the style of the Caritas we get a much clearer idea of the appearance of the early prototype on which all these busts depend.

Thus this one type of the madonna with the child on her arm can with great probability be derived from Ghiberti; the prototype certainly can be dated before 1427, perhaps in the last period of the first door, between 1416 and 1424. This one type only is meant, for there exist quite a number of other full figures and busts in terracotta or stucco, which commonly are brought into a more or less close connection with Ghiberti. Some of them may indeed belong to him or his atelier, although their types are somewhat different from the one dealt with. Two other groups (they are rather large) can be attributed to the Master of Modena and to the Master of the Pellegrini Chapel in St. Anastasia at Verona, who, although both were influenced by Ghiberti, are individualities, definitely different from him and from his atelier. Of a much greater interest, however, is one other group of terracotta virgins, which Bode has attributed also to Ghiberti. It seems, however, so different from the first group that this hypothesis can hardly be maintained. In this second type (examples of which are to be found in the National Gallery of Art, Washington, D.C. [formerly Kaiser Friedrich Museum, Berlin] [Fig. 122]; in the Museo Bardini in Florence; at S. Andrea in Siena, etc.) the boy, instead of sitting on the arm of his mother and pressing his face against her cheek, stands in front of her. He rests his left foot on the left side of his mother—perhaps on the arm of a chair or on a window sill—and steps toward her right side. Evidently he is afraid of something; he therefore presses himself against her breast while with his left (or sometimes with both hands he grasps her right shoulder; in most cases he has seized also a lappet of her headdress and sometimes he tries to draw it from her left shoulder over his breast. But he cannot get away: his mother holds with her left hand either his left foot or his left hip while with her right hand she slightly supports him under his left shoulder. Although variants occur more frequently in this second type than they do in the first one—the step of the boy varies in length, the mother sometimes bends her head slightly, sometimes the boy steps back rather than advances because his mother tickles his throat—the main features are so clear that here also a common prototype has to be assumed.

This prototype has evidently inspired also the features of the madonna and of the child in all the preserved instances of this second group. The face of the virgin is rather pointed, much more definitely triangular than are the faces of Ghiberti's women in any period. Compared with them, the forehead is more definitely curved, the eyes are larger and stand closer to each other, the mouth is more clearly defined, the nose is strong and very definite. The curls are rather short and much lighter than in Ghiberti's work (Figs. 120, 122). The hands of the Virgins in this second group are long and strong and they know how to grip and how to hold, in contrast to the soft and forceless hands that through the whole of his development remain so characteristic of Ghiberti and that characterize also the first group of the terracotta madonnas. The boy in the Ghiberti group is what one would call "such a pretty child" with a face that seems to apprehend the seriousness of his future life. In the second group he is just a "tough little fellow" without any kind of presentiment. Both groups are entirely different in composition as well as in the single features, and if the prototype of the first one is close to Ghiberti (as we believe), the second one certainly cannot be related to him. No similar type and no similar details can be found in the whole of his work.

The large and rather classical face—classical in spite of the fact that in the Washington group (Fig. 122) the artist has softened it somewhat—the long and strong hands, the short curls, the vigorous type of the boy all recall much more the sculpture of Siena in the second decade of the fifteenth century. Similar heads and curls, corresponding hands, analogous movements, and comparable draperies are characteristic of the work of Jacopo della Quercia, the great Sienese sculptor in the period between 1412 and 1419 when he did his Trenta Altar at Lucca and the Fonte Gaia at Siena. A comparison with the head of the Acca, the nude figure standing on the left corner of the Fonte Gaia or with any other figure of this period of Quercia will make this clear (Fig. 124).

Thus it might be worthwhile to consider whether the prototype (again we refer to the prototype, not to the examples preserved) of this second group was perhaps invented in the atelier of Quercia. This is an hypothesis which was already considered sixty years ago when *all* the different types of terracotta and stucco Virgins were attributed to Quercia (until Bode attributed them *all* to Ghiberti and to his atelier) in spite of the evident dissimilarities among the various groups. Both of these hypotheses overlooked these dissimilarities, and at the same time, both are too indistinct and unlimited; but it seems that among the vast number of Tuscan terracotta madonnas one group in its original prototype can be related to Ghiberti, while another one might go back to Quercia.

The most striking feature in all these types of the madonna is undoubtedly the intimate relation between mother and child. The mother carries the boy on her hand, the boy seems to be shy and presses his cheek against the face of his mother; or, in the second group, she holds him in front of her while he tries to escape from her arm and at the same time hides his head at her bosom; or else she tickles him and makes him lean back from her. No wonder that these motives have been praised as a characteristic element of the new style of the Quattrocento, as a sign of the new humanization which "makes the Early Renaissance the first modern style" and as a sign of the decisive place which Florence takes in this movement of humanization. Actually the way in which these motives are expressed may be new, but the motives themselves are much older, and the history of these motives is one of those characteristic features that illuminate in one flash the genesis of a whole period. For all these motives lead back from the Quattrocento to the Trecento and from there back to the Dugento and finally into Byzantine art.

The first type, the mother who presses her baby against her face, occurs several times in Florentine painting during the second half of the fourteenth century, for instance in a painting by Giovanni del Biondo in the Vatican Gallery of about 1370 to 1380 (all the paintings referred to are reproduced in van Marle, *History of Italian Painting,* Vols. I, II, III), in a painting in the Lehman Collection in New York (attributed by van Marle to a follower of Daddi), and in a third painting in the Corsini Gallery in Florence of about 1360 (attributed by Van Marle to another follower of Daddi). In the first of these paintings the Virgin stands holding the child with both arms against her left shoulder and just touching his forehead with her cheek; in the second painting she is seated, but the child stands on her left knee. Both paintings are similar to the later terracotta groups only in the one motive of the child pressing against the mother's face. In the third painting the connection seems to be closer since the child is seated on the left arm of the mother, his left leg dangling while his right leg crosses over her breast and seeks a hold on her right forearm. Even more similar is a painting formerly in the Kaiser Friedrich Museum in Berlin (attributed by van Marle to a Pistoian follower of Giotto about 1340–1350): the mother holds the child tightly in her right arm and bends her head. She presses the baby firmly against her face while he looks toward the spectator and leans his right leg against her left arm. This is a motive really akin to the terracotta madonnas of the first group, but it would be in vain to try to trace it farther back in Florentine painting to Giotto. It is connected much more closely with a virgin of the school of Pacino di Buonaguida in the Johnson collection in Philadelphia where the child's pose is exactly as in the terracotta virgins. From here the group can be traced only outside Florence. One trend continues to Siena where above all Ambrogio Lorenzetti uses the motif in his Madonnas. Before him the motive occurs in thirteenth-century madonnas in the Carmine Church at Siena and formerly in the Kaiser Friedrich Museum at Berlin. Another trend—and this trend may be even more important—goes back to Lucca, as far back as to a painting in the Academy in Florence of about 1250 attributed by van Marle to the school of Bonaventura Berlinghieri: again the mother presses the child against her face and again the child stretches his legs against her forearm. In these paintings of the thirteenth century the relation to Byzantine art becomes evident. Indeed it is this motive which is characteristic of one of the two Byzantine types of "Glykophilusa" or "Elëusa," the "tenderly loving" or "merciful" virgin. Quite common in Byzantine icons and manuscripts (Fig. 123), both these types must have been known at least since the eleventh century, since about 1085 they influenced one of the murals in the church of S. Clemente in Rome and not very much later a statue of the virgin at St. Maria im Kapitol in Cologne.

In a similar way the motives of the second, the Quercia group, can be traced back; again we find them in Florence in the sphere of Bernardo Daddi, in his triptych at the Bigallo of 1333. And again the motive ultimately goes back to Byzantine art, to the second type of the "Glykophilusa" as she is represented in a marble icon in San Marco at Venice where the child even grasps the headdress of the mother.

In other words, the seemingly new and realistic motives of the terracotta and stucco virgins of the early fifteenth century (both Florentine and Sienese) show perhaps a new humanized attitude. But the "realistic" feeling on which this attitude is based and which has created the motives is old: it has come to Italy from Byzantium and it has taken the way through those cities which have always been related to Byzantium, through Siena and Lucca (and probably also Pisa). Florence came in touch with it hardly before the middle of the fourteenth century. It is the route which we very often can trace where realistic motives of the fourteenth and fifteenth centuries are concerned; the seemingly realistic motive in many cases reveals itself as a Byzantine motive which is only developed on Italian soil, first in Siena and later in Florence. It is Byzantium that inspires the new art of the Italian Trecento and through it the Italian Renaissance. Whether Byzantium really created the new motive in the eleventh century remains rather doubtful; we would not be astonished if one day also the "Glykophilusa" and with it the terracotta madonnas of the early Quattrocento in Florence and Siena could be traced back from Byzantine art of the eleventh century to the Christian art of late antiquity.

Postscript

This was the first paper I wrote after coming to the United States, and I wish I could rewrite it in better English, more lucidly presented, with wider knowledge of the scattered material, and with a firmer grip on the many problems involved. Over the last thirty years excellent work has been done on the terracotta madonnas, notably by

John Pope-Hennessy. Even so, the problem still awaits comprehensive treatment: groupings as to regions, workshops, masters; prototypes and derivatives; dating; in some cases, authenticity; social background. Probably this is beyond the competence of anybody at this point. It is certainly beyond mine.

As I am going over the illustrations for this old essay, I am struck by another Ghibertian element in the Venetian well-head which had escaped me thirty years ago: the head of the youth with flying locks, to the right of the *Caritas*, is obviously, it seems to me, derived from a head on Ghiberti's bronze door, itself purloined from a Roman battle sarcophagus (Fig. 125).

Additional Bibliography

Since the paper was not provided with footnotes, I think it fair to include in the bibliography the most important works published prior to 1936 as well as those published since.

Bode, W. *Florentiner Bildhauer der Renaissance* (Berlin, 1921), pp. 73 ff.

Fiocco, G. "Michele da Firenze," *Dedalo,* XII (1932), 542 ff.

Hanson, A. C. *Jacopo della Quercia's Fonte Gaia* (Oxford-Warburg Series) (Oxford, 1965).

Krautheimer, R., and Krautheimer-Hess, T., *Lorenzo Ghiberti* (Princeton, 1956).

Offner, R. *Corpus of Florentine Painting* (New York, 1930 ff.).

Paoletti, P. *L'architettura e la scultura del Rinascimento in Venezia* (Venice, 1893).

Planiscig, L. "Die Bildhauer Venedigs in der ersten Hälfte des Quattrocento," *JKS,* n.f. IV (1930), 48 ff.

Pope Hennessy, J. *Italian Gothic Sculpture* (London-New York, 1955).

———, ed. *Catalogue of Italian Sculpture in the Victoria and Albert Museum,* I (London, 1964).

19

ALBERTI AND VITRUVIUS *

THE CLOSE TIES that link Leone Battista Alberti's *De re aedificatoria* to Vitruvius' *De architectura* hardly need enumerating. The near identity of the title and the identical division into ten books are obvious. Time and again Alberti names Vitruvius as his source of information, and even more frequently he refers to *De architectura* without naming it, either through direct quotation or paraphrase or by thinly veiled allusions. These references have been pointed out frequently: in 1912 by Theuer in his German translation of *De re aedificatoria;* in 1930 by P.-H. Michel; and more recently in the notes to Rykwert's reprint of James Leoni's English translation.[1] Likewise, it is easy to see—and this too has been pointed out—that in these passages Alberti drew on Vitruvius for information mainly in four areas: historical facts and fancy; technical details, such as the height of steps, the making of bricks and their sizes, the laying of pavements, the revetting of walls; the orders; and finally, antique building types poorly known to the Quattrocento, such as palaestrae, forums, theaters.

The purloinings from Vitruvius, then, while numerous, are limited in scope. At the same time—and this is no new discovery either—Alberti obviously was far from agreeing with Vitruvius on all points. To me it seems one might go further and state that on major points he was highly critical of the Roman author's work, the only writing on architecture to have come down from antiquity to the Quattrocento. Alberti has summed up some of the reasons for his criticism in the first chapter of Book VI. For one, he objects to the inelegance of Vitruvius' style, and especially to his interspersing the Latin text with Greek terms "so that the Latins thought he wrote Greek and the Greeks believed he spoke Latin. And this to such an extent that he writes neither Greek nor Latin and as far as we are concerned he need not have written at all since we cannot understand that kind of writing." At first glance this might seem to be no more than a criticism characteristic of the group of humanist *littérateur*-politicians among whom Alberti moved as a leading figure, intent on reviving Roman and Etruscan, not Greek, antiquity, and to this end striving toward the rebirth of a pure Latin style. But Alberti's criticism really probes much more deeply, for Vitruvius uses Greek exclusively to designate building types, architectural members, or standardized materials well-known to everybody in his time and, therefore, rarely in need of explanation: prostyle, amphiprostyle, peripteral temples, pyknostyle, systyle, aero-

*From *Acts of the Twentieth International Congress of the History of Art,* II (Princeton, 1963), 42–52.

style colonnades; sima, cymation, astragal; dydora, pentadora, tetradora bricks. Hence, Alberti really meant that in reading Vitruvius he was stumped and irked by an architectural terminology unintelligible to him and his fellow humanists, or at least hard to understand. He would have wanted more and clearer explanations. Their absence obviously was to be blamed not only on Vitruvius but at least in part on the ravages of time, for, as he says, Vitruvius' book has "come down to us so battered by time and damaged, that much is missing in many places" (did he think of the illustrations mentioned in the text, but lost?) "and at many points one would want a great deal more." To Alberti, the deficiencies of *De architectura,* whether Vitruvius' fault or caused by the ravages of time, were blatant, and his chapter is best understood as an explanation of the method he used to correct these shortcomings.

Vitruvius' terminology is transposed throughout into Latin: the title *De architectura* becomes *De re aedificatoria;* the *templum pycnostylum* becomes the *templum confertum; systylum* becomes *subconfertum; eustylum, elegans.* Where the Greek term seemed a needless flourish, Alberti replaced it by a short description: the prostyle becomes a *porticus pro fronte,* the amphiprostyle *a porticus pro fronte atque etiam in postico.* Or else, he created a new Latin term: for "one has to invent words where those in use are insufficient, and take them from similar objects" (Book VI, 13). Thus he calls the astragal *nextrum* "because that is what girls in Tuscany call the ribbon they wear in their hair."

Far more important, Alberti endeavored to interpret Vitruvius' text wherever it was obscure, and bound to be obscure, to a man of the Quattrocento. Good humanist that he was, he always approached antiquity first through its writings. The ancient authors were his guides to the lost world from which he wanted to resuscitate the brave new times and, for the architecture of the ancients, Vitruvius was his principal interpreter. Where Vitruvius was obscure, Alberti, as his fellow humanists would do in their own fields, first sought enlightenment in other writers of antiquity. Unlike his fellow humanists, however, he drew on another source as well: the monuments of ancient architecture which he knew in Rome and elsewhere. After all, he says right after his outcry over Vitruvius, from the old buildings, "one can learn a great deal as from the best masters" (Book VI, 1). It is quite possible that in the beginning he looked at these monuments as a mere complement to his reading, but they loomed ever more important as he wrote *De re aedificatoria.* Thus, an architectural term or the description of a building in Vitruvius, obscure when read, became clarified by a monument he knew. Conversely, a monument or an architectural member, otherwise unintelligible, became understandable in the light of a Vitruvius passage.

Where it was a question of interpreting the text on specific and clear details, such as the proportion of temples or the orders, it was easy to check, and if need be to correct Vitruvius by the monuments extant. But where the building types Vitruvius had in mind were unknown to Alberti, he had to reinterpret the text to make sense of it. The chapter on basilicas (Book VII, 14) is a case in point.

To Alberti the basilica is less impressive than the *templum;* it is timber-roofed, the nave is flanked by aisles and supported by columns; it has an apse, a *tribunal,* and this is preceded by a *causidica.* He obviously did not know forensic basilicas—except for the short façade of the Aemilia—and he apparently found Vitruvius' text hard to understand. However, the reference to the *causidica* makes clear what he had in mind, for he leaves no doubt that he means a transept. Alberti's allusion to a transept illuminates the interplay in his interpretation of classical architecture between the writings of the ancients and their monuments. He knew no Roman judiciary basilica, but he knew dozens of Early Christian and medieval transept basilicas in Rome. Classical as they looked to him—one thinks of Sta. Maria Maggiore—he explained them as Roman basilicas, taken over and later imitated by the Christians. Their transepts clarified for Alberti an obscure term used by Vitruvius: the *chalcidicum,* to be laid out, if there was sufficient space, at the ends of a basilica. For further clarification, Alberti replaced the term *chalcidicum* by *causidica,* "quod illic rhetorum turmae causidicique versarentur," because there lawyers and attorneys assemble.

Or he reinterpreted and bent the text of Vitruvius to make it conform to a building to which he felt it could be applied. Vitruvius' description of the Etruscan temple was, of course, unintelligible to Alberti. Yet he apparently thought Vitruvius might have had in mind a mausoleum (*templum* to him) resembling in plan the Maxentius basilica, although dark and on a small scale. Hence, he interpolated and amended the Vitruvius passage until it fitted the monument.

Whether limited to the terminology, or outright reinterpretation, emendation, and interpolation, such changes are signposts pointing to the differences between *De re aedificatoria* and *De architectura* and to Messer Battista's true intentions. Yet where Alberti really parts ways with Vitruvius is in his definition of the architect and of architecture. Vitruvius' architect is a strangely ambiguous being. As defined in chapter I of Book I, he is both a practitioner and a theoretician, and in this latter capacity, a walking encyclopedia: versed not only in draftsmanship, geometry, and arithmetic, but also an historian, a philosopher, and a scientist, with a good smattering of musical theory, of painting and sculpture, of medicine, jurisprudence, astronomy and astrology. Yet, as Vitruvius writes on, this *homo encyclopaedicus* fades into the background and what remains is a craftsman whose true love lies with the orders, with the techniques of construction, with theater design and interior decoration, with military engineering and ordnance. To Alberti, the architect is both less and more. He is no mere craftsman and no encyclopedist. "Him I call an architect," Alberti says in the preface—and every word counts in this definition—"who by sure and wonderful thought and method is able, both with intelligence and drive, to devise and with activity to execute whatever, by means of the moving of weights and the joining and massing of bodies, can be adapted with the greatest beauty for the most dignified needs of man." In short, Alberti's architect masterminds the technique of construction in order to create beautiful buildings for man both as an individual and as a social being, a *zoon politikon*. Concomitantly, his concept of architecture differs fundamentally from that sketched by Vitruvius in *De architectura.* To be sure, Vitruvius had set out to draw up definite rules, *prescriptiones terminatas,* so as to enable patrons of architecture to judge the quality of buildings, both in design and technique of construction. To this end he promises, in his preface, to set down all the principles of the field, *omnes disciplinae rationes.* Indeed, in the second chapter of Book I, he lists what to him are constituent principles of architectural practice and theory: propriety, planning, proportion, correspondence of parts, and layout. And he refers, needless to say, to the triad of *firmitas, utilitas, venustas* as fundamental to all architecture. But all these basic elements are listed at the beginning of the book, never to be taken up again. The place of architecture in the scheme of society or the interrelations of beauty, usefulness, and construction are never discussed. Whatever Vitruvius had set out to do, he ends up by writing a manual, a summary of contemporary and—as we know now—of often obsolete practice and theory. As a man who knows his craft he speaks competently not so much to patrons as through them to fellow craftsmen about the things that mattered to him; how to build a wall, how to lay a foundation, what paint to use. To Alberti, on the contrary, architecture is the supreme art, serviceable to mankind, dignified and enjoyable, but he does not write of it as a practitioner; in fact, I doubt that he thought of himself primarily as an architect, either when working on *De re aedificatoria* or even when designing and supervising his buildings in later years. In all his writing, in any event, he considers himself a counsellor-at-antiquity. Thus, he approaches architecture as a humanist, intent on finding out "the principles on which that art is based, the parts of which it consists, and how they can be executed" by the craftsman under the supervision of the humanist architect. Where Vitruvius listed principles only to forget them, Alberti views principles and the constituent parts of architecture as paramount— and it seems to me that a strong criticism of Vitruvius is implied, though not stated *expressis verbis.*

Alberti's position and his implied criticism of Vitruvius become manifest in the layout of *De re aedificatoria.* In *De architectura* Vitruvius proceeded carefully from point to point: his first book deals first with the definition of the architect and of architecture, then continues abruptly with city planning; the second book treats of the history of architecture and of materials; the third and fourth, of religious buildings, including principles of proportion, the orders, orientation, doors, Tuscan, round and peripteral temples, and altars, in that order. The fifth book discusses public architecture, from the forum to harbors, but mostly theaters. The sixth starts with a discussion of symmetry and proportion in domestic buildings, and follows this up by listing the parts and the diverse functions of residences. The seventh book is given to interior decoration. The eighth examines water engineering; the ninth, surveying and astronomy; the tenth is given over to mechanics, from pumps to water organs and artillery. It is hard to find a guiding principle —digressions are frequent. *Firmitas, utilitas, venustas*—construction, function, and design in modern parlance (or in Sir Henry Wotton's Elizabethan language, Firmness, Commodiousness, and Delight)—are inextricably intermingled. To Alberti, such looseness of concept and organization was bound to be repellent. The triad of *firmitas, utilitas* and *venustas* becomes for Alberti the organizing criterion of his book. The preface of *De re aedificatoria* defines the architect and the principles of architecture. Book I, *de lineamentis*—I should like to translate the term as "definitions"—analyzes the basic elements of any building, its parts from the site and foundations to the roof. Books II and III are given over to a discussion of *firmitas,* construction: Book II, *de materia,* treats of building materials; Book III, *de opere,* of workmanship. Books IV and V discuss *utilitas,* function: Book IV, *de universorum opere,* deals with public works; Book V, *de singulorum operibus,* discusses individual buildings for the commonwealth, and private building. Book VI starts out with one digressive chapter, the only digression in the whole work, on Alberti's reasons for and his difficulties in writing it. Chapter 2 speaks of beauty and ornament. Chapter 3 presents a history of architecture: an architecture of mass (*firmitas*) born in Asia merges in Greece with grace (*venustas*), and finally, in Rome, with usefulness (*utilitas*). The rest of the book, as announced in its title, *de ornamento,* deals with design, specifically the beauty of materials and workmanship. Correspondingly, Book VII treats of design in the realm of religious building (*de sacrorum ornamentis*); Book VIII, in public secular architecture (*de publici profani ornamento*); the first chapters of Book IX deal with design in domestic buildings (*de privatorum ornamento*). The last chapters, five through eight, of that book are given to the famous discussion of beauty and proportions, while the last chapter (divided by Bartoli into three) analyzes the duties of the architect and the relation to his patron. Books VI-IX, then, are given essentially to design and Book X (*de operum instauratione*) is but a collection of afterthoughts dealing with water supply and with possible building damage, its prevention and correction. Thus Alberti goes over the entire field of architecture, looking at the same subject—for example, public building—several times under different aspects. From general theoretical considerations he works up to construction, from there to function and then to design, to terminate finally by discussing beauty as a general and all-pervading principle found in God, that is, Nature. Where Vitruvius composes a manual for the practicing architect and the patron who orders and pays for the work and thus wants to check its quality, Alberti sets down a program. Nothing could be further from Vitruvius, and yet dozens of elements, even the triad of *firmitas, utilitas,* and *venustas,* are rooted in Vitruvius. (See tables, pp. 330 f.)

Alberti's relation to Vitruvius is, in fact, extraordinarily complex. The discovery in 1415 of a Vitruvius manuscript at St. Gall had created quite a stir among humanists—and one wonders why. Did Poggio, who had found the manuscript at St. Gall, believe it to be the Roman original—perhaps because of its Carolingian script? After all, Vitruvius manuscripts had been known and copied throughout the Middle Ages. To this day some fifty-odd manuscripts of Vitruvius are known, dating from the ninth through the fifteenth century. But despite the prolific copying, the Middle Ages made little use of Vitruvius. As pointed out by Paul Frankl recently, they exploited his chapter on human proportions; they drew on his geometrical solutions for establishing the values of irrational numbers; and they based themselves on his chapters on musical proportions.[2] But by the middle of the fifteenth century the approach had changed. To the new humanist generation, Vitruvius' book in its entirety was the only work on architecture surviving from classical antiquity. Humanist patrons wanted to build *all'antica* and their advisors were eager to know what he had to say about building. But his book remained sealed, its terminology unintelligible, its references to building types and extant monuments obscure. At the same time, Alberti was known in these humanist circles as a man steeped in the writings of the ancients, the best connoisseur of the ruins of ancient Rome, and the only humanist deeply concerned with the theory, the history, and the practice of art. What then was more natural than to turn to the author of the *Descriptio urbis Romae,* of *De pictura* and *De statua,* for information on the principles of good architecture exemplified by the ruins of Rome and to be found supposedly in Vitruvius? But Vitruvius was unintelligible, certainly to a layman. Thus, about 1440, when Lionello d'Este broached to Alberti the idea of writing on architecture, both may have thought of a Vitruvius commentary: the passage on Vitruvius in Book VI, chapter 1 of *De re aedificatoria* has often sounded to me as if Alberti had made and abandoned the attempt. Stumped by the difficulties encountered, and irked by the looseness of the presentation in *De architectura,* by the slightness of the concepts on which it was founded, Vitruvius' own disregard of them, and the paramount role assigned to craftsmanship, he would have set out to compose a treatise of his own. Chapter 1 of Book VI, out of place as it is, might well have been drafted as a preface at that point. Only as time went on did *De re aedificatoria* grow into final shape: tied to Vitruvius by a hundred details, employing even the Vitruvian triad of *firmitas, utilitas,* and *venustas,* but giving it a new and deeper significance. Yet it was critical of Vitruvius both on specific and on basic points, turning for information more and more both to the monuments of antiquity and to contemporary workshop practice. Decidedly, Alberti wrote not for architects but for patrons, the patrons of the new generation to be educated in humanist thought. It was, after all, not by chance that *De re aedificatoria* was written in Latin, the language of the educated, that its writing was instigated by Lionello d'Este, and that the finished work was presented after Lionello's death to Nicholas V.[3] *De re aedificatoria,* written for humanist patrons, was to be a new Vitruvius. The Roman author, like the buildings of antiquity, was to Alberti only a starting point. Whether monuments or writings, the works of the ancients had after all come down in fragments, battered and ravaged by time. Hence they had to be reconstructed, interpreted and improved, along the lines which to Alberti represented the true meaning of antiquity, the true meaning deduced from the totality of antiquity as he saw it: a consistent system of thought and life in which every thing and every action fell into place. On this basis Alberti established his program, his visionary yet precise interpretation of the role of architecture. Beauty, material, workmanship, and function coincide toward one end, to create dignified surroundings for the dignified actions of dignified people.

VITRUVIUS

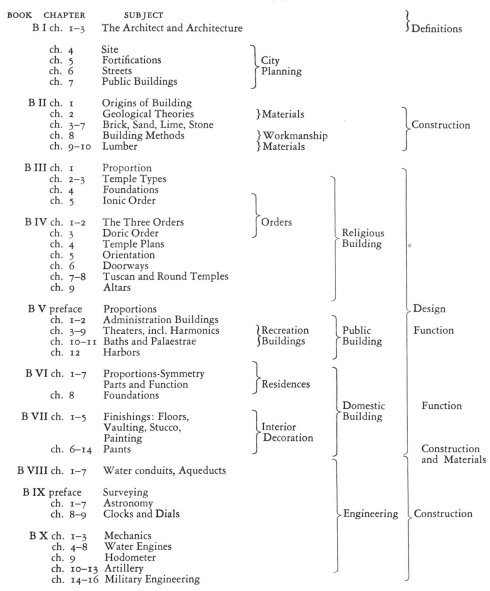

BOOK   CHAPTER   SUBJECT
  B I ch. 1–3   The Architect and Architecture   } Definitions

         ch. 4   Site   ⎫
         ch. 5   Fortifications   ⎬ City
         ch. 6   Streets   ⎪ Planning
         ch. 7   Public Buildings   ⎭

  B II ch. 1   Origins of Building   ⎫
         ch. 2   Geological Theories   } Materials   ⎫
         ch. 3–7 Brick, Sand, Lime, Stone   ⎬ Construction
         ch. 8   Building Methods   } Workmanship   ⎪
         ch. 9–10 Lumber   } Materials   ⎭

  B III ch. 1   Proportion
         ch. 2–3 Temple Types
         ch. 4   Foundations
         ch. 5   Ionic Order   ⎫
                                                     ⎬ Orders
  B IV ch. 1–2   The Three Orders   ⎭   ⎫
         ch. 3   Doric Order   ⎬ Religious
         ch. 4   Temple Plans   ⎪ Building
         ch. 5   Orientation   ⎪
         ch. 6   Doorways   ⎪
         ch. 7–8 Tuscan and Round Temples   ⎪
         ch. 9   Altars   ⎭

  B V preface   Proportions   } Design
         ch. 1–2 Administration Buildings
         ch. 3–9 Theaters, incl. Harmonics   } Recreation   ⎫ Public   Function
         ch. 10–11 Baths and Palaestrae   } Buildings   ⎬ Building
         ch. 12   Harbors   ⎭

  B VI ch. 1–7   Proportions-Symmetry   ⎫
                  Parts and Function   } Residences   ⎫
         ch. 8   Foundations   ⎬ Domestic   Function
                                                            ⎪ Building
  B VII ch. 1–5   Finishings: Floors,   ⎪
                  Vaulting, Stucco,   } Interior   ⎭
                  Painting   } Decoration
         ch. 6–14 Paints   } Construction
                                                                            and Materials
  B VIII ch. 1–7 Water conduits, Aqueducts

  B IX preface   Surveying
         ch. 1–7 Astronomy
         ch. 8–9 Clocks and Dials   } Engineering   } Construction

  B X ch. 1–3   Mechanics
         ch. 4–8 Water Engines
         ch. 9   Hodometer
         ch. 10–13 Artillery
         ch. 14–16 Military Engineering

ALBERTI

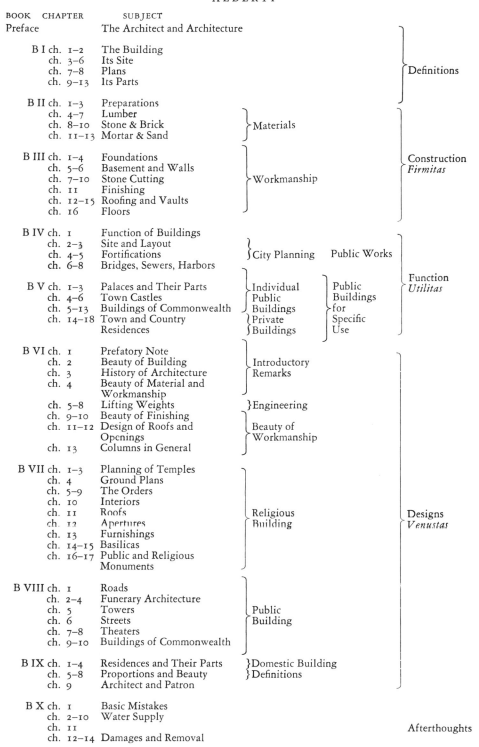

BOOK	CHAPTER	SUBJECT		
Preface		The Architect and Architecture		

B I ch. 1–2 The Building
ch. 3–6 Its Site
ch. 7–8 Plans
ch. 9–13 Its Parts — Definitions

B II ch. 1–3 Preparations
ch. 4–7 Lumber
ch. 8–10 Stone & Brick — Materials
ch. 11–13 Mortar & Sand

B III ch. 1–4 Foundations
ch. 5–6 Basement and Walls
ch. 7–10 Stone Cutting — Workmanship — Construction *Firmitas*
ch. 11 Finishing
ch. 12–15 Roofing and Vaults
ch. 16 Floors

B IV ch. 1 Function of Buildings
ch. 2–3 Site and Layout
ch. 4–5 Fortifications — City Planning   Public Works
ch. 6–8 Bridges, Sewers, Harbors

B V ch. 1–3 Palaces and Their Parts — Individual — Public — Function *Utilitas*
ch. 4–6 Town Castles — Public — Buildings
ch. 5–13 Buildings of Commonwealth — Buildings — for
ch. 14–18 Town and Country — Private — Specific
Residences — Buildings — Use

B VI ch. 1 Prefatory Note
ch. 2 Beauty of Building
ch. 3 History of Architecture — Introductory Remarks
ch. 4 Beauty of Material and Workmanship
ch. 5–8 Lifting Weights — Engineering
ch. 9–10 Beauty of Finishing
ch. 11–12 Design of Roofs and Openings — Beauty of Workmanship
ch. 13 Columns in General

B VII ch. 1–3 Planning of Temples
ch. 4 Ground Plans
ch. 5–9 The Orders
ch. 10 Interiors
ch. 11 Roofs
ch. 12 Apertures — Religious Building — Designs *Venustas*
ch. 13 Furnishings
ch. 14–15 Basilicas
ch. 16–17 Public and Religious Monuments

B VIII ch. 1 Roads
ch. 2–4 Funerary Architecture
ch. 5 Towers — Public Building
ch. 6 Streets
ch. 7–8 Theaters
ch. 9–10 Buildings of Commonwealth

B IX ch. 1–4 Residences and Their Parts — Domestic Building
ch. 5–8 Proportions and Beauty — Definitions
ch. 9 Architect and Patron

B X ch. 1 Basic Mistakes
ch. 2–10 Water Supply
ch. 11 — Afterthoughts
ch. 12–14 Damages and Removal

Notes

1. Leone Battista Alberti, *Zehn Bücher über die Baukunst,* ed. Max Theuer (Vienna-Leipzig, 1912); Paul-Henri Michel, *Un idéal humain au XVieme siècle; la pensée de L. B. Alberti* (Paris, 1930); L. B. Alberti, *Ten Books on Architecture,* tr. James Leoni, ed. J. Rykwert (London, 1955).

2. P. Frankl, *The Gothic,* (Princeton, 1960), 103 ff.

3. R. Krautheimer, *Lorenzo Ghiberti* (Princeton, 1956), 268 ff.

Postscript

Frank E. Brown (*Bucknell Review,* 1963) recently has presented Vitruvius' *De architectura* in a very different light: based on consistent philosophical principles and soundly constructed as a theory of architecture.

Far be it from me to quarrel with an authority such as Frank Brown on the subject of Vitruvius. It is Alberti who views *De architectura* as lacking in principles, loosely constructed and poorly presented. I *do* plead guilty of having let myself be persuaded too easily by Messer Battista to take his part in every respect. But then, *De re aedificatoria* is so crystal clear and so superior that I find it hard to find its equal anywhere in architectural theory.

The number of surviving Vitruvius manuscripts from the Middle Ages and the Quattrocento amounts to eighty-one rather than fifty, according to Carol Krinsky's list (1967) and a typewritten *addendum.*

Additional Bibliography

Brown, F. E., "Vitruvius and the Liberal Art of Architecture," *Bucknell Review*, II, 4, (1963), 99 ff.

Grayson, C., "The Composition of L. B. Alberti's Decem Libri de re aedificatoria," *Münch Jb*, 3rd ser., XI (1960), 152 ff.

Krinsky, C. H., "Seventy-eight Vitruvius manuscripts," *Journal of the Warburg and Courtauld Institutes,* XXX (1967), 36 ff.

20

ALBERTI'S TEMPLUM ETRUSCUM *

TEMPLES OCCUPY A KEY POSITION in Alberti's thinking, certainly at the time he wrote *De re aedificatoria* roughly in the five or six years prior to its presentation to Nicholas V in 1452.[1] Nearly the entire seventh book of *De Re Aedificatoria* centers on their design and their appurtenances; and time and again remarks on temples occur in the other nine books. Still the meaning to Alberti of the term *templum* (and we had better use Latin terms and the Latin text) [2] remains ambiguous as to its function and design. This is but natural in view of the complex components that went into the writing of *De re aedificatoria:* philosophical ideas and aesthetic theories, old and new; obsolete workshop practices and technical innovations; historical and archaeological fact and fiction; all this held together by the prophetic and programmatic vista of a new world populated by a new mankind which moves among buildings new in spirit and pattern. Yet this new world, its mankind and its architecture, are shaped in the image of classical antiquity, an image visionary and precise. The antique past, the present in which Alberti lives—both real and ideal—and the future he envisions are inextricably interwoven. Hence while *templa* are to him obviously places of worship, the divinity worshipped remains undefined; for it encompasses both gods of antiquity and the Supreme Being of Alberti's personalized Christian belief. Likewise the *templa* which actualize his concepts belong at the same time to the Roman past and to the program he established for the present and the future. Equally ambiguous remain the sources of his concept of the design of a *templum:* the writings of the ancients, from Herodotus to Vitruvius and Pliny; medieval traditions; the monuments—*bona fide templa* or other structures which Alberti and his contemporaries believed to be *templa*. Finally, it remains ever in doubt how far, if at all, the image of a *templum* as envisaged in *De re aedificatoria* about 1450 coincides with the *templa* Alberti designed in the twenty years between the completion of his architectural manifesto and the end of his life.

Templa, Alberti says, are to be designed and built with the greatest possible care, more so than any other type of building. They are to be the most perfect and the most outstanding ornament of a city,[3] having greater dignity than any

*This paper, from *MünchJb,* XII (1961), 65–72, was read at the symposium on L. B. Alberti held at the Zentralinstitut für Kunstgeschichte, Munich, in March 1960. My thanks are due to Mr. Walter Cahn, who assisted me in gathering some of the material, and to Miss Judith Levenson who went over the English, both of the Institute of Fine Arts, New York University.

other structures, public or private.[4] They are to rise in the middle of town, dominating the main square,[5] if possible raised from the ground.[6] They are always to be vaulted; *De re aedificatoria* VII, 11 leaves no doubt: Templis tectum dignitatis gratia atque etiam perpetuitatis maxime esse testudinatum velim." Likewise explicit is VII, 3, where vaulting is considered as an integral part of a *templum:* a timber roofed basilica has acoustic advantages over the "templum testudinatum." [7] *Templa* are to be dimly lit so as to evoke awe in the mind of the visitor; windows are to be small and high up.[8] The interiors should be decorated simply and with reticence.[9]

Book VII, 4 deals with the plans of *templa* in general. All *templa* have two components: a porch (*porticus*) and an interior room (*cella*). Otherwise they differ: they may be round, rectangular, or polygonal. Round and hexagonal shapes are preordained by nature, as witness the stars, tree trunks, and the cells of a honeycomb. But since octagons, decagons and dodecagons are derivatives of a circle, they can be easily constructed from it and were used by the ancients in their *templa* like circles and hexagons. Rectangular *templa* should be one and one-half or twice as long as wide. Whatever the shape of the *templum,* however, Alberti would like to see *tribunalia* added to it. In round or polygonal *templa,* one such tribunal should be joined to each or to alternating sides, in rectangular *templa* one to the end of the nave and possibly one to either of the long sides; grudgingly he will accept a larger odd number. *Tribunalia* may be rectangular or semicircular, or the two forms may alternate. Finally the chapter terminates with a discussion of what Alberti calls the *Templum Etruscum.*

"Nonnullis in templis hinc atque hinc vetusto Aetruscorum more pro lateribus non tribunal, sed cellulae minusculae habendae sunt. Eorum haec fiet ratio. Aream sibi sumpsere cuius longitudo in partes divisa sex, una sui parte latitudinem excederet; ex ipsa longitudine partes dabant duas latitudini porticus quae quidem pro vestibulo templi extabat. Reliquum dividebant in partes tris quae trinis cellarum latitudinibus darentur. Rursus latitudinem ipsam templi dividebant in partes decem. Ex his dabant partes tris cellis in dextram et totidem tris cellis in sinistram positis. Mediae vero ambulationi quattuor relinquebant. Ad caput templi unum medianasque ad cellas hinc atque hinc tribunal adigebant. Parietes pro faucibus cellarum efficiebant ex quinta vacui intervalli." [10]

The meaning is by and large clear, but a few explanations may be helpful. In contrast to other *templa,* so Alberti stresses, the *Templum Etruscum* has along its sides not *tribunalia,* but *cellulae minusculae;* we might retain for the moment the Latin terms, but in any event the contraposition of the two is as clear from the text as is the importance of the difference to Alberti. The area of the *templum,* Alberti continues, is to be laid out in a proportion of six to five, length to width. Two-sixths of the length are given to the porch, four to the cella. This latter is to be flanked on either side by three *cellulae.* The width of the *templum,* on the other hand, is to be divided into ten parts: three on either side are assigned to the *cellulae,* four parts in the middle to the nave, the *media ambulatio. Tribunalia,* clearly distinct from these *cellulae,* are to be joined, one to the end of the nave, the other two to the *cellae* occupying the middle of either side. The strength of the walls separating the *cellae* is to correspond to one-fifth the *cella* openings.

The difference between *tribunalia* and *cellae* is obviously a key point. The former throughout *De re aedificatoria* have the connotation of apses, mostly projecting from the main body of the building; *cellae,* on the other hand, are spaces—not necessarily projecting, but closely joined to each other, like the *cellae* of a honey comb, or of a hornet's nest. Niches hollowed out in the thickness of a wall but not adjoining each other, such as those of the Pantheon, are again something else: Alberti's term for them is *scafi,* literally troughs.[11] Text Fig. 16, then presents a rough sketch of the *Templum Etruscum* according to Alberti.

The literary source of Alberti's description of the *Templum Etruscum* has been pointed out before.[12] It is of course Vitruvius' description of the Tuscan shrine, Book IV, chapter 7, and again it may be helpful to quote the few sentences of the original text as far as Alberti uses them.

"Locus, in quo aedis constituetur, cum habuerit in longitudine sex partes, una adempta reliquum quod erit, latitudini detur. Longitudo autem dividatur bipertito, et quae pars erit interior, cellarum spatiis designetur, quae erit proxima fronti, columnarum dispositione relinquatur. Item latitudo dividatur in partes X. Ex his ternae partes dextra ac sinistra cellis minoribus sive ibi alae futurae sunt, dentur; reliquae quattuor mediae aedi attribuantur."[13]

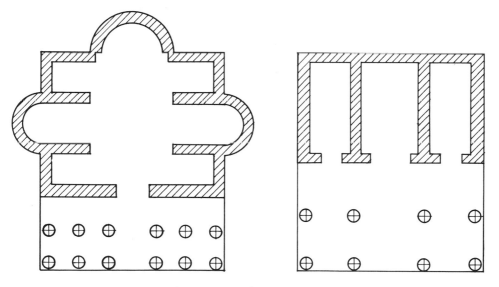

Text fig. 16. *Templum Etruscum* after Alberti and Vitruvius, reconstruction by Krautheimer

Obviously the Tuscan shrine as described by Vitruvius is very different from Alberti's *Templum Etruscum*. Only the overall proportion of the area, six by five, is the same. But the length is divided into two equal halves, *bipertitum;* the front half is to be given to a colonnaded porch, while the rear half is divided transversely into ten parts, corresponding to three *cellae,* those right and left each three-tenths, the one in the middle four-tenths wide. What Vitruvius then describes is a genuine *Templum Etruscum,* as we have known them these last 150 years from excavations: the temple at Lo Scasato may serve as an example. Certainly Vitruvius still knew such *templa,* and it is of small importance whether they really were Etruscan or late derivatives; in any event, he believed them to be Etruscan and described them carefully (Text Fig. 16).

It is only natural that Alberti would be fascinated by the Vitruvius passage. Not only did it concern a *templum* quite different from the other *templa* he had read of or seen: they all were Roman or Greek temples, the latter known to him from his readings. But here, in Vitruvius, was an Etruscan temple, a Tuscan one: a *templum* from the region which was close to his heart, both as the ancestral seat of his family and as the province where "the art of building had her ancient home among the Etruscans," who in their writings had laid down the rules for building *templa.*[14] It is equally understandable that he would be bewildered by Vitruvius' description of such a Tuscan shrine. Obviously he had never seen the like of it and he must have had to struggle to grasp the meaning of the text. Probably Vitruvius' description was to Alberti one of those passages which worried him so much in reading or commenting on the old master's *Decem Libri,* "the only writer on architecture, no doubt most instructive, whose work has been saved from the wreck of antiquity, but so ravaged by the passage of time and defective that much is missing in many places and in others elaboration is wanting."[15] The passage on the *Templum Etruscum* certainly wanted elaboration. It had to be interpreted. Alberti tried hard, but he could make sense of it only by bending Vitruvius' meaning. To be sure, the term *bipertitum* in Vitruvius' text was a perfectly good word and known to Alberti. But as he saw it, the division of the area into two equal parts was meaningless. A vestibule that deep was unthinkable; two parts out of six made better sense and even so it was a very deep vestibule. Similarly unimaginable to Alberti were the three *cellae* in Vitruvius' shrine, occupying on a transversal·axis the rear half of the area. Again the text made sense to him only if he could arrange the *cellae* lengthwise, on either side of the building. As a result he had to place in the middle a nave, not mentioned by Vitruvius. Finally the apses, the *tribunalia,* were—it seems at first glance—a gratuitous addition.

Such reinterpretation of Vitruvius might appear arbitrary. Seen within Alberti's overall approach to antiquity, it is quite consistent. Good humanist that he was, he always approached antiquity first through its writings. The ancient authors were his guides to that lost world from which he wanted to resuscitate the brave new times. For the architecture of the ancients Vitruvius was his principal interpreter. But as he complained, many passages in *De architectura* were obscure (and are still obscure to us) : he had to explain them to himself before presenting the results. This he tried to do, as his fellow humanists would in their fields, by referring to other writers of antiquity. Unlike his fellow humanists, however, he drew on yet another source as well: the monuments of ancient architecture which he knew in Rome and elsewhere. Indeed it is quite possible that in the beginning he looked at these monuments as a mere complement to his reading. But they loomed ever more important as his work progressed. *De re aedificatoria* leaves no doubt that by 1450 he knew them thoroughly and in fact had surveyed a great number in plan, elevation and details. Thus during the writing of his *magnum opus,* the monuments of the ancients and their writings mutually illuminated each other. An architectural term or the description of a building in Vitruvius, obscure when read, became clarified by a monument he knew. Conversely, a monument or an architectural member, otherwise unintelligible, became understandable in the light of a Vitruvius passage.

Not all of the monuments of antiquity Alberti knew could serve this end. They were too diversified. Thus, he selected among them those which fitted the image of ancient architecture as he envisaged it. This image was based on very clear criteria, drawn he thought from Vitruvius, but really his own. Criteria of function, construction and design, they were based on the concepts of *utilitas, firmitas, venustas* which were mentioned by Vitruvius, but never seriously applied in his work. For Alberti these criteria were basic. They determine the entire layout of *De re aedificatoria.* Specifically, they were applicable in different combinations to different categories of buildings. This was, he had taught himself to believe, how the ancients had and how he wanted to develop architectural types: cities, country houses, palaces, temples, basilicas. The palace of the legitimate ruler was to rise in the middle of town, easily accessible, beautiful in ornament and decor—elegant in design rather than overwhelming. The palace of the tyrant was to be set apart, strongly fortified and inspiring fear.[16] The *templum,* as we said, must be vaulted, dimly lit, beautifully designed, simply ornamented, filling the visitor with reverance and awe. The basilica, less impressive than the *templum,* was to be timber-roofed, the nave flanked by aisles and supported by columns; its *tribunal,* the apse, was to be preceded by a *causidicum,* and Alberti leaves no doubt that he means a transept. In fact, the reference to the transept illuminates the interplay in Alberti's interpretation of classical architecture between the writings of the ancients and their monuments. He was casting about for an explanation of the basilicas described by Vitruvius, but he knew no Roman judiciary basilica. On the other hand, he knew well dozens of Early Christian and medieval basilicas in Rome. Classical as they looked to him—one thinks of Sta. Maria Maggiore—he explained them as Roman basilicas, taken over and later imitated by the Christians. Some of these basilicas, Constantinian and medieval, were provided with transepts, and these transepts illuminated for Alberti an obscure term used by Vitruvius: the *chalcidicum* to be laid out if there was sufficient space at the ends of a basilica.[17] For further clarification, Alberti replaced the term *chalcidicum* by *causidica* "quod illic rhetorum turmae causidicique versarentur," [18] because there lawyers and attorneys assemble.

The contrast between basilica and *templum in De re aedificatoria* seems to us clear and strongly pointed.[19] In fact, we feel that it is pointed very specifically against the entire tradition of church building as Alberti knew it by 1450. All churches so far had been laid out as basilicas with a nave, well lit and flanked by aisles. This applied to contemporary church building as well, including churches such as S. Lorenzo or S. Spirito in Florence. Against this tradition Alberti maintains that the plan of the basilica had been used for churches by sheer default. Our ancestors—so he says—have occupied basilicas throughout for celebrating mass, and they did so for a number of reasons: they were used to meeting in private basilicas; the apse offered itself as a dignified location for an altar and for the choir, nave and aisles for the congregation; and the timber roof offered acoustic advantages.[20] But all this in Alberti's eyes was an historical error. His intention is to point out and to correct the thousand years of mistakes in church building. By implication, it is an attack also on Brunelleschi's great church buildings, except of course S. Maria degli Angeli which the grand master had designed after his return from Rome, where in 1432 he had met young Alberti.[21]

The monuments, then, which explained to Alberti the meaning of basilica are easily identified. Those by which he interpreted the concept of *templum* are less apparent. Obviously he knew dozens of *templa* in Rome and outside, as they had been known throughout the Middle Ages and listed in the *Mirabilia* and the *Graphia* and with little change still in the early fifteenth century in Poggio's *De varietate fortunae*.[22] However, he did not base his image of the *templum* indiscriminately on these Roman temples. Never in *De re aedificatoria* does he allude to any of the well-known timber-roofed temples, be it that of Antoninus and Faustina or the Temple of Nerva, unless it is to discuss their *pronaos* or the architectural membering. For plan and construction, he focuses primarily on vaulted structures: the Pantheon, the Temple of Venus and Roma, the Temple of Hadrian. In fact, aside from thermae rooms, apparently all vaulted structures were to him *templa:* they might be large *templa,* such as S. Costanza, the *Tempio di Bacco,* or the *tempietto* at the Clitumnus, or the mausoleum of Theodoric, "nobile id delubrum cui protecto integrum extat lapideum vas." [23] With all this the specific models are not easy to identify. What Alberti presents is an overall vision of the *templum.*

Since Theuer pointed it out, the consensus of opinion has agreed that the specific model for Alberti's *Templum Etruscum* is the Basilica of Maxentius.[24] It was known through the entire Middle Ages and as late as the nineteenth century as a *templum,* and only the name changed: *Templum Pacis, Templum Vespasiani, Templum Pacis et Latonae;* to Alberti it was the *Templum Latonae.*[25] Indeed the resemblances between the Basilica (Fig. 126) and Alberti's *Templum Etruscum* are striking: the proportion of the plan, width to length is roughly five to six; the entire structure is vaulted in all its parts; the nave is flanked on either side by three niches; their openings are roughly five times as wide as the separating piers; a vestibule leads from the short side into the nave; an apse terminates the nave to the east and a second apse is joined to the center niche to the north. Renaissance architects in their survey drawings added a corresponding third apse to the south. Francesco di Giorgio's, Giuliano da Sangallo's, Serlio's and Palladio's plans are examples of such graphic reconstructions.[26] To be sure, these reconstructions could have been based on an equation made *ex post facto* between Alberti's description of the *Templum Etruscum* and the Basilica of Maxentius; they do not necessarily prove that this equation was made by Alberti himself.

However, Theuer was no doubt right and the Basilica of Maxentius was certainly on Alberti's mind when he formulated his concept of the *Templum Etruscum*. Yet one wonders whether it was the only monument on which he based himself. At least one point gives cause to wonder whether the equation is quite that simple. Nobody in his senses would call the enormous niches of the Basilica, nearly thirteen meters deep and close to twenty meters wide, *cellulae minusculae*, tiny little cells, least of all Alberti, sensitive as he was to the intrinsic qualities of a work of art. One need only recall his description of a Roman relief, on which the corpse of Meleager was to be seen "dead down to the fingernails." [27] Nor do the huge windows in the Basilica of Maxentius correspond to the image of the *templum* as proffered by Alberti, dimly lit through small windows. The impression is rather that Alberti, when describing the *Templum Etruscum,* and indeed *templa* in general, thought of dark, small, compact buildings.

Such buildings would be found primarily not among temples of antiquity. Whether in Rome or elsewhere, they were too large and they were rarely vaulted. But they would be found among the mausolea, scattered all over the Roman countryside and far down into Campania. Alberti's remarks on *templa* of central plan leave no doubt. Time and again he alludes to hexagonal and octagonal *templa,* with projecting apses. But no such temples exist anywhere in Rome. Circular temples do exist, but none have *tribunalia,* projecting apses. On the contrary, dozens of circular, hexagonal, octagonal, decagonal, and dodecagonal mausolea rose in his time and rise today in the Roman Campagna, with apses projecting from their sides, dark or dimly lit by tiny windows high up in the walls, and vaulted. Square or rectangular mausolea are no less frequent, their *cellae* barrel-vaulted, terminated by an apse, and occasionally preceded by a vestibule, the side walls articulated by niches—at times alternatingly rectangular and semi-circular. The sketch books and publications of Renaissance architects from Francesco di Giorgio and Giuliano da Sangallo through Serlio and Palladio abound with the surveys of mausolea of all kinds. A glance through "Bramantino's" *Rovine di Roma* shows one after the other, round, polygonal, square or rectangular tombs known either to the draftsman directly or through earlier drawings, along the roads leading out of Rome: "a santo sebastiano," "fuori porta magiore," "dela dal li tre fontane," "dredo ala marana," "fuora san pranchacio," "fuori porta del popolo." [28] At times, but rarely, the draftsman may have tried to improve on the plan of the original building. By and large, however, he gives a reliable survey; this is confirmed by dozens of sketches which other architectural draftsmen have left of the same buildings: Baldassare Peruzzi, Antonio Sangallo the Younger, Sallustio Peruzzi, and the draftsman who around 1550 completed the Coner Sketchbook.[29]

Where they are rectangular, the majority of these mausolea were provided with simple niches, hollowed from the thickness of the walls, and just large enough to shelter an ash urn. Occasionally numbers of smaller urns may have been shelved in large niches, as in the Columbarium of the Freedmen of Livia;[30] but even there the niches remain confined within the thickness of the wall. To my knowledge, no mausoleum has survived with the plan of a *Basilica Maxentii* in miniature postulated by Alberti for the *Templum Etruscum* with *cellulae* flanking the nave on either side, and with three projecting apses. Such a gap in our knowledge does not prove that mausolea of that type did not exist, and were still known in the fifteenth and sixteenth centuries. Bastiano Sangallo shows a structure of just that plan (Fig. 127): [31] the nave is formed by three groin vaulted rectangular bays; it is flanked on either side by three square niches, those in the center with apses; a small apse terminates the nave in the rear, a short square vestibule precedes it in the front. The inscription on the sheet "palazo maiore," seems to assign the building to the Palatine, but no such structure has ever been found there; and the building on the plan looks small, rather like a mausoleum. Two other structures of similar plan, both unidentified, appear among Sallustio Peruzzi's drawings, on sheets filled otherwise with plans of identifiable mausolea (Figs. 128, 129).[32] Thus we think it at least possible that Alberti knew mausolea of the type he described as the *Templum Etruscum*. But it is equally possible that he transposed into the realm of mausoleum architecture and to a small scale the plan of the Basilica of Maxentius which, as he saw it, coincided with Vitruvius description of the *Templum Etruscum*.

Within the framework of humanistic thought, such transposition would be but natural. To any humanist, mausolea were temples, and conversely, the image of a temple grew naturally from the realm of funerary architecture. There is hardly any need to stress the equation established by the draftsmen of the sixteenth century between mausolea of any shape and "tèmpi" or "tempietti," where Francesco di Giorgio or Giuliano da Sangallo had simply spoken of "edifizi" or even of "sepulture." "Bramantino," Sallustio Peruzzi, Serlio, or the younger Coner draftsman testify in dozens of inscribed drawings to this equation between funerary and temple architecture. Invariably, mausolea are identified as "templum divi postunni," "in via appia verso albano erat templum valde ornatum," "tempio in opera lateritium." [33] One wonders whether this total equation of *templum* and mausoleum in the sixteenth century is linked with the increasing impact exerted on architectural theory by Alberti's *De re aedificatoria*. After all, Alberti was the guide of the sixteenth century far more than of the fifteenth in matters architectural and antiquarian. From the pages of his work it became obvious to the draftsmen of the sixteenth century that to Alberti the funeral buildings of Rome were *templa* and thus were determining elements in creating a sacred architecture.

Indeed it seems to us that among humanists, the equation of mausolea and *templa* was determined by a specific historical theory. They were perfectly aware that the mausolea which they termed *templa* had funerary connotations. Sarcophagi, urns, epitaphs found *in situ* and noted by them could leave no doubt. But just such finds may have led them to identify these mausolea as *templa*. After all, every humanist was well acquainted with the theory of Euhemeros.[34] Throughout the Middle Ages euhemerism had caused the transformation of the pagan gods into good sorcerers and bearers of inventions and gifts to mankind. In Early Christian times this theory had been presented by the Church Fathers in its original pure form, polemically but clearly: the gods of antiquity were but great men raised to heaven after their death. With the patristic revival of the mid-fifteenth century, the original theory of euhemerism was bound to gain renewed strength. A humanist like Alberti, steeped in patristic literature, was bound to be deeply impressed by it. To him, after all, all men of antiquity were godlike. If then the gods were but great men of old, the places of their burial were by necessity *templa*.

This equation of the funeral architecture of antiquity and *templa* becomes clear throughout the pages of *De re aedificatoria*. Among mausolea, the foremost are what Alberti calls *sacella,* chapels, and they are in his words, "pusilla templorum exemplaria," [35] small scale models of *templa*. Again he refers to mausolea, at least by implication, in the passage which states that the ancients made it a rule to turn the façades of their *sacella* toward the seashore or the riverbank or the highway.[36] What else could he think of but mausolea along the great Roman roads and rivers?

Alberti then, in our opinion, thought of mausolea as well as of the Basilica of Maxentius when offering in *De re aedificatoria* his concept of the *Templum Etruscum*. As he shifted from theory to practice during the following twenty years and started to build, the plans of his own *templa,* of the churches he designed on a large scale, invariably remained rooted in the funerary architecture of Roman antiquity. As early as 1450, when discussing thermae buildings in the eighth book of *De re aedificatoria,* he had pointed out that the *tepidaria* of the great imperial baths paralleled the outline of a *Templum Etruscum*. A *tepidarium* is—so he says—an "atrium amplissum et dignissimum cum cellis ex lineamento templi quod esse etruscum diximus," [37] a huge and dignified atrium with *cellae,* following the plan of the *templum* which we have called Etruscan. By 1470 he went much further; in that year he wrote a letter to Lodovico Gonzaga answering a request for suggestions for the church of S. Andrea, the marchese intended to build at Mantua. Alberti drew up a plan or a sketch and accompanied it by a cover letter. He points out that a project submitted by Antonio Manetti was beautiful but not what he had in mind. Then he continues:

"Pensai et congettai questo qual io ve mando. Questo sarà più capace più eterno più degno più lieto, costerà molto meno. Questa forma di tempio se nomina apud veteres Etruscum sacrum. . . ." [38]

In fact at S. Andrea the barrel vaulted nave is flanked on either side by three barrel vaulted chapels and is preceded by a portico. To be sure, the transept, its crossing, and the chancel with its apse are elements alien to the *Templum Etruscum* which Alberti had described in *De re aedificatoria*. But it remains an open question whether these elements were planned by Alberti. Certainly construction on them was not begun prior to 1597, more than a century after Messer Battista's death in 1472, and the dome was completed only after 1733.[39] Contemporary sources maintain that the new parts were laid out "conforme al modello antico," but such late statements can hardly be considered reliable. In any event, it seems to us quite possible and indeed likely that Alberti's original project envisioned only the nave and chapels, the former terminated presumably by an apse. Granted that S. Andrea is only not quite half as large as the Basilica of Maxentius; yet in planning it, Alberti thought on a scale very different from what he had in mind when discussing in *De re aedificatoria* the *Templum Etruscum*. Even so, it remains obvious that he did not think only of the Basilica of Maxentius when designing his church at Mantua. The proportions differ, there are no columns in front of the piers and the nave is covered not with groin vaults, but with a barrel vault. Comparatively small windows light the nave, and the chapels remain dark, thus producing the dim light Alberti demanded for a *templum*. Despite the large scale, S. Andrea conveys an impression of mass, darkness and awe, not unlike that which determines the design of the Roman mausolea which we think underlie Alberti's presentation of the *Templum Etruscum* in *De re aedificatoria*.

Notes

1. See my own *Lorenzo Ghiberti* (Princeton, 1956), pp. 268 ff., n. 28, and Cecil Grayson, "The Composition of L. B. Alberti's Decem libri de re aedificatoria," *MünchJb*, 3rd ser., XI (1960), 152 ff.

2. Translations of *De re aedificatoria* are even more treacherous than those of other writings of the fifteenth century. Misunderstandings of and even omissions from the original Latin text start with Bartoli's Italian translation of 1550. They continue through the English, French, and German translations, most of which are based on Bartoli's text and, needless to say, misinterpret it further. The translation of James Leoni (*Alberti's Ten Books on Architecture* [London, 1750]), used in all English-speaking countries to this day and indeed recently reprinted (ed. Joseph Rykwert [London, 1955]) is an example. M.

Theuer's translation into German (*Alberti's Zehn Bücher über die Baukunst*, [Vienna, 1912]) is exceptional in that it goes back to the Latin original, but even this translation is not free from misunderstandings. (See now, Leone Battista Alberti, *L'Architettura*, 2 vols. [Milan, 1966], with the Latin text and facing Italian translation by Giovanni Orlandi.)

3. *De re aedificatoria*, VII, 3. "Tota in re aedificatoria nihil est in quo maiore sit opus ingenio cura industria diligentia quam in templo constituendo atque exornando. Sino illud quod templum quidem bene cultum et bene ornatum perfecto maximum et primarium est urbis ornamentum."

4. *Ibid.*, VII, 3. "Quod, si regibus et magnis viris hospitibus aedes ornamus lautissimeque operamus: quid superis immotalibus faciemus?"

5. *Ibid.*, V, 6.

6. *Ibid.*, VII, 5. "Hoc alterum (scil.— the lack of steps ascending to the *templum*) a templi maiestate vehementer alienum est."

7. It is true that in one other passage, V, 6, Alberti seems to waver between timber-roofed and vaulted *templa*: "Testudinatum ab incendio erit tutius; contignatum ab terraemotibus illesius." However, the subsequent sentence indicates his preference: "Sed contra vetustatem hoc robustius; ad gratiam alterum hoc venustius." The terminating part of the sentence is missing from Bartoli's and the dependent translations.

8. *Ibid.*, VII, 12. "Apertiones fenestrarum in templis esse oportet modicas et sublimes; unde nihil praeter caelum spectes . . . Horror qui ex umbra excitatur natura sui auget in animis venerationem; et coniuncta quidem multa ex parte maiestati est austeritas . . ."

9. *Ibid.*, VII, 12.

10. *Ibid.*, VII, 4.

11. *Ibid.*, VII, 10, 12.

12. Theuer, *op. cit.*, 619 ff.; and J. Rykwert's notes to his edition of James Leoni's translation of the *Ten Books on Architecture*, p. 247, n. 154.

13. *Vitruvius on Architecture*, ed. Frank Granger ("Loeb Classical Library,") (London and New York, 1931) I, 238.

14. *De re aedificatoria*, VI, 3. "Nam quom in Italia vetus haberet hospitium ars aedificatoria praesertim apud Etruscos quorum praeter illa regum miracula quae leguntur, laberynthi et sepulchrorum, pervetusta et probatissima extant literis tradita templorum aedificandorum monimenta . . ."

15. *Ibid.*, VI, 1. "Ut vix unum ex tanto naufragio Vitruvium superstitem haberemus scriptorem procul dubio instructissimum, sed ita affectum tempestate atque lacerum ut multis locis multa desint et multis plurima desideres."

16. *Ibid.*, V, 3. "Nam regum quidem aedes in media urbis aditu facilis, ornatu venusta, lautitiae elegans, magis quam superba sit condecet. Tyranno non aedes magis quam arx locanda est . . ."

17. *De architectura*, V, 1 (*ed. cit.*, n. 13) I, p. 256. "Sin autem locus erit amplior in longitudine, chalcidica in extremis constituantur."

18. *De re aedificatoria*, VII, 14.

19. On this point, I part ways with Rudolf Wittkower, *Architectural Principles in the Age of Humanism* (London, 1949), p. 6 and n. 2, who would rather place less emphasis on the difference between *templum* and basilica.

20. *De re aedificatoria*, VII, 3. "At nostri quidem ad usum sacrificii passim basilicas usurparunt; id quidem tum quod a principio basilicis privatorum convocari et congruere consuessent; tum quod in eis summa cum dignitate pro tribunali ara collocaretur, et circum aras chorus bellissime haberetur. Reliquum basilicae uti est ambulatio et porticus populo . . . pateret. Accedebat quod concionantis pontificis vox commodius basilica audiretur materiata quam testudinato in templo."

21. L. H. Heydenreich, "Spätwerke Brunelleschi's," *JPKS*, LII (1931), 1 ff.

22. *Codex Urbis Romae Topographicus*, ed. C. L. Urlichs (Würzburg. 1871), *passim*, esp. pp. 107 ff. 121 f., 163 f., 237 f.

23. *De re aedificatoria*, I, 8.

24. Theuer, *op. cit.*, p. 356, and Pl. III, 5-6; pp. 618 ff., note 5; see also Rykwert, *op. cit.*, pp. 242, n. 30, and 247, n. 144.

25. *De re aedificatoria*, I, 8.

26. Francesco di Giorgio, *Trattato*,

Turin, Bibl. Naz.; *Il libro di Giuliano da San Gallo,* ed. C. Hülsen (Leipzig, 1910), f. 63 v; Sebastiano Serlio, *Cinque libri dell' architectura,* (Venice, 1566), Book III, fol. 8; Andrea Palladio, *I quataro libri dell' architettura* (Venice, 1570), Book IV, p. 12.

27. Alberti, *Della pittura,* Bk. II (H. Janitschek, *Leone Battista Alberti's kleinere kunsttheoretische Schriften* ["*Quellenschriften für Kunstgeschichte*"] [Vienna, 1877]), p. 113.

28. Bartolomeo Bramantino, *Le rovine di Roma,* ed. G. Mongeri (Milan, 1880), *passim.*

29. A. Bartoli, *Monumenti antichi nei disegni degli Uffizi* (Florence, 1914–22), *passim*; T. Ashby, "Sixteenth-century Drawings of Roman Buildings Attributed to Andreas Coner," *BSR,* II (1904), 26 ff., 27 f.

30. A. F. Gori, *Monumentum sive Columbarium Libertorum . . . Liviae Augustae* (Florence, 1727).

31. Bartoli, *op. cit.,* fig. 590 (Uffizi, dis. arch., 1720 *r*).

32. Bartoli, *op. cit.,* figs. 655 and 689 (Uffizi, dis. arch., 689 *v* and 669).

33. Bartoli, *op. cit.,* Figs. 652, 679, 691 (Uffizi, dis arch., 687 *r,* 664 *v,* 671 *r*) and *passim.*

34. J. Seznec, *The Survival of the Pagan Gods* (Bollingen Series, XXXVIII, New York, 1953), pp. 11 ff.; see also John Daniel Cooke, "Euhemerism: A Mediaeval Interpretation of Classical Paganism," *Speculum,* II (1927). 396 ff.

35. *De re aedificatoria,* VIII, 3.

36. *Ibid.,* V, 6.

37. *Ibid.,* VIII, 10.

38. *Leonis Baptistae Alberti Opera Inedita,* ed. H. Mancini (Florence, 1890), pp. 291 f.

39. A. E. Ritscher, "Die Kirche S. Andrea in Mantua," *Zeitschrift für Bauwesen,* XLIX (1899), cols. 1 ff., 181 ff.

Postscript

The concluding paragraph requires a word of caution. Contrary to prevailing opinion and to my own opinion at the time of writing, the transept of S. Andrea in Mantua turns out to have been begun long before 1597. Eugene J. Johnson, in his Ph.D. thesis, has established that it was planned as early as or before 1482. The late sixteenth-century statement to the effect that transept, chancel, and crossing conformed to the "modello antico" must then be taken seriously. This still leaves open the question whether this *modello,* including transept and chancel, originated as an afterthought of Alberti's between 1470 and 1472 or as a change of plan devised after his death in 1472. In neither case, it seems to me, can it have been on Alberti's mind when outlining to Lodovico Gonzaga the original project of the church as a *Templum Etruscum.*

Additional Bibliography

Buddensieg, T., "Die Konstantins Basilika in Einer Zeichnung Francesco di Giorgios . . ." *Münch]b,* 3rd ser., XIII (1962) 37 ff.

Francesco di Giorgio Martini, *Trattati,* ed. C. Maltese (Milan, 1967).

Hubala, H. "L. B. Albertis Langhaus von S. Andrea in Mantua," *Festschrift Kurt Badt* (Berlin, 1961), pp. 83–120.

Johnson, E. J. *S. Andrea in Mantua,* Ph.D. Diss., Institute of Fine Arts, New York University, in preparation.

21

THE TRAGIC AND COMIC SCENE
OF THE RENAISSANCE:
THE BALTIMORE AND
URBINO PANELS *

THE ARCHITECTURAL PERSPECTIVES in Urbino and Baltimore (Figs. 130, 131) need not be introduced to historians of art and architecture.[1] Twenty years ago they were masterfully analyzed by Fiske Kimball.[2] Their given date, sometime in the 1470's, is based on the remnants of an inscription which fifty years ago were half-legible on the Urbino panel. Their attribution to Luciano Laurana, based on the same half-effaced inscription, and generally though never definitely accepted,[3] has recently again been contested by ascribing them to Francesco di Giorgio Martini.[4] The question is moot. Indeed, the panels are not pendants, properly speaking, since they differ both in size and proportion: the Baltimore panel measures 0.91 × 2.19 m, the Urbino panel 1.09 × 3.82 m. It is not even quite certain that they were actually executed by the same hand.[5] But Kimball's principal thesis seems to remain beyond doubt: the architectures represented on the two panels are closely linked to Leone Battista Alberti's theories and, indeed, should be viewed as posthumous derivations from his architectural style.

This note regards neither the attribution of the panels nor their place in the history of Renaissance architecture. Its purpose is merely to attempt an explanation of their subject matter. They have been vaguely and alternately described as architectural perspectives and as stage designs.[6] To my knowledge no proof has ever been attempted one way or the other. I may be wrong, but I believe such proof is possible: in my opinion the panels are precisely the first representations of the *scena tragica* and the *scena comica* of the Renaissance.

Renaissance stage design, as is well known, was closely linked to the development of perspective. It was prepared during the second third of the fifteenth century by the large scale architectural backgrounds of paintings and reliefs in Florence, Perugia, Urbino and other progressive centers of Quattrocento art. Ghiberti's reliefs on the second door, especially the Queen of Sheba's visit to Solomon exemplify this type of design in which many-figured choirs support

*From *Gazette des Beaux-Arts*, XXXIII (1948), 327–346. The staff members of the Walters Art Gallery, Baltimore, especially Mr. Edward S. King, Miss Winifred Kennedy and Mr. David Rosen, have been most generous in providing information and photographs of the panel in that Gallery.

the action of the main actors, all standing against a highly developed architectural setting. The clear, correct, and impressive linear perspective of such architectural settings was transferred from these compositions into the newly developing art of theatre design, and, indeed, for almost three centuries perspective and stage design became nearly synonymous. Throughout the sixteenth and early seventeenth centuries, the principles of stage design are discussed simply as a sub-section of perspective design: witness, e.g., Sebastiano Serlio, *Il secondo libro di prospettiva,* Paris, 1545; Daniele Barbaro, *La pratica della perspettiva,* Venice, 1568; Nicolo Sabbatini, *Pratica di fabricar scene. . . . ,* Ravenna, 1638. This close alliance and, indeed, quasi-identity of stage design and perspective construction would explain also the great stress placed in both the Urbino and Baltimore panels on perspective design. The verticals and orthogonals of the construction are clearly visible in the main palaces on either side; and indeed, in the Baltimore panel, one can even see two rows of pin holes leading to the vanishing point, and obviously intended to hold in place a string used in the basic construction.[7]

Perspective construction, however, is but a means of stage design. It was used to realize, within the clearly defined and perceptible space of the Early and High Renaissance, the appropriate backgrounds for theatrical performances; appropriate, that is, not to the individual play (as with us) but to the species: tragedy, comedy or satire. In this concept the Renaissance is believed to follow the tradition of Roman and Greek antiquity.[8]

The Renaissance concept of the three types of stage sets—the tragic, the comic, and the satiric—goes back to Vitruvius' brief statement: "Tragic (scenes) are designed with columns, pediments (*fastigia*), statues and other regal surroundings; the comic have the appearance of private buildings with balconies (*moeniana*), and overhangs (*profectus*) with windows made to imitate reality after the fashion of ordinary buildings. Satiric settings are painted with trees, caves, mountains, and other country features designed to imitate landscapes."[9] On this basis Renaissance artists elaborated their types of scenes as first fully described by Serlio in the second book of his work. In this book, published in 1545,[10] he translates the Vitruvian generalizations into greater particulars which are too amusing not to be quoted. The tragic scene (Fig. 132) ". . . is to represent tragedies. Its settings want to be for great personalities since accidents of love, and unexpected events, and violent and cruel deaths have always taken place in the houses of great lords, of dukes and noble princes or even of kings. Therefore, there must be in these stage sets no building which has nothing noble . . ." In the comic scene (Fig. 133), on the other hand, "the settings . . . want to be those of private persons, such as citizens, lawyers, tradesmen, parasites and other similar people. In the first place the house of the procuress must not be omitted, also the scene must not be without a tavern, and a church (*tempio*) is highly necessary . . ."[11] He then exemplifies, with ". . . a pierced portico: behind which you may see another house like the first one, the arches of which are of Gothic design.[12] Balconies, some call them pergolas, others balustrades (*ringhiere*), contribute powerfully to the façades because of their foreshortening; likewise some cornices, the details of which jut out from the corner . . . are very effective. Likewise houses with strong outward projections (overhangs?) look well, such as the Tavern of the Moon down here (*sc.* in the wood cut). Especially one must choose the smaller houses and place them in front so that one sees other buildings above them . . ." (We omit the satirical scene which does not enter into our discussion.)

Serlio's woodcuts illustrate his descriptions: the tragic scene is flanked by palaces, leading towards a triumphal arch in the background. Obelisks and pyramids show behind it, far back. The palaces on both sides increase in height as they recede; but this increase is gradual and its slow progress is emphasized by placing the edifices throughout (or almost) on one straight line. Those to the right all open into porticoes toward the street and these porticoes are supported by arches on piers, or by architraves resting on columns; the upper floors have either arcaded windows or plain windows with mezzanine openings above. A small Roman temple is inserted between the palaces. To the left, another triumphal arch stands in the very foreground surmounted by two flaming urns; it is followed by palaces—one with a continuous balcony, the next with a small single one. A ruin, obviously Roman, appears in the middle ground. Statues and reliefs decorate the triumphal arch in the rear and the edifices in the forefront. All palaces are laid out in perfectly symmetrical designs: their axes number from three to five; the center axis is occupied by the entrance gate; and needless to say, all these gates face the street.

Just as one recognizes in Serlio's description and illustration of the tragic scene Vitruvius' "statues and regal surroundings," his comic scene embodies Vitruvius' directions. The houses change rapidly in size. To the left stands first the bawdy house, a small two-storied affair with an overhang sustained by wooden supports, and with pointed windows on the second floor. Behind it, and strongly protruding into the street, rises a tall palace with arched windows on the second floor, and an open pergola on the third. It is followed by a much lower building, again with a pergola on its upper, *i.e.* the second, floor. The corresponding buildings to the right are: a rather tall, two-storied structure with a pointed arched portico (*alla moderna*) below, and a wooden pergola above, overhung by a roof; a tall Renaissance palace follows next with four axes, its door to the right and surmounted by a balcony; again further back, the Tavern of the Moon juts out into the street, with its counter door on the ground floor, a pointed window on the second, and rectangular windows in the colossal overhang of the third; the roof is surmounted by some kind of lattice work. At the end of the street rises the façade of a church surmounted by a campanile: its top story is in ruins, and bushes grow from it; a flag pole sticks out from a lower story.

Compared to Vitruvius' sparse comments then, Serlio's representations of the two opposing types of scenes have become quite definite. Specific vocabularies, as it were, have been developed for both the tragic and the comic scenes and made recognizable by the recurrence of certain motives. The tragic scene is marked by the triumphal arch, the obelisks, the temple, the palaces, and by the overall use of classical forms and the perfect symmetry of design; the comic scene is characterized by the church façade, the tavern, the upper floor open loggia, the balconies, by Gothic arches and wooden construction, and throughout by buildings that are irregular in height and projection with an intentional lack of harmony and symmetry. The tragic scene represents a higher reality, a reality which is beyond the experience of daily life; its architecture is that of a never and nowhere land evolved from a free interpretation of antiquity. The comic scene, on the contrary, is one of everyday experience: diverse structures intermingle, from palaces to bawdy houses and taverns; a checkered array of construction methods are placed side by side, wood, brick, and stone; and the mixture of obsolete Gothic and of Renaissance houses conveys the impression of an historical development which for just this reason is natural to any old town. The bushes on the ruined top floor of the campanile only stress this element of daily experience which underlies the entire scene; it adds the element of natural decay to that of historical growth. Barbaro summarizes the contrast in clear words: "Tragic scenes are painted with tall palaces, beautiful porticoes, magnificent edifices, sumptuous arches, and military avenues; to the comic scenes are given private houses, taverns, alleys and narrow streets. . . ." [13]

Behind this elaboration of Vitruvius' spare stage directions lies the well known Renaissance concept of the social hierarchy of architecture. First formulated around 1450 in Alberti's *De re aedificatoria,* it implies that not only different building types but indeed different vocabularies and different styles of architecture correspond to the social position of a building.[14] The matter has not infrequently been treated before (most recently in an excellent essay by W. A. Eden)[15] and a few quotations from Alberti's writings will suffice: "Every man's house should certainly be suited to the condition of life which he is in . . ." (V, 6); "the magnitude of the building should be adapted to the dignity of the owner"; and "the Royal Palace or, in a free city, the house of the . . . Chief Magistrate ought to be the first in beauty and magnificence . . ." (XI, I). Churches, public buildings and private palaces, descending in that order, are to form a hierarchy in dignity and beauty. Below them are the houses of the common people: "they build only for necessity, the rich for pleasure and delight . . ." (V, 9); "their houses need not be beautiful but merely practical" (V, 18). This, indeed, is the tenet to be remembered throughout when reading over Alberti's precepts for design: that buildings must be of equal height; that they must be symmetrical; that they must have an odd number of axes with the entrance in the center; that orders of pilasters or columns are required to express the beauty of design, proportion, numbers and collocation. All of these precepts refer only to buildings of the higher class; in "middling houses" designed for "middling persons" (V, 18), they have to cede to the demands of practicality. This implies that they may have to be and, indeed, often are in practice irregular, simple and without ornament, and old-fashioned. For Alberti, and indeed for the entire Renaissance theory, architecture *all' antica* was an ideal design reserved for public buildings and for the palaces of a social and intellectual elite; the common people and their buildings had no part in it. Barbaro put this idea into a few words, with special reference to stage design: the comic scene "requires less knowledge of architecture than the tragic scene, since the buildings are of private persons who arrange themselves as best they can. . . ." [16] Already some years earlier in Serlio's stage design for the comic scene, this latter notion had come to mean that the architecture of the common people carried on the vocabulary *alla moderna, i.e.,* of Gothic architecture, and thus was both obsolete and slightly ridiculous.

The so-called Laurana panels at Urbino and Baltimore fall into place, it seems to me, when viewed anticipatorily and retrospectively under these two aspects: Alberti's concepts of a social hierarchy of architecture as formulated about 1450, and Vitruvius' description of the tragic and comic scenes, as interpreted in 1545 by Serlio. The Baltimore panel (Figs. 131, 134) shows in the foreground noble palaces, raised on high platforms. The fountain is flanked by four columns carrying images, a direct reminder, it would seem, of Vitruvius' formula. The marble pavement is laid out in a precious design. In the background rise, side-by-side, a miniature Colosseum, a triumphal arch, which becomes a significant prop of the tragic scenes of the High Renaissance (Fig. 134), and an octagonal building which can only be a temple. Further back, and hardly visible in the photographs, one distinguishes the towered entrance of what the fifteenth century would have called a *regia* and what we improperly call a castle, a number of palaces and, in a very subordinate position, some smaller houses. One might still be inclined to doubt the significance of the Baltimore panel within this argument. Turning to the Urbino panel, however, (Fig. 130), the situation becomes clear. To begin with, the Urbino "perspective" is designed in a far less solemn and fundamentally far less "antique" mood. The pavement of the plaza has a simple design: two octagonal well heads rise from it, very different from the basin *all'antica* of the Baltimore panel. The buildings, instead of keeping in line, project and recede along the plaza. The palaces in the foreground are Renaissance all right, but they have characteristics of their own: the first one to the left terminates with an upper loggia, its beams clearly showing—not as markedly, but definitely reminiscent of Serlio's comic scene. The second palace to the left has a balcony (Fig. 135). Further back, on either side of the picture, the houses grow small and decidedly petty-bourgeois. Their height varies, their roofs project strongly. Two buildings are linked by a garden wall; one house turns its short side without a door towards the street; in another one the quoins of the windows form pointed arches; to the right (Fig. 136) two houses show overhangs. Façades are irregular: one has only two axes, another, while having three, places the door asymmetrically in an outer bay. Throughout, plants hang from windows and grow from the corners of buildings, often

349

in disorder, and weeds or herbs rather than flowers (Fig. 136). To the left, a long vine hangs over the garden wall. In between, small dwarfed trees and flowerpots occupy window sills and balconies. Evidence of decay is visible on the buildings: water has left its mark on the corner of the loggia of the front palace to the left and on the ground floor of the palazzetto next to it; on the first palace to the right, pieces of stucco have broken off the false arcades of the top story.

All these elements find their counterparts in Serlio's stage set, two generations later, and other elements may be added to characterize the Urbino panel further: "classical," i.e. Roman, elements are entirely lacking; a church façade appears in the background, that is the very element which Serlio considered indispensable for the design of a comic scene. Even the round building in the center of the scene, at first hard to explain, is in reality an element which fits into and, indeed, characterizes the comic scene of the Renaissance (Fig. 137).

At first glance, this round structure looks like one of the many *tempietti* which Renaissance painters liked to set up in the midst of a plaza, and, indeed, the term used by the Renaissance for any such central building would have been *tempio* or *tempietto*. But what kind of a *tempietto* is the one at Urbino? It is round and covered with a low conical roof, surmounted by a small lantern. Its two stories are articulated by superimposed orders of Corinthian half columns. Windows open in the upper story, small loopholes beside that in the center right above the entrance porch. The ground floor, rising from a circular platform surrounded by steps, is open all around. Only low and thin walls of *opus reticulatum* are inserted between the piers with their half columns, almost as if they were stalls. Indeed, they are stalls—and the whole building is but a market hall, a strange type of structure which the fifteenth century appears to have considered an essential element of a market place *all'antica*.

We will have to make a little detour to understand how the humanists of the Early Renaissance hit upon the idea of placing such round halls in their pictures of marketplaces and how they came to give these halls their specific form. As we know today, market places in late Republican and Imperial times were called *macella*: a walled-in area was surrounded by shops which sometimes were protected by porticoes; a round structure, a *tholus* with a conical roof, rose in the center of the area, possibly a well-house and at the same time the shrine of the *genus macelli*; the Emperor's shrine opened as a niche from one wall of the area. The Renaissance obviously knew none of these archeological data. But they could rely on literary and pictorial sources. A *macellum* according to Varro (*De lingua latina*, V, 147) was a market where all kinds of viands were sold and for which a place had been built. ("*Haec omnia postquam contracta in unum locum quae ad victum pertinebant et aedificatus locus, appellatum macellum*."). Dio Cassius (LXI, 18, 3) confirmed this statement with a special reference to Nero's *Macellum Magnum*. Obviously then, a *macellum* was a building for market purposes—a supermarket as it were. One further detail seemed to be contained in a reference, likewise from Varro and known through Nonius' dictionary, to the *tholus macelli:* any domed structure obviously was round.

All these writers were known to the fifteenth-century humanists: Varro's fifth book; Nonius' excerpts; and Dio Cassius in translation.[17] Their references to *macella* and to the *tholus macelli* were common knowledge and they were bound to be misunderstood. A *tholus* was a dome; therefore a *tholus macelli* was a dome covering a *macellum* (rather than a dome rising in a *macellum* area); therefore a *macellum* was a round, domed structure, serving the business of the market. This misinterpretation was seemingly confirmed by a series of Neronian coins, frequent at that time;[18] they showed portions of the area with the surrounding porticoes and the *tholus* of the *Macellum Magnum* signed in big letters: MAC (ellum) AUG (usti). The *tholus* presented itself as a round, two-storied open pavilion, supported by superimposed orders of Corinthian columns, and accessible by steps. Grilles, shaped very much like *opus reticulatum,* link the columns to each other, at least on the upper floor. The columns, in most examples of the series, appear to carry architraves in both stories. A conical, tiled roof crowned by an *acroterium* and perhaps with a center opening, terminates the structure. The whole building rises against the background of a two-storied colonnade. These coins then would support the picture of a *macellum* which any good fifteenth-century humanist would have gained on the basis of the literary sources: round, two-storied, and with a conical roof or a dome. Since at the same time the sources seemed to imply that this *tholus* was the *macellum* itself and thus nothing but a market hall, any market place would have to be characterized by such a round structure. Its existence, in the eyes of the fifteenth-century humanists, would indeed characterize a square as a market place and set it off against other squares of a more aristocratic character such as the ones described by Alberti.

Traces of this link between round structures and market places are scattered through Renaissance descriptions and pictures. In a codex of 1465, belonging to and possibly illustrated by Giovanni Marcanova, M.D. from Bologna, a round structure occupies the center of the market place: its door is surmounted by a figure of Abundance holding a cornucopia in her arm. Vendors carry baskets with all kinds of edibles towards the building—another reference to Varro's etymologies (*forum* from *ferre*)—or offer their wares seated on the ground.[19] Another reminiscence of this same concept occurs in Filarete's dream city, Sforzinda (1460–64): the middle of the market place is taken up by a small central building. It is a church (*tempio*) but it is still crowned by a figure of the *Dea Copia.*[20]

But none of these buildings, in its design, is quite as close to the *macellum* as described and depicted by the ancients as the round structure in the Urbino panel.

Thus the round building in the center of the Urbino panel, rather than being an alien feature is, indeed, an essential element within the comic scene. The identity with a *macellum* would have been obvious to any Renaissance humanist.

Its presence would thus characterize the plaza as a market place, an everyday city square, surrounded by everyday buildings—some modern palaces, others petty bourgeois and obsolete. The elements of decay and of nature in and between these buildings would increase the "commonplace" character of the set. All this leads up to the fully developed Renaissance pattern of Serlio's stage designs —if due changes are taken into consideration. To begin with, Serlio develops his layouts in terms of proscenium, backstage, and backdrop, while the Urbino and Baltimore panels suggest mere backdrops. Secondly, and in addition to this fundamental difference in the technique of stage design, Serlio, in comparison with the Quattrocento panels, deepens the contrast between the comic and tragic scenes: in his comic scene the elements of decay, of everyday life and of obsolescence are more strongly marked; the Gothic elements, the low class of the structures, the eruption of ruin and nature into the town are stressed in an almost caricaturist way. Correspondingly he eliminates all those features of a "noble" Renaissance and Roman architecture which in the Urbino panel were still present and which thus tended to bridge the gap between the comic scene and its tragic counterpart, the Baltimore panel. Still, the Serlio designs are but a later and more clearly marked elaboration on a Renaissance interpretation of Vitruvian stage design—an interpretation of which the Baltimore and Urbino panels are, we submit, early examples.

Even so, a great number of questions remain to be answered: the two most important refer, first to the intermediary stages between the panels of the 1470's and Serlio's evolved patterns; and second to the milieu in which the panels in Urbino and Baltimore could originate. Too little is known of stage design before 1545 to give more than a cursory survey following the standard works on stage design.[21] In his research in perspective and stage design Serlio, according to his own statement, drew on Baldassare Peruzzi, Girolamo Genga, Raphael and Bramante. With the exception of Bramante these are also mentioned by Vasari as champions of stage design. To my knowledge, no drawing is known from Genga's hand; no stage drawing from Raphael's. Only some stage designs attributed to Peruzzi have been published.[22] The deplorable state of Peruzzi research makes it impossible at the moment either to judge the attributions or to enlarge the number of drawings in this group; but those published seem indeed to bridge the gap between the Serlio drawings and the Quattrocento panels. Of course, nobody can tell which, if any, of these drawings were done for the performance of Cardinal Bibbiena's comedy *Calandria* in October 1513, or for the other plays for which, according to Vasari, Peruzzi under the pontificate of Leo X made stage designs, with "palaces, . . . bizarre temples, loggias and various kinds of cornices. . . ." But it seems that among his drawings two groups can be distinguished. A stage scene, full of temples, grandiose palaces, obelisks and triumphal arches, appears to be sketched in a drawing in the *Taccuino senese,* evidently at the very end of Peruzzi's life. On the other hand two or three earlier drawings are characterized as stage sets for comedies: the

Turin drawing (Fig. 138), showing the left half of a backstage, reveals itself as a "comic" scene by the presence of a tavern and by the modest character of the surrounding houses with their large projecting roofs on long brackets. Likewise, the large sheet in the Uffizi (Fig. 139) must have been intended for a comedy. Again it shows a tavern, this time with pointed windows and with a covered balcony on the top floor; next to it rises a modest house with an asymmetrical façade and an overhanging bracketed roof; further in front stands a tiny palace with loggias on the lower and upper floors. There appear, moreover, the dome of a church, two or three campanili and a number of ruins such as the Castel S. Angelo, the Colosseum and the Torre delle Milizie, most of them with bushes growing from between their crumbling stones.

The majority of these elements anticipate Serlio's final pattern of the comic scene. At the same time, however, they clearly mark an earlier stage in the development. Indeed, the Gothic elements are hardly brought out. Renaissance features are more strongly stressed and are intermingled with architectural features from Roman antiquity which in Serlio's concept twenty years later, were reserved for the design of the tragic scene: Roman ruins and obelisks, triumphal arches and columns, and a small Roman temple. The separation of the vocabulary has, as it were, not yet been perfected. "Noble" elements are still interspersed with the overall "ignoble" architecture of the *scena comica*. We say still, for it seems as though the "ignoble" features—Gothic windows, balconies, small houses and an overall unclassical attitude—were between 1500 and 1540 gradually crowding out the Renaissance and classical elements which formerly had been present also in the comic scene. The stage design for a performance of the *Calandria* at Urbino in 1513, directed and described by Baldassare Castiglione, has often been quoted. It showed a street near the walls of the town (the low class character of the comedy is thus emphasized) with churches and taverns, both in backstage constructions and backdrop perspective; but intermingled with these "ignoble" elements were not only palaces, but (one thinks of the Urbino *macellum*) an octagonal *tempio* in the center and, on the left-hand side of the stage, a triumphal arch surmounted by an equestrian statue and decorated with other sculptures. On the other hand, the description of a stage set designed for a performance of Ariosto's *Cassaria* in Ferrara in 1508 mentions no classical elements, only "houses, belfries and gardens" (*"una contracta et prospettiva de una terra cum casa, chiesa, campanile et zardini. . ."*). Still, by and large, it would seem that the further back we go within the period of 1470–1520, the more the comic scene is still conceived in an overall classical design. Its architecture differs from the "noble" stage set only in certain features, such as balconies, overhangs and loggias and in their being intermingled with every-day elements, such as church façades and bell-towers, as well as in their dilapidation.

Back beyond 1500 the beginnings of stage design are even harder to trace. The engraved architectural perspective of a street with palaces, triumphal arches and campanile, signed with Bramante's name, seems indeed to compete with

Peruzzi's large drawing in the Uffizi. Like this it intermingles classical and Renaissance elements and clearly separates proscenium, backstage and backdrop; but it is now attributed to Cesariano and thus not necessarily earlier than Peruzzi's.[23] A drawing, likewise Bramantesque, in the Ambrosiana, is beyond doubt a comic scene, but it is hardly earlier than 1530.[24]

The one much quoted clue to an early stage perspective is a statement made by Giovanni Sulpizio da Veroli. In the dedication to Cardinal Raphael Riario which prefaces the first Vitruvius edition, Sulpizio lauds the Cardinal for having first presented on a regular stage an ancient tragedy, and for having erected to this end, between 1484 and 1486, a tent theatre in his own palace; and also for having first shown *"nostro saeculo . . . picturatae scenae faciem"* at the occasion of the performance of a comedy by Pomponius Laetus.[25] The date of this latter event is not given, but it must fall between Raphael Riario's election to the purple, December 1477, and the date of the dedication, ca. 1486. The term *facies picturatae scenae* can be interpreted correctly only within the context of Giovanni Sulpizio's entire preface. Sulpizio obviously thinks of a stage as consisting of a platform five feet high (corresponding to Vitruvius' *pulpitum*) and of a *facies*. The place and shape of this *facies* are not explained. Thus it might be located either at the entrance to the platform, framing it as a stage prospect, or at its end, terminating it as a backdrop.[26] Yet the term *facies* is explained again in another passage of the preface. There Sulpizio states that it would not be hard to construct a *facies* which could be turned around or pushed aside (*"versatilem et ductilem quando libuerit facies non difficulter"*); thus it cannot be a framing stage prospect, or a curtain, but only a backdrop. Such a backdrop might still have been designed as a *scaenae frons* (Vitruvius, V, 6, 7; VII, 10) with painted columns and three openings. Yet such a "correct interpretation" of Vitruvius appears in Italy first in Barbaro's illustrations in 1568.[27] The fifteenth and early sixteenth centuries speak only of stage sets with painted towers, palaces or landscapes. Thus Sulpizio's reference appears to be to a painted backdrop of this latter type.

The combination of these three figures, Raphael Riario, Giovanni Sculpizio da Veroli and Pomponius Laetus, spotlights the circle of problems which attended the origins of Renaissance stage design in the last decades of the fifteenth century. Riario, the brilliant and spendthrift nephew of Sixtus IV, was related through the marriage of his Rovere cousins to the princely houses of Ferrara and Urbino. In the 1480's and 1490's he had the Palazzo della Cancelleria designed as a residence by an Albertian architect, possibly from Alberti's Urbinate circle. He was a leading protector of the theatrical revival in Rome, a revival which paralleled the contemporary related movements at the dynastic courts of Ferrara, Urbino and Mantua. Pomponius Laetus was the outstanding figure in this revival: philologist, antiquarian, archeologist and one of the survivors of the unfortunate Roman Academy of the 1460's and the ensuing persecution—a martyr of antiquity. Resuscitated, as it were, he was the foremost theatrical producer of the 1480's;

Plautus' *Menaechmi* and *Epidicus,* Terence's *Andria,* Seneca's *Hippolytus* were among his productions performed in Rome both in public on the Capitoline Hill, and in private at the Castel S. Angelo and in Riario's palace. At the same time Pomponius Laetus was one of the outstanding authorities on technical Latin writers. Together with Sulpizio, he edited Frontinus' *On Aqueducts,* which is added to the first printed edition of Vitruvius, the very one dedicated to Cardinal Riario, and he seems to have assisted Sulpizio in preparing the Vitruvius edition as well.

Vitruvian studies, the theatrical revival of Plautus, Terence and Seneca, and the beginnings of stage design, thus formed an inseparable triad in late fifteenth-century Rome. Sulpizio's dedicatory letter to the young Cardinal reveals this interlocking. It is, in short, nothing but a harangue, imploring the Cardinal to support the theatrical revival by erecting a new theatre building. Vitruvius, if he were alive, so the argument runs, "would be working for you, building camps, villas, churches, porticoes, castles and palaces, but in the first place theatres. . . . Go ahead, then, and build a theatre! Yours compare with the achievements of the ancients, you have set up a theatre tent, and a painted scene. We need no gold or silver or ivory scene—just a modest place after the prescriptions of Vitruvius. . . . We need a theatre . . . Of churches we have a goodly number and you can build them when you are old. . . . The late Pope Sixtus, the present Pope Innocent have improved and are improving the looks of the city. What, then, is left for our time to do aside from bringing water to the town (an obvious allusion to Frontinus' work appended to the edition) and from setting up a theatre. . . ."

Vitruvian studies and the revival of the theatre were closely linked in the 1480's. The same circle of persons was involved. Indeed, it almost seems as though Vitruvius' work had been considered, at least partly, as an introduction to theatre design. His few sentences on the three types of scenes are, needless to say, of paramount importance, being determining factors in the development of stage design throughout the Renaissance. But perhaps one can go beyond this starting point. No doubt Vitruvius' remarks on perspective referred to stage design—specifically to the design of a *scaenae frons.*[28] In the Renaissance they would be interpreted as referring to stage backdrops; the very term *"scenographia"* would suggest such a link and, indeed, as pointed out before, the sixteenth century remained fully aware of this interpretation. At the same time an approach of still greater importance should be considered: Vitruvius' and altogether ancient architecture, could obviously be reconstructed on a stage set with the greatest ease, far easier, indeed, than it could be built. Antiquity, as interpreted by the Renaissance, was distinctly a never-never land—a higher reality which was fully consistent in itself. In a city such as Rome or Florence or Mantua an individual building, a church, a palace, perhaps a single house, could be set up to represent revived antiquity. It would stand out from the medieval surroundings, but it would stand out like a sore thumb. To remodel an entire town remained an ideal never achieved—aside from the very partial rebuilding of tiny Pienza—and obviously difficult to achieve where hard reality was concerned. But it could be done on the canvas of a stage set. This, we should say, is the real link between Vitruvian studies and stage design.

No doubt the two panels under discussion might be detailed sketches or models for actual stage design. But there is no need for such far-reaching assumptions; they may just as well be experiments in evolving scenes on the basis of Vitruvius —a kind of painted commentary to his chapter on the theatre. The difference between models and experiments is small, and certainly it was negligible in the circles in which, during the late fifteenth century, Vitruvius, Plautus and Terence were being interpreted, commented on, and revived. In any case, the two panels in Urbino and Baltimore are in our opinion early, and perhaps the earliest, attempts of the Renaissance to create an image of the comic and the tragic scene *al Vitruvio*. Urbino, in the 1470's, was, it seems, a focus of stage design. This is not strange if one remembers that during these very years it was a center of perspective studies, of architecture and of architectural theory: witness Piero della Francesca, Luciano Laurana, Francesco di Giorgio Martini and young Bramante.

Kimball has convincingly proved the dependence of the architectural design of the panels on the theories of Leone Battista Alberti. Indeed, the architecture of Urbino in this decade is largely dependent on his work, both in theory and practice: the main parts of the Ducal Palace; the church of S. Bernardino; and the related buildings in Jesi, Pesaro and Cortona. Could Alberti, then, also have stimulated the development of stage designs as first represented by the two panels? His remarks in *De re aedificatoria* (VIII, 7) are brief. Obviously they are excerpts from Vitruvius, but just for this reason they are worth quoting: "Since in the theatre three kinds of poets were active: the tragic kind who presented the miseries of the tyrants; the comic type who explained the worries and concerns of fathers of families; the satirical who sang the loveliness of the country, and the loves of the shepherds; there existed also an arrangement whereby, through a turning mechanism, a painted backdrop could be immediately produced, and there would appear either an *atrium* or a house (*casa*) or a forest, according to what they had to say and the stories they enacted." Thus Alberti thinks of stage design along three lines: first, there are no stage wings and the scene is limited to the mere painting of a backdrop. Second, this backdrop is limited to representing a courtyard or palace (*atrium* may mean either) or a single modest house (the term *casa* indicates its lowly condition) or a forest; and while Alberti does not expressly state so, the entire background of his writings and of his experiments with perspective peep-shows, allowed the inference that these representations were done in the form of architectural perspectives. Third, the three backdrops which were needed for tragedies, comedies and satires were envisaged as mounted on a turning device on which they could supposedly be wheeled about, according to what kind of play was performed.

This turning machine was obviously thought of as a triangular prism bearing one scene on each face; the *"versatilis facies"* of Sulpizio's preface immediately comes to mind. Obviously the device was a misinterpretation of the *periaktoi,* triangular prisms discussed and described by Vitruvius for use in the stage wings (the Latin translation of *periaktos* would be *versatilis*). Scenes like those on the panels in Urbino and Baltimore could easily have been painted on the sides of such a triangular prism. It is also obvious from his work that Alberti conceived the tragic and comic scenes in terms of "noble" and "ignoble" architecture respectively. But again it is obvious that at the time of writing *De re aedificatoria,* around 1450, he had not worked out the details of such a mechanism, or for that matter of the scenes. The simple *atrium* and *casa* are the barest indications of backdrops for the tragic and comic scenes respectively. They contrast a noble and an ignoble architecture, but it is a far cry from them to the highly developed plazas in the Baltimore and Urbino panels. Of course, one wants to remember that Alberti's concepts of stage design may well have changed into more elaborate schemes toward the end of his life. But it seems neither fair nor necessary to press this point. Certainly it was Alberti who first conceived the idea of using architectural perspectives for stage backdrops; certainly the architectures of the two panels were evolved from the background of Albertian theories and buildings; and certainly the development of Vitruvian studies and of theatrical experiments throughout the second half of the fifteenth century took place within a circle of which Alberti was a dominating figure—a circle which comprised the revived Roman Academy with Pomponius Laetus and Sulpicius Verulanus and which extended to the humanist courts of Central and Upper Italy—Mantua, Ferrara, Urbino.

Such is the background against which we want to place the two panels at Urbino and Baltimore—the first preserved experiments in stage design in the fifteenth century.

Notes

1. Galleria Nazionale delle Marche, Urbino, provenance unknown. The Walters Art Gallery, Baltimore, Md., no. 37,677, purchased from the Massarenti Collection.

2. F. Kimball, "Luciano Laurana and the High Renaissance," *AB,* X (1927–1928), 125 ff. We agree with Mr. Kimball in distinguishing from these two the panel formerly of the Kaiser Friedrich Museum, Berlin no. 1615. It differs from both the Urbino and Baltimore panels in size (1.23 x 2.34 m.) and particularly in the style of the architecture; see also: A. S. Weller, *Francesco di Giorgio* (Chicago, 1943), pp. 186 ff.; H. Posse, *Die Gemälde-Gallerie des Kaiser Friedrich Museums, Vollständiger beschreibender Katalog,* I, *Die romanischen Länder* (Berlin, 1909), p. 76, in comparing the Berlin panel with those in Urbino and Baltimore, suggests incorrectly that in the Massarenti Collection this latter had a companion piece; cf. E. von Esbroek, *Catalogue du Musée . . . au Palais Accoramboni* (Rome, 1897).

3. G. M. Richter, "Architectural Phantasies by Bramante," *GBA,* ser. VI,

XXXII (1943), 5 ff. was among recent authors favoring the Laurana attribution. M. Salmi, *Piero della Francesca e il Palazzo Ducale in Urbino* (Florence, 1943) (see U. Middeldorf's review, in *AB*, XXIX [1947], 141 ff.); and L. Serra, *Il Palazzo Ducale e la Galleria Nazionale di Urbino* (Rome, 1930), p. 108, attribute the panels to Piero della Francesca.

4. R. Papini, *Francesco di Giorgio Architetto* (Florence, 1946).

5. Suggestion by my late friend, Dr. F. Saxl, The Warburg Institute, London University.

6. V. Mariani, *La scenografia italiana* (Florence, 1930), reproduces the Urbino panel without further explanation; the editors of J. Burckhardt, *The Civilization of the Italian Renaissance* (Vienna, 1937), fig. 291, reproduce the Berlin panel as a "stage design." See also: R. Petrovitch, "Questi Schiavoni," *GBA, ser.* VI, XXX (1947), 47.

7. Compare for this use of a string, for example, Piero della Francesca, *De Prospectiva Pingendi,* ed. C. Winterberg (Strassburg, 1899). The panel shows, by the way, a marked *pentimento* in the perspective design of the octagonal building in the right background.

8. For the history of stage design in the Renaissance see the well known (and occasionally, rather repetitious) standard works: E. Flechsig, *Die Dekorationen der modernen Bühne in Italien* (Diss. Leipzig, 1892); G. Ferrari, *La scenografia* (Milan, 1902); M. Herrmann, *Forschungen zur deutschen Theatergeschichte* (Berlin, 1914); L. B. Campbell, *Scenes and Machines on the English Stage during the Renaissance* (Cambridge, 1923); C. A. Nissen, *Das Bühnenbild* (Bonn, 1924–1927); C. Ricci, *La scenografia italiana* (Milan, 1930); Mariani, *op. cit.*; G. Schoene, *Die Entwicklung der Perspektivbühne von Serlio bis Galli-Bibbiena ("Theatergeschichtliche Forschungen")* (Leipzig, 1933); H. Leclerq, *Les origines italiennes de l'architecture théatrale moderne* (Paris, 1946). Two most stimulating studies are: A. Scharff, *Beiträge zur Geschichte des Bühnenbildes von 15. bis zum 17. Jahrhundert* (Diss. Freiburg, 1925; typewritten ms. at the Warburg Institute, London University, London) and G. M. Kernodle, *From Art to Theater* (Chicago, 1944).

9. Lib. V, cap. 6. We follow the division and in general, the translation of the Loeb Classical Library edition, *Vitruvius, On Architecture,* ed. F. Granger (London and New York, 1931), I, 228 ff. Older editions of Vitruvius bring the passage as the begining of Lib. V, cap. 8.

10. Sebastiano Serlio, *Il secondo libro di prospettiva* (Paris, 1545); see: W. B. Dinsmoor, "The Literary Remains of Sebastiano Serlio," *AB,* XXIV (1942), 55 ff.; 115 ff. The woodcut of the comic scene in later editions (e. g. Venice, 1566 and 1619) shows occasionally right and left reversed (see our Fig. 133).

11. The Italian text says: ". . . uno tempio vi è molto necessario, per disporre li casamenti sopra il piano detto suolo: io ne ho dato il modo più dietro . . ." Obviously punctuation and text must be emendated into ". . . necessario; per disporre li casamenti sopra il piano detto il suolo, io ne ho dato il modo più dietro . . ."

12. Serlio, following a precedent set by Filarete, used the term "moderno" to mean "Gothic."

13. D. Barbaro, *La pratica della perspettiva* (Venice, 1568), p. 130; *Idem, I dieci libri dell'architettura di M. Vitruvio* (Venice, 1556), pp. 157 ff.

14. *Editio princeps* (Florence, 1486). We shall quote from the first still unsurpassed English translation, *Leone Battista Alberti, On Architecture,* trans. J. Leoni (London, 1755).

15. W. A. Eden, "Studies in Urban Theory, The 'De Re Aedificatoria' of Leon Battista Alberti," *The Town Planning Review,* XIX (1943), 10 ff.

16. *Op. cit.* (Venice, 1568), p. 157.

17. G. Voigt, *Die Wiederbelebung des classischen Alterthums,* 3rd ed. (Leipzig, 1893), I, 247, 352; *Varro, On the Latin Language* ed. R. Kent, I ("Loeb Classical Library" [London and Cambridge, Mass., 1938]), XII ff.

18. K. Wulzinger, "Die Macellum Dupondien des Nero," *Numismatik,* II (1933), 83 ff.; 116 ff.

19. C. Huelsen, *La Roma antica di Ciriaco d'Ancona* (Rome, 1907), p. 27, Pl. V.

20. *Antonio Averlino Filarete's Traktat über die Baukunst . . .*, ed. W. v. Oettingen (Vienna, 1890) ("*Quellenschriften für Kunstgeschichte und Kunsttechnik,*" N. F., III), (Vienna, 1890).

21. See note 8.

22. Nissen, *op. cit.,* Pl. 22; Ferrari, *op. cit.,* Pl. II.

23. F. Malaguzzi-Valeri, *La corte di Lodovico il Moro,* II (Milan, 1915), 309.

24. *Ibid.,* pp. 31 ff.

25. *L. Vitruvii Pollionis ad Caesarem Augustum de Architectura liber primus (-decimus),* ed. Joannes Sulpitius (Rome, ca. 1486).

26. Scharff, *op. cit.,* pp. 7 ff. as against Herrmann, *op. cit.,* pp. 295 ff., Leclerc, *op. cit.,* p. 71 and others.

27. Kernodle, *op. cit.,* pp. 174 ff.

28. See note 8 and A. M. G. Little, "Scaenographia," *AB,* XVIII (1936), 407 ff.; *idem,* "Perspective and Scene Painting," *ibid.,* XIX (1937), 487 ff.

Postscript

Discussion has continued on both the authorship and the function of the Baltimore and Urbino panels, but I am afraid it has not progressed much beyond the point it had reached twenty years ago.

To the names traditionally suggested as the possible authors of the panels—Luciano Laurana, Francesco di Giorgio, or Piero della Francesca—that of Giuliano Sangallo has been added by Sanpaolesi and Battisti. More recently Peter Murray returns to Piero della Francesca as the author of the Urbino panel, while attributing the one in Baltimore to "a pupil like Signorelli." I have never understood why the admittedly meager evidence of an inscription read in 1724 and again in 1902 and attributing the panels to Luciano Laurana should be disregarded *in toto.* But I am no *Attribuzler,* to use Burckhardt's expression.

Nor was this my concern when I wrote the paper twenty years ago. I was interested not in the author but in what the panels represented, and I took them to reflect not only stage sets—as had been previously suggested—but specifically the tragic and comic scene as interpreted by the Renaissance. I repeat "reflect" rather than "represent"; but I doubt that they were *cassone panels* (Chastel, 1961, 141, n. 7). My original proposal has been accepted by some of the more recent writers. But it has been rejected by Sanpaolesi, who views the panels as exercises in perspective, while Battisti sees in them representations of ideal cities and specifically of ancient cities designed for the stage. This latter seems to me a decisive point: as I pointed out in my paper, the ideal city of the Renaissance or for that matter of antiquity could be built in the fifteenth century not in stone but only on the canvas of a stage backdrop. Concomitantly—so much to Sanpaolesi's suggestion—stage design was the crowning achievement of perspective, as witness Serlio's Second Book. In brief, I am not prepared to change my opinion.

Additional Bibliography

Battisti, E. "La visualizzazione della scena classica nella commedia umanistica," *Commentari,* VIII (1957), 248 ff.

Chastel, A. *Art et humanisme* (Paris, 1961).

Magagnato, L. *Teatri italiani del Cinquecento* (Venice, 1954).

Murray, P. " 'Bramante milanese': The Printings and Engravings," *Arte lombarda,* VII (1962), 25 ff.

Sanpaolesi, P. "Le prospettive architettoniche di Urbino e di Filadelfia [*sic*]," *BdA,* ser. 4, XXXIV (1949), 322 ff.

Walton, G. *The Florentine Republican Representations of . . . Lucrezia,"* M.A. thesis. Institute of Fine Arts, New York University (1962), (unpublished).

INDEX

I

J

K

PLATES

Fig. 1. Dura-Europos, remains of Christian church, isometric view (Hopkins and Baur)

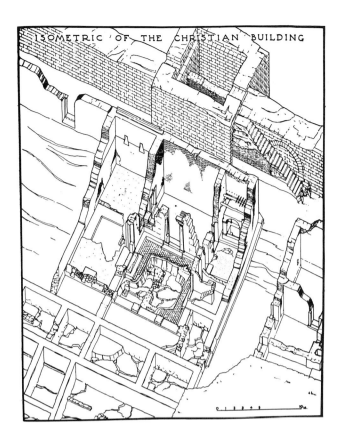

Fig. 2. Rome, Constantinian basilica of St. Peter, view of nave by Grimaldi, Rome, Vatican Library

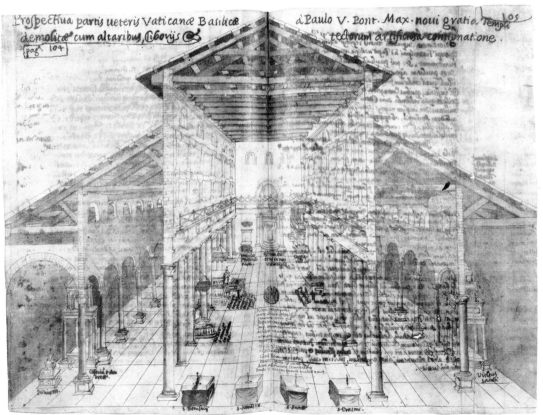

Fig. 4. Rome, S. Giovanni in Laterano, fourth-century window

Fig. 3. Rome, S. Giovanni in Laterano, fourth-century apse

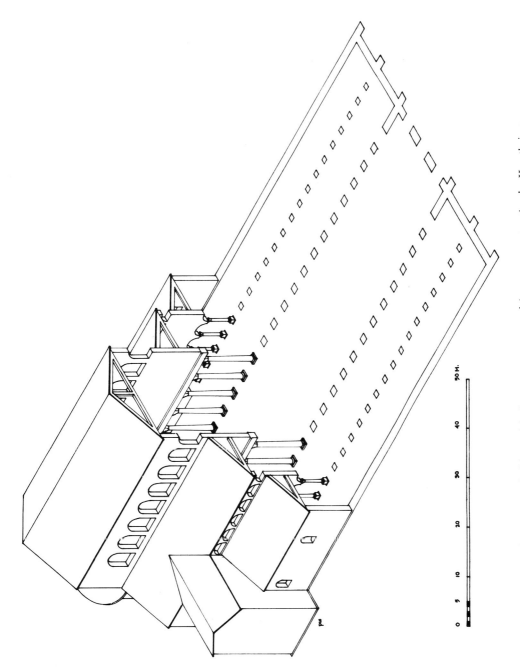

Fig. 5. Rome, S. Giovanni in Laterano, western end in 320, reconstruction by Krautheimer

Fig. 6a. Epitaph of Flavius Eurialus, 405.
Rome, ex-Lateran Museum

Fig. 6b. (top) Epitaph of unknown *"in basilica maxior,"* Rome, S. Lorenzo f.l.m. (bottom) Epitaph of Lucillus Pelio, ca. 400, Rome, S. Lorenzo f.l.m.

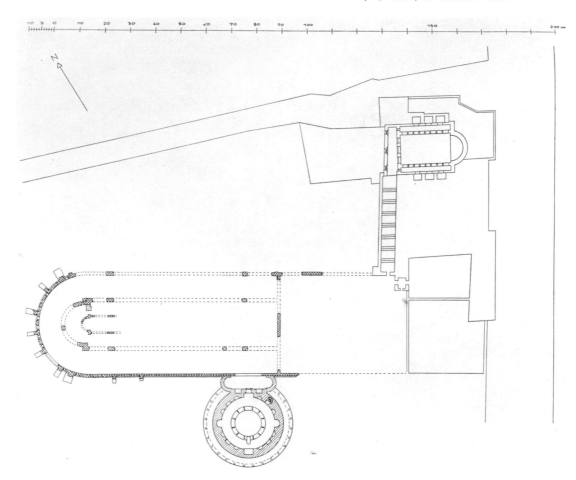

Fig. 7. Rome, Sant' Agnese f.l.m., *Coemeterium Agnetis,* ca. 350 and *basilica ad corpus,* 625-638, plan

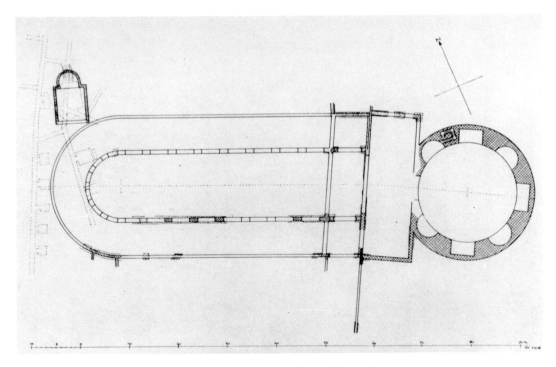

Fig. 8a. Rome, SS. Marcellino e Pietro, plan

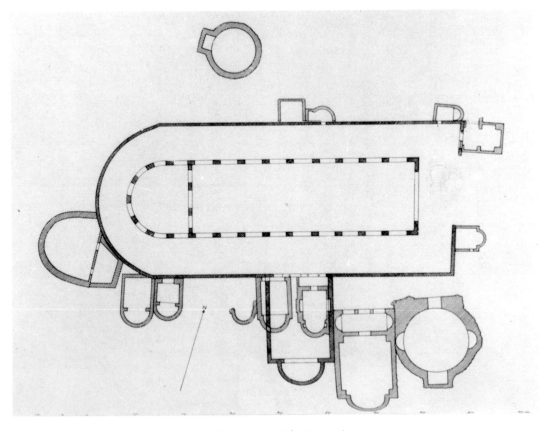

Fig. 8b. Rome, S. Sebastiano, plan

Fig. 9a. Rome, S. Sebastiano, model of reconstruction by Pacini, exterior

Fig. 9b. Rome, S. Sebastiano, model of reconstruction by Pacini, interior

Fig. 10. Rome, S. Lorenzo f.l.m., interior

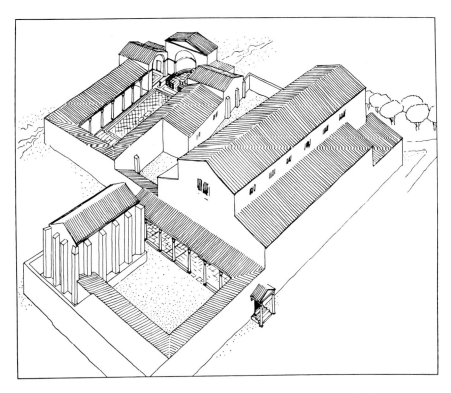

Fig. 11. Salona Marusinac, Anastasius complex, reconstruction by Dyggve

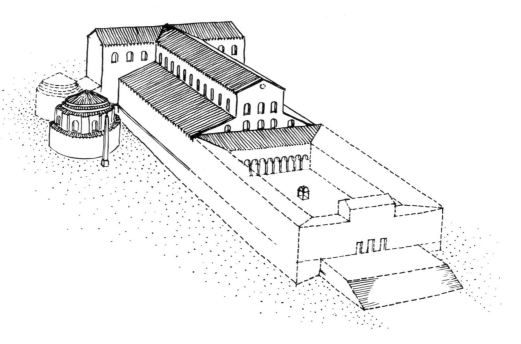

Fig. 12. Rome, Constantinian basilica of St. Peter, reconstruction by Frazer

Fig. 13. Rome, St. Peter's, Constantinian transept, drawing by Heemskerck, Stockholm, National Museum

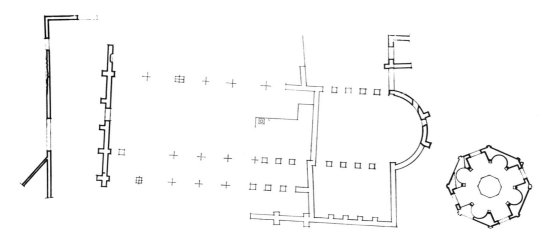

Fig. 14. Milan, Sta. Tecla, plan

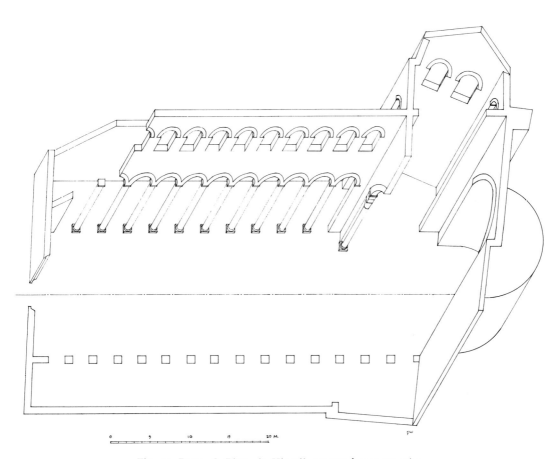

Fig. 15. Rome, S. Pietro in Vincoli, proposed reconstruction

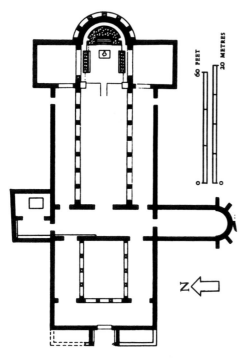

Fig. 17. Nikopolis, Basilica A, plan

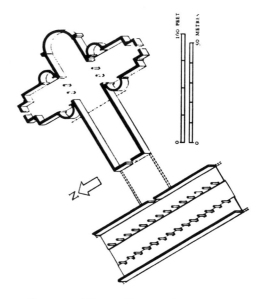

Fig. 19. Milan, Church of the Holy Apostles, isometric reconstruction by E. Villa

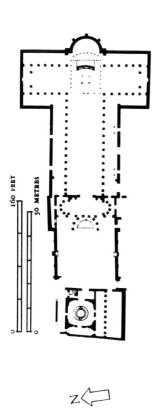

Fig. 16. Abu Mina, St. Menas, plan

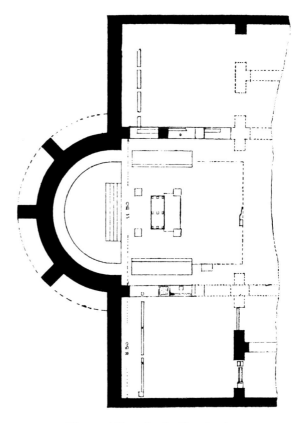

Fig. 18. Nikopolis, Basilica B, plan

386

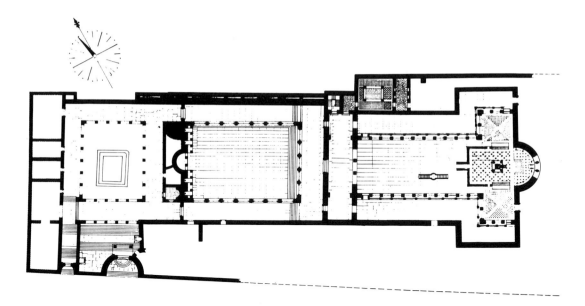

Fig. 20. Philippi, Basilica A, plan

Fig. 21. Salonika, S. Demetrius, perspective reconstruction by Orlandos

Fig. 22. Rome, Sto. Stefano Rotondo, exterior

Fig. 23. Rome, Sto. Stefano Rotondo, interior

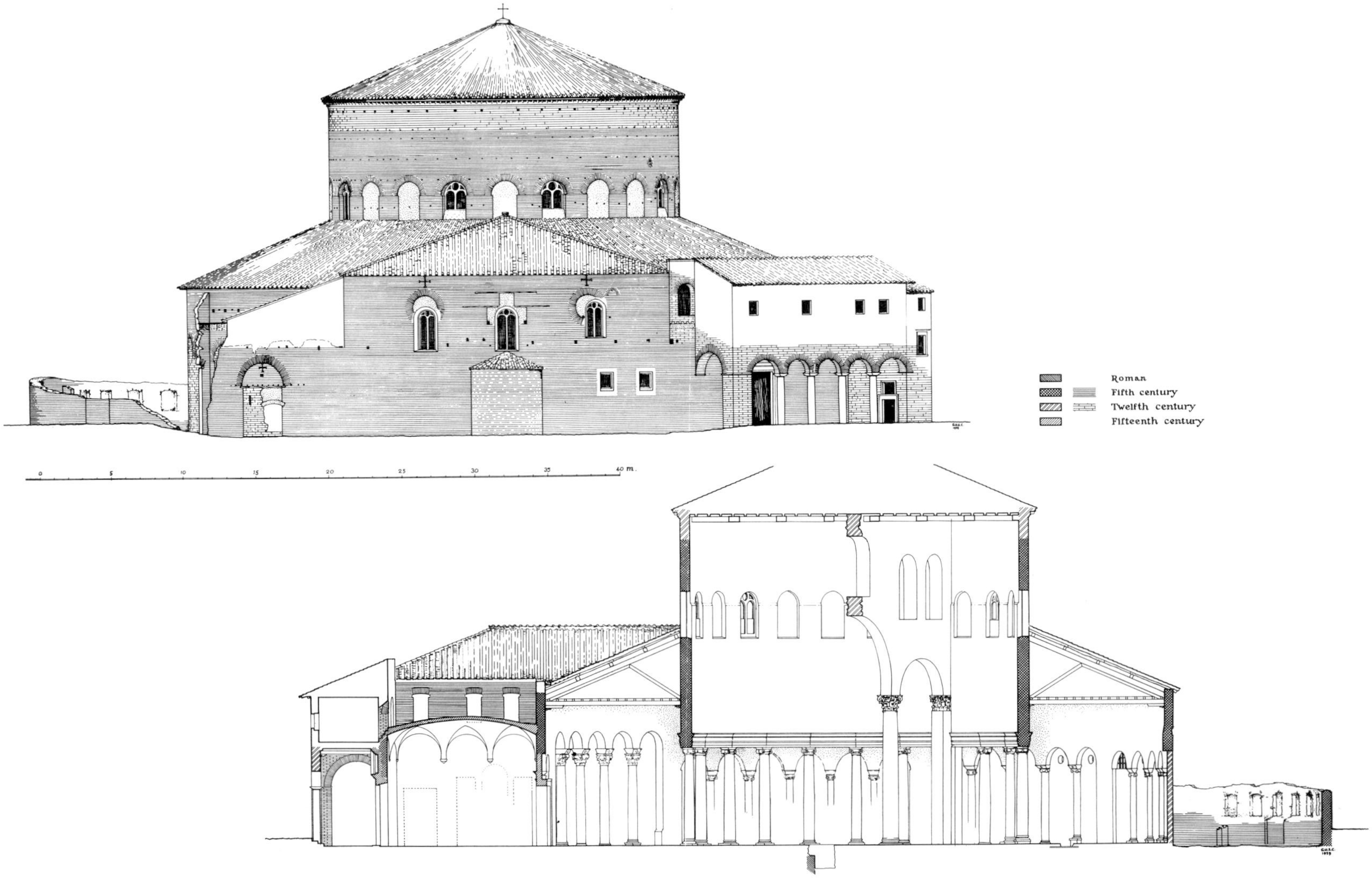
Roman
Fifth century
Twelfth century
Fifteenth century
0
5
10
15
20
25
30
35
40 m.

Fig. 24. Rome, Sto. Stefano Rotondo, elevation and transverse section

Fig. 25. Rome, Sto. Stefano Rotondo, elevation of side wall by Canina

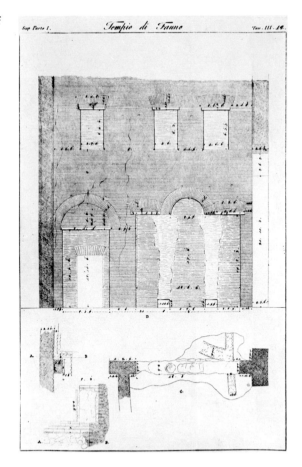

Fig. 26. Rome, Sto. Stefano Rotondo, interior prior to 1485, drawing by Cronaca, Florence, Uffizi

Fig. 27. Rome, Sta. Costanza, interior

Fig. 28. Rome, Sto. Stefano Rotondo, plan ca.
1570, drawing, Palladio workshop, London,
R.I.B.A.

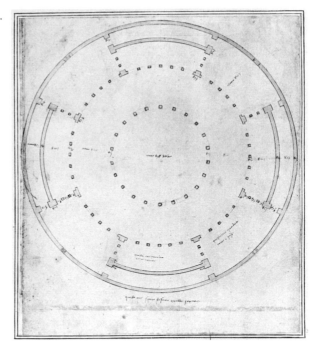

Fig. 29. Rome, Sta. Costanza, exterior, drawing by F. Giani, Rome, Bibliotheca Hertziana

Fig. 30. Jerusalem, Church of Holy Sepulchre, Anastasis rotunda, interior in 1609, engraving by J. Callot

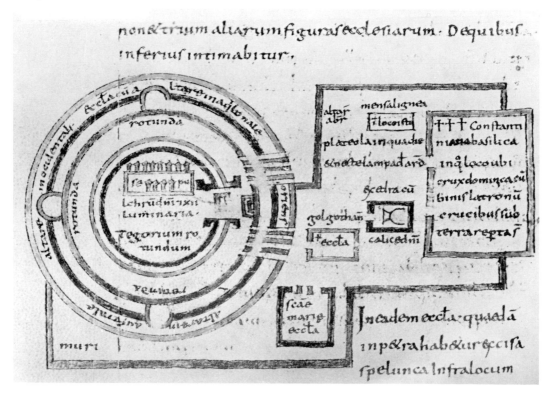

Fig. 31. Jerusalem, Church of Holy Sepulchre, Anastasis rotunda, plan ca. 670 by Arculf, Vienna

Fig. 33. Würzburg, Chapel of St. Mary, exterior

Fig. 32. Centula, S. Riquier and Chapel of St. Mary, seventeenth-
century engraving after lost eleventh-century representation

Fig. 34. Rome, Pantheon, interior in eighteenth-century, engraving by Pannini

Fig. 35. Ravenna, Mausoleum of Theodoric, later Church of Sta. Maria Rotunda

Fig. 36. Rome, Pantheon, exterior

Fig. 37. Ravenna, Mausoleum of Theodoric, later Church of Sta. Maria Rotunda and adjacent chapel, drawing by Piranesi, London, Courtauld Institute

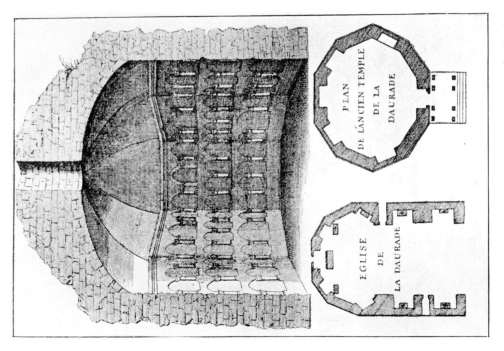

Fig. 39. Toulouse, La Daurade, interior, reconstruction by Martin

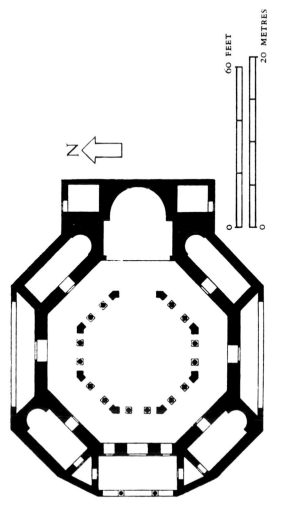

Fig. 38. Mount Garizim, Church of the Theotokos, plan

60 FEET

20 METRES

Fig. 40. Fulda, St. Michael, interior

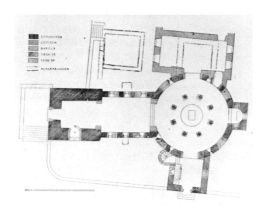

Fig. 41. Fulda, St. Michael, plan

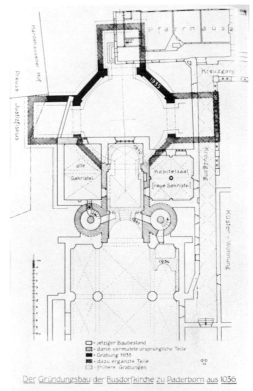

Der Gründungsbau der Busdorfkirche zu Paderborn aus 1036

232. Paderborn. Ausgrabungsplan der Busdorfkirche, gez. P. Mich

Fig. 42. Paderborn, Church of Holy Sepulchre, plan

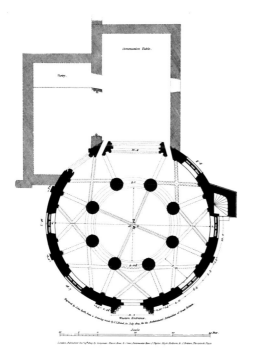

Fig. 43. Cambridge, Church of Holy Sepulchre, plan by Britton

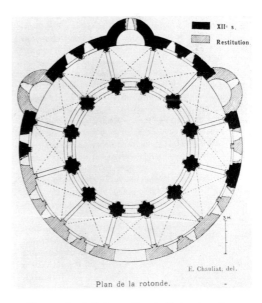

Plan de la rotonde.

Fig. 44. Lanleff (near Caen), Rotunda, plan

Fig. 45. Cambridge, Church of Holy Sepulchre, interior, engraving by Britton

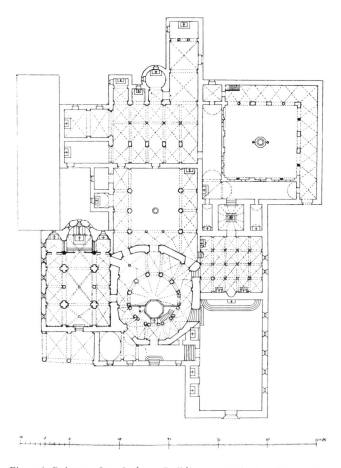

Fig. 46. Bologna, Sto. Stefano, Buildings at Holy Sepulchre, plan

Fig. 47. Bologna, Sto. Stefano, Rotunda of Holy Sepulchre, interior, engraving by Knight

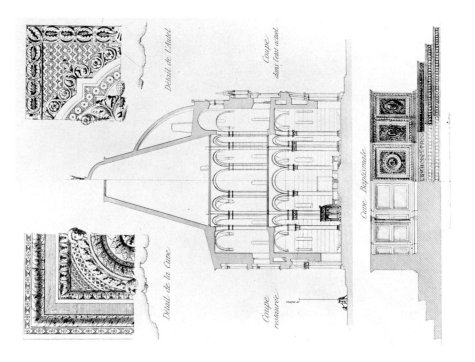

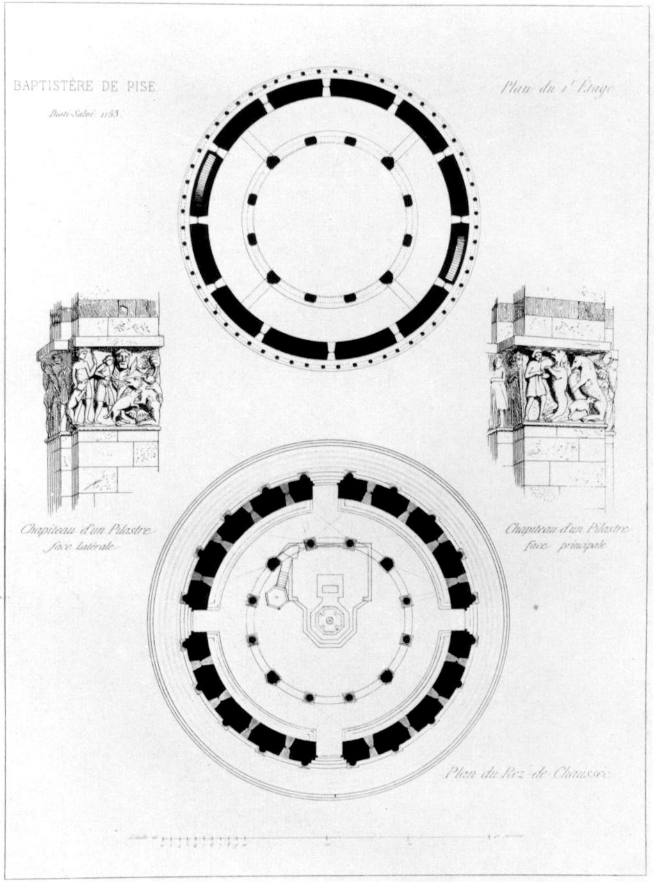

Fig. 49. Pisa, Baptistery, plan

Fig. 48. Pisa, Baptistery, interior

Fig. 50. Jerusalem, Church of Holy Sepulchre, Anastasis rotunda, *Sacramentary of Henry II,* Munich

Fig. 51. Jerusalem, Church of Holy Sepulchre, Anastasis rotunda, view on Wooden Casket of Sancta Sanctorum, Rome, Vatican Library

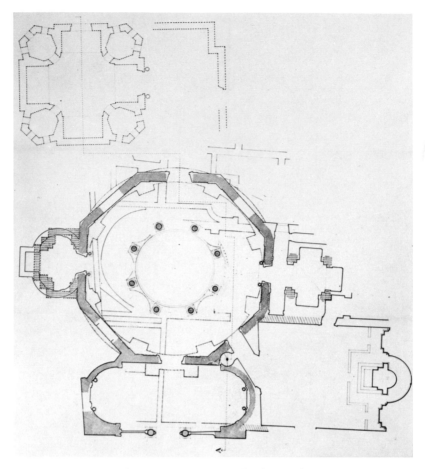

Fig. 52a. Rome, Lateran Baptistery, plan

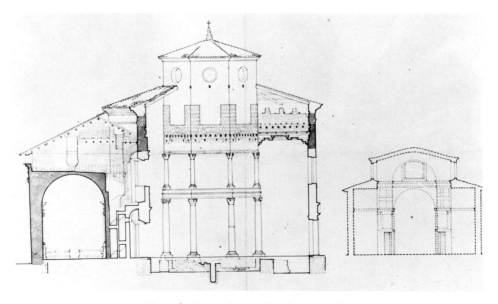

Fig. 52b. Rome, Lateran Baptistery, section

Fig. 54. Algeria, Djémila, Baptistery, ambulatory

Fig. 53. Syria, Kalat Siman, Baptistery, view

Fig. 55. Rome, Lateran Baptistery, interior, sixteenth-century reconstruction, engraving by Lafréri

Fig. 56. Nocera, Baptistery, interior, engraving by Saint-Non

Fig. 57. Rome, Villa dei Gordiani, Tor
de'Schiavi

Fig. 58. Rome, Villa dei Gordiani, Tor
de'Schiavi

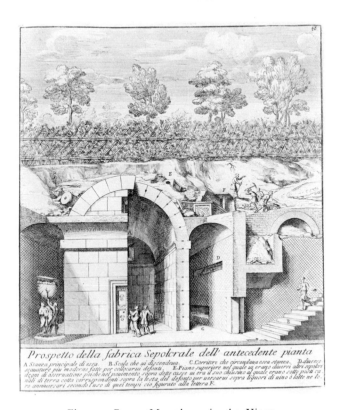

Fig. 59. Rome, Mausoleum in the Vigna
Cavalieri, engraving by Bartoli

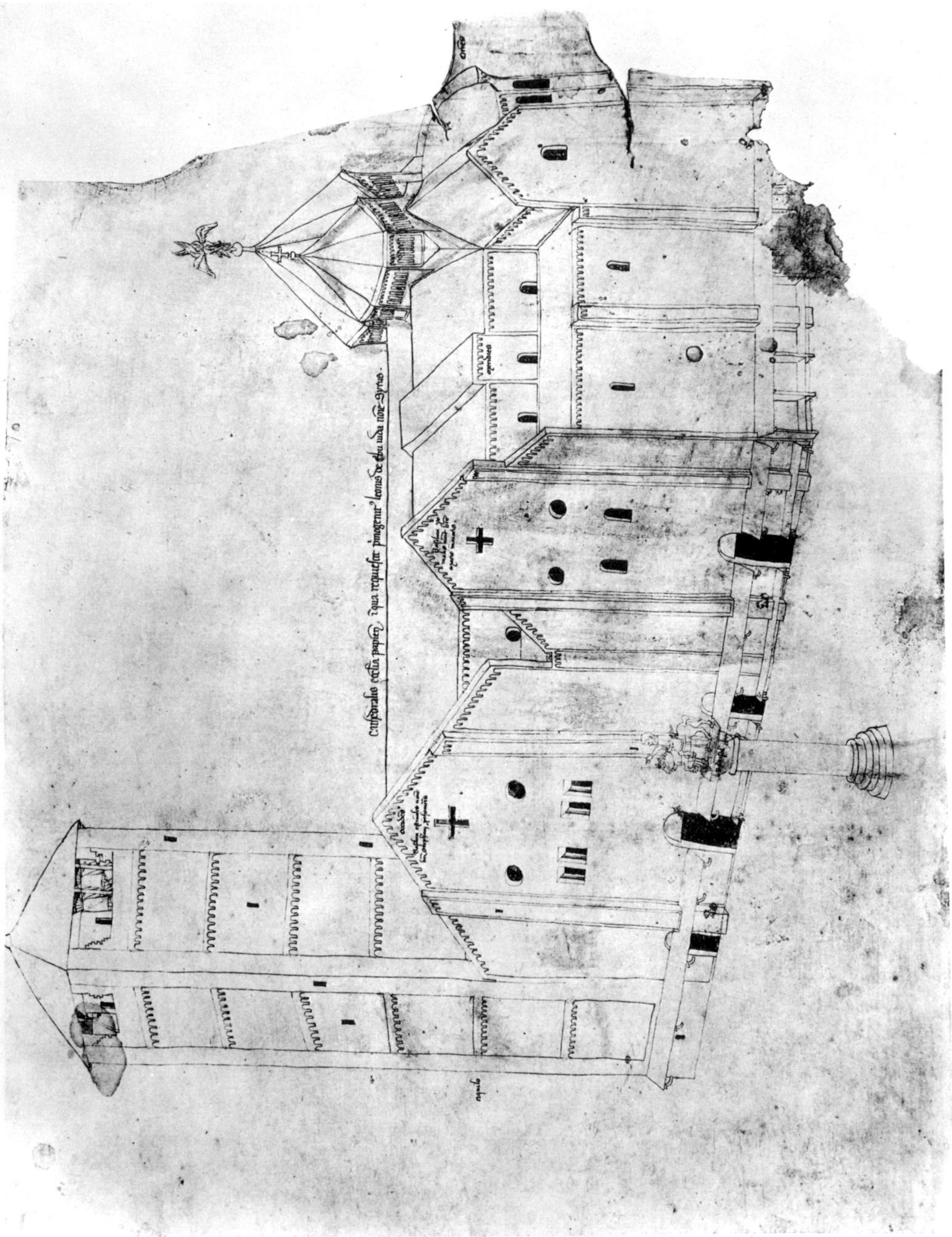

Fig. 60. Pavia, Double Cathedral, view by Opicinus de Canistris, Rome, Vatican Library

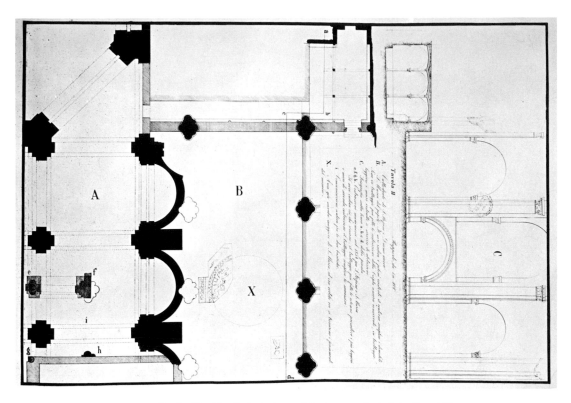

Fig. 61. Pavia, Double Cathedral, partial plan as of 1876 by Brambilla

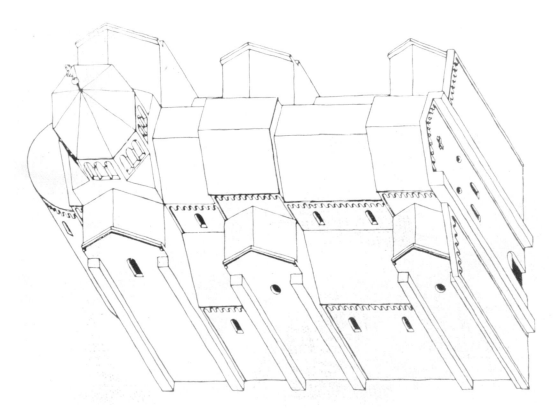

Fig. 62. Pavia, Sta. Maria Maggiore, reconstruction by Wachsmann

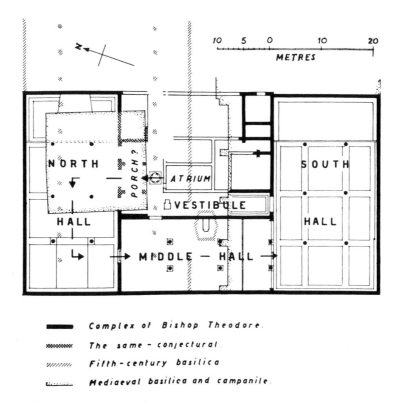

Complex of Bishop Theodore.

The same - conjectural.

Fifth-century basilica

Mediaeval basilica and campanile.

Fig. 63. Aquileia, Double Cathedral, plan, reconstruction by Corbett

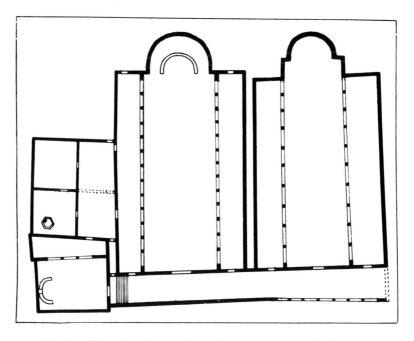

Fig. 64. Salona, Double Cathedral, plan, reconstruction by Dyggve

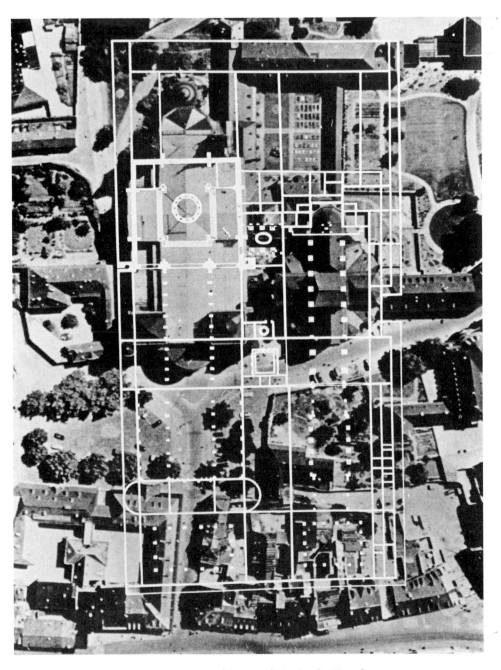

Fig. 65. Trier, Double Cathedral, plan by Kempf

Fig. 66. Rome, Sta. Maria Maggiore, interior, nave

Fig. 67. Rome, Sta. Maria Maggiore, interior, right aisle

415

Fig. 68. Rome, Sta. Maria Maggiore, nave elevation ca. 1480, anonymous drawing,
Rome, Vatican Library

Fig. 69. Rome, Sta. Maria Maggiore, partial elevation by Peruzzi, Florence, Uffizi

Fig. 70. Rome, Sta. Maria Maggiore, stucco frieze

Fig. 71. Rome, Sta. Maria Maggiore, fifth-century church, reconstruction by Corbett

Fig. 72. Rome, Basilica Ulpia, interior, reconstruction by Canina

Fig. 73. Rome, Lateran Baptistery, ambulatory wall, drawing by Giuliano da San Gallo, Rome, Vatican Library

Fig. 73. Rome, Lateran Baptistery, ambulatory wall, drawing by Giuliano da San Gallo, Rome, Vatican Library

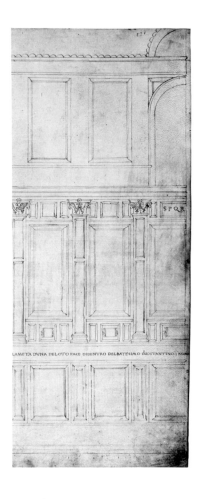

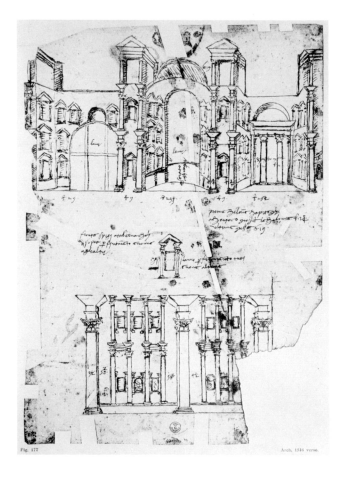

Fig. 74. Rome, Baths of Diocletian, interior, drawing by Antonio da San Gallo, Florence, Uffizi

Fig. 75. Constantinople, Church of Holy Apostles, late tenth-century
representation in *Menologium of Basil II,* Rome, Vatican Library

Fig. 76. Constantinople, Church of Holy Apostles, late tenth-century
representation in *Menologium of Basil II,* Rome, Vatican Library

Fig. 77. Constantinople, Church of Holy Apostles, late tenth-century representation in *Menologium of Basil II,* Rome, Vatican Library

Fig. 78. Constantinople, Church of Holy Apostles, early twelfth-century representation in *Homilies of James Kokkinobaphos,* Rome, Vatican Library

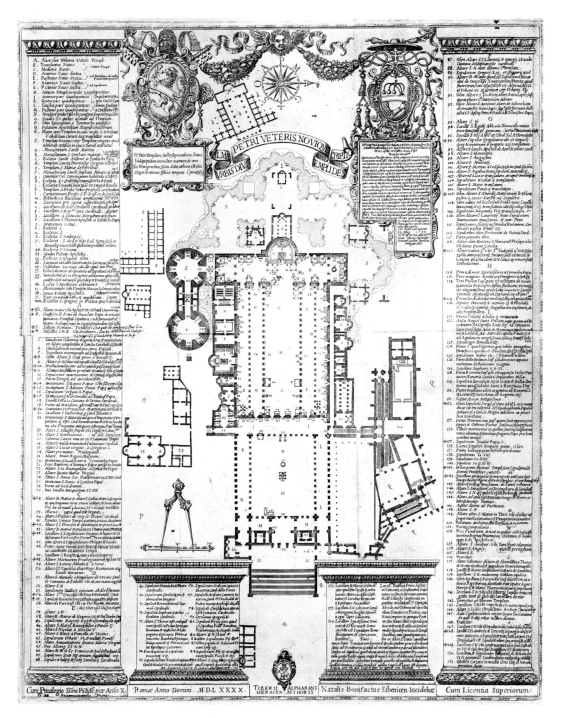

Fig. 79. Rome, Constantinian basilica of St. Peter, sixteenth-century plan by Alpharanus

423

Fig. 80. St. Peter's, drawing by Heemskerck, Berlin, Kupferstichkabinett

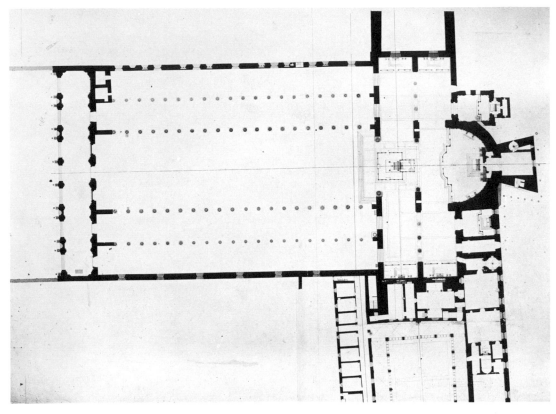

Fig. 81. Rome, S. Paolo f.l.m., plan before 1823, Rome, Palazzo Venezia

Fig. 82. Rome, S. Paolo f.l.m., air view

Fig. 83. Rome, S. Paolo f.l.m., interior in the eighteenth century, engraving by Piranesi

Fig. 84. Rome, S. Giovanni in Laterano, before seventeenth-century remodeling, reconstruction of interior, fresco in S. Martino ai Monti, 1637-1652

Fig. 85. Rome, Sta. Sabina, interior

Fig. 86. Vienne (Isère), St. Pierre, interior

Fig. 87. Fulda, Abbey Church, exterior from east, fifteenth-century woodcut by Sebastian Münster

Fig. 88. Fulda, Abbey Church, exterior from south, painting from Bishop's Palace, Fulda, 1648-1704

Fig. 89. Rome, Sant' Anastasia, exterior, drawing by Heemskerck, Berlin, Kupferstichkabinett

Fig. 90. Rome, Sto. Stefano degli Abessini, interior

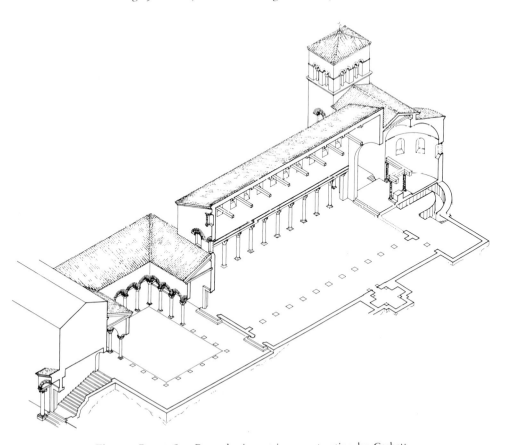

Fig. 91. Rome, Sta. Prassede, isometric reconstruction by Corbett

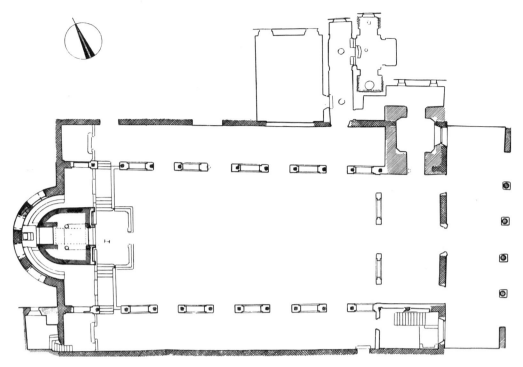

Fig. 93. Rome, Sta. Cecilia, plan

Fig. 92. Rome, Sta. Prassede, interior, engraving by Rossini

Fig. 94. Rome, S. Marco, interior

Fig. 95. Rome, S. Martino ai Monti, interior

Fig. 96. Rome, SS. Quattro Coronati, entrance tower

Fig. 97. Hersfeld, Abbey Church, interior

Fig. 98. Rome, S. Paolo f.l.m., nave after 1823, engraving by Rossini

Fig. 99. Lorsch, Torhalle, exterior

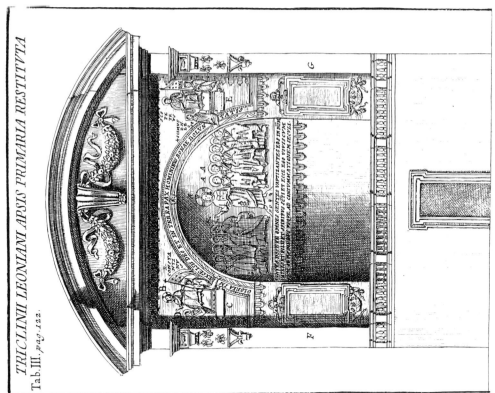

Fig. 101. Rome, Lateran, Triclinium of Leo III, engraving by Alemanni

Fig. 100. Lorsch, Torhalle, capital

Fig. 102. Sceptre of Charles V, Paris work-shop, ca. 1375, Paris, Louvre

Fig. 103. Orb on Sceptre of Charles V, detail of fig. 102

Fig. 104. Morse, French workshop, ca. 1400, Washington, National Gallery, Widener Collection

Fig. 105. God the Father holding Crucifix, detail of fig. 104

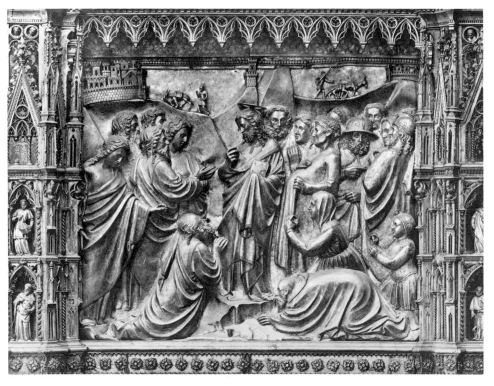

Fig. 106. Silver Altar of St. John the Baptist, Florentine workshop, 1367-1387, Florence, Museo dell' Opera del Duomo

Fig. 107. Lorenzo Ghiberti, *Sacrifice of Isaac,* Competition Panel, 1401-1403, Florence, Bargello

Fig. 108. Lorenzo Ghiberti, *Abraham and Isaac,* detail of fig. 107

Fig. 109. Lorenzo Ghiberti, *Sacrifice of Isaac,* detail of Competition Panel from side

Fig. 110. Lorenzo Ghiberti, *Two Servants,* detail of fig. 107

Fig. III. Lorenzo Ghiberti, *Christ on Mount of Olives,* ca. 1403-1407, North Doors, Florence, Baptistery

Fig. 112. Filippo Brunelleschi, *Sacrifice of Isaac,* Competition Panel, 1401-1403, Florence, Bargello

Fig. 113. Lorenzo Ghiberti, *Jesus among the Doctors,* ca. 1407-1414, North Doors, Florence, Baptistery

Fig. 114. French workshop, *Prophet,* ca. 1400, Paris, Louvre

Fig. 115. Lorenzo Ghiberti, Frame, details, 1403-1425, North Doors, Florence, Baptistery

Fig. 116. Jacopo della Quercia (?), *Saint,* Rotterdam, Museum
Boymans-van Beuningen

Fig. 117. Jacopo della Quercia, Trenta Altar, Lucca, S. Frediano

Fig. 118. Stucco after Jacopo della Quercia, Female Saint, Bologna, Museo Civico

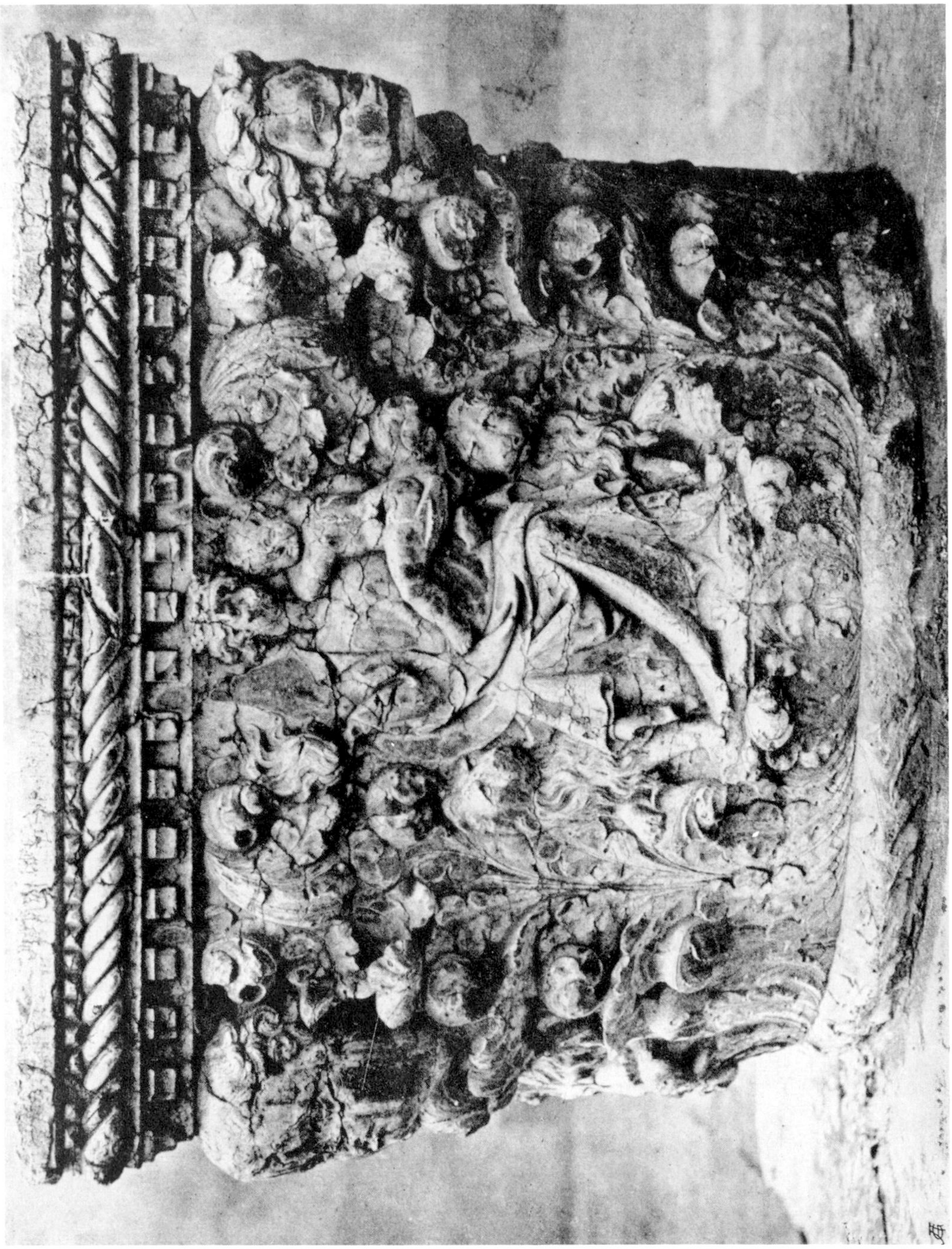

Fig. 119. Bartolommeo Buon, Well Head, 1427, Venice, Cà d'Oro

Fig. 120. *Madonna and Child,* fifteenth-century Florentine, Florence, Museo Bardini

Fig. 121. Lorenzo Ghiberti, Head of Girl, North Doors, Frame, Florence, Baptistery

Fig. 122. *Madonna and Child,* here attributed to Jacopo della Quercia, Washington, National Gallery, Kress Collection

Fig. 123. *Madonna and Child,* Italo-Byzantine, late thirteenth century, Siena, Carmine

Fig. 124. Jacopo della Quercia, *Acca,* detail of Fonte Gaia, 1414-1419, Siena

Fig. 125. Lorenzo Ghiberti, Head of Youth, North Doors, Frame, Florence, Baptistery

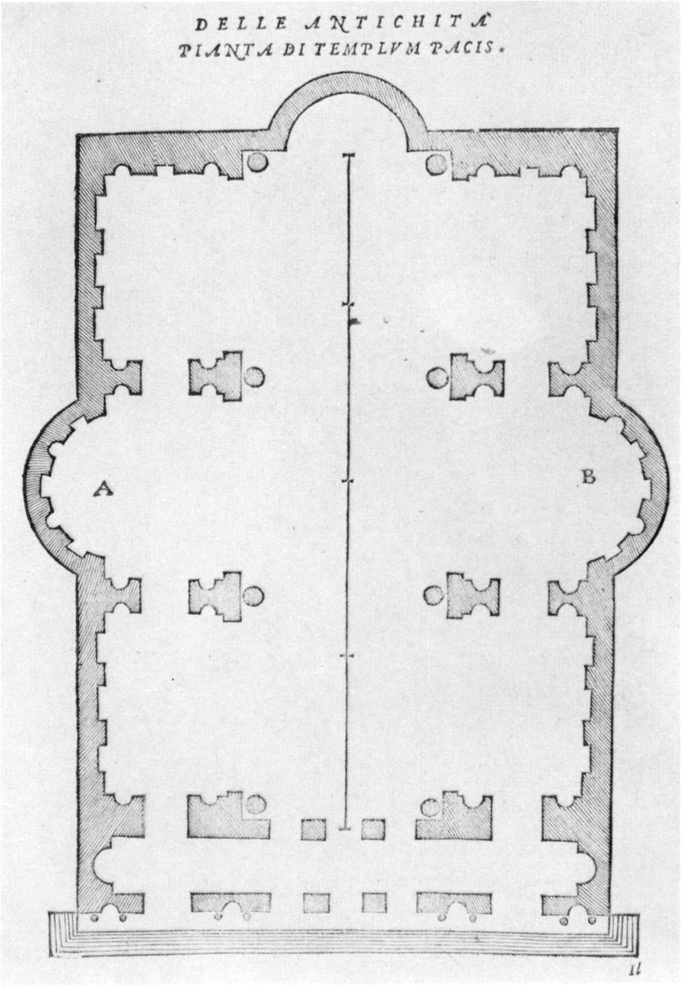

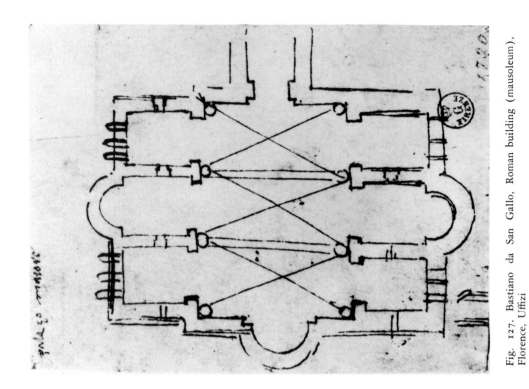

Fig. 127. Bastiano da San Gallo, Roman building (mausoleum), Florence, Uffizi

DELLE ANTICHITÀ
PIANTA DI TEMPLVM PACIS.

Fig. 126. Sebastiano Serlio, plan of Basilica of Maxentius

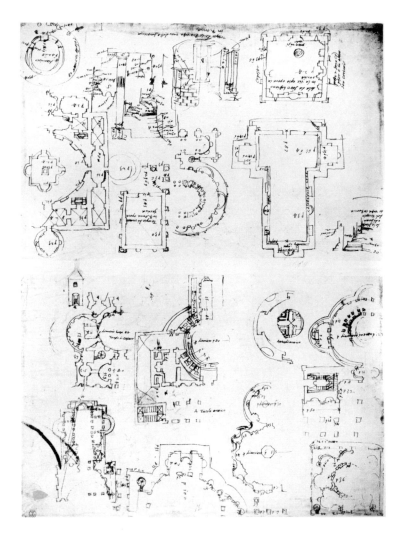

Fig. 128. Sallustio Peruzzi, Ancient buildings in Rome and Tivoli, Florence, Uffizi

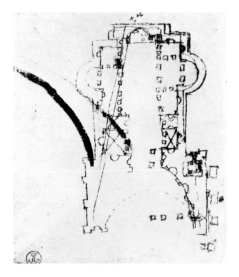

Fig. 129. Sallustio Peruzzi, Sketch of
Roman Mausoleum, detail of fig. 128

Fig. 130. Luciano Laurana (?), *Comic Scene*, Urbino, Galleria Nazionale delle Marche

Fig. 131. Luciano Laurana (?), *Tragic Scene*, Baltimore, Walters Art Gallery

Fig. 132. Sebastiano Serlio, *Tragic Scene*

Fig. 133. Sebastiano Serlio, *Comic Scene*

Fig. 134. Luciano Laurana (?), *Tragic Scene,* triumphal arch, detail of fig. 131

Fig. 135. Luciano Laurana, *Comic Scene,* buildings on left, detail of fig. 130

Fig. 136. Luciano Laurana, *Comic Scene,* buildings on right, detail of fig. 130

Fig. 137. Luciano Laurana, *Comic Scene*, central building, detail of fig. 130

463

Fig. 138. Baldassare Peruzzi, Stage Design, here identified as a *Comic Scene,* Turin, Palazzo Reale

Fig. 139. Baldassare Peruzzi, Stage Design, here identified as a *Comic Scene,* Florence, Uffizi